Mastering Computer Vision with PyTorch and Machine Learning

Online at: https://doi.org/10.1088/978-0-7503-6244-3

Mastering Computer Vision with PyTorch and Machine Learning

Caide Xiao
University of Calgary, Calgary, Canada

IOP Publishing, Bristol, UK

ISBN   978-0-7503-6244-3 (ebook)
ISBN   978-0-7503-6242-9 (print)
ISBN   978-0-7503-6245-0 (myPrint)
ISBN   978-0-7503-6243-6 (mobi)

DOI   10.1088/978-0-7503-6244-3

Supplementary material is available for this book from https://doi.org/10.1088/978-0-7503-6244-3.

Version: 20240401

IOP ebooks

British Library Cataloguing-in-Publication Data: A catalogue record for this book is available from the British Library.

Published by IOP Publishing, wholly owned by The Institute of Physics, London

IOP Publishing, No.2 The Distillery, Glassfields, Avon Street, Bristol, BS2 0GR, UK

US Office: IOP Publishing, Inc., 190 North Independence Mall West, Suite 601, Philadelphia, PA 19106, USA

This book is dedicated to my wife Rongju Sun and my mother Fengying Yin.

Contents

Preface

What this book is about

Mastering Computer Vision with Pytorch and Machine Learning is a book which provides a thorough and extensive guide for mastering advanced computer vision techniques for image processing by using Python and PyTorch from the ground up. Computer vision is a field of artificial intelligence and computer science that focuses on enabling computers to interpret and understand visual information from the world around them. Computer vision and machine learning are closely related fields. Machine learning is used in computer vision to enable computers to automatically find patterns and relationships in large datasets of images and videos. With a focus on practical applications, this book covers essential concepts such as Kullback Leibler divergence, maximum likelihood, convolutional neural networks (CNN), generative adversarial networks (GAN), Wasserstein generative adversarial networks (WGAN), WGAN with gradient penalty (WGAN-GP), information maximizing generative adversarial networks (infoGAN), variational autoencoders (VAE), and their applications for image classification/image generation. Readers will also learn how to leverage the latest computer vision techniques like Yolov8 for object detection, stable diffusion models for image generation, vision transformers for zero-shot object detection, knowledge distillation for compression of neural networks, DINO for self-supervised learning, segment anything models (SAM), NeRF and 3D Gaussian Splatting for 3D scenes synthesis. This book is a valuable resource for professionals, researchers, and students who want to expand their knowledge of advanced computer vision techniques using PyTorch. With clear explanations, practical examples, and real-world use cases, readers will learn how to apply computer vision techniques to image analysis tasks, and develop skills necessary to build and train their own models for advanced image analysis. Whether you are a beginner or an experienced data scientist, this book will provide you with the knowledge and tools you need to succeed.

Prerequisites to readers

Computer vision projects use neural network models or vision transformers as mathematical functions to process images. The outputs of these functions could be integers for image classification, or new images similar to images in train datasets for image generation, or bounding boxes with class identities and probabilities for objection detection. Neural networks in models are mathematical operators organized in special sequences. Large-scale computer vision models may have billions of parameters to learn from training datasets. Model training time is dependent on the sizes of the input data, Python codes, and computer hardware to process the data. This book is written for readers with linear algebra knowledge about matrix calculations and basic ideas about statistics. With such mathematics background, readers can write their codes even they have no idea about Python which is a simple yet powerful programming language with excellent functionality for machine learning. Kaggle and Google Colab provide free GPUs for any people with a Google account. In those two free internet platforms, powerful computer hardware and software are ready to use. Most codes listed in the book can run on either of the two free internet platforms. Readers do not need to buy expensive computers.

Because of some limits in Kaggle and Google Colab, it's better to have your own computer with the following open-source software. The first is Microsoft Visual Studio Code (VS Code). It is a free code editor provided by Microsoft for Windows, Linux, and macOS. It has many features and extensions for editing, debugging, and developing codes in many programming languages. It is a popular choice for people of all skill levels due to its ease of use, customizability, and community-driven development. In a VS Code terminal, we can then install many extensions, such as Python, Jupyter notebook, PyTorch, Torchvision, NumPy, Pandas, Matplotlib, OpenCV, tqdm, and more. The development of computer science is very fast. We need to have more than one virtual workspace in VS Code for different versions of Python and other libraries. Most codes in the book can run with Python v3.6, and many codes in the last six chapters must run with Python v3.9 to v3.11 for the latest computer vision techniques, such as Ultralytics Yolov7 to Yolov9, Hugging Face zero-shot object detection, Facebook DINO and SAM.

Structure of the book

There are twelve chapters in this book. Chapter 1 introduces mathematical concepts and tools about computer vision and machine learning; these are probability, maximum likelihood, Shannon entropy, gradients, activation functions, loss functions, datasets, dataloaders and learning rate etc. Nine pairs of numbers about Celsius and Fahrenheit temperature conversion are used in different projects of this chapter to introduce those mathematical concepts step by step. Chapter 2 introduces deep convolution neuron networks for image classifications of three datasets: MNIST, CIFAR10 and Vegetable Images. These are supervised learning projects where models learn to make predictions based on labeled training data. Chapters 3–6 are about image generation with different algorithms: GANs, VAEs, WGANs, and infoGANs. Using conditional GANs, infoGANs, VAEs, or VAE-GANs, we can generate the desired images with special styles. VAEs and infoGANs are used in unsupervised learning projects. The main advantage of unsupervised learning is that it can be used to uncover hidden patterns and structure in data without any prior knowledge or labeled data.

Codes in all projects listed in the book are in the same style with four parts: data input, data display, data process and output data visualization. A simple dataset for quadratic curve generation is used in chapters 2–9 to help readers understand complex algorithms in new models. In many projects, readers only need to focus on the third part which is about how to construct and use models to process data. Chapters 7–12 introduce the latest computer vision techniques (up to February of 2024) for image classification, image generation, object detection, object segmentation and synthesis of 3D scenes. YOLOv8 from Ultralytics is one of the latest techniques for object detection and segmentation. It is easy to install and use for image analysis tasks. OpenAI, Hugging Face, Meta AI and Intelligent Systems Lab provide us with new tools for image analysis. With their libraries, we only need to write codes in a few lines to generate photo-realistic images, to detect/segment/classify objects, to retrieve images, and to estimate image relative depth without model training (zero-shot). The last chapter is about synthesis of 3D scenes by NeRF or 3D Gaussian splatting. Many detailed mathematics derivations are put in the appendices. Many extra project codes can also be found in the appendices.

Keywords

Computer vision, Machine Learning, Kullback Leibler Divergence, maximum likelihood, PyTorch, CNN, GAN, WGAN, WGAN-GP, infoGAN, VAE, image classification, object detection, image segmentation, image generation, image retrieve, YOLO, U-Net, Stable Diffusion, zero-shot, ViT, Knowledge Distillation, DINO, SAM, fastSAM, MiDaS, NeRF, 3D scenes and 3D Gaussian Splatting.

Acknowledgements

I wish to express my sincere appreciation to the professional editors of the Institute of Physics Publishing (IOPP) Ltd. They are Senior Commissioning Manager John Navas, eBooks Coordinator Phebe Hooper and Production Editor Chris Benson. It would have been almost impossible to finish the book in two years without my wife Rongju Sun's support and patience. I also received help about subjects in the book from my PhD supervisor, Professor Senfang Sui. In the early 1980s, I began to learn to write computer codes in BASIC. Comparing with other computer languages such as BASIC, Fortran, Java, C, I found Python is the best. It is free (open source) for people, and it is easy to use if you know English words and Algebra. Many smart people publicly released their Python and Pytorch libraries for people to use. These free libraries are just like transistors, capacitors, inductors and resistors in electronics. We can use them to construct computer vision models which would work day and night to generate photorealistic images. Many kind people have published their Python codes on GitHub, and even teach people how to use their codes by YouTube videos. Many of my codes in the book were inspired by these people. I have much to thank those teachers for in the great YouTube University on Earth, and can only mention some of them: Dr Sreenivas Bhattiprolu (DigitalSreeni), Aladdin Persson, Aarohi Singla, FreedomWebTech, Rob Mulla and OutofAi. Many free and publicly available image datasets and pre-trained weights files were used in computer vision projects of this book. They were generated by Torchvision, Hugging Face, Roboflow, OpenAI, Meta AI. Professor Ziwei Liu gave me permission to use CelebA dataset, and Dr Alex Krizhevsky gave me permission to use CIFA10 dataset in the book.

Author biography

Dr Caide Xiao

 **Dr Caide Xiao** was born on 25 October 1961. He was a physics teacher at Yunyang Medical College in China after he received his Batchelor degree in 1983 from the Physics Department of Central China Normal University in Wuhan, where he learnt to write computer codes on Apple II. From 1990 to 1996, he was a postgraduate student in Professor Senfang Sui's laboratory for optical biosensors in Tsinghua University, Beijing. Then he worked as a visiting scholar in many Biophysics laboratories in Italy, Canada and United States of America. Now, he has established his home in Calgary, Canada. Many photos in the book came from Calgary Stampede Parades and Banff National Park.

Chapter 1

Mathematical tools for computer vision

This chapter is about mathematical tools and a Python/PyTorch platform for computer vision projects. Section 1.1 introduces some mathematical concepts about information entropy, statistics probability distribution functions, Kullback–Leibler divergence, Jensen's inequality and an overfitting issue in nonlinear regression. The remaining four sections are about the gradient descent algorithm for model training in machine learning, Python/PyTorch libraries (tools) for datasets, dataloaders, activation functions, GPU usage and model training/saving. A simple data file is used many times in this chapter to introduce these concepts and libraries.

Humans have the ability to imagine, create and build new things that have never existed before. The ability to innovate and invent is one of the key characteristics of human intelligence and has led to significant advancements in various fields, such as science, technology, engineering and the arts. We build skyscrapers in cities to live in, make cellphones to keep in our pockets for communication and launch rockets to carry satellites to the edge of our solar system to explore our universe. All these engineering achievements are based on laws of physics and mathematics, such as Newton's law of universal gravitation, Maxwell's electromagnetic law, Einstein's theory of relativity, quantum mechanics, etc. These laws are the foundations of our civilization. They are keys for us to understand and modify our world. However, knowing these physics and mathematics laws is not enough, experts or professionals also have to do work based on their experiences. Those experiences come from lifetime practices. Once, when an expert passed away, all of the experiences of that expert were lost. Now it is possible for professionals to train computers with machine learning algorithms, so that human experiences can be inherited and stored in computers forever. The goal of computer vision research is to enable computers to have humanlike perception capabilities. Machine learning is a branch of artificial intelligence (AI) that deals with the development of algorithms and statistical models. Machine learning allows computers to 'learn' from data without being explicitly programmed. In machine learning, models based on algorithms are trained

doi:10.1088/978-0-7503-6244-3ch1

on datasets to find patterns in the datasets to predict new data. There are several types of machine learning, including supervised learning, unsupervised learning, semi-supervised learning, and reinforcement learning, each having a unique set of algorithms and approaches.

1.1 Probability, entropy and Kullback–Leibler divergence

Images are composed of pixels, which are minuscule dots on a screen. When numerous pixels are arranged in a specific configuration (pattern), they form an image. The resolution of an image is determined by the number of pixels it contains. Higher image resolutions give us clearer and more detailed visuals. From the pattern or probability of an image's pixels distributed in a space, we can generate new images. To begin our study of computer vision, it is essential to embrace the concept of statistics, particularly probability. Utilizing the Bayesian probability theorem and Shannon's information entropy theory, we can derive loss functions for model training. These models would be so smart that they can not only tell us if there are dogs or cats in an image, but also can generate photorealistic images/videos according to our text prompts.

1.1.1 Probability and Shannon entropy

To a fair coin, its 'head' and 'tail' sides have the same probability (50%) to appear when you toss it. In the coin system, we have a discrete random variable X within a space of {'head', 'tail'}, and its probability mass function (PMD) is $P(X) = \{1/2, 1/2\}$. In case when a coin is not fair, its head probability is $p = 0.45$, and we toss the coin ten times ($n = 10$), what is the probability of getting four heads ($x = 4$)? This unfair coin system has a discrete random variable X within a space of {0, 1, ..., 10} with the binomial dstribution function. Taking those parameters into equation (1.1), you will obtain the answer: 23.8%.

$$P(X = x) = \frac{n!}{x!(n-x)!}p^x(1-p)^{n-x} \tag{1.1}$$

The height variable (X) of our bodies is a continuous random number with a Gaussian distribution function which is the most important probability density function (PDF) for machine learning. Although probability density functions of many image datasets are too complex to write down explicitly, we can still try to use Gaussian distribution functions to approximate them.

$$P(X = x) = N(x; \mu, \sigma^2) = \frac{1}{\sqrt{2\pi\sigma^2}}e^{-\frac{1}{2}\left(\frac{x-\mu}{\sigma}\right)^2} \tag{1.2}$$

In equation (1.2), μ is the **mean** or expected value of X, σ is the standard deviation of X and σ^2 is the **variance** of X. For any random variable X with a known PDF, its expected value $E_p[X]$ and variance $E_p[(X-\mu)^2]$ are:

$$\mu = \sum_{i=1}^{n} x_i p(x_i) \xrightarrow{or} \int_{-\infty}^{\infty} xp(x)dx \tag{1.3}$$

$$\sigma^2 = \sum_{i=1}^{n}(x_i - \mu)^2 p(x_i) \overset{or}{\to} \int_{-\infty}^{\infty}(x - \mu)^2 p(x)dx \tag{1.4}$$

Shannon '**Entropy**' of information is the 'amount of information' contained in a random variable, or the minimum bits to encode information of a system.

$$H(p) = -\sum_{i=1}^{n}p_i \log_2(p_i) \overset{or}{\to} -\int_{-\infty}^{\infty}p(x)\log_2 p(x)dx \tag{1.5}$$

A fair coin system's entropy is $H(p) = -2\frac{1}{2}\log_2\left(\frac{1}{2}\right) = 1$ bit, and a fair dice system's entropy is $H(p) = -6\frac{1}{6}\log_2\left(\frac{1}{6}\right) = 2.585$ bits. For mathematical convenience in machine learning, we usually use natural logarithm, and the entropy unit is 'nit'. The coin's entropy and the dice's entropy are 0.69 nits and 1.79 nits respectively.

1.1.2 Kullback–Leibler divergence and cross entropy

In the case where there are two distribution functions p and q for a same random variable X, their log likelihood ratio is a function $f(x) = \ln\left[\frac{p(x)}{q(x)}\right]$. The expected value of the log likelihood ratio is called **Kullback–Leibler divergence** (D_{KL}):

$$D_{KL}(p||q) = E_p\left[\ln\frac{p(X)}{q(X)}\right] = \sum_{i=1}^{n}p(x_i)\ln\frac{p(x_i)}{q(x_i)} \tag{1.6}$$

D_{KL} is used to measure the difference between two PDFs of a system with the same random variable X. If p and q are the same, we have $D_{KL} = 0$. Cross entropy is another index to quantify the difference between two PDFs, and it is often used as a loss function in machine learning.

$$H(p, q) = -\sum_{i=1}^{n}p(x_i)\ln(q(x_i)) = D_{KL}(p||q) + H(p) \tag{1.7}$$

The following scenario is used to enable us to understand these formulae. On a big desk in a casino, a coin is used as a gambling machine. At the beginning of a game, a gambler asks to verify if the coin is fair and the request is permitted. The target PMD is $P(X) = \{1/2, 1/2\}$. After tossing the coin 10 000 times, the gambler finds the real PMD is $Q(X) = \{0.65, 0.35\}$. The D_{KL} of the two distributions is $D_{KL} = 0.5\ln(0.5/0.65)+0.5\ln(0.5/0.35) = 0.047$; and the cross entropy is obtained with $H(p,q) = -0.5\ln(0.65)-0.5\ln(0.35) = 0.740$. With the fair coin's entropy $H(p) = 0.693$ nit, we would be sure that equation (1.7) is correct. When two distributions of a system are the same, their cross entropy has the minimum value: $H(p)$. That is why cross entropy can be used as a loss function in model training for machine learning.

Kullback–Leibler divergence is not symmetry: $D_{KL}(p||q) \neq D_{KL}(q||p)$, and it is a positive number: $D_{KL}(p||q) \geqslant 0$. The first property is obvious, and the second property can be proved with $(x-1) \geqslant \ln(x)$ in a condition $x \geqslant 0$. Based on this information, we have $[q(x)/p(x)-1] \geqslant \ln[q(x)/p(x)]$ or $-\ln[q(x)/p(x)] \geqslant -[q(x)/p(x)-1]$, and then we get:

$$D_{KL}(p||q) = -\int_x p(x)\ln\left(\frac{q(x)}{p(x)}\right)dx \geqslant -\int_x p(x)\left(\frac{q(x)}{p(x)} - 1\right)dx = 0$$

Jensen–Shannon divergence (D_{JS}) is a symmetry divergence. You can calculate the D_{JS} of the unfair coin found by the gambler with equation (1.8) (using a discrete sum but not by an integration), and it should be 0.0128 nit. It is obvious that we have $0 \leqslant D_{JS}(p||q) \leqslant \ln(2)$. By replacing both $p/(p+q)$ and $q/(p+q)$ with 1.0 in the following equation, you can prove it, because those two fractions are less than 1.0

$$D_{JS}(p \parallel q) = \frac{1}{2}\int\left(p(x)\ln\left(\frac{2p(x)}{p(x) + q(x)}\right) + q(x)\ln\left(\frac{2q(x)}{p(x) + q(x)}\right)\right)dx \quad (1.8)$$

We know the univariate Gaussian distributions from equation (1.2). In computer vision projects, we also need to use **multivariate normal distributions** to create fake images. For mathematical convenience, we just handle a multivariate normal distribution system with three independent random variables x_1, x_2 and x_3 whose means are μ_1, μ_2 and μ_3 and standard deviations are σ_1, σ_2 and σ_3 respectively. Their variances construct a diagonal matrix Σ whose inverse matrix is Σ^{-1}

$$X = \begin{bmatrix} x_1 \\ x_2 \\ x_3 \end{bmatrix} \quad \Sigma = \begin{bmatrix} \sigma_1^2 & 0 & 0 \\ 0 & \sigma_2^2 & 0 \\ 0 & 0 & \sigma_3^2 \end{bmatrix} \quad \Sigma^{-1} = \begin{bmatrix} \frac{1}{\sigma_1^2} & 0 & 0 \\ 0 & \frac{1}{\sigma_2^2} & 0 \\ 0 & 0 & \frac{1}{\sigma_3^2} \end{bmatrix} \quad |\Sigma|^{1/2} = (\sigma_1^2\sigma_2^2\sigma_3^2)^{1/2}$$

$$p(X = x) = \prod_{i=1}^{3} N\left(x_i; \mu_i, \sigma_i^2\right) = \frac{1}{(2\pi)^{3/2}\,|\Sigma|^{1/2}}e^{-\frac{1}{2}(x-\mu)^T\Sigma^{-1}(x-\mu)} \quad (1.9)$$

If there is another multivariate normal distribution $q(X = x)$ whose means are zeros and the Σ matrix is a 3×3 identity matrix I, it is not difficult to obtain $D_{KL}(p||q)$ with all the above information (appendix A)

$$D_{KL}(p||q) = \frac{1}{2}\sum_{i=1}^{3}\left[\mu_i^2 + \sigma_i^2 - 1 - \ln\left(\sigma_i^2\right)\right] \quad (1.10)$$

1.1.3 Conditional probability and joint entropies

Sometimes there are two or more random variables in a system. Each of them has its own PDF. These variables combine together to create a joint PDF. For example, in a gamble machine there is a fair coin and fair dice, and they are independent. The dice number variable is X with a uniform probability mass function $P(X) = \{1/6, 1/6, 1/6, 1/6, 1/6, 1/6\}$; a variable about the coin's sides is Y with another uniform probability mass function $P(Y) = \{1/2, 1/2\}$. The joint PDF of the coin and the dice is also a uniform probability distribution $P(X, Y)$ with twelve statuses, and the probability of any status is equal to 1/12 as shown in table 1.1.

The sum of the six joint probabilities $p(x_i, y_1)$ on the first row titled 'Head(y_1)' is equal to $p(y_1) = 1/2$, and the sum of other six joint probabilities $p(x_i, y_2)$ on the second row for 'Tail(y_2)' is $p(y_2) = 1/2$, where $i = 1,2,...,6$. The coin's PMF $P(Y)$ is constructed by the two numbers in a 1D array: $P(Y) = \{p(y_1), p(y_1)\}$. The sum of a column titled 'One(x_1)' is $p(x_1) = 1/6$. The sum of each of the rest five columns is also equal to $p(x_i) = 1/6$ where $i = 2, 3, ..., 6$. The dice's PMF $P(X)$ is constructed by the six numbers in a 1D array: $P(X) = \{p(x_1), p(x_2), ..., p(x_6)\}$. The sum of all the 12 joint probabilities $p(x_i, y_j)$, the sum of the dice's six probabilities $p(x_i)$ and the sum of the coin's two probabilities $p(y_j)$ are all equal to one ($i = 1,2,...,6, j = 1,2$). $P(X)$ and $P(Y)$ are marginal probabilities.

A conditional probability of an event Y is the coin's probability when a dice event X has already happened or is known. It is written as $P(Y|X)$ for the probability of Y given X. For example, the dice was tossed with the digit five on its top, and then the coin will be tossed. The conditional probabilities of the coin are still half and half: $p(y_1|x_i = 5) = \frac{1}{2}$ and $p(y_2|x_i = 5) = \frac{1}{2}$ as shown in table 1.2. The conditional probability table $P(Y|X)$ could be obtained by normalizations of each of the six columns in table 1.1 by a $P(X)$ element at the bottom of the joint $P(X, Y)$ table respectively. Each of the 12 elements in the $P(Y|X)$ table 1.2 is the same: $\frac{1}{2}$. A conditional probability table $P(X|Y)$ could also be obtained by normalizations of each of the two rows of the joint $P(X, Y)$ table by a $P(Y)$ element on the right side respectively. Each of the 12 elements of the $P(X|Y)$ table 1.3 is also the same: 1/6 as

Table 1.1. Joint probabilities $P(X, Y)$ of a system with a fair coin and fair dice.

$P(X, Y)$ Coin side(Y)	Dice numbers (X)						$P(Y)$
	One(x_1)	Two(x_2)	Three(x_3)	Four(x_4)	Five(x_5)	Six(x_6)	
Head(y_1)	1/12	1/12	1/12	1/12	1/12	1/12	1/2
Tail(y_2)	1/12	1/12	1/12	1/12	1/12	1/12	1/2
$P(X)$	1/6	1/6	1/6	1/6	1/6	1/6	1

Table 1.2. Conditional possibilities $P(Y|X)$.

$P(Y|X)$ Coin side (Y)	Dice numbers (X)					
	One (x_1)	Two (x_2)	Three (x_3)	Four (x_4)	Five (x_5)	Six (x_6)
Head(y_1)	1/2	1/2	1/2	1/2	1/2	1/2
Tail (y_2)	1/2	1/2	1/2	1/2	1/2	1/2

Table 1.3. Conditional possibilities $P(X|Y)$.

$P(X\|Y)$ Coin side (Y)	Dice numbers(X)					
	One (x_1)	Two (x_2)	Three (x_3)	Four (x_4)	Five (x_5)	Six (x_6)
Head (y_1)	1/6	1/6	1/6	1/6	1/6	1/6
Tail (y_2)	1/6	1/6	1/6	1/6	1/6	1/6

Table 1.4. Probabilities of smokers among men and women on an island.

$P(Y\|X)$	Women (x_1)	Men (x_2)	$P(X,Y)$	x_1	x_2	$P(Y)$	$P(X\|Y)$	x_1	x_2
Smokers (y_1)	$p(y_1\|x_1) = 0.10$	$p(y_1\|x_2) = 0.30$	y_1	0.055	0.135	0.19	y_1	0.289	0.711
Non-smokers (y_2)	$p(y_2\|x_1) = 0.90$	$p(y_2\|x_2) = 0.70$	y_2	0.495	0.315	0.81	y_2	0.611	0.389
$P(X)$	0.55	0.45	$P(X)$	0.55	0.45	1.00			

shown in table 1.3. According to **Bayes' theorem**, the element-wise relationship among $p(x,y)$, $p(x|y)$, $p(y|x)$, $p(x)$ and $p(y)$ is set by equation (1.11).

$$p(y|x) = \frac{p(x,y)}{p(x)} = \frac{p(x|y)}{p(x)}p(y) \qquad (1.11)$$

In the above formula, $p(x)$ and $p(y)$ are marginal probabilities or prior probabilities, $p(x|y)$ is the likelihood of x given y, and $p(y|x)$ is the posterior probability of y given x. I use the following example to explain these probability names. Among the people on a small island, 55% (= $p(x_1)$) are women and 45% (= $p(x_2)$) are men. Among those women, 10% (= $p(y_1|x_1)$) are smokers, and among the men, 30% (= $p(y_1|x_2)$) are smokers. The variables for smokers and non-smokers are y_1 and y_2 respectively. From the sound and the smell in the air, you know a person is smoking. What is the probability that the smoker is a woman? To answer this question, we need to construct a posterior probability $P(X|Y)$ sub-table shown by three columns on the right side of in table 1.4 based on the above data. We start our work from a likelihood sub-table about $P(Y|X)$ constructed by the three columns on the left side of the table. Values in cells of the row 'Smokers(y_1)' and in cells of the marginal $P(X)$ row are known. Values in cells of the row 'Non-smokers(y_2)' are obtained logically. Among women on the island, 90% are non-smokers, and among men, 70% are non-smokers.

From the likelihood $P(Y|X)$ sub-table, we are able to construct the joint probability sub-table $P(X,Y)$ shown in the middle three columns of table 1.4. The values of four cells in the $P(X,Y)$ table are obtained according to equation (1.11) with $p(x,y) = p(y|x)p(x)$. Now we know that among all the people on the island, 5.5% of the smokers are women; 13.5% of the smokers are men; 49.5% of the non-smokers are women; and 31.5% of the non-smokers are men. The marginal possibilities $p(y_1)$ and $p(y_2)$ for smokers and non-smokers are 19% and 81% respectively. With the joint possibility sub-table, we can calculate the values in the four cells of the posterior probability $P(X|Y)$ shown on the right side of table 1.4. These calculations are also based on equation (1.11) with $p(x|y) = p(x,y)/p(y)$. For example, the probability of a smoker who is a woman is $p(x_1|y_1) = p(x_1, y_1) /p(y_1) = 28.9\%$.

The above explanations about the posterior probability calculations are very complex even for the simple question with four variables: men, women, smokers, non-smokers. Aren't they? Since we had limited life-time and limited resources, we only could explore a part of our world which is accessible for us. With information from the accessible data and Bayes' theorem, we could deduce information of the whole system. In the above simple example, the joint probability table $P(X, Y)$ is about the probabilities relative to the whole population on the island. The prior possibility table $P(Y|X)$ came from our investigation or exploration. It is about probabilities relative to each sub-population: men and women. The posterior probability table $P(X|Y)$ has information derived from the prior probability table and the joint probability table. It is about probabilities relative to each sub-group: smokers and non-smokers. In fact, it is not necessary to construct those three sub-tables shown in table 1.4. According to Bayes' theorem, we have $p(x_1|y_1) = p(y_1|x_1)p(x_1)/p(y_1) = p(y_1|x_1)p(x_1)/[p(y_1|x_1)p(x_1)+ p(y_1|x_2)p(x_2)] = 28.9\%$. You see that prior probabilities or likelihood are known data, and the posterior probability is the inference from these known data. From probabilities in table 1.4, we can calculate the joint entropy $H(X, Y)$, the prior conditional entropy $H(X|Y)$, the posterior conditional entropy $H(Y|X)$ and the mutual information $I(X, Y)$ with the following formulae

$$H(X, Y) = -\sum_{i=1}^{2}\sum_{j=1}^{2}p(x_i, y_j) \ln\left(p(x_i, y_j)\right) = 1 \tag{1.12}$$

$$H(X|Y) = -\sum_{i=1}^{2}\sum_{j=1}^{2}p(x_i, y_j) \ln\left(p(x_i|y_j)\right) = 0 \tag{1.13}$$

$$H(Y|X) = -\sum_{i=1}^{2}\sum_{j=1}^{2}p(x_i, y_j) \ln\left(p(y_i|x_j)\right) = 0.454 \tag{1.14}$$

$$I(X, Y) = I(Y, X) = \sum_{i=1}^{2}\sum_{j=1}^{2}p(x_i, y_j) \ln\left(\frac{p(y_i, x_j)}{p(y_i)p(x_j)}\right) = 0.032 \tag{1.15}$$

$$H(X) = -\sum_{j=1}^{2}p(x_j) \ln\left(p(x_j)\right) = 0.688 \tag{1.16}$$

$$H(Y) = -\sum_{j=1}^{2}p(y_j) \ln\left(p(y_j)\right) = 0.486 \tag{1.17}$$

$$I(X, Y) = H(X) - H(X|Y) = H(Y) - H(Y|X) = 0.032 \qquad (1.18)$$

$$H(X, Y) = H(X) + H(Y|X) = H(Y) + H(X|Y) = 1.142 \qquad (1.19)$$

If random variables X and Y are not independent, the mutual information $I(X, Y)$ is a positive number. Using tables 1.1–1.3, you will find that the mutual information I (X, Y) of the gambling machine with a fair coin and a fair dice is equal to zero. In chapter 6, the mutual information $I(X, Y)$ will enable us to control what images to generate.

1.1.4 Jensen's inequality

If a function $g(x)$ is a **convex function** in a range $x \in X$ with $E[g(X)]$ and $g[E(X)]$ are finite, then the average of the function's values in the range is bigger or equal to the function's value at the average of X: $E[g(X)] \geqslant g[E(X)]$. The PDF of x can be a normal distribution or another kind of distribution.

Example 01: There is a convex function $g(x) = x^2$ with $x \in [-1,1]$ and PDF $p(x) = 1/2$

$$\mu = E_p[X] = \overline{X} = \int_{-1}^{1} x p(x) dx = 0, \ g\left(E_p[X]\right) = (\mu)^2 = 0$$

$$E_p[g(X)] = \overline{X^2} = \int_{-1}^{1} x^2 p(x) dx = \frac{1}{3}, \qquad E_p[g(X)] \geqslant g\left(E_p[X]\right)$$

Example 02: There is another convex function $g(x) = -\ln(x)$ with $x \in [0.5, 4.5]$ and PDF $p(x) = 1/4$

$$\mu = E_p[X] = \int_{0.5}^{4.5} x p(x) dx = \frac{5}{2}, \ g(E_p[X]) = -\ln(\mu) = -\ln\left(\frac{5}{2}\right) = -0.92$$

$$E_p[g(X)] = -\int_{0.5}^{4.5} \ln(x) p(x) dx = -0.78, \ E_p[g(X)] \geqslant g\left(E_p[X]\right)$$

1.1.5 Maximum likelihood estimation and over fitting

In machine learning, we need to know probability density functions of datasets for image generation. From a PDF of a dataset, we can generate new data (images). In most cases, we only have data (images), how can we find a PDF hidden in the dataset? Maximum likelihood estimation (MLE) is a method which allows us to find a PDF in a dataset if we have a set of data $\{x_i\}$, where $i = 1, 2, \ldots, n$. For example, the dataset is about body heights of students, and the data in the dataset follow a Gaussian distribution $N(x; \mu, \sigma)$. Using MLE, we will find the PDF's parameters: μ and σ. Likelihood is the probability of an event which has happened with an unknown PDF. The body height x_i of a student is a sample from a likelihood function $N(x;\mu,\sigma)$ in which each student's body height is independent. The likelihood function is the joint probability of the dataset:

$$\text{likelihood}(\mu, \sigma^2 | x_1, x_2, \ldots x_n) = \prod_{i=1}^{n} N(x_i; \mu, \sigma^2) \quad (1.20)$$

The above likelihood function should be maximized by optimizing its two parameters: μ, and σ^2. For mathematics convenience in the Python and PyTorch coding environment, we need to minimize the negative log likelihood, and use it as a **loss function** $L = -\ln\left(\prod_{i=1}^{n} N(x_i; \mu, \sigma^2)\right)$ as shown in equation (1.21). Then from $\partial L/\partial \mu = 0$ and $\partial L/\partial \sigma = 0$, it is easy to get the PDF's mean $\mu = \overline{X}$, and the variance $\sigma^2 = \overline{X^2} - \overline{X}^2$

$$L = \frac{n}{2}\ln(2\pi) + \frac{n}{2}\ln(\sigma^2) + \frac{1}{2\sigma^2}\sum_{i=1}^{n}(x_i - \mu)^2 \quad (1.21)$$

The mean squared error (MSE) loss function can be derived from the maximum likelihood estimation. For a set of data pairs $\{x_i, y_i\}$, we assume that each target y_i of a given x_i is a random number coming from an independent Gaussian distribution $p_i(y_i|x_i) = \mathbb{N}(y_i; \mu_i, \sigma^2)$. All those Gaussian distributions have the same variance ($\sigma^2 = 1/\beta$), where β has a name 'precision', and the mean of each Gaussian distribution is a predicted value (μ_i) of the target y_i, where $i = 1, 2, \ldots, n$. We suppose μ is a linear function of weights: $\mu_i = f(x_i, W) = w_0 + \sum_{j=1}^{m} w_j x_i^j$ or $\mu = X \cdot W$.

$$\begin{bmatrix} \mu_1 \\ \mu_2 \\ \cdots \\ \mu_n \end{bmatrix} = \begin{bmatrix} 1 & x_1 & \cdots & x_1^m \\ 1 & x_2 & \cdots & x_2^m \\ \cdots & \cdots & \cdots & \cdots \\ 1 & x_n & \cdots & x_n^m \end{bmatrix} \cdot \begin{bmatrix} w_0 \\ w_1 \\ \cdots \\ w_m \end{bmatrix} \quad (1.22)$$

From the joint likelihood of these random variables $\text{likelihood}(Y|X) = \prod_{i=1}^{n} p_i(y_i|x_i)$, we have a loss function $L = -\ln\left(\prod_{i=1}^{n} \frac{1}{\sqrt{2\pi\sigma^2}} e^{-\frac{1}{2}\left(\frac{y_i-\mu_i}{\sigma}\right)^2}\right)$

$$L = \frac{\beta}{2}\sum_{i=1}^{n}(\mu_i - y_i)^2 - \frac{n}{2}\ln(\beta) + \frac{n}{2}\ln(2\pi) \quad (1.23)$$

To obtain W and β, we need to maximize the likelihood function. The reults are the same to minimize the loss function. From $\nabla_W L = 0$ and $\nabla_\beta L = 0$, we get:

$$W = (X^T \cdot X)^{-1} \cdot X^T \cdot Y \quad (1.24)$$

$$\beta = \frac{1}{N}\sum_{i=1}^{N}(\mu_i - y_i)^2 \qquad (1.25)$$

If $\beta = 1$, equation (1.23) becomes a MSE loss function. The constant in the loss function doesn't affect the loss function's gradients. In fact, in Ridge regression (Hilt *et al* 1977) we add a constant to the MSE loss function to fight overfitting issues by adjusting a parameter λ in $L = \frac{1}{2}\sum_{i=1}^{N}(\hat{y}_i - y_i)^2 + \frac{\lambda}{2}||W||^2$, where $||W||^2 = w_0^2 + w_1^2 + \ldots + w_M^2$

$$W = (X^T \cdot X + \lambda I)^{-1} X^T \cdot Y \qquad (1.26)$$

The code in project 1.1.1 is an application of using MLE for a nonlinear regression about $y = x^4 + x^2 - 1$, which is defined in Cell 01 of a Jupyter notebook in VS Code as a lambda function named f. If you are having issues understanding the codes in the project, you can skip them and just remember the overfitting issue shown in figure 1.1. We will not use the codes again. The tools for the project are libraries from NumPy and Matplotlib. **NumPy** is an open-source Python library for scientific computing and data analysis. From the library, we can import many high-level mathematical functions for linear algebra and nonlinear algebra calculations. Since its core is a well-optimized C code, NumPy is easy to handle with the speed of compiled codes. **Matplotlib** is a data visualization Python library. There are many Matplotlib functions for use in creating different kinds of plots.

Nonlinear regression results are shown in figure 1.1. The green curve in the figure has 101 points generated by the function as a ground truth for the regression

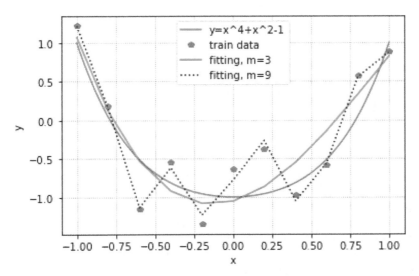

Figure 1.1. Nonlinear regression results with maximum likelihood estimation algorithm. Overfitting can be seen from the dashed zig-zag line (*m*: the order of a univariate polynomial function for nonlinear regression).

results. The eleven blue dots come from a train dataset used for the nonlinear regression. The y value of each blue dot at its x position is assumed to be a random number with an independent Gaussian distribution whose mean is μ according to equation (1.22). All the eleven Gaussian distributions have the same variance. Based on equation (1.25), a function y_hat defined in Cell 02 returns mu and W. The inputs of the function are 11 data pairs $\{x_i, y_i\}$ of the train dataset, and the order (m) is the univariate polynomial (equation (1.22))

```
# Project 1.1.1: Nonlinear regressions over fitting------------------Python v3.6
import numpy as np
from numpy.linalg import inv       # for matrix inverse
import matplotlib.pyplot as plt
n = 11    # number of train data pairs (xi,yi) for nonlinear regression
scale=0.7 # The amplitude of noise added to the 11 train data pairs (xi,yi)
f = lambda x: x**4+x**2-1 # function for a smooth curve as a ground Truth
x_true = np.linspace(-1.0,1,101) # The ground Truth curve's X
y_true = f(x_true)              # The ground Truth curve's Y=f(x)
x_train = np.linspace(-1,1,n)    # Train data X
y_train = (f(x_train)+          # Train data Y: noisy curve
           np.random.uniform(-scale, scale, size=x_train.shape))
# Cell 02: A function for calculations of y_hat (mu) and Weights--------------
def y_hat(x, y, m):    # m: the order of a univariate polynomial (Eq.1.1.22)
    ones = np.ones(len(x)) # ones=[1,1,...,1], len(ones) = n = 11
    for i in range(1,m+1):
        ones = np.vstack((ones, x**i))
    X = ones.T
    W = inv(X.T@X)@(X.T@y)       #--------------------Eq.1.1.24
    mu = X@W                     #--------------------Eq.1.1.22
    return mu, W
Y3hat, W3 = y_hat(x_train, y_train, 3)
Y9hat, W9 = y_hat(x_train, y_train, 9)
# Cell 03: Showing regression results-----------------------------------------
fig, ax = plt.subplots()
ax.plot(x_true, y_true, 'g-', label='y=x^4+x^2-1')
ax.plot(x_train, y_train, 'bp', label='train data')
ax.plot(x_train, Y3hat, 'r-', label='fitting, m=3')
ax.plot(x_train, Y9hat, 'k:', label='fitting, m=9')
ax.set(xlabel='x', ylabel='y')
ax.grid(color='g', linestyle=':')
ax.legend();
print(((Y3hat-y_train)**2).mean()) #beta3=0.1247
print(((Y9hat-y_train)**2).mean()) #beta9=0.0012
#-----------------------------------------------------------------------The End
```

Codes in Cell 03 are used to display the nonlinear regression results. Using an order $m = 3$ univariate polynomial function to numerically simulate an order 4 univariate polynomial function, we know the regression result (the red curve) would not be good enough. In real world cases, we often do not know the ground truth as shown by the green curve in figure 1.1. We have to try many times to get what we need. With an order $m = 9$ univariate polynomial, we obtained a dashed zig-zag line which goes through each blue dot. From the black dashed line, we see an overfitting issue. Although the loss function value or beta value is close to zero, the order 9 nonlinear regression result is worser than the result of order 3. Overfitting is a big issue in machine learning. We will try to avoid it. The email symbol @ in Cell 02 denotes a dot production between two matrices in algebra.

1.1.6 Application of expectation-maximization algorithm to find a PDF

In many machine learning projects we need to find a PDF of a dataset in a high dimensional space. The **expectation-maximization algorithm** (Dempster *et al* 1977) is a useful method to perform maximum likelihood estimation for these projects. In a scenario where a teacher gives his students a 1D dataset in a csv text file for homework to find a PDF, the first thing the student should do is plot a histogram of the data with the codes in project 1.1.2. From the histogram shown in figure 1.2(A), the student can guess that the teacher generated the data file with three Gaussian distributions, and their contributions to a DPF of the dataset are the same (weight = 1/3). From the histogram, the student can also guess that the means and variances of the three normal distributions are: [−5.5, 0.0, 4.0], [1.0, 1.0, 1.0]. If the student finished the homework just by guessing, the teacher would not award the student a pass.

The dataset $X = \{x_1, x_2, ..., x_n\}$ in the project could be generated from a 3D latent space $Z = \{z_1, z_2, z_3\}$. The likelihood of each point (x_j) in the dataset is obtained by equation (1.27) with those parameters guessed about the three Gaussian distributions, and they are listed in table 1.5, in which $P(Z)$ is for marginal probability with $p(z_i) = 1/3$. Each element of $P(Z)$ is the weight of a Gaussian distribution contributed to the PDF of the dataset X. The parameters of the three Gaussian distributions and their weights would be updated at each step or epoch of model training of the project.

$$p(x_j|z_i) = \frac{1}{\sqrt{2\pi\sigma_i^2}} e^{-\frac{1}{2}\left(\frac{x_j-\mu_i}{\sigma_i}\right)^2}, \ (i = 1, 2, 3, j = 1, 2, ..., n) \qquad (1.27)$$

Each point x_j could be treated as a random number with a marginal possibility $p(x_j)$ which is obtained with equation (1.28). The joint probability density function of

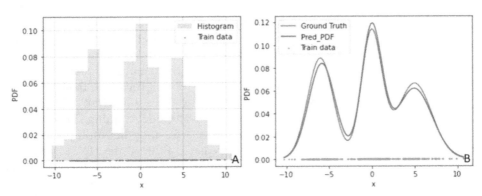

Figure 1.2. (A) Histogram of 1D dataset from a csv file with 300 numbers (output of Cell 02). (B) A PDF of the 1D dataset found by expectation-maximization algorithm (output of Cell 04).

Table 1.5. Likelihood $P(X|Z)$ and marginal possibilities $P(Z)$.

$P(X|Z)$	x_1	x_2	...	x_n	$P(Z)$
z_1	$p(x_1|z_1)$	$p(x_2|z_1)$	...	$p(x_n|z_1)$	$p(z_1) = 1/3$
z_2	$p(x_1|z_2)$	$p(x_2|z_2)$	...	$p(x_n|z_2)$	$p(z_2) = 1/3$
z_3	$p(x_1|z_3)$	$p(x_2|z_3)$	...	$p(x_n|z_3)$	$p(z_3) = 1/3$

Table 1.6. Posterior possibility $P(Z|X)$ and marginal possibilities $P(X)$.

$P(Z|X)$	x_1	x_2	...	x_n
z_1	$p(z_1|x_1)$	$p(z_1|x_2)$	...	$p(z_1|x_n)$
z_2	$p(z_2|x_1)$	$p(z_2|x_2)$	...	$p(z_2|x_n)$
z_3	$p(z_3|x_1)$	$p(z_3|x_2)$	...	$p(z_3|x_n)$
$P(X)$	$p(x_1)$	$p(x_2)$	...	$p(x_n)$

the dataset is $P(X) = p(x_1)p(x_2)...p(x_n)$. The loss function of model training for the dataset is:

$$L = -\ln(P(X)) = \ln \prod_{i=1}^{n} p(x_j) = -\sum_{j=1}^{n} \ln\left(\sum_{i=1}^{m=3} p(x_j|z_i)p(z_i)\right) \qquad (1.28)$$

Then we can calculate the posterior possibilities $P(Z|X)$ according to equation (1.29). The calculation results are shown in table 1.6 in which $p(z_i|x_j)$ is the posterior possibility at z_i of a given x_j

$$p(z_i|x_j) = \frac{p(x_j|z_i)p(z_i)}{p(x_j)} = \frac{p(x_j|z_i)p(z_i)}{\sum_{k=1}^{3} p(x_j|z_k)p(z_k)} \qquad (1.29)$$

By setting the gradients of the loss function to be equal to zero, we can obtain optimized parameters of the three Gaussian distributions and their weights $P(Z)$. It is easy to get μ_i and σ_i. There is a trick to getting $p(z_i)$. With the condition $p(z_1)+p(z_2)+p(z_3) = 1$ in table 1.5, we know that only two of the three marginal probabilities are independent. Using derivations in appendix B, we obtain formulae from equations (1.30)–(1.32). From them, we will update those three Gaussian distributions' parameters for tables 1.5–1.6 in the second epoch of model training. This updating process repeats many times ($n\_epochs = 5000$) in a for-loop iteration on line 02 of Cell 04. The blue curve in figure 1.2(B) is a predicted PDF of the 1D dataset. After getting the student's homework, the teacher told the student that three Gaussian distributions with equal weights were used to generate the data of the csv file. Codes to generated the csv file are listed in Cell 06. The original parameters of these Gaussian distributions were $\mu = [-6, 0, 5]$ and $\sigma = [1.5, 1.2, 2]$. For comparison, the student drew the true PDF curve (green curve) in figure 1.2(B). From the simple project about finding a PDF of a dataset, we now know how to calculate posterior possibilities for data predications. In chapter 5, we will use posterior possibilities to generate images. You can skip the codes if they are not easy to understand, because this is not the way to write machine learning codes

$$p(z_i) = \frac{1}{n} \sum_{j=1}^{n} p(z_i | x_j) \tag{1.30}$$

$$\mu_i = \frac{\sum_{j=1}^{n} x_j p(z_i | x_j)}{\sum_{j=1}^{n} p(z_i | x_j)} \tag{1.31}$$

$$\sigma_i^2 = \frac{\sum_{j=1}^{n} (x_j - \mu_i)^2 p(z_i | x_j)}{\sum_{j=1}^{n} p(z_i | x_j)} \tag{1.32}$$

```python
# Project 1.1.2: Application of Expectation-Maximization Algorithm----Python v3.6
import numpy as np; import pandas as pd; import matplotlib.pyplot as plt
X = np.loadtxt('d:/TeachersData.csv', skiprows=1, delimiter=',')   #input data
n_samples = X.size      #n_samples=300
# Cell 02: Data visualization with a histogram------------------------Cell 02
fig, ax = plt.subplots(figsize=(5,4))
ax.hist(X, bins=15, density=True, color = "skyblue", label="Histogram")
ax.scatter(X, [0] * len(X), s=5, c='r', marker='.', label="Train data")
ax.set(xlabel="x", ylabel="PDF", ylim=[-0.005,0.11]); ax.legend()
ax.grid(which='major', axis='both', color='g', linestyle=':')
plt.show()
# Cell 03: Set parameters of 3 Gaussians to simulate the True PDF-------Cell 03
k = 3       # Using 3 Gaussian distributions to simulate a true PDF
u = np.array([-5.5, 0, 3.5])       # 3 means by guess
variances = np.ones((k))           # 3 variances by guess
s = variances**0.5                 # 3 standard deviations
pz = np.array([1/3, 1/3, 1/3])     # marginal possibility P(Z)=[1/3, 1/3, 1/3]
def pdf(x, u, s):                  # Gaussian distribution PDF
    pi = np.pi
    return 1/(2*pi*s**2)**0.5*np.exp(-0.5*((x-u)/s)**2)
bins = np.linspace(np.min(X),np.max(X), n_samples)
# Cell 04: Fitting with Expectation-maximization algorithm--------------Cell 04
n_epochs = 5000
for step in range(n_epochs):
```

```
    likelihood = np.empty((k, len(X)))      #likelihood p(xj|zi) for Table 1.5
    for i in range(k):
        likelihood[i] = pdf(X, u[i], s[i]) # p(xj|zi), i=1,2,3, j=1,2,..,n
    px = np.sum(         # px: marginal possibility: px=[p(x1), p(x2),...,p(xn)]
            [likelihood[i] * pz[i] for i in range(k)], axis=0)
    b = np.empty((k, len(X)))
    for i in range(k):      #posterior possibility b for p(zi|xj) for Table 1.6
      p_xj_zi = likelihood[i] * pz[i] #p(xj, zi)=p(xj|zi)p(zi), j=1,2,...,n
      b[i] = p_xj_zi / px            #p(zi|xj)=p(xj, zi)/p(xj)
      # update mean and variance
      u[i] = np.sum(b[i] * X) / (np.sum(b[i])+1e-7)         #----------Eq.1.31
      variances[i] = np.sum(b[i] * np.square(X - u[i])) / (np.sum(b[i])+1e-7)
      s[i] = variances[i]**0.5                #--------------Eq.1.32
      # update the weights
      pz[i] = np.mean(b[i])                    #---------------Eq.1.30
# Cell 05: Show fitting results--------------------------------------------Cell 05
fig, ax = plt.subplots(figsize=(5,4))
y = pdf(bins, -6, 1.5)/3+pdf(bins, 0, 1.2)/3+pdf(bins, 5, 2)/3  #---Ground Truth
ax.set(xlabel="x", ylabel="PDF")
ax.scatter(X, [0] * len(X), s=5, c='r', marker='.', label="Train data")
ax.plot(bins, y, color='g', label='True PDF')
plt.plot(bins, pz[0]*pdf(bins, u[0], s[0])+
            pz[1]*pdf(bins, u[1], s[1])+
            pz[2]*pdf(bins, u[2], s[2]),
            'b', label='fit PDF')
plt.legend(loc='upper left');
print('original means=', -6,0,5)
print('fitting means=', u)
print('original sigmas=', 1.5,1.2,2)
print('fitting sigms=', s)
#--------------------------------The End----------------------------------------
# Cell 06: Data Generated by 3 Gaussians for Expectation-maximization fitting
import numpy as np; import pandas as pd; import matplotlib.pyplot as plt
n_samples = 100
k = 3      # Using 3 Gausian distributions to simulate a true pdf
u1, s1 = -6, 1.5 #u: mean; s: sigma for 3 Normal distributions to generate data
u2, s2 = 0, 1.2
u3, s3 = 5, 2
x1 = list(np.random.normal(loc=u1, scale=s1, size=n_samples)) #len(x1)=100
x2 = list(np.random.normal(loc=u2, scale=s2, size=n_samples)) #len(x2)=100
x3 = list(np.random.normal(loc=u3, scale=s3, size=n_samples)) #len(x3)=100
X = np.array(x1 + x2 + x3)  # len(X)=300, concatenation of x1, x2 and x3
my_DF = pd.DataFrame({'X': X})
my_DF.to_csv('d:/TeachersData.csv', index=False)
#------------------------------------------------------------------------------
```

1.2 Using a gradient descent algorithm for linear regression

We will finish a linear regression project by using a gradient descent algorithm, the way to write machine learning codes. In project 1.2.1, we need to find a linear relationship between two temperature scales: Fahrenheit (F) and Celsius (C). One array is for temperatures measured in Celsius: $C = [-20, -15, -10, -5, 0, 5, 10, 15, 20]$, and another array is generated by using a function F = 32 + 9C/5 for temperatures in Fahrenheit: $F = [-4, 5, 14, 23, 32, 41, 50, 59, 68]$. This is very easy homework. Just type those numbers in array C and array F into two columns of a Microsoft Excel sheet, a straight line and a linear regression function $F = 30.0 + 1.8C$ would be displayed on screen by a few mouse clicks. But we have to do extra work by using a Jupyter Notebook file in VS Code as an integrated development environment (IDE).

Many computer vision projects are very complex. They are not 'as easy as a cakes, but 'as hard as a nut'. We have to have to use powerful tools to solve problems in those projects. Jupyter Notebook is an open-source web-based interactive computational environment which supports a wide range of programming languages, including Python, R, Julia, and more. Jupyter Notebook files are saved with a suffix '*ipynb*' and can be opened in any web browser, where users can run codes in cells to get results. VS Code is a free, open-source code editor. It supports a wide range of programming languages, including Python, C++, JavaScript, etc. It provides features such as syntax highlighting, debugging, code completion, and GitHub integration. In a Jupyter notebook, we can create a mathematical model or models with parameters of millions or even billions to extract information hiding in a large amount of data for computer vision projects. The data can be images, videos, voices, text, time series graphs such as stock prices. The sizes of the data files can be a few hundred megabytes (MB) to many gigabytes (GB). It is impossible and unnecessary for us to type those data into our computer. We only need to know how to download data files into computers. Python and PyTorch have many libraries or tools to use to help with data input into VS code.

Usually, a machine learning model has many neural layers. Those digital neurons are different from the biological neurons in our brains. In a computer vision model, a neuron layer is a set of artificial neurons that process input data and produce output data. Those layers can be treated as a series of filters that successively extract and refine the information contained in the input data. The digital neurons are mathematical operators. Each neuron layer has some learnable parameters. All of these parameters in a model are automatically updated during model training, and they are called model **parameters**. For example, finishing the project about the relationship between array C and array F, we will obtain a slope 1.8 and an intercept or bias 32.0 in a linear function. They are the linear model's two parameters. To obtain a model's parameters by model training, we need a criterion to evaluate how good the model is by comparing the model's outputs with the original data. A criterion is also called a loss function in machine learning. In each step or epoch of model training, we use a gradient descent algorithm to reduce the value of the loss function. We need to set learning rate and training steps (epochs) to train the model. These parameters set by ourselves are different from model parameters, and we call them the model's **hyperparameters**. A train process could take a few seconds, hours, days or even weeks. The training time is dependent on data size, codes and computer hardware. One or more graphics processing units (GPU) in a computer are needed to reduce model training time. Optimized for parallel processing, GPUs can perform many computation tasks simultaneously.

It is easy to find the minimum or maximum of a function $y = f(x)$ with $y' = 0$. We can set the gradient of a function such as $y = x^2 + 2x + 3$ to be equal to zero ($y' = 2x + 2 = 0$) to find the function's minimum at $x = -1$. Usually, there are hundreds, thousands, even billions of parameters distributed in many neural layers of a model. Most of those parameters are in arrays or matrices, not scalars. It is not easy for us to explicitly write down formulae of a loss function's gradients for those arrays. You know how hard it is to get equations (1.30)–(1.32) from the loss function (equation (1.28)) in appendix B. Now, we create a *Jupyter Notebook* file and name it 'LinearRegression.ipynb' in VS Code. In the notebook, we can add many cells. In each cell, we write codes to do a specific job. Codes in all the cells are like specific machines on an assembly line. Working together, these codes can handle a huge amount of data. Codes in the first cell of all projects in the book are used to import Python and PyTorch libraries as tools. Hyperparameters for model training are also listed in the first cell. Codes in Cell 02 of each project are used to read and pack data. In Cell 02 of project 1.2.1, a 'comma separated values' text file 'd:/C2F.csv' is loaded into computer memory.

```python
# Project 1.2.1, Linear Regression by Gradient Descent Algorithm------Python v3.6
import numpy as np                #a library for data operations------line 01
import matplotlib.pyplot as plt   #a library for data visualization---line 02
n_epochs = 20000                  # training steps
lr = 5e-3                         # learn_rate
# Cell 02: Input data from a csv file ----------------------------------Cell 02
CF = np.loadtxt('d:/C2F.csv', skiprows=1, delimiter=',')   #----line 01
C = CF[:, 0]                                                #----line 02
F = CF[:, 1]                                                #----line 03
print('C =', C)                                             #----line 04
print('F =', F)                                             #----line 05
X = np.vstack((C, np.ones(len(C)))).T                       #----line 06
print('X=', '\n', X)
Y= F.reshape(-1,1)
print('Y=', '\n', Y)
# Cell 03: Definition of a model, a loss function and a gradient function--------
def model(X, W):            #X.shape=(9,2), W.shape=(2,1)
    return X@W              #(X@W).shape=(9,1)
def criterion(y_hat, Y):    # MSE oss function
    return ((y_hat-Y)**2).mean()
def gradient(X, Y, y_hat):  #gradient of MSE to W
    return 2*(X.T@(y_hat-Y))/X.shape[0]
#-------------------------------------------------------------------------------
```

With codes on line 01–02 of Cell 01 (the line number starting with a hash symbol # is line 0), two Python libraries are imported for the linear regression project. To save pages of typing, we will use them with their abbreviated names: np and plt. A NumPy function '*np.loadtxt*' in Cell 02 loads a csv file on hard disk and stores data as a 9×2 array named 'CF' in the computer memory. If you open the csv file with MS Excel, you will see two columns and each column has a name. We do not need the column names in model training, so we set the option *skiprows = 1* for the function on line 01 of Cell 02. If you open the file in a text editor, you will see all data are separated by commas, so we set another option of the function to read data with *delimiter* = ',', The second and third line of Cell 02 are used to separate the 9×2 NumPy array into a 1D array C and a 1D array F. Finally array C and array F are printed on screen with codes on the fourth and fifth lines. Checking the numbers of the two arrays on screen, you need to make sure that there are no mistakes in data loading.

On the sixth line of Cell 2, the length of the C array is obtained with a NumPy function $np.len(C)$. From this number, a 1D ONES array is created by another NumPpy function $np.ones(len(C))$. Each element of the ONES array is equal to 1.0. Array C and the ONES array are vertically stacked into a 2×9 array which is then transposed into a 9×2 array X as shown in equation (1.33). The Python function $reshape(-1,1)$ changes the shape of array F from 1D to 9×1. With '-1' in the reshape function, the computer automatically counts the row or column numbers

$$X = \begin{bmatrix} x_{0,0} & 1 \\ x_{1,0} & 1 \\ \cdots & \cdots \\ x_{8,0} & 1 \end{bmatrix} = \begin{bmatrix} -20 & 1 \\ -15 & 1 \\ \cdots & \cdots \\ 20 & 1 \end{bmatrix}, \quad Y = \begin{bmatrix} y_0 \\ y_1 \\ \cdots \\ y_8 \end{bmatrix} = \begin{bmatrix} -4 \\ 5 \\ \cdots \\ 68 \end{bmatrix}, \quad \hat{y} = \begin{bmatrix} x_{0,0} & 1 \\ x_{1,0} & 1 \\ \cdots & \cdots \\ x_{8,0} & 1 \end{bmatrix} \cdot \begin{bmatrix} w_0 \\ w_1 \end{bmatrix} \quad (1.33)$$

To obtain a linear relationship ($F = kC + b$) about the two 1D arrays, we need two parameters: the slope k and the intercept b. For mathematical convenience, we pack them into a weight array $W = [w_0, w_1]^T = [k, b]^T$. The superscript T on an array means a transpose operation to the array, so the weight array has two rows and one column. The model of the project is defined as y_hat = $X@W$ on the second line of Cell 03, where X is a 9×2 array (equation (1.33)). The first column of array X is the array C in a column, and each element of its second column is equal to 1.0. The @ operation result of X and W gives us an array y_hat with a shape of 9×1, and each element of y_hat is a prediction of the model. Each parameter of array W is initialized to be zero by a code on line 03 of Cell 04. With these settings, we obtain the initial prediction array y_hat with all nine elements to be zeros at epoch = 0. We need the model's prediction y_hat to be as close as to the target Y by using a MSE criterion or loss function during model training.

$$L(X, w) = \frac{1}{(n+1)} \sum_{i=0}^{n} (\hat{y}_i - y_i)^2 \quad (1.34)$$

$$\nabla L = \begin{bmatrix} \dfrac{\partial L}{\partial w_0} \\ \dfrac{\partial L}{\partial w_1} \end{bmatrix} = \frac{2}{n+1} \begin{bmatrix} x_{0,0} & x_{1,0} & \cdots & x_{n,0} \\ 1 & 1 & \cdots & 1 \end{bmatrix} \cdot \begin{bmatrix} \hat{y}_0 - y_0 \\ \hat{y}_1 - y_1 \\ \cdots \\ \hat{y}_{n-1} - y_{n-1} \end{bmatrix} \quad (1.35)$$

The formula of the loss function and the formula of the gradient of the loss function to the weights are shown in equation (1.34) and (1.35), where $n = 9$ (appendix C). The MSE loss function sets a 3D digital valley with a lowest point, or a minimum of zero. The weight matrix is then updated in a direction opposite to the direction of the gradient of the loss function: $w_{i+1} = w_i - lr \cdot \nabla L$, where '*lr*' is a small number for learning rate. In this way, the model can be trained in each epoch with a step of '*lr*' to approach the lowest point. This is an optimization algorithm to train models and it is called the 'gradient descent algorithm'.

In Cell 03, three functions are defined according to equations (1.33)–(1.35). They are the model, the MSE criterion and the gradient function. A square array operation in the criterion function is not a regular mathematic operation in linear algebra. There are many of this kind of non-algebra operations in NumPy and PyTorch for element-wise operations without for-loops to accelerate calculations. The learning rate hyperparameter in Cell 01 should be set before model training. If the learning rate is too small, the model training may take longer to reach its minimum. Or if the learning rate is too big, the model's loss values may oscillate around the loss function's minimum, and the training process will never be finished. With an optimized learning rate, the training loss would decrease significantly at the beginning of model training, and then decreases slowly. We will use variable learning rates by using learning rate schedulers provided by PyTorch later.

```
# Cell 04: Definition of the training function----------------------------------
from tqdm import trange
def fit(x, y, epochs, learn_rate):
    W = np.zeros((x.shape[1], 1))   #x.shape[1]=2
    progress_bar = trange(epochs)
    for i in progress_bar:
        y_hat = model(x,W)
        loss = criterion(y_hat, y)
        progress_bar.set_description(f"loss={loss.item():.9f}" )
        progress_bar.set_postfix({'k': W[0,0], 'd': W[1,0]})
        W -= learn_rate*gradient(x, y, y_hat)
    return W
W = fit(X, Y, n_epochs, lr)
#---------------------------------------------------------------------------------
```

A fit function for the linear regression project is defined in Cell 04. This function needs four inputs. The first two are input data with specific array shapes shown in equation (1.33). The remaining two are the training epochs and learning rate. They are hyperparameters of the model. A small Python module *tqdm* is used to show a progress bar during model training. For a big computer vision project, model running time may be hours or even weeks. This tool will tell us how long we should wait. In a for-loop of the fit function with a progress bar, the model's prediction y_hat and loss function values are calculated. On the progress bar, we can see the epoch, the loss, the slope w[0,0] and the intercept w[1,0]. Then the weight array is updated with the gradient descent algorithm. After model training, the fit function returns the weight array. This fit function is used on the last line of Cell 04, and its output is the weight array. This is a simple machine learning project with 20 000 training epochs. My computer finishes calculations of the project in less than 24 s. Later, you will see that big projects could take more than 60 min for 20 epochs. Even for the model training with 20 000 epochs, the slope of the linear regression is still about 10^{-8} less the 1.80. If the learning rate is bigger than 7×10^{-3}, the linear regression would fail to find the right slope and intercept. After copying and pasting Cell 01 to 04 to your VS code notebook and running them, you will finish the linear regression project, and will find the two parameters of the model.

Using codes in Cell 05 to replace codes in Cell 04, we can see a trace of the loss function in a 3D digital space created by codes in Cell 06. From the trace of the loss function in the 3D digital valley shown in figure 1.3, we can see how the program automatically finds the minimum point of the valley. Since this is a simple project model with only two parameters, it is possible to display the surface of the digital valley in a 3D space with the x-axis for the intercept b, y-axis for the slope k, and z-axis for the loss values. Models in big machine learning projects have millions, even billions, of parameters, we can't see their loss surfaces directly with our eyes. In the training function defined in Cell 05, a block memory is reserved for a floating array Z on the third line of the function. If the hyperparameter for epochs is equal to 20 000, the array Z will have 20 000 rows and three columns. In each training step or epoch, the slope, the intercept and a loss value would be stored in a row of the array Z. After model training, the function returns the array Z which recorded the trace of the loss values during model training.

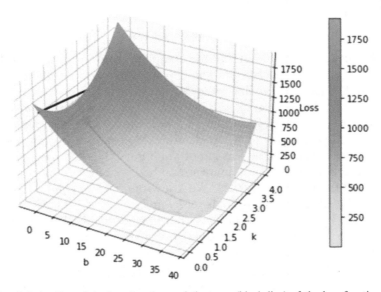

Figure 1.3. The digital valley of the loss function and the trace (black line) of the loss function in 20 000 training steps.

```
# Cell 05 Training data for a 3D surface plot. Using Cell 05 to replace Cell 04
from tqdm import trange
def train3d(x, y, epochs, learn_rate):
    Z = np.empty((epochs, 3))   # to record [[k, b, loss], []...[]]-----line 3
    w = np.zeros((x.shape[1], 1))   # to initialize w -----------x.shape[1]=2
    progress_bar = trange(epochs)
    for i in progress_bar:
        Z[i, 0] = w[0,0]          # slope k
        Z[i, 1] = w[1,0]          # intercept b
        y_hat = model(x,w)
        loss = criterion(y_hat, y)
        Z[i, 2] = loss
        progress_bar.set_description(f"loss={loss.item():.5f}" )
        progress_bar.set_postfix({'k': w[0,0], 'd': w[1,0]})
        w -= learn_rate*gradient(x, y, y_hat)
    return Z
Z = train3d(X, Y, epochs=n_epochs, learn_rate=lr)
#Cell 06: Plot a 3D surface with data from training----------------------Cell 06
fig, ax = plt.subplots(subplot_kw={"projection": "3d"}, figsize=(16,6))
b_col = np.float32(np.linspace(-2, 38, 801))
k_row = np.float32(np.linspace(0, 4, 401))
b, k = np.meshgrid(b_col, k_row)               #--------------------line 04
L = np.empty((len(k_row), len(b_col)))
w = np.zeros((X.shape[1], 1))
for i, ki in enumerate(k_row):
    for j, bj in enumerate(b_col):
        w = [[ki], [bj]]
        y_hat = model(X,w)
        L[i,j] = criterion(y_hat, Y)     # creating a loss surface
surf = ax.plot_surface(b, k, L, cmap='cool')   #loss surface
ax.plot3D(Z[:,1], Z[:,0], Z[:,2], 'k-', lw=2, label='loss')   #loss trace
ax.set(xlabel='b', ylabel='k', zlabel='Loss')
plt.colorbar(surf, shrink=0.8);
#----------------------------- The End ------------------------------------
```

Although codes in Cell 06 are a little complex, the outputs of the cell shown in figure 1.3 are easy to understand. The colored surface is the digital valley's top surface, and the black zig-zag line is the loss function's trace in 20 000 epochs. If you choose a smaller learning rate, the learning trace would be a smooth line. To understand the code in Cell 06, you need a little more knowledge about the Python library *matplotlib.pyplot* for data visualization. You can learn what you need from many YouTube websites about this important library. The codes in the cell set a plot for a 3D projection and the plot figure size to be 16×6 square inches. Then a mesh grid is created for the digital valley. We know the intercept should be 32, and the slope should be 1.8. An array b_col is set by *np.linspace(−2, 38, 801)*, and an array k_row is set by *np.linspace(0,4,401)*. With a function *np.meshgrid()*, the above two 1D arrays were converted into two 2D arrays named b and k. Their sizes are the same: 401×801. If you add an extra cell in the VS code notebook and print them out, you will see that each column of array k is the same, and each row in array b is the same. The two for-loops in Cell 06 combine the two array elements at each mesh grid point into a 2×1 array for the weight array w. The Python function *enumerate()* to any 1D array can provide the array's index value and the array's element value at that index. With the weight array w and array X and Y, the loss function value can be calculated at each grid point. The digital valley surface is then plotted by *ax. plot_surface( )*, and the loss value trace is plotted by another function *ax.plot3D( )*.

This simple project has a direct solution with $\nabla L = 0$ in equation (1.35) to get $w = (X^T \cdot X)^{-1} \cdot X^T \cdot Y$. Although it is easy to finish this simple project with this explicit formula in milliseconds, we should learn how to use the gradient descent algorithm to do this kind of work because we do not have direct solutions for many complex computer vision projects. Those complex projects have millions, or even billions of parameters to train, and we are not able to write down mathematics formulae for gradients of any loss function to model parameters. PyTorch can help us to calculate those gradients. PyTorch is an open-source machine learning framework based on its Torch library. It provides tensor computation with strong GPU supports, and deep neural networks built on a tape-based auto-grad system. PyTorch is developed by Facebook's AI Research lab and is widely used for computer vision and natural language processing tasks. TensorFlow is another open-source machine learning framework developed by Google. Pytorch is more popular than TensorFlow today.

1.3 Automatic gradient calculations and learning rate schedulers

In each computer vision project, we must calculate gradients for at least one loss function to parameters during model training. In a model with a billion parameters distributed in many neural layers, it is almost impossible to derive gradient formulae manually. PyTorch can be used to automatically calculate these gradients without providing gradient formulae. We know that the gradient of a scalar function $f(x,y,z)$ to a vector $V = [x,y,z]$ is still a vector whose components are partial derivatives: $\nabla f = [\partial f/\partial x, \partial f/\partial y, \partial f/\partial z]$. For example, a function $f(x,y,z) = x^2 + y^2 + z^2$ at a point $V = [1,2,3]$, the gradient is: $\nabla f = [2x, 2y, 2z] = [2, 4, 6]$. The following VS Codes are used to calculate the gradients automatically by PyTorch. The torch package is imported on the first line of Cell 01. It supports data structures of multi-dimensional tensors, and provides mathematical operations for these tensors. Torch tensors are similar to NumPy's array, and they can be converted to each other. The main advantage of using torch tensors is that torch tensors can be moved to NVIDIA GPU for parallel computations to save time.

```
# Cell 01: Auto-grad for gradient calculations-----------------------Python v3.6
import torch                          #------------------------line 01
V = torch.tensor([1.0, 2, 3], requires_grad=True)   #------------line 02
print('V=', V)
for i in range(3):
    f = torch.sum(V**2)     #f=x^2+y^2+z^2
    f.backward()
    print(i,'\t', V.grad) #df/dV = [2*x, 2*y, 2*z]
    #V.grad.zero_()          # reset df/dV=0                #------------line 08
# Outputs which should NOT be copied and pasted in a cell of VS Code to Run------
V= tensor([1., 2., 3.], requires_grad=True)
0       tensor([2., 4., 6.])
1       tensor([4., 8., 12.])
2       tensor([6., 12., 18.])
#-------------------------------------------------------------------------------
```

To calculate gradients of a scalar function, a vector as a torch tensor must have its attribute 'requires_grad' to be True (line 02). With this setting, all mathematics operations of the vector are recorded by PyTorch. In the for-loop of Cell 01, the f function must be inside the loop, and then the $f.backward()$ function must be called to compute the gradients in all operations. The gradient of the function is then accumulated with $V.grad$. About the outputs of Cell 01, the gradient calculations in the first iteration are right, the other two are wrong. Only if you delete the hash tag symbol # in front line 08 are all the calculations correct. Every time you use PyTorch to calculate gradients automatically, you need to reset gradients to be zero by $grad.$ $zero\_()$ or use other methods mentioned later.

```
# Cell 02: Automatic gradient calculations with detach()---------------------
import torch
x = torch.arange(1,4).to(torch.float)
x.requires_grad=True
print('x=', x)              # x = tensor([1., 2., 3.], requires_grad=True)
y=x**2  #y=[x1^2, x2^2, x3^2]=tensor([1., 4., 9.], grad_fn=<PowBackward0>)
z=x**3  #z=[x1^3, x2^3, x3^3]=tensor([ 1.,  8., 27.], grad_fn=<PowBackward0>)
print('y=', y); print('z=', z)
R=(y.detach()+z).sum()    #---------------------------set dR/dy=0 by y.detach()
print('R=', R)  #R=(x1)^2+(x2)^2+(x3)^2+(x1)^3+(x2)^3+(x3)^3=50
R.backward()
print('dR/dx=', x.grad)   #dr/dx=[3(x1)^2, 3(x2)^2, 3(x3)^2]
x.grad.zero_()
print('R.requires_grad=', R.requires_grad)
#--Outputs which should NOT be copied and pasted in a cell of VS Code to Run----
x= tensor([1., 2., 3.], requires_grad=True)
y= tensor([1., 4., 9.], grad_fn=<PowBackward0>)
z= tensor([ 1., 8., 27.], grad_fn=<PowBackward0>)
R= tensor(50., grad_fn=<SumBackward0>)
dR/dx= tensor([ 3., 12., 27.])
R.requires_grad= True
#---------------------------------------------------------------------------
```

For a scalar function with more than one variable, we may need to ignore one variable's contributions to the function's gradient. The codes in the above Cell 02 could be used for learning more about the $backward()$ function and a $detach()$ function of PyTorch for automatic gradient calculations. Here is another function $R = y + z$, where $y = x_1^2 + x_2^2 + x_3^2$, $z = x_1^3 + x_2^3 + x_3^3$ at $x = [x_1, x_2, x_3] = [1,2,3]$. We can calculate the gradient $\nabla_x R = \frac{\partial R}{\partial y}\frac{\partial y}{\partial x} + \frac{\partial R}{\partial z}\frac{\partial z}{\partial x}$ with a formula $[2x_1 + 3x_1^2, 2x_2 + 3x_2^2, 2x_3 + 3x_3^2]$. Using PyTorch, we do not need to know the gradient formula. Just by calling the function $R.backward()$, all intermediate gradients of $\nabla_x R$ will be recorded and tracked by a back propagation algorithm of PyTorch. Then by calling $x.grad$, $\nabla_x R$ is obtained by an acumulation of all the intermediate gradients.

By setting $\partial R/\partial y = 0$, we can ignore the contribution of y to $\nabla_x R$. In generative adversarial networks (GANs) projects in chapter 3, we will meet this kind of task. In this case, we have $\nabla_x R = [3 \times 1^2, 3 \times 2^2, 3 \times 3^2]$. In the above Cell 02, $y.detach()$ is used for $\partial R/\partial y = 0$. You can change $y.detach()$ to $z.detach()$ to see the difference of the gradient outputs. Based on the knowledge of automatic gradient calculations in

PyTorch, we can write codes of project 1.3.1 for the simple linear regression about the temperature conversion in a different way.

```python
# Project 1.3.1: Using PyTorch Auto-grad for linear regression--------Python v3.6
import torch; import torch.nn as nn; from tqdm import trange
import torch.optim.lr_scheduler as lr_scheduler
import numpy as np; import pandas as pd; import matplotlib.pyplot as plt
n_epochs = 20000
lr = 1.5                    #initial learning rate
#Cell 02: Read data from a csv file and convert array into tensor---------cell 02
CF = np.loadtxt('d:/C2F.csv', delimiter=',', skiprows=1)
X = torch.FloatTensor(CF[:, 0]).view(-1,1)
Y = torch.FloatTensor(CF[:, 1]).reshape(-1,1)
#--------------------------------------------------------------------------------
```

More libraries or tools are imported in Cell 01. Torch is a PyTorch package for multi-dimensional tensors and their mathematical operations. Torch also provides many utilities for neural network construction and model training. We will use *torch. nn* to construct our linear regression model, and a module named *lr_scheduler* for a variable learning rate. A pandas dataframe will be used to record model training history. Pandas is a Python package. A pandas dataframe is a 2D data structure with rows and columns. Did you notice that in Cell 02 for data input, variables X and Y are torch FloatTensors? A tensor is a data container which can be used to store a 1D, 2D, 3D and even more than 4D array or matrix. A batch of color photos with a batch size of 64 and an image resolution 256×256 can be stored in a 4D PyTorch tensor whose shape is $64 \times 3 \times 256 \times 256$. In Cell 02, data from the csv file are stored in a NumPy 2D array. Each of its two columns is then converted into a float32 tensor with a shape of 9×1 respectively. Here the 'view(−1, 1)' and 'reshape(−1, 1)' do the same work. We do not need to concatenate a ONES tensor with X. PyTorch will take care of the extra work. If you add an extra cell below Cell 01, and run CF. dtype or X.dtype in the extra cell, you will find that the data type of array CF is 'floating64', and the data type of tensor X is torch.float32. There are many kinds of tensor data type. Sometimes we need to convert one type into another type. Most times we will deal with torch.float32 in computer vision projects. Occasionally, we will us torch.float16 to save memory and model training time.

```python
#Cell 03: Model, Criterion, Optimizer and learning rate scheduler--------Cell 03
model = nn.Linear(1,1)
criterion = nn.MSELoss()
optimizer = torch.optim.Adam(model.parameters(), lr=lr)
my_lambda  = lambda i: 1/10000*i+1e-5 if i<10000 else (
                2-1/10000*i if i<17000 else
                    0.3-5e-5*(i-17000))
scheduler = lr_scheduler.LambdaLR(optimizer, lr_lambda=my_lambda )   #--line 07
#scheduler = lr_scheduler.ReduceLROnPlateau(optimizer,               #--line 08
#               mode='min', factor=0.5, patience=2000, verbose=False) #line 09
print(optimizer.state_dict())
print('initial learning rate=', optimizer.param_groups[0]['lr'])
#--------------------------------------------------------------------------------
```

The torch class *nn.Linear(1,1)* is used to create a fully connected neural network layer in a model with one variable input and one variable output. Mathematically, this model is designed to do the job of the linear regression model: $X@w^T$. By default, the weight tensor w is a tensor with the shape 1×2. The first and the second element of the tensor is the slope and the intercept or bias respectively. This torch model does more work than the mathematical operation $X@w^T$. It initializes the weight array w, and stores the weight parameters of the model. Please read the output of Cell 03 carefully. It prints out parameters of the optimizer. In Cell 04, we will use an item *optimizer.param_groups[0]['lr']* to get the learning rate during model training. By default, the class *nn.MSELoss()* does the job according to equation (1.34). The division by n can be avoided to reduce model training time with *nn.MSELoss(reduction = 'sum')*. After running the code in Extra-Cell-01 about the loss function, you would know the average loss is equal to 4.0 (loss $= [3 \times (2 - 0)^2]/3$) in the example.

```
# Extra-Cell-01: Practice for Learning nn.MSELoss()----------------------------
import torch; import torch.nn as nn
criterion = nn.MSELoss(reduction='mean')
y_hat = 2*torch.ones(3, 1, requires_grad=True)
y = torch.zeros(3, 1)
print(y_hat, '\n', y)
loss = criterion(y_hat, y)
print(loss) #loss=4
#-----------------------------------------------------------------------------
```

There are many kinds of optimizers which are used to calculate gradients of the loss function, and update the model weight array automatically by *optimizer.step()* during model training. The Adam (adaptive moment estimation) optimizer is the most popular. It is not easy and not necessary to go through mathematical algorithms of optimizers.

```
# Extra-Cell-02: Definitions of seven learning rate lambda functions----------
my_lambda = lambda i: 0.5              # CONSTANT learning_rate=lr0*0.5
my_lambda = lambda i: 1-0.99/20000*i  # learning_rate=lr0*(1-0.99/20000*i)
my_lambda = lambda i: 0.9999 ** i      # learning_rate=lr0*0.9999^i
my_lambda = lambda i: np.exp(-i/5000) #learning_rate=lr0*exp(-i/5000)
my_lambda = lambda i: 0.1+0.4*(1+np.cos(i/20000*np.pi)) #CosineAnnealingLR
my_lambda = lambda i: 1/10000*i+1e-5 if i<10000 else (
          2-1/10000*i if i<17000 else 0.3-5e-5*(i-17000))
lr_list = [1.0, 0.5, 0.25, 0.125, 0.06]
my_lambda = lambda i: lr_list[i//5000] #StepLR
#-----------------------------------------------------------------------------
```

Learning rate is the most important hyperparameter for model training. PyTorch provides many learning rate schedulers to change learning rate during model training. The most versatile scheduler is the LambdaLR. You can define any function with the training epoch (i) as its variable. The initial learning rate (lr_0) is usually set in Cell 01 for the optimizer, and the learning rate at epoch (i) is equal to lr_0 times the Lambda function value. In Extra-Cell-02, the first function is for a constant learning rate: $lr_i = 0.5 \times lr_0$. With the second lambda function, the learning rate decreases linearly during model training for 20 000 epochs. If the third or the fourth function is chosen, the learning rate decreases exponentially. The fifth lambda function is the same as *CosineAnnealingLR* scheduler in PyTorch. The sixth lambda function has three segments: for $i < 10\,000$, for i between $10\,000$ and $17\,000$, and for $i > 17\,000$. The last lambda function is like *StepLR* scheduler in PyTorch. It picks out a number from a list named lr_list at an index of $i//5000$.

```
#Cell 04 Definition of the training function----------------------------cell 04
def fit(x, y, epochs):
    df = pd.DataFrame(np.empty([epochs, 2]), index = np.arange(epochs),
                      columns=['lr', 'Loss'])
    progress_bar = trange(epochs)
    for i in progress_bar:
        y_hat = model(x)                                #model prediction
        loss = criterion(y_hat, y)                      #calculate loss value
        df.iloc[i,0] = optimizer.param_groups[0]['lr']  #record learning rate
        df.iloc[i,1] = loss.item()                      #record loss
        optimizer.zero_grad()                           # gradient initializations
        loss.backward()                                 # gradient calculations
        optimizer.step()                                # update model parameters
        scheduler.step()                # update learining rate-----------line 13
        #scheduler.step(loss.item())    # for ReduceLROnPlateau scheduler--line 14
        progress_bar.set_description("loss=%.9f" % df.iloc[i,1])
        progress_bar.set_postfix({'leraning rate': df.iloc[i,0]})
    return df
train_history = fit(X, Y, n_epochs)
#Cell 05: Showing training results with graphs--------------------------Cell 05
df = train_history
fig, ax = plt.subplots(1,3, figsize=(12,3))             # for 3 graphs in a row
ax[0].plot(X, Y, 'ro', label='Y')                       # Y plot
ax[0].plot(X, model(X).detach(), 'b:+', label='y_hat')  # y_hat plot
ax[0].set(xlabel='Celsius(deg)', ylabel='Fahrenheit(deg)')
ax[1].plot(X, model(X).detach()-Y, 'r:d', label='y_hat-Y')
ax[1].ticklabel_format(style='sci', axis='y', scilimits=(0,0));
ax[1].set(xlabel='Celsius(deg)', ylim=[-1e-8,1e-8])
ax[2].plot(df.iloc[:,0], label='lr'); ax[2].set(xlabel='epoch')
#df.plot(ax=ax[2], y=[0]) #--------Pandas' data visualization code---line 11
for i in range(3):
    ax[i].legend()
    ax[i].grid(which='major', axis='both', color='g', linestyle=':')
plt.show()
#Cell 06: Check the model parameters------------------------------------Cell 06
p=list(model.named_parameters())
for i in range(len(p)):
    print(p[i][0], '=', p[i][1].item(), '\tshape =', p[i][1].shape)
#---Outputs of Cell 06--------------------------------------------------------
#weight = 1.7999999523162842 shape = torch.Size([1, 1])
#bias = 32.0 shape = torch.Size([1])
#----------------------------------------------------------------------------
```

A pandas dataframe named df in Cell 04 is used to record the learning rate and loss function value for each epoch during model training. The dataframe can be obtained by calling the fit function on the last line of Cell 04. The model *nn.Linear (1,1)* takes care of all its parameters. In each training epoch, the gradients of the loss function to all its parameters are reset to be equal to zero by *optimizer.zero_grad()* on line 10. Just as the *optimizer.step()* updates the model parameters for every epoch, *scheduler.step()* updates the optimizer's learning rate.

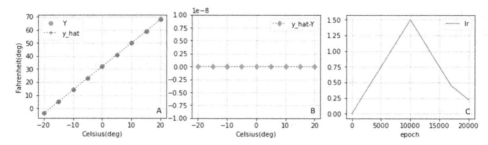

Figure 1.4. Model training output graphs. (A) original data Y and predicted data y_hat, (B): The difference between y_hat and Y, (C): The learning rate curve with three segments set by a lambda learning scheduler.

From figure 1.4(A), we could not tell the difference between the model's prediction y_hat and the original data Y by just looking. Running the codes in Cell 06, you would see the difference is less than 10^{-8} as shown in figure 1.4(B). The learning rate graph shown in figure 1.4(C) is what we set by *my_lambda* function in Cell 03. Pandas has powerful data visualization tools. You can use line 11 to replace line 10 in Cell 05 to plot the learning rate curve. PyTorch has smarter schedulers for us to change learning rates. One of them is the ReduceLROnPlateau(). It automatically reduces learning rate when a loss function's value or another value has stopped improving for a 'patience' number of epochs. There are two learning schedulers in Cell 03. By moving a hash tag symbol # in front of line 08 to line 07, and delete a # symbol in front of line 09 in Cell 03, you can try the smarter scheduler in Cell 07 for a 3D loss function surface.

```
#Cell 07: Model training for 3D graphs---- to replace Cell 04-------------Cell 07
def train3D(x, y, epochs):
    df = pd.DataFrame(np.empty([epochs, 4]), index = np.arange(epochs),
                      columns=['slope', 'bias', 'Loss', 'lr'])
    progress_bar = trange(epochs)
    for i in progress_bar:
        p = list(model.parameters())    # ----------line 06
        y_hat = model(x)
        loss = criterion(y_hat, y)
        df.iloc[i, 0] = p[0].detach().item()              # slope
        df.iloc[i, 1] = p[1].detach().item()              # bias
        df.iloc[i, 2] = loss.detach().item()              # loss
        df.iloc[i, 3] = optimizer.param_groups[0]['lr']   # lr
        optimizer.zero_grad()     # gradients initialzation
        loss.backward()           # gradients calculation
        optimizer.step()          # model update
        #scheduler.step()              #for lr of LambdaLR-----------line 18
        scheduler.step(loss.item()) #for lr of ReduceLROnPlateau --line 19
        progress_bar.set_description("loss=%.9f" % df.iloc[i,2])
        progress_bar.set_postfix({'leraning rate': df.iloc[i,3]})
    return df
train_history = train3D(X, Y, n_epochs)
#----------------------------------------------------------------------------
```

We can use Cell 07 to replace Cell 04, and re-train the model for a 3D graph output. The option *loss.item( )* in the *scheduler.step( )* on line 19 in Cell 07 specifically instructs the scheduler to monitor the loss function's value. If the minimum of the loss function's value does not change in 2000 epochs (patience number), the learn rate will be halved (factor = 0.5). On line 06 of Cell 07, the model's parameters are assigned to a list named p. The values of two elements of the list, the slope and bias are recorded in the pandas dataframe during model training. After the model is trained, the dataframe is returned for plotting of a 3D Graph shown in figure 1.5. Inside the two for-loops of Cell 08, we must use *nn. Parameter( )* to assign a tensor to a parameter of the model. You can try different initial learning rates and schedulers to see the trace of the loss function.

```
#Cell 08: Plot a Loss function surface and a model training trace---------Cell 08
import matplotlib.pyplot as plt
import numpy as np
fig, ax = plt.subplots(subplot_kw={"projection": "3d"}, figsize=(12,8))
b_col = np.float32(np.linspace(-2, 38, 401))
k_row = np.float32(np.linspace(0, 4, 201))
b, k = np.meshgrid(b_col, k_row)
L = np.empty((len(k_row), len(b_col)))
for i, ki in enumerate(k_row):
    for j, bj in enumerate(b_col):
        model.weight = nn.Parameter(torch.tensor([[ki]], requires_grad=False))
        model.bias = nn.Parameter(torch.tensor([bj], requires_grad=False))
        y_hat = model(X)
        L[i,j] = criterion(y_hat, Y)      # creating a loss surface
surf = ax.plot_surface(b, k, L, cmap='cool')
ax.plot3D(z[:,1], z[:,0], z[:,2], 'k-', lw=2)
ax.set(xlabel='b', ylabel='k', zlabel='Loss')
plt.colorbar(surf, shrink=0.7);
#-----------------------------------------------------------------------------
```

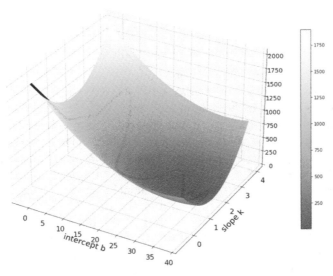

Figure 1.5. The digital valley (color) of the loss function and the trace (black) of the loss function during model training.

1.4 Dataset, dataloader, GPU and models saving

Data for model training in computer vision projects should be packed into datasets. Usually, sizes of datasets are huge. Many datasets are already packed into datasets by many selfless dataset creators. After downloading a dataset, we need to slice each dataset into a dataloader with many batches, because our computer memory is not big enough to handle all data of a dataset in a single batch. Just like eating a big cake, we have to cut it with a knife into small pieces so that each piece can fit into our mouths. We will learn how to pack the data in the temperature csv file into a dataset and slice it into a dataloader in project 1.4.1. They are all extra jobs for the simple project, but are essential steps for big datasets in computer vision projects.

```python
# Project 1.4.1 Dataset, Dataloader and GPU for linear regression-----Python v3.6
import torch; import torch.nn as nn
from torch.utils.data import Dataset, DataLoader
import torch.optim.lr_scheduler as lr_scheduler; from tqdm import trange
import numpy as np; import pandas as pd; import matplotlib.pyplot as plt
n_epochs = 20000
batch_size = 3
lr = 0.1                          # initial learning rate
# Cell 02: A class used to read a data file and pack data into a dataset--------
class C2F(Dataset):
    def __init__(self, filename):
        xy = np.loadtxt(filename, delimiter=',', skiprows=1, dtype=np.float32)
        self.x = torch.from_numpy(xy[:, 0])
        self.y = torch.from_numpy(xy[:, 1])
        self.n_samples = xy.shape[0]
    def __getitem__(self, index):
        return self.x[index], self.y[index]
    def __len__(self):
        return self.n_samples
# Cell 03: Applications of the class C2F to a text data file 'd:/C2F.csv'--------
my_dataset = C2F('d:/C2F.csv')
n_samples = len(my_dataset)              # n_samples = 9
print(my_dataset[0])                     #(tensor(-20.), tensor(-4))
#----------------------------------------------------------------------------
```

More Python and PyTorch libraries are imported in Cell 01 as tools for us to pack our data into a dataset and slice the dataset into a dataloader. How is data packed inside a dataset? Or what is the dataset structure? Codes in Cell 02 of project 1.4.1 are used as an example to show you how to pack data into a dataset. With a subclass Dataset imported from *torch.utils.data* in PyTorch, a class named C2F is defined. The __init__ function in the C2F class uses the *np.loadtxt* function to input date from the csv file with a string as its file name. The option 'np.float32' is important because we need it to convert the data into float32 tensors. Then each of the two columns and the length of each column are recorded. The second function in the C2F class named __getitem__ can be used to pick out a single pair of data in the dataset at a specific index. With the last function __len__ in the class C2F, we can find how many data pairs are in the dataset. In Cell 03, the csv file with a name string 'd:/C2F.csv' is used for an instance of the C2F class. You can see the class C2F does its jobs just as we want. In *my_dataset[0]* of Cell 03, if you change the '0' to ':', you will print out all nine elements in the array x and all nine elements of the array y.

```
#Cell 04: Slicing the dataset into a dataloader with a batch size of 3----------
dataloader=DataLoader(dataset=my_dataset, batch_size=batch_size, shuffle=False)
for x, y in dataloader:
    print('x=', x);  print('y=', y)
    break
batch_per_epoch = int(n_samples/batch_size)      #batch_per_epoch=3
#------------------------------------------------------------------------------
```

It is easy to use a subclass DataLoader from *torch.utils.data* in PyTorch to slice a dataset into many small batches. With an option *shuffle = False* in Cell 04, the data sequence would not be changed. To an image dataloader for model training in the future, we need this option to be True to reduce 'overfitting'. A for-loop in Cell 04 prints out the first batch of the dataloader. Of course, if you remove the 'break', you will print out all three batches.

```
# Cell 05: Model definition---------------------------------------------Cell 05
class LinearRegression(nn.Module):
    def __init__(self):
        super().__init__()
        self.net = nn.Sequential(nn.Linear(1, 1),
                    )
    def forward(self,x):
        return self.net(x)
model = LinearRegression().cuda()
#Cell 06: Model training criterion, optimizer and learning rate scheduler--------
criterion = nn.MSELoss()
optimizer = torch.optim.Adam(model.parameters(), lr=lr)
scheduler = lr_scheduler.OneCycleLR(optimizer,
                max_lr=lr, anneal_strategy='cos',
                steps_per_epoch=batch_per_epoch, epochs=n_epochs, pct_start=0.3)
#------------------------------------------------------------------------------
```

In sections 1.2 and 1.3, we defined a linear regression model as *X@w*, or *nn. Linear (1,1)*. In Cell 05 of this project, we write extra codes to define the simple model. Usually, computer vision projects use many neural layers in their neural network models. The *nn. Sequential( )* in Cell 05 can contain many kinds of mathematical operations to process and extract information from data. This is the way to define all computer vision models in big projects of this book. The function 'forward' in the class accepts input data and returns output data. In the last line of Cell 05, a model was defined as an instance of the LinearRegression class, and the model was moved to the memory of a graphics processing unit (GPU) by 'cuda()'. CUDA's ability of parallel computing can significantly reduce model training time. In Cell 06, a loss function (criterion), model optimizer and learning rate scheduler are defined. A learning rate scheduler OneCycleLR is used here. This scheduler changes learning rate along all iterations of all epochs. Since there are three batches in each epoch, the 20 000 epochs have 60 000 iterations for the model training.

```
#Cell 07 Model Training function----------------------------------------------
def fit(epochs):
    iterations = epochs*batch_per_epoch
    df = pd.DataFrame(np.empty([iterations, 2]),
                      index = np.arange(iterations),
                      columns = ['lr', 'Loss'])
    progress_bar = trange(epochs)
    for i in progress_bar:
        for j, (x, y) in enumerate(dataloader):
            x = x.view(-1,1).cuda()
            y = y.view(-1,1).cuda()
            optimizer.zero_grad()
            y_hat = model(x)
            loss = criterion(y_hat, y)   #loss for a batch
            df.iloc[i*3+j, 0] = optimizer.param_groups[0]['lr']
            df.iloc[i*3+j, 1] = loss.item()
            progress_bar.set_description("loss=%.9f" % loss.item())
            progress_bar.set_postfix({'lr': df.iloc[i*3+j, 0]})
            loss.backward()
            optimizer.step()
            scheduler.step()
    return df
train_history = fit(n_epochs)
k, b = list(model.parameters())
print('k =', k.item())   #k=1.7999999523162842
print('b =', b.item())   #b=32.0
#------------------------------------------------------------------------------
```

In Cell 07, each batch of data x and y coming from the dataloader is sent to GPU by *cuda*(), because the model is in GPU. Model parameters k and b are printed out by codes on the last two lines in Cell 07. With the codes in Cell 08, the model training results are shown in three graphs (figure 1.6). For the y_hat calculations on line 06 of Cell 08, Data X in the dataset must be sent to GPU. Using matplotlib to plot y_hat in figure 1.6(A), we have to send y_hat back to CPU. It is no surprise that the running time for this project with GPU is much longer than the running time of project 1.2.1. Many extra codes added to the project take extra time. For huge datasets, it is guaranteed that GPU saves model training time significantly.

```
#Cell 08: Showing training results with graphs----------------------------------
df = train_history
fig, ax = plt.subplots(1, 3, figsize=(12,3))
x_dataset, y_dataset = my_dataset[:]
X = x_dataset.view(-1,1)
Y = y_dataset.view(-1,1)
y_hat = model(X.cuda()).detach().cpu()     #---X to GUP and y_hat to CPU line 06
ax[0].plot(X, Y, 'ro', label='Y')
ax[0].plot(X, y_hat, 'b:+', label='y_hat')
ax[0].set(xlabel='Celsius(deg)', ylabel='Fahrenheit(deg)')
ax[1].plot(df.iloc[:, 1], 'r-', label='Loss')
ax[1].set(xlabel='interation')
ax[2].plot(df.iloc[:, 0], 'k-', label='learning rate')
ax[2].set_xlabel('interation')
for i in range(3):
    ax[i].legend()
    ax[i].grid(which='major', axis='both', color='g', linestyle=':')
plt.show()
#-----------------------------------------------------------------------End
```

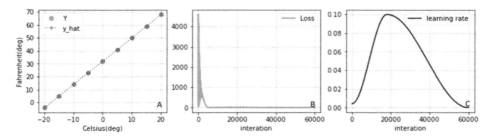

Figure 1.6. Model training output graphs. (A): original data Y and predicted data y_hat. (B): loss curve, (C): learning rate curve with OneCycleLR learning rate scheduler.

Training models with a huge amount of data takes hours, days or even weeks. After your computer is turned off, all those good parameters of your trained models disappear. It is painful to take a long time to train the model again. We need to save parameters of trained models so that we can use them for later applications. To save a trained model, you need a file name, for example: File_name = 'd:/model4LR.pth', and then use the code 'torch.save(model, File_name)'. The trained linear regression model defined in Cell 05 would be saved by codes in Cell 09.

```
# Cell 09: save a trained model------------------------------------model saving
File_name = 'd:/model4LR.pth'
torch.save(model, File_name)
# Cell 10: load a saved model---------------------------- saved model loading--
saved_model = torch.load(File_name)
saved_model.eval()
print(saved_model.state_dict())
# Cell 11: Verify the loaded model works--------------saved model applications--
x_dataset, y_dataset = my_dataset[:]
y_hat = saved_model(x_dataset.view(-1,1).cuda())
y_hat
#------------------------------------------------------------------------------
```

To avoid confusion, I use 'saved_model' as the name of the model loaded from the saved file in Cell 10. Before using the loaded model, we have to set the saved model for evaluation by the code *saved_model.eval( )* after the model is loaded. With the last line in Cell 10, the trained model's parameters are printed out. You can see that the two parameters are right, and the saved model is in GPU. Using codes in Cell 11, you will find that the loaded model works. There are more methods to save trained models. The second method is only saving the model parameters to a file. Just by reloading those parameters in the file to the model, we can reuse the trained model. You can try the second method by running Cell 12–14.

```
# Cell 12: The second method to save a trained model---------------------------
torch.save(model.state_dict(), 'd:/model4LR2.pth')
# Cell 13: Reload the saved model parameters to the model
saved_model = LinearRegression()
saved_model.load_state_dict(torch.load('d:/model4LR2.pth'))
saved_model.cuda().eval()
# Cell 14: Verify the loaded model works-----------------saved model applications
x_dataset, y_dataset = my_dataset[:]
y_hat = saved_model(x_dataset.view(-1,1).cuda())
y_hat
#------------------------------------------------------------------------------
```

The third method is to save a check-point of a trained model during training. Big computer vision projects need many days for model training. We have to restart model training from a check-point saved on a previous day. In Cell 15, you can see that the model's parameters, the optimizer's parameters, the loss function, and learning rate scheduler are all saved in a file. You can reload those parameters by running codes in Cell 16.

```
# Cell 15: Saving a check point during training ---------------check point saving
state = {'epochs': 20000,
         'model_state': model.state_dict(),
         'optimizer_state': optimizer.state_dict(),
         'criterion': nn.MSELoss(),
         'scheduler': lr_scheduler.OneCycleLR(
                 optimizer, max_lr=0.1, anneal_strategy='cos',
                 steps_per_epoch=3, epochs=n_epochs, pct_start=0.3)}
torch.save(state, 'd:/model4LR3.pth')
# Cell 16: Loading the saved check point--------------------check point loading
model = LinearRegression().cuda()
optimizer = torch.optim.Adam(model.parameters(), lr=1.0)
checkpoint = torch.load('d:/model4LR3.pth')
model.load_state_dict(checkpoint['model_state'])
optimizer.load_state_dict(checkpoint['optimizer_state'])
epochs = checkpoint['epochs']
criterion= checkpoint['criterion']
scheduler = checkpoint['scheduler']
# Cell 17: Verify the loaded model works--------verification of saved check point
print(model.state_dict())
x_dataset, y_dataset = my_dataset[:]
y_hat = model(x_dataset.view(-1,1).cuda())
y_hat
#--------------------------------------------------------------------------------
```

1.5 Activation functions for nonlinear regressions

Our world is beautiful because many phenomena are nonlinear. In computer vision projects, we have to use multiple neural layers to handle nonlinear mathematical problems. However, multiple linear layers in a sequence of a model work just like a single linear layer. For example, in case our model has two fully connected linear layers: $Y_1 = w_1X+b_1$ and $Y_2 = w_2Y_1+b_2$, we will get $Y_2 = w_2w_1X+(w_2b_1+ b_2)$ which is still a linear layer. To avoid the mathematical issue, we have to add an activation function between two linear layers. There are many kinds of activation functions, and they are all nonlinear. The following are four commonly used classes for activating functions:

1. sigmoid class nn.Sigmoid(): $f(x) = \frac{1}{1+e^{-x}}$

2. hyperbolic class class nn.Tanh(): $f(x) = \frac{e^x - e^{-x}}{e^x + e^{-x}}$

3. rectified linear unit class nn.ReLU(): $f(x) = \begin{cases} x \ (x \geqslant 0) \\ 0 \ (x < 0) \end{cases}$

4. leaky ReLU class nn.LeakyReLU(0.1): $f(x) = \begin{cases} x \ (x \geqslant 0) \\ 0.1x \ (x < 0) \end{cases}$

We will use the sigmoid class for a activate function in a nonlinear regression for $y(x) = e^{-5x}$ in project 1.5.1. The variable x in all the activation functions can be a scalar or an array. If the input of the sigmoid function is an array or matrix, the sigmoid function element-wisely acts on the array. Each element's value of the sigmoid function's output is in the range [0,1]. In the project, a csv data file was created from the function $y(x) = e^{-5x}$, where x is between 0.0 and 1.0. The length of the x array is 51. We would like to use a model with two fully connected layers to simulate this exponential function.

```python
# Project 1.5.1 None-linear regression with an activation function----Python v3.6
import torch; import torch.nn as nn
from torch.utils.data import Dataset, DataLoader
import torch.optim.lr_scheduler as lr_scheduler; from tqdm import trange
import numpy as np; import pandas as pd; import matplotlib.pyplot as plt
n_epochs = 20000
batch_size = 17
lr = 0.1
# Cell 02:  A class to read a data file and pack data into a dataset-----Cell 02
class My_Dataset(Dataset):
    def __init__(self, filename):
        xy = np.loadtxt(filename, delimiter=',', skiprows=1, dtype=np.float32)
        self.x = torch.from_numpy(xy[:, 0])
        self.y = torch.from_numpy(xy[:, 1])
        self.n_samples = xy.shape[0]
    def __getitem__(self, index):
        return self.x[index], self.y[index]
    def __len__(self):
        return self.n_samples
# Cell 03: Dataset and Dataloader------------------------------------------Cell 03
dataset = My_Dataset('d:/nonlinearF.csv')   #y(x)=exp(-5x), x=[0,1], len(x)=51
n_samples = len(dataset)                     #n_samples= 51
dataloader = DataLoader(dataset=dataset, batch_size=batch_size)
batch_per_epoch = int(n_samples/batch_size)          #batch_per_epoch=3
# Cell 04: Show the data of the dataset in a graph----------------------Cell 04
x, y = dataset[:]
fig, ax = plt.subplots()
ax.plot(x,y)
ax.set(xlabel='x', ylabel='y', title='y=exp(-5x)')
ax.grid(which='major', axis='both', color='g', linestyle=':');
# Cell 05: A model with two layers and an active function--------------Cell 05
class NonLinearRegression(nn.Module):
    def __init__(self):
        super().__init__()
        self.net = nn.Sequential(nn.Linear(1,4), nn.Sigmoid(), nn.Linear(4,1))
    def forward(self, x):
        return self.net(x)
model = NonLinearRegression().cuda()
criterion = nn.MSELoss(reduction='mean')
optimizer = torch.optim.Adam(model.parameters(), lr=lr)
scheduler = lr_scheduler.OneCycleLR(
    optimizer, max_lr=lr, anneal_strategy='linear',
    steps_per_epoch=batch_per_epoch, epochs=n_epochs, pct_start=0.3)
#----------------------------------------------------------------------------
```

A csv file named 'd:/nonlinearF.csv' was input and converted into a dataset in Cell 03. With the batch size being set to be equal to 17, the dataset is sliced into three batches in a dataloader. The data in the dataset is shown in a graph by codes in Cell 04. A model in Cell 05 with two layers is defined. The first layer and the last layer are fully connected layers. Between them is a sigmoid activation class which has no parameters. A learning rate scheduler OneCycleLR is used in the project, and its option 'anneal_strategy' is set to be 'linear', not 'cos' as before.

```python
# Cell 06: Training Function------------------------------------Cell 06
def fit(epochs):
    iterations = epochs*batch_per_epoch
    df = pd.DataFrame(np.empty([iterations, 2]),
                        index = np.arange(iterations),
                        columns = ['lr', 'Loss'])
    progress_bar = trange(epochs)
    for i in progress_bar:
        for j, (x, y) in enumerate(dataloader):
            x = x.view(-1,1).cuda()
            y = y.view(-1,1).cuda()
            optimizer.zero_grad()
            y_hat = model(x)
            loss = criterion(y_hat, y)  #loss for one batch
            df.iloc[i*3+j, 0] = optimizer.param_groups[0]['lr']
            df.iloc[i*3+j, 1] = loss.item()
            progress_bar.set_description("loss=%.9f" % loss.item())
            progress_bar.set_postfix({'lr': df.iloc[i*3+j, 0]})
            loss.backward()
            optimizer.step()
            scheduler.step()
    return df
train_history = fit(n_epochs)
#Cell 07: Showing training results with graphs----------------------Cell 07
df = train_history
fig, ax = plt.subplots(1, 3, figsize=(12,3))
x_dataset, y_dataset = dataset[:]
X = x_dataset.view(-1,1)
Y = y_dataset.view(-1,1)
y_hat = model(X.cuda()).detach().cpu()
ax[0].plot(X, Y, 'r-', label='Y=exp(-5x)')
ax[0].plot(X, y_hat, 'b:+', label='y_hat')
ax[0].set(xlabel='x', ylabel='y')
ax[1].plot(df.iloc[:, 1], 'r-', label='Loss')
ax[1].set(xlabel='interation')
ax[2].plot(df.iloc[:, 0], 'k-', label='learning rate')
ax[2].set_xlabel('interation')
for i in range(3):
    ax[i].legend()
    ax[i].grid(which='major', axis='both', color='g', linestyle=':')
plt.show()
#------------------------------------------------------------------
```

Model training results are shown in figures 1.7. From figure 1.7(A), we can see that the nonlinear regression is very good. Between the model outputs y_hat and the target y, the absolute maximum difference is about 7.5×10^{-4}. By using the code 'p = list(model.parameters()); print(p)' in Cell 08, we get four tensors. The first two

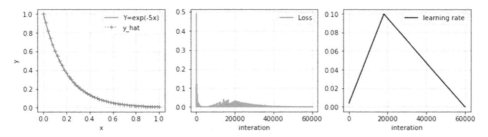

Figure 1.7. Nonlinear regression results for y(x) = exp(−5x). (A) Ground truth Y and the predicted curve y_hat. (B) Loss curve. (C) Learning rates of OneCycleLR with anneal_strategy = 'linear'.

are the weight p[0] and bias p[1] of the first fully connected layer. The last two are the weight p[2] and bias p[3] of the last fully connected layer. All of them are stored in GPU, and their 'requires_grad' options are true. The following formula is what we obtained from the model training. Running codes in Cell 08, you would know how the model parameters are used in the following formula. Neural networks are very powerful to simulate any mathematical functions. In bigger projects, models have many neural layers and many parameters. We are not able to give the right side of the following formula, and it is not necessary.

$$e^{-5X} = \text{model}(X) = [\sigma(X@p[0]^T + p[1])]@p[2]^T + p[3]$$

```
# Cell 08: verify the nonlinear regression------------------------------Cell 08
s = nn.Sigmoid()
p = list(model.parameters()); print(p)
X, Y = dataset[:]
X = X.cuda().view(-1, 1); Y = Y.cuda().view(-1, 1)
z1 = X@p[0].T+p[1]
(s(z1)@p[2].T + p[3]-Y).T
#(model(X)-Y).T
#------------------------------------------------------------------ The End
```

References

Dempster A P, Laird N M and Rubin D B 1977 Maximum likelihood from incomplete data via the EM algorithm *J. Royal Stat. Soc. Ser. B (Methodol.)* **39** 1–38

Hilt D E, Seegrist D W, United States Forest S and Northeastern Forest Experiment S 1977 *Ridge, a Computer Program for Calculating Ridge Regression Estimates* (Upper Darby, PA: Dept. of Agriculture, Forest Service, Northeastern Forest Experiment Station)

IOP Publishing

Mastering Computer Vision with PyTorch and Machine Learning

Caide Xiao

Chapter 2

Image classifications by convolutional neural networks

This chapter is about constructing and using convolution neural networks (models) to classify images in two simple labeled datasets: MNIST and CIFAR-10. Transfer learning is introduced to use pre-trained models for the Vegetable Images dataset image classification. A confusion matrix obtained in the MNIST image classification project is used to show how to calculate some metrics of model training: recall, precision, f1_score and intersection over union (IOU).

It is easy for human babies to know what they are seeing (image classification), even though they may be confused by their parents' 'twin'. Image classification is a branch of computer vision which started in the 1960s. After more than 60 years, the intelligence of computers on image classification has surpassed human beings. Today, smart cameras beside traffic lights in cities can read the licence plates of moving cars; cell phones can recognize users' faces. Image classification is used in a wide range of applications, including self-driving cars and biomedical diagnosis systems. We should attribute the successes of computer vision to the artificial intelligence theories of many pioneers, more powerful computer hardware, and many free datasets with huge amounts of data. Three datasets are used to train image classification algorithms or models in this chapter. They are MNIST, CIFAR-10 and Vegetable Images. These image datasets have labels with which we train our models for supervised learning. Just like showing animal pictures in a book to a three-year old child, you tell the child: 'that is a dog, that is a cat, or that is a bird.' The child's brain is trained by the labeled pictures. Later, the child is taken outside and shown real animals and is then asked many times: 'What is the name of that animal?' in different environments. The right percentage of the child's answers is a benchmark that indicates how well the child was trained. In the same way, after training of an image classification model with an image dataset, your model can predict if there is a cat, a dog, a bird or a digit '5' on a photo in a dataset. A well-trained model may have a million parameters. These parameters and the structure of the model can be saved and written into integrated circuit (IC) chips for specific applications.

2.1 Classification of hand written digits in the MNIST database

MNIST (Modified National Institute of Standards and Technology) is the most famous database (LeCun *et al* 1998) for computer vision. It is often used as a benchmark for testing machine learning algorithms. We should keep in mind that the MNIST dataset is a very simple dataset, even a model with two fully connected neural layers can achieve 98% accuracy. A model that performs well on MNIST does not mean it works well on other datasets. The MNIST dataset is often used as a starting point for testing and developing machine learning models. The MNIST dataset has a train dataset and a test dataset, and they have 60 000 and 10 000 black and white images, respectively. All images have a same resolution: 28×28. The train dataset is used to train a model, and the test dataset is used to check if the trained model has 'overfitting' issues. Having this issue, a trained model has higher predication accuracy for the train dataset, but lower accuracy for its test dataset. This phenomenon may happen because our computers are very powerful in remembering detailed structures (noises) in our train datasets. Those detailed structures could be different in different images. To avoid overfitting, we even slice the MNIST train dataset into a smaller train dataset with 50 000 images and a validation dataset with 10 000 images for model training.

Before the ancient Egyptians built their pyramids, they must have their tools ready for measuring, cutting and moving those big cubic stones. For our MNIST image classification codes in project 2.1, we also need tools ready. Those tools are the Python and PyTorch libraries. With them, we can load datasets into computers from the internet, slice a dataset into a dataloader, and display them on computer screens. Codes in Cell 01 of the following project provide these tools. Among those tools, Torchvision is new to us. Torchvision is a library and is a part of PyTorch. In this library, there are many popular datasets to download, many pre-trained models to use, and many image transformation operations to reduce overfitting issues. Torchvision was installed after PyTorch was installed in VS Code. Many hyperparameters such as batch size and learning rate are also set in Cell 01. How can our model be trained to read digitals in MNIST images? Our model really doesn't read 2D images in the same way that our eyes read. In this project, our model has two fully connected layers. Those 28×28 pixels of each image are flattened into a 1D tensor with 784 elements. The simple model only extracts statistic information (probabilities) from these data. With the statistics information, the model's prediction accuracy will be more than 98%.

With codes in Cell 02, the MNIST database can be downloaded from the internet if the data path on your hard disk is empty and the MNIST option is set to be 'download = True' on line 01 and 04. The total size of compressed MNIST image files downloaded from the MNIST dataset source is about 116 MB. If the database is already downloaded on your computer, you should set the download option to be 'False', and the image data would then be read from a file path set on the last line of Cell 01. A dot in the data path string on the last line of Cell 01 means the current working directory of VS Code. You can find it by running 'import os; os. getcwd()' in an extra cell. You can also use an absolute data path. With the train option to be 'True', images of the train dataset inside the compressed file would be loaded; or if 'train = False', images of the test dataset inside the compressed file would be loaded. Each image pixel in the MNIST images is an 8-bit integer (0–255). With a transform function on line 02 and 05 in Cell 02, pixel values of each image are converted into float32 tensors in a range [0.0, 1.0].

```
# Project 2.1 MNIST Image Classification ---------------------------Python v3.6
import torch; import torch.nn as nn; from torch.utils.data import DataLoader
from torchvision import transforms as T; from torchvision.datasets import MNIST
from torchvision.utils import make_grid; import matplotlib.pyplot as plt
import numpy as np; import pandas as pd; from tqdm import tqdm
from sklearn.metrics import confusion_matrix
class_names = ['Zero', 'One', 'Two', 'Three', 'Four', 'Five', 'Six', 'Seven',
               'Eight', 'Nine']
n_epochs = 25
batch_size = 32
lr = 1e-2        #initial learning rate
img_size = 28; n_class = 10; n_hidden = 100
data_path = './OCR/data/'
# Cell 02: MNIST train_dataset and test_dataset ------------------------------
train_dataset = MNIST(data_path, train=True, download=False,    #--------line 01
                  transform=T.Compose([T.ToTensor()]))
n_samples = len(train_dataset)        #n_samples = 60000
test_dataset = MNIST(data_path, train=False, download=False,    #--------line 04
                  transform=T.Compose([T.ToTensor()]))
n_tests = len(test_dataset)           #n_tests = 100000
# Cell 03: Dataloaders----------------------------------------------------Cell 03
train_dataloader=DataLoader(train_dataset, batch_size=batch_size, shuffle=True,
                      num_workers=4, pin_memory=True)
test_dataloader=DataLoader(test_dataset, batch_size=batch_size, shuffle=False,
                      num_workers=4, pin_memory=True)
for imgs, labels in train_dataloader:
    #print('labels=', '\n', labels)
    print('batch_imgs.shape=', imgs.shape)   #torch.Size([32, 1, 28, 28])
    break
# Cell 04: Show images in the first dataloader------------------------Cell 04
def show_images(my_imgs):
    fig, ax = plt.subplots(figsize=(12,8))
    input = make_grid(my_imgs, nrow=16, padding=2)          #---------line 03
    ax.imshow(input.permute(1,2,0), cmap='gray'); ax.set(xticks=[], yticks=[])
    plt.show()
show_images(imgs)
#-----------------------------------------------------------------------------
```

Using codes in Cell 03, we slice the two datasets into two dataloaders, respectively, by using a PyTorch DataLoader class. With a smaller batch size, we need a longer time for model training, and we get better training results. When you have GPU memory issues (out of memory), reducing the batch size parameter is a solution. To reduce the 'overfitting' issue of model training, we set the shuffle option to be True on the first line of Cell 03, so the train dataloader is constructed with samples randomly chosen from the dataset. The test dataloader is used to verify if the trained model has overfitting issues, and it does not need to be randomly packed. From the outputs of Cell 04, we can see that a batch of the train dataloader has 32 images, each image has

Figure 2.1. MNIST images in a batch of the train dataloader with a batch size of 32. Reproduced from Deng (2012) CC BY 3.0.

one channel, and the resolution of each image is 28×28. An image with one channel is a black and white image, and an image with three channels is a color image. Also, each image in the dataset has a label which is the number shown by the photo. We can display the last image of the test dataset by using codes in an extra cell after Cell 04: 'img, _ = test_dataset[-1]; plt.imshow(img.permute(1,2,0));'.

A function named 'show_images' is defined in Cell 04. The input of the function is a batch of images from a dataloader. In a for-loop of Cell 03, only the first batch of images is picked out to display. Using a *torchvision.utils* module *make_grid*, we combine all small images in the batch into a bigger image. The number of small images in each row of the bigger image is set by an option 'nrow' on line 03 of Cell 04. The space around each small image is set by another parameter 'padding'. By default, 'padding' is equal to 2 pixels. Every time you run the function 'show_images', you will see a different bigger image such as one shown in figure 2.1, because of the option *shuffle = True* setting for the train dataloader in Cell 02. By using the test dataloader as an input of the function, you will see that the bigger image does not change.

Running the two following extra cells after Cell 04, you will know more about the *make_grid* and *permute* operations for displaying images. In Extra Cell ONE, a tensor named 'my_imgs' is generated by 16 integers from 0 to 15. These 16 integers are packed into a tensor with a shape of $4 \times 1 \times 2 \times 2$. We can say that the tensor has four rows and one column, and each element of the 4×1 tensor is a 2×2 tensor. In computer vision, we would say that the image tensor contains four images, each image has one channel and the image resolution is 2×2. It is a surprise to see that the bigger image named 'big_img' in the Extra Cell ONE has the same three channels, and the shape of the bigger image is $3 \times 4 \times 4$. If you change the padding parameter to 1 or 2, the shape of the bigger image would be changed to $3 \times 7 \times 7$ or $3 \times 10 \times 10$. Each element's value of those extra rows and columns is zero. Keeping the padding set to zero and changing the 'nrow' parameter from 1 to 5, you would see some things you would not know.

```
# Extra Cell ONE: The usage of make_grid() ------------------------------------
import torch
from torchvision.utils import make_grid
my_imgs = torch.arange(16).view(4,1,2,2)
print('my_imgs=\n', my_imgs)
big_img = make_grid(my_imgs, nrow=2, padding=0)
print('big_img.shape=', big_img.shape)
print('big_img=\n', big_img)
# Extra Cell TWO after Cell 04 ------------------------------------------------
x = torch.arange(18).view(2,3,3)
print(x)
print(x.permute(1, 2, 0))
print(x)
#----------------------------------------------------------------------------
```

$$\begin{bmatrix} 0 & 1 \\ 2 & 3 \end{bmatrix}$$

$$\begin{bmatrix} 4 & 5 \\ 6 & 7 \end{bmatrix} \begin{bmatrix} 0 & 1 & 4 & 5 \\ 2 & 3 & 6 & 7 \\ 8 & 9 & 12 & 13 \\ 10 & 11 & 14 & 15 \end{bmatrix} \begin{bmatrix} 0 & 1 & 4 & 5 \\ 2 & 3 & 6 & 7 \\ 8 & 9 & 12 & 13 \\ 10 & 11 & 14 & 15 \end{bmatrix} \begin{bmatrix} 0 & 1 & 4 & 5 \\ 2 & 3 & 6 & 7 \\ 8 & 9 & 12 & 13 \\ 10 & 11 & 14 & 15 \end{bmatrix}$$

$$\begin{bmatrix} 12 & 13 \\ 14 & 15 \end{bmatrix}$$

Now we can explain why the shape of the bigger image is $3 \times 62 \times 482$ in Cell 04. Any black and white image processed by module *make_grid( )* would become an image with the same three channels. By arranging 32 MNIST images into a 2×16 array with padding = 2 for a bigger image, the height and the width of the big image should be $[(28 + 2) \times 2 + 2]$ and $[(28 + 2) \times 16 + 2]$, respectively. Using the *imshow( )* function from *matplotlib.pyplot* to show the big image with a shape $3 \times 62 \times 482$, we have to permute the big image so that its shape is changed to $62 \times 482 \times 3$. With codes in the above Extra Cell TWO, we practice how to view a 3D tensor at different angles by the permutation function. The permutation operation to a tensor does not change the tensor, but only the view shape of the tensor.

In the above Extra Cell TWO, 18 integers were reshaped into a $2 \times 3 \times 3$ tensor. This 3D tensor has three axes Dim_0, Dim_1 and Dim_2 as shown in figure 2.2. The directions of the three axes follow a left-hand role: if the thumb, the index finger and the middle finger of your left hand are perpendicular to each other, the index finger

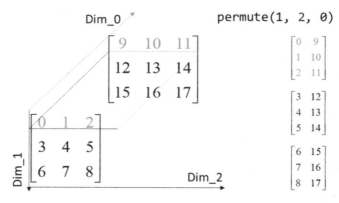

Figure 2.2. (Left) A normal view for a 3D tensor created by codes in extra cell two: your eyes look along Dim_0, your nose is along Dim_1, and a line linked your two eyes is parallel with Dim_2. (Right) Three sub-tensors of the permuted tensor are on three planes perpendicular to Dim 1.

points to Dim_0, the middle finger points to Dim_1, and the thumb points to Dim_2. We view the tensor along the direction of the Dim_0 axis; our noses are in the Dim_1 direction; and the direction of a line linking your left eye to our right eye is in the direction of Dim_2. The 3D tensor is sliced on planes perpendicular to the Dim_0. This is the normal view angle to the 3D tensor. With the code *x.permute(1,2,0)*, we should look at the tensor from the top along Dim_1. The tensor should be sliced by horizontal planes, and the top plane is shown in the figure. With our noses in the Dim_2 direction, we obtain three sub-tensors and each of them has three rows and two columns.

```
# Cell 05: Model, Criterion, Optimizer Definitions-----------------------Cell 05
class Model(nn.Module):
    def __init__(self):
        super().__init__()
        self.net = nn.Sequential(
                nn.Linear(img_size*img_size, n_hidden),
                nn.ReLU(),
                nn.Linear(n_hidden, n_class)
        ) #output.shape = batch_size x n_class
    def forward(self, images):        #images.shape = batch_size x 1 x 28^2
        input = images.view(images.shape[0], -1)
        output = self.net(input)           # input.shape = batch_size x 784
        return output                      # output.shape = batch_size x 10
model = Model().cuda()
criterion = nn.CrossEntropyLoss(reduction='sum')
optimizer = torch.optim.SGD(model.parameters(), lr=lr)
#-----------------------------------------------------------------------------
```

In the model defined in Cell 05, there are two fully connected layers. One of them is *nn.Linear(784, 100)* and the other is *nn.Linear(100, 10)*. Between them is an activation class *nn.ReLU()*. It is not *nn.Sigmoid()*. You can still use the sigmoid class for an activation function, if you want. The ReLU activation function sets all negative numbers to be zero, and keeps any positive number as it is. It works well and takes less time for calculations. The model does not really analyze 2D images. Each 2D image's 28×28 pixels are converted into a 1D tensor with 784 elements in the forward function of the model. For each batch of the train dataloader with 32 images, the input of the model is a tensor with a shape of 32×784. The output of the first layer is a tensor of shape 32×100, and the output of the last layer is a tensor of shape 32×10.

In chapter 1, we used an MSE loss function for continuous variables. For the MNIST image classification project, the targets are discrete integers 0, 1, ..., 9 about image class identities. A cross-entropy loss function is used for image classifications. Codes of the following Extra Cell THREE are used to show you how a cross-entropy loss function works. In the extra cell, a 1D tensor [2,1,0] named 'targets' is supposed to be a 1D tensor of image labels from a batch of a dataloader (line 03), and a 3×4 tensor named 'y_hat' is supposed to be an output of a model (line 06). In this example, the batch size of a dataloader is three and the total number of image classes in the dataset is four. With them, the criterion or loss function nn. CrossEntropyLoss() directly gives you the loss function value on the last line of the extra cell. We should know that the cross-entropy loss function does some extra work to the outputs of any image classification model.

```
# Extra Cell THREE after Cell 05: Example of CrossEntropyLoss Calculations-------
import torch; import torch.nn as nn; import torch.nn.functional as F
criterion = nn.CrossEntropyLoss(reduction='mean')
targets = torch.tensor([2, 1, 0])
print('targets=', targets) #targets are image labels in a dataloader---line 03
y_hat = torch.randn(3, 4, requires_grad=True)
print('y_hat=\n', y_hat)          #y_hat is the output of a model -------line 06
loss = criterion(y_hat, targets)
print('CrossEntropyLoss=', loss)        # CrossEntropyLoss= tensor(1.5229)

# Extra Cell FOUR after Cell 05: Manual Calculations of CrossEntropyLoss --------
Y_hat = y_hat.softmax(dim=1)    # the softmax function to each row of y_hat
print('Y_hat=\n', Y_hat)         # the sum of each sy_hat row is equal to 1.0
p = F.one_hot(targets, num_classes=y_hat.shape[1])      #-----------line 03
print('one_hot=\n', p)           # the sum of each sy_hat row is equal to 1.0
L = -torch.sum(p*torch.log(Y_hat))/len(targets)
print('my_CrossEntropyLoss =', L)       # my_CrossEntropyLoss = tensor(1.5229
#-----------------------------------------------------------------------------
```

$$s\left(\begin{bmatrix} \hat{y}_{1,1} & \hat{y}_{1,2} & \cdots & \hat{y}_{1,m} \\ \hat{y}_{2,1} & \hat{y}_{2,2} & \cdots & \hat{y}_{2,m} \\ \cdots & \cdots & \cdots & \cdots \\ \hat{y}_{n,1} & \hat{y}_{n,2} & \cdots & \hat{y}_{n,m} \end{bmatrix}\right) = \begin{bmatrix} \dfrac{e^{\hat{y}_{1,1}}}{\sum_{k=1}^{m} e^{\hat{y}_{1,k}}} & \dfrac{e^{\hat{y}_{1,2}}}{\sum_{k=1}^{m} e^{\hat{y}_{1,k}}} & \cdots & \dfrac{e^{\hat{y}_{1,m}}}{\sum_{k=1}^{m} e^{\hat{y}_{1,k}}} \\ \dfrac{e^{\hat{y}_{2,1}}}{\sum_{k=1}^{m} e^{\hat{y}_{2,k}}} & \dfrac{e^{\hat{y}_{2,2}}}{\sum_{k=1}^{m} e^{\hat{y}_{2,k}}} & \cdots & \dfrac{e^{\hat{y}_{2,m}}}{\sum_{k=1}^{m} e^{\hat{y}_{2,k}}} \\ \cdots & \cdots & \cdots & \cdots \\ \dfrac{e^{\hat{y}_{n,1}}}{\sum_{k=1}^{m} e^{\hat{y}_{n,k}}} & \dfrac{e^{\hat{y}_{n,2}}}{\sum_{k=1}^{m} e^{\hat{y}_{n,k}}} & \cdots & \dfrac{e^{\hat{y}_{n,m}}}{\sum_{k=1}^{m} e^{\hat{y}_{n,k}}} \end{bmatrix} = \hat{Y} \qquad (2.1)$$

$$H(p, q) = -\sum_{i=1}^{n}\sum_{j=1}^{m} p_{i,j} \ln\left(\hat{Y}_{i,j}\right) \qquad (2.2)$$

On the left hand side of equation (2.1), a $\hat{y}$ tensor is an output of a model for a batch of images in a dataloader, where n is the batch size. In the example of the Extra Cell THREE, the batch size is three. The $\hat{y}$ tensor has m columns for m classes in the dataset. In the same example of the Extra Cell THREE, m is equal to 4. The first line of the Extra Cell FOUR uses a SoftMax function which acts on each element of each row of the $\hat{y}$ tensor with an option dim = 1 as shown in equation (2.1). In this way, the sum of each row of the $\hat{Y}$ tensor on the right side of equation (2.1) is equal to one. The tensor $\hat{Y}$ is used to represent the result of the SoftMax operation to the $\hat{y}$ tensor. Then the $1 \times n$ tensor 'targets = [2,1,0]' is hot-coded into a $(n \times m)$ target tensor named 'p' on line 03 in Extra Cell FOUR. The values of most elements in tensor p are zeros, and only p[0,2], p[1,1], p[2,0] are set to be 1. The cross entropy is then calculated according to equation (1.7) which is modified as equation (2.2). The only non-zero element on each row of tensor p is used to pick out an element at the same location of $\hat{Y}$ for cross-entropy calculations. Since these mathematical operations are automatically finished by the cross-entropy loss function, we do not need to mention the SoftMax operation in image classification models.

```python
# Cell 06: Training all batches of images in one epoch----------------------
def training():
    total_loss = 0.0; n_correct = 0.0
    model.train()
    for images, labels in train_dataloader:
        targets = labels.cuda()
        y_hat = model(images.cuda())
        predictions = torch.argmax(y_hat, dim=1)          #===========line 07
        n_correct += torch.sum(predictions==targets).item()
        loss = criterion(y_hat, targets)
        total_loss += loss.item()
        optimizer.zero_grad()
        loss.backward()
        optimizer.step()
    return total_loss/n_samples, 100*n_correct/n_samples
# Cell 07: Evaluation of all batches of images in one epoch------------------
def evaluation():
    total_loss = 0.0; n_correct = 0
    with torch.no_grad():
        model.eval()
        for images, labels in test_dataloader:
            targets = labels.cuda()
            y_hat = model(images.cuda())
            predictions = torch.argmax(y_hat, dim=1)   #===========line 08
            n_correct += torch.sum(predictions==targets).item()
            loss = criterion(y_hat, targets)
            total_loss += loss.item()
    return total_loss/n_tests, 100*n_correct/n_tests
# Cell 08: Training Function with a pandas DataFrame-------------------------
def fitting(epochs):
    df = pd.DataFrame(np.empty([epochs, 4]),
            index = np.arange(epochs),
            columns=['loss_train', 'acc_train', 'loss_test', 'acc_test'])
    progress_bar = tqdm(range(epochs))
    for i in progress_bar:
        df.iloc[i,0], df.iloc[i,1] = training()
        df.iloc[i,2], df.iloc[i,3] = evaluation()
        progress_bar.set_description("train_loss=%.5f" % df.iloc[i,0])
        progress_bar.set_postfix(
                {'train_acc': df.iloc[i,1], 'test_acc': df.iloc[i,3]})
    return df
train_history = fitting(n_epochs)
#--------------------------------------------------------------------------
```

In Cell 06, the 'model.train()' function sets the model for training, so that gradients of the loss function to model parameters will be calculates. In a for-loop, each batch of images and labels in the train dataloader are loaded into GPU memory by '*cuda()*'. After being processed by the SoftMax function on each row of the model's output, the $\hat{Y}$ tensor has a maximum number on each row. With the *torch.argmax* function, we can find a column index on each row at which the maximum number can be found. These indices are stored in a 1×32 tensor named *predictions* on line 07 of Cell 06. On the next line, the sum of correct prediction numbers is found with *torch.sum(predictions = = targets)*. Running the codes in an extra cell 'a = torch.tensor([1,0,3,2]); b = torch.tensor([1,2,3,1]); torch.sum(a = = b)', you will know how to find the sum of matched elements in two 1D tensors. The remaining codes in Cell 06 are not new. Since the loss function has an option 'reduction = 'sum'', the value of the variable named 'total_loss' was divided by 60 000, the total images in the train dataset. Also, the variable 'n_correct' records the number of correct predictions for labels in the dataset. The returned value of 100*n_correct/60000 gives an accurate prediction percentage. Cell 07 is used for 'test_dataloader' to check if the trained model has overfitting issues. The code *model.eval( )* in the cell sets the model for evaluation (without gradient calculations). The outputs of Cell 07 are test loss and test accuracy. In Cell 08, a pandas dataframe is used to record training history. A returned dataframe is used in Cell 09 to plot train results.

```
# Cell 09: Display training results by graphs------------------------------
df = train_history
fig, ax = plt.subplots(1,2, figsize=(10,4), sharex=True)
df.plot(ax=ax[0], y=[1,3], style=['r-o', 'b-+'])
df.plot(ax=ax[1], y=[0,2], style=['r-o', 'b-+'])
for i in range(2):
    ax[i].grid(which='major', axis='both', color='g', linestyle=':')
ax[0].set(xlabel='epoch', ylabel='accuracy(%)')
ax[1].set(xlabel='epoch', ylabel='loss');
# Cell 10: How to use the parameters of the trained model---------------
p_list = [p.numel()  for p in model.parameters()]
print(np.sum(p_list), 'parameters = sum', p_list ) #79510=sum[78400,100,1000,10]
#---------------------------------------------------------------------
```

We have to use a test dataset for model training to find the overfitting issues for the classification accuracies. The test accuracy should be lower than the train accuracy. Figure 2.3 shows that the prediction accuracy for the test dataset is about 2% lower than that of the train dataset. At the beginning of the model training, model parameters are randomly set by PyTorch, and the model was not well-trained, so the test accuracy may be higher than the train accuracy. The model training has some overfitting issues based on the accuracy and loss graphs. This is normal for model training. Both Adam and SGD optimizers could be used for the model training, and the test accuracies are about 98%. If the model only has one neural layer with code *nn.Linear(784,10)*, the test accuracy is over 92%. If the model has three fully connected layers and two activation functions, the test accuracy is still around 98%. From the output of Cell 10, you will find that the simple model has 79 510 parameters. To increase the test classification accuracy, we need to use a model with different algorithms and more parameters.

In computer vision projects for image classification, image segmentation, and object detection, the first metrics used to evaluate model training is accuracy, but it is

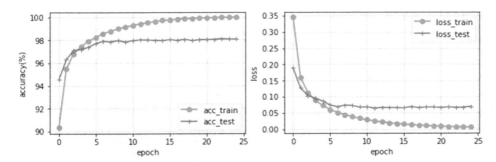

Figure 2.3. Model training results with SGD optimizer. (Left) MNIST classification accuracies, (Right): Loss curves.

Table 2.1. A confusion matrix for test dataset.

Class		Prediction									
		Zero	One	Two	Three	Four	Five	Six	Seven	Eight	Nine
Ground truth	Zero	969	1	1	0	2	2	2	1	1	1
	One	0	1122	3	2	0	1	2	1	3	1
	Two	4	3	1006	4	3	1	2	4	5	0
	Three	0	0	7	987	0	3	0	2	5	6
	Four	1	0	2	0	962	0	4	4	1	8
	Five	2	0	0	8	1	870	5	0	5	1
	Six	3	2	1	1	5	6	939	1	0	0
	Seven	1	2	7	1	0	0	0	1006	6	5
	Eight	4	0	2	2	2	1	0	2	958	3
	Nine	2	2	0	2	7	2	1	5	3	985

not enough. From a confusion matrix (table 2.1) obtained by codes in Cell 11 about the test dataset, four more metrics (table 2.2) can be obtained for detailed information about model training results. In the confusion matrix table, class names in the left column are for labels of ground truth, and class names in the top row are for predicted labels from the trained model. We will only use the row with the class name 'Five' about the digit 5 as an example to explain the confusion matrix. Out of 892 images for the digit 5, only 870 predicted correctly. Two digit 5 were predicted as 0, eight digit 5 were predicted as 3, ..., one digit 5 was predicted as 9. For a confusion table about the train dataset, all numbers are zeros except10 numbers on the diagonal. Those 10 numbers on the diagonal of the confusion matrix in table 2.1 are true positive (TP) values of 10 classes. The summation of a row of the table has the name 'support' which is equal to the total ground truth of a class. A support has two parts: the true positive (TP) and false negative (FN) of the class. A metric named **'recall'** is equal to the ratio of TP and (TP+FN). It is about the percentage of correct predictions out of the ground truth of a class.

Table 2.2. Evaluation metrics for test dataset.

Class	precision	recall	f1_score	IOU	support
Zero	0.983	0.989	0.986	0.972	980
One	0.991	0.989	0.990	0.980	1135
Two	0.978	0.975	0.976	0.954	1032
Three	0.980	0.977	0.979	0.958	1010
Four	0.980	0.980	0.980	0.960	982
Five	0.982	0.975	0.979	0.958	892
Six	0.983	0.980	0.982	0.964	958
Seven	0.981	0.979	0.980	0.960	1028
Eight	0.971	0.984	0.977	0.955	974
Nine	0.975	0.976	0.976	0.953	1009
macro_avg	0.980	0.980	0.980	0.961	10 000
weighted_avg	0.981	0.981	0.981	0.962	Acc = 0.98

```
# Cell 11: confusion matrix for image classification----------------------------
def matrics(my_dataloader):
    y_true = []; y_pred = []
    for imgs, labels in my_dataloader:
        y_true += labels
        model_output = model(imgs.cuda())
        y_hat = torch.argmax(model_output, dim=1)
        y_pred += y_hat.cpu()
    return confusion_matrix(y_true, y_pred)
cf = matrics(test_dataloader)
print('confusion_matrix=\n', cf)
#-------------------------------------------------------------------------------
```

The summation of a column of the confusion matrix has the name 'Prediction' which also has two parts: the true positive (TP) and false positive (FP) of the class. A metric named '**precision**' is equal to the ratio of TP and (TP+FP). It is the percentage of correct predictions in the predictions for a class. A harmonic mean of the precision and the recall is a metric called **F1 score**: 2TP/(2TP+FP+FN). The last metric is intersection over union (**IOU**) which also has another name: **Jaccard score**: TP/(TP+FP+FN). It is an important evaluation metric for object detection. The above four evaluation metrics are listed in table 2.2 for all 10 classes in the test dataset. They are the outputs of a function defined in Cell 12 applied to the test dataset. There are two kinds of average for the four metrics. The **macro average** of a metric is the average of 10 numbers of a class in a column of table 2.2. The metric value of each class has the same weight. The lower-right corner cell of the metrics table is for the accuracy of model training. Its value matches the last point of a corresponding accuracy curve shown in figure 2.3(A). Above the cell of the accuracy number is the number of total samples in the test dataset: 10 000. A support number of a class in the right column divided by the total sample number is the weight of a class for the **weighted average** calculations.

```
# Cell 12: Metrics of confusion matrix for image classification-----------------
def metrics(cf, target_names):
    n = len(target_names)
    df = pd.DataFrame(
        np.zeros([n+2, 5]),
        index = target_names + ['macro_avg', 'weighted_avg'],
        columns=['precision', 'recall', 'f1_score', 'IoU', 'support'])
    for i in range(n):       # i for row: ground truth labels=============line 07
        TP = cf[i,i]                        # TP
        support = cf[i,:].sum()             # TP + FN, sum of a cf row
        recall = TP/support                 # TP/(TP+FN)
        preds = cf[:n,i].sum()              # TP + FP, sum of a cf column
        precision = TP/preds                # TP/(TP+FP)
        f1_score = 2*TP/(preds + support)   # 2TP/(2TP+FN+FP)
        IoU = TP/(preds + support -TP)      # TP/(TP+FN+FP)
        df.iloc[i, 0:5] = [np.round(precision, 3), np.round(recall, 3),
                np.round(f1_score, 3), np.round(IoU, 3), np.round(support, 0)]
        for j in range(4):       # for macro_average =================== line 17
            df.iloc[n, j] = np.round(df.iloc[:n, j].mean(), 3)
        df.iloc[n, 4] = np.round(cf.sum(),0)   #Total samples========== line 19
        for j in range(4):       # for weighted_average ================ line 20
            df.iloc[n+1, j] = np.round(np.sum(
                [df.iloc[i, j]*df.iloc[i, 4]/df.iloc[n, 4] for i in range(n)]),3)
        df.iloc[n+1, 4] = np.round(           # for accuracy ========== line 23
                        np.sum([cf[i,i] for i in range(10)])/cf.sum(), 3)
    return df
df = metrics(cf, class_names)
print(df)
#--------------------------------------------------------------------------------
```

2.2 Mathematical operations of a 2D convolution

A convolutional neural network (CNN) uses a small 4D tensor to extract important local patterns on images, such as horizontal lines '-', vertical lines '|', cross lines ' × ', etc. The small 4D tensor is the kernel of a 2D convolution. Convolutional kernels are digital sensors. Before you know how a convolutional neural network works, I would like to show you how powerful a CNN is in the above MNIST classification project. Using the following codes to replace those codes in Cell 05 of project 2.1, you will find that the classification accuracy for the test dataset is up to 99.5%.

```
# Cell 05-2: ResNet6 Model, Criterion, Optimizer: n_epochs=15, test_acc=99.53%
def basic(in_channels, out_channels):
    return nn.Sequential(
        nn.Conv2d(in_channels, out_channels,
                  kernel_size=3, padding=1, bias=False),
        nn.BatchNorm2d(out_channels),
        nn.ReLU(inplace=True))
class Rs_Block(nn.Module):
    def __init__(self, in_channels):
        super().__init__()
        self.resnet = nn.Sequential(
                      basic(in_channels, in_channels),
                      basic(in_channels, in_channels))
    def forward(self, x):
        return x + 0.5*self.resnet(x)
class ResNet6(nn.Module):
    def __init__(self, in_channels=1, num_classes=10):
        super().__init__()
        self.net =  nn.Sequential(
            basic(in_channels, 64), nn.MaxPool2d(2), #Nx64x14^2 layer 01
            basic(64, 128), nn.MaxPool2d(2),   #Nx128x7^2     layer 02
            Rs_Block(128),  nn.MaxPool2d(2),   #Nx128x3^2     layer 03-04
            basic(128, 256), nn.MaxPool2d(3),  #Nx256x1^2     layer 05
            nn.Flatten(),
            nn.Linear(256, num_classes)  #      Nx10          layer 06
            )
    def forward(self, x):
        return self.net(x)
model = ResNet6().cuda()
criterion = nn.CrossEntropyLoss(reduction='sum')
optimizer = torch.optim.SGD(model.parameters(), lr=lr)
#-------------------------------------------------------------------------
```

In the above CNN model, a PyTorch class *nn.Conv2d*() is used. It has many options to set, such as: input channels, output channels, kernel size, stride, padding, bias, etc. There are many YouTube videos teaching the mathematics of convolution operators. I would like to use the following two examples to make it easier to understand the complex convolution operations. For mathematical convenience, we just use square tensors whose row number and column number are the same. The convolution class is also powerful to handle rectangular tensors

$$X = \begin{bmatrix} 0 & 1 & 2 & 3 \\ 4 & 5 & 6 & 7 \\ 8 & 9 & 10 & 11 \\ 12 & 13 & 14 & 15 \end{bmatrix}, \ K = \begin{bmatrix} 0 & 1 \\ 2 & 3 \end{bmatrix}, \ \text{conv2d}(X, K) = \begin{bmatrix} 24 & 30 & 36 \\ 48 & 54 & 60 \\ 72 & 78 & 84 \end{bmatrix}$$

The sizes of the above tensor X and K are 4×4 and 2×2 respectively. The underlined digits in the tensor K are used to distinguish the digits from the digits in the tensor X. Two constants n and f are used to represent sizes of X and K, respectively $(n = 4, f = 2)$. At the beginning of a manual convolution operation, the tensor K is moved on top of the tensor X with an element $K(0)$ and an element $X(0)$ at the same position. Then each of the four elements of tensor K is multiplied by an element of tensor X in the same position. The sum of these products is the first element of the convolution: $24 = 0 \times 0 + 1 \times 1 + 2 \times 4 + 3 \times 5$. Then tensor K is shifted to the right side by a step of one column with $K(0)$ on the top of $X(1)$. The moving distance (s) has a name 'stride'. By default, s is equal to one. After calculations, tensor K is moved again with $K(0)$ on the top of $X(2)$. The maximum steps that the tensor K can be moved horizontally is equal to $[(n - f)/s + 1]$ which sets the size of the convolution operator's output to be three for this example. Then tensor K is moved to a position where $K(0)$ is on the top of $X(4)$. These moving and calculation processes continue to the last block where $K(0)$ is on top of $X(10)$: $84 = 0 \times 10 + 1 \times 11 + 2 \times 14 + 3 \times 15$. The following code is used to do the above job.

```
# Extra Cell ONE: Definition of conv2d() for convolution operations-----------
import torch
X = torch.arange(16).to(torch.float).view(4,4); print('X=\n', X)
K = torch.tensor([[0.,1],[2,3]]); print('K=\n', K)
def conv2d(X, K):
    n = X.shape[0]              # n=4
    f = K.shape[0]              # f=2
    s = 1                       # s: stride
    m = int((n - f)/s + 1)      # m=3: convolution output size
    Y = torch.empty(m, m)       # Y: convolution output
    for i in range(m):
        for j in range(m):
            Y[i, j] = (X[i: i + f, j: j + f] * K).sum()
    return Y
print('conv2d(X,K)=\n', conv2d(X,K))
#------------------------------------------------------------------------------
```

If the value of $[(n - f)/s$ is a fraction, we just take the integer part of the fraction. To avoid an issue of image size shrinking from convolution operators, we can add extra rows and columns filled with zeros around tensor X. This operation is called 'padding'. A constant named p is used for the padding. If p is set to be one for the above tensor X, then the sizes of the above convolution output should be $[(n - f + 2 \times 1)/s + 1]$. By default, the stride is equal to one, but stride could be two, three or a bigger integer. Using a bigger stride number, we may reduce model training time, but would lose detailed information about images. Considering all these parameters, we have the output size of a convolution:

$$m = \frac{n - f + 2p}{s} + 1 \tag{2.3}$$

It is not necessary for us to define our own convolution functions. PyTorch has a class *nn. Conv2d()* for image convolution operations, and we just need to know how to use it. The following example is about using a PyTorch convolution for another tensor X and another tensor K. The convolution results are also shown below. The names of subunits of these tensors are written on their lower-right corners for readers, not for Python codes. For example, the tensor X has two channels or subunits: X_0 and X_1. The shape of tensor X is: X.shape $= 1 \times 2 \times 4 \times 4$, and the shape of the kernel K is: K.shape $= 3 \times 2 \times 2 \times 2$. The shape of the convolution output Y is: Y.shape $= 1 \times 3 \times m^2$, where m is set by equation (2.3). The dimensional relationships of these tensors are: Y.shape[0] = X.shape[0], Y.shape[1] = K.shape

[0] and X.shape[1] = K.shape[1]. Dimension ONE of X and K should be the same for convolutions. The last two dimensions of a kernel could be 1×1, 2×2, 3×3, 4×4 or even 7×7 for bigger images.

```
# Extra Cell TWO: Convolution(in_channels=2, out_channels=3, n=4, f=2, s=1, p=0)
import torch
import torch.nn as nn
X = torch.arange(32).view(1,2,4,4).to(torch.float)   #--------------------line 03
print('X.shape=', X.shape)
#print('X=\n', X)
conv = nn.Conv2d(in_channels=2,out_channels=3, kernel_size=2)   #--------line 06
K = torch.arange(24).view(3,2,2,2).to(torch.float)            #-------line 07
print('K.shape=', K.shape)
print('K=\n', K)
conv.weight = nn.Parameter(K)                           #--------------------line 10
conv.bias = nn.Parameter(torch.tensor([0.0, 0, 0])) #--------------------line 11
output = conv(X)                                        #--------------------line 13
print(output.shape)
output
#---------------------------------------------------------------------------
```

$$X = \left[\left[\begin{array}{cccc} 0 & 1 & 2 & 3 \\ 4 & 5 & 6 & 7 \\ 8 & 9 & 10 & 11 \\ 12 & 13 & 14 & 15 \end{array} \right]_{X_0} \left[\begin{array}{cccc} 16 & 17 & 18 & 19 \\ 20 & 21 & 22 & 23 \\ 24 & 25 & 26 & 27 \\ 28 & 29 & 30 & 31 \end{array} \right]_{X_1} \right]$$

$$K = \left[\left[\begin{array}{cc} 0 & 1 \\ 2 & 3 \end{array} \right]_{K_{00}} \left[\begin{array}{cc} 4 & 5 \\ 6 & 7 \end{array} \right]_{K_{01}} \right. \\ \left[\begin{array}{cc} 8 & 9 \\ 10 & 11 \end{array} \right]_{K_{10}} \left[\begin{array}{cc} 12 & 13 \\ 14 & 15 \end{array} \right]_{K_{11}} \\ \left. \left[\begin{array}{cc} 16 & 17 \\ 18 & 19 \end{array} \right]_{K_{20}} \left[\begin{array}{cc} 20 & 21 \\ 22 & 23 \end{array} \right]_{K_{21}} \right]$$

$$Y = \left[\left[\begin{array}{ccc} 440 & 468 & 496 \\ 552 & 580 & 608 \\ 664 & 692 & 720 \end{array} \right]_{C_0} \left[\begin{array}{ccc} 1112 & 1204 & 1296 \\ 1480 & 1572 & 1664 \\ 1848 & 1940 & 2032 \end{array} \right]_{C_1} \left[\begin{array}{ccc} 1784 & 1940 & 2096 \\ 2408 & 2564 & 2720 \\ 3032 & 3188 & 3344 \end{array} \right]_{C_2} \right]$$

On the third line of the Extra Cell TWO, 32 integers from 0 to 31 were packed into a $1 \times 2 \times 4 \times 4$ tensor X. Because the convolution class only accepts a 4D float32 tensor, tensor X has to be converted into this type by an option *to(torch.float)*. On the sixth line of the Cell, an instance named 'conv' is defined for the class *nn.Conv2d ()*. Its 'in_channels' option is set to be equal to X.shape[1] = 2, its 'out_channels' option is set to be equal to K.shape[0] = 3, and the kernel size option (f) is set to be equal to K.shape[-1] = 2. Default values are used for other options of the convolution, such as $s = 1$, $p = 0$, and bias = True. With these settings, we get

$m = 3$. PyTorch automatically initializes weights and biases of the class's instance with random numbers for kernels. These parameters are learnable. With codes on lines from 07 to 10, we manually set the kernel with 24 integers by $nn.Parameter()$. Also, a 1×2 zero tensor is assigned to the bias of the convolution instance.

Only after being able to manually calculate the above convolution results, would you be comfortable using the convolution class. To manually obtain the first element of the first channel of the convolution's output $C_0(440)$, we move K_{00} and K_{01} on top of X_0 and X_1 respectively, with $K_{00}(0)$ and $X_0(0)$ in the same position, also with $K_{01}(4)$ and $X_1(16)$ in the same position. The sum of eight multiplications with elements on the same locations is: $440 = (0 \times 0 + 1 \times 1 + 2 \times 4 + 3 \times 5) + (4 \times 16 + 5 \times 17 + 6 \times 20 + 7 \times 21)$. After K_{00} and K_{01} synchronously scanning over X_0 and X_1 respectively, the subunit C_0 of the convolution is obtained. The second and the third channel of the kernel repeat the same operations of the first channel of K to X. Finally, with $K_{20}(16)$, $X_0(10)$ in the same position, and $K_{21}(20)$, $X_1(26)$ in the same position, the last element of the convolution is obtained in this way: $C_2(3344) = (16 \times 10 + 17 \times 11 + 18 \times 14 + 19 \times 15) + (20 \times 26 + 21 \times 27 + 22 \times 30 + 23 \times 31)$.

Codes in the following Extra Cell THREE are used to show you how to use kernels to find local patterns in images. An image tensor X in the cell is constructed by four 3×3 patches. The first one is for a horizontal line '-' pattern; the second one is for a vertical line '|' pattern; the third one is for a cross ' $\times$ ' pattern; and the last one is for a pattern which is the combination of the above three patterns. Those 3×3 patches for the first three patterns in tensor X are used as three filters of a kernel tensor K with a shape of $3 \times 1 \times 3 \times 3$. The outputs of the convolution of X with K and a MaxPool2d are shown below.

```
# Extra Cell THREE: Convolution and MaxPool2d()-------------------------------
import torch
import torch.nn as nn
X=torch.tensor([[[[0,0,0,0,1,0],
                  [1,1,1,0,1,0],
                  [0,0,0,0,1,0],
                  [1,0,1,1,1,1],
                  [0,1,0,1,1,1],
                  [1,0,1,1,1,1.]]]])
K = torch.tensor([[[0,0,0],
                   [1,1,1],
                   [0,0,0.]],
                  [[0,1,0],
                   [0,1,0],
                   [0,1,0.]],
                  [[1,0,1],
                   [0,1,0],
                   [1,0,1.]]])
K = K.unsqueeze(dim=1)      #K = K.view(3,1,3,3)
print('X.shape=', X.shape)  # [1,1,6,6]
print('K.shape=', K.shape)  # [3,1,3,3]
conv = nn.Conv2d(in_channels=1, out_channels=3, kernel_size=3, padding=1)
conv.weight = nn.Parameter(K)
conv.bias = nn.Parameter(torch.tensor([0, 0, 0.]))
output = conv(X)
print(output)
torch.nn.functional.max_pool2d(output, 2)
#-------------------------------------------------------------------------------
```

$$X_{0,0} = \begin{bmatrix} 0 & 0 & 0 & 0 & 1 & 0 \\ 1 & 1 & 1 & 0 & 1 & 0 \\ 0 & 0 & 0 & 0 & 1 & 0 \\ 1 & 0 & 1 & 1 & 1 & 1 \\ 0 & 1 & 0 & 1 & 1 & 1 \\ 1 & 0 & 1 & 1 & 1 & 1 \end{bmatrix}$$

$$K = \begin{bmatrix} \begin{bmatrix} 0 & 0 & 0 \\ 1 & 1 & 1 \\ 0 & 0 & 0 \end{bmatrix}_{K_0} & \begin{bmatrix} 0 & 1 & 0 \\ 0 & 1 & 0 \\ 0 & 1 & 0 \end{bmatrix}_{K_1} & \begin{bmatrix} 1 & 0 & 1 \\ 0 & 1 & 0 \\ 1 & 0 & 1 \end{bmatrix}_{K_2} \end{bmatrix}^T$$

$$Y = \begin{bmatrix} \begin{bmatrix} 0 & 0 & 0 & 1 & 1 & 1 \\ 2 & 3 & 2 & 2 & 1 & 1 \\ 0 & 0 & 0 & 1 & 1 & 1 \\ 1 & 2 & 2 & 3 & 3 & 2 \\ 1 & 1 & 2 & 2 & 3 & 2 \\ 1 & 2 & 2 & 3 & 3 & 2 \end{bmatrix}_{C_0} & \begin{bmatrix} 1 & 1 & 1 & 0 & 2 & 0 \\ 1 & 1 & 1 & 0 & 3 & 0 \\ 2 & 1 & 2 & 1 & 3 & 1 \\ 1 & 1 & 1 & 2 & 3 & 2 \\ 2 & 1 & 2 & 3 & 3 & 3 \\ 1 & 1 & 1 & 2 & 2 & 2 \end{bmatrix}_{C_1} & \begin{bmatrix} 1 & 2 & 1 & 2 & 1 & 1 \\ 1 & 1 & 1 & 2 & 1 & 2 \\ 1 & 4 & 2 & 4 & 3 & 2 \\ 2 & 0 & 3 & 3 & 3 & 3 \\ 0 & 5 & 0 & 5 & 5 & 3 \\ 2 & 0 & 3 & 2 & 3 & 0 \end{bmatrix}_{C_2} \end{bmatrix}^T$$

$$\text{Maxpool2}D(Y, 2) = \begin{bmatrix} \begin{bmatrix} 3 & 2 & 1 \\ 2 & 3 & 3 \\ 2 & 3 & 3 \end{bmatrix}_{M_0} & \begin{bmatrix} 1 & 1 & 3 \\ 2 & 2 & 3 \\ 2 & 3 & 3 \end{bmatrix}_{M_1} & \begin{bmatrix} 2 & 2 & 2 \\ 4 & 4 & 3 \\ 5 & 5 & 5 \end{bmatrix}_{M_2} \end{bmatrix}^T$$

After running the codes in Extra Cell THREE, you will see the above results. Since the padding is set to be one, the sizes of the three channels of the convolution's output are the same as the sizes of tensor X. A sub-tensor C_1 is the convolution result of X with K_1. The maximum value of elements in C_1 is 3.0. From the locations of the maximum value in C_1, you can find the locations of the vertical line '|' pattern in the tensor X. The local pattern information is then concentrated by a PyTorch function 'max_pool2d()' with a stride option of size 2. A PyTorch class named 'nn. MaxPool2d(2)' is used in the ResNet6 model in Cell 05-2 in the last section. The sub-tensor M_1 of the output of the 'max_pool2d' function came from C_1. In machine learning, we do not need to find or search for patterns. By using the gradient decedent algorithm to loss functions, we can train our models to find local patterns automatically in images, and these patterns are recorded in filters of kernels of each CNN layer. The ResNet6 model defined in Cell 05-2 has five CCN layers and one fully connected layer or a dense layer. The PyTorch class *nn. BatchNorm2d( )* in the function named 'basic' of the model normalizes its input of a 4D tensor. The basic function of ResNet6 has one CNN layer. A class in the model named 'Rs_Block()' has two CNN layers.

2.3 Using ResNet9 for CIFAR-10 classification

In any computer vision project with CNN models, information flows through CNN layers sequentially in one direction. These types of models are 'plain' models. It is a common sense that the more layers a model has, the smarter the model will be. What is the limit of the maximum layers of a CNN model: 10, 100 or even more than 1000 layers? In 2015, Kaiming He and his three colleagues published a paper (He *et al* 2016) titled 'Deep residual learning for image recognition'. They found that a 'plain' model with 20 layers was more accurate than another 'plain' model with 56 layers. They found that this strange issue was caused by a mathematical issue called 'gradient vanishing', and they solved the problem by using residual neural networks (**ResNet**). With their solution, a ResNet model could have more than a thousand CNN layers.

The input of a computer vision project about image classification is a batch of images: a 4D tensor X. If a plain model has three layers, each layer works like a mathematical function. Using a 'forward propagation' algorithm, the output of the model is: $\hat{y} = f_3(f_2(f_1(X)))$. Values of a loss function are also obtained from another function $L = g(X, f_1, f_2, f_3)$. Using the gradient descent algorithm to optimize the model, we calculate the gradients of the loss function to the input tensor X with a 'backward propagation' algorithm: $\nabla_X L = \frac{\partial L}{\partial f_3} \frac{\partial f_3}{\partial f_2} \frac{\partial f_2}{\partial f_1} \frac{\partial f_1}{\partial X}$. In machine learning, we frequently handle float32 tensors. In cases where the values of all the partial gradients in $\nabla_X L$ are less than one, and the layers of the plain model are 100 or even 1000, the gradient of L to X will be very close to zero. This is the 'gradient vanishing' issue. In this case, the model parameters cannot be updated, and model training results will not be improved.

To avoid the 'gradient vanishing' issue, Kaiming He and his colleagues let information flow through model layers with branches. In the ResNet6 model of section 2.1, the third and fourth layers came from a class *Rs_Block* which has two branches to process input information. One branch bypasses layer 03 and layer 04, another branch was processed by the two layers. Since the shapes of the tensors of the two branches are the same, they could be added together directly for the output of the *Rs_Block*. From those examples of convolution operations in the last section, we saw that the element values of convolution outputs were bigger because of multiplication and sum operations in convolutions. The output of the second branch was reduced by half, and the reduced output was added to the first branch's output for the output of the *Rs_Block* class.

In more complex ResNet models, we have to use *nn.Conv2d( )* with kernels of filter size one and other PyTorch classes to modify data channels and resolutions in the two branches. Before jumping deeper in ResNet networks, let us to use the above knowledge to classify images in CIFAR-10 dataset (Krizhevsky and Hinton 2009). This database was created by a Toronto research organization: Canadian Institute for Advanced Research. The CIFAR-10 database has 60 000 color images in

10 different classes. The resolution of these images is 32 × 32. The codes in Cell 01 are used to import Python and PyTorch libraries for the CIFAR-10 image classification project. Hyperparameters are also set in the cell. With codes in Cell 02, we input the CIFAR-10 database for two datasets. By using four image transformation operations, the difference between image classification accuracies about the train and validation datasets are small. Otherwise, the classification accuracy for the train dataset quickly increases to almost 100%, but the one for the validation datasets is much lower. These augmentations can significantly reduce the overfitting issue.

In Cell 02, a dataset with 50 000 images was randomly split into a train dataset and a validation dataset, and they have 40 000 and 10 000 images, respectively. These two datasets are used for model training and validation. The test dataset will be used at the end to evaluate the trained model. With codes in Cell 03, the three datasets are sliced into three dataloaders. Running codes in Cell 04, we can see 100 images in a batch of the train dataloader, but only the first 40 images are displayed in figure 2.4 to save page.

Figure 2.4. CIFA-10 images (outputs of Cell 04). Reproduced with permission from Krizhevsky and Hinton (2009) courtesy of Alex Krizhevsky.

```
# Project 2.3 Image Classification for CIFAR10 with ResNet9-----------Python v3.6
import torch; import torch.nn as nn; from torch.utils.data import DataLoader
import torch.optim.lr_scheduler as lr_scheduler
from torch.utils.data.dataset import random_split as split
import torchvision.transforms as T; from torchvision.utils import make_grid
from torchvision.datasets import CIFAR10
import pandas as pd; import numpy as np; import matplotlib.pyplot as plt
from tqdm import trange; from sklearn.metrics import confusion_matrix
n_epochs = 30
batch_size = 100
img_size = 32
img_channels = 3
n_class = 10
lr = 5e-3
n_train= 40000
n_val = 10000
s_p_e = int(n_train/batch_size) #steps per epoch = 400 for lr_scheduler
data_path = './OCR/data/cifar10'
class_names = ['airplanes', 'cars', 'birds', 'cats', 'deer', 'dogs', 'frogs',
               'horses', 'ships', 'trucks']
# Cell 02: CIFAR-10 Datasets----------------------------------------------Cell 02
dataset =CIFAR10(data_path, train=True, download=False, transform=T.Compose([
                T.RandomCrop(img_size, padding=4, padding_mode='reflect'),
                T.RandomHorizontalFlip(),
                T.ToTensor(),
                T.Normalize([0.5, 0.5, 0.5], [0.5, 0.5, 0.5])]))
test_dataset = CIFAR10(data_path, train=False, download=False,
                transform=T.Compose([T.ToTensor(),
                        T.Normalize([0.5, 0.5, 0.5], [0.5, 0.5, 0.5])]))
train_dataset, val_dataset = split(dataset, [n_train, n_val],
                                generator=torch.manual_seed(999))
# Cell 03: Slice datasets into dataloaders---------------------------------
train_dl = DataLoader(train_dataset, batch_size=batch_size, shuffle=True,
                    num_workers=4, pin_memory=True)
val_dl = DataLoader(val_dataset, batch_size=batch_size, shuffle=False,
                    num_workers=4, pin_memory=True)
test_dl = DataLoader(test_dataset, batch_size=batch_size, shuffle=False,
                    num_workers=4, pin_memory=True)
for imgs, labels in train_dl:
        print(labels.view(-1,10))
        print('imgs.shape=', imgs.shape)
        break                   #pick out the 1st batch of the train dataloader
# Cell 04: Show images in a batch of dataloader----------------------------
def denorm(img_tensors):     # Shift image pixel values to [0,1]
    return img_tensors * 0.5 + 0.5
def show_imgs(images):
    fig, ax = plt.subplots(figsize=(16,12))
    inputs = make_grid(denorm(images), nrow=10, padding=1)
    ax.imshow(inputs.permute(1,2,0))
    ax.set(xticks=[], yticks=[]);
show_imgs(imgs)
#-------------------------------------------------------------------------
```

```python
# Cell 05: ResNet9 model, criterion, optimizer and learning rate scheduler
def basic(in_channels, out_channels):
    return nn.Sequential(
        nn.Conv2d(in_channels, out_channels,
                kernel_size=3, padding=1, bias=False),
        nn.BatchNorm2d(out_channels),
        nn.ReLU(inplace=True)
        )
class Rs_Block(nn.Module):
    def __init__(self, in_channels):
        super().__init__()
        self.resnet = nn.Sequential(
                basic(in_channels, in_channels),
                basic(in_channels, in_channels)
                )
    def forward(self, x):
        return x + self.resnet(x)
class ResNet9(nn.Module):
    def __init__(self, in_channels=img_channels, num_classes=n_class):
        super().__init__()
        self.net =  nn.Sequential(
                basic(in_channels, 64),              #batch_size x 64 x 32^2
                basic(64, 128), nn.MaxPool2d(2),     #batch_size x 128 x 16^2
                Rs_Block(128),                       #batch_size x 128 x 16^2
                basic(128, 256), nn.MaxPool2d(2),    #batch_size x 256 x 8^2
                basic(256, 512), nn.MaxPool2d(2),    #batch_size x 512 x 4^2
                Rs_Block(512),                       #batch_size x 512 x 4^2
                nn.MaxPool2d(4),                     #batch_size x 512 x 1^2
                nn.Flatten(),
                nn.Linear(512, num_classes)          #batch_size x 10
            )
    def forward(self, images):
        output = self.net(images) #images.shape=batch_size x 3 x 32^2
        return output               #output.shape = batch_size x 10
model = ResNet9().cuda()
criterion = nn.CrossEntropyLoss(reduction='sum')
optimizer = torch.optim.SGD(model.parameters(), lr=lr)
scheduler = lr_scheduler.OneCycleLR(optimizer, max_lr=lr,
                steps_per_epoch=s_p_e, epochs=n_epochs, pct_start=0.4)
# Cell 06: Model Training for the train_dataloader----------------------Cell 06
def training(my_dataloader):
    total_loss = 0.0; n_correct = 0.0
```

```
    n_samples = len(my_dataloader.dataset)
    model.train()
    for i, (images, labels) in enumerate(my_dataloader):
        labels = labels.cuda(non_blocking=True)
        outputs = model(images.cuda(non_blocking=True))
        predictions = torch.argmax(outputs, dim=1)
        n_correct += torch.sum(predictions==labels).item()
        loss = criterion(outputs, labels)
        total_loss += loss.item()
        loss.backward()
        nn.utils.clip_grad_value_(model.parameters(), clip_value=0.1)
        optimizer.step()
        scheduler.step()
        optimizer.zero_grad()
    return total_loss/n_samples, 100*n_correct/n_samples
# Cell 07: Model Evaluation for val_dataloader and test_dataloader------Cell 07
def evaluation(my_dataloader):
    n_samples = len(my_dataloader.dataset)
    with torch.no_grad():
        total_loss = 0.0; n_correct = 0
        model.eval()
        for i, (images, labels) in enumerate(my_dataloader):
            labels = labels.cuda(non_blocking=True)
            outputs = model(images.cuda(non_blocking=True))
            predictions = torch.argmax(outputs, dim=1)
            n_correct += torch.sum(predictions==labels).item()
            loss = criterion(outputs, labels)
            total_loss += loss.item()
    return total_loss/n_samples, 100*n_correct/n_samples
# Cell 08: The main training function-----------------------------Cell 08
def fitting(epochs):
    df = pd.DataFrame(np.empty([epochs, 5]),
        index = np.arange(epochs),
        columns=['loss_train', 'acc_train', 'loss_val', 'acc_val', 'lr'])
    progress_bar = trange(epochs)
    for i in progress_bar:
        df.iloc[i,0], df.iloc[i,1] = training(train_dl)
        df.iloc[i,2], df.iloc[i,3] = evaluation(val_dl)
        df.iloc[i,4] = optimizer.param_groups[0]['lr']
        progress_bar.set_description("train_loss=%.5f" % df.iloc[i,0])
        progress_bar.set_postfix(
                    {'train_acc': df.iloc[i,1], 'test_acc': df.iloc[i,3]})
    return df
train_history = fitting(n_epochs)
# Cell 09: Graphs of Model training outputs-------------------------Cell 09
import matplotlib.pyplot as plt
df= train_history
fig, ax = plt.subplots(1,3, figsize=(12,3), sharex=True)
df.plot(ax=ax[0], y=[1,3], style=['r-+', 'b-d'])
df.plot(ax=ax[1], y=[0,2], style=['r-+', 'b-d'])
df.plot(ax=ax[2], y=[4], style=['r-+'])
for i in range(3):
```

```
    ax[i].set_xlabel('epoch')
    ax[i].grid(which='major', axis='both', color='g', linestyle=':')
ax[0].set_ylabel('accuracy(%)')
ax[2].ticklabel_format(style='sci', axis='y', scilimits=(0,0));
# Cell 10: Using test dataloader to test the trained model-------------Cell 10
n = 580
loss, accuracy = evaluation(test_dl)
print('test dataloader accuracy (%)=', accuracy)
img, label = test_dataset[n]
def predict_image(img, model):
    print('img.shape=', img.shape)
    x = img.unsqueeze(0).cuda()
    print('img.unsqueeze(0).shape=', x.shape)
    y_hat = model(x); print('y_hat =', y_hat)
    pred_idx = torch.argmax(y_hat, dim=1); print('pred_idx =', pred_idx.item())
    return dataset.classes[pred_idx[0].item()]
print('Prediction is: {0}; Label is {1}'.format(
        predict_image(img, model), dataset.classes[label]))
plt.imshow(denorm(img).permute(1,2,0));
# Cell 11: save a trained model---------------------------------model saving
File_name = 'C:/Users/xiaoc/Python/Exercises/GroundingDINO/teacher.pth'
torch.save(model, File_name)
#----------------------------------------------------------------------------
```

The structure of the model ResNet9 and the model NesRet6 are almost the same. The only difference is that ResNet9 has three more neural layers. There are two ResNet blocks in the ResNet9 model. From figure 2.5, outputs of Cell 08 and Cell 09, you can find that the image classification accuracies for the train dataset and the valuation dataset are over 99% and 92%, respectively. After running the code *evaluation(test_dl)* on the second line of Cell 10, we will get the accuracy for the test dataset that is also over 92%.

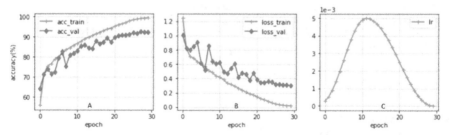

Figure 2.5. CIFAR-10 image classification results. (A) Accuracy curves. (B) Loss curves. (C) Learning rate curve. Model training time is 23 min.

2.4 Transfer learning with ResNet for a dataset of Vegetable Images

Inventing a CNN model to solve problems in a computer vision project is not an easy job. The architecture of the ResNet9 model came from Jovian. It is the simplest and the most efficient model for image datasets with lower resolutions. For datasets with high resolution images, we have to use more powerful models. Fortunately, there are many very smart models which had been trained with millions of images. We do not need to reinvent 'wheels'. Transfer learning is about using pre-trained models to new datasets for image classifications or other computer vision projects. By running codes *import torchvision; import torchvision.models; dir(models)* in an extra cell before Cell 06 in Project 2.4, you will see more than a hundred pre-trained models, such as resnet18, resnet34, resnet50, resnet101, resnet152 and vgg16, etc. These pre-trained models were designed for bigger images (224×224). We will modify and use resnet18, resnet50 and resnet152 in the project for a dataset of Vegetable Images classification. Using CC BY-SA 4.0 license, Shahriyar Mahmud Mamun (the author of the dataset) in Bangladesh kindly gives people freedom to share and adapt the dataset.

The project for Vegetable Images classification has three parts. Cell 01 to 04 combined together is the first part. It imports datasets, slices datasets into dataloaders and displays a batch of images and their labels. The size of a zip file downloaded from Kaggle is around 560 MB. After unzipping the file in my computer to a folder named 'VegetableImgs', I got three sub-folders named 'train', 'test' and 'validation'. Under each of these sub-folders, there are 15 sub-folders. The name of each of the second level sub-folders is the name of a kind of vegetable. Using a torchvision datasets tool, *ImageFolder*, to pack these images into three datasets, I obtained the names of 15 classes in these datasets. By running *train_dataset.classes* in an extra cell after the Cell 04, you will see a list of names of the 15 classes: Bean, Bitter_Gourd, Bottle_Gourd, Brinjal, Broccoli, Cabbage, Capsicum, Carrot, Cauliflower, Cucumber, Papaya, Potato, Pumpkin, Radish and Tomato. The sizes of images in the datasets are not the same. Image resolutions of most images are 224×224. We have to resize all images to the same resolution for datasets. To save the model training time, we can resize images from 224×224 to 128×128.

The three datasets were then sliced into three dataloaders, respectively, in Cell 03 with a batch size of 64. A quarter of images in the first batch of the train dataloader are displayed in figure 2.6. Some of the images are upside down in the figure. That is the effect of the *RandomVerticalFlip* in the image transform operations. Cell 05 is the second part, in which there is a pre-trained model, a criterion, an optimizer and a learning rate scheduler. The last part of the project (Cell 06 to Cell 09) is used to train the model and display training results.

Figure 2.6. Sixteen vegetable images in a batch of the train_dataloader (the output of Cell 04). Reproduced from Shahriyar Mahmud Mamun's Vegetable Images Dataset, CC BY-SA 4.0 license,

```
# Project 2.4: Vegetable image classification with ResNet18 model-----Python v3.6
import torch; import torch.nn as nn; from torch.utils.data import DataLoader
import torch.optim.lr_scheduler as lr_scheduler
from torchvision.utils import make_grid; from torchvision import models
from torchvision.datasets import ImageFolder
from torchvision import transforms as T;
from  matplotlib import pyplot as plt
import numpy as np; import pandas as pd; from tqdm import tqdm, trange
n_epochs = 10
img_size = (224, 224); img_channels = 3
batch_size=64
lr =1e-2
data_path = 'D:/ImageSets/VegetableImgs/'
# Cell 02: Flowers Dataset --------------------------------------------Cell 02
train_dataset = ImageFolder(root=data_path+'train/', transform=T.Compose([
                    T.Resize(img_size),
                    T.RandomVerticalFlip(0.5),
                    T.RandomHorizontalFlip(p=0.5),
                    T.ToTensor(),
                    T.Normalize([0.5,0.5,0.5], [0.5,0.5,0.5])]))
val_dataset = ImageFolder(root=data_path+'validation/', transform=T.Compose([
                    T.Resize(img_size),
                    T.ToTensor(),
                    T.Normalize([0.5,0.5,0.5], [0.5,0.5,0.5])]))
test_dataset = ImageFolder(root=data_path+'test/', transform=T.Compose([
                    T.Resize(img_size),
                    T.ToTensor(),
                    T.Normalize([0.5,0.5,0.5], [0.5,0.5,0.5])]))
classes = train_dataset.classes; n_class = len(classes)
s_p_e = int(len(train_dataset)/batch_size); n_samples=s_p_e * batch_size
# Cell 03: Flowers DataLoader------------------------------------------Cell 03
train_dataloader = DataLoader(train_dataset, batch_size=batch_size, shuffle=True,
                    num_workers=4, pin_memory=True, drop_last=True)
val_dataloader = DataLoader(val_dataset, batch_size=batch_size, shuffle=False,
                    num_workers=4, pin_memory=True, drop_last=True)
test_dataloader = DataLoader(test_dataset, batch_size=batch_size, shuffle=False,
                    num_workers=4, pin_memory=True, drop_last=True)
n_batch = len(train_dataloader) #113
# cell 04: Display the 1st batch of the train_dataloader---------------Cell 04
for imgs, labels in train_dataloader:
    print(imgs.shape, '\nlables=', labels); break
def denorm(img_tensors): # Shift image pixel values to [0,1]
    return img_tensors * 0.5 + 0.5
def show_imgs(images):
    fig, ax = plt.subplots(figsize=(16,10))
    inputs = make_grid(denorm(images[:16]), nrow=8)
    ax.imshow(inputs.permute(1,2,0))
    ax.set(xticks=[], yticks=[]);
show_imgs(imgs)
#------------------------------------------------------------------------------
```

```
# Cell 05: Use a pre-trained ResNet------------------------------Cell 05
model = models.resnet18(pretrained=True)        #------------line 01
#print(model)                                    #------------line 02
model.eval()                                     #------------line 03
#for param in model.parameters():                #------------line 04
#    param.requires_grad = False                 #------------line 05
num_ftrs = model.fc.in_features                  #------------line 06
model.fc = nn.Linear(num_ftrs, n_class)          #------------line 07
model = model.cuda()
criterion = nn.CrossEntropyLoss(reduction='sum')
optimizer = torch.optim.SGD(model.parameters(), lr=lr)
scheduler = lr_scheduler.OneCycleLR(optimizer, max_lr=lr,
        steps_per_epoch=s_p_e, epochs=n_epochs, pct_start=0.4)
# Cell 06: A function to train the train_dataloader--------------------Cell 06
def training(my_dataloader):
    total_loss = 0.0; n_correct = 0.0
    n_samples = len(my_dataloader.dataset)
    model.train()
    for images, labels in my_dataloader:
        labels = labels.cuda(non_blocking=True)
        outputs = model(images.cuda(non_blocking=True))
        predictions = torch.argmax(outputs, dim=1)
        n_correct += torch.sum(predictions==labels).item()
        loss = criterion(outputs, labels)
        total_loss += loss.item()
        loss.backward()
        nn.utils.clip_grad_value_(model.parameters(), clip_value=0.1)
        optimizer.step()
        scheduler.step()
        optimizer.zero_grad()
    return total_loss/n_samples, 100*n_correct/n_samples
#------------------------------------------------------------------------
```

By default, all these pre-trained models from torchvision are used for image datasets with 1000 classes. If you use *print(model)* on the second line of Cell 05, you will find that the last layer of the resnet18 model is a fully connected layer: *nn.Linear(1024,1000, bias=False)*. It was used for ImageNet dataset with 1000 classes, so we have to change the parameters of the last layer for the vegetable image dataset with only 15 classes. The codes on line 06-07 of Cell 05 do the work. Then running the code *print(model)* in an extra cell after Cell 05, you will find the last fully connected layer is changed to *nn.Linear (1024, 15, bias=False)*. We can also import optimized parameters with an option *pretrained=True* on line 01 of Cell 05 for the pre-trained model. I tried with another option 'False', and found the classification accuracies were lower. If you remove hashtag # symbols in front of lines 04 and 05, the codes on the two lines will freeze all parameters coming with the trained model. Since the last fully connected layer is modified, only the parameters in the last layer will be updated during model training. In this case, the classification accuracies were not good enough. With codes in Cell 05 to update all parameters in the pre-trained resnet18 model, the classification accuracies were around 98% for the test dataloader (figure 2.7). With resnet50 and resnet101, the accuracies would be improved a little more, but the training time would be doubled and tripled, respectively. Codes in Cell 10 can be used to classify a single image with an index in the test dataset. It prints out that image for you to verify the classification.

```
# Cell 07: Evaluation function for val_dataloader and test_dataloader----Cell 07
def evaluation(my_dataloader):
    n_samples = len(my_dataloader.dataset)
    with torch.no_grad():
        total_loss = 0.0; n_correct = 0
        model.eval()
        for images, labels in my_dataloader:
            labels = labels.cuda(non_blocking=True)
            outputs = model(images.cuda(non_blocking=True))
            predictions = torch.argmax(outputs, dim=1)
            n_correct += torch.sum(predictions==labels).item()
            loss = criterion(outputs, labels)
            total_loss += loss.item()
    return total_loss/n_samples, 100*n_correct/n_samples
# Cell 08: Main training function with pandas DataFrame----------------Cell 08
def fitting(epochs):
    df = pd.DataFrame(np.empty([epochs, 5]),
        index = np.arange(epochs),
        columns=['loss_train', 'acc_train', 'loss_val', 'acc_val', 'lr'])
    progress_bar = trange(epochs)


    for i in progress_bar:
        df.iloc[i,0], df.iloc[i,1] = training(train_dataloader)
        df.iloc[i,2], df.iloc[i,3] = evaluation(val_dataloader)
        df.iloc[i,4] = optimizer.param_groups[0]['lr']
        progress_bar.set_description("train_loss=%.5f" % df.iloc[i,0])
        progress_bar.set_postfix(
                    {'train_acc': df.iloc[i,1], 'val_acc': df.iloc[i,3]})
    return df
train_history = fitting(n_epochs)
# Cell 09: Graphs of Model training outputs---------------------------Cell 09
df= train_history
fig, ax = plt.subplots(1,3, figsize=(12,3), sharex=True)
df.plot(ax=ax[0], y=[1,3], style=['r-+', 'b-d'])
df.plot(ax=ax[1], y=[0,2], style=['r-+', 'b-d'])
df.plot(ax=ax[2], y=[4], style=['r-+'])
for i in range(3):
    ax[i].set_xlabel('epoch')
    ax[i].grid(which='major', axis='both', color='g', linestyle=':')
ax[0].set_ylabel('accuracy(%)')
ax[2].ticklabel_format(style='sci', axis='y', scilimits=(0,0));
# Cell 10: Using test dataloader to test the trained model-------------Cell 10
loss, accuracy = evaluation(test_dataloader)
print('test dataloader accuracy (%)=', accuracy)
n = 1300
img, label = test_dataset[n]
def predict_image(img, model):
    print('img.shape=', img.shape)
    x = img.unsqueeze(0).cuda()
    print('img.unsqueeze(0).shape=', x.shape)
    y = model(x)
    preds = torch.argmax(y, dim=1)
    return train_dataset.classes[preds[0].item()]
print('Prediction is: {0}; Label is {1}'.format(
        predict_image(img, model), train_dataset.classes[label]))
plt.imshow(denorm(img).permute(1,2,0));
#---------------------------------The End------------------------------------
```

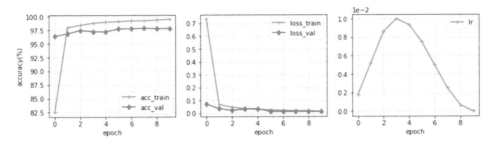

Figure 2.7. Vegetable image classification results by ResNet18. (Left) accuracy curves (train dataset: 99.4%, validation dataset: 97.6%, test dataset: 97.9%). (Middle) loss curves. (Right) the learning rate curve. Model training time is 7 min.

What codes are inside those pre-trained ResNet models? From the flowing ResNet18 model, you would know other models with more than 100 layers, but it is not necessary. The function named 'basic' has two convolution layers. The input of the function is a 4D tensor, and the output of the function is also a 4D tensor, but its channels and resolution could be different from the input. A class titled 'Id_Block' has two branches. Its basic branch's input and output have the same shape; another branch's output is the input tensor itself. The outputs from the two branches directly add together as the output of the class. A class named 'Rs_Block' also has two branches. Comparing it with the shape of its input tensor, the output from the basic branch (stride = 2) has different channels and resolutions. A branch named 'shortcut' with a convolution of kernel size one is used to modify its input tensor, so the second branch's output shape can match with the output shape of the basic branch. These blocks are used to build the ResNet18 model.

```python
# ResNet18 Codes -----------------------------------------------------
import torch.nn as nn
def basic(in_channels, out_channels, stride=1):
    return nn.Sequential(
        nn.Conv2d(in_channels, out_channels, kernel_size=3,
                stride=stride, padding=1, bias=False),
        nn.BatchNorm2d(out_channels),
        nn.ReLU(inplace=True),
        nn.Conv2d(out_channels, out_channels, kernel_size=3,
                stride=1, padding=1, bias=False),
        nn.BatchNorm2d(out_channels))
class Id_Block(nn.Module):
    def __init__(self, in_channels, out_channels, stride=1):
        super().__init__()
        self.basic_block = basic(in_channels, out_channels, stride=stride)
        self.relu = nn.ReLU()
    def forward(self, x):
        return self.relu(x + self.basic_block(x))
class Rs_Block(nn.Module):
    def __init__(self, in_channels, out_channels, stride=2):
        super().__init__()
        self.basic_block = basic(in_channels, out_channels, stride=2)
        self.shortcut = nn.Sequential(
            nn.Conv2d(in_channels, out_channels, kernel_size=1,
                stride=stride, padding=0, bias=False),
            nn.BatchNorm2d(out_channels))
        self.relu = nn.ReLU()
    def forward(self, x):
        return self.relu(self.shortcut(x) + self.basic_block(x))
class ResNet(nn.Module):          #ResNet18 layer=[2,2,2,2]
    def __init__(self, image_channels=3, num_classes=10):
        super().__init__()
        self.net = nn.Sequential(#------layer0 out_shape=64x48^2
            nn.Conv2d(in_channels=image_channels, out_channels=64,
                kernel_size=7, stride=2, padding=3, bias=False),
            nn.BatchNorm2d(64),
            nn.ReLU(),
            #------layer1 out_shape=64x24^2
            nn.MaxPool2d(kernel_size=3, stride=2, padding=1),
            Id_Block(64, 64, 1), Id_Block(64, 64, 1),
            #------layer2 out.shape=128x12^2
            Rs_Block(64, 128, 2),Id_Block(128, 128, 1),
            #------layer3 out_shape=256x6^2
            Rs_Block(128, 256, 2),Id_Block(256, 256, 1),
            #------layer4 out_shape=512x3^2
            Rs_Block(256, 512, 2),Id_Block(512, 512, 1),
            nn.AdaptiveAvgPool2d(1),
            nn.Flatten(),
            nn.Linear(512, num_classes))
    def forward(self, x):
        return self.net(x)
model = ResNet().cuda()
#--------------------------------------------------------------------
```

There are 17 convolution layers and a fully connected layer in the ResNet18 model. That is why it has the name 'ResNet18'. Running *p_list = [p.numel() for p in model.parameters()]; print(sum(p_list),' = ', p_list)*, you will find the total parameter number (11 181 642) in the resnet18, and also the numbers of parameters in each layer. Then changing to another pre-trained model and checking those parameter numbers, you will find that the parameter number in the resnet50 model is 23 528 522. We can print out all parameter names and their shapes by running the following short codes. From the first line of the outputs of the Extra Cell 01, we get a parameter named 'conv1.weight' and its shape: torch.size([64, 3, 7, 7]). It is the weight tensor of the convolution operation in the first convolution layer of the ResNet18 model.

```
# Extra Cell 01 After Cell 11-----------------------------------------------
for name, parameter in model.named_parameters():
    print(name, '\t\t', parameter.shape)
#---------------------Outputs of Extra Cell 01-----------------------------
conv1.weight                  torch.size([64, 3, 7, 7])
bn1.weight                    torch.Size([64])
bn1.bias                      torch.Size([64])
layer1.0.conv1.weight         torch.Size([64, 64, 3, 3])
......
#-------------------------------------------------------------------------
```

The weight tensor of the convolution could be treated as a batch of images with 64 samples, three channels and a resolution of 7 × 7. We can display this batch of images with codes in the following Extra Cell 02. Each element's value of the weight tensor is sifted to [0, 1]. The left image in figure 2.8 came from the pre-trained ResNet18 model with optimized parameters; the right one also came from the same model but with randomly initialized parameters. In section 2.2 we generated patterns with matrices for convolutions. Now we see real convolution patterns. A ResNet model with deeper layers would pick out more detail pattern information about images.

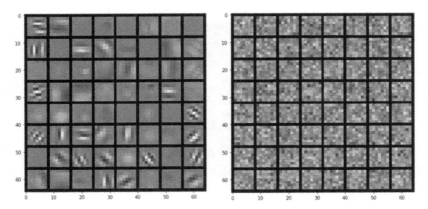

Figure 2.8. Images of the convolution kernel weights in layer 1 of resnet18. (Left): Pre-trained ResNet50 model with optimized parameters. (Right): Pre-trained model with randomly initialized parameters

```
# Extra Cell 02: Show kernel patterns of the model's 1st convolution------------
fig, ax = plt.subplots(figsize=(7, 7))
w = model.conv1.weight.cpu() # move w from GPU to CPU
min_w=torch.min(w)           # find the minimum number of the w tensor
w1 = (-1/(2*min_w))*w + 0.5  #Shift w elements to [0,1]
img_grid = make_grid(w1, nrow=8, padding=1) # Combine 64 images into one
ax.imshow(img_grid.permute(1,2,0));
#---------------------------The End--------------------------------- ----------
```

References

Coates A, Ng A and Lee H 2011 An analysis of single-layer networks in unsupervised feature learning *J. Mach. Learn. Res.—Proc. Track* **15** 215–23

He K, Zhang X, Ren S and Sun J 2016 Deep residual learning for image recognition *Proc. of the IEEE Conf. on Computer Vision and Pattern Recognition* 770–8

Krizhevsky A and Hinton G 2009 Learning multiple layers of features from tiny images. Technical Report TR-2009, University of Toronto https://www.cs.toronto.edu/~kriz/learning-features-2009-TR.pdf

Lecun Y, Cortes C and Burges C J C 1998 The MNIST database of handwritten digits.

Deng L 2012 The MNIST database of handwritten digit images for machine learning research *IEEE Signal Process. Mag.* **29** 141–2

IOP Publishing

Mastering Computer Vision with PyTorch and Machine Learning

Caide Xiao

Chapter 3

Image generation by GANs

This chapter is about using generative adversarial networks (GANs) and conditional GANs to generate fake images similar to images in the six datasets: MNIST, Fashion MNIST, Anime Face, CelebA and Rock Paper Scissors. A simple quadratic curve dataset is used to make it is easy to understand the mathematical principle of GANs.

Image generation is more difficult than image classification. This is true both for human beings and for computers. After Ian Goodfellow and his colleagues published a paper (Goodfellow *et al* 2014) titled 'Generative adversarial nets' in 2014, many algorithms were developed based on GANs. Today, computers can be trained to create photo-realistic images of human faces. Just by searching 'this person does not exist', you will find a website where you can see astonishing fake photos of human faces. A GAN has two neural networks or models: a generator and a discriminator. The generator creates fake data samples from pure noises. The discriminator uses fake samples and real samples as its inputs, and evaluates them to find the fake. During model training, the two networks compete with each other. The generator tries to produce data (images) to fool the discriminator and the discriminator manages to correctly identify the generated data. The training process continues until the generator creates data that is so realistic that the discriminator can't distinguish it from real data. At the end of model training, the GAN can find a PDF of image pixels in the dataset. Using parameters of the PDF, computers can generate fake images which are similar to real images.

3.1 The GAN theory

One GAN model is used as a generator (G) which is trained to generate fake images from 1D noisy vectors. The number of elements in a noisy vector could be 1, 2, or even more than 100. Those vectors came from a standard normal distribution function (section 1.1.1). Model G has many parameters (θ_g) to be trained. Another model is used as a discriminator (*D*) which is trained to distinguish fake images from real images in a dataset. It also has many parameters (θ_d) to be trained. Model G is just like an art student who is taught to paint by his teacher Leonardo da Vinci, the model D. After watching his teacher's many masterpieces, the student paints his first picture. The teacher tells his student what he has painted incorrectly, and how to improve his skill. The student then paints a second picture. The teacher checks the picture again and gives the student more advice; the process is repeated many times. Finally, the student is able to paint another Mona Lisa and nobody can say that it is a fake. This is an ideal result. However, what happens if the student is not smart enough to understand his master's ideas and suggestions, or if the teacher is not Leonardo da Vinci, but an ordinary man? The training will be a failure in both cases.

GAN model training is still a challenge. One big issue of GAN's model training is 'mode collapse'. For example, you took 120 min to train your models to generate MNIST images for ten digits, but the outputs only had one digit. There are many parameters in the two models, and there are also many hyperparameters in your codes. How can you adjust them to get what you want in a short time? Before we face those model training challenges, we need to build our training machine for GANs. There are four parts to the machine. The first part is for data input, the second part is for constructions of the two models, the third part is for model training, and the fourth part is for data visualization. Only the second part is new for us. Model D and model G are trained in a for-loop for each batch of real images in a dataloader with a batch size *m*:

1. From the dataloader, take a batch of image samples: $\{x_1, x_2..., x_m\}$.
2. Using model D to convert x_i into a scalar $\hat{y}_i = D(x_i) \in [0,1]$, ($i = 1, 2..., m$).
3. Set any real image's target as ONE: $y_i = 1$, ($i = 1, 2, ..., m$).
4. Calculate BCE loss between the targets and the predictions by $\frac{-1}{m}\sum_{i=1}^{m} \ln (D(x_i))$.
5. Generate a batch of noise vectors from a standard normal distribution: $\{z_1, z_2..., z_m\}$.
6. Create a batch of fake images from the noise vectors: $\tilde{x}_i = G(z_i)$, ($i = 1, 2..., m$).
7. Convert any fake image into a scalar $D(\tilde{x}_i) \in [0,1]$ as a fake prediction.
8. Set each fake image's target as ZERO.
9. Calculate BCE loss by $\frac{-1}{m}\sum_{i=1}^{m} \ln (1 - D(\tilde{x}_i))$ without updating model G.
10. Calculate model D's loss:

$$L_D(\theta_d) = \frac{-1}{m}\sum_{i=1}^{m} \ln (D(x_i)) - \frac{1}{m}\sum_{i=1}^{m}(1 - \ln (D(\tilde{x}_i))) \tag{3.1}$$

$$L_D(\theta_d) = - E[\ln(D(X))] - E[\ln(1 - D(G(Z)))]$$

$$\rightarrow -\int p_r(x)\ln\left[D(x)\right]dx - \int p_z(z)\ln\left[1 - D(G(z))\right]dz$$

$$\rightarrow -\int p_r(x)\ln\left[D(x)\right]dx - \int p_g(x)\ln\left[1 - D(x)\right]dx$$

$$= -\int\left(p_r(x)\ln[D(x)] + p_g(x)\ln[1 - D(x)]\right)dx$$

This is the training criterion for the discriminator D with a given generator G. In the condition of G is given, it is possible to find an optimized discriminator D^* to minimize the loss function by $\frac{d}{dD(x)}\left(p_r(x)\ln\left[D(x)\right] + p_g(x)\ln\left[1 - D(x)\right]\right) = 0$ at a fixed x. The optimized discriminator D^* is found to be: $D_G^*(x) = \frac{p_r(x)}{p_r(x) + p_g(x)}$, where we have:

$$L_D(\theta_d) = 2\ln(2) - 2D_{JS}(p_r\|p_g)$$

Based on equation (1.8): $0 \leqslant D_{JS}(p_r \mid p_g \leqslant \ln(2))$, we have $0 \leqslant L_D(\theta_d) \leqslant 2\ln(2)$. In case $p_r = p_g$, model D's loss achieves a maximum: $2\ln(2)$.

11. Update D's parameters θ_d without changing θ_g: $\theta_d \leftarrow \theta_d - \eta\nabla_{\theta_d}L_D(\theta_d)$.
12. Then with a new batch of noises from a normal distribution: $\{z_1, z_2..., z_m\}$.
13. Create a new batch of fake images from the noises: $\tilde{x}_i = G(z_i)$.
14. Convert each $\tilde{x}_i$ into a scalar $D(\tilde{x}_i)\in[0,1]$ as a real prediction.
15. Set each fake image's target as ONE.
16. Calculate BCE loss:

$$L_G(\theta_g) = \frac{-1}{m}\sum_{i=1}^{m}\ln\left(D(\tilde{x}_i)\right) \tag{3.2}$$

17. Update G's parameters with $\theta_g \leftarrow \theta_g - \eta\nabla_{\theta_g}L_G(\theta_g)$.

3.1.1 Implement a GAN for quadratic curve generation

It is better to implement GAN theory to a simple dataset in the beginning. In the following project 3.1.1, only two fully connected layers are used in the generator model (G) and the discriminator model (D) shown in figure 3.1(A). These models handle data in three spaces. The first space is the observed space or real space with 21 dimensions for real quadratic curves. The data of each real curve in a batch of a dataloader come from a quadratic function $y = ax^2 + b$, where x is a 1D array generated by a NumPy function: *np.linspace(−1, 1, 21)*. The factor 'a' in the function is also a 1D array generated by a uniform distribution function: *np.random. uniform(1, 2, size = 64)* and is reshaped into a 64 × 1 NumPy array. Another constant b in the function is set to be equal to $(a -1)$. A batch in a dataloader

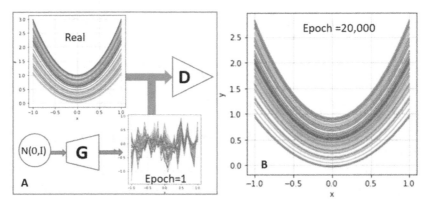

Figure 3.1. (A) The information flow chart for the two models of a GAN. The real curves are outputs of Cell 03. (B) Fake curves at epoch = 20 000, the outputs of Cell 10. Model training time is 11 min.

generated by a function *training_data( )* defined in Cell 02 is a 64 × 21 array. The output of Cell 03 is a graph with 64 real quadratic curves. When printing out data of the last curve $y[63]$ in an extra cell after Cell 01, we would see a 1D NumPy array with 21 floating numbers.

The second space is a latent space with two dimensions (z_dim = 2). Each batch of noise vectors in the latent space is generated by a standard normal distribution function $N(0,I)$ as shown in figure 3.1(A). In Cell 01, the shape of a batch of noise vectors named 'latent_noise' is 64 × 2. The third space is a 1D space named 'critical space' created by the discriminator model D with elements of the batch size. Because the last activate function of model D is a Sigmoid activation function, the value of each element of the critical space is in the range [0,1]. Using a batch of curves (real or fake) as input, model D outputs a batch of scalars. In an extra cell after Cell 09 running the code $D(torch.cuda.FloatTensor(y)).T$, you will get a batch of scalars: tensor ([[0.5777, 0.5896, 0.5465, 0.5909, 0.5825, 0.5710, 0.5672, 0.5742, 0.5858, 0.5727, 0.5582, 0.5435, 0.5661, 0.5390, 0.5611, 0.5673, 0.5926, 0.5957, 0.5521, 0.5668, 0.5571, 0.5948, 0.5742, 0.5589, 0.5634, 0.5714, 0.5482, 0.5927, 0.5947, 0.5880, 0.5490, 0.5582, 0.5575, 0.5450, 0.5552, 0.5678, 0.5504, 0.5413, 0.5415, 0.5648, 0.5715, 0.5896, 0.5489, 0.5505, 0.5711, 0.5963, 0.5747, 0.5426, 0.5622, 0.5399, 0.5580, 0.5820, 0.5600, 0.5616, 0.5605, 0.5636, 0.5526, 0.5724, 0.5752, 0.5728, 0.5491, 0.5960, 0.5571, 0.5436]], device = 'cuda:0', grad_fn = <PermuteBackward0>). Each scalar came from a real image.

Running code $D(G(latent noise)).T$ after Cell 09, you will get another batch of scalar: tensor([[0.5378, 0.5387, 0.5648, 0.5501, 0.5448, 0.5204, 0.5447, 0.5554, 0.5333, 0.5341, 0.5489, 0.5313, 0.5729, 0.5398, 0.5922, 0.5367, 0.5377, 0.5413, 0.5610, 0.5572, 0.5356, 0.5419, 0.5526, 0.5290, 0.5886, 0.5620, 0.5499, 0.5300, 0.5167, 0.5296, 0.5286, 0.5235, 0.5418, 0.5266, 0.5280, 0.5531, 0.5223, 0.5587, 0.5294, 0.5362, 0.5281, 0.5256, 0.5597, 0.5408, 0.5471, 0.5292, 0.5576, 0.5494, 0.5363, 0.5348, 0.5214, 0.5245, 0.5607, 0.5234, 0.5366, 0.5475, 0.5375, 0.5464, 0.5228, 0.5498, 0.5216, 0.5309, 0.5654, 0.5702]], device = 'cuda:0', grad_fn = <PermuteBackward0>). Each scalar is for a fake image. Model D will be trained to increase the scalar of each real curve as close as possible to one, and decrease the scalar of each fake curve as close as possible to zero with a BCE loss function (equation (3.1)). While mode D is trained or model D's parameters are updated, model G's parameters are not touched. Then model G is trained with a new batch of noise vectors by another BCE loss function (equation (3.2)) which tries to increase the scalar of each fake curve as close as possible to one. Model D and model G are trained alternately many times until, and the results of the competition between the two models are $D(X) = D(G(Z)) = 0.5$.

```python
# project 3.1.1 Generate y=ax^2+b curves by GAN ---------------------Python v3.6
import torch; import torch.nn as nn; import numpy as np; import pandas as pd
import matplotlib.pyplot as plt; from tqdm import trange
import torch.optim.lr_scheduler as lr_scheduler
n_epochs = 20000
batch_size = 64
z_dim = 2          # latent space dimensions---------------------------line 06
n_hidden = 256     # number of neurons in the only hidden layer of the GAN
n_points = 21      # number of points on each curve of training_data
n_batch = 5        # Data_loader batch number per epoch
lr = 1e-4          # learning rate
latent_noise = torch.randn(        # latent_noise.shape = 64 x 2
    batch_size, z_dim, requires_grad=True, device='cuda')      #------line 12
# Cell 02: Creating training data from y=a*x^2+(a-1)--------------------Cell 02
x = np.linspace(-1, 1, n_points)    # x=[-1.0, -0.9, ..., 1.0]
def training_data():        # create a batch of dataloader for training
    a = np.random.uniform(1, 2, size=batch_size).reshape(-1,1)  #a.shape=64x1
    points = a*x*x + (a-1)  # points.shape = 64 x 21
    return points
y = training_data()
# Cell 03: Show curves-------------------------------------------------Cell 03
def show_curves(x, y):
    fig, ax = plt.subplots(figsize=(4,4))
    for i in range(batch_size):
        ax.plot(x, y[i,:])
    ax.set(xlabel='x', ylabel='y', xticks=np.arange(-1.0, 1.1, 0.5))
    ax.grid(color='g', linestyle=':')
    plt.show()
show_curves(x,y)
#----------------------------------------------------------------------------
```

Running codes in Cell 01–03, we would see 64 beautiful quadratic curves (figure 3.1(A)), just like the rings of Saturn through a telescope. The variable 'z_dim' in Cell 01 is the dimension of each 2D noisy vector which goes through two layers of model G to generate 21 points for a fake curve. The input of model D defined in Cell 05 is a batch of 64 curves. Each curve with 21 points is processed by model D to become a positive scalar tensor whose value is in the range [0,1]. An activate function LeakyReLU(0.2) is used between those two fully connected layers. This function multiplies a factor 0.2 to each negative number, and keeps each positive number as it is for the outputs of the first layer. Both of these models are sent to GPU by 'cuda()'.

```
# Cell 04: Generator class------------------------------------------Cell 04
class generator(nn.Module):
    def __init__(self):
        super().__init__()
        self.net = nn.Sequential(nn.Linear(z_dim, n_hidden),
                                 nn.ReLU(True),
                                 nn.Linear(n_hidden, n_points))
    def forward(self, z):
        fake_curves = self.net(z)    #z.shape = batch_size x z_dim = 64 x 2
        return fake_curves           #fake_curves.shape = batch_size x n_points
G = generator().cuda()
# Cell 05: Discriminator Class-------------------------------------Cell 05
class discriminator(nn.Module):
    def __init__(self):
        super().__init__()
        self.net = nn.Sequential(nn.Linear(n_points, n_hidden),
                                 nn.LeakyReLU(0.2, inplace=True),
                                 nn.Linear(n_hidden, 1),
                                 nn.Sigmoid())
    def forward(self, curves):
        output = self.net(curves)    # curves.shape = batch_size x n_points
        return output                # outputs.shape = batch_size x 1
D = discriminator().cuda()
# Cell 06 Gradient-penalty function------------for future projects-------Cell 06
# Cell 07: Model optimizers and BCELoss training criterion--------------Cell 07
optimizer_D = torch.optim.Adam(D.parameters(), lr=lr)
optimizer_G = torch.optim.Adam(G.parameters(), lr=lr)
criterion = nn.BCELoss(reduction='mean')
scheduler = lr_scheduler.OneCycleLR(optimizer_D, max_lr=lr, #=============
                  steps_per_epoch=n_batch, epochs=n_epochs, pct_start=0.6)
# Cell 08: Model D's training function for a batch of dataloader----------Cell 08
def train_D(curves, optimizer_D):
    # Using a batch of real images to calculate BCE loss with a target of ONEs
    batch_size = curves.shape[0]
    real_preds = D(curves)
    ones_target = torch.ones(batch_size, 1, device='cuda')
    real_loss = criterion(real_preds, ones_target)
    real_score = torch.mean(real_preds).item()
    # Generating a batch of fake images for BCE loss with a target of ZEROs
    noise = torch.randn(batch_size, z_dim, requires_grad=True, device='cuda')
    curves_fake = G(noise)
    fake_preds = D(curves_fake.detach()) # detach() for without training G
    zeros_target = torch.zeros(batch_size, 1, device='cuda')
    fake_loss = criterion(fake_preds, zeros_target)
    fake_score = torch.mean(fake_preds).item()

    loss_D = real_loss + fake_loss
    optimizer_D.zero_grad()
    loss_D.backward()
    optimizer_D.step()
    scheduler.step()    #========================================================
    return loss_D.item(), real_score, fake_score
```

```
# Cell 09: Definition of a training function for the generator-----------Cell 09
def train_G(optimizer_G):
    noise = torch.randn(batch_size, z_dim, requires_grad=True, device='cuda')
    curves_fake = G(noise)
    fool_preds = D(curves_fake)
    ones_targets = torch.ones(batch_size, 1).cuda()
    loss_G = criterion(fool_preds, ones_targets)
    optimizer_G.zero_grad()
    loss_G.backward()
    optimizer_G.step()
    return loss_G.item()
# Cell 10: Fitting function--------------------------------------------Cell 10
def fit(epochs):
    torch.cuda.empty_cache()
    df = pd.DataFrame(np.empty([epochs, 4]), index = np.arange(epochs),
                      columns=['Loss_G', 'Loss_D', 'D(X)', 'D(G(Z))'])
    for i in trange(epochs):
        loss_G = 0.0; loss_D = 0.0; real_sc = 0.0; fake_sc = 0.0
        for _ in range(n_batch):
            curves_real = torch.cuda.FloatTensor(training_data())
            loss_d, real_score, fake_score = train_D(curves_real, optimizer_D)
            loss_D += loss_d; real_sc += real_score; fake_sc += fake_score
            loss_g = train_G(optimizer_G)
            loss_G += loss_g
        df.iloc[i, 0:3] = loss_G/n_batch, loss_D/n_batch, real_sc/n_batch
        df.iloc[i, 3] = fake_sc/n_batch
        if i==0 or (i+1)%4000==0:
            print(
            "Epoch={:5}, Ls_G={:.3f}, Ls_D={:.3f}, D(X)={:.3f}, D(G(Z))={:.3f}"
            .format(i+1, df.iloc[i,0], df.iloc[i,1], df.iloc[i,2], df.iloc[i,3]))
            fake_curves = G(latent_noise).cpu()
            show_curves(x, fake_curves.detach().numpy())
    return df
train_history = fit(n_epochs)
# Cell 11: Show the training history in Graph-------------------------Cell 11
#import matplotlib.pyplot as plt; import matplotlib.ticker as ticker
df= train_history
fig, ax = plt.subplots(1,2, figsize=(9,4), sharex=True)
df.plot(ax=ax[0], y=[0,1], style=['r:', 'b:'])
df.plot(ax=ax[1], y=[2,3], style=['b:', 'r:'])
for i in range(2):
    ax[i].set_xlabel('epoch')
    ax[i].grid(which='major', axis='both', color='g', linestyle=':')
ax[0].set(ylim=[0.4, 1.6], ylabel='Loss')
ax[0].axhline(y=2*np.log(2), color='k', linestyle='--') #Theory D loss Value
ax[0].axhline(y=np.log(2), color='k', linestyle='--')   #Theory G loss Value
ax[1].axhline(y=0.5, color='k', linestyle='--') #Theory D(X), D(G(Z)) values
ax[1].set_ylim([0, 1.0])
plt.show()
#------------------------------ The End ----------------------------------
```

Cell 06 is reserved for future use. Since the project has two models, Cell 07 defines two Adam optimizers. The two models use the same criterion function: BCELoss(). A tensor named 'noise' in Cell 08 and Cell 09 is used as an input for model G to generate 64 fake curves. The codes for model D training were written following the GAN theory. There are three parts in this cell. The first part is used to calculate the real samples' BCE loss, the second part is to calculate the fake samples' BCE loss. The function 'detach()' in the calculations for 'fake_preds' is very important. With

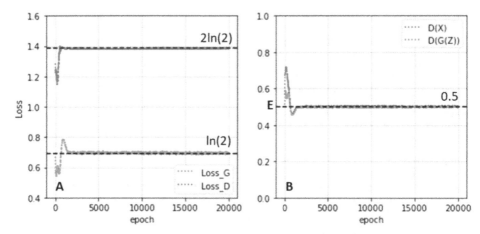

Figure 3.2. (A) Curves of two loss functions, the outputs of Cell 11. (B) Averages of D(X) and D(G(Z)). Three straight dashed lines were drawn based on theoretical values: 2ln(2), ln(2) and 0.5.

this, only model D's parameters are updated in the third part of the cell, and model G's parameters are untouched. The outputs of the cell are model D's loss, real_score (average of D(X)) and fake_score (average of D(G(Z))). One cycle learning rate scheduler is better than a fixed learning rate scheduler for the project.

Codes in Cell 08–09 were written following the GAN theory. It is necessary to mention that the target to train model G in Cell 09 is a tensor with all elements equal to 1.0. In Cell 10, a pandas dataframe is used to record model training history. During the training for 20 000 epochs, only at the beginning and every 4000 epochs will the training results be shown. These results are 'Loss_G', 'Loss_D', 'D(X)' and 'D(G(Z))'. Fake curves are also shown. Cell 11 is used to display the pandas dataframe in graphs (figure 3.2). The two dash lines in figure 3.2(A) were drawn based on theoretical values of Loss_D and Loss_G. Those training loss curves are very close to their theory values respectively. The dashed line in (B) is for the theory value of average D(X) and average D(G(Z)). Training curves overlap with the theoretical line. Only for this simplest project we can train those models for 20 000 epochs in about 11 min.

3.1.2 Using a GAN with two fully connected layers to generate MINST Images

A GAN with the two simple models shown in section 3.1.1 will be used in the following project 3.1.2 to generate fake MNIST images. The two models are not powerful enough to handle data in this project. We cannot generate crystal clear fake images similar to real MNIST images. The easier project is used as a contrast to demonstrate the power of deep convolution GANs in the next section. In Cell 01 of project 3.1.2, tools for the project are imported from Python and PyTorch, also hyperparameters are set. Codes in Cell 02–04 are used to import the MNIST datasets, to slice datasets into dataloaders with a batch size 100, and to pick out and display the first batch images in figure 3.3(A). The values of image pixels were normalized to [−1, 1] in Cell 02. Pixel values of images generated by model G are also in the same range by an activation function Tanh(). Using *imgs.min( )* or *imgs. max( )* in an extra cell after Cell 04, you can verify these limits of pixel values.

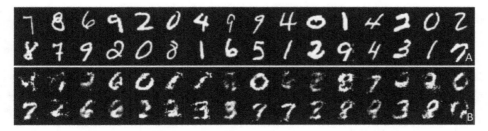

Figure 3.3. (A) Real MNIST images from the output of Cell 04. (B) Fake MNIST images generated by the simple GAN. Model training time is 11 min. The MNIST image dataset is from Deng (2012) with a license CC BY 3.0.

Although VS Code can display these kinds of images with a notice of 'clipping input data to the valid range [0,1]', it is better to shift those pixel values to [0,1] by using a function named *denorm( )* in Cell 04. Cell 05 is reserved for future usage. In Cell 06 and Cell 07, model D and model G are defined with two fully connected layers. Their structures are almost the same as those in section 3.1.1. Only the input variable number of model D and output variable number of G were changed.

```python
# Project 3.1.2: Generate MNIST images by a GAN ---------------------Python v3.6
import torch; import torch.nn as nn; from torch.utils.data import DataLoader
import torch.optim.lr_scheduler as lr_scheduler
import torchvision.transforms as T; from torchvision.datasets import MNIST
from torchvision.utils import make_grid; import matplotlib.pyplot as plt
import numpy as np; import pandas as pd; from tqdm import trange
n_epochs = 50
batch_size = 100
img_size = 28
img_channels = 1
n_hidden = 128
n_class = 10
z_dim = 100            # Latent space dimensions
lr = 2e-4             # initial learning rate
k = 20                # k=G_lr/D_lr
fixed_latent = torch.randn(48, z_dim, device='cuda')
path = './OCR/data/'
# Cell 02: MNIST DataSet ------------------------------------------------Cell 02
trainData = MNIST(path, train=True, download=False,
            transform=T.Compose([T.ToTensor(),
                        T.Normalize([0.5],[0.5])]))
n_samples = len(trainData) #len(trainData)=60000
# Cell 03: Create a DataLoader (trainLoader)----------------------------Cell 03
train_dataloader = DataLoader(trainData, batch_size=batch_size, shuffle=True)
n_batch = len(train_dataloader) #n_batch=n_sample/batch_size=600
for imgs, labels in train_dataloader: # for the 1st batch on the train dataloader
    print('batch_imgs.shape=', imgs.shape)
    #print('labels=\n', labels[:48].view(-1,16))
    break
# Cell 04: Show the images in the 1st batch of the train dataloader-------Cell 04
def denorm(img_tensors):        # Shift the value of each image pixel to [0,1]
    return img_tensors * 0.5 + 0.5
def show_imgs(imgs):
    fig, ax = plt.subplots(figsize=(12,8))
    input = make_grid(denorm(imgs[:48]), nrow=16, padding=2) #display 48 images
    ax.imshow(input.permute(1,2,0), cmap='gray')
    ax.set(xticks=[], yticks=[])
    plt.show()
show_imgs(imgs)
#-----------------------------------------------------------------------------
```

```python
# Cell 06: Discriminator Class------------------------------------------Cell 06
class Discriminator(nn.Module):
    def __init__(self):
        super().__init__()
        self.model = nn.Sequential(
            nn.Flatten(),              #shape = batch_size x 784
            nn.Linear(img_size*img_size, n_hidden),
            nn.LeakyReLU(0.01),
            nn.Linear(n_hidden, 1),
            nn.Sigmoid())
    def forward(self, images):
        output = self.model(images)  #images.shape = batch_size x 1 x 28^2
        return output                #output.shape = batch_size x 1
D = Discriminator().cuda()
# Cell 07: Generator Class---------------------------------------------Cell 07
class Generator(nn.Module):
    def __init__(self):
        super().__init__()
        self.model = nn.Sequential(
            nn.Linear(z_dim, n_hidden),
            nn.LeakyReLU(0.01),
            nn.Linear(n_hidden, img_size*img_size),
            nn.Tanh())
    def forward(self, z):            # z.shape = batch_size x z_dim
        output = self.model(z)       # output.shape = batch_size x 784
        fake_imgs = output.view(-1, 1, 28, 28)
        return  fake_imgs            #fake_imgs = batch_size x 1 x 28^2
G = Generator().cuda()
# Cell 08: Definitions of optimizers, criterion, learning rate scheduler
optimizer_D = torch.optim.Adam(D.parameters(), lr=lr, betas=(0.5, 0.999))
optimizer_G = torch.optim.Adam(G.parameters(), lr=k*lr, betas=(0.5, 0.999))
criterion = nn.BCELoss(reduction='sum')
v = lambda i: np.exp(-0.046*i)
scheduler = lr_scheduler.LambdaLR(optimizer_D, lr_lambda=v)
# Cell 09: Model D's training function --------------------------------Cell 09
def train_D(inputs, optimizer_D):
    real_preds = D(inputs)
    batch_size = inputs.shape[0]
    one_targets = torch.ones(batch_size, 1, device='cuda')
    real_loss = criterion(real_preds, one_targets)
    real_score = torch.mean(real_preds).item()

    z = torch.randn(batch_size, z_dim).cuda()
    fake_images = G(z)
    zero_targets = torch.zeros(batch_size, 1, device='cuda')
    fake_preds = D(fake_images.detach())
    fake_loss = criterion(fake_preds, zero_targets)
    fake_score = torch.mean(fake_preds).item()

    loss = real_loss + fake_loss
    optimizer_D.zero_grad()
    loss.backward()
```

```
        optimizer_D.step()
        return loss.item(), real_score, fake_score
# Cell 10: Model G's training function --------------------------------Cell 10
def train_G(optimizer_G):
        z = torch.randn(batch_size, z_dim).cuda()
        fake_images = G(z)    # Create fake images
        preds = D(fake_images)
        one_targets = torch.ones(batch_size, 1).cuda()
        # Try to fool the discriminator
        loss = criterion(preds, one_targets)
        optimizer_G.zero_grad()
        loss.backward()
        optimizer_G.step()
        return loss.item()
# Cell 11: The definition of a fitting function to train G and D---------Cell 11
def fit(epochs):
        torch.cuda.empty_cache()
        df = pd.DataFrame(np.empty([epochs, 5]),
            index = np.arange(epochs),
            columns=['Loss_G', 'Loss_D', 'D(X)', 'D(G(Z))', 'LearningRate'])
        for i in trange(epochs):
            loss_G = 0.0; loss_D = 0.0; real_sc = 0.0; fake_sc = 0.0
            for real_images, _ in train_dataloader:
                inputs = real_images.cuda()
                loss_d, real_score, fake_score = train_D(inputs, optimizer_D)
                loss_D += loss_d; real_sc += real_score; fake_sc += fake_score
                loss_g = train_G(optimizer_G)
                loss_G += loss_g
            df.iloc[i, 0] = loss_G/n_samples
            df.iloc[i, 1:4] = loss_D/n_samples, real_sc/n_batch, fake_sc/n_batch
            df.iloc[i, 4] = optimizer_D.param_groups[0]['lr']      #Record lr_D
            scheduler.step()                                       #Update lr_D
            optimizer_G.param_groups[0]['lr'] = df.iloc[i,4]*k #------------line 18
            if i==0 or (i+1)%5==0:
                print(
                "Epoch={}, Ls_G={:.4f}, Ls_D={:.4f}, D(X)={:.4f}, D(G(Z))={:.4f}"
                .format(i+1, df.iloc[i,0], df.iloc[i,1], df.iloc[i,2], df.iloc[i,3]))
                fake_images = G(fixed_latent)
                show_imgs(fake_images.detach().cpu())
        return df
train_history = fit(n_epochs)    #dt = 10 min, n_epochs=50
#--------------------------------------------------------------------------
```

```
# Cell 12: Graphs of Model training outputs-------------------------Cell 12
df= train_history
fig, ax = plt.subplots(1,3, figsize=(15,4), sharex=True)
df.plot(ax=ax[0], y=[0,1], style=['r-+', 'b-'])
df.plot(ax=ax[1], y=[2,3], style=['b-', 'r-+'])
df.plot(ax=ax[2], y=[4], style=['r-+'])
for i in range(3):
    ax[i].set_xlabel('epoch')
    ax[i].grid(which='major', axis='both', color='g', linestyle=':')
ax[0].set(ylabel='Loss', ylim=[0.4,1.8])
ax[0].axhline(y=2*np.log(2), color='k', linestyle='--') #Theory D loss Value
ax[0].axhline(y=np.log(2), color='k', linestyle='--')   #Theory G loss Value
ax[1].axhline(y=0.5, color='k', linestyle='--')   #Theory D(X), D(G(Z)) values
ax[1].set_ylim([0.48, 0.6])
ax[2].set_ylim([0, 2.2e-4])
ax[2].ticklabel_format(style='sci', axis='y', scilimits=(0,0));
# Cell 13: Verify if the generator works for inputs-----------------------Cell 13
inputs = torch.randn(1, z_dim).cuda()
fake_images = G(inputs) #generat a fake image
print('inputs.shap=', inputs.shape)
print('fake_images.shape=', fake_images.shape)
show_imgs(fake_images.detach().cpu())
#-------------------------------------The End---------------------------------
```

Using $k = 1$ and a constant lambda function, we use a constant learning rate for both models, and find that model D is smarter than model G. A lambda learning rate scheduler $e^{-0.046i}$ is used and is shown in figure 3.4(C). With the ratio k to be 20, model G's learning rate is a function: $G\_lr = k \times lr \times e^{-0.046i}$. Model training curves of Loss_D, G_loss, D(X) and D(G(Z)) are all tuned to their theory values. It is a trick to train the two models with their own learning rate scheduler. Please pay attention to *df.iloc[i,4]*k* on line 18 of in Cell 11.

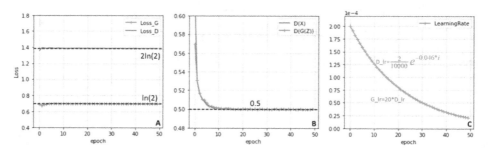

Figure 3.4. (A) Loss curves for model D and G. (B) The D(X) curve and the D(G(Z)) curve. (C) A lambda learning rate scheduler with an exponential function for model D. Black dashed lines are drawn based on theory values.

3.2 Applications of deep convolutional GANs

The fake MNIST images shown in figure 3.3(B) are not crystal clear because model G and model D with only two fully connected layers are not smart enough. We will use a powerful deep convolutional GAN (DCGAN) to repeat the project. In a

DCGAN, model D uses convolution neural layers to convert each image into a scalar, and model G uses transposed convolution neural layers to restore each image from a scalar. We need to know the mathematical operations of a transposed convolution.

3.2.1 Mathematical operations of ConvTranspose2D

Using convolution operations, a DCGAN's discriminator model shrinks an image in a batch of a dataloader into a scalar tensor. From equation (2.3), we know that the output size of a 2D convolution is: $m = (n - f + 2p)/s + 1$. A DCGAN's generator model uses transposed convolution operations to convert a scalar back to an image. This operation also has many options, such as: input channels, output channels, kernel size, stride, padding, bias, etc. The output size of a transposed convolution operation can be derived from equation (2.3), where m is the input tensor size, and n is the output tensor size of a transposed convolution operation.

$$n = (m - 1)s + f - 2p \qquad (3.3)$$

Running codes in the following Extra Cell ONE, you will discover how a ConvTranspose2d class works. Nine integers from 0 to 8 are used to construct a $1 \times 1 \times 3 \times 3$ tensor X in which $m = 3$. Tensor X is an input of an instance of the ConvTranspose2d class. The input's batch size is one, the resolution of the only image in the batch is 3×3, and the image channel is one. The integer tensor is then converted into a float32 tensor, because the transposed convolution instance accepts this type of tensor, not an integer tensor. Usually, the weight and bias of the instance named 'CT' are randomly initialized by PyTorch. The weight of the operator is then assigned with a $1 \times 1 \times 3 \times 3$ ONES tensor by using $nn.Parameter()$, and the bias of the instance is assigned with a scalar ZERO tensor.

```
# Extra Cell ONE: A single Channel ConvTranspose2d operation----------------
X = torch.arange(9).view(1,1,3,3).to(dtype=torch.float32)
print('X=\n', X.data)
CT = nn.ConvTranspose2d(in_channels = 1,
                        out_channels = 1,
                        kernel_size = 3,
                        stride = 3,
                        padding = 0,
                        bias = True)
CT.weight = torch.nn.Parameter(torch.ones(1,1,3,3))
print('K.weight=\n', CT.weight.data)
CT.bias = torch.nn.Parameter(torch.zeros(1))
print('K.bias=', CT.bias.data)
output = CT(X)
print('Y=\n', output.data)
#--------------------------------------------------------------------------
```

$$X_{00} = \begin{bmatrix} 0 & 1 & 2 \\ 3 & 4 & 5 \\ 6 & 7 & 8 \end{bmatrix}, \quad K_{00} = \begin{bmatrix} 1 & 1 & 1 \\ 1 & 1 & 1 \\ 1 & 1 & 1 \end{bmatrix}, \quad Y_{00}(s=1) = \begin{bmatrix} 0 & 1 & 3 & 3 & 2 \\ 3 & 8 & 15 & 12 & 7 \\ 9 & 21 & 36 & 27 & 15 \\ 9 & 20 & 33 & 24 & 13 \\ 6 & 13 & 21 & 15 & 8 \end{bmatrix}$$

$$Y_{00}(s=3) = \begin{bmatrix} 0 & 0 & 0 & 1 & 1 & 1 & 2 & 2 & 2 \\ 0 & 0 & 0 & 1 & 1 & 1 & 2 & 2 & 2 \\ 0 & 0 & 0 & 1 & 1 & 1 & 2 & 2 & 2 \\ 3 & 3 & 3 & 4 & 4 & 4 & 5 & 5 & 5 \\ 3 & 3 & 3 & 4 & 4 & 4 & 5 & 5 & 5 \\ 3 & 3 & 3 & 4 & 4 & 4 & 5 & 5 & 5 \\ 6 & 6 & 6 & 7 & 7 & 7 & 8 & 8 & 8 \\ 6 & 6 & 6 & 7 & 7 & 7 & 8 & 8 & 8 \\ 6 & 6 & 6 & 7 & 7 & 7 & 8 & 8 & 8 \end{bmatrix}, \quad Y_{00}(s=2) = \begin{bmatrix} 0 & 0 & 1 & 1 & 3 & 2 & 2 \\ 0 & 0 & 1 & 1 & 3 & 2 & 2 \\ 3 & 3 & 8 & 5 & 12 & 7 & 7 \\ 3 & 3 & 7 & 4 & 9 & 5 & 5 \\ 9 & 9 & 20 & 11 & 24 & 13 & 13 \\ 6 & 6 & 13 & 7 & 15 & 8 & 8 \\ 6 & 6 & 13 & 7 & 15 & 8 & 8 \end{bmatrix}$$

Taking $m = 3$, $f = 3$, $s = 3$ and $p = 0$ to equation (3.3), we get $n = 9$. It is true that the shape of the output $Y(s = 3)$ of the above codes in Extra Cell ONE is $1 \times 1 \times 9 \times 9$. Each element of tensor X is converted into a 3×3 subunit in the output Y, and each subunit is equal to the X's element times the kernel tensor K. With $p = 1$ or 2 in the above codes, the output is obtained by peeling off one or two outside layers from the $Y(s = 3)$ tensor. In the following discussion, the padding parameter p is set to be equal to ZERO. It is a little difficult to understand those operations for stride settings ($s = 2$ and $s = 1$). We know that dimensional indices of a tensor in PyTorch starts from ZERO. To get the output tensor $Y(s = 2)$, we combine rows 2 and 3, rows 5 and 6 in $Y(s = 3)$ at first by a summation of two elements at the same column index, and then combine columns 2 and 3, columns 5 and 6 by adding operations to each pair of elements at the same row index. Since two rows and two columns are lost during these operations, the shape of the $Y(s = 2)$ tensor is $1 \times 1 \times 7 \times 7$. The red and blue colors in the $Y(s = 3)$ tensor are used to show elements on rows 2 and 3 and rows 5 and 6. To get $Y(s = 1)$ from $Y(s = 3)$, we combine rows 1 and 3, rows 2 and 4 at first to obtain a middle tensor with the shape $1 \times 1 \times 7 \times 9$. Then in the middle tensor, we combine rows 2 and 4, rows 3 and 5. Finally, we do the same combination operations for the columns. These operations are not easy to handle manually; fortunately, PyTorch takes cares of them.

Codes in Extra Cell TWO are for applications of a 2D transposed convolution operator in the second example. The input image's shape is X.shape = [1,2,3,3], the kernel tensor's shape is K.shape = [2,3,2,2], and the output tensor's shape of the transposed convolution is Y.shape = [X.shape[0], K.shape[1], n, n], where n is set by equation (3.3). Taking $m = 3$, $f = 2$, $s = 2$, $p = 0$ into the CT instance, we get $n = 6$. The *in_channels* and the *out_channels* of the CT instance are equal to X.shape[1] and K.shape[1], respectively. In the example, 18 integers are used to construct an input image tensor X which is then converted into a $1 \times 2 \times 3 \times 3$ float32 tensor.

The kernel tensor K has two rows and three columns. The shape of each of its six subunits is 2×2. The shape of the output tensor is $Y(X,K)$.shape = [1,3,6,6]. A sub-tensor in the middle of $Y(X,K)$ is obtained by using summation results of two ConvTranspose2d operations for (X_0, K_{01}) and (X_1, K_{11}). For example, the element 17 in the middle sub-tensor of Y was obtained by $17 = 4 \times 1 + 13 \times 1$.

$$X = \begin{bmatrix} \begin{bmatrix} 0 & 1 & 2 \\ 3 & 4 & 5 \\ 6 & 7 & 8 \end{bmatrix}_{X_0} \\ \begin{bmatrix} 9 & 10 & 11 \\ 12 & 13 & 14 \\ 15 & 16 & 17 \end{bmatrix}_{X_1} \end{bmatrix}^T , \quad K = \begin{bmatrix} \begin{bmatrix} 0 & 0 \\ 0 & 0 \end{bmatrix}_{K_{00}} & \begin{bmatrix} 1 & 1 \\ 1 & 1 \end{bmatrix}_{K_{01}} & \begin{bmatrix} 2 & 2 \\ 2 & 2 \end{bmatrix}_{K_{02}} \\ \begin{bmatrix} 1 & 0 \\ 0 & 1 \end{bmatrix}_{K_{10}} & \begin{bmatrix} 1 & 0 \\ 0 & 1 \end{bmatrix}_{K_{11}} & \begin{bmatrix} 1 & 0 \\ 0 & 1 \end{bmatrix}_{K_{12}} \end{bmatrix}$$

$$Y(X, K) = \begin{bmatrix} \begin{bmatrix} 9 & 0 & 10 & 0 & 11 & 0 \\ 0 & 9 & 0 & 10 & 0 & 11 \\ 12 & 0 & 13 & 0 & 14 & 0 \\ 0 & 12 & 0 & 13 & 0 & 14 \\ 15 & 0 & 16 & 0 & 17 & 0 \\ 0 & 15 & 0 & 16 & 0 & 17 \end{bmatrix} & \begin{bmatrix} 9 & 0 & 11 & 1 & 13 & 2 \\ 0 & 9 & 1 & 11 & 2 & 13 \\ 15 & 3 & 17 & 4 & 19 & 5 \\ 3 & 15 & 4 & 17 & 5 & 19 \\ 21 & 6 & 23 & 7 & 25 & 8 \\ 6 & 21 & 7 & 23 & 8 & 25 \end{bmatrix} & \begin{bmatrix} 9 & 0 & 12 & 2 & 15 & 4 \\ 0 & 9 & 2 & 12 & 4 & 15 \\ 18 & 6 & 21 & 8 & 24 & 10 \\ 6 & 18 & 8 & 21 & 10 & 24 \\ 27 & 12 & 30 & 14 & 33 & 16 \\ 12 & 27 & 14 & 30 & 16 & 33 \end{bmatrix} \end{bmatrix}$$

```
# Extra Cell TWO: ConvTranspose2d for 2-channel in 3-channel out----------------
X = torch.arange(18).view(1,2,3,3).to(dtype=torch.float32)
print('X.shape =', X.shape)
print('X =\n', X)
CT = nn.ConvTranspose2d(2, 3, 2, stride=2, padding=0)
k = torch.ones(2,3,2,2).to(dtype=torch.float32)
for i in range(3):
    k[0,i] = i*k[0,i]        # reset k[0,i]
    k[1,i] = torch.eye(2)    # reset k[1,i]
CT.weight = torch.nn.Parameter(k)
CT.bias = torch.nn.Parameter(torch.zeros(3))
print('Kernel',  CT.weight)
Y = CT(X)
print('Y.shape=', Y.shape)
Y.data
#-----------------------------------------------------------------------------
```

3.2.2 Applications of a DCGAN for MNIST and fashion MNIST

The DCGAN architecture for project 3.2.2 to generate fake MNIST images is based on the paper by Alec Radford and Luke Metz (Radford *et al* 2016) published on 2016 with modification. Without instructions from the paper, it is almost impossible to adjust each hyperparameter of the DCGAN models for good results. Codes in that paper were written for color images with a resolution of 64×64. If images in the

MNIST database were resized from $1 \times 28 \times 28$ to $1 \times 64 \times 64$, the training time of the model would be significantly longer. By keeping the original MNIST image resolution, both the generator model and the discriminator model only need four neural layers, not five neural layers. Since MNIST and Fashion MNIST have the same structure, the codes of the following project can be used for either of the two datasets by changing the dataset name on line 04 of Cell 01 and line 01 in Cell 02. Fake images in figures 3.5(B) and (D) are outputs of the DCGAN project with a learning rate scheduler shown in figure 3.6(C). The quality of these fake images is good, but not good enough, especially for the fake Fashion MNIST images. It is not easy to generate detailed patterns on those fake Fashion MNIST images with alphabets and trademarks.

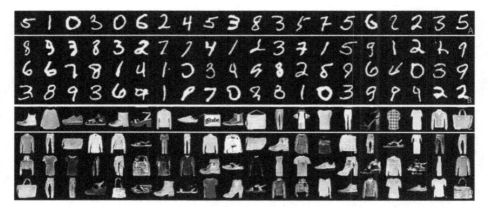

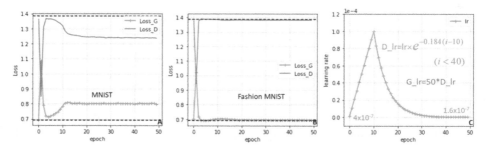

Figure 3.5. (A, C) Real MNIST and real Fashion MNIST images. (B, D) Fake MNIST and fake Fashion MNIST images generated by a DCGAN with a lambda learning rate for model D and lr_G/lr_D = 50. Model training time is 28 min. Reproduced from Deng (2012). CC BY 3.0.

Figure 3.6. Model training history (A) MNIST dataset loss curves for model D and G. (B) Fashion MNIST dataset loss curves for model D and G. Reproduced from Xiao *et al* (2017) CC BY 3.0. (C) A lambda learning rate scheduler with three segments for D_lr and G_lr = 50*D_lr. Black dashed lines were drawn based on theory values.

```python
# Project 3.2.2 Applications of DCGAN for MNIST or Fashion MNIST------Python v3.6
import torch; import torch.nn as nn
from torch.utils.data import DataLoader
import torchvision.transforms as T; from torchvision.utils import make_grid
import torch.optim.lr_scheduler as lr_scheduler
from torchvision.datasets import MNIST       #MNIST FashionMNIST ----line 04
import matplotlib.pyplot as plt; from tqdm import trange
import numpy as np; import pandas as pd
n_epochs = 50
batch_size = 100
img_size = 28
img_channels = 1
n_class = 10
z_dim = 100
lr = 1e-4
k=50        # k=G_lr/D_lr
fixed_latent = torch.randn(batch_size, z_dim, device='cuda')
path = './OCR/data/'
# Cell 02: MNIST DataSet --------------------------------------------------Cell 02
trainData = MNIST(path, train=True, download=False,
                transform=T.Compose([T.ToTensor(), T.Normalize([0.5],[0.5])]))
n_samples = len(trainData) #len(trainData)=60000
# Cell 03: Create a DataLoader (trainLoader)-------------------------------Cell 03
train_dataloader = DataLoader(trainData, batch_size=batch_size, shuffle=True)
n_batch = len(train_dataloader) #n_batch=n_sample/batch_size=600
# Cell 04: Show the images in the 1st batch of the train dataloader-------Cell 04
for imgs, labels in train_dataloader: # for the 1st batch on the train dataloader
    print('imgs_batch.shape=', imgs.shape)
    #print('labels=', labels[:40])
    break
def denorm(img_tensors):          # Shift the value of each image pixel to [0,1]
    return img_tensors * 0.5 + 0.5
def show_imgs(imgs):
    fig, ax = plt.subplots(figsize=(12,8))
    input = make_grid(denorm(imgs[:60]), nrow=20, padding=2) #display 48 images
    ax.imshow(input.permute(1,2,0), cmap='gray')
    ax.set(xticks=[], yticks=[])
    plt.show()
show_imgs(imgs)
# Cell 05: Model parameters initialization ------------------------------Cell 05
def weights_init(m):
    if(type(m) == nn.ConvTranspose2d or type(m) == nn.Conv2d):
        nn.init.normal_(m.weight.data, 0.0, 0.02)
    elif(type(m) == nn.BatchNorm2d):
        nn.init.normal_(m.weight.data, 0.0, 0.02)
        nn.init.constant_(m.bias.data, 0)
# Cell 06: Definition of an image discriminator class-------Model D-------Cell 06
def basic_D(in_channels, p=1):
    return nn.Sequential(nn.Conv2d(in_channels, 2*in_channels, kernel_size=4,
                                stride=2, padding=p, bias=False),
                    nn.BatchNorm2d(2*in_channels),
                    nn.LeakyReLU(0.2, inplace=True)
```

```
        )
class Discriminator(nn.Module):
    def __init__(self):
        super().__init__()
        self.net = nn.Sequential(
            nn.Conv2d(img_channels, 64, kernel_size=4, stride=2, padding=1),
            nn.LeakyReLU(0.2, inplace=True),
            # layer 01 outputshape=batch_size x 64 x 14^2
            basic_D(64, p=2),
            # layer 02 output.shape=batch_size x 128 x 8^2
            basic_D(128, p=1),
            # layer 03 output.shape=batch_size x 256 x 4^2
            nn.Conv2d(256, 1, kernel_size=4, stride=1, padding=0),
            nn.Flatten(),
            nn.Sigmoid()
        )   # layer 04 output.shape=batch_size x 1
    def forward(self, images):
        output = self.net(images)    # input.shape=batch_size x 1 x 28^2
        return output                # output.shape=batch_size x 1
D = Discriminator().cuda()
D.apply(weights_init)
# Cell 07: The definition of a generator Class------------Model G------Cell 07
def basic_G(out_channels, f=4):
    return nn.Sequential(nn.ConvTranspose2d(2*out_channels, out_channels,
                    kernel_size=f, stride=2, padding=1, bias=False),
                nn.BatchNorm2d(out_channels),
                nn.ReLU(True))
class Generator(nn.Module):
    def __init__(self):
        super().__init__()
        # input_latent_tensor.shape=batch_size x z_dim x 1^2
        self.net = nn.Sequential(
            nn.ConvTranspose2d(z_dim, 256, 4, 1, 0, bias=False),
            nn.BatchNorm2d(256),
            nn.ReLU(True),
            #layer 01 output.shape = batch_size x 256 x 4^2
            basic_G(128, f=3),
            #layer 02 output.shape = batch_size x 128 x 7^2
            basic_G(64, f=4),
            #layer 03 output.shape = batch_size x 64 x 14^2
            nn.ConvTranspose2d(64, img_channels, 4, 2, 1),
            nn.Tanh()
        )   #layer 04 output.shape = batch_size x 1 x 28^2
    def forward(self, z):        # z.shape=batch_size x z_dim
        input = z.unsqueeze(dim=-1).unsqueeze(dim=-1)
        fake_imgs = self.net(input)    #input.shape = batch_size x z_dim x 1^2
        return fake_imgs               #fake_imgs.shape = batch_size x 1 x 28^2
G = Generator().cuda()
G.apply(weights_init)
#-------------------------------------------------------------------------
```

The generator model class defined in Cell 07 has four transposed convolution layers. Its last layer has no batch normalization operation according the DCGAN paper. Model G's input is a 2D tensor with size of *batch_size* × *z_dim*. According to the paper, the latent dimension *z_dim* was set to be equal to 100. Noise tensors are generated during model training, and they will be filled with random numbers generated by a standard normal distribution. A 2D noise tensor was first converted into a 4D tensor in the 'forward' function by two *unsqueeze(dim = −1)* functions, and was then processed by the four transposed convolution layers. Because the activation function of the model is *Tanh( )*, the pixel values of output images from model G is in the range [−1,1]. In another extra cell after Cell 07, running 'D(G (fixed_latent))', you will verify that the two models are functional.

```python
# Cell 08: Definitions of optimizers, criterion, learning rate scheduler
optimizer_D = torch.optim.Adam(D.parameters(), lr=lr, betas=(0.5, 0.999))
optimizer_G = torch.optim.Adam(G.parameters(), lr=0.01*k*lr, betas=(0.5, 0.999))
criterion = nn.BCELoss(reduction='sum')
v=lambda i: 0.099*i+0.01 if i<10 else (np.exp(-0.184*(i-10)) if i<40 else 0.004)
#v=lambda i: 1
scheduler = lr_scheduler.LambdaLR(optimizer_D, lr_lambda=v)
# Cell 09: Model D's training function ---------------------------------Cell 09
def train_D(inputs, optimizer_D):
    real_preds = D(inputs)
    ones_targets = torch.ones(inputs.shape[0], 1, device='cuda')
    real_loss = criterion(real_preds, ones_targets)
    real_score = torch.mean(real_preds).item()
    latent = torch.randn(inputs.shape[0], z_dim, device='cuda')
    fake_images = G(latent)
    zeros_targets = torch.zeros(fake_images.shape[0], 1, device='cuda')
    fake_preds = D(fake_images.detach())
    fake_loss = criterion(fake_preds, zeros_targets)
    fake_score = torch.mean(fake_preds).item()

    loss = real_loss + fake_loss
    optimizer_D.zero_grad()
    loss.backward()
    optimizer_D.step()
    return loss.item(), real_score, fake_score
# Cell 10: Model G's training function ---------------------------------Cell 10
def train_G(optimizer_G):
    latent = torch.randn(batch_size, z_dim, device='cuda')
    fake_images = G(latent)   # Create fake images
    preds = D(fake_images)
    targets = torch.ones(batch_size, 1, device='cuda')
    # Try to fool the discriminator
    loss = criterion(preds, targets)
    optimizer_G.zero_grad()
    loss.backward()
    optimizer_G.step()
    return loss.item()
# Cell 11: The definition of a fitting function to train G and D---------Cell 11
def fit(epochs):
    torch.cuda.empty_cache()
    df = pd.DataFrame(np.empty([epochs, 5]),
        index = np.arange(epochs),
        columns=['Loss_G', 'Loss_D',
            'D(X)', 'D(G(Z))', 'lr'])
    for i in trange(epochs):
        loss_G = 0.0; loss_D = 0.0; real_sc = 0.0; fake_sc = 0.0
        for real_images, _ in train_dataloader:
            inputs = real_images.cuda()
            loss_d, real_score, fake_score = train_D(
                inputs, optimizer_D)
            loss_D += loss_d
            real_sc += real_score; fake_sc += fake_score
```

```
        loss_g = train_G(optimizer_G)
        loss_G += loss_g
    df.iloc[i, 0] = loss_G/n_samples
    df.iloc[i, 1] = loss_D/n_samples
    df.iloc[i, 2] = real_sc/n_batch
    df.iloc[i, 3] = fake_sc/n_batch
    df.iloc[i, 4] = optimizer_D.param_groups[0]['lr']        #Record lr_D
    scheduler.step()                                          #Update lr_D
    optimizer_G.param_groups[0]['lr'] = df.iloc[i,4]*k       #G_lr=k*G_lr
    if i==0 or (i+1)%10==0:
        print(
        "Epoch={}, ls_G: {:.4f}, ls_D: {:.4f}, r_sc: {:.4f}, f_sc: {:.4f}"
        .format(i+1, df.iloc[i,0], df.iloc[i,1], df.iloc[i,2], df.iloc[i,3]))
        fake_images = G(fixed_latent)
        show_imgs(fake_images.detach().cpu())
    return df
train_history = fit(n_epochs)      #de=24min, n_epoch=50
# Cell 12: Graphs of Model training outputs-----------------------Cell 12
df= train_history
fig, ax = plt.subplots(1,3, figsize=(15,4), sharex=True)
df.plot(ax=ax[0], y=[0,1], style=['r-+', 'b-'])
df.plot(ax=ax[1], y=[2,3], style=['b-+', 'r-'])
df.plot(ax=ax[2], y=[4], style=['r-+'])
for i in range(3):
    ax[i].set_xlabel('epoch')
    ax[i].grid(which='major', axis='both', color='g', linestyle=':')
ax[0].set_ylabel('Loss')
ax[0].axhline(y=2*np.log(2), color='k', linestyle='--') #Theory D loss Value
ax[0].axhline(y=np.log(2), color='k', linestyle='--')    #Theory G loss Value
ax[1].axhline(y=0.5, color='k', linestyle='--')  #Theory D(X), D(G(Z)) values
#ax[1].set_ylim([0.45, 0.55])
ax[2].set(ylabel='learning rate', ylim=[-1e-5, 1.2e-4])
ax[2].ticklabel_format(style='sci', axis='y', scilimits=(0,0))
plt.show()
# Cell 13: Verify if the generator works for inputs-------------------------
inputs = torch.randn(1, z_dim).cuda()
fake_images = G(inputs) #create images
print('inputs.shap=', inputs.shape)
print('fake_images.shape=', fake_images.shape)
show_imgs(fake_images.detach().cpu())
#--------------------------------------------------------------------------
```

In the DCGAN paper, a constant learning rate was set to be equal to 2×10^{-4} for both models. Although this setting works, I tried to tune the loss curves to match theoretical curves with a lambda learning rate scheduler shown in figure 3.6(C). Since model D is smarter than model G, the learning rate of model G was set to be $50 \times$ D_lr. The following equation is the lambda function. If the initial learning rate and k were set to be 4×10^{-5} and 500, respectively, the loss curves of MNIST's model training could also be tuned to follow theoretical curves

$$lr = lr_0 \times \begin{cases} 0.099i + 0.01 & (i < 10) \\ e^{-0.184 \times (i-10)} & (10 \leqslant i < 40) \\ 0.004 & (i \geqslant 40) \end{cases}$$

For the epoch in the range [0, 10), D_lr linearly increases from 4×10^{-7} to 4×10^{-5}; for the epoch in the range [10, 40), the D_lr exponentially decreases to 1.6×10^{-7}, and then keeps the rate in the last ten epochs. The Loss_D and Loss_G curves are almost straight lines for the Fashion MNIST dataset. With bigger G_lr, it is easier and faster to generate good MNIST images. Codes in Cell 13 can be used to generate and show a single fake MNIST image. Every time you run it, you will see a different image. Occasionally, we cannot find a digit in a noisy image.

3.2.3 Using a DCGAN to generate fake anime-faces and fake CelebA images

Anime-faces Dataset (Chao 2019) was created by Brian Chao with a Database Contents License (DbCL). After downloading a zip file and unzipping it (7.7 GB) in your computer, you will see 63 632 high-quality face images of carton characters. These color images have no labels, and their resolutions vary from 27×27 to 120×120. We used the tool named *ImageFolder* from Torchvision to pack these images into a dataset. All the images in the dataset were then resized to a resolution of 64×64, and the value of each pixel was shifted to a range [−1, 1]. Both model D and model G have five layers. The DCGAN codes for the Anime-faces dataset can also be used for the CelebFaces Attributes Dataset (CelebA) Dataset) (Liu *et al* 2015) by just changing the image file path on the last line in Cell 01. This dataset contains 202 599 high resolution (178×218) color photos. Fake images generated by the DCGAN model are shown in figure 3.7. The model training time of the two datasets were around 44 and 150 min, respectively.

Figure 3.7. (A) Fake anime-faces dataset images generated by DCGAN at the 20th epoch of model training with a learning rate scheduler shown in figure 3.8(C). Real images for model training are reproduced from Churchill and Chao (2019) with a license DbCL v1.0. (B) Fake CelebA images generated by DCGAN at the 16th epoch of model training. The CelebA dataset is used with permission from Liu *et al* (2015) courtesy of Ziwei Liu.

```
# Project 3.2.3 Using DCGAN to Generate Anime Faces or CelebFaces-----Python v3.6
import torch; import torch.nn as nn; from torch.utils.data import DataLoader
import torch.optim.lr_scheduler as lr_scheduler
from torchvision.utils import make_grid; import torchvision.transforms as T
from torchvision.datasets import ImageFolder
import matplotlib.pyplot as plt; from tqdm import trange
import pandas as pd; import numpy as np
n_epochs = 20
batch_size = 64
img_size = 64
img_channels = 3
z_dim = 100
lr = 1e-4
k = 18          # k=G_lr/D_lr
fixed_latent = torch.randn(48, z_dim, device='cuda') #  A batch of random numbers
data_path = './OCR/data/AnimeFaces'
#data_path = './OCR/data/CelebA/img_align_celeba/'
# Cell 02: Anime-face Dataset-----------------------------------------------Cell 02
train_dataset = ImageFolder(data_path, transform=T.Compose([
                    T.Resize(img_size), T.CenterCrop(img_size),
                    T.ToTensor(), T.Normalize([0.5]*3, [0.5, 0.5, 0.5])]))
n_samples = len(train_dataset) #n_sample=63566
# Cell 03: Dataloader-------------------------------------------------------Cell 03
train_dataloader = DataLoader(train_dataset, batch_size=batch_size,
                        shuffle=True, num_workers=2, pin_memory=True)
n_batch = len(train_dataloader) #n_batch=994
for imgs, _ in train_dataloader:
    print("imgs_batch.shape=", imgs.shape)
    break
# Cell 04: Show images of in the 1st the batch of train_dataloader--------Cell 04
def denorm(img_tensors):
    return img_tensors*0.5 + 0.5
def show_imgs(images):
    fig, ax = plt.subplots(figsize=(16,12))
    input = make_grid(denorm(images[:48]), nrow=16)
    ax.imshow(input.permute(1,2,0))
    ax.set(xticks=[], yticks=[])
    plt.show()
show_imgs(imgs)
# Cell 05: Model parameters initialization -----------------------------Cell 05
def weights_init(m):
    if(type(m) == nn.ConvTranspose2d or type(m) == nn.Conv2d):
        nn.init.normal_(m.weight.data, 0.0, 0.02)
    elif(type(m) == nn.BatchNorm2d):
        nn.init.normal_(m.weight.data, 0.0, 0.02)
        nn.init.constant_(m.bias.data, 0)
# Cell 06: Discriminator class----------------------------------------------Cell 06
def basic_D(in_channels):
    return nn.Sequential(nn.Conv2d(in_channels, 2*in_channels, kernel_size=4,
                            stride=2, padding=1, bias=False),
                    nn.BatchNorm2d(2*in_channels),
                    nn.LeakyReLU(0.2, inplace=True))
```

```
class Discriminator(nn.Module):
    def __init__(self):
        super().__init__()
        self.net = nn.Sequential(
                        nn.Conv2d(img_channels, 64, 4, 2, 1),
                        nn.LeakyReLU(0.2, inplace=True),
                        # layer01 output.shape=batch_size x 64 x 3 x 32^2
                        basic_D(64),
                        # layer 02 output.shape=batch_size x 128 x 16^2
                        basic_D(128),
                        # layer 03 output.shape=batch_size x 256 x 8^2
                        basic_D(256),
                        # layer 04 output.shape=batch_size x 512 x 4^2
                        nn.Conv2d(512, 1, 4, 1, 0),
                        nn.Flatten(),
                        nn.Sigmoid()
        )               # layer 05 output.shape=batch_size x 1
    def forward(self, images):
        output = self.net(images)   # images.shape = batch_size x 3 x 64^2
        return output               # output.shape = batch_size x 1
D = Discriminator().cuda()
D.apply(weights_init)
# Cell 07: Generator Class--------------------------------------------------Cell 07
def basic_G(out_channels):
    return nn.Sequential(nn.ConvTranspose2d(2*out_channels, out_channels,
                         kernel_size=4, stride=2, padding=1, bias=False),
                         nn.BatchNorm2d(out_channels),
                         nn.ReLU(True))
class Generator(nn.Module):
    def __init__(self):
        super().__init__()
        self.net = nn.Sequential(
            # Input_latent.shape=batch_size x z_dim x 1^2
            nn.ConvTranspose2d(z_dim, 512, 4, 1, 0, bias=False),
            nn.BatchNorm2d(512),
            nn.ReLU(True),
            # layer01 output.shape = batch_size x 512 x 4^2
            basic_G(256),
            # layer02 output.shape = batch_size x 256 x 8^2
            basic_G(128),
            # layer03 output.shape = batch_size x 128 x 16^2
            basic_G(64),
            # layer04 output.shape = batch_size x 64 x 32^2
            nn.ConvTranspose2d(64, img_channels, 4, 2, 1),
            nn.Tanh()
        )   # layer05 output.shape = batch_size x 3 x 64^2
    def forward(self, z):
        input = z.view(-1, z_dim, 1, 1)    #z.shape = batch_size x z_dim
        output = self.net(input)       #input.shape = batch_size x z_dim x 1^2
        return output                  #output.shape = batch_size x 3 x 64^2
G = Generator().cuda()
G.apply(weights_init)
# Cell 08: Choose optimizers and a criterion-------ANIME FACES------------Cell 08
optimizer_D = torch.optim.Adam(D.parameters(), lr=lr, betas=(0.5, 0.999))
optimizer_G = torch.optim.Adam(G.parameters(), lr=k*lr, betas=(0.5, 0.999))
criterion = nn.BCELoss(reduction='sum')
v = lambda i: 1 if i<5 else 0.72**(i-5)
scheduler = lr_scheduler.LambdaLR(optimizer_D, lr_lambda = v)
#---------------------------------------------------------------------------
```

According the GAN paper (Goodfellow *et al* 2014), a constant learning rate (2×10^{-4}) is used for model training. During each training process with 20 epochs, model G's loss function values increase to above 5.0, and model D's loss decreases to below 0.2. The fake images generated by the system were worse and worse with the constant learning rate on my computer. Finally, you only get one kind of face with one eye in all fake images. That is a phenomenon called 'model collapse' in GAN's model training. It is caused by a weaker mode G and a smarter model D. Just as with a student who is not smart enough to understand his teacher's instruction to improve his homework, their teacher will find it easy to see mistakes in the student's homework. Still using constant learning rates, I adjusted model G's learning rate to 800% of the model D's learning rate. Although the quality of those fake images was improved, we could easily distinguish them by eye from those real images in the dataset. From figure 3.8, you can see that a lambda scheduler was used for training of model D. Its learning rate was 10^{-4} in the first five epochs, and then the learning rate exponentially decreased to 10^{-6} at the end of model training. Model G's learning rate was set to be 18 times model D's learning rate. Other ratios for G_lr and D_lr such as 10, 15, 20 and 21 were tested with good results.

```python
# Cell 09: Model D's training function --------------------------------Cell 09
def train_D(inputs, optimizer_D):
    real_preds = D(inputs)
    real_targets = torch.ones(inputs.shape[0], 1, device='cuda')
    real_loss = criterion(real_preds, real_targets)
    real_score = torch.mean(real_preds).item()

    latent = torch.randn(inputs.shape[0], z_dim, device='cuda')
    fake_images = G(latent)
    fake_targets = torch.zeros(fake_images.shape[0], 1, device='cuda')
    fake_preds = D(fake_images.detach())
    fake_loss = criterion(fake_preds, fake_targets)
    fake_score = torch.mean(fake_preds).item()

    loss = real_loss + fake_loss
    optimizer_D.zero_grad()
    loss.backward()
    optimizer_D.step()
    return loss.item(), real_score, fake_score
# Cell 10: Model G's training function --------------------------------Cell 10
def train_G(optimizer_G):
    latent = torch.randn(batch_size, z_dim, device='cuda')
    fake_images = G(latent)    # Create fake images
    preds = D(fake_images)
    targets = torch.ones(batch_size, 1, device='cuda')
    loss = criterion(preds, targets)
    optimizer_G.zero_grad()
    loss.backward()
    optimizer_G.step()
    return loss.item()
# Cell 11: The definition of a fitting function to train G and D---------Cell 11
def fit(epochs):
    torch.cuda.empty_cache()
    df = pd.DataFrame(np.empty([epochs, 5]),
        index = np.arange(epochs),
```

```
        columns=['Loss_G', 'Loss_D', 'D(X)', 'D(G(Z))',
'LearningRate'])
    for i in trange(epochs):
        loss_G = 0.0; loss_D = 0.0; real_sc = 0.0; fake_sc = 0.0
        for real_images, _ in train_dataloader:
            inputs = real_images.cuda()
            loss_d, real_score, fake_score = train_D(inputs, optimizer_D)
            loss_D += loss_d
            real_sc += real_score; fake_sc += fake_score
            loss_g = train_G(optimizer_G)
            loss_G += loss_g

        df.iloc[i, 0] = loss_G/n_samples
        df.iloc[i, 1] = loss_D/n_samples
        df.iloc[i, 2] = real_sc/n_batch
        df.iloc[i, 3] = fake_sc/n_batch
        df.iloc[i, 4] = optimizer_D.param_groups[0]['lr']       #Record lr_D
        scheduler.step()                                        #Update lr_D
        optimizer_G.param_groups[0]['lr'] = df.iloc[i,4]*k       #Update lr_G
        if i==0 or (i+1)%2==0:
            print(
            "Epoch={}, Ls_G={:.4f}, Ls_D={:.4f}, D(X)={:.4f}, D(G(Z))={:.4f}"
            .format(i+1, df.iloc[i,0], df.iloc[i,1], df.iloc[i,2], df.iloc[i,3]))
            fake_images = G(fixed_latent)
            show_imgs(fake_images.detach().cpu())
    return df
train_history = fit(n_epochs) #dt=38min, 46min, 43min
# Cell 12: Graphs of Model training outputs--------------------------Cell 12
df= train_history
fig, ax = plt.subplots(1,3, figsize=(15,4), sharex=True)
df.plot(ax=ax[0], y=[0,1], style=['r-+', 'b-d'])
df.plot(ax=ax[1], y=[2,3], style=['b-+', 'r-d'])
df.plot(ax=ax[2], y=[4], style=['r-+'])
for i in range(3):
    ax[i].set_xlabel('epoch')
    ax[i].grid(which='major', axis='both', color='g', linestyle=':')


#ax[0].set_ylabel('Loss')
ax[0].set(ylabel='Loss', ylim=[0,2])
ax[0].axhline(y=2*np.log(2), color='k', linestyle='--') #Theory D loss Value
ax[0].axhline(y=np.log(2), color='k', linestyle='--')   #Theory G loss Value
ax[1].axhline(y=0.5, color='k', linestyle='--')  #Theory D(X), D(G(Z)) values
ax[1].set_ylim([0, 1]); ax[2].set_ylim([-2e-5, 1.2e-4])
ax[2].ticklabel_format(style='sci', axis='y', scilimits=(0,0))
plt.show()
# Cell 13: Verify if the generator works for inputs--------------------Cell 13
inputs = torch.randn(1, z_dim).cuda()
fake_images = G(inputs) #create images
print('inputs.shap=', inputs.shape)
print('fake_images.shape=', fake_images.shape)
show_imgs(fake_images.detach().cpu())
#---------------------------------The End---------------------------------
```

In a project of the last section for MNIST image generation, lambda functions with three segments were used to fine tune model loss values. Changing the ratio k ($= $ G_lr/D_lr) from 4, 8, 10, 20, 50, 200, 400, 500 and 1000, we could obtain crystal

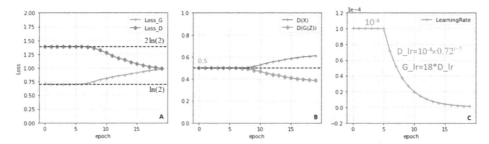

Figure 3.8. Training loss curves with a Lambda learning rate scheduler for the Anime-faces Dataset. (A) Loss curves. (B) Average of D(X) and D(G(Z)). (C) Model D's Lambda learning rate scheduler with G_lr = 18 × D_lr. Black dash lines were drawn based one theory values.

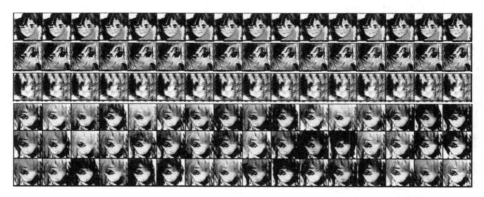

Figure 3.9. Fake Anime-faces dataset images generated by the DCGAN with model collapse issues in four model training explorations. In each of the first three explorations, all 48 fake images were the same, and only images in the first row were shown.

clear fake MNIST images. What is the best ratio of the two learning rates? Images from the anime-faces dataset are very good samples for us to search the best ratio k, because they contain more detailed information. From eye sizes, color, nose and mouth positions on fake images, our eyes can see very small differences. Twenty is a critical number for the ratio k with the initial learning rate set to be equal to 10^{-4}, although the loss function curves of the two models are not straight lines. With small fluctuations on those loss values around theory values, the GAN models can generate fake images with detailed information. With higher ratio k, those loss curves could be tuned to straight lines, but the DCGAN models learnt slowly, and fake images were noisier, and even had ghost faces. With lower ratio k, the DCGAN's model D is smarter than its mode G, so the loss values of model G will increase epoch by epoch. If mode G's loss value is above six, the GAN system will have 'model collapse' issues as shown in figure 3.9. Fake images from the lower ratio k are also noisier.

3.3 Conditional deep convolutional GANs

Although DCGANs can generate high-quality fake images, it is impossible to generate fake images with a specific class or style set by us. After Mehdi Mirza and Simon Osindero published their paper (Mirza and Osindero 2014) titled 'Conditional generative adversarial nets' in 2014, we have a powerful tool: conditional deep convolutional GANs (cDCGAN), which can generate fake images according to our requirements. We can even use text or sound prompts to instruct a cDCGAN to generate any kind of fake images similar to real images in a train dataset. In a project of the last section for MNIST image generation, we discarded label information. Now we will encode each label of each image as an extra channel of the image. Then, a batch of images with label information is packed into a 4D tensor as the input of model D in a cDCGAN. In the last section, we used a 1×100 noise tensor as the input of model G to generate a fake image. Now we will use a 1×110 tensor for model G to generate a fake image. The extra 10 elements come from a fake label in range [0,9] for MNIST dataset. The codes for training the two models are almost the same as those in DCGANs. Parameters of models will be updated during model training, so that our models are smart enough to generate realistic fake images with the specific digits we asked for. An embedding class of PyTorch is used to encode information of the label with its image.

On line 02 of the following Extra Cell ONE is a 1D tensor with five labels in a batch images of a MNIST dataloader. An instance of the embedding class on line 04 would embed the 1D tensor into a 5×3 tensor filled with random numbers before model training. The first parameter of the instance is the class number (10) of MNIST. The maximum value of the 1D tensor should be nine. The second parameter of the instance is the embedding output's column number. The embedding output's row number is equal to the length of the 1D label tensor. Since the first and the last elements in the 1D tensor are the same in the example, the first row and the last row of the embedding output are the same. The parameters of the embedding instance will be updated during model training.

```
# Extra Cell ONE: An example nn.Embedding() class application--------------------
import torch; import torch.nn as nn
labels=torch.tensor([2, 7, 4, 9, 2])         #---------- line 02
print('labels=', labels)
emb = nn.Embedding(10, 3)                     #---------- line 04
print("embedded_labels=\n", emb(labels).data)
#---------Outputss of Extra Cell 01-----------------------------------------------
labels= tensor([2, 7, 4, 9, 2])
embedded_labels=
tensor([[ 0.8012, -0.9888, -0.3108],
        [-0.3597,  0.4291, -0.0490],
        [ 1.4051, -0.9362,  0.8602],
        [-0.1518,  0.1342,  0.8762],
        [ 0.8012, -0.9888, -0.3108]])
#--------------------------------------------------------------------------------
```

3.3.1 Applications of a cDCGAN to MNIST and fashion MNIST datasets

Fashion-MNIST (Xiao *et al* 2017) is a dataset created by the German company Zalando. It has the same structure as the MNIST dataset: a training dataset and a test dataset containing 60 000 and 10 000 labeled black and white images, respectively. The resolution of those images is 28 × 28. The images are categorized into ten classes (0 to 9) for t-shirt/top, trouser, pullover, dress, coat, sandal, shirt, sneaker, bag and ankle boot. Running a code *train_Dataset.classes* in an extra cell after Cell 04 in project 3.3.1, you will see these category names. Since the dataset structures of MNIST and Fashion MNIST are the same, the codes in the project can be used for the two datasets, respectively, by changing the dataset name in Cell 01 and Cell 02. Fake MNIST images and Fake fashion MNIST images generated by the cDCGAN are shown in figure 3.10. Their quality is good enough compared with real images.

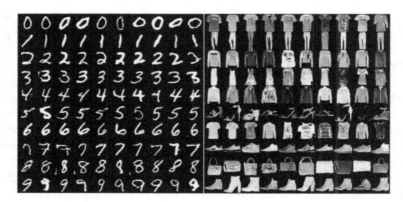

Figure 3.10. Fake MNIST images (left) and Fake Fashion MNIST images (right) generated by cDCGAN. They are the outputs of Cell 11. Model training time is 11 min.

```
Project 3.3.1: Using a cDCGAN for MNIST or Fashion MNIST-------------Python v3.6
import torch; import torch.nn as nn; from torch.utils.data import DataLoader
import torch.optim.lr_scheduler as lr_scheduler
from torchvision import transforms as T
from torchvision.datasets import MNIST     # MNIST, FashionMNIST
from torchvision.utils import make_grid
import numpy as np; import pandas as pd; from tqdm import trange
import matplotlib.pyplot as plt
n_epochs = 20
batch_size = 100
img_size = 28
img_dim = img_size*img_size # img_dim = 28x28=784
img_channels = 1
n_class = 10
z_dim = 100
lr = 2e-4
k = 5          # k = G_lr/D_lr
#  Generate a batch of random number with a shape of 100 x 100
fixed_latent = torch.randn(batch_size, z_dim, device='cuda')
# Generate a long tensor: [0,0,0,0,0,0,0,0,0,1, ..., 8,9,9,9,9,9,9,9,9,9]
fixed_labels = torch.cuda.LongTensor(
              [i for i in range(n_class) for j in range(n_class)])
```

```
# Cell 02: MNIST DataSet -------------------------------------------------Cell 02
trainData = MNIST('./OCR/data/', train=True, download=False,
                transform=T.Compose([T.ToTensor(), T.Normalize([0.5],[0.5])]))
n_samples = len(trainData) #len(trainData)=60000
# Cell 03: Create a DataLoader (trainLoader)-----------------------------Cell 03
train_dataloader = DataLoader(trainData, batch_size=batch_size, shuffle=True)
n_batch = len(train_dataloader) #n_batch=n_sample/batch_size=600
for imgs, labels in train_dataloader: # for the 1st batch on the train dataloader
    print('imgs_batch.shape=', imgs.shape)
    print('labels=', labels.view(-1, 10))
    break
# Cell 04: Show the images in the 1st batch of the train dataloader-------Cell 04
def denorm(img_tensors):        # Shift the value of each image pixel to [0,1]
    return img_tensors * 0.5 + 0.5
def show_imgs(imgs):
    fig, ax = plt.subplots(figsize=(12,8))
    input = make_grid(denorm(imgs), nrow=10, padding=0) #display 48 images
    ax.imshow(input.permute(1,2,0), cmap='gray')
    ax.set(xticks=[], yticks=[])
    plt.show()
show_imgs(imgs)

# Cell 05: Model parameters initialization ------------------------------Cell 05
def weights_init(m):
    if(type(m) == nn.ConvTranspose2d or type(m) == nn.Conv2d):
        nn.init.normal_(m.weight.data, 0.0, 0.02)
    elif(type(m) == nn.BatchNorm2d):
        nn.init.normal_(m.weight.data, 1.0, 0.02)
        nn.init.constant_(m.bias.data, 0)
# Cell 06: Discriminator class-------------------------------------------Cell 06
def basic_D(in_channels, p=1):
    return nn.Sequential(nn.Conv2d(in_channels, 2*in_channels, kernel_size=4,
                                   stride=2, padding=p, bias=False),
                        nn.BatchNorm2d(2*in_channels),
                        nn.LeakyReLU(0.2, inplace=True))
class Discriminator(nn.Module):
    def __init__(self): # real images and labels combination (batch x 2 x 28^2)
        super().__init__()
        self.model = nn.Sequential(
            nn.Conv2d(img_channels+1, 64, kernel_size=4, stride=2, padding=1),
            nn.LeakyReLU(0.2, inplace=True),
            # layer 01 output.shape = batch_size x 64 x 14^2
            basic_D(64, p=2),
            # layer 02 output.shape = batch_size x 128 x 8^2
            basic_D(128, p=1),
            # layer 03 output.shape = batch_size x 256 x 4^2
            nn.Conv2d(256, 1, kernel_size=4, stride=1, padding=0),
            nn.Flatten(),
            nn.Sigmoid()
        )   # layer 04 output.shape = batch_size x 1
        # Encode a batch of labels as an extra channel of images
        self.label_emb = nn.Embedding(n_class, img_dim)      #************line 22
    def forward(self, images, labels):     #images.shape = batch_size x 1 x 28^2
        x = images.view(-1, img_dim)        # x.shape = batch_size x 784
        c = self.label_emb(labels)          # c.shape = batch_size x 784
        x_c = torch.cat([x, c], dim=1)      #x_c.shape = batch_size x (784+784)
        input = x_c.view(-1, img_channels+1, img_size, img_size)
        out = self.model(input)             #input.shape = batch_size x 2 x 28^2
        return out                          #output.shape = batch_size x 1
D = Discriminator().cuda()
D.apply(weights_init)
#----------------------------------------------------------------------------
```

The code on line 22 of Cell 06 is the embedding class's instance *nn.Embedding(10, 784)*. With the first line of the forward function in the model D, each image in a batch of a dataloader is reshaped into a 1D tensor with 784 elements. Using the embedding instance, the second line of the forward function encodes each label in the batch into a 1D tensor with 784 elements. Now we have two tensors, and they have the same shape: batch_size × 784. These two tensors are concatenated along the row direction (dim = 1). The result is a longer tensor with a shape of batch_size × 1568. Then, it is reshaped into a 4D tensor with a shape of batch_size × 2 × 28 × 28, and it is then processed through the convolution network of model D as usual. The output of model D is an 1D tensor with batch size elements. Each of the elements is a positive number with a value between 0 and 1 because of the sigmoid activation function in model D. According the GAN paper, batch normalization in layer 01 and layer 04 is not used. With this setting, the bias options of the two convolutions are set to be 'True' by default.

```
# Cell 07: Generator Class-----------------------------------------------Cell 07
def basic_G(out_channels, f=4):
    return nn.Sequential(nn.ConvTranspose2d(2*out_channels, out_channels,
                        kernel_size=f, stride=2, padding=1, bias=False),
                    nn.BatchNorm2d(out_channels),
                    nn.ReLU(True))
class Generator(nn.Module):
    def __init__(self):
        super().__init__()
        self.model = nn.Sequential(
                    nn.ConvTranspose2d(z_dim+10, 256, 4, 1, 0, bias=False),
                    nn.BatchNorm2d(256),
                    nn.ReLU(True),
                    # Layer 01 output.shape = batch_size x 256 x 4^2
                    basic_G(128, f=3),
                    # Layer 02 output.shape = batch_size x 128 x 7^2
                    basic_G(64, f=4),
                    # Layer 03 output.shape = batch_size x 64 x 14^2
                    nn.ConvTranspose2d(64, 1, 4, 2, 1),
                    nn.Tanh()
                )   # Layer 04 output.shape = batch_size x 1 x 28^2
        self.label_emb = nn.Embedding(n_class, 10)      #**************line 21
        # Encode each label in a batch into 10 trainable random numbers
    def forward(self, z, labels):
        z = z.view(-1, z_dim)            # z.shape = batch_size x z_dim
        c = self.label_emb(labels)       # c.shape = batch_size x 10
        z_c = torch.cat([z, c], dim=1)   #z_c.shape = batch_size x (z_dim+10)
        input = z_c.view(-1, z_dim+10, 1, 1)
        out = self.model(input)          # input.shape = batch_size x 110 x 1^2
        return out                       # out.shape = batch_size x 1 x 28^2
G = Generator().cuda()
G.apply(weights_init)
#----------------------------------------------------------------------------
```

Model G's forward function needs two inputs. One is a tensor for a batch of latent vectors as usual, and another is a 1D fake label tensor which is then embedded into a tensor with a shape of batch_size × 10. The two tensors are then concatenated along the row direction (dim = 1). The result is a tensor with a shape of batch_size × 110.

Then it is reshaped into a 4D tensor with a shape of batch_size $\times$ 110 $\times$ 1 $\times$ 1, and is then processed through a transposed convolution network in model G as usual. The output of model G is a batch of images. Layer 04 of model G also has no batch normalization operation.

```python
# Cell 08: Choose optimizers and a criterion------------------------Cell 08
optimizer_D = torch.optim.Adam(D.parameters(), lr=lr, betas=(0.5, 0.999))
optimizer_G = torch.optim.Adam(G.parameters(), lr=k*lr, betas=(0.5, 0.999))
criterion = nn.BCELoss(reduction='sum')
v = lambda i: 1
#v = lambda i: 1 if i<5 else (np.exp(-0.384*(i-5)) if i<17 else 0.01)
scheduler = lr_scheduler.LambdaLR(optimizer_D, lr_lambda = v)
# Cell 09: Model D's training function ----------------------------Cell 09
def train_D(inputs, labels, optimizer_D):
    # The inputs are real images & labels in a DataLoader batch
    batch_size = inputs.shape[0]
    real_preds = D(inputs, labels)
    one_targets = torch.ones(batch_size, 1, device='cuda')
    real_loss = criterion(real_preds, one_targets)
    real_score = torch.mean(real_preds).item()
    # create fake images and labels with random numbers
    latent = torch.randn(batch_size, z_dim, device='cuda')
    fake_labels = torch.LongTensor(
                torch.randint(0, 10, (batch_size,))).cuda()
    fake_images = G(latent, fake_labels)
    # Set the fake images & labels to be fake by the fake_loss
    zero_targets = torch.zeros(batch_size, 1, device='cuda')
    fake_preds = D(fake_images.detach(), fake_labels.detach())
    fake_loss = criterion(fake_preds, zero_targets)
    fake_score = torch.mean(fake_preds).item()
    # Train the optimizer_D with real_loss and fake_loss
    loss = real_loss + fake_loss
    optimizer_D.zero_grad()
    loss.backward()
    optimizer_D.step()
    return loss.item(), real_score, fake_score
# Cell 10: Model G's training function ----------------------------Cell 10
def train_G(optimizer_G):
    # Create fake images and labels
    latent = torch.randn(batch_size, z_dim, device='cuda')
    fake_labels = torch.LongTensor(
        torch.randint(0, 10, (batch_size,))).cuda()
    fake_images = G(latent, fake_labels)
    # Try to fool the discriminator
    preds = D(fake_images, fake_labels)
    one_targets = torch.ones(batch_size, 1, device='cuda')
    loss = criterion(preds, one_targets)
    optimizer_G.zero_grad()
    loss.backward()
    optimizer_G.step()
    return loss.item()
# Cell 11: The definition of a fitting function to train G and D---------Cell 11
def fit(epochs):
    torch.cuda.empty_cache()
    df = pd.DataFrame(np.empty([epochs, 5]),
        index = np.arange(epochs),
        columns=['Loss_G', 'Loss_D', 'D(X)', 'D(G(Z))', 'lr'])
```

```
for i in trange(epochs):
    loss_G = 0.0; loss_D = 0.0; real_sc = 0.0; fake_sc = 0.0
    for real_images, labels in train_dataloader:
        inputs = real_images.cuda()
        labels = labels.cuda()
        loss_d, real_score, fake_score = train_D(inputs, labels, optimizer_D)
        loss_D += loss_d; real_sc += real_score; fake_sc += fake_score
        loss_g = train_G(optimizer_G)
        loss_G += loss_g
    df.iloc[i, 0] = loss_G/n_samples
    df.iloc[i, 1] = loss_D/n_samples
    df.iloc[i, 2] = real_sc/n_batch
    df.iloc[i, 3] = fake_sc/n_batch
    df.iloc[i, 4] = optimizer_D.param_groups[0]['lr']     #Record lr_D
    scheduler.step()                                      #Update lr_D
    optimizer_G.param_groups[0]['lr'] = df.iloc[i,4]*k    #G_lr=k*G_lr
    if i==0 or (i+1)%5==0:
        print(
        "Epoch={}, Ls_G={:.4f}, Ls_D={:.4f}, D(X)={:.4f}, D(G(Z))={:.4f}"
        .format(i+1, df.iloc[i,0], df.iloc[i,1], df.iloc[i,2], df.iloc[i,3]))
        print('G_lr=', optimizer_G.param_groups[0]['lr'])
        fake_images = G(fixed_latent, fixed_labels)
        show_imgs(fake_images.detach().cpu())
return df
train_history = fit(n_epochs) #epochs=20, dt=10min


# Cell 12: Graphs of Model training outputs----------------------------Cell 12
import matplotlib.pyplot as plt; import matplotlib.ticker as ticker
history= train_history
fig, ax = plt.subplots(1,3, figsize=(15,4), sharex=True)
history.plot(ax=ax[0], y=[0,1], style=['r-+', 'b-d'])
history.plot(ax=ax[1], y=[2,3], style=['b-+', 'r-d'])
history.plot(ax=ax[2], y=[4], style=['r-+'])
for i in range(3):
    ax[i].set_xlabel('epoch')
    ax[i].grid(which='major', axis='both', color='g', linestyle=':')
#ax[0].set_ylabel('Loss')
ax[0].set(ylabel='Loss', ylim=[0,2.5])
ax[0].axhline(y=2*np.log(2), color='k', linestyle='--') #Theory D loss Value
ax[0].axhline(y=np.log(2), color='k', linestyle='--')   #Theory G loss Value
ax[1].axhline(y=0.5, color='k', linestyle='--')  #Theory D(X), D(G(Z)) values
ax[1].set_ylim([0, 1]); ax[2].set_ylim([-0.25e-4, 2.5e-4])
ax[2].ticklabel_format(style='sci', axis='y', scilimits=(0,0));
# Cell 13: Verify if the generator works for inputs----------------------Cell 13
def generate_image(G, digital):
    z = torch.randn(1, 100).cuda()
    N = len(trainData.classes)-1
    if digital <= N:
        label = torch.LongTensor([digital]).cuda()
        img = G(z, label).data.cpu()
        show_imgs(img)
    else:
        print("Your label is bigger than ", N)
#---------------------------------The End-------------------------------------
```

Codes from Cell 08 to Cell 13 are almost the same as those in the last section. The only difference is that the label information is added to the system. On the last two lines of Cell 01, a 1D long tensor named 'fixed_labels' is created by '[i for i in range

(10) for j in range(10)])'. There are 100 digits in the 1D long tensor. This 1D tensor and another 100×100 tensor named 'fixed_latent' in Cell 01 are used in Cell 11 to generate fake MNIST images during model training for us to check fake image quality. Training the two models is easy. Using a constant lambda scheduler (v = lambda i: 1) and the ratio $k = 5$, I obtained high-quality fake MNIST images in about 10 min. The cDCGAN uses a variable learning rate shown in figure 3.11(F) for the fashion MNIST dataset. Those loss curves, D(X) and D(G(Z)) curves are almost straight lines.

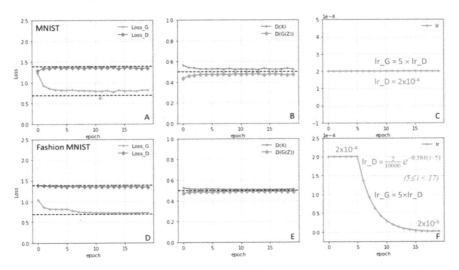

Figure 3.11. (Top) Training history of a cDCGAN for MNIST with two constant learning rates. (Bottom) for Fashion MNIST with a lambda learning rate scheduler shown in (F). Black dashed lines were based on theory values.

3.3.2 Applications of a cDCGAN to generate fake Rock Paper Scissors images

There are many datasets with beautiful color photos, but they are very big and take very long time for model training by ordinary laptops. In the following project 3.3.2, the Rock Paper Scissors dataset is used. The dataset was created by Laurence Moroney. He kindly permits people to share and adapt the dataset for all uses: commercial or non-commercial under a license of Attribution 2.0 Canada. It is a small color image dataset with three classes. Images of three hand shapes from different races, ages and genders were saved in three folders: test, train and validation. In the train folder there are three sub-folders for hands in shapes of rock, paper and scissors, a game that originated in China. A hand in the 'rock' shape is a closed fist (label 1); a hand in the 'paper' shape is an open fist (label 0), and a hand in the 'scissors' shape is a fist with the thumb, the index finger and the middle finger extended (label 2). When Torchvision ImageFolder packs those images from the train folder into a dataset, the name of each sub-folder will be used to label images in the sub-folder. There are three classes in the train dataset, and each class

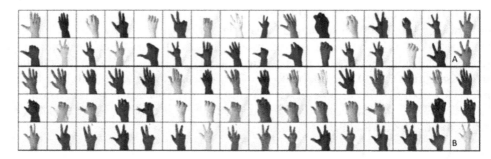

Figure 3.12. (A) Real images in the Rock Paper Scissors dataset, the output of Cell 04. Model training time is 20 min. Reproduced from Moroney (2021) CC BY 3.0. (B) Fake images, images in each row belong to a class (0: paper, 1: rock, 2: scissors), the output of Cell 11.

contains 840 images with a resolution of 300×300. Codes in Cell 01 to 04 input and pack the dataset, slice images of the dataset into a dataloader, and display a batch of images shown figure 3.12(A). Fake images generated by a cDCGAN in the project are shown in figure 3.12(B), the outputs of Cell 11.

```python
# Project 3.3.2 Using cDCGAN for Rock Paper Scissors Dataset---------Python v 3.6
import torch; import torch.nn as nn; from torch.utils.data import DataLoader
import torch.optim.lr_scheduler as lr_scheduler
import torchvision.transforms as T; from torchvision.utils import make_grid
from torchvision.datasets import ImageFolder
import numpy as np; import pandas as pd; from tqdm import trange
import matplotlib.pyplot as plt
n_epochs = 50
batch_size=32
z_dim = 100
n_class = 3
lr = 4e-4
k = 25          # k=G_lr/D_lr
img_size = 128
img_dim = img_size*img_size
img_channels = 3
# Generate a batch of noise with a shape of 48 x z_dim
fixed_latent = torch.randn(48, z_dim, device='cuda')
# Generate a long tensor for fake labels: [[0]*16+[1]*16+[2]*16]
fixed_labels = torch.cuda.LongTensor(
                [i for i in range(n_class) for _ in range(16)])
# Cell 02: Import Rock Paper Scissors dataset-------------------------Cell 02
train_dataset = ImageFolder('./OCR/data/RockPaperScissors/train',
                transform=T.Compose([T.Resize(img_size),
                        T.ToTensor(),
                        T.Normalize([0.5]*3, [0.5]*3)]))
n_samples = len(train_dataset) # n_samples=2520
# Cell 03: DataLoader ------------------------------------------------Cell 03
train_dataloader = DataLoader(train_dataset, batch_size=batch_size,
                    shuffle=True, num_workers=4, pin_memory=True)
n_batch = len(train_dataloader) #n_batch=79
for imgs, labels in train_dataloader:
    print('imgs.shape=', imgs.shape)
    print('labels=', '\n', labels.view(-1, 16))
```

```
        break
# Cell 04: Show a batch of images in the train_dataloader---------------Cell 04
def denorm(img_tensors): # Shift image pixel values to [0,1]
    return img_tensors * 0.5 + 0.5
def show_imgs(images):
    fig, ax = plt.subplots(figsize=(16,10))
    inputs = make_grid(denorm(images), nrow=16)
    ax.imshow(inputs.permute(1,2,0))
    ax.set(xticks=[], yticks=[])
    plt.show()
show_imgs(imgs)
# Cell 06: Discriminator class-------------------------1024-------------Cell 06
def basic_D(in_channels):
    return nn.Sequential(
        nn.Conv2d(in_channels, 2*in_channels, 4, 2, 1, bias=False),
        nn.BatchNorm2d(2*in_channels),
        nn.LeakyReLU(0.2, inplace=True)
        )
class Discriminator(nn.Module):
    def __init__(self):
        super().__init__()
        self.net = nn.Sequential(
            nn.Conv2d(img_channels+1, 64, kernel_size=4, stride=2, padding=1),
            nn.BatchNorm2d(64),
            nn.LeakyReLU(0.2, inplace=True),
            # layer 01 output.shape = batch_size x 64 x 64^2
            basic_D(64),
            # layer 02 output.shape = batch_size x 128 x 32^2
            basic_D(128),
            # layer 03 output.shape = batch_size x 256 x 16^2
            basic_D(256),
            # layer 04 output.shape = batch_size x 512 x 8^2
            basic_D(512),
            # layer 05 output.shape = batch_size x 1024 x 4^2
            nn.Conv2d(1024, 1, kernel_size=4, stride=1, padding=0),
            nn.Flatten(),
            nn.Sigmoid()
            )    # layer 06 output.shape = batch_size x 1
        self.label_code = nn.Embedding(n_class, 1*img_dim)
        # Encode a batch of labels as an extra image channel
    def forward(self, images, labels): # images.shape = batch_size x 3 x 128^2
        x = images.view(-1, img_channels*img_dim) #x.shape= batch_size x 3*16384
        c = self.label_code(labels)           # c.shape = batch_size x 1*16384
        x_c = torch.cat([x, c], dim=1)        #x_c.shape = batch_size x 4*16384
        input = x_c.view(-1, img_channels+1, img_size, img_size)
        out = self.net(input)              #input.shape = batch_size x 4 x 128^2
        return out                         #output.shape = batch_size x 1
D = Discriminator().cuda()
D.apply(weights_init)
# Cell 07: Generator Class---------------------------------------------Cell 07
def basic_G(in_channels):
    return nn.Sequential(
```

```python
            nn.ConvTranspose2d(in_channels, int(in_channels/2), 4, 2, 1, bias=False),
                nn.BatchNorm2d(int(in_channels/2)),
                nn.ReLU(True))
class Generator(nn.Module):
    def __init__(self):
        super().__init__()
        self.net = nn.Sequential(
                        basic_G(512),
                        # Layer 01 output.shape = batch_size x 256 x 8^2
                        basic_G(256),
                        # Layer 02 output.shape = batch_size x 128 x 16^2
                        basic_G(128),
                        # Layer 03 output.shape = batch_size x 64 x 32^2
                        basic_G(64),
                        # Layer 04 output.shape = batch_size x 32 x 64^2
                        nn.ConvTranspose2d(32, img_channels, 4, 2, 1),
                        nn.Tanh()
                    )   # Layer 05 output.shape = batch_size x 3x 128^2
        self.label_emb = nn.Embedding(n_class, 1*4*4)   #for fake labels
        self.latent = nn.Linear(z_dim, 511*4*4)         #for noise z
    def forward(self, z, labels):               #z.shape = batch_size x z_dim
        x = self.latent(z)                      #x.shape = batch_size x 511*4*4
        c = self.label_emb(labels)              #c.shape = batch_size x 1*4*4
        x_c = torch.cat([x, c], dim=1)          #x_c.shape = batch_size x 512*4*4
        input = x_c.view(-1, 512, 4, 4)
        output = self.net(input)                # input.shape = batch_size x 512 x 4^2
        return output                           #output.shape = batch_size x 3 x 128^2
G = Generator().cuda()
G.apply(weights_init)
# Cell 08: Definitions of optimizers, criterion, learning rate scheduler
criterion = nn.BCELoss(reduction='sum')
optimizer_D = torch.optim.Adam(D.parameters(), lr=lr, betas=(0.5, 0.999))
optimizer_G = torch.optim.Adam(G.parameters(), lr=k*lr, betas=(0.5, 0.999))
v = lambda i: 0.91
scheduler = lr_scheduler.MultiplicativeLR(optimizer_D, lr_lambda=v)
# Cell 09: Model D's training function --------------------------------Cell 09
def train_D(images, labels, optimizer_D):
    batch_size = images.shape[0]
    real_preds = D(images, labels)
    one_targets = torch.ones(batch_size, 1, device='cuda')
    real_loss = criterion(real_preds, one_targets)
    real_score = torch.mean(real_preds).item()
    # create fake images and labels with random numbers
    latent = torch.randn(batch_size, z_dim, device='cuda')
    fake_labels = torch.randint(0, 3, (batch_size,), device='cuda')
    fake_images = G(latent, fake_labels)
    # Set the fake images & labels to be fake by the fake_loss
    zero_targets = torch.zeros(fake_images.shape[0], 1, device='cuda')
    fake_preds = D(fake_images.detach(), fake_labels.detach())
    fake_loss = criterion(fake_preds, zero_targets)
    fake_score = torch.mean(fake_preds).item()
    # Train the optimizer_D with real_loss and fake_loss
```

```
        loss = real_loss + fake_loss
        optimizer_D.zero_grad()
        loss.backward()
        optimizer_D.step()
        return loss.item(), real_score, fake_score
# Cell 10: Model G's training function ---------------------------------Cell 10
def train_G(optimizer_G):
    # Create fake images and labels
    latent = torch.randn(batch_size, z_dim, device='cuda')
    fake_labels = torch.randint(0, 3, (batch_size,), device='cuda')
    fake_images = G(latent, fake_labels)
    # Try to fool the discriminator
    preds = D(fake_images, fake_labels)
    one_targets = torch.ones(batch_size, 1, device='cuda')
    loss = criterion(preds, one_targets)
    optimizer_G.zero_grad()
    loss.backward()
    optimizer_G.step()
    return loss.item()
# Cell 11: The definition of a fitting function to train G and D---------Cell 11
def fit(epochs):
    torch.cuda.empty_cache()
    df = pd.DataFrame(np.empty([epochs, 5]),
        index = np.arange(epochs),
        columns=['Loss_G', 'Loss_D', 'D(X)', 'D(G(Z))', 'lr_D'])
    for i in trange(epochs):
        loss_G = 0.0; loss_D = 0.0; real_sc = 0.0; fake_sc = 0.0
        for real_images, labels in train_dataloader:
            inputs = real_images.cuda()
            labels = labels.cuda()
            loss_d, real_score, fake_score = train_D(inputs, labels, optimizer_D)
            loss_D += loss_d; real_sc += real_score; fake_sc += fake_score
            loss_g = train_G(optimizer_G)
            loss_G += loss_g
        df.iloc[i, 0] = loss_G/n_samples
        df.iloc[i, 1] = loss_D/n_samples
        df.iloc[i, 2] = real_sc/n_batch
        df.iloc[i, 3] = fake_sc/n_batch
        df.iloc[i, 4] = optimizer_D.param_groups[0]['lr']       #Record lr_D
        scheduler.step()                                        #Update lr_D
        optimizer_G.param_groups[0]['lr'] = df.iloc[i, 4]*k     #G_lr=k*G_lr
        if i==0 or (i+1)%10==0:
            print(
            "Epoch={}, Ls_G={:.2f}, Ls_D={:.2f}, D(X)={:.2f}, D(G(Z))={:.2f}"
            .format(i+1, df.iloc[i,0], df.iloc[i,1], df.iloc[i,2], df.iloc[i,3]))
            fake_images = G(fixed_latent, fixed_labels)
            show_imgs(fake_images.detach().cpu())
    return df
train_history = fit(n_epochs)     #n_epochs=50, dt=20min
# Cell 12: Graphs of Model training outputs------------------------------Cell 12
history= train_history
fig, ax = plt.subplots(1,3, figsize=(15,4), sharex=True)
```

```
history.plot(ax=ax[0], y=[0,1], style=['r-+', 'b-'])
history.plot(ax=ax[1], y=[2,3], style=['b-+', 'r-'])
history.plot(ax=ax[2], y=[4], style=['r-+'])
for i in range(3):
    ax[i].set_xlabel('epoch')
    ax[i].grid(which='major', axis='both', color='g', linestyle=':')
ax[0].set(ylabel='Loss')#, ylim=[0,2])
ax[0].axhline(y=2*np.log(2), color='k', linestyle='--') #Theory D loss Value
ax[0].axhline(y=np.log(2), color='k', linestyle='--')   #Theory G loss Value
ax[1].axhline(y=0.5, color='k', linestyle='--')  #Theory D(X), D(G(Z)) values
ax[2].set(ylabel='learning rate of D')
ax[2].ticklabel_format(style='sci', axis='y', scilimits=(0,0))
plt.show()
# Cell 13: Verify if the generator works for inputs----------------------Cell 13
def generate_image(G, digital):
    z = torch.randn(1, 100).cuda()
    N = len(train_dataset.classes)-1
    if digital <= N:
        label = torch.LongTensor([digital]).cuda()
        img = G(z, label).data.cpu()
        show_imgs(img)
    else:
        print("Your label is bigger than ", N)
generate_image(G, 0)
#--------------------------------The End-----------------------------------
```

The code structure for this project is almost the same as the one in section 3.3.1. This project is for color images with a resolution of 128×128 and three image classes. Model D in Cell 06 has six convolution layers, and model G in Cell 07 has five transposed convolution layers. Because of the layer number difference, model D is smarter than model G. In Cell 08, a multiplicative learning rate scheduler is used for model training. The learning rate function curve is shown in figure 3.13(C). Starting from 4×10^{-4}, the learning rate exponentially decreases according to a function: $4 \times 10^{-4} \times (0.91)^{epoch}$. The multiplicative learning rate scheduler prevents the issue of explosion of loss function values. Running codes in Cell 13, you will generate a single big fake color image with the desired label for an integer from 0 to 2 in the function: *generate_image(G, 0)*, and you will find its quality is not good enough comparing with real images.

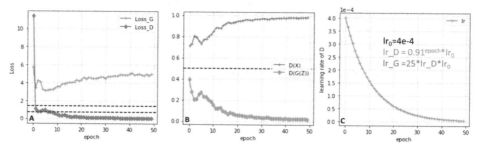

Figure 3.13. Model training history. (A) Loss curves for model D and G. (B) $D(X)$ curves and $D(G(Z))$ curves. (C) The learning rate scheduler for model D, and model G's learning is equal to 25*lr_D.

References

Churchill S and Chao B 2019 Anime face dataset: a collection of high-quality anime faces. https://www.kaggle.com/datasets/splcher/animefacedataset

Deng L 2012 The MNIST database of handwritten digit images for machine learning research 141–2 *IEEE Signal Process. Mag.* **29** 141–2

Goodfellow I, Pouget-Abadie J, Mehdi Mirza B X, Warde-Farley D, Ozair S, Courville A and Bengio Y 2014 Generative adversarial nets *Proc. of the Int. Conf. on Neural Information Processing Systems* 2672–80

Liu Z, Luo P, Wang X and Tang X 2015 Deep learning face attributes in the wild *Proc. of the IEEE Int. Conf. on Computer Vision* 3730–8

Liu Z, Luo P, Wang X and Tang X 2015 *Proc. of Int. Conf. on Computer Vision (ICCV)* https://liuziwei7.github.io/papers/faceattributes_poster.pdf

Mirza M and Osindero S 2014 Conditional generative adversarial nets *arXiv preprint arXiv:1411.1784.*

Moroney L 2021 Rock Paper Scissors Dataset https://universe.roboflow.com/landada/rock-paper-scissors-hchrz (accessed 29 November 2023)

Radford A, Metz L and Chintala S 2016 Unsupervised representation learning with deep convolutional generative adversarial networks *CoRR*, abs/1511.06434.

Xiao H, Rasul K and Vollgraf R 2017 Fashion-mnist: a novel image dataset for benchmarking machine learning algorithms *arXiv preprint arXiv:1708.07747.*

Xiao H, Rasul K and Vollgraf R 2017 Fashion-MNIST: a novel image dataset for benchmarking machine learning algorithms https://github.com/zalandoresearch/fashion-mnist.

Chapter 4

Image generation by WGANs with gradient penalty

Wasserstein generative adversarial networks (WGANs) and WGANs with gradient penalty (WGAN-GP) are introduced in this chapter to solve model collapse issues in GAN model training. The quadratic curve dataset, MNIST, Anime Face, and CelebA datasets are used. A conditional WGAN-GP is implemented to the Rock Paper Scissors dataset to generate images according to our settings. Although model training time is longer, the quality of fake images generated in this chapter is higher.

Using GANs, we can generate photo-realistic fake images, but it is not easy to train GAN models because of model collapse issues. From our projects in previous chapters, we know that the discriminator model D is usually smarter than model G in most GANs. It is easy for model D to see the difference between fake images and real images, and model G is not powerful enough to improve its skill to fool model D. In model training of many GAN projects the values of model D's loss function would decrease step by step to zero and the values of model G's loss function would increase to above 6 in less than 20 epochs. We then have model collapse issues at the end of model training. By choosing different learning rate schedulers with different initial learning rates, we can tune models to prevent model collapse. However, it takes a long time (hours and days) to adjust model hyperparameters and learning rate schedulers for each GAN project.

In 2017, Martin Arjovsky (Arjovsky *et al* 2017) and his colleagues introduced a WGAN to stablilize model training and to prevent issues such as model collapse. In a WGAN, a generator G and a discriminator D are used as usual in a GAN. A difference is that no activation function is used at the end of WGAN's discriminator D. The output of the discriminator D for an image in a batch of a dataloader is a real number which can be in a range from negative infinite to positive infinite $(-\infty, +\infty)$. From a batch of real images (X), we obtain a batch of 1D vectors $D(X)$. A batch of fake images $G(Z)$ is generated from a batch of noise vectors (Z) in a latent space with z_dim dimensions. Using the batch of fake images as input, model D outputs another batch of 1D vectors $D(G(Z))$. Model D's loss function is the average of $D(G(Z))$ subtracts the average of $D(X)$ as shown in equation (4.1), and model G's loss function is shown as equation (4.2)

$$L_D(\theta_d) = \frac{1}{n}\sum_{i=1}^{n}D(G(z_i)) - \frac{1}{n}\sum_{i=1}^{n}D(x_i) \tag{4.1}$$

$$L_G(\theta_g) = -\frac{1}{n}\sum_{i=1}^{n}D(G(z_i)) \tag{4.2}$$

According to the WGAN paper (Arjovsky *et al* 2017), there is a mathematical condition (1-Lipschitz continuity) to use the above loss functions in a WGAN: the absolute values of derivatives of model D's loss function should be less than 1.0. This condition could be fulfilled by clipping model D's weights in the range [−0.01, 0.01]. However, in the following project 4.1.1 the quality of fake images generated by WGAN is worse than DCGAN, even WGAN codes run a longer time with more epochs. In 2017, Ishaan Gulrajani and his colleagues improved WGAN with a new method published in their paper (Gulrajani *et al* 2017) titled 'Improved training of Wasserstein GANs'. The paper proposed an alternative way to enforce the 1-Lipschitz continuity by adding a penalty to model D's loss function as shown in equation (4.3). This modified WGAN is called Wasserstein GAN with gradient penalty (WGAN-GP)

$$L_D(\theta_d) = \frac{1}{n}\sum_{i=1}^{n}D(\tilde{x}_i) - \frac{1}{n}\sum_{i=1}^{n}D(x_i) + \frac{\lambda}{n}\sum_{i=1}^{n}[(\|\nabla_{\hat{x}_i}D(\hat{x}_i)\|_2 - 1)^2] \tag{4.3}$$

In the formula, x_i is a real image in a batch of a dataloader, $\tilde{x}_i$ is a fake image generated by the generator model $G(z_i)$ from a noisy vector z_i, and $\hat{x}_i$ is an interpolation between x_i and $\tilde{x}_i$ by $\hat{x}_i = \varepsilon x_i + (1 - \varepsilon)\tilde{x}_i$, where ε is a random number uniformly distributed within [0,1), and λ is a penalty coefficient which was set to be equal to 10 in the WGAN-GP paper (Gulrajani *et al* 2017). Before we introduce the WGAN-GP theory, we need to know how to calculate $\nabla_{\hat{x}_i}D(\hat{x}_i)$ which is a gradient of a scalar function to a vector. Suppose we have a 1D tensor $x = [0, 0.5, 1.5, 2.0]$, and a scalar function f is defined as the sum of squares of the tensor's elements: $f(x) = x_0^2 + x_1^2 + x_2^2 + x_3^2$. The gradient of the function to the vector x is $\nabla f(x)$, and its norm $\|\nabla f(x)\|_2$ to the given vector x at $x = [0, 0.5, 1.5, 2.0]$ are listed below:

$$\nabla f(x) = \left[\frac{\partial f}{\partial x_0}, \frac{\partial f}{\partial x_1}, \frac{\partial f}{\partial x_2}, \frac{\partial f}{\partial x_3}\right] = [2x_0, 2x_1, 2x_2, 2x_3] = [0, 1, 3, 4]$$

$$\|\nabla f(x)\|_2 = (0^2 + 1^2 + 3^2 + 4^2)^{1/2} = 5.1$$

The gradient norm $\|\nabla f(x)\|_2$ is the Euclidean norm for each row in a gradient tensor. Since there is only one row in the above gradient tensor $\nabla f(x)$, there is one element in the norm. Each element of the norm is equal to the square root of the sum of each element's square in the gradient's row. Imported from PyTorch, an autograd.grad class in the following Extra Cell ONE can do the above job automatically. The output of the class's instance is a tuple with the gradient tensor as its only element.

Using '[0]' at the end of the output of the class instance, we picked out the gradient tensor from the tuple. According the last part of equation (4.3), the gradient penalty of the following codes is: $\lambda(5.1 - 1)^2 = 168$.

```
# Extra Cell ONE: torch.autograd.grad, norm()-----------------------------------
import torch; import torch.nn as nn; from torch.autograd import grad
x = torch.FloatTensor([0, 0.5, 1.5, 2])
x.requires_grad=True
print('x =', x)
f = (x*x).sum()        # f = x[0]^2 + x[1]^2 + x[2]^2 + x[3]^2
print('f =', f)        # f= tensor(6.5000)
df2dx = grad(outputs=f,
             inputs=x,
             grad_outputs=torch.ones_like(f),
             create_graph=True,
             retain_graph=True)[0]
print('df2dx = ', df2dx)                    #df2dx= tensor([0., 1., 3., 4.])
grad_norm = df2dx.norm(p=2, dim=0)
print('grad_norm=', grad_norm)                      #grad_norm= tensor(5.1)
gradient_penalty = 10*torch.mean((grad_norm - 1) ** 2)
print('gradient_penalty=', gradient_penalty) #gradient_penalty=tensor(168.02)
#-------------------------------------------------------------------------------
```

4.1 Using a WGAN or a WGAN-GP for generation of fake quadratic curves

The detailed mathematical principles of WGAN and WGAN-GP are very complex. Codes for the following project 4.1.1 about quadratic curve generation are used to help us understand them. Open a new Jupyter notebook in the VS Code, copy Cells 01-5 from section 3.1.1, and paste them in the new notebook. You should delete the activate class *nn.Sigmoid( )* at the end of Cell 05 for the discriminator D. Some hyperparameters are added or modified specially for the new project. The following codes are for WGAN-GP. If you remove hash tag symbols # in front of line 04, 05 and 12 in Cell 08, and add # symbols in front of line 10 and 11 in the same Cell, the codes are modified for WGAN. Figure 4.1 shows the outputs of the project. You can

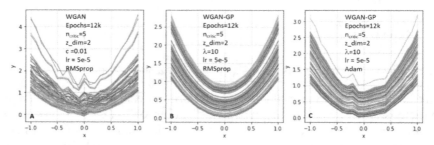

Figure 4.1. (A) Fake curves generated by WGAN. (B) Fake curves generated by WGAN-GP with the RMSprop optimizer. (C) Fake curves generated by WGAN-GP with the Adam optimizer. Some hyperparameters are listed in graphs ($12k = 12\ 000$). Model training time is 24 min.

see that the quality of fake curves generated by WGAN-GP with RMSprop optimizer is better.

```python
# Project 4.1.1: Using WGAN-GP for fake quadratic curves-------------Python v3.6
import torch; import torch.nn as nn; import numpy as np; import pandas as pd

import matplotlib.pyplot as plt; from tqdm import trange
n_epochs = 12000
batch_size = 64
z_dim = 2          # latent space dimensions 2
n_hidden = 256     # number of neurons in a only hidden layer
n_points = 21      # number of points on each curve of training_data
n_batch = 5
lr = 5e-5          # learning rate: 5e-5
n_critic = 5       # iteration number for WGAN and WGAN-GP
lambda_gp = 10     # the gradient penalty coefficient only for WGAN-GP
c = 0.01           # the clipping parameter only for WGAN
# Cell 02: Creating training data from y=a*x^2+(a-1)----------------------Cell 02
x = np.linspace(-1, 1, n_points)
def training_data():
    a = np.random.uniform(1, 2, size=batch_size).reshape(-1,1)
    points = a*x*x + (a-1)
    return points
y = training_data()
# Cell 03: Show curves----------------------------------------------------Cell 03
def show_curves(x, y):
    fig, ax = plt.subplots(figsize=(4,4))
    for i in range(batch_size):
        ax.plot(x, y[i,:])
    ax.set(xlabel='x', ylabel='y')#, ylim=[-0.1,3.5])
    ax.set(xticks=np.arange(-1.0, 1.1, 0.5))
    ax.grid(color='g', linestyle=':')
    plt.show()
show_curves(x,y)
#-----------------------------------------------------------------------------

# Cell 04: Generator class------------------------------------------------Cell 04
class Generator(nn.Module):
    def __init__(self):
        super().__init__()
        self.net = nn.Sequential(nn.Linear(z_dim, n_hidden),
                        nn.ReLU(True),
                        nn.Linear(n_hidden, n_points))
    def forward(self, z):
        fake_curves = self.net(z)    #noisy vectors z.shape = batch_size x z_dim
        return fake_curves           #fake_curves.shape = batch_size x n_points
G = Generator().cuda()
# Cell 05: Discriminator Class--------------------------------------------Cell 05
class Discriminator(nn.Module):
    def __init__(self):
        super().__init__()
        self.net = nn.Sequential(nn.Linear(n_points, n_hidden),
                        nn.LeakyReLU(0.2, inplace=True),
                        nn.Linear(n_hidden, 1))
    def forward(self, curves):       # cureves could be real or fake
        outputs = self.net(curves)   # curves.shape = batch_size x n_points
        return outputs               # outputs.shape = batch_size x 1
D = Discriminator().cuda()
```

```
# Cell 06 Gradient-penalty function----------------------------------Cell 06
def gradient_penalty(D, real_data, fake_data):
    batch_size = real_data.size(0)
    eps = torch.rand(batch_size, 1, device='cuda') #rand: uniform PDF in [0,1)
    eps = eps.expand_as(real_data)  #eps.shape = batch_size x n_points
    # Interpolation between real data and fake data.
    interpolations = eps * real_data + (1 - eps) * fake_data
    interp_logits = D(interpolations)     # shape = batch_size x 1
    gradients = torch.autograd.grad(
                    outputs = interp_logits,
                    inputs = interpolations,
                    grad_outputs = torch.ones_like(interp_logits),
                    create_graph = True,
                    retain_graph = True)[0]

    gradients = gradients.view(batch_size, -1)  # get Gradient
    grad_norm = gradients.norm(2, dim=1)         # get Gradient Norm
    gradient_penalty = lambda_gp*torch.mean((grad_norm - 1) ** 2)
    return gradient_penalty
# Cell 07: Model optimizers----------------------------------------------Cell 07
optimizer_D = torch.optim.RMSprop(D.parameters(), lr=lr)
optimizer_G = torch.optim.RMSprop(G.parameters(), lr=lr) #RMSprop, Adam
#---------------------------------------------------------------------------
# Extra Cell TWO: about interpolation of real and fake curves---Extra Cell TWO
curves_real = torch.cuda.FloatTensor(training_data())         #-------line 1
noise = torch.randn(batch_size, z_dim, requires_grad=True)  #-------line 2
curves_fake = G(noise.cuda())                               #-------line 3
eps = torch.rand(64, 1).cuda()         #----------------------------line 4
print('eps.T=\n', eps.T)
eps = eps.expand_as(curves_real)       #----------------------------line 6

print('eps[63]=', eps[-1])
# Interpolation between real curves and fake curves.
interpolation = eps * curves_real + (1 - eps) * curves_fake #-------line 9
print('curves_real[63]=', curves_real[-1])
print('curves_fake[63]=', curves_fake[-1])
print('interpolation[63]=', interpolation[-1])  #-----------------line 12
eps[63,20]*curves_real[63,20]+(1-eps[63,20])*curves_fake[63, 20] #-line 13
#---------------------------------------------------------------------------
```

Within the seven cells of project 4.1.1, only Cell 06 is new. The function *gradient_penalty* needs three inputs: the discriminator model D, a batch of real curves (64×21 tensor) and a batch of fake curves (64×21 tensor). The above Extra Cell TWO is used to help us to understand how to construct an interpolation curve from a real curve and a fake curve. The first three lines in the extra cell generate a 64×21 tensor for a batch of 64 real curves and a same size tensor for a batch of 64 fake curves. The code on the fourth line generates a 64×1 random tensor named 'eps' which is then expanded by the code on the sixth line into a 64×21 tensor. Each element in a row of the expanded eps tensor is a same random number. The *eps* [63] printed on screen is an example of the last row of the expanded tensor. With codes in the last four lines in the extra cell, you will know how to calculate the interpolation tensor. Each interpolation curve is obtained by element-wise calculations according to the formula on line 9: *interpolation = eps * curves_real + (1−eps) * curves_fake*. The output of line 13 is the result of manual calculations about the last element of the last interpolation curve. It is the same as the last element of the output of line 12. A batch of interpolations will be used as an input of model D which outputs a batch of scalars (line 07 in Cell 06). The batch of scalars has a name 'interp_logits' and its gradients to the interpolation are obtained by codes on line 08 in Cell 06 for the gradient penalty.

```
# Cell 08: Model Training -----------------------------------------------Cell 08
def train_D(curves_real, optimizer_D):                              # line 01
    batch_size = curves_real.shape[0]
    for _ in range(n_critic):
        #for parm in D.parameters():      #only for WGAN             # line 04
        #    parm.data.clamp_(-c, c)      #only for WGAN             # line 05
        real_score = D(curves_real).mean()
        z = torch.randn(batch_size, z_dim, requires_grad=True, device='cuda')
        curves_fake = G(z)
        fake_score = D(curves_fake.detach()).mean()
        gp = gradient_penalty(D, curves_real, curves_fake) #WGAN-GP line 10
        loss_D = fake_score - real_score + gp     #only for WGAN-GP line 11
        #loss_D = fake_score - real_score         #only for WGAN line 12
        optimizer_D.zero_grad()
        loss_D.backward(retain_graph=True)
        optimizer_D.step()
    return loss_D.item(), real_score.item(), fake_score.item()
# Cell 09: GAN Definition of a training function for the generator------Cell 09
def train_G(optimizer_G):
    noise = torch.randn(batch_size, z_dim, requires_grad=True, device='cuda')
    curves_fake = G(noise)
    loss_G = -D(curves_fake).mean()
    optimizer_G.zero_grad()
    loss_G.backward()
    optimizer_G.step()
    return loss_G.item()
# Cell 10: Fitting function---------------------------------------------Cell 10
def fit(epochs):
    torch.cuda.empty_cache()
    df = pd.DataFrame(np.empty([epochs, 4]),
                        index = np.arange(epochs),
                        columns=['Loss_G', 'Loss_D', 'D(X)', 'D(G(Z))'])
    for i in trange(epochs):
        loss_G = 0.0; loss_D = 0.0; real_sc = 0.0; fake_sc = 0.0
        for _ in range(n_batch):
            curves_real = torch.cuda.FloatTensor(training_data())
            loss_d, real_score, fake_score = train_D(curves_real, optimizer_D)
            loss_D += loss_d
            real_sc += real_score
            fake_sc += fake_score
            loss_g = train_G(optimizer_G)
            loss_G += loss_g
        df.iloc[i, 0] = loss_G/n_batch
        df.iloc[i, 1] = loss_D/n_batch
        df.iloc[i, 2] = real_sc/n_batch
        df.iloc[i, 3] = fake_sc/n_batch
        if i==0 or (i+1)%2000==0:
            print(
            "Epoch={:5}, Ls_G={:.3f}, Ls_D={:.3f}, D(X)={:.3f}, D(G(Z))={:.3f}"
            .format(i+1, df.iloc[i,0], df.iloc[i,1], df.iloc[i,2], df.iloc[i,3]))
            z = torch.randn(batch_size, z_dim, requires_grad=True, device='cuda')
            fake_curves = G(z).cpu()
```

```
        show_curves(x, fake_curves.detach().numpy())
    return df
train_history = fit(n_epochs)
# Cell 11: Show the training history in Graph--------------------------Cell 11
df= train_history
fig, ax = plt.subplots(1,2, figsize=(8,4))#, sharex=True)
df.plot(ax=ax[0], y=[0,1], style=['b:', 'k-'])
df.plot(ax=ax[1], y=[2,3], style=['b-', 'k:'])
gp = df.iloc[:,1]+df.iloc[:,2]-df.iloc[:,3]
ax[0].plot(gp, label='Gradient Penalty', color='r')
for i in range(2):
    ax[i].set_xlabel('epoch')
    ax[i].grid(which='major', axis='both', color='g', linestyle=':')
ax[0].set(ylabel='Loss')
ax[0].legend()
plt.show()
#---------------------------The End-----------------------------------
```

According to the WGAN paper (Arjovsky *et al* 2017), the RMSprop optimizer should be used. You can try the Adam optimizer in Cell 07, but there is not much difference about the quality of the fake curves generated by the WGAN. At the end of the Extra Cell TWO, if you add and run the following code $D(torch.FloatTensor$ $(y).cuda()).T$, you will get a 1×64 tensor listed below, where y is a 64×21 numpy array generated by Cell 02 for real curves. Each real curve was compressed by model D into a real number in the 1D critical space

tensor([[−0.0117, 0.0057, −0.0153, −0.0998, −0.1126, −0.0682, −0.0417, −0.0155,
    −0.0779, −0.1115, 0.0053, 0.0025, 0.0029, −0.1112, −0.0124, −0.1099,
    −0.0176, −0.0806, −0.0436, −0.0785, −0.0720, −0.0747, −0.0176, −0.0962,
    −0.0622, −0.0094, −0.0295, −0.0681, −0.0810, −0.0414, −0.0492, −0.0683,
    −0.0849, −0.0824, −0.0509, −0.0292, −0.1097, −0.0534, −0.0341, −0.1099,
    −0.1024, −0.0659, −0.0413, −0.0531, 0.0039, −0.0964, −0.0046, −0.0288,
    −0.0428, −0.0430, −0.0190, −0.0657, −0.1021, −0.0610, −0.0137, −0.0826,
    −0.0550, −0.0018, −0.0918, −0.0722, −0.0053, −0.0519, −0.0776, −0.0334]],
    device = 'cuda:0', grad_fn = <PermuteBackward0>)

There is a probability distribution function hidden in these numbers in the 1D critical space. We only care about the mean of the PDF with a hypothesis that the PDF follows a normal distribution with a constant variance. Changing the 'T' in the above code to mean() for the above 64 numbers, you will get the average of those 64 numbers $D(X) = -0.1803$. It is a scalar tensor. WGAN uses the average number as a statistic location for these real curves in the 1D critical space. Using the code: $D (G$ $(torch.randn(batch\_size, z\_dim, requires\_grad = True).cuda())).mean()$, you will get the average of another 1D tensor with 64 elements: $D(G(Z)) = 0.0046$. This is the statistic location of a batch of fake curves. The WGAN's model D wants to maximize the distance between $D(X)$ and $D(G(Z))$, so it is possible for model D to distinguish true curves from fake curves. The distance is called the 'Wasserstein distance' or 'Earth moving distance'. In computer vision projects, we always use a gradient descendent algorithm to find the minimum of a loss function during model training. We have to use the loss function shown in equation (4.1) to minimize the negative Wasserstein distance for model D. The WGAN's model G wants to fool model D by maximizing $D(G(Z))$. With the same mathematical reasoning, we choose model G's loss function as shown in equation (4.2).

The mathematical concept of Wasserstein distance is not easy to understand. Suppose you want to remove a pyramid from Giza in Egypt to Athens in Greece and build the exact same pyramid, there are many ways to move the stone blocks of the pyramid. One way is towards China, across the Pacific Ocean to America, and then across the Atlantic Ocean and Mediterranean Sea to Athens. A shorter path is north across the Mediterranean Sea to Athens. The shortest path is the 'Earth moving distance' on which we finish a project with the shortest time and the minimum cost. Jensen–Shannon divergence is used in the loss function of GAN's model D (section 3.1.1). If real samples' PDF and the fake samples' PDF do not overlap, the value of the loss function will be a constant (zero), and the gradients of the loss function will also be zero. Model D will not be trained with vanished gradients. Wasserstein distance is introduced to solve this issue.

For stable model trainings, the WGAN paper instructed that the model D is trained more times ($n_{\text{critic}} = 5$) than model G. In the first for-loop in Cell 08, each batch of real curves and fake curves are trained n_{critic} times. These extra calculations significantly increase training time. But if we are sure that our model training will provide good results in hours or days, we would like to wait. Another for-loop in Cell 08 is used to limit model D's weights by clipping ($c = 0.01$) specifically for WGAN. The paper instructs us to do so for model D's 1-Lipschitz continuity. Figure 4.1 shows the outputs of the above codes in three conditions. The WGAN-GP paper (Gulrajani *et al* 2017) instructs us to use the Adam optimizer. But from figure 4.1(B), we can see the RMSprop optimizer is better than Adam for this project. Loss function curves and WGAN-GP's gradient penalty curves are shown in figure 4.2.

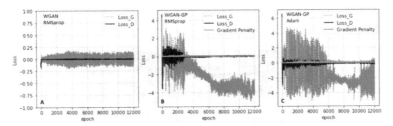

Figure 4.2. Loss function curves for WGAN and GAN-GP. Hyper-parameter settings for these loss function curves are the same as those shown in figure 4.1.

4.2 Using a WGAN-GP for Fashion MNIST

Since projects with the MNIST dataset are too easy, we will focus on using WGAN-GP for the Fashion MNIST dataset. If you want, you can change dataset name in Cell 02 of the following project 4.2.1 to get a comparison of the results of the two datasets. Although Fashion MNIST and MNIST have the same structure, images in the first dataset have detailed patterns, such as trade marks on shoes and T-shirts. The detailed information is not easy to restore on fake images. Because ResNet9 did a good job for image classification in the projects in chapter 2, perhaps ResNet9 has the ability to keep detailed image structure information for fake image generation. Only after using a modified ResNet9 in model D could better fake images be generated, but they were still not good enough compared with real images. My model training time with ResNet9 was over two hours in 30 epochs. Fake fashion MNIST images are shown in figure 4.3.

```
# Project 4.2.1: WGAN-GP for Fashion MNIST---------------------------Python v3.6
import torch; import torch.nn as nn
from torchvision import transforms as T; from torch.utils.data import DataLoader
from torchvision.datasets import FashionMNIST #FashionMNIST, MNIST
from torchvision.utils import make_grid; from tqdm import trange
import numpy as np; import pandas as pd; from matplotlib import pyplot as plt
n_epochs = 30
batch_size = 100
img_channels = 1
z_dim = 100
lr = 2e-4          # Learning rate in cell 08
k = 5              #lr_G = k*lr_D
lamda_gp = 10
n_critic = 1
fixed_latent = torch.randn(batch_size, z_dim, device='cuda') #a batch of noises
# Cell 02: MNIST of Fashion DataSet ----------------------------------Cell 02
path = './OCR/data/'
train_Dataset = FashionMNIST(path, train=True, download=False,
        transform=T.Compose([T.ToTensor(), T.Normalize([0.5],[0.5])])
        )
n_samples = len(train_Dataset) #len(trainData)=60000
# Cell 03: Create a DataLoader (train_dataloader)------------------------Cell 03
train_dataloader = DataLoader(train_Dataset, batch_size=batch_size, shuffle=True)
n_batch = len(train_dataloader) #n_batch=n_sample/batch_size=600
# Cell 04: Show the images in a batch of the train dataloader------------Cell 04
for imgs, labels in train_dataloader: # for the 1st batch on the train dataloader
    print('imgs_batch.shape=', imgs.shape)
    #print('labels=', labels[:40])
    break
def denorm(img_tensors):        # Shift the value of each image pixel to [0,1]
    return img_tensors * 0.5 + 0.5
```

Figure 4.3. Fake Fashion MNIST images generated by a WGAN-GP (epochs = 30, n_{critic} = 1, λ = 10, lr_D = 2 $\times$ 10^{-4}, lr_G = 10^{-3}, RMSprop optimizer, model training time = 124 min). The Fashion MNIST dataset is from Xiao *et al* (2017) with a license CC BY 3.0.

```python
def show_imgs(imgs):
    fig, ax = plt.subplots(figsize=(12,8))
    input = make_grid(denorm(imgs), nrow=10, padding=2)
    ax.imshow(input.permute(1,2,0), cmap='gray')
    ax.set(xticks=[], yticks=[])
    plt.show()
show_imgs(imgs)
# Cell 05: Model parameters initialization --------------------------------Cell 05
def weights_init(m):
    if(type(m) == nn.ConvTranspose2d or type(m) == nn.Conv2d):
        nn.init.normal_(m.weight.data, 0.0, 0.02)
    elif(type(m) == nn.BatchNorm2d):
        nn.init.normal_(m.weight.data, 1.0, 0.02)
        nn.init.constant_(m.bias.data, 0)
# Cell 06: Discriminator model D-------------------------------------------Cell 06
def basic(in_channels, out_channels, f=3, s=1, p=1):
    return nn.Sequential(
        nn.Conv2d(in_channels, out_channels,
                kernel_size=f, stride=s, padding=p, bias=False),
        nn.InstanceNorm2d(out_channels),
        nn.LeakyReLU(0.2, inplace=True)
        )
class Rs_Block(nn.Module):
    def __init__(self, in_channels):
        super().__init__()
        self.resnet = nn.Sequential(
                basic(in_channels, in_channels, 3, 1, 1),
                basic(in_channels, in_channels, 3, 1, 1)
                )
    def forward(self, x):
        return x + self.resnet(x)
class ResNet9(nn.Module):
    def __init__(self, in_channels=img_channels):
        super().__init__()
        self.net =  nn.Sequential(
                basic(img_channels, 64, 3, 1, 1), #batch_size x 64 x 28^2
                basic(64, 128, 4, 2, 1),          #batch_size x 128 x 14^2
                Rs_Block(128),                    #batch_size x 128 x 14^2
                basic(128, 256, 4, 2, 2),         #batch_size x 256 x 8^2
                basic(256, 512, 4, 2, 1),         #batch_size x 512 x 4^2
                Rs_Block(512),                    #batch_size x 512 x 4^2
                nn.Conv2d(512, 1, 4, 1, 0),       #batch_size x 512 x 1^2
                nn.Flatten()
            )
    def forward(self, images):
        output = self.net(images) #images.shape=batch_size x 1 x 28^2
        return output             #output.shape = batch_size x 1
D = ResNet9().cuda()
D.apply(weights_init)
# Cell 07: Generator model G-----------------------------------------------Cell 07
def basic_G(in_channels, out_channels, f=4,s =2, p =0):
    return nn.Sequential(
```

```
                nn.ConvTranspose2d(in_channels, out_channels,
                        kernel_size=f, stride=s, padding=p, bias=False),
                nn.BatchNorm2d(out_channels),
                nn.ReLU(True)
        )
class Generator(nn.Module):
    def __init__(self):
        super().__init__()
        self.net = nn.Sequential(
            basic_G(z_dim, 256, 4, 1, 0),
            #layer 01 output.shape = batch_size x 256 x 4^2
            basic_G(256, 128, 3, 2, 1),
            #layer 02 output.shape = batch_size x 128 x 7^2
            basic_G(128, 64, 4, 2, 1),
            #layer 03 output.shape = batch_size x 64 x 14^2
            nn.ConvTranspose2d(64, 1, 4, 2, 1),
            nn.Tanh()
        )   #layer 04 output.shape = batch_size x 1 x 28^2
    def forward(self, z):
        input = z.view(-1, z_dim, 1, 1) #z.shape = batch_size x z_dim
        output = self.net(input)  #input.shape = batch_size x z_dim x 1^2
        return output              #output.shape = batch_size x 1 x 28^2
G = Generator().cuda()
G.apply(weights_init)
# Cell 08: Optimizers------------------------------------------------Cell 09
#optimizer_D = torch.optim.Adam(D.parameters(), lr=lr, betas=(0.5, 0.9))
#optimizer_G = torch.optim.Adam(G.parameters(), lr=lr, betas=(0.5, 0.9))
optimizer_D = torch.optim.RMSprop(D.parameters(), lr=lr)
optimizer_G = torch.optim.RMSprop(G.parameters(), lr=k*lr)
# Cell 09 Gradient-penalty function---------------------------------cell 09
def gradient_penalty(D, real_data, fake_data):
    batch_size = real_data.size(0)      #real_data.shape = batch_size x 1 x 28^2
    eps = torch.rand(batch_size, 1, 1, 1, device='cuda') # batch_size x 1 x 1^2
    eps = eps.expand_as(real_data)            #eps.shape=batch_size x 1 x 28^2
    # Sample Epsilon from a uniform distribution
    interpolation = eps * real_data + (1 - eps) * fake_data
    # Interpolation of real data and fake data,   shape = batch_size x 1 x 28^2
    interp_logits = D(interpolation)
    # get logits for interpolated images
    gradients = torch.autograd.grad(
                outputs=interp_logits,
                inputs=interpolation,
                grad_outputs=torch.ones_like(interp_logits),
                create_graph=True,
                retain_graph=True,
            )[0]    # Compute Gradients
    # Compute and return Gradient Norm
    gradients = gradients.view(batch_size, -1)
    grad_norm = gradients.norm(2, dim=1)
    gradient_penalty = torch.mean((grad_norm - 1) ** 2)
    return gradient_penalty
# Cell 10: Model D's training function------------------------------Cell 10
```

```
def train_D(inputs, optimizer_D):
    for _ in range(n_critic):
        batch_size = inputs.shape[0]
        real_preds = D(inputs)
        real_score = torch.mean(real_preds)
        z = torch.randn(batch_size, z_dim, device='cuda')
        fake_images = G(z)
        fake_preds = D(fake_images.detach())
        fake_score = torch.mean(fake_preds)
        gp = gradient_penalty(D, inputs, fake_images)
        loss = fake_score - real_score + lamda_gp*gp
        optimizer_D.zero_grad()
        loss.backward(retain_graph=True)
        optimizer_D.step()
    return loss.item(), real_score.item(), fake_score.item()
# Cell 11: Model G's training function--------------------------------Cell 11
def train_G(optimizer_G):
    z = torch.randn(batch_size, z_dim, device='cuda')
    fake_images = G(z)    # Create fake images
    preds = D(fake_images)
    loss = -torch.mean(preds)
    optimizer_G.zero_grad()
    loss.backward()
    optimizer_G.step()
    return loss.item()
# Cell 12: The main training function---------------------------------Cel2
def fit(epochs):
    torch.cuda.empty_cache()
    df = pd.DataFrame(np.empty([epochs, 4]),
                      index = np.arange(epochs),
                      columns=['loss_G', 'loss_D',
                               'real_scores', 'fake_scores'])
    for i in trange(epochs):
        loss_G = 0.0; loss_D = 0.0; real_sc = 0.0; fake_sc = 0.0
        for real_images, _ in train_dataloader:
            inputs = real_images.cuda()
            loss_d, real_score, fake_score = train_D(inputs, optimizer_D)
            loss_D += loss_d
            real_sc += real_score
            fake_sc += fake_score
            loss_g = train_G(optimizer_G)
            loss_G += loss_g
        df.iloc[i, 0] = loss_G/n_batch
        df.iloc[i, 1] = loss_D/n_batch
        df.iloc[i, 2] = real_sc/n_batch
        df.iloc[i, 3] = fake_sc/n_batch
        if i==0 or (i+1)%5==0:
            print(
            "loss_G={:.3f}, loss_D={:.3f}, real_score={:.3f}, fake_score={:.3f}"
            .format(df.iloc[i, 0], df.iloc[i, 1], df.iloc[i, 2], df.iloc[i, 3]))
            fake_images = G(fixed_latent)
            show_imgs(fake_images.detach().cpu())
```

```
        return df
history = fit(n_epochs)
# Cell 13: Show the training history-------------------------------------Cell 13
df = history
fig, ax = plt.subplots(1,2, figsize=(9,4), sharex=True)
df.plot(ax=ax[0], y=[0,1], style=['r-', 'b-+'])
gp = df.iloc[:,1] - df.iloc[:,3] + df.iloc[:,2]
ax[0].plot(gp, label='Gradient Penalty', color='k', linestyle=':')
ax[0].set(ylabel='loss')
ax[0].legend()

df.plot(ax=ax[1], y=[2,3], style=['r-+', 'b-'])
for i in range(2):
    ax[i].grid(which='major', axis='both', color='g', linestyle=':')
    ax[i].set(xlabel='epoch')
plt.show()
# Cell 14: Verify if the generator works for inputs----------------------Cell 14
def generate_image(G, digital):
    z = torch.randn(1, z_dim).cuda()
    N = len(train_Dataset.classes)-1
    if digital <= N:
        label = torch.LongTensor([digital]).cuda()
        img = G(z, label).data.cpu()
        show_imgs(img)
    else:
        print("Your label is bigger than ", N)
generate_image(G, 4)
#-------------------------The End-----------------------------------------------
```

4.3 WGAN-GP for CelebA dataset and Anime Face dataset

By changing the dataset path name in Cell 01 of project 4.3.1, you can use the following WGAN-GP codes for the CelebA dataset or the anime-faces dataset. The model training time for the two datasets are 274 and 85 min, respectively, with epochs = 25 and n_critic = 1. The model training time would be tripled if n_critic = 5. Figure 4.4 shows fake CelebA images randomly generated by the following WGAN-GP codes. Their quality is much better than those generated by DCGAN in section 3.2.3. Although the model training is much longer, WGAN-GP saves us a lot of time because we do not need to adjust many hyperparameters to avoid model collapse issues. After model training, you can use Cell 14 to generate a single fake image, and you will find its quality is still not good enough. It is possible to obtain high quality fake images by setting image size to be equal to 256 in Cell 01. In that case, model training time on a laptop with a single GPU would be very long.

Figure 4.4. Fake CelebA images generated by WGAN-GP at epoch = 25 with model training time of 274 min. They are outputs of Cell 12. CelebA dataset is used with permission from Liu *et al* (2015) courtesy of Ziwei Liu.

```python
# Project 4.3.1 WGAP-GP for Anime-faces Dataset or CelebA Dataset ----Python v3.6
import torch; import torch.nn as nn; from torch.utils.data import DataLoader
from torchvision.utils import make_grid; import torchvision.transforms as T
from torchvision.datasets import ImageFolder; import matplotlib.pyplot as plt
import pandas as pd; import numpy as np; from tqdm import trange
n_epochs = 25
image_size = 64
img_channels = 3
batch_size = 64
z_dim = 128
lr = 1e-4
n_critic = 1
lamda_gp = 10
fixed_latent = torch.randn(48, z_dim, device='cuda')  # A batch of random
numbers
# Cell 02: Anime-face Dataset-----------------------------------------------Cell 02
#data_path = './OCR/data/AnimeFaces'
data_path = 'OCR/data/CelebA/img_align_celeba'
train_dataset = ImageFolder(data_path,
            transform=T.Compose([T.Resize(image_size),
                        T.CenterCrop(image_size),
                        T.ToTensor(),
                        T.Normalize([0.5]*3, [0.5, 0.5, 0.5])]))
n_samples = len(train_dataset) #n_sample=63566
# Cell 03: Dataloader-------------------------------------------------------Cell 03
train_dataloader = DataLoader(train_dataset, batch_size=batch_size,
                    shuffle=True, num_workers=3, pin_memory=True)
n_batch = len(train_dataloader) #n_batch=994
for imgs, _ in train_dataloader:
    print("imgs_batch.shape=", imgs.shape)
    break
# Cell 04: Show images of in the 1st the batch of train_dataloader--------Cell 04
def denorm(img_tensors):
    return img_tensors*0.5 + 0.5
def show_imgs(images):
    fig, ax = plt.subplots(figsize=(16,12))
    input = make_grid(denorm(images[:48]), nrow=16)
    ax.imshow(input.permute(1,2,0))
    ax.set(xticks=[], yticks=[])
    plt.show()
show_imgs(imgs)
# Cell 05: Model parameters initialization ---------------------------------Cell 05
```

```
def weights_init(m):
    if(type(m) == nn.ConvTranspose2d or type(m) == nn.Conv2d):
        nn.init.normal_(m.weight.data, 0.0, 0.02)
    elif(type(m) == nn.BatchNorm2d):
        nn.init.normal_(m.weight.data, 0.0, 0.02)
        nn.init.constant_(m.bias.data, 0)
# Cell 06: Definition of an image discriminator class-------------------Cell 06
def basic_D(in_channles, out_channels, f=4, s=2, p=1):
    return nn.Sequential(
                nn.Conv2d(in_channles, out_channels,
                        kernel_size=f, stride=s, padding=p, bias=False),
                nn.InstanceNorm2d(out_channels, affine=True),
                nn.LeakyReLU(0.2, inplace=True)
    )
class Discriminator(nn.Module):
    def __init__(self):
        super().__init__()
        self.net = nn.Sequential(
            nn.Conv2d(img_channels, 64, 4, 2, 1),
            nn.LeakyReLU(0.2, inplace=True),
            # layer01 output.shape=batch_size x 64 x 32^2
            basic_D(64, 128, 4, 2, 1),
            # layer 02 output.shape=batch_size x 128 x 16^2
            basic_D(128, 256, 4, 2, 1),
            # layer 03 output.shape=batch_size x 256 x 8^2
            basic_D(256, 512, 4, 2, 1),
            # layer 04 output.shape=batch_size x 512 x 4^2
            nn.Conv2d(512, 1, 4, 1, 0),
            nn.Flatten()
        )   # layer 05 output.shape=batch_size x 1
    def forward(self, images):
        scalars = self.net(images) # images.shape=batch_size x 3 x 64^2
        return scalars              #scalars.shape=batch_size x 1
D = Discriminator().cuda()
D.apply(weights_init)
# Cell 07: Generator class------------------------------------------------Cell 07
def basic_G(in_channles, out_channels, f=4, s=2, p=1):
    return nn.Sequential(
                nn.ConvTranspose2d(in_channles, out_channels,
                    kernel_size=f, stride=s, padding=p, bias=False),
                nn.BatchNorm2d(out_channels),
                nn.ReLU(True)
            )
class Generator(nn.Module):
    def __init__(self):
        super().__init__()
        self.net = nn.Sequential(
            basic_G(z_dim, 512, 4, 1, 0),
            # layer01 output.shape = batch_size x 512 x 4^2
            basic_G(512, 256, 4, 2, 1),
            # layer02 output.shape = batch_size x 256 x 8^2
            basic_G(256, 128, 4, 2, 1),
```

```
            # layer03 output.shape = batch_size x 128 x 16^2
            basic_G(128, 64, 4, 2, 1),
            # layer04 output.shape = batch_size x 64 x 32^2
            nn.ConvTranspose2d(64, 3, 4, 2, 1),
            nn.Tanh()
        )   # layer05 output shape = batch_size x 3 x 64^2
    def forward(self, z):
        input = z.view(-1, z_dim, 1, 1)   # z.shape = batch_size x z_dim
        images = self.net(input)      # input.shape = batch_size x z_dim x 1^2
        return images                 #images.shape = batch_size x 3 x 64^2
G = Generator().cuda()
G.apply(weights_init)
# Cell 08: Choose optimizers-----------------------------------------Cell 08
optimizer_D = torch.optim.RMSprop(D.parameters(), lr=lr)
optimizer_G = torch.optim.RMSprop(G.parameters(), lr=lr)
#optimizer_G = torch.optim.Adam(G.parameters(), lr=lr, betas=(0.0, 0.9))
#optimizer_D = torch.optim.Adam(D.parameters(), lr=lr, betas=(0.0, 0.9))
# Cell 09: Gradient penalty function----------------------------------cell
09
def gradient_penalty(D, real_data, fake_data):
        batch_size = real_data.size(0)
        eps = torch.rand(batch_size, 1, 1, 1).cuda()# uniform distribution
        eps = eps.expand_as(real_data)  # eps.shape=batch_size x 3 x 64^2
        # Interpolation between real data and fake data.
        interpolation = eps * real_data + (1 - eps) * fake_data
        logits = D(interpolation)  #logits for interpolated images
        gradients =
torch.autograd.grad(outputs=logits,
                                    inputs=interpolation,
                                    grad_outputs=torch.ones_like(logits),
                                    create_graph=True,
                                    retain_graph=True
                        )[0]
        gradients = gradients.view(batch_size, -1)
        grad_norm = gradients.norm(2, 1)
        gradient_penalty = torch.mean((grad_norm - 1) ** 2)
        return gradient_penalty
# Cell 10: Definition of a train function for the discriminator--------Cell 10
def train_D(inputs, optimizer_D):
    for _ in range(n_critic):
        # The inputs are real images from a batch of DataLoader loaded in cuda
        batch_size = inputs.shape[0]
        real_preds = D(inputs)
        real_score= torch.mean(real_preds)
        # create fake images with random numbers
        latent = torch.randn(batch_size, z_dim).cuda()
        fake_images = G(latent)
        fake_preds = D(fake_images.detach())
        fake_score = torch.mean(fake_preds)
        # Update discriminator weights
        gp = gradient_penalty(D, inputs, fake_images)
        loss = fake_score - real_score + lamda_gp*gp
```

```
    optimizer_D.zero_grad()
        loss.backward()
        optimizer_D.step()
    return loss.item(), real_score.item(), fake_score.item()
# Cell 11: Train the generator to fool the discriminator---------------Cell 11
def train_G(optimizer_G):
    latent = torch.randn(batch_size, z_dim).cuda()
    fake_images = G(latent) # Create fake images from latent
    preds = D(fake_images)
    loss = -torch.mean(preds)
    optimizer_G.zero_grad()
    loss.backward()
    optimizer_G.step()
    return loss.item()
# Cell 12: Definition of a fitting function to train D&G-----------------Cell 12
def fit(epochs):
    torch.cuda.empty_cache()
    # The DataFrame df is a recorder of the training history
    df = pd.DataFrame(np.empty([epochs, 4]),
        index = np.arange(epochs),
        columns=['Loss_G', 'Loss_D', 'D(X)', 'D(G(Z))'])
    for i in trange(epochs):
        loss_G = 0.0; loss_D = 0.0; real_sc = 0.0; fake_sc = 0.0
        for real_images, labels in train_dataloader:
            inputs = real_images.cuda()
            labels = labels.cuda()
            loss_d, real_score, fake_score = train_D(inputs, optimizer_D)
            loss_D += loss_d; real_sc += real_score; fake_sc += fake_score
            loss_g = train_G(optimizer_G)
            loss_G += loss_g
        # Record losses & scores
        df.iloc[i, 0] = loss_G/n_batch
        df.iloc[i, 1] = loss_D/n_batch
        df.iloc[i, 2] = real_sc/n_batch
        df.iloc[i, 3] = fake_sc/n_batch
        if i==0 or (i+1)%5==0:
            print(
            "Epoch={:2}, Ls_G={:.2f}, Ls_D={:.2f}, D(X)={:.2f}, D(G(Z))={:.2f}"
            .format(i+1, df.iloc[i,0], df.iloc[i,1], df.iloc[i,2], df.iloc[i,3]))
            fake_images = G(fixed_latent)
            show_imgs(fake_images.detach().cpu())
    return df
history = fit(n_epochs) #n_epochs=25, Anime-faces dt=85min; CelebA dt=274min
# Cell 13: Show the training history------------------------------------Cell 13
df = history
fig, ax = plt.subplots(1,2, figsize=(9,4), sharex=True)
df.plot(ax=ax[0], y=[0,1], style=['r-', 'b-+'])
gp = df.iloc[:,1] - df.iloc[:,3] + df.iloc[:,2]
ax[0].plot(gp, label='Gradient Penalty', color='k', linestyle=':')
ax[0].set(ylabel='loss')
ax[0].legend()
df.plot(ax=ax[1], y=[2,3], style=['r-+', 'b-'])
```

```
for i in range(2):
    ax[i].grid(which='major', axis='both', color='g', linestyle=':')
    ax[i].set(xlabel='epoch')
plt.show()
# Cell 14: Verify if the generator works for inputs----------------------Cell 14
n_images = 1    # the number of fake images: 1 <= n_images <= 100
z = torch.randn(n_images, z_dim).cuda()
img = G(z).data.cpu()
show_imgs(img)
#-----------------------------The End -------------------------------------
```

4.4 Implementation of a cWGAN-GP for Rock Paper Scissors dataset

WGAN-GPs only randomly generate fake images. Using a conditional WGAN-GP (cWGAN-GP) system, we can generate fake images for a dataset with class labels set by us. To save model training time, the small Rock Paper Scissors dataset is chosen to demonstrate the application of cWGAN-GP for color images. The model training time of the following project 4.4.1 is about 64 min for 100 epochs. Figure 4.5 shows real images from the dataset, and fake images generated by the following cWGAN-GP codes. It is better to use *nn.InstanceNorm2d( )* to replace *nn. BatchNorm( )* in model D. Otherwise, the loss function values in figure 4.6 would be higher than 10 000, and the quality of the fake images would be poor. It seems that the Adam optimizer is better than the RMSprop optimizer for this project. When a gradient penalty is calculated in Cell 09, we must generate an interpolation image

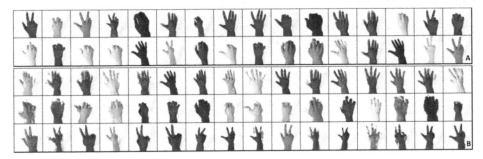

Figure 4.5. (A) Real images in the Rock Paper Scissors dataset. (B) Fake images generated by cWGAN-GP (images in row 1, 2, 3 are for paper: 0, rock: 1 and scissors: 2 respectively). The Rock Paper Scissors dataset is from Moroney (2021) with a license CC BY 3.0.

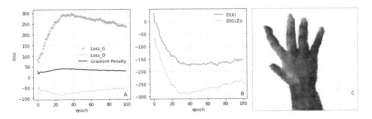

Figure 4.6. Model raining history of cWGAN-GP. (A) Loss curves and the gradient penalty curve, outputs of Cell 13. (B) $D(X)$, $D(G(X))$ curves. (C) A single fake image with label 0 generated by codes in Cell 14.

4-18

from a real image and a fake image. Should we use the real label of the real image, or the fake label of the fake image? It is found that using fake labels is the right choice. Using real labels to replace fake labels resulted in model collapse issues. Codes for applications of a cWGAN-GP system for MNIST or Fashion MNIST are listed in appendix E.

```python
# Project 4.4.1 cWGAN-GP for the Rock-Paper- Scissors Dataset --------Python v3.6
import torch; import torch.nn as nn; from torch.utils.data import DataLoader
import torchvision.transforms as T; from torchvision.utils import make_grid
from torchvision.datasets import ImageFolder; from tqdm import trange
import numpy as np; import pandas as pd; import  matplotlib.pyplot as plt
n_epochs = 100
batch_size=32
z_dim = 100
lr = 4e-4
n_critic = 1
lamda_gp = 10
img_size = 128
img_channels = 3
n_class = 3
fixed_latent = torch.randn(48, z_dim).cuda() # noises.shape = 48 x z_dim
# Generate a long tensor for fake labels with 3 classes
fixed_labels = torch.LongTensor([i for i in range(3) for j in range(16)]).cuda()
# Cell 02: Import Rock Paper Scissors dataset--------------------------Cell 02
train_dataset = ImageFolder('./OCR/data/RockPaperScissors/train',
        transform=T.Compose([T.Resize(img_size),
                             T.ToTensor(),
                             T.Normalize([0.5,0.5,0.5], [0.5,0.5,0.5])]))
n_samples = len(train_dataset) # n_samples=2520
# Cell 03: DataLoader ------------------------------------------------Cell 03
train_dataloader = DataLoader(train_dataset, batch_size=batch_size,
        shuffle=True,num_workers=4, pin_memory=True)
n_batch = len(train_dataloader) #n_batch=79
for imgs, labels in train_dataloader:
    print("imgs.shape=", imgs.shape)
    print('labels=', '\n', labels.view(-1,16))
    break
# Cell 04: Show a batch of images in the train_dataloader-------------Cell 04
def denorm(img_tensors): # Shift image pixel values to [0,1]
    return img_tensors * 0.5 + 0.5
def show_imgs(images):
    fig, ax = plt.subplots(figsize=(16,10))
    inputs = make_grid(denorm(images), nrow=16)
    #inputs = make_grid(images, nrow=16)
    ax.imshow(inputs.permute(1,2,0))
    ax.set(xticks=[], yticks=[])
    plt.show()
show_imgs(imgs)
# Cell 05: Model parameters initialization ---------------------------Cell 05
def weights_init(m):
    if(type(m) == nn.ConvTranspose2d or type(m) == nn.Conv2d):
        nn.init.normal_(m.weight.data, 0.0, 0.02)
    elif(type(m) == nn.BatchNorm2d):
        nn.init.normal_(m.weight.data, 1.0, 0.02)
        nn.init.constant_(m.bias.data, 0)
# Cell 06: Discriminator class----------------------------------------Cell 06
def basic_D(in_channels):
    return nn.Sequential(
```

```
            nn.Conv2d(in_channels, 2*in_channels, 4, 2, 1, bias=False),
            nn.InstanceNorm2d(2*in_channels),
            nn.LeakyReLU(0.2, inplace=True)
            )
class Discriminator(nn.Module):
    def __init__(self):
        super().__init__()
        self.net = nn.Sequential(
            nn.Conv2d(img_channels+1, 64, 4, 2, 1),
            nn.LeakyReLU(0.2, inplace=True),
            # layer 01 output.shape = batch_size x 64 x 64^2
            basic_D(64),
            # layer 02 output.shape = batch_size x 128 x 32^2
            basic_D(128),
            # layer 03 output.shape = batch_size x 256 x 16^2
            basic_D(256),
            # layer 04 output.shape = batch_size x 512 x 8^2
            basic_D(512),
            # layer 05 output.shape = batch_size x 1024 x 4^2
            nn.Conv2d(1024, 1, kernel_size=4, stride=1, padding=0),
            nn.Flatten()
        )   # layer 06 output.shape = batch_size x 1
        self.label_code = nn.Embedding(n_class, 1*img_size*img_size)
        # Encode a batch of labels
    def forward(self, images, labels):        # x.shape = batch_size x 49152
        x = images.view(-1, img_channels*img_size*img_size)
        c = self.label_code(labels)          # c.shape = batch_size x 16384
        x_c = torch.cat([x, c], dim=1)       #x_c.shape = batch_size x 65536
        input = x_c.view(-1, img_channels+1, img_size, img_size)
        out = self.net(input)                 #input.shape = batch_size x 4 x 128^2
        return out                            #output.shape = batch_size x 1
D = Discriminator().cuda()
D.apply(weights_init)
# Cell 07: Generator Class-------------------------------------------------Cell 07
def basic_G(in_channels):
    return nn.Sequential(
        nn.ConvTranspose2d(in_channels, int(in_channels/2), 4, 2, 1, bias=False),
            nn.BatchNorm2d(int(in_channels/2)),
            nn.ReLU(True)
        )
class Generator(nn.Module):
    def __init__(self):
        super().__init__()
        self.net = nn.Sequential(
            basic_G(512),
            # Layer 01 output.shape = batch_size x 256 x 8^2
            basic_G(256),
            # Layer 02 output.shape = batch_size x 128 x 16^2
            basic_G(128),
            # Layer 03 output.shape = batch_size x 64 x 32^2
            basic_G(64),
            # Layer 04 output.shape = batch_size x 32 x 64^2
```

```
                nn.ConvTranspose2d(32, 3, kernel_size=4, stride=2, padding=1),
                nn.Tanh()
        )    # Layer 05 output.shape = batch_size x 3x 128^2
        self.label_emb = nn.Embedding(n_class, 4*4)  #for fake labels
        self.latent = nn.Linear(z_dim, 511*4*4)      #for noise z
    def forward(self, z, labels):        #z.shape = batch_size x z_dim
        y = self.latent(z)               #y.shape = batch_size x 511*4*4
        c = self.label_emb(labels)       #c.shape = batch_size x 1*4*4
        y_c = torch.cat([y, c], dim=1)   #y_c.shape = batch_size x 512*4*4
        input = y_c.view(-1, 512, 4, 4)  #input.shape = batch_size x 512 x 4^2
        output = self.net(input)         #output.shape = batch_size x 3 x 128^2
        return output
G = Generator().cuda()
G.apply(weights_init)
# Cell 08: Learning rate, Optimizers, latent tensor and labels-----------Cell 08
optimizer_D = torch.optim.Adam(D.parameters(), lr=lr, betas=(0, 0.9))
optimizer_G = torch.optim.Adam(G.parameters(), lr=lr, betas=(0, 0.9))
#optimizer_D = torch.optim.RMSprop(D.parameters(), lr=lr)
#optimizer_G = torch.optim.RMSprop(G.parameters(), lr=lr)
# Cell 09 Gradient-Penalty function-------------------------------------Cell 09
def gradient_penalty(D, real_data, fake_data, fake_labels):
    batch_size = real_data.size(0) #real_data.shape = batch_size x 3 x128^2
    # Sample Epsilon from uniform distribution
    eps = torch.rand(batch_size, 1, 1, 1).cuda()
    eps = eps.expand_as(real_data)            #eps.shape=batch_size x 3 x 128^2
    # Interpolation between real data and fake data.
    interpolation = eps * real_data + (1 - eps) * fake_data
    # get logits for interpolated images
    logits = D(interpolation, fake_labels)  #shape = batch_size x 1
    gradients =
torch.autograd.grad(outputs=logits,
                                inputs=interpolation,
                                grad_outputs=torch.ones_like(logits),
                                create_graph=True,
                                retain_graph=True
                    )[0]    # Gradients
    gradients = gradients.view(batch_size, -1)
    grad_norm = gradients.norm(2, 1)
    gradient_penalty = torch.mean((grad_norm - 1) ** 2)
    return gradient_penalty        # Compute and return the gradient norm
# Cell 10: Definition of a train function for the discriminator--------Cell 10
def train_D(inputs, labels, optimizer_D):
    for _ in range(n_critic):
        real_preds = D(inputs, labels)
        real_score = torch.mean(real_preds)
        # create fake images and labels with random numbers
        latent = torch.randn(inputs.shape[0], z_dim).cuda()
        fake_labels = torch.LongTensor(
                torch.randint(0, n_class, (inputs.shape[0],))).cuda()
        fake_images = G(latent, fake_labels)
        fake_preds = D(fake_images.detach(), fake_labels.detach())
        fake_score = torch.mean(fake_preds)
```

```
            # Train the optimizer_D with real_loss and fake_loss
            gp = gradient_penalty(D, inputs, fake_images, fake_labels)
            loss = fake_score - real_score + lamda_gp*gp
            optimizer_D.zero_grad()
            loss.backward()
            optimizer_D.step()
        return loss.item(), real_score.item(), fake_score.item()
# Cell 11: Train the generator to fool the discriminator------------------Cell 11
def train_G(optimizer_G):
    # Create fake images and labels
    latent = torch.randn(batch_size, z_dim).cuda()
    fake_labels = torch.LongTensor(
        torch.randint(0, n_class, (batch_size,))).cuda()
    fake_images = G(latent, fake_labels)
    # Try to fool the discriminator
    preds = D(fake_images, fake_labels)
    loss = -torch.mean(preds)
    optimizer_G.zero_grad()
    loss.backward()
    optimizer_G.step()
    return loss.item()
# Cell 12: Definition of a fitting function to train D&G------------------Cell 12
def fit(epochs):
    torch.cuda.empty_cache()
    # The DataFrame df is a recorder of the training history
    df = pd.DataFrame(np.empty([epochs, 4]),
                    index = np.arange(epochs),
                    columns=['Loss_G', 'Loss_D', 'D(X)', 'D(G(Z))'])
    for i in trange(epochs):
        loss_G = 0.0; loss_D = 0.0; real_sc = 0.0; fake_sc = 0.0
        for real_images, labels in train_dataloader:
            inputs = real_images.cuda()
            labels = labels.cuda()
            loss_d, real_score, fake_score = train_D(inputs, labels, optimizer_D)
            loss_D += loss_d; real_sc += real_score; fake_sc += fake_score
            loss_g = train_G(optimizer_G)
            loss_G += loss_g
        # Record losses & scores
        df.iloc[i, 0] = loss_G/n_batch
        df.iloc[i, 1] = loss_D/n_batch
        df.iloc[i, 2] = real_sc/n_batch
        df.iloc[i, 3] = fake_sc/n_batch
        if i==0 or (i+1)%5==0:
            print(
            "Epoch={:2}, Ls_G={:.2f}, Ls_D={:.2f}, D(X)={:.2f}, D(G(Z))={:.2f}"
            .format(i+1, df.iloc[i,0], df.iloc[i,1], df.iloc[i,2], df.iloc[i,3]))
            fake_images = G(fixed_latent, fixed_labels)
            show_imgs(fake_images.detach().cpu())
    return df
history = fit(n_epochs)
# Cell 13: Show the training history------------------------------------Cell 13
df = history
```

```
fig, ax = plt.subplots(1,2, figsize=(9,4), sharex=True)
df.plot(ax=ax[0], y=[0,1], style=['r+', 'b:'])
gp = df.iloc[:,1] - df.iloc[:,3] + df.iloc[:,2]
ax[0].plot(gp, label='Gradient Penalty', color='k', linestyle='-')
ax[0].set(ylabel='loss')
ax[0].legend()
df.plot(ax=ax[1], y=[2,3], style=['r-', 'b:'])
for i in range(2):
    ax[i].grid(which='major', axis='both', color='g', linestyle=':')
    ax[i].set(xlabel='epoch')
plt.show()
# Cell 14: Verify if the generator works for inputs--------------------Cell 14
def generate_image(G, digital):
    z = torch.randn(1, 100).cuda()
    N = len(train_dataset.classes)-1
    if digital <= N:
        label = torch.LongTensor([digital]).cuda()
        img = G(z, label).data.cpu()
        show_imgs(img)
    else:
        print("Your label is bigger than ", N)
generate_image(G, 0)
#--------------------------------The End----------------------------------
```

References

Arjovsky M, Chintala S and Bottou L 2017 Wasserstein generative adversarial networks *Int. Conf. on Machine Learning* (PMLR) pp 214–23

Gulrajani I, Ahmed F, Arjovsky M, Dumoulin V and Courville A C 2017 Improved training of wasserstein gans *Adv. Neural Inform. Process. Syst.* **30** 5769–79

Liu Z, Luo P, Wang X and Tang X 2015 Proc. of Int. Conf. on Computer Vision (ICCV) https://liuziwei7.github.io/papers/faceattributes_poster.pdf

Moroney L 2021 Rock Paper Scissors Dataset https://universe.roboflow.com/landada/rock-paper-scissors-hchrz (accessed 29 November 2023)

Xiao H, Rasu K and Vollgraf R 2017 Fashion-MNIST: a novel image dataset for benchmarking machine learning algorithms https://github.com/zalandoresearch/fashion-mnist

Chapter 5

Image generation by VAEs

This chapter introduces variational autoencoders (VAEs) for unsupervised learning to generate fake quadratic curves and fake MNIST images. It is easy to train models in VAEs, but the quality of the images from VAEs is not as good as that from GANs. VAE-GANs are a hybrid of the two techniques, and they are implemented for MNIST, Fashion MNIST and Anime datasets.

In chapter 3, we used generative adversarial networks to generate fake images. Model training of DCGANs and cDCGANs is still a challenge because of model collapse and other issues. It takes a long time to adjust initial learning rates, learning rate schedulers and other hyperparameters to achieve successful model training. In chapter 4, WGAN-GPs were used to stablize model training. We can also use an unsupervised learning algorithm to generate images. Generative models (Kingma and Welling 2013) based on the algorithm are variational autoencoders (VAEs) which are easy to train. They can be used to generate new data samples (images) that are similar to images in a given dataset by learning a compact representation of the dataset's underlying structure. There are also two models in a VAE system. An encoder model or network maps the input data to a low-dimensional representation (compresses each image into a lower dimensional latent vector). The latent vector can have 1D, 2D, 3D and even more than a hundred dimensions. For example, a MNIST image could be compressed into a vector with only two elements in a 2D latent space. Then a decoder network in the system uses the latent vector to generate an image similar to the original MNIST image. The image compression ratio is 392 (= 784/2). However, VAE is not designed for image compression, because the VAE algorithm is not as good as the JPEG algorithm. VAEs were invented earlier than GANs. The theory is more difficult to understand, and the quality of fake images generated by a VAE are usually not as sharp as those by GAN. So, why should we waste our time learning VAEs?

What we are interested is not the fake images, but those lower dimensional latent vectors generated by a VAE system. Each element in a latent vector is an image characteristic learnt by the VAE system. By tuning values of these elements in the latent vector, we can edit images to generate new images. For example, it is possible for us to change human facial expressions in images from angry to smiling, and change moon phases in images from full moon to new moon. With new techniques based on the VAE algorithm, such as vector quantized variational autoencoders (VQ-VAE), we can achieve state-of-the-art results in unsupervised learning. We can combine VAE with GAN to take advantage of the two techniques for model training. VAEs have been used in many areas, including image generation, anomaly detection, and reinforcement learning.

5.1 VAE and beta-VAE

In applications of a VAE system for image generation, each image in a dataset is a point in a high dimensional observed space. For example, each MNIST image is a point in a 784-dimensional space. Usually, our computer memory is not big enough to handle all images in a dataset. We have to slice an image dataset into a dataloader with many batches. Their batch size is a constant n. Images in a batch are observed data: x_1, x_2, ..., x_n. Each image is generated by a latent vector with elements: z_1, z_2, ..., z_m, where $m \ll n$. Table 5.1 shows the unknown joint probabilities of the observed data points and the unknown latent vectors. The marginal possibilities of p (x_j) are also unknown ($j = 1, 2, ..., n$). We assume that the prior distribution $p(z_i)$ follows a standard normal distribution $N(0,I)$, where I is an identity matrix. According to equation (1.28), we have $p(x_j) = \sum_{i=1}^{m} p(x_j, z_i) = \sum_z p(x_j, z)$. From the negative likelihood of the dataset, we have a loss function:

$$L = -\ln(P(X)) = -\ln \prod_{j=1}^{n} p(x_j) = -\sum_{j=1}^{n} \ln\left(\sum_z p(x_j, z)\right) \tag{5.1}$$

Since the joint probabilities are unknown, we cannot do anything about the loss function directly with the above equation. Luckily, we can build an encoder network which uses each batch of images in a dataloader as the encoder's input to obtain a mean vector and a variance vector for each image in a batch of images. The mean

Table 5.1. Unknown joint probabilities of a VAE system.

$P(X,Z)$	x_1	x_2	...	x_n	$P(Z)$
z_1	$p(x_1,z_1)$	$p(x_2,z_1)$	...	$p(x_n,z_1)$	$p(z_1)$
z_2	$p(x_1,z_2)$	$p(x_2,z_2)$	...	$p(x_n,z_2)$	$p(z_2)$
...	...	...	...	...	...
z_m	$p(x_1,z_m)$	$p(x_2,z_m)$	...	$p(x_n,z_m)$	$p(z_m)$
$P(X)$	$p(x_1)$	$p(x_2)$	...	$p(x_n)$	1.00

vector and the variance vector are then used to construct a multivariate normal distribution $q(z|x)$ for each image. Each element of the latent vector of the image is then obtained by sampling from $q(z|x)$. With the VAE encoder's prior possibilities and Jensen's inequality about $g(x) = -\ln(x)$ in section 1.1.4, we can indirectly find the minimum of the loss function of the VAE system. Inside the following minus logarithm function is the average of (p/q) about z, and it should be less than or equal to the average of $-\ln(p/q)$

$$L = -\sum_{j=1}^{n} \ln \sum_{z} q(z \mid x_j) \frac{p(x_j, z)}{q(z \mid x_j)} \leqslant -\sum_{j=1}^{n} \sum_{z} q(z \mid x_j) \ln \frac{p(x_j, z)}{q(z \mid x_j)}$$

$$L \leqslant \sum_{j=1}^{n} \left[\sum_{z} q(z \mid x_j) \ln \frac{q(z \mid x_j)}{p(z)} - \sum_{z} q(z \mid x_j) \ln \left(p(x_j \mid z) \right) \right]$$

$$L \leqslant \sum_{j=1}^{n} \left(D_{\mathrm{KL}}(q(z \mid x_j) \| p(z)) - E_{z \sim q(z|x_j)} \ln \left(p(x_j \mid z) \right) \right) \tag{5.2}$$

We can also build a decoder network (P) for the VAE system. The decoder uses latent vectors from the encoder's model Q to generate a fake image ($\hat{x}$). We train the decoder for a distribution $p(x|z)$ as a normal distribution with an identity variance: $p(x_j \mid z) = \frac{1}{\sqrt{(2\pi)^m \mid I \mid}} e^{-\frac{1}{2}(x_j - \mu_\theta(z))^T I(x_j - \mu_\theta(z))}$, where θ is a group of parameters of the decoder, and $\hat{x}_j = \mu_\theta(z)$ is the output of the decoder. With the above information, the loss function of the VAE system can be written as the following equation (constants are ignored):

$$L \leqslant \sum_{j=1}^{n} \sum_{i=1}^{m} \left(\mu_{i,j}^2 + \sigma_{i,j}^2 - \ln\left(\sigma_{i,j}^2\right) - 1 \right) + \frac{1}{2} \sum_{j=1}^{n} \| x_j - \hat{x}_j \|^2 \tag{5.3}$$

If we can minimize the right hand side of equation (5.3), it is logical that we can minimize the left hand size of the equation, because the left hand side is equal to or less than the right hand side. The first part of the right hand side in equation (5.3) is called 'regularization loss', and the second part is called 'reconstruction loss'. In the above tables and equations, we treated the latent z as a discrete variable. In fact, the latent z could be a continuous variable in a VAE system. We can also get the same result about the VAE loss function from the following mathematical derivations with $\int_z q(z \mid x_j) dz = 1$ and $D_{\mathrm{KL}} \geqslant 0$

$$L = -\ln\left(P(X)\right) = -\ln\prod_{j=1}^{n} p(x_j) = -\sum_{j=1}^{n}\left[\ln\left(p(x_j)\right)\int_z q(z \mid x_j)dz\right]$$

$$L = -\sum_{j=1}^{n}\int_z q(z \mid x_j)\ln\left(p(x_j)\right)dz = -\sum_{j=1}^{n}\int_z q(z \mid x_j)\ln\left(\frac{p(z, x_j)}{p(z \mid x_j)}\right)dz$$

$$L = -\sum_{j=1}^{n}\int_z q(z \mid x_j)\ln\left(\frac{p(z, x_j)}{q(z \mid x_j)}\frac{q(z \mid x_j)}{p(z \mid x_j)}\right)dz$$

$$L = -\sum_{j=1}^{n}\int_z q(z \mid x_j)\ln\left(\frac{p(z, x_j)}{q(z \mid x_j)}\right)dz - \sum_{j=1}^{n}\int_z q(z \mid x_j)\ln\left(\frac{q(z \mid x_j)}{p(z \mid x_j)}\right)dz$$

$$L = -\sum_{j=1}^{n}\int_z q(z \mid x_j)\ln\left(\frac{p(z, x_j)}{q(z \mid x_j)}\right)dz - \sum_{j=1}^{n} D_{\mathrm{KL}}\big(q(z \mid x_j)\|p(z \mid x_j)\big)$$

$$L \leqslant -\sum_{j=1}^{n}\int_z q(z \mid x_j)\ln\left(\frac{p(x_j \mid z)p(z)}{q(z \mid x_j)}\right)dz$$

$$L \leqslant \sum_{j=1}^{n}\int_z q(z \mid x_j)\ln\left(\frac{q(z \mid x_j)}{p(z)}\right)dz - \sum_{j=1}^{n}\int_z q(z \mid x_j)\ln\left(p(x_j \mid z)\right)dz$$

$$L \leqslant \sum_{j=1}^{n}\Big(D_{\mathrm{KL}}(q(z \mid x_j)\|p(z)) - E_{z \sim q(z|x_j)}\ln\left(p(x_j \mid z)\right)\Big)$$

This is an issue about the two parts of the loss function (5.3). The values of the two parts are not the same scale. Higgins and his colleagues in 2017 proposed a solution in their paper (Higgins *et al* 2017) with a hyperparameter β to balance the contributions of the two parts of the loss function. They named the VAE with a modified loss function (equation (5.4)) 'beta-VAE'. If $\beta = 1.0$, we have a regular VAE system; if $\beta > 1.0$, the regularization loss (D_{KL}) would quickly decrease to zero, and we would have the 'model collapse' issue for fake image generations in the following projects; if $\beta = 0.0$, our VAE system becomes an autoencoder system. Using bigger β, we would have very blurred fake images, but we would have more power to tune new fake images in different phases.

$$L = \beta\sum_{j=1}^{n}\sum_{i=1}^{m}\left(\mu_{i,j}^2 + \sigma_{i,j}^2 - \ln\left(\sigma_{i,j}^2\right) - 1\right) + \frac{1}{2}\sum_{j=1}^{n}\|x_j - \hat{x}_j\|^2 \qquad (5.4)$$

5.2 Application of beta-VAE for fake quadratic curves

In the following project 5.2.1 for generation of fake quadratic curves, only two fully connected layers are used in both the encoder model (Q) and the decoder model (P) of a beta-VAE system. In Cell 01, the hyperparameter z_dim is set to be equal to 2 for convenience of data visualization. That means that each curve with 21 points is generated from a 2D latent vector. The decoder of the system will use two numbers sampled from a 2D Gaussian distribution to restore each curve with 21 points. The hyperparameter beta is set to be equal to 0.5 so we can balance the contributions of the two parts in the loss function. Noises are added to the quadratic curves (line 04 of Cell 02). In figure 5.1(A), the 64 real curves are not smooth because of the noises. We do not have a dataset for the project. The data for model training is generated whenever we need a batch of data in a dataloader, and the batch number per epoch is set to be 5.

The architecture of a VAE system is shown in figure 5.1(A). Each real curve in a batch with noise was processed by the encoder model Q to obtain two vectors for a multivariate Gaussian distribution: a mean vector (μ) and a standard deviation vector (σ). Then a latent vector z is generated by $z = \mu + \sigma\varepsilon$ for each real curve, where ε is a random number generated from a standard multivariate normal distribution $N(0,I)$. In the following project codes, you will see a trick which shows how to calculate the standard deviation vector (σ) in which each element must be a positive number. The decoder's model P uses a batch of the latent vectors Z to generate a batch of fake images ($\hat{X}$). Those fake curves shown in figure 5.1(A) are very noisy at the beginning of model training. Then at epoch 20 000, noises are filtered out and the fake curves shown in figure 5.1(C) are smooth.

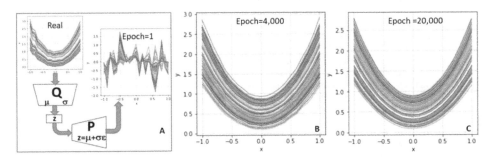

Figure 5.1. (A) VAE information flow chart (real curves are outputs of Cell 03). (B and C) fake quadratic curves generated by a beta-VAE with $\beta = 0.5$ (outputs of Cell 07). Model training time is 9 min

```python
# Project 5.2.1 Application of beta-VAE for fake quadratic curves ----Python v3.6
import torch; import torch.nn as nn; from tqdm import trange
import torch.optim.lr_scheduler as lr_scheduler
import numpy as np; import pandas as pd; import matplotlib.pyplot as plt
n_epochs = 20000
batch_size = 64
z_dim = 2          # latent space dimensions
n_hidden = 256     # number of neurons in the only hidden layer
n_points = 21      # number of points on each curve of training_data
lr = 1e-4          # learning rate 1e-4 ok epochs=12000-20000
beta = 0.5         # to balance Dkl and reconstruction loss      beta = 0.5 ok
n_batch = 5        # batch number per epoch
n_samples = n_batch*batch_size       #for loss calcualtions in Cell 07
# Cell 02: Creating a batch of training data ---------------------------Cell 02
x = np.linspace(-1, 1, n_points) # x =[-1.0, -0.9, ... ,1.0]
def training_data():    # data generator with y=a*x^2+(a-1)
    a = np.random.uniform(1, 2, size=batch_size).reshape(-1,1)
    noises = 0.015*np.random.randn(n_points)    # add noises to images--line 04
    y_values = a*(x+noises)**2 + (a-1)
    return y_values
y = training_data()      #y.shape=64 x 21
# Cell 03: Show a batch of curves---------------------------------------Cell 03
def show_curves(x, y):
    fig, ax = plt.subplots(figsize=(4,4))
    for i in range(batch_size):
        ax.plot(x, y[i,:])
    ax.set(xlabel='x', ylabel='y')#, ylim=[-0.1,3.5])
    ax.set(xticks=np.arange(-1.0, 1.1, 0.5))
    ax.grid(color='g', linestyle=':')
    plt.show()
show_curves(x,y)
# Cell 04: Encoder Class-----------------------------------------------Cell 04
class encoder(nn.Module):
    def __init__(self):
        super().__init__()
        self.net = nn.Sequential(
                nn.Linear(n_points, n_hidden),
                nn.LeakyReLU(0.2, inplace=True)) #outputs for 2 branchs
        self.mu = nn.Linear(n_hidden, z_dim)        #branch 1/2 for mu
        self.logvar = nn.Linear(n_hidden, z_dim)    #branch 2/2 for logvar
    def forward(self, curves):      # curves.shape = batch_size x n_points
        outputs = self.net(curves)  # outputs.shape = batch_size x n_hidden
        mu = self.mu(outputs)       # mu = mean of ~N(mean, std)
        logvar = self.logvar(outputs) # logvar = ln(std^2)
        std = torch.exp(0.5*logvar)   # std =(e^(ln(std^2)))**0.5 =(std^2)**0.5
        epsilon = torch.randn_like(std) # epsilon: ~N(0,I)
        z = mu + std*epsilon          #  noises constructed from ~N(mu, std)
        return z, mu, logvar          # z.shape = batch_size x 2
Q = encoder().cuda()
# Cell 05: Generator class---------------------------------------------Cell 05
class decoder(nn.Module):
    def __init__(self):
```

```
            super().__init__()
            self.net = nn.Sequential(
                        nn.Linear(z_dim, n_hidden),
                        nn.ReLU(True),
                        nn.Linear(n_hidden, n_points))
    def forward(self, z):
            fake_curves = self.net(z)     # z.shape = batch_size x z_dim
            return fake_curves            # fake_curves.shape = batch_size x n_points
P = decoder().cuda()
# Cell 06: Loss function and Optimizer-------------------------------Cell 06
def loss_function(fake, real, mu, logvar):
    MSE = 0.5*torch.nn.functional.mse_loss(fake, real, reduction='sum')
    Dkl = torch.sum(mu.pow(2) + logvar.exp() - logvar - 1)
    return MSE, Dkl    #MSE: reconstruction loss; Dkl: regularisation loss
optimizer = torch.optim.Adam([{'params': P.parameters()},
                {'params': Q.parameters()}], lr=lr)
scheduler = lr_scheduler.OneCycleLR(optimizer, max_lr=lr, #==============
                steps_per_epoch=n_batch, epochs=n_epochs, pct_start=0.6)
#-------------------------------------------------------------------------
```

The encoder class defined in Cell 04 uses a batch of real curves as its input which is processed by a fully connected layer. The encoder outputs a latent vector z, a mean (μ) tensor, and a log variance ($\ln(\sigma^2)$) tensor. The latent vector z is sampled from a normal distribution $N(\mu,\sigma^2)$ by $z = \mu + \sigma\varepsilon$, where ε is a random number generated by a standard normal distribution $\sim N(0,I)$. This is the trick to calculate standard deviations (std) which must be positive numbers. From the log variance, we can get the standard deviation by $\sigma = \sqrt{e^{\ln(\sigma^2)}}$. The decoder P defined in Cell 05 has two fully connected layers as usual. It uses a batch of latent vectors as its input. The output of the decoder is a batch of fake curves. According to equation (5.4), the loss function is defined in Cell 06. If the two parts in the loss function are calculated with 'mean' instead of 'sum', we have to adjust the β value to be around 0.01. The Adam optimizer is used for model training. The training function defined in Cell 07 uses a pandas dataframe to record loss values during model training. In each epoch, five batches of real curves are generated for model training. Each batch of the training data is processed by the encoder model Q. The output z of model Q is the input of model P to generate fake curves. Then loss values are calculated, and the parameters of the two models are updated by the Adam optimizer. Loss function curves are shown in figure 5.2(A).

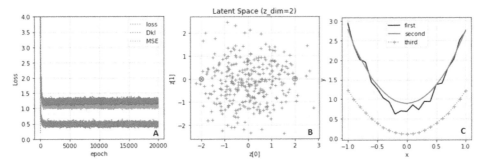

Figure 5.2. Model training history and applications of trained models to generate fake curves from latent vectors. (A) Total-loss, D_{kl} loss and reconstruction loss curves (outputs of Cell 08). (B) Distribution of latent vectors in a 2D latent space (outputs of Cell 09). (C) Fake curves generated from latent vectors ($z = [-2, 0]$, $z = [2, 0]$, $z = [-2, 15]$) by mode P (outputs of Cell 10).

```
# Cell 07: Training function---------------------------------------------Cell 07
def fit(epochs):
    torch.cuda.empty_cache()
    # The DataFrame df is a recorder of the training history
    df = pd.DataFrame(np.empty([epochs, 3]),
        index = np.arange(epochs), columns=['loss','Dkl', 'MSE'])
    for i in trange(epochs):        #trange from tqdm for a progress bar
        loss_total = 0.0; loss_prior=0; loss_rec=0
        for _ in range(n_batch):    #training with 5 batches of training data
            real_curves = torch.cuda.FloatTensor(training_data())
            z, mu, logvar = Q(real_curves)
            fake_curves = P(z)
            MSE, Dkl = loss_function(fake_curves, real_curves, mu, logvar)
            loss = MSE + beta*Dkl
            loss_total += loss.item()
            loss_prior += Dkl.item()
            loss_rec += MSE.item()
            optimizer.zero_grad()
            loss.backward()
            optimizer.step()
            scheduler.step()
        df.iloc[i, 0] = loss_total/n_samples
        df.iloc[i, 1] = loss_prior/n_samples
        df.iloc[i, 2] = loss_rec/n_samples
        if i==0 or (i+1)%4000==0:
            print(
            "Epoch={:2}, Loss={:.2f}, Dkl_Loss={:.2f}, Rec_Loss={:.2f}"
            .format(i+1, df.iloc[i,0], df.iloc[i,1], df.iloc[i,2]))
            y2cpu = fake_curves.detach().cpu()
            show_curves(x, y2cpu)
    return df
train_history = fit(n_epochs)
# Cell 08: Show the training history------------------------------------Cell 08
history = train_history
fig, ax = plt.subplots(figsize=(4,4))
history.plot(ax=ax, color=['r', 'b', 'g'], style=[':', ':', ':'])
ax.grid(which='major', axis='both', color='g', linestyle=':')
ax.set( xlabel='epoch', ylim=[0, 4], ylabel='Loss');
# Cell 09: 2D latent space graph----------------------------------------Cell 09
torch.cuda.empty_cache()
Q.eval()
m = 64
X= np.empty(m*n_batch)      #X for z[0]
Y= np.empty(m*n_batch)      #Y for z[1]
Z = np.empty((m*n_batch,2))    #Z for z
for i in range(n_batch):
    curves_real = torch.cuda.FloatTensor(training_data())
    z, mu, logvar = Q(curves_real)
    Z = z.detach().cpu().numpy()
    X[i*m: (i+1)*m]= Z[:,0]
    Y[i*m: (i+1)*m]= Z[:,1]
fig, ax = plt.subplots(figsize=(4,4))
```

```
ax.plot(X, Y, 'g+')
ax.grid(which='major', axis='both', color='g', linestyle=':')
ax.set(xlim=[-3,3], ylim=[-3,3], xlabel ='z[0]', ylabel='z[1]',
       title ='Latent Space (z_dim=2)')
plt.show()
# Cell 10: Using P(z|x) to generate fake curves-------------Cell 10
fig, ax = plt.subplots(figsize=(4,4))
noise1 = torch.FloatTensor([-2, 0]).cuda()
latent_curve1 = P(noise1).detach().cpu().numpy()
ax.plot(x, latent_curve1, 'k-', label='first')

noise2 = torch.FloatTensor([2, 0]).cuda()
latent_curve2 = P(noise2).detach().cpu().numpy()
ax.plot(x, latent_curve2, 'b-', label='second')

noise3 = torch.FloatTensor([0, -9]).cuda()
latent_curve3 = P(noise3).detach().cpu().numpy()
ax.plot(x, latent_curve3, 'r:+', label='third')
ax.legend()
ax.set(xlabel='x', ylabel='y', xticks=np.arange(-1.0, 1.1, 0.5))
ax.grid(color='g', linestyle=':');
#---------------------------------------------------------------------
```

Codes in Cell 09 calculate the trained Q's outputs with five batches of training data for mu, std and z. The latent vectors (z) are then plotted in figure 5.2(B), and their distribution pattern follows a 2D standard normal distribution function. If $\beta = 4.0$, each element of the mu array is very close to 0.0, and each element of the std array is very close to 1.0. If $\beta = 0.0$, the dots in figure 5.2(B) are in a straight line, and each element of the std vectors is very close to zero. The hyperparameter β can be used to compress the latent vectors into an area following a standard normal distribution. That is the job of the autoencoder network. In figure 5.2(B), coordinates of two latent vectors marked by $\otimes$ and $\oplus$ are $[-2,0]$ and $[2,0]$ respectively. From them, two smooth fake curves were generated by the decoder P, and are shown in figure 5.2(C). The value $z[0]$ of a latent vector can be used to tune vertical positions of fake curves. The value of $z[1]$ gives us power to adjust the smoothness of fake curves. The zig-zag fake curve in figure 5.2(C) was generated with a latent vector $z = [-2, 15]$. Every time you run the codes of the project, the controllers for fake curves would be different. Sometimes, value of $z[1]$ could control the positions of fake curves on the y-axis.

5.3 Application of beta-VAE for the MNIST dataset

The beta-VAE architecture for the MNIST project to generate fake images is almost the same as that one in the last section for fake quadratic curve generation. The main difference is the usage of deep convolution networks for the encoder Q and the decoder P. We know that neural networks with two fully connected layers are not powerful enough to handle MNIST images. The real and fake MNIST images (figure 5.3(B)) generated by codes in project 5.3.1 should be the same. We can see that fake MNIST images are blurry and some digits are wrong. These issues were caused by the setting of $z\_dim = 2$ in Cell 02 for data visualization. When an MNIST image was compressed by the encoder from 784 pixels into a latent vector with only two elements, a fraction of information was lost, so the decoder could not correctly restore the original image information. Figure 5.4 shows other training results: a 2D latent space with points of latent vectors, loss curves and fake images generated by p $(x|z)$ with $z[0]\in[-10,10]$ and $z[1]\in[-10,10]$. By tuning the β value from 0 to 10, you could see that the points in the latent space would be compressed from a big

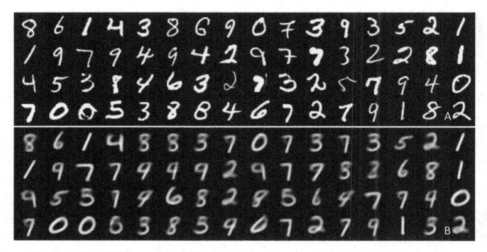

Figure 5.3. (A) Real MNIST images. (B) Fake MNIST images generated by β-VAE with z_dim = 2 and β = 0.01. These images are blurry and some digits are wrong. If z_dim = 20, fake images are as good as real images, and there are no digital mistakes. Model training time is 9 min. The MNIST image dataset is from Deng (2012) with a license CC BY 3.0.

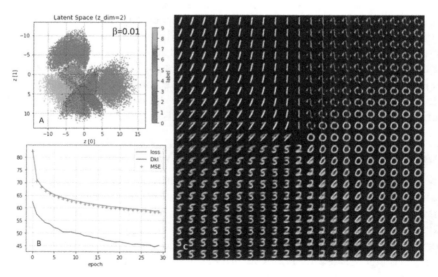

Figure 5.4. Model training results of a beta-VAE with β = 0.01. (A) 2D latent space: the output of Cell 12. (B) Loss curves: the output of Cell 09 (total-loss, regularization loss D_{kl} and reconstruction loss MSE). (C) Fake images generated by p(x|z): the output of cell 13 with $-10\leqslant z[0]\leqslant 10$ and $-10\leqslant z[1]\leqslant 10$.

irregular area into a round area with a radius of about three. Our models could really be trained to force $q(z|x)$ into $N(0, I)$ by a big value of β, but fake digital images generated by $p(x|z)$ would be too blurry to read. We need the power of Kullback–Leibler divergence in model training, but not too much. Changing z_dim from 2 to 20 in Cell 01, we would get crystal clear fake MNIST images, but the latent space in figure 5.4(A) cannot be shown. Using VAE, we are able to generate the desired fake images without label information from image datasets.

```python
# Project 5.3.1 Using beta-VAE to generate fake MNIST images----------Python v3.6
import torch; import torch.nn as nn; from torch.utils.data import DataLoader
import torchvision.transforms as T; from torchvision.datasets import MNIST
from torchvision.utils import make_grid; import matplotlib.pyplot as plt
import numpy as np; import pandas as pd; from tqdm import trange
n_epochs = 30
batch_size = 100
img_channels = 1
img_size = 28
img_dim = img_size*img_size
n_class = 10
z_dim = 2          #Dimensions of the latent space
lr = 5e-4          #Learning rate
beta = 0.01        #beta is used to tune the power of Dkl(q(z|x), N(0,I))
# Cell 02: MNIST DataSet -------------------------------------------------Cell 02
trainData = MNIST('./OCR/data/', train=True, download=False,
                transform=T.Compose([T.ToTensor(), T.Normalize([0.5],[0.5])]))
n_samples = len(trainData) #len(trainData)=60000
# Cell 03: Create a DataLoader (train_dataloader)------------------------Cell 03
train_dataloader = DataLoader(trainData, batch_size=batch_size, shuffle=True)
n_batch = len(train_dataloader) #n_batch=n_sample/batch_size=600
for imgs, labels in train_dataloader: # for the 1st batch on the train dataloader
    print('imgs_batch.shape=', imgs.shape)
    #print('labels=', labels[:40])
    break
# Cell 04: Show the images in the 1st batch of the train dataloader-------Cell 04
def denorm(img_tensors):        # Shift the value of each image pixel to [0,1]
    return img_tensors * 0.5 + 0.5
def show_imgs(imgs):
    fig, ax = plt.subplots(figsize=(12,8))
    input = make_grid(denorm(imgs[:64]), nrow=16, padding=2)
    ax.imshow(input.permute(1,2,0), cmap='gray')
    ax.set(xticks=[], yticks=[])
    plt.show()
show_imgs(imgs)
# Cell 05: Model parameters initialization ----------------------------Cell 05
def weights_init(m):
    if(type(m) == nn.ConvTranspose2d or type(m) == nn.Conv2d):
        nn.init.normal_(m.weight.data, 0.0, 0.02)
    elif(type(m) == nn.BatchNorm2d):
        nn.init.normal_(m.weight.data, 1.0, 0.02)
        nn.init.constant_(m.bias.data, 0)
# Cell 06: Encoder Class-----------------------------------------------Cell 06
def basic_E(in_channels, out_channels, f=4, p=1):
    return nn.Sequential(
            nn.Conv2d(in_channels, out_channels,
                    kernel_size=f, stride=2, padding=p, bias=False),
            nn.BatchNorm2d(out_channels),
            nn.LeakyReLU(0.2, inplace=True))
class Encoder(nn.Module):
```

```python
    def __init__(self):
        super().__init__()
        self.net = nn.Sequential(
            basic_E(1, 64, f=4, p=1),      #shape=batch_size x 64 x 14^2
            basic_E(64, 128, f=4, p=2),    #shape=batch_size x 128 x 8^2
            basic_E(128, 256, f=4, p=1),)  #shape=batch_size x 256 x 4^2
        self.mu = nn.Conv2d(256, z_dim,
                        kernel_size=4, stride=1, padding=0, bias=True)
        self.logvar = nn.Conv2d(256, z_dim,
                        kernel_size=4, stride=1, padding=0, bias=True)
    def forward(self, images):          # images.shape = batch_size x 1 x 28^2
        outputs = self.net(images)  # outputs.shape = batch_size x 4
        mu = self.mu(outputs).squeeze()       # mu.shape = batch_size x z_dim
        logvar = self.logvar(outputs).squeeze() # logvar = ln(std^2)
        std = torch.exp(0.5*logvar) # std=(e^(ln(std^2)))**0.5=(std^2)**0.5
        epsilon = torch.randn_like(std) # epsilon: ~N(0,I)
        z = mu + std*epsilon             # noises constructed from ~N(mu, std)
        return z, mu, logvar             # z.shape = batch_size x z_dim
Q = Encoder().cuda()
Q.apply(weights_init)
# Cell 07: Decoder Class----------------------------------------------Cell 07
def basic_D(in_channels, out_channels, f=4, p=1):
    return nn.Sequential(
            nn.ConvTranspose2d(in_channels, out_channels,
                    kernel_size=f, stride=2, padding=p, bias=False),
            nn.BatchNorm2d(out_channels),
            nn.ReLU(inplace=True))
class Decoder(nn.Module):
    def __init__(self):
        super().__init__()
        self.net = nn.Sequential(
            basic_D(z_dim, 256, f=4, p=0),      #shape = batch_size x 256 x 4^2
            basic_D(256, 128, f=3, p=1),        #shape = batch_size x 128 x 7^2
            basic_D(128, 64, f=4, p=1),         #shape = batch_size x 64 x 14^2
            nn.ConvTranspose2d(64, img_channels,
                kernel_size=4, stride=2, padding=1),
            nn.Tanh())                          # output.shape = batch_size x 1 x 28^2
    def forward(self, z):               #z.shape = batch_size x z_dim
        output = self.net(z.view(-1, z_dim, 1, 1))
        return output                   # output.shape = batch_size x 1 x 28^2
P = Decoder().cuda()
P.apply(weights_init)
# Cell 08: Loss functions and Adam optimizer----------------------------Cell 08
def loss_function(fake, real, mu, logvar):
    MSE = 0.5*torch.nn.functional.mse_loss(fake, real, reduction='sum')
    Dkl = torch.sum(mu.pow(2) + logvar.exp() - logvar - 1)
    return MSE, Dkl    #MSE: reconstruction loss; Dkl: regularisation loss
optimizer = torch.optim.Adam([{'params': P.parameters()},
                {'params': Q.parameters()}], lr=lr, betas=(0.5, 0.999))
# Cell 09: Definition of a fitting function
def fit(epochs):
    torch.cuda.empty_cache()
```

```python
    # The DataFrame df is a recorder of the training history
    df = pd.DataFrame(np.empty([epochs, 3]),
                        index = np.arange(epochs),
                        columns=['loss','Dkl', 'MSE'])
    for i in trange(epochs):
        loss_total = 0.0; loss_prior=0; loss_rec=0
        for real_images, _ in train_dataloader:
            inputs = real_images.cuda()
            z, mu, logvar = Q(inputs)
            real = inputs.reshape(-1, img_dim) #flatten real images
            fake = P(z).reshape(-1, img_dim)    #flatten fake images
            MSE, Dkl = loss_function(fake, real, mu, logvar)
            loss = MSE + beta*Dkl
            loss_total += loss.item()
            loss_prior += Dkl.item()
            loss_rec += MSE.item()
            optimizer.zero_grad()
            loss.backward()
            optimizer.step()
        df.iloc[i, 0] = loss_total/n_samples
        df.iloc[i, 1] = loss_prior/n_samples
        df.iloc[i, 2] = loss_rec/n_samples
        if i==0 or (i+1)%10==0:
            print(
                "Epoch={:4}, Loss={:.2f}, Dkl_Loss={:.2f}, Rec_Loss={:.2f}"
                    .format(i+1, df.iloc[i,0], df.iloc[i,1], df.iloc[i,2]))
            show_imgs(real_images)
            show_imgs(P(z).detach().cpu())
    return df
train_history = fit(n_epochs)
# Cell 10: Show the training history------------------------------------Cell 10
df = train_history
fig, ax = plt.subplots(figsize=(5,4))
df.plot(ax=ax, style=['-','-', '+'], color=['r','b','g'])
ax.grid(which='major', axis='both', color='g', linestyle=':')
ax.set(xlabel='epoch');
# Cell 11: 2D latent space data-----------------------------------------Cell 11
torch.cuda.empty_cache()
Q.eval()
x= np.empty(n_samples);  y= np.empty(n_samples); c= np.empty(n_samples)
for i, (img, label) in enumerate(train_dataloader):
    m = len(label)
    real_img = img.cuda()
    latent, _, _ = Q(real_img)
    logits = latent.squeeze().detach().cpu()
    x[i*m: (i+1)*m]= logits[:,0].numpy()
    y[i*m: (i+1)*m]= logits[:,1].numpy()
    c[i*m: (i+1)*m]= label
# Cell 12: 2D latent space----------------------------------------------cell 12
fig, ax = plt.subplots(figsize=(5,4))
plt.scatter(x=x, y=y, c=c, s=0.5, cmap="brg")
ax.grid(which='major', axis='both', color='k', linestyle=':')
```

```
ax.invert_yaxis()       #-----------------------------attention for invert yaxis
ax.set(xlabel ='z [0]', ylabel ='z [1]',
       title ='Latent Space (z_dim=2)')
cbar = plt.colorbar(label="label", orientation="vertical",shrink=0.9)
cbar.set_ticks(np.arange(10))
cbar.set_ticklabels(np.arange(10));
# Cell 13: Create fake images from P(x|z) with data from Cell 12-----------Cell
13
fig, ax = plt.subplots(figsize=(10,8))
big_image = np.empty((21*28,21*28))
b=10            #z, latent space  -b< z[0]<=b, -b< z[1]<=b, step dz[0]=2*b/20
for i in np.arange(0, 21, 1):
    x_p = -b+i*0.1*b
    for j in np.arange(0, 21, 1):
        y_p = -b+j*b*0.1
        noise = torch.tensor([[y_p, x_p]], dtype=torch.float).cuda()
        latent_img = P(noise).detach().cpu()
        big_image[28*i:28*(i+1), 28*j:28*(j+1)] = latent_img
plt.imshow(big_image, cmap='gray')
ax.set(xticks=[], yticks=[]);
#-------------------------------The End-----------------------------------
```

5.4 Using VAE-GAN for MNIST, Fashion MNIST & Anime-Face Dataset

Compares with GANs, VAE systems are easy to train. They can automatically find characteristics of images in datasets without labels. Those characteristics of images in a latent space with low dimensions can be tuned to generate new images. However, the quality of fake images generated by a VAE system is usually not as good as the quality of those generated by a GAN. The issue is caused by the VAE's reconstruction loss function based on element-wise errors, the second part of equation (5.3). For example, if pixels of an MNIST image are horizontally shifted one pixel to the left, the VAE's reconstruction loss values would be huge, but to our eyes there is no difference between the original image and shifted image. In 2016, Larsen and his colleagues published a paper (Larsen *et al* 2016) titled 'Autoencoding beyond pixels using a learned similarity metric'. With a hybridization of VAE and GAN, they 'replace element-wise errors with feature-wise errors to better capture data distributions while offering invariance towards, e.g. translation.' A VAE-GAN system is a generative model that combines the two popular generative systems: a VAE system and a GAN system. The VAE component of the system is used to learn a compact, continuous representation of a dataset, while the GAN component is used to generate new, synthetic data instances. Using the strengths of the two systems, VAE-GANs are able to generate high-quality fake images while also learning a compact, continuous representation of datasets. This makes VAE-GANs are useful in many areas, such as image synthesis, unsupervised representation learning, and data generation for deep reinforcement learning.

In the VAE-GAN system shown in figure 5.5, there are three models: an encoder model Q, a decoder model P and a discriminator model D. The first two models belong to a VAE system. The decoder also works as a generator for the GAN system which has the discriminator model D. Each real image (x) in a batch of a dataloader

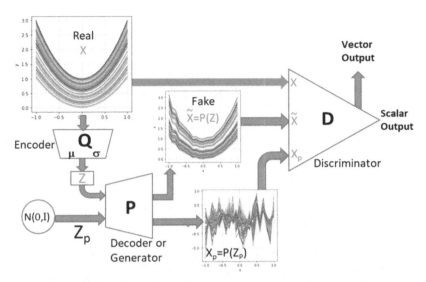

Figure 5.5. A VAE-GAN's architecture and its information flow chart with three models: an encoder Q, a decoder P and a discriminator D. Each quadric curve represents a real sample (x) in a batch (X) of a dataloader.

X is processed by the encoder Q to create a multivariate normal distribution $q(z|x)$ in a latent space with dimensions of z_dim. Then by sampling from those multivariate normal distributions, a batch of latent vectors (Z) is generated as an input of the decoder P, which restores the batch of latent vectors Z to a batch of fake images $(\widetilde{X})$ in the real image space, and the discriminator model D compresses each of the fake images into a scalar in range [0,1] as usual. The batch of real images can also be directly processed by model D as shown by the longest arrow in figure 5.5. A batch of noise (Z_p) sampled from a multivariate standard normal distribution $N(0,I)$ is processed by P and D. The model D's three scalar batches are used to calculate loss values (L_{GAN}) with a BCE loss function

$$L_{GAN} = \ln\left(D(X)\right) + \ln\left(1 - D(\widetilde{X})\right) + \ln\left(1 - D\left(X_p\right)\right) \qquad (5.5)$$

The VAE-GAN's model D does one more job than an ordinary GAN's model D. From a neural layer just before the last layer of the model D, the VAE-GAN's model D outputs two batches of vectors. The dimensions of each vector in a batch could be in thousands. A batch of vectors (V_X) from real images and a batch of vectors $(V_{\widetilde{X}})$ from fake images are used to replace real images and fake images in the reconstruction loss function of a VAE system. This modified reconstruction loss function has the name $L_{llike}^{Dis_l}$ according to the VAE-GAN paper, and it is a part of the decoder's loss function and also a part of the encoder's loss function. The L_{prior} in equation (5.7) is the Kullback–Leibler divergence between the $q(Z|X)$ and the multivariate standard normal distribution $N(0,I)$

$$L_P = L_{llike}^{Dis_l} - L_{GAN} = \text{MSELoss}(V_X, V_{\widetilde{X}}) - L_{GAN} \qquad (5.6)$$

$$L_Q = L_{\text{llike}}^{\text{Dis}_l} + L_{\text{prior}} = \text{MSELoss}(V_X, V_{\tilde{X}}) + D_{\text{KL}}(q(Z \mid X)\|p(Z)) \qquad (5.7)$$

Mode D, P and Q are trained with their own loss functions. The values of the three models' loss functions are not to the same scale, especially if those values are calculated with summation in each batch. Many people calculate the values of the three loss functions by summation with average loss in each batch, and use $L_P = \gamma L_{\text{llike}}^{\text{Dis}_l} - L_{\text{GAN}}$ and/or $L_Q = 5L_{\text{llike}}^{\text{Dis}_l} + L_{\text{prior}}$ to balance those loss values, where $\gamma = 15$ or 25. In the following VAE-GAN project, loss function values are calculated with summation of each batch. Because values of L_{GAN} and L_{prior} are very small compared with $L_{\text{llike}}^{\text{Dis}_l}$, the hyperparameter γ in front of $L_{\text{llike}}^{\text{Dis}_l}$ is set to be 1.0. The latent dimension is set to be two by z_dim = 2, so that we can show the latent space in figure 5.7(A). During model training in every five epochs, Cell 11 will output a batch of real images and a batch of fake images as shown in figure 5.6.

Figure 5.6. (A and B) Real MNIST images (outputs of Cell 11). (C and D) Fake MNIST images generated by VAE-GAN with z_dim = 2 and 20 respectively. (C) is noisy with wrong digits comparing with (A), and the fake images in (D) are as good as the real images in (B) without digital mistakes. Model training time is 36 min. The real images were reproduced from MNIST dataset of Deng (2012) with a license CC BY 3.0.

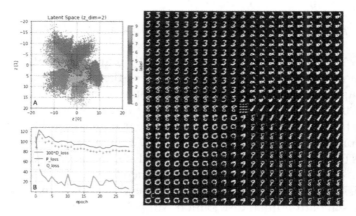

Figure 5.7. VAE_GAN model training results. (A) 2D latent space: the output of Cell 14. (B) Curves of loss functions: the output of Cell 12. (C) Fake images generated by $p(x|z)$: the output of Cell 15 with $-10 \leqslant z[0] \leqslant 10$ and $-10 \leqslant z[1] \leqslant 10$.

```
# Project 5.4.1 Cell 01: Using VAE-GAN for MNIST--------------------Python v3.6
import torch; import torch.nn as nn; from torch.utils.data import DataLoader
from torchvision import transforms as T; from torchvision.utils import make_grid
from torchvision.datasets import MNIST   # FashionMNIST, MNIST
import numpy as np; import pandas as pd; from tqdm import trange
import matplotlib.pyplot as plt
n_epochs = 30
batch_size = 100
img_size = 28
img_dim = img_size * img_size
img_channels = 1
n_class = 10
z_dim = 2
lr = 3e-4
alpha = 10    # for the discriminator model D's learning in Cell 09: lr_D=10*lr
# Cell 02: MNIST DataSet ------------------------------------------------Cell 02
trainData = MNIST('./OCR/data/', train=True, download=False,
              transform=T.Compose([T.ToTensor(), T.Normalize([0.5],[0.5])]))
n_samples = len(trainData) #len(trainData)=60000
# Cell 03: Create a DataLoader (trainLoader)-----------------------------Cell 03
train_dataloader = DataLoader(trainData, batch_size=batch_size, shuffle=True)
n_batch = len(train_dataloader) #n_batch=n_sample/batch_size=600
for imgs, labels in train_dataloader: # for the 1st batch on the train dataloader
    print('imgs_batch.shape=', imgs.shape)
    #print('labels=', labels[:40])
    break
# Cell 04: Show the images in the 1st batch of the train dataloader-------Cell 04
def denorm(img_tensors):        # Shift the value of each image pixel to [0,1]
    return img_tensors * 0.5 + 0.5
def show_imgs(imgs):
    fig, ax = plt.subplots(figsize=(12,8))
    input = make_grid(denorm(imgs[:64]), nrow=16, padding=2)
    ax.imshow(input.permute(1,2,0), cmap='gray')
    ax.set(xticks=[], yticks=[])
    plt.show()
show_imgs(imgs)
# Cell 05: Model parameters initialization ----------------------------Cell 05
def weights_init(m):
    if(type(m) == nn.ConvTranspose2d or type(m) == nn.Conv2d):
        nn.init.normal_(m.weight.data, 0.0, 0.02)
    elif(type(m) == nn.BatchNorm2d):
        nn.init.normal_(m.weight.data, 1.0, 0.02)
        nn.init.constant_(m.bias.data, 0)
# Cell 06: Encoder Class----------------------------------------Model Q------Cell 06
def conBL(in_channels, out_channels, f=4, s=2, p=1):
    return nn.Sequential(      # convolution-BatchNormalization-LeakReLU block
            nn.Conv2d(in_channels, out_channels,
                   kernel_size=f, stride=s, padding=p, bias=False),
            nn.BatchNorm2d(out_channels),
            nn.LeakyReLU(0.2, inplace=True))
class Encoder(nn.Module):
    def __init__(self):
```

```python
            super().__init__()
            self.net = nn.Sequential(
                conBL(img_channels, 64, f=4, s=2, p=1),#shape=batch_size x 64 x 14^2
                conBL(64, 128, f=4, s=2, p=2),         #shape=batch_size x 128 x 8^2
                conBL(128, 256,f=4, s=2,  p=1))        #shape=batch_size x 256 x 4^2
            self.mu = nn.Conv2d(256, z_dim, 4, 1, 0, bias=False)
            self.logvar = nn.Conv2d(256, z_dim, 4, 1, 0, bias=False)
        def forward(self, images):              #images.shape=batch_size x 1 x 28^2
            output = self.net(images)           #output.shape=batch_size x 256 x 4^2
            mu = self.mu(output).squeeze()          #mu.shape=batch_size x z_dim
            logvar = self.logvar(output).squeeze() #logvar.shape=batch_size x z_dim
            std = torch.exp(0.5*logvar)             #std.shape=batch_size x z_dim
            z = (mu + std*torch.randn_like(std))    #rand_like(std): ~N(0, I)
            return z, mu, logvar
Q = Encoder().cuda()
Q.apply(weights_init)
# Cell 07: Definition of an image discriminator class-------Model D-------Cell 07
class Discriminator(nn.Module):
    def __init__(self):
        super().__init__()
        self.net = nn.Sequential(
            nn.Conv2d(img_channels, 32, 4, 2, 1),
            nn.LeakyReLU(0.2, inplace=True),        #shape=batch_size x 32 x 14^2
            conBL(32, 64, 4, 2, 2),                 #shape=batch_size x 64 x 8^2
            conBL(64, 128, 4, 2, 1),                #shape=batch_size x 128 x 4^2
            conBL(128, 256, 2, 2, 0)) #layer 04, shape=batch_size x 256 x 2^2
        self.scalar = nn.Sequential(
            nn.Conv2d(256, img_channels, kernel_size=2, stride=1, padding=0),
            nn.Flatten(),
            nn.Sigmoid())                           #shape=batch_size x 1
    def forward(self, images):          #images.shape = batch_size x 1 x 28^2
        output = self.net(images)       #output.shape = batch_size x 256 x 2^2
        scalars = self.scalar(output)   #scalars.shape = batch_size x 1
        return scalars, output.view(-1, 256*2*2)
D = Discriminator().cuda()
D.apply(weights_init)
# Cell 08: Decoder Class-----------------------------------Model P------Cell 08
def basic_P(in_channels, out_channels, f=4, s=2, p=1):
    return nn.Sequential(
        nn.ConvTranspose2d(in_channels, out_channels,
            kernel_size=f, stride=s, padding=p, bias=False),
        nn.BatchNorm2d(out_channels),
        nn.ReLU(True))
class Decoder(nn.Module):
    def __init__(self):
        super().__init__()
        self.net = nn.Sequential(
            basic_P(z_dim, 256, 4, 1, 0),          #shape = batch_size x 256 x 4^2
            basic_P(256, 128, 3, 2, 1),            #shape = batch_size x 128 x 7^2
            basic_P(128, 64, 4, 2, 1),             #shape = batch_size x 64 x 14^2
            nn.ConvTranspose2d(64, img_channels, 4, 2, 1, bias=False),
            nn.Tanh())              # layer 04 output.shape = batch_size x 1 x 28^2
```

```
    def forward(self, z):
        input = z.view(-1, z_dim, 1, 1)      #z.shape=batch_size x z_dim
        output = self.net(input)             #input.shape=batch_size x z_dim x 1^2
        return output                        #output.shape=batch_size x 1 x 28^2
P = Decoder().cuda()
P.apply(weights_init)
# Cell 09: Criterion and optimizers------------------------------------Cell 09
criterion=nn.BCELoss(reduction='sum') # 'sum' is better than 'mean', for Model D
loss = nn.MSELoss(reduction='sum')    # for Model Q and P
optimizer_Q=torch.optim.RMSprop(Q.parameters(), lr=lr)
optimizer_P=torch.optim.RMSprop(P.parameters(), lr=lr)
optimizer_D=torch.optim.RMSprop(D.parameters(), lr=alpha*lr) --------line 05
#------------------------------------------------------------------------------
```

The discriminator D in Cell 07 is a little different from a GAN's model D in section 3.2.2. It has two outputs. One output is a batch of scalars in the range [0,1] as usual; another output is a batch of vectors from layer 04, and each vector has 1024 elements. The second output is used to replace images (real or fake) for reconstruction loss calculations. The higher the vector's element number is, the longer the time needed for model training, and the better the quality of fake images will be. Since we are using GAN again, we meet the same issue about choosing learning rates to balance the smartness between an image generator and an image discriminator. In Cell 01, an initial learning rate (lr) was set to be 10^{-3} for all three models. Model Q and P use the same learning rate. In model training for GANs, we usually use a smaller learning rate for model D. But in VAE-GAN we have to use a bigger learning rate ($10 \times$ lr) for model D to make the fake images sharper (line 05 of Cell 09).

```
# Cell 10: Loss functions----------------------------------------------Cell 10
def loss_gan(inputs, z):      #GAN loss, inputs are real images, z comes from Q
    batch_size = inputs.shape[0]
    preds_real = D(inputs)[0]       # scalars of real images from model D
    one_targets = torch.ones(batch_size, 1, device='cuda')
    loss_real = criterion(preds_real, one_targets) #BCELoss for real images
    pred_fake = D(P(z))[0]          # scalars from fake images from model D
    zero_targets = torch.zeros(batch_size, 1, device='cuda')
    loss_fake = criterion(pred_fake, zero_targets) #BCELoss for fake images
    z_p = torch.randn(batch_size, z_dim, device='cuda') #samples from N(0,I)
    x_p = P(z_p)
    pred_x_p =D(x_p)[0]
    loss_noises = criterion(pred_x_p, zero_targets)  #BCELoss for noise z_p
    loss_gan = loss_real + loss_fake + loss_noises
    return loss_gan
def loss_rec(inputs, z):          #Reconstruction loss
    pixel_real = D(inputs)[1]
    pixel_fake = D(P(z))[1]
    #rec_loss =((pixel_real - pixel_fake)**2).sum()
    rec_loss = 0.5*loss(pixel_real, pixel_fake)
    return rec_loss
# Cell 11: Definition of a fitting function----------------------------Cell 11
def fit(epochs):
    torch.cuda.empty_cache()
    df = pd.DataFrame(np.empty([epochs, 3]),
                index = np.arange(epochs),
                columns=['D_loss', 'P_loss', 'Q_loss'])
    for i in trange(epochs):
        loss_q = 0.0; loss_d = 0.0; loss_p = 0.0
```

```
        for real_images, _ in train_dataloader:
            inputs = real_images.cuda()
            z, mu, logvar = Q(inputs)
            D_loss = loss_gan(inputs, z)       #---- Discriminator Loss
            loss_d += D_loss.item()
            optimizer_D.zero_grad()
            D_loss.backward(retain_graph=True)
            optimizer_D.step() #--------------------Training for model D

            D_loss = loss_gan(inputs, z)
            rec_loss =loss_rec(inputs, z)
            P_loss = rec_loss - D_loss          # ---------Decoder Loss
            loss_p += P_loss.item()
            optimizer_P.zero_grad()
            P_loss.backward(retain_graph=True)
            optimizer_P.step() #--------------------Training for model P

            Dkl = mu.pow(2) + logvar.exp()- logvar - 1
            prior_loss = torch.mean(Dkl)
            rec_loss =loss_rec(inputs, z)
            Q_loss =  rec_loss + prior_loss # --Encoder Loss
            loss_q += Q_loss.item()
            optimizer_Q.zero_grad()


            Q_loss.backward(retain_graph=True)
            optimizer_Q.step() #--------------------Training for model Q

        df.iloc[i, 0] = loss_d/n_samples
        df.iloc[i, 1] = loss_p/n_samples
        df.iloc[i, 2] = loss_q/n_samples
        if i==0 or (i+1)%5==0:
            print('Dkl=', prior_loss.item())
            print(
                "Epoch={}, D_loss: {:.4f}, loss_P: {:.4f}, loss_Q: {:.4f}"
                .format(i+1, df.iloc[i,0], df.iloc[i,1], df.iloc[i,2]))
            show_imgs(real_images)
            fake_images = P(z)
            show_imgs(fake_images.detach().cpu())
    return df
train_history = fit(n_epochs)
# Cell 12: Show the training history------------------------------------Cell 12
df = train_history.copy()
df.iloc[:,0] =100*df.iloc[:,0]
fig, ax = plt.subplots(figsize=(4.5,3))
#history.plot(ax=ax, style=['-','-', '+'], color=['r','b','g'])
df.columns=['100*D_loss', 'P_loss', 'Q_loss']
df.plot(ax=ax, style=['-','-', '+'], color=['r','b','g'])
ax.grid(which='major', axis='both', color='g', linestyle=':')
ax.set(xlabel='epoch')#, ylim=[0, 800])
plt.show()
# Cell 13: Data for 2D latent space------------------------------------Cell 13
torch.cuda.empty_cache()
D.eval()
x= np.empty(n_samples);  y= np.empty(n_samples); z= np.empty(n_samples)
```

```
for i, (img, label) in enumerate(train_dataloader):
    m = len(label)
    real_img = img.cuda()
    latent, _, _ = Q(real_img)
    logits = latent.squeeze().detach().cpu()
    x[i*m: (i+1)*m]= logits[:,0].numpy()    # z[0]=x
    y[i*m: (i+1)*m]= logits[:,1].numpy()    # z[1]=y
    z[i*m: (i+1)*m]= label
# Cell 14: 2D latent space graph--------------------------------------Cell 14
fig, ax = plt.subplots(figsize=(5,4))
plt.scatter(x=x,y=y,c=z,s=0.5,cmap="brg")
ax.grid(which='major', axis='both', color='k', linestyle=':')
ax.set(xlabel ='z [0]', ylabel ='z [1]', ylim=[-20, 20], xlim=[-20, 20],
        title ='Latent Space (z_dim=2)')
ax.invert_yaxis()
cbar = plt.colorbar(label="label", orientation="vertical",shrink=0.9)
cbar.set_ticks(np.arange(10))
cbar.set_ticklabels(np.arange(10))
plt.show()
#-------------------------------The End-----------------------------------
```

Codes in Cell 11 are used to train the three models. A pandas dataframe with three columns records loss function values of model Q, P and D during training. Since D_loss values are smaller comparing with values of Q_loss and P_loss, D_loss values are multiplied by 100 just for plotting in figure 5.7(B). There are four parts in Cell 11. Part one to three are used to train model D, P and Q, respectively. The last part is for recording and showing training results. During model training, two loss functions defined in Cell 10 would be called. A loss function named 'loss_gan' is for the L_{GAN}. There are three items in L_{GAN}: loss_real, loss_fake and loss_noises. Their calculations are based on BCE loss function as usual in GAN projects. The loss function named 'loss_rec' is a modified reconstruction loss function $L_{llike}^{Dis_l}$ according to equation (5.6). This loss function has two inputs: one is a batch of real images, and the other is a batch of latent vectors of the real images. The two batches of data are processed by model D to output two batches of vectors, respectively. Then the two batches of vectors are used as the inputs of $L_{llike}^{Dis_l}$. Model training results are shown in figure 5.7. Comparing this with figure 5.4, you can see those digits in the 2D latent space are disentangled more.

The MNIST dataset is the simplest dataset widely used in computer vision projects. If your codes work for the dataset, it does not mean that your codes are functional for other datasets. By choosing the latent space dimensions to be 20, we can generate crystal clear fake MNIST images. Just change the dataset name from MNIST to Fashion MNIST, the results would be very different. Even z_dim was set to be equal to 256, detailed patterns, such as Nike's trademark '$\sqrt{}$' on shoes, 'N.Y.' on t-shirt could not be found on fake Fashion MNIST images. On the right hand side of a real image shown in figure 5.8(A), there is a black square block which was blurred in a fake image at the same position.

VAE-GANs were successfully applied to datasets with black and white images of lower resolutions. We need to see how VAE-GANs handle color image datasets. Codes in appendix D are used to generate color fake anime-faces dataset images. Because the image resolution of the Anime-face Dataset is higher, more neural layers are used in the three models of the VAE-GAN system. The model training time for

Figure 5.8. (A) Real fashion MNIST images. (B) Fake fashion MNIST images generated by VAE_GAN with z_dim = 256. Detailed patterns on real images were lost or blurred on the fake images. The Fashion MNIST dataset is from Xiao *et al* (2017) with a license CC BY 3.0.

Figure 5.9. Fake anime-face dataset images generated VAE_GAN codes with z_dim = 128, lr = 1e-4 and epochs = 25.

each epoch is about 8 min on my laptop. With a batch size set of 64 and the training epoch number of 25, the model training time is about 210 min. Although the model training time is longer, we do save time because it is not necessary to waste time tuning hyperparameters for high-quality fake images. The quality of fake images shown figure 5.9 is not as good as the quality of real anime-face dataset images, but is good enough. Using Kaggle's free GPU P100, the model training time is about 90 min.

References

Deng L 2012 The MNIST database of handwritten digit images for machine learning research *IEEE Signal Process. Mag.* **29** 141–1

Higgins I, Matthey L, Pal A, Burgess C P, Glorot X, Botvinick M M, Mohamed S and Lerchner A 2017 *beta-VAE: Learning Basic Visual Concepts with a Constrained Variational Framework* (ICLR)

Kingma D P and Welling M 2013 Auto-encoding variational bayes. *arXiv preprint arXiv:*1312.6114

Larsen A B L, Sønderby S K, Larochelle H and Winther O 2016 Autoencoding beyond pixels using a learned similarity metric *Int. Conf. on Machine Learning* (PMLR) pp 1558–66

Xiao H, Rasul K and Vollgraf RM 2017 Fashion-MNIST: a novel image dataset for benchmarking machine learning algorithms https://github.com/zalandoresearch/fashion-mnist

Chapter 6

Image generation by infoGANs

An information maximizing generative adversarial net (infoGAN) is also an unsupervised computer vision technique with which we can generate specific style images, similar to images in training datasets, without using labels. The quadratic curve dataset is used to explain the infoGAN principle at first, and then this technique is used for the MNIST, Anime-face and Rock Paper Scissors datasets.

Although it is important to randomly generate realistic fake images with vanilla GANs, it is more important to use conditional GANs to generate desired fake images. Since conditional GANs can encode label information with images in datasets, they have the ability to generate specific images with labels pre-set by ourselves. Unfortunately, many datasets are not labeled, because dataset labeling is very expensive. What can we do for unsupervised learning? Using variational autoencoders is a solution to generate desired fake images for datasets without labels. However, fake images generated by VAE systems are usually blurry, not crystal clear. In 2016, Xi Chen and his collaborators published a paper (Chen *et al* 2016) titled 'InfoGAN: Interpretable representation learning by information maximizing generative adversarial nets'. With an infoGAN system, our codes are smart enough to automatically find different characteristics of images in datasets during model training, and enable us to change some parameters linked with those characteristics, so we can generate fake images with desired classes and effects.

6.1 Using infoGAN to generate quadratic curves

In the infoGAN architecture shown in figure 6.1(A), there are four models: model G, model D0, model D1 and model Q. The first one is the generator model G which has the same structure as a generator model in an ordinary GAN. The last one is an 'auxiliary model' Q. D0 and D1 are two parts of the discriminator model D of a GAN in section 3.1.1. There are two fully connected layers in the model D. Its last neural layer is taken away to construct model D1, and another neuron layer is used for model D0. The outputs of model D0 are shared by model D1 and model Q. The

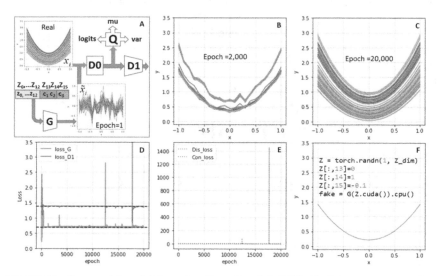

Figure 6.1. (A) The four models and information flow of an infoGAN. (B) Fake curves at epoch = 2000. (C) Fake curves at epoch = 20 000. (D) Loss curves for model D and G. (E) Loss curves for model Q's outputs. (F) A fake curve generated with $Z[:,13] = 0$, $Z[:,14] = 1$ and $Z[:,15] = -0.1$. Model training time is 21 min.

three outputs of model Q are named 'logits', 'mu' and 'var'. The input of model G in the GAN of section 3.11 is a batch of noise vectors generated by a multivariate standard normal distribution, and each noise vector is represented by a lowercase letter z with z_dim elements. In the infoGAN system, we use a capital letter Z to represent a noise vector for model G's input. The vector Z is a concatenation result of an incompressible noise vector, a label vector and a style vector. The incompressible noise vector is the noise vector (z) in a GAN system, and we cannot tune them to get any desired effect for fake images. The elements of the label vector are discrete numbers (integers) in a uniform distribution for the quadratic curve project. The element in the style vector is a continuous number uniformly distributed in the range $[-1,1]$ for the quadratic curve project. In the infoGAN paper, the concatenation of the last two vectors is called latent code c with elements named c_1, c_2, ...c_L. The element number of the incompressible noise vector, the element number of labels and the element number of styles for the simple project were arbitrarily chosen as $z\_dim = 13$, $n\_class = 2$ and $n\_styles = 1$, respectively. As shown in figure 6.1(A), the noise vector Z's dimensional number is $Z\_dim = (13 + 2 + 1)$. Each batch of Z vectors is generated by a function defined in Cell 09 of Project 6.1.

We do the extra work described above to obtain desired fake curves or images. Just for another example of the MNIST dataset without using its label information, we want to use infoGAN to generate desired fake digital images. In that case, the number of the label vector is set to be $n\_class = 10$ for its 10 classes, and $n\_styles = 2$ for two image styles. Since each MNIST image has 28×28 pixels, we choose $z\_dim = 62$ for the element number of an incompressible noise vector z. For the simple quadratic curve project, each curve has 21 numbers, so we could set $z\_dim = 13$. We really have no information about labels and styles of those quadratic curves, and want to see what an infoGAN can learn from data of quadratic curves with $n\_class = 2$ and $n\_styles = 1$. Based on the infoGAN paper, the latent code name 'c' is used to denote the concatenation of all latent variables c_1, c_2 and c_3 for the quadratic curve project. We can use a factored probability distribution for the latent code

$$P(c_1, c_2, \ldots, c_L) = \prod_{i=1}^{L=3} p(c_i) \tag{6.1}$$

Each batch of noise vectors (Z) is used by model G to generate a batch of fake images as shown in figure 6.1(C). Model D0 uses a batch of fake curves or a batch of real curves as its input. The output of D0 is a $m \times n\_hidden$ tensor, where $m =$ batch size and $n\_hidden = 128$. This output is shared by model D1 and model Q. Model D1 is trained to ensure that the fake images have good quality comparing with real images by using the following BCE loss function L_{D1} which is the same of an ordinary GAN

$$L_{D1} = \frac{-1}{m} \sum_{i=1}^{m} \ln\left[D1(D0(x_i))\right] - \frac{1}{m} \sum_{i=1}^{m} \ln\left[1 - D1(D0(\tilde{x}_i))\right] \tag{6.2}$$

The output tensor of model D0 is also used by model Q which has three outputs: a $m \times 2$ logits tensor, a $m \times 1$ mean tensor μ, and a $m \times 1$ variance tensor σ^2. There are three parts in the loss function L_G shown in the following equation (6.3). The first part is a BCE loss function with which model G is trained to generate fake images as good as real images to fool model D1; the second part is a cross-entropy loss function about labels in the latent code and the logits of model Q's output; the third part is a Gaussian negative log-likelihood loss function which establishes a mathematical link between a batch of c_3 in Z vectors and model Q's two outputs (μ and σ^2). As the infoGAN paper mentioned, a hyperparameter λ in equation (6.3) should be a small number, because the loss function values from the style variable may be very big. A mathematical link between fake images and the latent code is the mutual information $I(c, G(z, c))$ mentioned in section 2.1.3. We can use the link just like a dial to tune model G to generate fake images with desired effects

$$L_G = \frac{-1}{m} \sum_{i=1}^{m} \ln\left[D1(D0(\tilde{x}_i))\right] + \mathrm{CrossE_{Loss}(logits,labels)} + \frac{\lambda}{2m} \sum_{i=1}^{m} \left(\ln \sigma_i^2 + \frac{((c_3)_i - \mu_i)^2}{\sigma_i^2} \right) \tag{6.3}$$

In the gambling machine mentioned in chapter 1, section 1.1.3, a fair coin and a fair dice are independent, so their mutual information is equal to zero. We cannot predict the coin's side from the digit of a dice tossed on a table. To use the latent code to tune the fake images with the desired effects, we should maximize the mutual information between the latent code c and the fake images: $I(c,G(z,c)) = H(c) - H(c|G(z,c))$ according to equation (1.18). We know the PDF of c from equation (6.1), so we can calculate to find its entropy $H(c)$. But we do not know the PDF of fake images $G(z,c)$, and it is impossible to directly calculate $I(c,G(z,c))$. By introducing the auxiliary model Q, the authors of the infoGAN paper circumvented the problem, and they found the low bound of the mutual information: $L_I(G,Q)$

$$I(c,\,G(z,\,c)) \geqslant L_I(G,\,Q) = E_{x \sim G(z,\,c)}\Big[E_{c' \sim P(c,\sim,x)}[\ln\,[Q(c',\,\sim\,,x)]]\Big] + H(c) \quad (6.4)$$

It is logical that you can maximize the mutual information by maximizing its low bound. With the gradient descent algorithm, we need to find the minimum of the negative of the low bound. That is why the Gaussian negative log-likelihood loss function is used in model G's loss function (6.3). In the codes of the following infoGAN project 6.1 for the quadric curve project, most hyperparameters and all libraries are listed in Cell 01. As usual, Cell 02 generates data, and Cell 03 uses those data to draw real quadric curves. Figure 6.1(B) and (C) show fake curves generated by the infoGAN codes. Values of model D1's loss function is very close to its theory numbers. But model G's loss curve is very noisy. These noises come from the Gaussian negative log-likelihood loss 'loss_con' shown in figure 6.1(E). The hyperparameter 'lambda_info' is used to limit contribution of 'loss_con' to model G's loss.

```python
# Project 6.1 InforGAN for Quadric Curve Generation ------------------Python v3.6
import torch; import torch.nn as nn; from tqdm import trange
import numpy as np; import pandas as pd; import matplotlib.pyplot as plt
n_epochs = 20000        # traing epochs
n_points = 21           # nummber of points on each curve
batch_size = 64         # total 64 curves in a batch
n_batch = 5             # batchs per epoch for model trainig in Cell 12
n_hidden = 128          # number of neurons in the only hidden layer
z_dim = 13              # dimensions of incompressible noise vector z
n_class = 2             # dimensions oflabels for latent code
n_styles = 1            # dimensions of styles for latent code
Z_dim = z_dim + n_class + n_styles    # Z_dim = 16
lr = 5e-5               # initial learning rate, 1e-4, 5e-5 ok
k = 25                  # k = lr_G / lr_D in optimizer_G of Cell 08:
lambda_info = 0.01      # for loss_G in Cell 11
# Cell 02: Creating training data from y=a*x^2+(a-1)----------------------Cell 02
x = np.linspace(-1, 1, n_points)        # x=[-1, -0.9,...,1]
def training_data():
    a = np.random.uniform(1, 2, batch_size).reshape(-1,1)
    points = a*x*x + (a-1)
    return points
y = training_data()
# Cell 03: Show curves--------------------------------------------------Cell 03
def show_curves(x, y):
    fig, ax = plt.subplots(figsize=(4,4))
    batch_size = y.shape[0]
    for i in range(batch_size):
        ax.plot(x, y[i,:])
    ax.set(xlabel='x', ylabel='y', ylim=[-0.1,3.5])
    ax.set(xticks=np.arange(-1.0, 1.1, 0.5))
    ax.grid(color='g', linestyle=':')
    plt.show()
show_curves(x,y)
# Cell 04: Generator class----------------------------------------------Cell 04
class Generator(nn.Module):
    def __init__(self):
        super().__init__()
        self.net = nn.Sequential(nn.Linear(Z_dim, n_hidden),
                            nn.ReLU(True),
```

```
                              nn.Linear(n_hidden, n_points))
    def forward(self, input):      # input.shape = batch_size x Z_dim
        output = self.net(input)    # output.shape = batch_size x n_points
        return output
G = Generator().cuda()
# Cell 05: The 1st part of the Discriminator Class----------------------Cell 05
class Discriminator0(nn.Module):
    def __init__(self):
        super().__init__()
        self.net = nn.Sequential(nn.Linear(n_points, n_hidden),
                                 nn.LeakyReLU(0.2, inplace=True))
    def forward(self, input):      # input.shape = batch_size x n_points
        output = self.net(input)    # output.shape = batch_size x n_hidden
        return output
D0 = Discriminator0().cuda()
# Cell 06: Discriminator Class-------------------------------------------Cell 06
class Discriminator1(nn.Module):
    def __init__(self):
        super().__init__()
        self.net = nn.Sequential(nn.Linear(n_hidden, 1),
                                 nn.Sigmoid())
    def forward(self, input):      # input.shape = batch_size x n_hidden
        return self.net(input)      # output.shape = batch_size x 1
D1 = Discriminator1().cuda()
# Cell 07: Q model after model D0 to get 3 more outputs-----------------Cell 07
class Auxillary(nn.Module):
    def __init__(self):
        super().__init__()
        self.net = nn.Sequential(nn.Conv2d(n_hidden, 64, 1, bias=False),
                                 nn.BatchNorm2d(64),
                                 nn.LeakyReLU(0.1, inplace=True))
        self.conv_disc = nn.Conv2d(64, n_class, 1)
        self.conv_mu = nn.Conv2d(64, n_styles, 1)
        self.conv_var = nn.Conv2d(64, n_styles, 1)
    def forward(self, x):                      # x.shape = batch_size x 128
        input = x.unsqueeze(-1).unsqueeze(-1)  #input.shape=batch_sizex128x1^2
        y = self.net(input)                    # y.shape=batch_size x 64 x 1^2
        logits = self.conv_disc(y).squeeze()   # logits.shape=batch_size x 2
        mu = self.conv_mu(y).squeeze()         # mu.shape=batch_size x 1
        var = torch.exp(self.conv_var(y).squeeze())
        return logits, mu, var                 # var.shape=batch_size x 1
Q = Auxillary().cuda()
# Cell 08: criteria, optimizers-----------------------------------------Cell 08
criterionD1 = nn.BCELoss()              # D Loss for real and fake images.
criterionQ_dis = nn.CrossEntropyLoss()  # for latent labels code and logits
criterionQ_con = nn.GaussianNLLLoss()   # Loss function for model Q's mu&var
optimizer_D1 = torch.optim.Adam([{'params': D0.parameters()},
              {'params': D1.parameters()}], lr=lr, betas=(0.5, 0.999))
optimizer_G = torch.optim.Adam([{'params': G.parameters()},
              {'params': Q.parameters()}], lr=k*lr, betas=(0.5, 0.999))
# Cell 09: Noise function for the generator ----------------------------Cell 09
def noise4G_input(m=batch_size, noise_size=z_dim, n=n_class):
```

```
    z = torch.randn(m, noise_size, device='cuda') #z.shape = batch_size x 13
    labels = torch.cat(      # Categorical latent code [0,1]*32: len(labels) = 64
        (torch.arange(n).repeat(m//n), torch.arange(m%n)), dim=0)
    # Create integer labels in the latent code:   dis_c.shape = batch_size x 2
    dis_c = torch.nn.functional.one_hot(labels, n).cuda()
    # Create styles in the latent code:          con_c.shape = batch_size x 1
    con_c = torch.Tensor(m, n_styles).uniform_(-1.0, 1.0).cuda()
    Z = torch.cat([z, dis_c, con_c], dim=1)
    return Z, labels, con_c                      #Z.shape=batch_size x 16
# Cell 10: Model D1 training function----------------------------------Cell 10
def train_D1(inputs, Z, optimizer_D1):       #z: noise vectors rom Cell 09
    batch_size = inputs.shape[0]         #input: real curves
    real_preds = D1(D0(inputs))
    ones_targets = torch.ones(batch_size, 1, device='cuda')
    real_loss = criterionD1(real_preds, ones_targets)
    fake_curves = G(Z)
    fake_preds = D1(D0(fake_curves.detach()))
    zeros_targets = torch.zeros(batch_size, 1, device='cuda')
    fake_loss = criterionD1(fake_preds, zeros_targets)

    loss_D1 = real_loss + fake_loss
    optimizer_D1.zero_grad()
    loss_D1.backward()
    optimizer_D1.step()
    return loss_D1.item()
# Cell 11: Train the generator to fool the discriminator------------Cell 11
def train_G(Z, labels, con_c, optimizer_G):
    # Create fake curves and labels
    batch_size = Z.shape[0]
    fake_curves = G(Z)        #fake_curves.shape = batch_size x 21
    preds0 = D0(fake_curves)
    preds = D1(preds0)
    ones_targets = torch.ones(batch_size, 1, device='cuda')
    loss_fake = criterionD1(preds, ones_targets)          # to fool D1
    logits, mu, var = Q(preds0)
    target = labels.cuda()
    dis_loss = criterionQ_dis(logits, target)   #for label information
    con_loss = criterionQ_con(con_c, mu, var)   #for style information
    loss_G = loss_fake + dis_loss + con_loss*lambda_info
    optimizer_G.zero_grad()
    loss_G.backward()
    optimizer_G.step()
    return loss_G.item(), dis_loss.item(), con_loss.item()
# Cell 12: Definition of a fitting function-----------------------------Cell 12
def fit(epochs):
    torch.cuda.empty_cache()
    # The DataFrame df is a recorder of the training history
    df = pd.DataFrame(np.empty([epochs, 4]),
                    index=np.arange(epochs),
                    columns=['loss_G', 'loss_D1', 'Dis_loss', 'Con_loss'])
    for i in trange(epochs):
        loss_G = 0.0; loss_D1 = 0.0; loss_Dis = 0.0; loss_Con = 0.0
```

```
    for _ in range(n_batch):
        inputs = torch.cuda.FloatTensor(training_data())     #real curves
        Z, labels, con_c = noise4G_input()           #outputs of Cell 09
        loss_d = train_D1(inputs, Z, optimizer_D1)
        loss_D1 +=   loss_d
        loss_g, loss_dis, loss_con = train_G(Z, labels, con_c, optimizer_G)
        loss_G += loss_g
        loss_Dis += loss_dis
        loss_Con += loss_con
    # Record losses & scores
    df.iloc[i, 0] = loss_G/n_batch
    df.iloc[i, 1] = loss_D1/n_batch
    df.iloc[i, 2] = loss_Dis/n_batch
    df.iloc[i, 3] = loss_Con/n_batch
    if i==0 or (i+1)%2000==0:
        print(
        "Epoch={:5},Ls_G={:.2f},Ls_D1={:.2f},loss_dis={:.2f},loss_con={:.2f}"
        .format(i+1, df.iloc[i,0], df.iloc[i,1], df.iloc[i,2], df.iloc[i,3]))
        fake_curves = G(Z).cpu()
        show_curves(x, fake_curves.detach().numpy())
    return df
train_history = fit(n_epochs)
# Cell 13: Show the training history in Graph-----------------------Cell 13
history= train_history
fig, ax = plt.subplots(1,2, figsize=(8,4), sharex=True)
history.plot(ax=ax[0], y=[0,1], style=['r-', 'b-'])
history.plot(ax=ax[1], y=[2,3], style=['r:', 'b:'])
for i in range(2):
    ax[i].set_xlabel('epoch')
    ax[i].grid(which='major', axis='both', color='g', linestyle=':')
ax[0].set(ylim=[0,3], ylabel='Loss')
ax[0].axhline(y=2*np.log(2), color='k', linestyle='--') #Theory D loss Value
ax[0].axhline(y=np.log(2), color='k', linestyle='--')   #Theory G loss Value
plt.show()
# Cell 14: Generate a single tunable fake curve--------------------Cell 14
Z = torch.randn(1, Z_dim)
Z[:,13]=1
Z[:,14]=0
Z[:,15]=0
print(Z)
fake_curve = G(Z.cuda()).cpu()
show_curves(x, fake_curve.detach().numpy())
fake_curve.min()
#---------------------------The End----------------------------------------
```

In Cell 09, the noise tensor generator function named 'noise4G_input' is new to us. It generates three random tensors and concatenates them into a $m \times 16$ tensor Z which is the first output of the function. This tensor will be used to generate a batch of fake curves. The other two outputs ('labels' and 'con_c') of this function will be updated during model training and can be used to tune those fake images for our desired effects. The 'train_D1' function in Cell 10 is as usual in an ordinary GAN. In Cell 11 about a function named 'train_G', the loss function has three parts. The first part is BCE loss used to fool model D1; the second part is the cross-entropy loss used to establish links between the logits output of model Q and latent labels; the third part is Gaussian negative log-likelihood loss. It is used to insure the styles in the latent code with a normal distribution $N(c_3; mu, \sigma^2)$, where *mu* and *var* $= \sigma^2$ are two outputs of model Q. We use a class of Pytorch named `'nn.GaussianNLLLoss'` to calculate of the loss values.

Codes from Cell 12 to 14 are used to train models and display the model training results. After model training, a single fake curve is generated which is shown in figure 6.1(F). Its data was generated by $Z = torch.randn(1, Z\_dim)$ and then set by Z $[:,13] = 0$, $Z[:,14] = 1$ and $Z[:,15] = -0.1$. With label code $c_1 = 0$ and $c_2 = 1$, the infoGAN system generates a fake curve whose lowest point is below $y = 0.5$; and with label $c_1 = 1$ and $c_2 = 0$, the infoGAN system generates a fake curve whose lowest point is above $y = 0.5$. The style variable c_3 can be used to tune the lowest point of a fake curve moving along the y-axis continuously. If $|c_3|$ is too big ($\gg 1$), the fake curve will not be smooth. The extra work based on infoGAN theory gives us the power to tune fake images without label information in datasets.

6.2 Implementation of infoGAN for the MNIST dataset

With the knowledge about the DCGAN MNIST project in section 3.2.2 and the infoGAN structure about fake quadratic curve generation in the last section, it should be easy for us to understand the following codes in project 6.2.1 about using an infoGAN to generate fake MNIST images. What we should pay attention to is the parameter 'k' in Cell 01. It is the ratio between the learning rate of model G and that of model D1. In the infoGAN paper, it was set to be 5. As mentioned in section 3.2.2, we know that model G is not as smart as model D. We should use a bigger number ($k = 25$) for the ratio so the two models have the same intelligence to compete with each other. It took a long time to adjust both the initial learning rate (*lr*) and the ratio (*k*) to generate high quality fake images shown in figure 6.2(A) which are outputs of Cell 15. These fake images are crystal clear and could not be distinguished from real images output by Cell 04. Each column of those fake images has the same digits. This means that our infoGAN algorithm works.

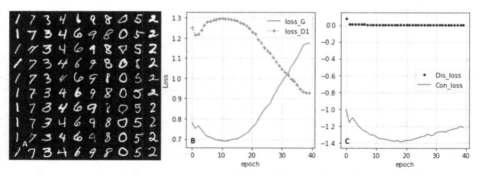

Figure 6.2. (A) Fake MNIST images generated by an infoGAN at the end of model training, outputs of Cell 15. (B and C) Curves of Loss functions, the outputs of Cell 16 about the model training history (model training time: 21 min).

```
# Project 6.2.1 inforGAN for MNIST dataset --------------------------Python v3.6
import torch; import torch.nn as nn; from torch.utils.data import DataLoader
from torchvision import transforms as T; from torchvision.utils import make_grid
from torchvision.datasets import MNIST; from tqdm import trange
import numpy as np; import pandas as pd; import matplotlib.pyplot as plt
img_size = 28
img_channels = 1
n_epochs =40
batch_size = 100
z_dim = 62        # incompressible noise elements z0-z61 or Z0 to Z61
n_class = 10      # for labels of latent code c1 to c10 or Z62 to Z71
n_styles = 2      # for styles of the latent code c11 and c12 or Z72, Z73
Z_dim = z_dim + n_class + n_styles       # Z_dim = 74
lr = 1e-4         # learning rate
k = 25            # k = G_lr/D_lr
lambda_info = 0.1 # for negtive Gaussian loss in Cell 14
#Cell 02: Input MNIST DataSet--------------------------------------------Cell 02
path = './OCR/data/'
trainData = MNIST(path, train=True, download=False,
    transform=T.Compose([T.ToTensor(), T.Normalize([0.5], [0.5])]))
n_samples = len(trainData)  #len(trainData)=60000
# Cell 03: MNIST DataLoader (trainLoader)--------------------------Cell 03
train_dataloader = DataLoader(trainData,
    batch_size=batch_size, shuffle=True)
n_batch = len(train_dataloader)  #len(trainLoader) = n_samples/n_batch
for imgs, labels in train_dataloader:
    print('imgs.shape=', imgs.shape)
    print(labels.view(-1,10))
    break
# Cell 04: Show the images of the 1st batch of trainLoader ---------Cell 04
def denorm(img_tensors):
    return img_tensors*0.5 + 0.5
def show_imgs(imgs):
    fig, ax = plt.subplots(figsize=(12,8))
    input = make_grid(denorm(imgs), nrow=10, padding=2)
    ax.imshow(input.permute(1,2,0), cmap='gray')
    ax.set(xticks=[], yticks=[])
    plt.show()
show_imgs(imgs)
# Cell 05: Model parameters initialization  -----------------------------Cell 07
def weights_init(m):
    if(type(m) == nn.ConvTranspose2d or type(m) == nn.Conv2d):
        nn.init.normal_(m.weight.data, 0.0, 0.02)
    elif(type(m) == nn.BatchNorm2d):
        nn.init.normal_(m.weight.data, 1.0, 0.02)
        nn.init.constant_(m.bias.data, 0)
# Cell 06: Genetor class-------------------------------------------------Cell 06
def basic_G(in_channels, outchannels, f=4, s=2, p=1):
    return nn.Sequential(nn.ConvTranspose2d(in_channels, outchannels,
                         kernel_size=f, stride=s, padding=p, bias=False),
                    nn.BatchNorm2d(outchannels),
                    nn.ReLU(True))
```

```python
class Generator(nn.Module):
    def __init__(self):
        super().__init__()
        self.net = nn.Sequential(
            basic_G(Z_dim, 256, 1, 1, 0),
            #layer 01 output.shape=batch_size x 256x 1^2
            basic_G(256, 128, 7, 1, 0),
            #layer 02 output.shape=batch_size x 128 x 7^2
            basic_G(128, 64, 4, 2, 1),
            #layer 03 output.shape=batch_size x 64 x 14^2
            nn.ConvTranspose2d(64, img_channels, 4, 2, 1),
            nn.Tanh()
        )    #layer 04 output.shape=batch_size x 1 x 28^2
    def forward(self, images):
        output = self.net(images)  #images.shape = batch_size x Z_dim x 1^2
        return output              # output.shape = batch_size x 1 x 28^2
G = Generator().cuda()
G.apply(weights_init)
# Cell 07: The 1st part of the Discriminator Class --------------------Cell 09
def basic_D(in_channels, out_channels, f=4, s=2, p=1):
    return nn.Sequential(nn.Conv2d(in_channels, out_channels,
                            kernel_size=f, stride=s, padding=p, bias=False),
                        nn.BatchNorm2d(out_channels),
                        nn.LeakyReLU(0.1, inplace=True)
                        )
class Discriminator0(nn.Module):
    def __init__(self):
        super().__init__()
        self.net = nn.Sequential(
            basic_D(img_channels, 32, 4, 2, 1),
            # layer 01 outputshape=batch_size x 32 x 14^2
            basic_D(32, 64, 4, 2, 2),
            # layer 02 output.shape=batch_size x 64 x 8^2
            basic_D(64, 128, 4, 2, 1),
            # layer 03 output.shape=batch_size x 128 x 4^2
            basic_D(128, 256, 4, 2, 0)
        )    #layer 04 output.shape = batch_size x 256 x 1^2
    def forward(self, x):
        output = self.net(x)    # x.shape=batch_size x 1 x 28^2
        return output           # output.shape = batch_size x 256 x 1^2
D0 = Discriminator0().cuda()
D0.apply(weights_init)
# Cell 08: Continuous of Model D0 to get a number for each image--------Cell 08
class Discriminator1(nn.Module):
    def __init__(self):
        super().__init__()
        self.net = nn.Sequential(
            nn.Conv2d(256, 1, kernel_size=1),
            nn.Flatten(),
            nn.Sigmoid()
        )
    def forward(self, x):
```

```
        output = self.net(x)   # x.shape = batch_size x 256 x 1^2
        return output        # output.shape = batch_size x 1
D1 = Discriminator1().cuda()
D1.apply(weights_init)
# Cell 09: Continuous of D0 to get 3 more outputs --------------------Cell 09
class Auxillary(nn.Module):
    def __init__(self):
        super().__init__()
        self.net = nn.Sequential(
            nn.Conv2d(256, 128, kernel_size=1, bias=False),
            nn.BatchNorm2d(128),
            nn.LeakyReLU(0.1, inplace=True)
        )
        self.conv_disc = nn.Conv2d(128, n_class, kernel_size=1)
        self.conv_mu = nn.Conv2d(128, n_styles, kernel_size=1)
        self.conv_var = nn.Conv2d(128, n_styles, kernel_size=1)
    def forward(self, x):   #x.shape = batch_size x 256 x 1^2
        y = self.net(x)      #y.shape = batch_size x 128 x 1^2
        logits = self.conv_disc(y).squeeze()       #batch_size x 10
        mu = self.conv_mu(y).squeeze()             #batch_size x 2
        var = torch.exp(self.conv_var(y).squeeze()) #batch_size x 2
        return logits, mu, var
Q = Auxillary().cuda()
Q.apply(weights_init)
# Cell 10: Criteria functions for loss calculations----------------------Cell 10
criterionD1 = nn.BCELoss()                # Loss function for model D1
criterionQ_dis = nn.CrossEntropyLoss()  # Loss function for model Q's logits
criterionQ_con = nn.GaussianNLLLoss()   #-Loss function for model Q's mu&var
# Cell 11: Adam optimiser is used for D1, G and Q.----------------------Cell 11
optimizer_D1 = torch.optim.Adam([{'params': D0.parameters()},
                    {'params': D1.parameters()}], lr=lr, betas=(0.5, 0.999))
optimizer_G = torch.optim.Adam([{'params': G.parameters()},
                    {'params': Q.parameters()}], lr=k*lr, betas=(0.5, 0.999))
# Cell 12: Noise function for model G's inputs-------------------------Cell 12
def noise4G_input(m=batch_size, noise_size=z_dim, n=n_class):
    noise = torch.randn(m, noise_size).cuda()  # create incompressible noise z
    # Create integer labels in the latent code for c1, c2,..., c10
    labels = torch.cat((torch.arange(n).repeat(m//n),
                    torch.arange(m%n)), dim=0).cuda()
    dis_c = torch.nn.functional.one_hot(labels, n_class)  #hot code for labels
    # Create styles in the latent code: c11, c12
    con_c = torch.Tensor(m, n_styles).uniform_(-1.0, 1.0).cuda()
    Z = torch.cat([noise, dis_c, con_c], 1).view(-1, Z_dim, 1, 1)
    return Z, labels, con_c          #Z.shape = batch_size x Z_dim x 1^2
fixed_Z = noise4G_input(batch_size, z_dim, n_class)[0].cuda()
# Cell 13: Training function for Model D0 and D1------------------------Cell 13
def train_D1(inputs, Z, optimizer_D1):
    batch_size = inputs.shape[0]
    real_preds = D1(D0(inputs)) #--------------------for real images
    one_targets = torch.ones(batch_size, 1).cuda()
    real_loss = criterionD1(real_preds, one_targets)
    fake_images = G(Z)           # -------------------for fake images
```

```python
        fake_preds = D1(D0(fake_images.detach()))
        zero_targets = torch.zeros(batch_size, 1).cuda()
        fake_loss = criterionD1(fake_preds, zero_targets)
        loss_D1 = real_loss + fake_loss # --------------model D1's loss
        optimizer_D1.zero_grad()
        loss_D1.backward()
        optimizer_D1.step()
        return loss_D1.item()
# Cell 14: Training for Model G and Q-----------------------------------Cell 14
def train_G(Z, labels, con_c, optimizer_G):
        batch_size = Z.shape[0]
        fake_images = G(Z)                      # Create fake images and labels
        preds0 = D0(fake_images)
        preds = D1(preds0)                      # Try to fool model D1
        one_targets = torch.ones(batch_size, 1).cuda()
        loss_fake = criterionD1(preds, one_targets)
        logits, mu, var = Q(preds0)
        target = labels        # latent code labels: Z62, Z63, ..., Z71
        dis_loss = criterionQ_dis(logits, target)
        con_loss = criterionQ_con(con_c, mu, var)
        loss_G = loss_fake + dis_loss + con_loss*lambda_info
        optimizer_G.zero_grad()
        loss_G.backward()
        optimizer_G.step()
        return loss_G.item(), dis_loss.item(), con_loss.item()
# Cell 15: Definition of a fitting function----------------------------Cell 15
def fit(epochs):
        torch.cuda.empty_cache()
        # The DataFrame df is a recorder of the training history
        df = pd.DataFrame(np.empty([epochs, 4]), index = np.arange(epochs),
                    columns=['loss_G', 'loss_D1', 'Dis_loss', 'Con_loss']
        )
        for i in trange(epochs):
            loss_G = 0.0; loss_D1 = 0.0; Dis_loss = 0.0; Con_loss = 0.0
            for real_images, _ in train_dataloader:
                inputs = real_images.cuda()
                batch_size = inputs.shape[0]
                Z, labels, con_c = noise4G_input(batch_size, z_dim, n_class)
                loss_d = train_D1(inputs, Z, optimizer_D1)
                loss_D1 += loss_d
                loss_g, dis_loss, con_loss= train_G(Z, labels, con_c, optimizer_G)
                loss_G += loss_g
                Dis_loss += dis_loss
                Con_loss += con_loss
            # Record losses & scores
            df.iloc[i, 0] = loss_G/n_batch
            df.iloc[i, 1] = loss_D1/n_batch
            df.iloc[i, 2] = Dis_loss/n_batch
            df.iloc[i, 3] = Con_loss/n_batch
            if i==0 or (i+1)%10==0:
                print(
                "Epoch={},loss_G={:.2f},loss_D1={:.2f},Dis_ls={:.2f},Con_ls={:.2f}"
```

```
            .format(i+1,df.iloc[i,0],df.iloc[i,1],df.iloc[i,2],df.iloc[i,3]))
            fake_images = G(fixed_Z)
            show_imgs(fake_images.detach().cpu())
    return df
train_history = fit(n_epochs) #training time=17min
# Cell 16: Show the training history---------------------------------Cell 16
df =train_history
import matplotlib.pyplot as plt
fig, ax = plt.subplots(1,2, figsize=(8,4), sharex=True)
df.plot(ax=ax[0], y=[0,1], color=['r', 'b'], style=['-',':+'])
ax[0].set(ylabel='Loss')
df.plot(ax=ax[1], y=[2,3], color=['k', 'm'], style=['.','-'])
for i in range(2):
    ax[i].grid(which='major', axis='both', color='g', linestyle=':')
    ax[i].set(xlabel='epoch')
plt.show()
# Cell 17: Using latent code to tune fake images---------------------Cell 17
G.eval()
c = [1,7,3,4,6,9,8,0,5,2]
digitals = np.empty(10, dtype=np.int32)
for i, ci in enumerate(c):
    digitals[ci] = i
Z, _, _ = noise4G_input()
Z[:,z_dim:(z_dim+10)]=0
for i in range(10):
    Z[10*i:(10*i+10), digitals[i]+z_dim, :, :] = 1
fake_images = G(Z)
show_imgs(fake_images.detach().cpu())
# Cell 18: Using the last style variable to tune fake images-----------Cell 18
Z1 = torch.clone(Z)
Z1[:,-1]= 2 # digital angles
fake_images = G(Z1)
show_imgs(fake_images.detach().cpu())
# Cell 19: Using the first style variable to tune fake images-----------Cell 19
Z2 = torch.clone(Z)
Z2[:,-2]= 1.5  # Stride thickness
fake_images = G(Z2)
show_imgs(fake_images.detach().cpu())
#----------------------------The End---------------------------------------
```

With codes in Cell 12 to generate noise tensors for fake images, we use integer numbers from 0 to 9 as labels in the latent code to generate fake images. Each column of those fake images in figure 6.2(A) has the same latent digital label. From left to right in figure 6.2(A), the latent code labels on each row are 0, 1, ..., 9. However, real labels of real images of each row are 1, 7, 3, 4, 6, 9, 8, 0, 5, 2, respectively. From the figure, we see that the latent code labels (0, 1...,9) are not the real labels of images in the MNIST dataset. After running codes from Cell 01 to 15, the models are trained. Then using the instructions of the infoGAN paper and with many tests, the following table 6.1 was obtained to tune the fake images for desired results. Using Cell 17, we can generate fake images shown in figure 6.3(A) with digits sorted from low to high in rows. The two continuous style variables in the latent code could be used to tune the image stride width and digit angles of fake images, respectively. Every time you run the codes of the project, the function of each element of the latent code to tune fake images is different.

In Cell 17, a list named 'c' is used to establish links between MNIST labels and their latent code shown in table 6.1. The list was obtained by reading digits from left to right

Table 6.1. Latent code for tuning fake MNIST images.

Latent code	c_1	c_2	c_3	c_4	c_5	c_6	c_7	c_8	c_9	c_{10}	c_{11}	c_{12}
MNIST label	1	7	3	4	6	9	8	0	5	2	Angle	Width
Z: noise for G	Z_{64}	Z_{68}	Z_{62}	Z_{66}	Z_{67}	Z_{65}	Z_{70}	Z_{71}	Z_{63}	Z_{69}	Z_{72}	Z_{73}

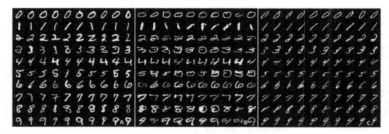

Figure 6.3. By tuning latent code c1 to c12 to get desired fake MNIST images with codes in Cell 17. (A) Normal fake images in rows sorted from 0 to 9 by changing latent code label sequence with codes in Cell 17. (B) $c_{11} = 1.5$, tuning the stride width of fake images by codes in Cell 18. (C) $c_{12} = -1.5$, tuning the digital angles of fake images by codes in Cell 19.

in any row of figure 6.2(A). Then the noise generator in Cell 12 generated a $100 \times 74 \times 1 \times 1$ tensor Z. From column 62 to column 71, each element in these 10 columns is reset to zero. With a for-loop for every 10 rows of the tensor Z, the value of an element in a column is set to be one, and the column index is obtained according to table 6.1. For example, from row 0 to 9 at the beginning, each element of the noise tensor Z at column 71 is set to be one. All 10 fake images of the first 10 rows of the tensor are digital zero images. The *show_imgs* function in Cell 04 display the 100 fake digital images of the tensor as a bigger image with those same 10 digits on each row. In this way, we can choose which digit should be in a row. We can also change the display angles and stride widths of those images with Z[:,−2] and Z[:,−1], respectively. Although the value of each element in the last two columns (Z_{72}, Z_{73}) can be any real number, fake digital images are readable only if they are in the range [−2,2],

I have to admit that there is a cheat in the project. Ten integers were chosen for the latent code for labels because we know there are 10 classes in the MNIST dataset. If we do not have MNIST label information, and choose five digitals or 20 digitals for the latent code label, what will happen? If you change the variable 'n_class' in Cell 01 to five, you will find that there will be more than one digit in each column of figure 6.2(A), in that case you display five MNIST images on each of ten rows. You would see 7&1, 5&8, 0&3, 2&6 and 4&9 are in five different columns. If the variable 'n_class' in Cell 01 is 20 and 20 digital images are displayed on each of five rows in figure 6.2(A), you will see one digit in two or even three columns with slightly different styles. I also changed the variable 'styles' from 2 to 4, but could not get more than two control dials to tune fake images. Changing the dataset name in Cell 01, we can use the above infoGAN codes for the FashionMNIST dataset. You can see that the style variable c_{11} could be used to tune the brightness of fake images, and another variable c_{12} could be used to tune the contrast of those fake images.

6.3 infoGAN for fake Anime-face dataset images

The Anime-face dataset has no label information. From the outputs of Cell 03 in project 6.3.1, you will see all image labels are the same: 1. The variable for the number of latent labels *n_class* in Cell 01 is arbitrarily set to be equal to 10. We will separate Anime-face images into 10 classes. The number of latent styles is set to be equal to 2, so we have two dials to tune fake images. With the dimension number of the incompressible noise (z) is set to be equal to 116, the number of dimensions of a noise vector (Z) for fake image generation is 128. Figure 6.4 shows some fake images. They are half of the outputs of Cell 14. The quality of fake images is good, but still not good enough comparing with real images. Each column of those fake images belongs to a class. Figure 6.5 shows loss curves and tuned fake images. The outputs of Cell 16 are 10×10 fake images, but only three rows are shown in figure 6.5(C). Images in each row belong to a class. The last style variable c_{12} can be used to tune the hue of fake images from yellow to blue by changing c_{12} from positive to negative. Figure 6.5(D)

Figure 6.4. Fake anime images, half of the outputs of Cell 14, and each column is a class (model training time: 48 min).

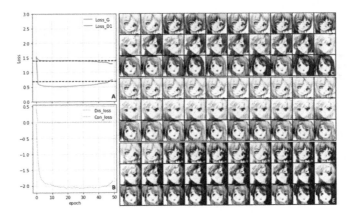

Figure 6.5. (A and B) Curves of Loss functions, the outputs of Cell 15. (C) Fake anime images, the first three rows of the outputs of Cell 16. (D) Fake images tuned by the last style variable $Z[:,-1]$ which changes the fake image hue from yellow to blue, the output of Cell 17. (E) Fake images tuned by the first style variable $Z[:,-2]$ which changes the image shadow from left side to right side, the output of Cell 18.

was generated by codes in Cell 17 with c_{12} or $Z[:,-1] = 1$. The first style variable c_{11} can be used to tune the light direction or the side in shadow of fake images. Shadows in the fake images in figure 6.5(E) are on the right hand side. These images were generated by codes in Cell 18 with c_{11} or $Z[:,-2] = 3$.

```python
# Project 6.3.1 InfoGAN for Anime-Face Dataset----------------------Python v3.6
import torch; import torch.nn as nn; from torch.utils.data import DataLoader
from torchvision.datasets import ImageFolder; import torchvision.transforms as T
from torchvision.utils import make_grid; import matplotlib.pyplot as plt
from tqdm import trange; import numpy as np; import pandas as pd
n_epochs = 50
batch_size = 100
img_size = 64
img_channels = 3
z_dim = 116          # z: imcompressive noise
n_class = 10         # number of classes for labels in the latent code
n_styles = 2         # number of styles for latent code
Z_dim = z_dim + n_class + n_styles  # Z: input for model G
lr = 5e-5
k = 10               #k = G_lr/D_lr
lambda_info = 0.1 # for negtive Gaussian loss in Cell 14
# Cell 02: AnimeFace Dataset----------------------------------------Cell 02
data_dir = './OCR/data/AnimeFaces'
train_dataset = ImageFolder(data_dir, transform=T.Compose([
               T.Resize(img_size), T.CenterCrop(img_size),T.ToTensor()]))
n_samples = len(train_dataset) #63566
# Cell 03: DataLoader ---------------------------------------------Cell 03
train_dataloader = DataLoader(train_dataset, batch_size=batch_size,
               shuffle=True, num_workers=3, pin_memory=True)
n_batch = len(train_dataloader) #636
for imgs, labels in train_dataloader:
    print("imgs.shape=", imgs.shape)
    print('lebels=\n', labels.view(5,-1))
    break
# Cell 04: show images --------------------------------------------Cell 04
def show_imgs(images):
    fig, ax = plt.subplots(figsize=(14,10))
    #input = make_grid(denorm(images), nrow=16)
    input = make_grid(images, nrow=10, padding=1)
    ax.imshow(input.permute(1,2,0))
    ax.set(xticks=[], yticks=[])
    plt.show()
show_imgs(imgs)
# Cell 05: Model parameters initialization ------------------------Cell 05
def weights_init(m):
    if(type(m) == nn.ConvTranspose2d or type(m) == nn.Conv2d):
        nn.init.normal_(m.weight.data, 0.0, 0.02)
    elif(type(m) == nn.BatchNorm2d):
        nn.init.normal_(m.weight.data, 1.0, 0.02)
        nn.init.constant_(m.bias.data, 0)
# Cell 06: Generator class(parameters 2,298,624)------------------Cell 06
def basic_G(in_channels, out_channels, f=4, s=2, p=1):
    return nn.Sequential(nn.ConvTranspose2d(in_channels, out_channels,
                        kernel_size=f, stride=s, padding=p, bias=False),
                    nn.BatchNorm2d(out_channels),
                    nn.ReLU(True))
```

```
class Generator(nn.Module):
    def __init__(self):
        super().__init__()
        self.net = nn.Sequential(
                        basic_G(Z_dim, 256, 1, 1, 0),
                        # layer 01 output.shape=batch_size x 256 x 1^2
                        basic_G(256, 128, 8, 1, 0),
                        # layer 02 output.shape=batch_size x 128 x 8^2
                        basic_G(128, 64, 4, 2, 1),
                        # layer 03 output.shape=batch_size x 64 x 16^2
                        basic_G(64, 32, 4, 2, 1),
                        # layer 04 output.shape=batch_size x 32 x 32^2
                        nn.ConvTranspose2d(32, 3, 4, 2, 1),
                        nn.Sigmoid()
                    ) # layer 05 output.shape=batch_size x 3 x 64^2
    def forward(self, Z):
        output = self.net(Z)    # Z.shape=batch_size x Z_dim x 1^2
        return output       # output.shape=batch_size x 3 x 64^2
G = Generator().cuda()
G.apply(weights_init)
# Cell 07: The 1st part of discriminator--------------------------------Cell 07
def basic_D(in_channels, out_channels):
    return nn.Sequential(nn.Conv2d(in_channels, out_channels,
                         kernel_size=4, stride=2, padding=1, bias=False),
                         nn.BatchNorm2d(out_channels),
                         nn.LeakyReLU(0.1, inplace=True)
                         )
class Discrinimator0(nn.Module):
    def __init__(self):
        super().__init__()
        self.net = nn.Sequential(
            nn.Conv2d(3, 32, 4, 2, 1),
            nn.LeakyReLU(0.1, inplace=True),
            # Layer 1 output.shape = batch_size x 64 x 32^2
            basic_D(32, 64),
            # Layer 2 output.shape = batch_size x 64 x 16^2
            basic_D(64, 128),
            # Layer 3 output.shape = batch_size x 128 x 8^2
            basic_D(128, 256),
        ) # Layer 4 output.shape = batch_size x 256 x 4^2
    def forward(self, x):       # x is a batch of images
        output = self.net(x)    # x.shape = batch_size x 3 x 64^2
        return output       #output.shape = batch_size x 256 x 4^2
D0 = Discrinimator0().cuda()
D0.apply(weights_init)
# Cell 08: The rest of the Discriminator class--------------------------Cell 08
class Discriminator1(nn.Module):
    def __init__(self):
        super().__init__()
        self.net = nn.Sequential(nn.Conv2d(256, 1, 4),
                                 nn.Flatten(),
                                 nn.Sigmoid()
                                 ) #output.shape = batch_size x 1
    def forward(self, x):           # x is the output of model D0
        output = self.net(x)    # x.shape = batch_size x 256 x 4^2
        return output       #output.shape = batch_size x 1
D1 = Discriminator1().cuda()
D1.apply(weights_init)
# Cell 09: Auxiliary class----------------------------------------------Cell 09
```

```
class Auxillary(nn.Module):
    def __init__(self):
        super().__init__()
        self.net = nn.Sequential(
            nn.Conv2d(256, 128, 4, bias=False),
            nn.BatchNorm2d(128),
            nn.LeakyReLU(0.1, inplace=True)
        )
        self.conv_disc = nn.Conv2d(128, n_class, 1)
        self.conv_mu = nn.Conv2d(128, n_styles, 1)
        self.conv_var = nn.Conv2d(128, n_styles, 1)
    def forward(self, x):    # x is the output of model D0
        y = self.net(x)      # y.shape = batch_size x 128 x 4^2
        disc_logits = self.conv_disc(y).squeeze()   # batch_size x n_class
        mu = self.conv_mu(y).squeeze()              # batch_size x n_styles
        var = torch.exp(self.conv_var(y).squeeze()) # batch_size x n_styles
        return disc_logits, mu, var
Q = Auxillary().cuda()
Q.apply(weights_init)
# Cell 10: Criteria and Optimizers----------------------------------------Cell 10
criterionD1 = nn.BCELoss()                  # D Loss for real and fake images.
criterionQ_dis = nn.CrossEntropyLoss()   # for latent labels code and logits
criterionQ_con = nn.GaussianNLLLoss()    # Loss function for model Q's mu&var
optimizer_D1 = torch.optim.RMSprop([{'params': D0.parameters()},
                                    {'params': D1.parameters()}], lr=lr)
optimizer_G = torch.optim.RMSprop([{'params': G.parameters()},
                                   {'params': Q.parameters()}], lr=k*lr)
# Cell 11: Noise function for the generator ---------------------------Cell 11
def noise4G_input(m=batch_size, z_noise=z_dim, n=n_class):
    noise = torch.randn(m, z_noise).cuda() # for incompressible noise z
    # Create categorical latent code
    labels = torch.cat((torch.arange(n).repeat(m//n),
                        torch.arange(m%n)), dim=0).cuda()
    dis_c = torch.nn.functional.one_hot(labels, n)
    con_c = torch.Tensor(m, n_styles).uniform_(-1.0, 1.0).cuda()
    Z = torch.cat([noise, dis_c, con_c], dim=1).view(-1, Z_dim, 1, 1)
    return Z, labels, con_c
fixed_Z= noise4G_input()[0].cuda()
# Cell 12: Discrinimator training function whose-----------------------Cell 12
def train_D1(inputs, Z, optimizer_D1):
    batch_size = inputs.shape[0]        # the input is a batch of real images
    real_preds = D1(D0(inputs))
    ones_targets = torch.ones(batch_size, 1).cuda()
    real_loss = criterionD1(real_preds, ones_targets)
    fake_images = G(Z)                  # Create a batch of fake images
    zeros_targets = torch.zeros(batch_size, 1).cuda()
    fake_preds = D1(D0(fake_images.detach()))
    fake_loss = criterionD1(fake_preds, zeros_targets)
    loss_D1 = real_loss + fake_loss     # Model D1's loss
    optimizer_D1.zero_grad()
    loss_D1.backward()
    optimizer_D1.step()
```

```
        return loss_D1.item()
# Cell 13: Train the generator to fool the discriminator----------------Cell 13
def train_G(Z, labels, con_c, optimizer_G):
    batch_size = Z.shape[0]
    fake_images = G(Z)                  # Create a batch of fake images
    preds0 = D0(fake_images)            # Try to fool the discriminator
    preds = D1(preds0)
    ones_targets = torch.ones(batch_size, 1).cuda()
    loss_fake = criterionD1(preds, ones_targets)

    logits, mu, var = Q(preds0)
    target = labels
    dis_loss = criterionQ_dis(logits, target)
    con_loss = criterionQ_con(con_c, mu, var)

    loss_G = loss_fake + dis_loss + con_loss*lambda_info
    optimizer_G.zero_grad()
    loss_G.backward()
    optimizer_G.step()
    return loss_G.item(), dis_loss.item(), con_loss.item()
# Cell 14: Definition of a fitting function----------------------------Cell 14
def fit(epochs):
    torch.cuda.empty_cache()
    # The DataFrame df is a recorder of the training history
    df = pd.DataFrame(np.empty([epochs, 4]), index = np.arange(epochs),
        columns=['Loss_G', 'Loss_D1', 'Dis_loss', 'Con_loss']
        )
    for i in trange(epochs):
        loss_G = 0.0; loss_D1 = 0.0; Dis_loss = 0.0; Con_loss = 0.0
        for real_images, _ in train_dataloader:
            inputs = real_images.cuda()
            batch_size = inputs.shape[0]
            Z, labels, con_c = noise4G_input(batch_size, z_dim, n_class)
            loss_d= train_D1(inputs, Z, optimizer_D1)
            loss_D1 += loss_d
            loss_g, dis_loss, con_loss = train_G(Z, labels, con_c, optimizer_G)
            loss_G += loss_g
            Dis_loss += dis_loss
            Con_loss += con_loss
        # Record losses & scores
        df.iloc[i, 0] = loss_G/n_batch
        df.iloc[i, 1] = loss_D1/n_batch
        df.iloc[i, 2] = Dis_loss/n_batch
        df.iloc[i, 3] = Con_loss/n_batch
        if i==0 or (i+1)%10==0:
            print(
            "Epoch={}, Ls_G={:.4f}, Ls_D={:.4f}, Dis_ls={:.4f}, Con_ls={:.4f}"
            .format(i+1,df.iloc[i,0],df.iloc[i,1],df.iloc[i,2],df.iloc[i,3]))
            fake_images = G(fixed_Z)
            #fake_images = G(z)
            show_imgs(fake_images.detach().cpu())
    return df
```

```
train_history = fit(n_epochs)    #epoch=50 dt=40min
# Cell 15: Show the training history in Graph--------------------------Cell 15
df= train_history
fig, ax = plt.subplots(1,2, figsize=(8,4), sharex=True)
df.plot(ax=ax[0], y=[0,1], style=['r-', 'b-'])
df.plot(ax=ax[1], y=[2,3], style=['r:', 'b:'])
for i in range(2):
    ax[i].set_xlabel('epoch')
    ax[i].grid(which='major', axis='both', color='g', linestyle=':')
ax[0].set(ylim=[0,3], ylabel='Loss')
ax[0].axhline(y=2*np.log(2), color='k', linestyle='--') #Theory D loss Value
ax[0].axhline(y=np.log(2), color='k', linestyle='--')   #Theory G loss Value
plt.show()
#-----------------------------------------------------------------------


# Cell 16: Using latent code to tune fake images----------------------Cell 16
G.eval()
c = [0,1,2,3,4,5,6,7,9,9]
digitals = np.zeros(10, dtype=np.int32)
for i, ci in enumerate(c):
    digitals[ci] = i
Z = noise4G_input()[0]
Z[:,z_dim:(z_dim+10)]=0
for i in range(10):
    Z[10*i:(10*i+10), digitals[i]+z_dim, :, :] = 1
fake_images = G(Z)
show_imgs(fake_images.detach().cpu())
# Cell 17: Using the last style variable to tune fake images-------------Cell 17
Z1 = torch.clone(Z)
Z1[:,-1]= 1# hue
fake_images = G(Z1)
show_imgs(fake_images.detach().cpu())
# Cell 18: Using the first style variable to tune fake images------------Cell 17
Z2 = torch.clone(Z)
Z2[:,-2]= 3   #light direction
fake_images = G(Z2)
show_imgs(fake_images.detach().cpu())
#-------------------------------The End--------------------------------
```

6.4 Implementation of infoGAN to the rock paper scissors dataset

Project 6.4.1 is not easy. All those hyperparameters in Cell 01 were found by trying in a few days. Using a laptop with a few gigabytes of GPU memory (6 GB) to the dataset with bigger image size (128×128), I had to choose a small batch size (36). The incompressible noise dimensions (z_dim), the initial learning rate (lr), and the ratio (k) of lr_G to lr_D1 are all critical. The RMSprop optimizer is better than the Adam optimizer for this project. If model D in section 3.3.2 was modified for model D0 and Model D1 in this project, fake images would have broken fingers and swollen fingers. With the powerful residual neural network (ResNet9) in section 2.3, it is possible to generate fake images with good enough quality shown in figure 6.6(B).

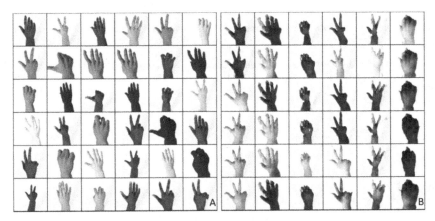

Figure 6.6. (A) Real images are the outputs of Cell 04. (B) Fake images are the outputs of Cell 14, and each column is a class (model training time: 9 min). The real images were reproduced with permission from Laurence Moroney, the author of the rock paper scissors dataset.

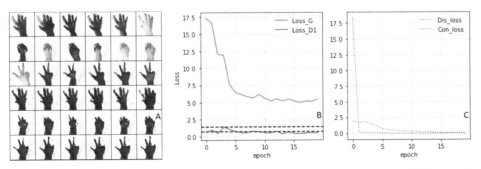

Figure 6.7. (A) Fake images generated by tuning the latent label code and the style variable. (B) Curves of loss functions for model G and D1. (C) Loss function curves for model Q.

We know that there are three classes in the dataset, but the hyperparameter (n_class) for the number of classes was intentionally set to be six. In figure 6.6(B), images in each column belong to a class. The column sequence is [0,1,2,3,4,5]. Two columns in the figure are for label rock, three columns are for label scissors, and one column is for label paper (open hand). With codes in Cell 16, fake images in column 1, 2, and 0 of figure 6.6(B) were displayed in row 0, 1 and 2 of figure 6.7(A). Using infoGAN, we can generate the desired images by tuning the latent labels. The dark fake images on rows 3 to 5 in figure 6.7(A) are the same as those on rows 0, 1 and 2 respectively. However, the style variable of the last three rows was set to be equal to 30. The only style variable in the project could be used to tune the contrast of fake images.

```python
# Project 6.4.1 infoGAN for the Rock-Paper- Scissors Dataset----------Python v3.6
import torch; import torch.nn as nn; from torch.utils.data import DataLoader
import torch.optim.lr_scheduler as lr_scheduler; import matplotlib.pyplot as plt
import torchvision.transforms as T; from torchvision.utils import make_grid
from torchvision.datasets import ImageFolder; from tqdm import trange
import numpy as np; import pandas as pd
n_epochs = 20        #30
batch_size=36
z_dim = 57   #100, 11, no 2, 123ok,
n_class = 6
n_styles = 1
Z_dim = z_dim + n_class + n_styles
lr = 1e-4
k = 30        # k=32 1e-4 ok,
lambda_info = 0.1
img_channels = 3
img_size = 128
# Cell 02: Import Rock Paper Scissors dataset--------------------------Cell 02
train_dataset = ImageFolder('./OCR/data/RockPaperScissors/train',
        transform=T.Compose([T.Resize(img_size),
                             T.ToTensor(),
                             T.Normalize([0.5,0.5,0.5], [0.5,0.5,0.5])]))
n_samples = len(train_dataset) # n_samples=2520
# Cell 03: DataLoader --------------------------------------------------Cell 03
train_dataloader = DataLoader(train_dataset, batch_size=batch_size,
                              shuffle=True, num_workers=4, pin_memory=True)
n_batch = len(train_dataloader) #n_batch=79
for imgs, labels in train_dataloader:
    print('imgs.shape=', imgs.shape)
    print('labels=', '\n', labels.view(-1, 6))
    break
# Cell 04: Show a batch of images in the train_dataloader--------------Cell 04
def denorm(img_tensors): # Shift image pixel values to [0,1]
    return img_tensors * 0.5 + 0.5
def show_imgs(images):
    fig, ax = plt.subplots(figsize=(16,10))
    inputs = make_grid(denorm(images), nrow=6)
    #inputs = make_grid(images, nrow=16)
    ax.imshow(inputs.permute(1,2,0))
    ax.set(xticks=[], yticks=[])
    plt.show()
show_imgs(imgs)
#----------------------------------------------------------------------------
```

```
# Cell 05: Model parameters initialization -----------------------------Cell 05
def weights_init(m):
    if(type(m) == nn.ConvTranspose2d or type(m) == nn.Conv2d):
        nn.init.normal_(m.weight.data, 0.0, 0.02)
    elif(type(m) == nn.BatchNorm2d):
        nn.init.normal_(m.weight.data, 1.0, 0.02)
        nn.init.constant_(m.bias.data, 0)
# Cell 07: The 1st part of discrinimator--------------ResNet9----------Cell 07
def basic(in_channels, out_channels):
    return nn.Sequential(
        nn.Conv2d(in_channels, out_channels,
                kernel_size=3, padding=1, bias=False),
        nn.BatchNorm2d(out_channels),
        nn.ReLU(inplace=True)
        )
class Rs_Block(nn.Module):
    def __init__(self, in_channels):
        super().__init__()
        self.resnet = nn.Sequential(
                basic(in_channels, in_channels),
                basic(in_channels, in_channels)
                )
    def forward(self, x):
        return x + self.resnet(x)
class ResNet9(nn.Module):
    def __init__(self, in_channels=3, num_classes=10):
        super().__init__()
        self.net =  nn.Sequential(
                basic(in_channels, 64),
                nn.MaxPool2d(2),                     #64x64^2
                basic(64, 128), nn.MaxPool2d(2),     #128x32^2
                Rs_Block(128), nn.MaxPool2d(2),      #128x16^2
                basic(128, 256), nn.MaxPool2d(2),    #256x8^2
                basic(256, 512), nn.MaxPool2d(2),    #512x4^2
                Rs_Block(512)                        #512x4^2
                )
    def forward(self, x):        #x.shape=batch_size x 3 x 128^2
        output  = self.net(x)    #output.shape = batch_size x 512 x 4^2
        return output
D0 = ResNet9().cuda()
D0.apply(weights_init)

# Cell 08: The rest of the Discriminator class--------------------------Cell 08
class Discriminator1(nn.Module):
    def __init__(self):
        super().__init__()
        self.net = nn.Sequential(
            nn.Conv2d(512, 1, 4),
            nn.Flatten(),
            nn.Sigmoid()
            ) #output.shape = batch_size x 1
    def forward(self, x):            # x is the output of model D0
```

```
            output = self.net(x)          # x.shape = batch_size x 512 x 4^2
            return output             #output.shape = batch_size x 1
D1 = Discriminator1().cuda()
D1.apply(weights_init)
# Cell 09: Auxillary class----------------------------------------------Cell 09
class Auxillary(nn.Module):
    def __init__(self):
        super().__init__()
        self.net = nn.Sequential(
            nn.Conv2d(512, 256, 4, bias=False),
            nn.BatchNorm2d(256),
            nn.LeakyReLU(0.1, inplace=True)
        )
        self.conv_disc = nn.Conv2d(256, n_class, 1)
        self.conv_mu = nn.Conv2d(256, n_styles, 1)
        self.conv_var = nn.Conv2d(256, n_styles, 1)
    def forward(self, x):   # x is the output of model D0
        y = self.net(x)       # y.shape = batch_size x 256 x 1^2
        disc_logits = self.conv_disc(y).squeeze()   # batch_size x n_class
        mu = self.conv_mu(y).squeeze()              # batch_size x n_styles
        var = torch.exp(self.conv_var(y).squeeze()) # batch_size x n_styles
        return disc_logits, mu, var
Q = Auxillary().cuda()
Q.apply(weights_init)

# Cell 09: Generator Class----------------------------------------------Cell 07
def basic_G(in_channels):
    return nn.Sequential(
        nn.ConvTranspose2d(in_channels, int(in_channels/2), 4, 2, 1, bias=False),
            nn.BatchNorm2d(int(in_channels/2)),
            nn.ReLU(True))
class Generator(nn.Module):
    def __init__(self):
        super().__init__()
        self.net = nn.Sequential(
                    nn.ConvTranspose2d(Z_dim, 512, 4, 1, 0, bias=False),
                    nn.BatchNorm2d(512),
                    nn.ReLU(True),
                    # layer 01 output.shape=batch_size x 512 x 4^2
                    basic_G(512),
                    # Layer 01 output.shape = batch_size x 256 x 8^2
                    basic_G(256),
                    # Layer 02 output.shape = batch_size x 128 x 16^2
                    basic_G(128),
                    # Layer 03 output.shape = batch_size x 64 x 32^2
                    basic_G(64),
                    # Layer 04 output.shape = batch_size x 32 x 64^2
                    nn.ConvTranspose2d(32, img_channels, 4, 2, 1),
                    nn.Tanh()
            )       # Layer 05 output.shape = batch_size x 3x 128^2
    def forward(self, Z):
        output = self.net(Z)              #Z.shape = batch_size x Z_dim x 1^2
```

```
return output            # output.shape = batch_size x 3 x 128^2
G = Generator().cuda()
G.apply(weights_init)
# Cell 10: Definitions of optimizers, criterion, learning rate scheduler
criterionD1 = nn.BCELoss()              # D Loss for real and fake images.
criterionQ_dis = nn.CrossEntropyLoss()  # for latent labels code and logits
criterionQ_con = nn.GaussianNLLLoss()   # Loss function for model Q's mu&var
optimizer_D1 = torch.optim.RMSprop([{'params': D0.parameters()},
                                    {'params': D1.parameters()}], lr=lr)
optimizer_G = torch.optim.RMSprop([{'params': G.parameters()},
                                   {'params': Q.parameters()}], lr=k*lr)
# Cell 11: Noise function for the generator ---------------------Cell 11
def noise4G_input(m=batch_size, z_noise=z_dim, n=n_class):
    noise = torch.randn(m, z_noise).cuda() # for incompressible noise z
    # Create categorical latent code
    labels = torch.cat((torch.arange(n).repeat(m//n),
                        torch.arange(m%n)), dim=0).cuda()
    dis_c = torch.nn.functional.one_hot(labels, n)
    con_c = torch.Tensor(m, n_styles).uniform_(-1.0, 1.0).cuda()
    Z = torch.cat([noise, dis_c, con_c], dim=1).view(-1, Z_dim, 1, 1)
    return Z, labels, con_c
fixed_Z= noise4G_input()[0].cuda()
# Cell 12: Discriminator training function --------------------------Cell 12
def train_D1(inputs, Z, optimizer_D1):
    batch_size = inputs.shape[0]        # the input is a batch of real images
    real_preds = D1(D0(inputs))
    ones_targets = torch.ones(batch_size, 1).cuda()
    real_loss = criterionD1(real_preds, ones_targets)
    fake_images = G(Z)                  # Create a batch of fake images
    zeros_targets = torch.zeros(batch_size, 1).cuda()
    fake_preds = D1(D0(fake_images.detach()))
    fake_loss = criterionD1(fake_preds, zeros_targets)
    loss_D1 = real_loss + fake_loss     # Model D1's loss
    optimizer_D1.zero_grad()
    loss_D1.backward()
    optimizer_D1.step()
    return loss_D1.item()
# Cell 13: Train the generator to fool the discriminator----------------Cell 13
def train_G(Z, labels, con_c, optimizer_G):
    batch_size = Z.shape[0]
    fake_images = G(Z)                  # Create a batch of fake images
    preds0 = D0(fake_images)            # Try to fool the discriminator
    preds = D1(preds0)
    ones_targets = torch.ones(batch_size, 1).cuda()
    loss_fake = criterionD1(preds, ones_targets)

    logits, mu, var = Q(preds0)
    target = labels
    dis_loss = criterionQ_dis(logits, target)
    con_loss = criterionQ_con(con_c, mu, var)

    loss_G = loss_fake + dis_loss + con_loss*lambda_info
```

```
        optimizer_G.zero_grad()
        loss_G.backward()
        optimizer_G.step()
        return loss_G.item(), dis_loss.item(), con_loss.item()
# Cell 14: Definition of a fitting function----------------------------Cell 14
def fit(epochs):
    torch.cuda.empty_cache()
    # The DataFrame df is a recorder of the training history
    df = pd.DataFrame(np.empty([epochs, 4]), index = np.arange(epochs),
        columns=['Loss_G', 'Loss_D1', 'Dis_loss', 'Con_loss']
        )
    for i in trange(epochs):
        loss_G = 0.0; loss_D1 = 0.0; Dis_loss = 0.0; Con_loss = 0.0
        for real_images, _ in train_dataloader:
            inputs = real_images.cuda()
            batch_size = inputs.shape[0]
            Z, labels, con_c = noise4G_input(batch_size, z_dim, n_class)
            loss_d= train_D1(inputs, Z, optimizer_D1)
            loss_D1 += loss_d
            loss_g, dis_loss, con_loss = train_G(Z, labels, con_c, optimizer_G)
            loss_G += loss_g
            Dis_loss += dis_loss
            Con_loss += con_loss
        # Record losses & scores
        df.iloc[i, 0] = loss_G/n_batch
        df.iloc[i, 1] = loss_D1/n_batch
        df.iloc[i, 2] = Dis_loss/n_batch
        df.iloc[i, 3] = Con_loss/n_batch
        if i==0 or (i+1)%5==0:
            print(
            "Epoch={}, Ls_G={:.4f}, Ls_D={:.4f}, Dis_ls={:.4f}, Con_ls={:.4f}"
            .format(i+1,df.iloc[i,0],df.iloc[i,1],df.iloc[i,2],df.iloc[i,3]))
            fake_images = G(fixed_Z)
            #fake_images = G(z)
            show_imgs(fake_images.detach().cpu())
    return df
train_history = fit(n_epochs)
# Cell 15: Show the training history in Graph----------------------------Cell 15
history= train_history
fig, ax = plt.subplots(1,2, figsize=(8,4), sharex=True)
history.plot(ax=ax[0], y=[0,1], style=['r-', 'b-'])
history.plot(ax=ax[1], y=[2,3], style=['r:', 'b:'])
for i in range(2):
    ax[i].set_xlabel('epoch')
    ax[i].grid(which='major', axis='both', color='g', linestyle=':')
ax[0].set( ylabel='Loss')
ax[0].axhline(y=2*np.log(2), color='k', linestyle='--') #Theory D loss Value
ax[0].axhline(y=np.log(2), color='k', linestyle='--')   #Theory G loss Value
plt.show()
# Cell 16: Using latent code to tune fake images-------------------------Cell 16
G.eval()
c = [1,2,0]
```

```
Z = fixed_Z
Z[:,z_dim:(z_dim+n_class)]=0    # reset for c1=0, c2=0, c3=0
Z[0:6,z_dim+c[0],:]= 1          # paper
Z[6:12,z_dim+c[1],:]=1          # rock
Z[12:18,z_dim+c[2],:]=1          # scissors
Z[18:24,z_dim+c[0],:]= 1        # paper
Z[24:30,z_dim+c[1],:]=1          # rock
Z[30:36,z_dim+c[2],:]=1            # scissors
Z[18:36,-1,:,:]=-20             # style
fake_images = G(Z)
show_imgs(fake_images.detach().cpu())
#----------------------------The End----------------------------------------
```

Reference

Chen X, Duan Y, Houthooft R, Schulman J, Sutskever I and Abbeel P 2016 Infogan: interpretable representation learning by information maximizing generative adversarial nets *Adv. Neural Inform. Process. Syst* **29** 2172–80

IOP Publishing

Mastering Computer Vision with PyTorch and Machine Learning

Caide Xiao

Chapter 7

Object detection by YOLOv1/YOLOv3 models

This is the hardest chapter in the book. YOLO is the most powerful computer vision technique for object detection, object counting, object tracking and image segmentation, etc. It will be helpful for you to understand models of later YOLO versions by YOLOv1 codes which are written from the ground up in this chapter with many help functions. You can skip YOLOv1 if it is too hard for you, because the latest YOLOv8 models are easy to use without knowing YOLOv1. Two Python functions for YOLOv3 in section 7.5 are used in the rest of the book to display images or video frames processed by other computer vision models just by changing the model's name in the two functions.

Most of our information comes to us from our eyes, and most of our actions/ behaviors are responses to what we see. With only a glance at an image, we instantly know the categories, locations and relationships of objects on the image. We are on the way to having our computers with artificial intelligence to do the same thing. In chapter 2, ResNet models were used to tell us what an object was on a photo. This kind of computer vision work is image classification: to identify the category of an object on an image. But the intelligence of those neural networks is only at the level of human babies. In practical applications of computer vision, such as the applications of auto-driving software, we not only need to identify multiple objects on each photographic frame, but also need to know where those objects are on the frame using bounding boxes. This kind of computer vision work is object detection: the combination of object classification and object location. The outputs for an object detection project provide spatial information about objects using bounding boxes. From that information, we will know what the coordinates of the top-left corner and the lower-right corner of each bounding box are, or the center coordinates plus width and height of each bounding box. We also will know what object is in each bounding box and what the probability is of that object in the bound box.

With neural networks for image classification, object detection should be a very easy job for us. Suppose the image resolution in an image dataset or a video camera is 640 × 480, we could use a 64 × 48 window to slide across an image from left to right and top to bottom, so the object detection job for the image is separated into 100 image classification jobs on these 10 × 10 small areas of the image. The location information of any area with an object is obtained from the location of the sliding window. But this simple algorithm has a number of issues to overcome. The first one is how to choose the size of the small window so that there is only one object within it. Different objects have different sizes. Even a same object has different sizes on an image depending on the distance between the object and the camera taking the image. The second issue is the height/width ratio of the window. Some objects, e.g. trees are taller and some objects, e.g. buses are wider. To consider these issues, we have to use multiple sliding windows with different sizes and different ratios. The computation job of the simple algorithm is too heavy to handle with contemporary computer hardware for real-time object detection. For example, a car driven by auto-driving software needs eight cameras to get a 3D view around the car, and each camera takes 24 images per second. Even if the computer in the car could finish object detection in one second for those 24 × 8 images, the car will have moved 10 meters at a speed of 36 km h^{-1} (the speed limit within a school zone). To avoid car accidents, we need the car's computer to do object detection calculations in a few milliseconds.

In 2014, Ross Girshick and his colleagues in UC Berkeley proposed a region-based convolutional network (R-CNN) algorithm (Girshick *et al* 2014) for object detection. It is a two-stage detection algorithm: the first stage is used to find sub-regions on an image with objects, the second stage is then used with neural networks to classify each object in a sub-region that might contain objects. Computing time is saved by handling only those regions with probabilities of containing objects. Based on this algorithm, Fast R-CNN (Girshick 2015) in 2015, Faster R-CNN (Ren *et al* 2015) in 2016 were proposed to improve object detection speed and accuracy. Although Faster R-CNN's detection accuracy is higher, it is still not quick enough for real-time object detection. Then in 2016, we had algorithms of one-stage object detection: Single-Shot Detector (SSD) (Liu *et al* 2016) and You Only Look Once (YOLO) (Redmon *et al* 2016). Using an image as an input, a model with either of the two algorithms uses a convolutional neural network to find objects on images. They are fast enough for real-time object detection with good enough accuracies. After Redmon *et al* introduced the first YOLO version, we then had YOLOv2, YOLOv3, YOLOv4, YOLOv5, YOLOv6, YOLOv7, YOLOv8 and YOLOv9.

7.1 Bounding boxes of Pascal VOC database for YOLOv1

To understand YOLOv1, we need to know the data structure of Pascal VOC 2012 database (Everingham *et al* 2012). Images in the database were selected from Flickr, an image source contributed by many individuals with different licenses. The database can be used for object classification, detection, and segmentation. The images and labels can be downloaded from Kaggle. After setting up a Kaggle account from my Google account, I downloaded a 2 GB compressed file named 'VOCtrainval_11-May-2012.tar', and then unzipped the file onto my laptop. The uncompressed files in five sub-folders occupied more than 5.6 GB in my laptop's hard driver. We only need to use two sub-folders for object detection. One sub-folder is named *JPEGImages*, and the other sub-folder is named *Annotations*. In the first sub-folder, there are 17 125 images in 20 classes. In the second sub-folder, there are 17 125 xml files containing information about bounding boxes for each image. The prefix of each JPEG image file name is the same as those for the XML file labeling the image (XML is the abbreviation of extensible markup language). XML files are also used for storing, transmitting and reconstructing arbitrary data. They can be opened and edited with any web browser or any text editor, e.g. Notepad in MS Windows. The code below is the structure of a XML file opened in a web browser. From the data in the XML file, we know the image's shape is $600 \times 540 \times 3$. On the image, there are three objects: two people and a dog. The coordinates of two corners of each object are listed in the XML file. These coordinates are pixels relative to the top-left corner [0,0] of the image. To avoid copyright issues, many of the images used in chapters 7–12 are from my own camera.

```xml
<annotation>
    <folder>d:/VOC</folder>
    <filename>Fig7_1.jpg</filename>
    <size>
        <width>600</width>
        <height>540</height>
        <depth>3</depth>
    </size>
    <segmented>1</segmented>
    <object>
        <name>person</name>
        <pose>Right</pose>
        <truncated>0</truncated>
        <difficult>0</difficult>
        <bndbox>
            <xmin>76</xmin>
            <ymin>98</ymin>
            <xmax>160</xmax>
            <ymax>376</ymax>
        </bndbox>
    </object>
    <object>
        <name>dog</name>
        <pose>Left</pose>
        <truncated>0</truncated>
        <difficult>0</difficult>
        <bndbox>
            <xmin>170</xmin>
            <ymin>350</ymin>
            <xmax>332</xmax>
            <ymax>530</ymax>
        </bndbox>
    </object>
```

```
<object>
        <name>person</name>
        <pose>Left</pose>
        <truncated>0</truncated>
        <difficult>0</difficult>
        <bndbox>
                <xmin>390</xmin>
                <ymin>0</ymin>
                <xmax>600</xmax>
                <ymax>510</ymax>
        </bndbox>
</object>
</annotation>
```

To manipulate XML data in Python, we need to install a python module named *xmltodict* to use as a tool. A function defined in the following Utility 01 can be used to read XML files for information about bounding boxes for any Pascal VOC image. The output of the *xmltodict* module on line 03 of the cell is a list with more than one element, and each element is an OrderedDict if there is more than one object in an image. But when there is only one object in an image, the output of the module is just an OrderedDict. Codes on line 05–06 of the cell were used to pack the output into a list for any image with only one object. Without these codes, our program would give error message and stop its work occasionally. You can change the index variable from 8 to 8888 on line 01 in the App-Cell after Utility 02 to see the issue. Running these codes in the free Kaggle GPU platform, I found the output of the *xmltodict* module was a Python dictionary, so the condition on line 05 of Utility 01 was changed for both cases. Codes on line 04–05 in the App-Cell are used to replace codes on line 02–03 to display my own image files. Figure 7.1 showed my image with its three bounding boxes for two people and a dog. The object class name of each bounding box was printed at its center. A 7 × 7 grid was also printed over the image.

Figure 7.1. An image and its three bounding boxes with their VOC class labels printed at their centers respectively (the outputs of the following App-Cell). Information of the three bounding boxes came from the above XML file.

Different images have different resolutions in VOC dataset. The coordinates of the top-left corner and lower-right corner of each bounding box on an image are relative to the top-left corner [0, 0] of the image. Using codes on line 01-03 and deleting codes on line 04-05 in the App-Cell, you will see a VOC image (index = 54) with rider on a white horse.

```python
# Utility Functions for images and bounding boxes--------------------Python v3.9
import torch; import xmltodict    # -----------a Python module to read xml data
import glob; import numpy as np; from collections import OrderedDict; import cv2
import matplotlib.pyplot as plt; import matplotlib.patches as patches; import os
import albumentations as A; import pandas as pd; from PIL import Image
root = 'D:/ImageSets/VOC/VOCdevkit/VOC2012/'
img_dir = root + 'JPEGImages/'
mxl_dir = root + 'Annotations/'
img_files = sorted(glob.glob(os.path.join(img_dir, "*.*"))) # VOC img file list
xml_files = sorted(glob.glob(os.path.join(mxl_dir, "*.*"))) # VOC xml file list
classes = ['aeroplane', 'bicycle', 'bird', 'boat', 'bottle', 'bus', 'car', 'cat',
           'chair', 'cow', 'diningtable', 'dog', 'horse', 'motorbike',
           'person', 'pottedplant', 'sheep', 'sofa', 'train', 'tvmonitor']
C = len(classes)
def denorm(img_tensors): return img_tensors*0.5 + 0.5
# Utility 01: Read a xml file data for bounding boxes information --------------
def xml_bboxes(xml_file_path):
    f = open(xml_file_path)
    doc = xmltodict.parse(f.read())            #---------------------------line 03
    objects = doc['annotation']['object']
    if isinstance(objects, OrderedDict or dict): # ----------------------line 05
            tmp = []; tmp.append(objects); objects = tmp
    bbox_info = []
    for object in objects:
        bbox_info.append([                      #---------------------------line 09
            float(object['bndbox']['xmin']), float(object['bndbox']['ymin']),
            float(object['bndbox']['xmax']), float(object['bndbox']['ymax']),
            classes.index(object['name'])])
    return np.array(bbox_info) #[[xmin, ymin, xmax, ymax, class_id], [],...[]]
# Utility 02: Show an image with its bounding boxes---------------------------
def show_imgBboxes(image, bboxes_info):
    fig, ax = plt.subplots(figsize=(8, 6))
    ax.imshow(image)                 # ------------------------------show an image
    H, W, _ = image.shape
    for i, bbox in enumerate(bboxes_info):    # -----------draw bounding boxes
        x, y, X, Y = bbox[:4]                 # w=X-x,      h=Y-y
        class_label = classes[int(bbox[4])]   # class_id -> class name
        ax.add_patch(patches.Rectangle((x,y), (X-x), (Y-y),
            linestyle='-', linewidth=1.5, edgecolor='y', facecolor='none'))
        plt.text((x+X)/2, (y+Y)/2, class_label, color='r', fontsize=14)
    majorXticks = np.linspace(0, W, 8); majorYticks = np.linspace(0, H, 8)
    ax.set_xticks(majorXticks); ax.set_yticks(majorYticks)
    ax.grid(which='both', color='r', linestyle=':', alpha=0.9)
    plt.show()
# App-Cell: Applications of Utility 01-02 to display an image -----------------
#index = 54     #---------try any file index < 17,125 for an VOC image----line 01
#image = plt.imread(img_files[index])              #--------------------line 02
#bbox_info = xml_bboxes(xml_files[index])          #--------------------line 03
image = plt.imread('d:/Fig7_1.jpg')                #--------------------line 04
bbox_info = xml_bboxes('d:/Fig7_1.xml')            #--------------------line 05
print('Original image.shape =', image.shape)
print('Bounding box info: \n', bbox_info)
show_imgBboxes(image, bbox_info)
```

According to the YOLOv1 paper (Redmon *et al* 2016), grid cells in an array of 7 × 7 are used to encode bounding boxes on each image. In a Cartesian coordinate system, we usually use a pair of numbers (x, y) as coordinates of an object on a plane (2D space), and the positive direction of the y-axis is bottom-up. For NumPy arrays and torch tensors, we also use a pair of numbers (row_idx, column_idx) to locate a matrix element. Both the row index and the column index start from zero, but the positive direction of the row-axis is upside down. You can find the center of the woman (person) in figure 7.1 is in the grid cell (2, 1) or [2,1], and the dog's center is in the grid cell [5,2]. There are 20 classes in the VOC dataset. The names of those classes can be found by searching web sites. In a list above the Utility 01 Cell are names of the 20 classes. If you count one by one, you will find the index of the category of 'person' is 14. You can verify your counting by a Python code's output of *classes[14]*. Sometimes we know the name of an object, for example 'dog', and Python can find its index is equal to 11 by the code's output: *classes.index('dog')*.

7.2 Encode VOC images with bounding boxes for YOLOv1

Computers really do not know anything about image objects but only understand the digits '0' and '1'. After model training, it appears that a computer has the intelligence to tell us something about our images in a dataset, because we trained models in the computer using data in a special format with special loss functions. Neural networks are so powerful that they remember many details about images so that they can fool us by 'overfitting'. We have to do more work on image augmentations to avoid overfitting issues.

7.2.1 VOC image augmentations with bounding boxes

When the image shown in figure 7.1 is resized to 448 × 448 for YOLOv1 model training, the coordinates of those three bounding boxes also need to be transformed accordingly. In the YOLOv1 model training, the width and height of each bounding box in a transformed image is normalized by 448. The coordinates of the center of each bounding box [x_c, y_c] are normalized by 64. Since the value of x_c or y_c could be any integer from 0 to 448, the normalization to 64 should be a number whose value is in the range 0–7. An integer part of the number is used as a grid cell's row index or column index; the value of the remainder of the normalization is less than 64 pixels. The remainder is then normalized by 64 again as a center coordinate of the bounding box relative to the top-left corner of the grid cell. In this way, all four parameters of each bounding box are positive numbers with their values less than one. We do these extra works to reduce the possibility of explosions of loss function values.

To fight overfitting issues in model training, we have to do a random horizontal flip, a random vertical flip, a random rotation and more augmentations to each image. The bounding boxes of each image with augmentations must also have the same transformations, so that each bounding box would not lose its target. By the end of those augmentations, the left and right sides of each bounding box should be vertical, and the top and bottom sides of the bounding box should be horizontal even if the image was rotated. This work employs very tedious mathematics. We can use a Python module named 'albumentations' to do these complex jobs automatically with a function defined in the following Utility 03. The augmentation function uses any VOC image and its bounding boxes from Utility 01 as inputs. The outputs of the function are the transformed image and its transformed bounding boxes. The format option of the augmentation transforms on line 15 of Utility 03 could be 'pascal_voc', 'coco' or 'yolo' for different bounding box styles in different datasets. More augmentations could be added between line 01 to 15. Each augmentation would increase the model training time. Figure 7.2 shows a transformed image and it bounding boxes. Comparing this with figure 7.1, you will find that the original image is rotated and horizontally flipped.

```
# Utility 03: Albumentation function for an image and its bounding boxes--------
def imgBboxesTransforms(image, bbox_info):   # --------------------------line 01
    bboxes_voc = bbox_info[:,:4]    #bboxes coordinates of objects on an image
    class_idx=list(bbox_info[:,4])  # class indices of objects on an image
    class_labels = [classes[int(idx)] for idx in class_idx]  # class names
    transform = A.Compose([
        A.Resize(width=448, height=448),
        A.VerticalFlip(p=0.5),
        A.HorizontalFlip(p=0.5),
        A.Rotate(limit=90, p=0.95, border_mode=cv2.BORDER_CONSTANT),
        A.RGBShift(r_shift_limit=20, g_shift_limit=20, b_shift_limit=20),
        A.RandomBrightnessContrast(p=0.5),
        A.Normalize(mean=(0.5, 0.5, 0.5), std=(0.5, 0.5, 0.5)),
        A.PixelDropout(dropout_prob=0.01),
        A.ColorJitter(brightness=0.2, contrast=0.2, saturation=0.2, hue=0.2),
        ], bbox_params=A.BboxParams(format="pascal_voc",    #---------line 15
            min_area=25, min_visibility=0.1, label_fields=['class_labels']))
    transf_instance = transform(
            image=image, bboxes=bboxes_voc, class_labels=class_labels)
    transformed_image = transf_instance['image']
    transformed_bboxes = transf_instance['bboxes']
    transformed_class_labels = transf_instance['class_labels']
    transformed_class_idx = [[classes.index(label)]
                        for label in transformed_class_labels]
    transf_bboxes = [(list(t_bbox)) + transformed_class_idx[j]
                for j, t_bbox in enumerate(transformed_bboxes)]
    return transformed_image, transf_bboxes

# Application of Utility 01-03 to a transformed image with it bounding boxes----
transf_image, transf_bboxes = imgBboxesTransforms(image, bbox_info)
df = pd.DataFrame(transf_bboxes, columns = [            # for print out bboxes
        'x_min','y_min', 'x_max','y_max', 'class_idx'])
pd.options.display.float_format = '{:,.0f}'.format; print(df)
if transf_image.min() < 0: transf_image = denorm(transf_image)
show_imgBboxes(transf_image, transf_bboxes)
#------------------------------------------------------------------------------
```

Figure 7.2. Augmentations of an image with its bounding boxes by codes in Utility 03. The coordinates of the three bounding boxes are [0, 0, 206, 404, 14], [307, 107, 418, 346, 14] and [154, 284, 305, 448, 11] respectively. The centers of the three objects are in grid cell [3, 1], [3, 5] and [5, 3] respectively.

7.2.2 Encoding bounding boxes to grid cells for YOLOv1 model training

Figure 7.2 will be used as an example for encoding bounding boxes to grid cells on a transformed image by a function defined in the following Utility 04. The input of the function is the second output of Utility 03. First, a tensor named 'label_matrix' is defined with a shape [S, S, C + 5B] for any transformed VOC image with a resolution 448×448, where S, C and B are equal to 7, 20 and 2 respectively. The value of each element in the label_matrix tensor is initialized to be equal to zero. We can treat the label_matrix tensor as a 3D object with S × S squares on a plane and behind each square there are 30 cubes. Cubes from 0 to 19 of a grid cell are used to hot-code the class label of an object whose center is in the grid cell. For example, we find the center of the boy (person) in figure 7.2 is in grid cell [3, 1]. Since the index for person in the VOC classes is 14, we then set: label_matrix[3, 1, 14] = 1 by using a code on line 22 of Utility 04. Also, the dog class's index in the VOC classes is 11 and the dog is in grid cell [5, 3], so we set the value of a cube: label_matrix [5, 3, 11] = 1. Cube 20 of each grid cell in the label_matrix is used to record the probability of an object in the cell. For our training dataset, the probability is set to be one, so we have label_matrix[3, 1, 20] = 1 and label_matrix[5, 3, 20] = 1.

Any grid cell's cubes from 21 to 22 are used to record the center coordinates of an object relative to the top-left corner of the grid cell from which we can find the center of the object. The same grid cell's cubes from 23 to 24 are used to store the width and height of the bounding box relative to the transformed image. By reading the second outputs of Utility 03 with codes starting from line 04 in Utility 04, we get the boy's bounding box information [0, 0, 206, 404, 14]. They are x_min, y_min, x_max, y_max and class_id respectively. The center coordinates (X_c, Y_c), the width (W) and height (H) of the bounding box relative to the transformed images are easy to obtain with the following formulae in which the lower-case variables are parameters relative to the grid cell. The column index of the grid cell is the integer part of $(X_c/64)$, and the remainder of the division normalized by 64 again is x_c. The row index and column index of the grid cell with the boy's center are 3 and 1 respectively. The coordinates of the boy's center relative to the top-left corner of the grid cell are [0.61, 0.16]. Now we can fill the cubes from 21 to 24 for grid cell [3, 1] with $[x_c, y_c, w, h]$. The value of each of the last five cubes of any grid cell is zero for any image in a training dataset. The encoding results of grid cell [3, 1] is a list: label_matrix [3, 1, :] = [0, 0, 0, 0, 0, 0, 0, 0, 0, 0, 0, 0, 0, 0, 1, 0, 0, 0, 0, 0, 1.0, 0.61, 0.16, 0.46, 0.90, 0, 0, 0, 0, 0]. The dog's bounding box information in the same image is [154, 284, 305, 448, 11]. You can use this to encode the grid cells [5, 3] for the dog. The function defined in Utility 04 does the above job automatically. A NumPy function *np.where( )* can be used to find any grid cell with an object on an image. The function outputs two 1D arrays for those grid cells' row indices and column indices. Codes from line 16 to line 22 are used to ensure that one grid cell on a VOC image only encodes one object. The maximum objects detected by a YOLOv1 model on any image is 49. This is a limit of YOLOv1 model.

$$X_c = \frac{1}{2}(x_{max} + x_{min}) \qquad X_c = \frac{1}{2}(206 + 0) = 103 \qquad x_c = (X_c\%64)\frac{1}{64} = 0.61$$

$$Y_c = \frac{1}{2}(y_{max} + y_{min}), \qquad Y_c = \frac{1}{2}(404 + 0) = 202 \qquad y_c = (Y_c\%64)\frac{1}{64} = 0.16$$

$$W = x_{max} - x_{min} = 206 \qquad w = \frac{W}{448} = 0.46 \qquad column_{idx} = int(\frac{X_c}{64}) = 1$$

$$H = y_{max} - y_{min} = 404 \qquad h = \frac{H}{448} = 0.90 \qquad row_{idx} = int(\frac{Y_c}{64}) = 3$$

```
# Utility 04: A function to encode bounding box for yolov1 model training-------
def encoded_bboxes(bboxes_info):                      #---------------------line 01
    S=7; B=2; C=len(classes); cell_size=64    # cell_size = 448/S--------line 02
    label_matrix = torch.zeros((S, S, (C+5*B))) #----------------------line 03
    for object in bboxes_info:
        x_min, y_min, x_max, y_max, class_idx = object        #----------line 05
        #center of the bbox relative to (0,0) a transformed image
        Xc = (x_min + x_max)/2; W = x_max - x_min
        Yc = (y_min + y_max)/2; H = y_max - y_min
        w = W/448; h = H/448          # normalize W and H by 448
        #coordinates of the bbox center in the cell[grid_row, grid_column]
        grid_column, x_cell = divmod(Xc, cell_size) #x_cell's unit in pixel
        grid_row, y_cell = divmod(Yc, cell_size)
        grid_row, grid_column = [int(grid_row), int(grid_column)]
        x_c = x_cell/cell_size # Normalize the bbox's coordinates by 64
        y_c = y_cell/cell_size
        if label_matrix[grid_row, grid_column, C] == 0:       #----------line 16
            label_matrix[grid_row, grid_column, C] = 1  # 1 object per cell
            bbox_coordinates = torch.tensor(           # Box coordinates
                [round(x_c,2), round(y_c,2), round(w,2), round(h,2)])
            label_matrix[grid_row, grid_column, (C+1):(C+5)] = bbox_coordinates
            # Set one hot encoding for the class_label
            label_matrix[grid_row, grid_column, class_idx] = 1  #------line 22
    return label_matrix


# Applications of Utility 01-04 to encode bounding boxes of a transformed image
label_matrix=encoded_bboxes(transf_bboxes)  #---transf_bboxes from  Utility 03
row_idx, column_idx = np.where(label_matrix[:,:, C]) #grid cells with objects
print('Objects in grid cells with row_idx and column_idx:', row_idx, column_idx)
print(f'The object in grid cell [{row_idx[0]},{column_idx[0]}] is encoded as:\n'
    , label_matrix[row_idx[0],column_idx[0],:])
#------------------------------------------------------------------------------
```

7.2.3 Chess pieces dataset from Roboflow

The Pascal VOC 2012 database is not a dataset. With the above auxiliary functions defined in Utility 01–04, it is possible for us to pack those images and their labels into a dataset for YOLOv1 model training. However, the Pascal VOC 2012 dataset is too big for my laptop to handle. According to Redmon *et al* 2016, the YOLOv1 model's first 20 convolutional layers were trained with ImageNet dataset in one week. Four more convolutional layers and two fully connected layers were then added, and the YOLOv1 model was trained by images from PASCAL VOC 2007 and 2012 with more time. To demonstrate YOLOv1 model training, I have to use a small dataset: Chess Pieces Dataset. In February 2021, Roboflow kindly released this dataset free on a public license. Inside a 17 MB zip file, there are 693 images in 13 classes for YOLOv7 model training. Bounding box information about chess piece images is in the text files, not in the XML files. From those files, you can see each object's class index, object center coordinates, its bounding box width and height normalized by 416. Here is an example of a label text file for the first test image about a white bishop chess piece: 7 0.5120192307692307 0.0829326923076923 0.04567307692307692 0.13341346153846154. All the image files and label files are in three sub-folders: train, test and valid in a folder named Chess. Codes in Utility 05 could be used to convert text files in each of the three sub-folders into XML files for YOLOv1 model training. Since the original file names are too long to remember, the file names were changed to integers with three digitals by a code on line 20 in the following Utility 05. The XML file converted from a text file about the white bishop is listed below. The XML file's structure is simpler than the one in the VOC dataset. Under the <object> item, there is no <bndbox> item. When we pack these files for a dataset, we have to delete ['bndbox'] on line 10 to 11 in Utility 01 for the chess dataset. Please pay attention to an integer in *str(idx + I)* on line 20. Using Utility 05, all 693 samples in the train, valid and test sub-folders are converted and moved into a folder named chess4yolov1 with two sub-folders: *Annotations* and *JPEGimages*. File names of converted samples have three digitals from 000 to 692. If the root folder on line 03 of Utility 05 is set for the sub-folder train, the integer I in *str(idx + I)* on line 20 is equal to 0; for the sub-folder valid, the integer I is equal to 606; and for the sub-folder test, the integer I is equal to 664. A sample with name 688 was deleted because 688.xml is empty. With an object empty sample in the dataset, my codes had issues during model training. Codes in Utility 05 can run in VS Code with Python 3.9, not Python 3.6 which does not support writing a pandas DataFrame to an XML file.

```
<annotation>
    <object>
        <name>white-bishop</name>
        <xmin>203.49999999999997</xmin>
        <ymin>6.750000000000007</ymin>
        <xmax>222.49999999999997</xmax>
        <ymax>62.24999999999999</ymax>
    </object>
</annotation>
```

```
# Utility 05: Convert text files to xml files: works in Python 3.9.5 not in 3.6-
import numpy as np; import pandas as pd; from PIL import Image
import os; import glob
root = 'D:/ImageSets/Chess/Chess/test/'  #dataset's folder: train, test, valid
img_dir = root + 'images/'
txt_dir = root + 'labels/'
xml_dir = root + 'xml/' #creat a xml folder under root before running the codes
def txt_xml(txt_files):
    for idx, txt_file in enumerate(txt_files):
        df = pd.read_csv(txt_file, sep=' ',  #read a text file into a dadaframe
                names= ['name', 'xc', 'yc', 'w', 'h'])
        DF = pd.DataFrame(np.empty((len(df), 5)), #set DF for output a xml file
                columns=['name', 'xmin', 'ymin', 'xmax', 'ymax'])
        df.iloc[:,1:] = np.array(416*df.iloc[:,1:]) #all bboxes on an image
        DF.iloc[:,0] = [classes[int(label)] for label in list(df.iloc[:,0])]
        xc=df.iloc[:,1]; yc=df.iloc[:,2]; w=df.iloc[:,3]; h=df.iloc[:,4]
        DF.iloc[:,1] = xc-w/2; DF.iloc[:,2]=yc-h/2   # xmin and ymin of bboxes
        DF.iloc[:,3] = xc+w/2; DF.iloc[:,4] = yc+h/2 # xmax and ymax of bboxes
        my_xml = DF.to_xml(row_name = 'object',      # DF -> xml data structure
                    index = False, root_name='annotation')
        file_prefix = str(idx+664).zfill(3)   # --------------------- line 20
        with open(xml_dir+file_prefix+'.xml', 'w') as file:
            file.write(my_xml)  · # write xml data to a xml file-------line 22
        img_file = img_files[idx]
        my_image = Image.open(img_file) #open & rename an image file---line 24
        my_image = my_image.save(xml_dir+file_prefix+'.jpg')
    return None
classes = ['bishop', 'black-bishop', 'black-king', 'black-knight', 'black-pawn',
           'black-queen', 'black-rook', 'white-bishop', 'white-king',
           'white-knight', 'white-pawn', 'white-queen', 'white-rook']
txt_files = sorted(glob.glob(os.path.join(txt_dir, "*.*")))
img_files = sorted(glob.glob(os.path.join(img_dir, "*.*")))
txt_xml(txt_files)
#-------------------------------------------------------------------------------
```

After running codes in Utility 05 for files in the three sub-folders: train, test and valid, image files were obtained and moved to the sub-folder *JPEGimages*, and all XML files were moved to the *Annotations* folder. Before packing these files into a dataset in the following project 7.1, all modules or tools necessary for the project are imported in Cell 01, in which hyperparameters are also set. For my 6 GB memory in a RTX 2060 GPU, the maximum batch size is eight. With Kaggle's free 16 GB GPU memory, the maximum batch size could be 128. Usually, training results with a small batch size are better. The last two lines of Cell 01 are for a list of XML files and a list of image files respectively. I have to list the Utility 01 after Cell 01, because the Chess dataset's XML file structure is different from VOC dataset's XML file structure. The Chess dataset constructed in Cell 02 is randomly split into three datasets, and from them we have a train dataloader, a valid dataloader and a test dataloader. Their sample sizes are 560, 80 and 52 respectively. Codes in Cell 04 are used to display some images in a dataloader. A function named 'grid2bboxes' defined in the Cell 03 extracts encoded grid cells' information of images for parameters of bounding boxes.

```python
# Project 7.1 Application of YOLOv1 for Chess Piece Dataset-----------Python v3.9
import xmltodict; import albumentations as A; import torch; import torch.nn as nn
from torch.utils.data import DataLoader, Dataset, random_split
import torch.optim.lr_scheduler as lr_scheduler
from torchvision import models; import torchvision.transforms as T
import torchvision.transforms.functional as TF
import numpy as np; import pandas as pd; from tqdm import trange
import os; import cv2; import glob; from PIL import Image
from collections import OrderedDict, Counter
import matplotlib.pyplot as plt; import matplotlib.patches as patches
batch_size = 8
lr = 4e-4
n_epochs =100
seed = 42; np.random.seed(seed); torch.manual_seed(seed)
epsilon = 1e-6          # for stability in numerical calcualtions
root = 'D:/ImageSets/Chess/chess4yolov1/'
img_dir = root + 'JPEGimages/'
xml_dir = root + 'Annotations/'
classes = ['bishop', 'black-bishop', 'black-king', 'black-knight', 'black-pawn',
           'black-queen', 'black-rook', 'white-bishop', 'white-king',
           'white-knight', 'white-pawn', 'white-queen', 'white-rook']
B=2; C=len(classes); S=7; cell_size=64  #parameters of grid cells
def denorm(img_tensors): return img_tensors*0.5 + 0.5
xml_files = sorted(glob.glob(os.path.join(xml_dir, "*.*"))) #xml file list
img_files = sorted(glob.glob(os.path.join(img_dir, "*.*"))) #img file list
# Utility 01: read a xml file data for bounding boxes information --------------
def xml_bboxes(xml_file_path):
    f = open(xml_file_path)
    doc = xmltodict.parse(f.read())          #-------------------------line 03
    objects = doc['annotation']['object']
    if isinstance(objects, dict or OrderedDict): # --------------------line 05
        tmp = []; tmp.append(objects); objects = tmp
    bbox_info = []
    for object in objects:
        bbox_info.append([
            float(object['xmin']), float(object['ymin']), #line10
            float(object['xmax']), float(object['ymax']), #line11
            classes.index(object['name'])])
    return np.array(bbox_info)
# Cell 02: Dataset and 3 Dataloaders-------------------------------------Cell 02
class ChessDataset(Dataset):
    def __init__(self, img_files, xml_files):
        self.xml_files = xml_files
        self.img_files = img_files
    def __len__(self):
        return len(self.xml_files)
    def __getitem__(self, index):
        xml_file = self.xml_files[index] #a single file from total samples
        img_file = self.img_files[index]
        my_image = np.array(Image.open(img_file))     #PIL image to numpy array
        my_bboxes = xml_bboxes(xml_file)              #----------Utility  01
        transf_img, trandf_bboxes = imgBboxesTransforms(
```

```
                              my_image, my_bboxes)    #----------Utility  03
            label_matrix = encoded_bboxes(trandf_bboxes)  #----------Utility  04
            return TF.to_tensor(transf_img), label_matrix
Chess = ChessDataset(img_files, xml_files)
# split the original dataset into 3 datasets
n_train = 560; n_valid=80; n_test=len(Chess)-n_train-n_valid
train_dataset, valid_dataset, test_dataset = random_split(
                    dataset=Chess, lengths=[n_train, n_valid, n_test],
                    generator=torch.Generator().manual_seed(0))
train_dataloader = DataLoader(train_dataset, batch_size, shuffle=True)
valid_dataloader = DataLoader(valid_dataset, batch_size, shuffle=True)
test_dataloader = DataLoader(test_dataset, batch_size, shuffle=True)
# Cell 03: A function to convert grid cells to bboxes of an encoded image-------
def grid2bboxes(target):                  #-------target.shape = 7 x 7 x 30
    grid_rows, grid_columns = np.where(target[:, :, C])
    n_bboxes = len(grid_rows)
    bboxes = np.zeros((n_bboxes, 6)).astype(np.float32())
    for j in range(n_bboxes):
        class_idx=np.where(target[grid_rows[j], grid_columns[j],0:C])[0].item()
        possibility = target[grid_rows[j], grid_columns[j], C]
        x, y, w, h = target[grid_rows[j], grid_columns[j], (C+1):(C+5)]
        W = w*448; H= h*448
        x_min = (grid_columns[j] + x)*64 - W/2
        y_min = (grid_rows[j] + y)*64 - H/2
        bboxes[j, :] = [class_idx, possibility, x_min, y_min, W, H]
    return bboxes
# Cell 04: Display images and bboxes in a batch of a dataloader--------Cell 04
def img_show(images, targets, n=batch_size):
    fig, ax = plt.subplots(1, n, figsize=(12,8))
    majorTicks = np.linspace(0, 448, 8)
    for i, img in enumerate(images[:n]):
        ax[i].imshow(img.cpu().numpy().transpose((1,2,0)))
        ax[i].set_xticks(majorTicks); ax[i].set_yticks(majorTicks)
        ax[i].grid(which='both', color='r', linestyle=':', alpha=0.8)
        bboxes = grid2bboxes(targets[i])
        for j, bbox in enumerate(bboxes):
            class_label = classes[int(bbox[0])]    # class name
            x_min, y_min, W, H = bbox[2:]
            ax[i].add_patch(patches.Rectangle(
                    (x_min, y_min), W, H, linestyle='-',
                    linewidth=1.5, edgecolor='y', facecolor='none'))
            ax[i].text(x_min+W/2, y_min+H/2, class_label, color='r')
    plt.show()
images, targets=next(iter(train_dataloader)) #-------------------- line 17
if images.min() < 0:                   #images.shape=8 x 3 x 448 x 448
    images=denorm(images)              #targets.shape=8 x 7x 7 x 23
img_show(images=images,targets=targets,n=2) # only 2/8 images are displayed
#-----------------------------------------------------------------------------
```

7.3 ResNet18 model, IOU and a loss function

7.3.1 Using ResNet18 to replace YOLOv1 model

There is no super power in the YOLOv1 model which is just a linear CNN model with 24 convolutional layers followed by two fully connected layers. In July 2022, we had YOLOv7 models (Wang *et al* 2022). In January 2023, Ultralytics released a more powerful YOLOv8 models. The simple YOLOv1 is still useful for us to understand the YOLO algorithm. The original YOLOv1 model did not use batch normalizations because batch normalization (Ioffe and Szegedy 2015) was invented a year later than YOLOv1. In Aladdin Persson's GitHub, the original YOLOv1 model was modified by adding a batch normalization after each convolutional operation. However, the modified YOLOv1 is still not powerful enough for the Pascal VOC dataset on my laptop, so a pre-trained ResNet18 (section 2.4) is used as a model for the Chess dataset. On the first line of Cell 05, the pre-trained ResNet18 model was imported from models in torchvision. Then the number of output variables of the last fully connected layer in the ResNet18 was changed from 1000 to 1127 (= $7 \times 7 \times 23$) for predicted values in 23 cubes of each 7×7 grid cells. I only used the pre-trained ResNet18 model in the first 100 eopochs of model training. At the end of the first 100 epochs of model training, I saved a trained model to a file named *Chess-Yolo-01.pth*, and moved the ''''' symbols on line 09 to the front of line 01. In this way, I could use the trained model for the next 100 epochs. The trained model file name should be changed by increasing the last digital of the previous file name. With Python v3.6, model training takes about 54 min for every 100 epochs by running codes in Cell 09. With Python v3.9, the model training time for the same codes is 37 min. In about 20 h within two days, the model training gave me good enough results (figure 7.3). It seems that the Adam optimizer is better than the SGD optimizer in the Chess project. During model training, the learning rate was changed by *ReduceLROnPlateau* scheduler. The mean average precision (mAP) is an important index of model training for object detection. If mAP is above 0.5, our

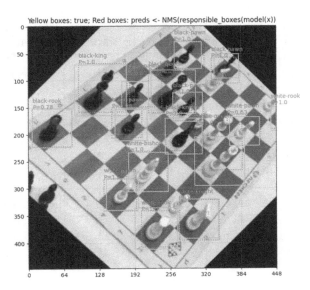

Figure 7.3. A test image with its true bounding boxes (yellow) and predicted bounding boxes (red) at the end of model training with 100×21 epochs. Final mAP for the train, validation and test dataloaders is 0.76, 0.62 and 0.66, respectively. Model training time is 37 min for every 100 epochs. The Chess Pieces Dataset is from Roboflow (2001) with a license CC BY 4.0.

model training is good enough; mAP around 0.7 is good; and mAP above 0.9 is excellent. For an excellent model training, the true and the predicted bounding boxes in figure 7.3 should be the same.

```
# Cell 05: Use the pre-trained ResNet18 to replace yolov1 model-----------Cell 05
  model = models.resnet18(pretrained=True)        #-------------line 01
model.eval()                                      #-------------line 02
num_ftrs = model.fc.in_features         #num_ftrs=512----------line 03
model.fc = nn.Linear(num_ftrs, S*S*(C+5*B)) # =7*7*23=1127 ---line 04
model = model.cuda()
'''
File_name = root + '/Chess-Yolo-20-new.pth'
saved_model = torch.load(File_name)
model= saved_model.eval()                 #----------------line 09'''
optimizer = torch.optim.Adam(model.parameters(), lr=lr)
scheduler = lr_scheduler.ReduceLROnPlateau(optimizer,   #-----line 12
            mode='min', factor=0.5, patience=10, verbose=False)
y_hat = model(images.cuda())              #-----------------line 15
print(y_hat.shape)  #------------------------- y_hat.shape=[8, 1127]
#-------------------------------------------------------------------------------
```

7.3.2 Intersection over union (IOU) and the loss function

The bounding boxes for each image are encoded by 7×7 grid cells. For the Chess dataset with 13 classes, there are $(13 + 5 \times 2)$ cubes for each grid cell. The last five cubes (from 18 to 22) of each grid cell in a model prediction are used for the bounding box of another predicted object. Each grid cell of the model's predictions could predict two bounding boxes. However, we only use one bounding box which had a higher IOU value with a true bounding box in the same grid cell for calculations of loss function values. We have to recap IOU for image classification in chapter 2.

Suppose we have two pieces of paper, and they have the same size: 10×10 cm^2. If the paper on top covers 1/4 the area of the other paper, the intersection area of the two pieces of paper is 25 cm^2. Then we can calculate the IOU of the two pieces of paper: IOU = 25/$(100 + 100 - 25) = 1/7$. In the case when they completely overlap each other, the IOU value is one. Computers do the job in a different way. Using the code on line 17 of Cell 04, we get a batch of transformed images and their bounding boxes encoded in grid cells for a batch of samples in a train dataloader. The batch of bounding boxes are our targets. Taking the batch of transformed images into the ResNet18 model on line 15 of Cell 05, we can obtain the model's output y_hat with a shape of N $\times$ 1127, where N is the batch size: 8. The y_hat and the targets are then taken into a loss class defined in Cell 06 (line 07) in section 7.3.3. From the codes on line 10, 12 and 14 of Cell 06, we have a batch of true bounding boxes, two batches of predicted bounding boxes. The following IOU function defined in *Utility_fn(1/5)* will use each bounding box's center coordinates (x_c, y_c), width (*w*) and height (*h*) to calculate IOU values according to the following formulae

$$x_{1\min} = x_{1c} - \frac{1}{2}w_1 \quad x_{2\min} = x_{2c} - \frac{1}{2}w_2$$

$$y_{1\min} = y_{1c} - \frac{1}{2}h_1 \quad y_{2\min} = y_{2c} - \frac{1}{2}h_2$$

$$x_{1\max} = x_{1c} + \frac{1}{2}w_1, \quad x_{2\max} = x_{2c} + \frac{1}{2}w_2$$

$$y_{1\max} = y_{1c} + \frac{1}{2}h_1 \quad y_{2\max} = y_{2c} + \frac{1}{2}h_2$$

$$x_{3\,min} = \max\left(x_{1\,min}, x_{2\,min}\right)$$
$$w_3 = x_{3\,max} - x_{3\,min}$$
$$y_{3\,min} = \max\left(y_{1\,min}, y_{2\,min}\right)$$
$$h_3 = y_{3\,max} - y_{3\,min}$$
$$x_{3\,max} = \min\left(x_{1\,max}, x_{2\,max}\right), \quad A_{12} = w_1 h_1 + w_2 h_2$$
$$y_{3\,max} = \min\left(y_{1\,max}, y_{2\,max}\right) \quad IOU = \frac{w_3 h_3}{A_{12} - w_3 h_3}$$

The IOU function's inputs are the parameters of true bounding boxes and predicted bounding boxes. They have the same structure: [..., x_c, y_c, w, h]. The three dots indicate an image's index in a batch of dataloader, row index and column index of a grid cell on an image's 7 × 7 grid cells. The intersection area of two rectangles is still a rectangle. The coordinates of the top-left corner and the lower-bottom corner of the intersection could be obtained from the above formulae in which the variables' subscript number 1, 2, and 3 are used for a predicted bounding box, a true bounding box and their intersections respectively. To use these formulae, we should have each bounding box's four parameters at the same scale. However, each bounding box's center coordinates are normalized by 64, and the width and height of the box are normalized by 448. A constant *self.S* on line 10, 12 and 14 in Cell 06 is used to set them to the same scalar. To calculate the IOU of two bounding boxes in different grid cells of an image, we also need to consider each grid cell's row index and column index to y_c and x_c respectively. Please pay attention to the data structure: 'boxes_preds[..., 0:1]' in the IOU function. With this kind of tensor structure, we keep the original tensor's shape, so we can do calculations for 4D tensors without for-loops to save computation time. If the data structure is like this 'boxes_preds[..., 0]', we will lose the last dimension of the original tensor, and waste time in many for-loops. The average IOU values of all classes on all images of a dataset is the mAP metrics or index. Aladdin Persson has very helpful YouTube videos about IOU, mAP, Non Max Suppression (NMS) and more. Some of the following codes were inspired by his GitHub codes with MIT license.

```
# Utility_fn(1/5): intersection_over_union (IOU) calculations------------fn(1/5)
def IOU(boxes_preds, boxes_labels): # boxes_preds=[[Xc, Yc, W, H],...]
    box1_x1 = boxes_preds[..., 0:1] - (boxes_preds[..., 2:3]) / 2
    box1_y1 = boxes_preds[..., 1:2] - (boxes_preds[..., 3:4]) / 2
    box1_x2 = boxes_preds[..., 0:1] + (boxes_preds[..., 2:3]) / 2
    box1_y2 = boxes_preds[..., 1:2] + (boxes_preds[..., 3:4]) / 2
    # -----up-left and lower-right conners of all prediction bboxes
    box2_x1 = boxes_labels[..., 0:1] - (boxes_labels[..., 2:3]) / 2
    box2_y1 = boxes_labels[..., 1:2] - (boxes_labels[..., 3:4]) / 2
    box2_x2 = boxes_labels[..., 0:1] + (boxes_labels[..., 2:3]) / 2
    box2_y2 = boxes_labels[..., 1:2] + (boxes_labels[..., 3:4]) / 2
    # ----up-left and lower-right corners of all ground true bboxes
    x3min = torch.max(box1_x1, box2_x1)
    y3min = torch.max(box1_y1, box2_y1)
    x3max = torch.min(box1_x2, box2_x2)
    y3max = torch.min(box1_y2, box2_y2)
```

```
# ----up-left and lower-right corners of all ground true bboxes
x3min = torch.max(box1_x1, box2_x1)
y3min = torch.max(box1_y1, box2_y1)
x3max = torch.min(box1_x2, box2_x2)
y3max = torch.min(box1_y2, box2_y2)
#-----intersection corners of the prediction and true boxes
intersection = (x3max - x3min).clamp(0) * (y3max - y3min).clamp(0)
# clamp(0) is for the case when they do not intersect
box1_area = abs((box1_x2 - box1_x1) * (box1_y2 - box1_y1))
box2_area = abs((box2_x2 - box2_x1) * (box2_y2 - box2_y1))
return intersection / (box1_area + box2_area - intersection + 1e-6)
#-------------------------------------------------------------------------------
```

During model training, five parts of the following loss function (Redmon *et al* 2016) are optimized by the mean squared error algorithm. It is easy to see that the first part is for errors of center coordinates of the bounding boxes, and the second part is for errors of square roots of sizes (widths and heights) of bounding boxes. The square roots of sizes are used to balance errors between bigger and smaller bounding boxes. Because the size values of bounding boxes are less than 1.0 in YOLO encoding, the square root operations will amplify size errors nonlinearly, and errors from smaller sizes are amplified more. From the values of $(0.1)^{1/2}$ and $(0.01)^{1/2}$, you would have an idea why not directly use the sizes of bounding boxes in the second part of the loss function. A bigger hyperparameter $\lambda_{coord} = 5$ is used to enhance the bounding boxes' coordinate errors and size errors.

$$L = \lambda_{coord}\sum_{i=0}^{48}\sum_{j=0}^{1}\mathbb{1}_{ij}^{obj}\left[(x_i - \hat{x}_i)^2 + (y_i - \hat{y}_i)^2\right] + \lambda_{coord}\sum_{i=0}^{48}\sum_{j=0}^{1}\mathbb{1}_{ij}^{obj}\left[\left(\sqrt{w_i} - \sqrt{\hat{w}_i}\right)^2 + \left(\sqrt{h_i} - \sqrt{\hat{h}_i}\right)^2\right]$$

$$+ \sum_{i=0}^{48}\sum_{j=0}^{1}\mathbb{1}_{ij}^{obj}(\hat{C}_i - C_i)^2 + \lambda_{noobj}\sum_{i=0}^{48}\sum_{j=0}^{1}\left(1 - \mathbb{1}_{ij}^{obj}\right)(\hat{C}_i - C_i)^2 + \sum_{i=0}^{48}\mathbb{1}_{ij}^{obj}\sum_{c\in classes}\left(p_i(c) - \hat{p}_i(c)\right)^2$$

On each image, there are 7×7 grid cells ($i = 0, 1, ..., 48$), and the model predicts two bounding boxes ($j = 0, 1$) for each grid cell. The two upper case sigma symbols are shorthand notation to indicate the sum of errors of all 49×2 bounding boxes. However, only a few grid cells on an image have objects. The variable $\mathbb{1}_{ij}^{obj}$ in the loss function is equal to 1.0 only if a grid cell (i) has an object and a responsible bounding box (j) which has a higher IOU value to its ground truth bounding box. Otherwise, the variable in the loss function is equal to 0.0. We have to use codes in Cell 06 to explain the above ideas. An instance of the loss function class defined in the cell needs two inputs. The first one is a batch of predictions which came from a batch of images processed by the model: preds $\hat{y}$. The second one is a batch of encoded bounding boxes: target y. On line 07 and 08, both of them are shaped to $N \times 49 \times 23$, where N is the batch size. Each of them is a 3D object with height N, width 49 and depth 23. Using codes on line 15 and 16 of Cell 06, we get IOU values of two predicted bounding boxes of an image on a grid cell to a ground truth, and then search to find the best (responsible) bounding box identity (j) on line 19 for each of the 49 grid cells on the image. The tensor named 'bestbox' on line 19 is used to do a part of the job for $\mathbb{1}_{ij}^{obj}$ on line 21–23.

Taking a batch of images with only a white bishop image into the ResNet18 model by a code on line 15 of Cell 05, we will have the model's prediction $\hat{y}$ whose shape is [1, 1127]. The prediction is then reshaped to [1, 49, 23]. We know the resized shape of the target of the white bishop in the batch is the same: [1, 49, 23]. In the 49 grid cells of the target, only one is not empty: y_i = [00000, 00100, 000, 1$x_c y_c$wh, 00000]. Codes between line 09 to 22 of Cell 06 calculate values of IOU to set one predicted bounding box as a responsible bounding box for each of 49 grid cells. The tensor named 'exists_box' on line 20 does another part of the job for 1^{obj}_{ij}. It is a $N \times 49 \times 1$ tensor . The tensor is a map of grid cells with objects on an image. When this tensor is used to multiply another tensor, the result is about grid cells with objects. Using the targets of a batch of images generated on line 17 of Cell 04 and running the codes in an extra cell: *exists_box = targets[..., 13:14][0]; exists_box.squeeze( )*, you would see a 7×7 tensor with only a few elements that are not zeros. The exists_box tensor is used as a mask to pick out responsible boxes as box_preds on line 23. The value of box_loss on line 28 is the sum of the first two parts of the loss function without λ_{coord}. On line 28, a function torch.flatten(X, end_dim = −2) changes the shape of a tensor X from $8 \times 49 \times 4$ to 392×4. Lines 33, 39 and 43 are for object loss, no object loss and class loss respectively. Detailed information about the loss function can be found in the YOLOv1 paper (Redmon *et al* 2016). You can use the following codes inside the quote markers to learn how to calculate 3D tensors in batches: 'x = torch. zeros(2,3,1); x[0,1,0]=1; print(x); y = torch.arange(24).reshape(2,3,4); print(y); x*y'.

```
# Cell 06: Loss function-----------------------------------------------------
class YoloLoss(nn.Module):
    def __init__(self, S=S, B=B, C=C):
        super().__init__()
        self.S =S; self.B =B; self.C =C; self.mse = nn.MSELoss(reduction="sum")
        self.lambda_noobj = 0.5; self.lambda_coord = 5
    def forward(self, preds, target):         #----------------------------line 06
        preds = preds.reshape(-1, self.S*self.S, (self.C+5*self.B))  # Nx49x23
        target = target.reshape(-1, self.S*self.S, (self.C+5*self.B)) # Nx49x23
        true_bb = target[..., (C+1):(C+5)].clone()      # true bboxes,   line 09
        true_bb[..., 2:4] = self.S * true_bb[..., 2:4]  # relative to 64 pixels
        pred1bb = preds[..., (C+1):(C+5)].clone()       # pred bboxes 1
        pred1bb[..., 2:4] = self.S * pred1bb[..., 2:4]  #----------------line 12
        pred2bb = preds[..., (C+6):(C+10)].clone()      # pred bboxes 2
        pred2bb[..., 2:4] = self.S * pred2bb[..., 2:4]  #----------------line 14
        IOU4Box_1 = IOU(pred1bb, true_bb)               #----------------line 15
        IOU4Box_2 = IOU(pred2bb, true_bb)               #----------------line 16
        ious = torch.cat([IOU4Box_1.unsqueeze(0),       #----------------line 17
                IOU4Box_2.unsqueeze(0)], dim=0)     # ious.shape=2xNx49x1 line 18
        bestbox = torch.argmax(ious, dim=0)       # bestbox.shape=Nx49x1  line 19
        exists_box = target[..., C:(C+1)]         # exists_box.shape=Nx49x1 line 20
```

```
            responsible_bboxes = (bestbox * preds[..., (C+6):(C+10)] +        #line 21
                            (1 - bestbox) * preds[..., (C+1):(C+5)])
            box_preds =exists_box*responsible_bboxes # box_preds.shape=Nx49x4 line 23
            box_preds[..., 2:4] = torch.sign(box_preds[..., 2:4])*(        #line 24
                    torch.sqrt(torch.abs(box_preds[..., 2:4] + 1e-6)))
            box_targets = exists_box * target[..., (C+1):(C+5)]    #---Nx49x4, line 26
            box_targets[..., 2:4] = torch.sqrt(box_targets[..., 2:4])        #--line 27
            box_loss = self.mse(torch.flatten(box_preds, end_dim=-2),        #--line 28
                    torch.flatten(box_targets, end_dim=-2)
                    ) # Nx49x4 flatten @ end_dim=-2-> 392x4) ============== box loss
            p_box = (bestbox * preds[..., (C+5):(C+6)] + #p_box.shape=Nx49x1 line 31
                    (1 - bestbox) * preds[..., C:(C+1)])
            object_loss = self.mse(torch.flatten(exists_box * p_box),        #----line 33
                    torch.flatten(exists_box * target[..., C:(C+1)])
                    ) #Nx49x1 flatten -> 8x49============================== object loss
            no_object_loss = self.mse(                          #----line 36
                torch.flatten((1-exists_box)*preds[...,C:(C+1)],start_dim=1),
                torch.flatten((1-exists_box)*target[...,C:(C+1)],start_dim=1))
            no_object_loss += self.mse(                          #----line 39
                torch.flatten((1-exists_box)*preds[...,(C+5):(C+6)],start_dim=1),
                torch.flatten((1-exists_box)*target[...,C:(C+1)],start_dim=1)
                ) # Nx49x1 flatten @ start_dim=1 -> 8x49 ============ no_object loss
            class_loss = self.mse(                              #----line 43
                torch.flatten(exists_box * preds[..., :C], end_dim=-2,),
                torch.flatten(exists_box * target[...,:C], end_dim=-2,)
                )  # Nx49x20 flatten @ end_dim=-2 -> 392x20 ============= class loss
            total_loss = (self.lambda_coord * box_loss + object_loss +    #---line 47
                    self.lambda_noobj * no_object_loss + class_loss)
            return total_loss
    loss_fn = YoloLoss()
    #---------------------------------------------------------------------------
```

7.4 Utility functions for model training

Using codes in Cell 07 to 10, we can train the ResNet18 model with the chess dataset. Since these codes for model training have been used many times, it is not necessary to explain them again. It took me a long time to solve the overfitting issue by using those augmentations listed in Utility 03. Augmentations of image rotation and normalization are very helpful to fight the issue. With only resize transformation in Utility 03 for the Pascal VOC images, it was easy to get the train dataset's mAP above 99.8%, but never obtained the valid dataset' mAP over 1%. The mAP metrics are the most important metrics used to evaluate how good a deep learning model is trained for object detection. The following Utility_fn(2/5) to Utility_fn(5/5) should be copied and pasted in front Cell 06 in VS Code.

```
# Cell 07: Training function--------------------------------------------------
def train_fn(train_dataloader, model, optimizer, loss_fn):
    model.train()
    train_loss = 0.0
    for x, y in train_dataloader:
        y_hat = model(x.cuda())
        loss = loss_fn(y_hat, y.cuda())
```

```
        train_loss += loss.item()
        optimizer.zero_grad()
        loss.backward()
        optimizer.step()
    return train_loss/len(train_dataloader)
# Cell 08: Evaluation function------------------------------------------------------
def eval_fn(valid_dataloader, model, loss_fn):
    model.eval()
    valid_loss = 0.0
    for batch_idx, (x, y) in enumerate(valid_dataloader):
        with torch.no_grad():
            y_hat = model(x.cuda())
        loss = loss_fn(y_hat, y.cuda())
        valid_loss += loss.item()
    return valid_loss/len(valid_dataloader)
# Cell 09: Fitting function ---------------------------------------------------------
def fit(epochs):
    torch.cuda.empty_cache()
    df = pd.DataFrame(np.empty([epochs, 3]), index = np.arange(epochs),
                        columns=['Train_Loss', 'Valid_Loss', 'learn_rate'])
    progress_bar = trange(epochs)
    for i in progress_bar:
        Train_Loss = train_fn(train_dataloader, model, optimizer, loss_fn)
        Valid_Loss = eval_fn(valid_dataloader, model, loss_fn)
        df.iloc[i, 0] = Train_Loss
        df.iloc[i, 1] = Valid_Loss
        df.iloc[i, 2] = optimizer.param_groups[0]['lr']       #Record lr
        scheduler.step(Valid_Loss)                #---------update learning rate
        progress_bar.set_description("train_loss=%.5f" % df.iloc[i,0])
        progress_bar.set_postfix(
                    {'valid_loss': df.iloc[i,1], 'lr': df.iloc[i,2]})
    return df
train_history = fit(n_epochs)
# Cell 10: Show the training history----------------------------------------Cell 10
df = train_history
fig, ax = plt.subplots(1,2, figsize=(12,4), sharex=True)
df.plot(ax=ax[0], y=[0, 1], style=['b-+', 'r-'])
df.plot(ax=ax[1], y=[2], style=['r-'])
for i in range(2):
    ax[i].set_xlabel('epoch')
    ax[i].grid(which='major', axis='both', color='g', linestyle=':')
ax[1].ticklabel_format(style='sci', axis='y', scilimits=(0,0));
plt.show()
# Cell 11: save the trained model------------------------------------------Cell 11
File_name = root + '/Chess-Yolo-21-new.pth'
torch.save(model, File_name)
```

```
# Cell 12: mAP of model training results--------------------------------Cell 12
iou_threshold=0.5; threshold=0.4
pred_bboxes, true_bboxes = get_bboxes(train_dataloader,
                                model, iou_threshold, threshold)
my_mAP = mAP(pred_bboxes, true_bboxes, iou_threshold=0.5, num_classes=C)
print(my_mAP)
# Cell 13: Using the trained model to detect objects with bounding boxes---------
idx = 1        # idx for an image in a dataloader: [0,1,..., batch_size-1]
images,targets=next(iter(test_dataloader))   # get a batch of samples
true_bboxes = grid2bboxes(targets[idx])       # true bounding boxes of the samples
image=images[idx]
y_hat = model(images.cuda())                   # a batch of predictions
pred_bboxes = responsible_boxes(y_hat)
good_bboxes = NMS(pred_bboxes[idx], 0.5, 0.5)
def predBbox_show(image, good_bboxes):
    fig = plt.figure(figsize=(12,8))
    ax = fig.add_subplot(1, 1, 1)
    ax.imshow(image.cpu().numpy().transpose((1,2,0)))
    for j, bbox in enumerate(good_bboxes):
        class_label = classes[int(bbox[0])]+'\nP='+str(round(bbox[1],2))
        Xc, Yc, W, H = bbox[2:]
        x = Xc-W/2; y = Yc-H/2
        ax.add_patch(patches.Rectangle((x,y), W, H, linestyle=':',
                    linewidth=1.5,edgecolor='r',facecolor='none'))
        plt.text(x, y, class_label, color='r')   # print in center
        ax.set_xticks(np.linspace(0, 448, 8))    # grid settings
    for i, tbbox in enumerate(true_bboxes):
        X, Y, W, H = tbbox[2:]
        ax.add_patch(patches.Rectangle((X,Y), W, H, linestyle='-',
                    linewidth=1.5,edgecolor='y',facecolor='none'))
    ax.grid(which='both', color='y', linestyle=':', alpha=0.8)
    ax.set_title(
        'Yellow boxes: true; Red boxes: preds <-
NMS(responsible_boxes(model(x)))')
    plt.show()
if image.min() < 0:                            #targets.shape=8x7x7x23
    image=denorm(image)
predBbox_show(image, good_bboxes)
#----------------------------------------------------------------------------
```

After model training, codes in Cell 11 save the trained model to a file which will be used for the next 100-epoch model training, and codes in Cell 12 are used to calculate mAP. A function defined in Utility_fn(5/5) uses all true bounding boxes and predicted bounding boxes in a dataset to calculate mAP. Those bounding boxes come from a function defined in Utility_fn(4/5): get_bboxes. Each of the two outputs of Utility_fn(4/5) is a list, and each element in the list is a list with seven elements: an image's index in a dataset, a class index, the probability of an object belonging to the class, center coordinates and sizes of a bounding box relative to sizes of a transformed image (448×448). For example, the valid dataset has 80 samples, so an image index of a bounding box would be an integer from 0 to 79. Using codes on line 08 and 11 of the mAP function in Utility_fn(5/5), we could get predicted and true bounding boxes belonging to a class on all images in a dataset. With codes between lines 12 to 15 in Utility_fn(5/5), numbers of true bounding boxes on each image are encoded by a tensor with elements of zeros. If the first and last images of the valid dataset have three and two true bounding boxes, a dictionary name 'amount_bboxes' on line 15 in Utility_fn(5/5) would be {0: torch.tensor(0,0,0), ..., 79: torch.tensor(0,0)}.

Using the code on line 16 in Utility_fn(5/5), we reverse sort all predicted bounding boxes in the dataset according to their probabilities: the bounding box with the maximum probability is on top. Then according to an IOU threshold of the mAP function, we would decide if a predicted bounding box is true positive (TP) or false positive (FP). The IOU threshold parameter of the mAP function could be 0.50 to 0.95. With a higher the IOU threshold, we would have a smaller number of TP of bounding boxes. Codes in a for-loop from line 22 to 39 make the decision for us. After picking out a predicted bounding box whose image index is detection[0], all true bounding boxes of the same class on the same image are used to find a best true bounding box having the highest IOU. If the IOU is bigger than the IOU threshold and the true bounding box has never been used, the predicted bounding box is a true positive. The used true bounding box is then marked as used on line 35 in Utility_fn (5/5). Otherwise, the predicted bounding box is false positive. The results of these judgments are recorded by an 1D tensor TP and an 1D tensor FP respectively. Operations of cumulative sum are then acting on the two 1D tensors on line 40 and 41. For example, to a 1D tensor [1,0,1,0,1], the result of the cumulative sum operation on dimension zero is [1,1,2,2,3]. The results of the two cumulative sum operations are two 1D tensors: TP_cumsum and FP_cumsum. From them, we can calculate two more metrics for object detection: recall and precision on line 42 to 45 with the following formulae

$$recall = \frac{TP_{cumsum}}{Total_{truebboxes}} \quad precision = \frac{TP_{cumsum}}{TP_{cumsum} + FP_{cumsum}}$$

On a 2D plane with *recall* as its x-axis and *precision* as its y-axis, we add one point at [0,1] and draw a curve about the relationship between *recall* and *precision*. The area between the curve and the x-axis for each class is recorded in a list, and the average of the areas of all classes is the mean average precision (mAP) at an IOU threshold.

The title of figure 7.3 told us that yellow rectangles were true bounding boxes, and the dashed red rectangles were predicted bounding boxes. From the trained model's prediction y_hat = model(images) to each batch images (batch size N), we obtained two batches of predicted bounding boxes, but most of them are empty. A function defined in Utility_fn(3/5) picks out $N \times 49$ responsible bounding boxes for a batch of images. Each bounding box is a list with six elements. They are the class index of a responsible object, its probability, the center coordinates and sizes of the object's predicted bounding box. Then, a few of these bounding boxes are selected by a non-max suppression (NMS) function defined in Utility_fn(2/5).

The title of figure 7.3 also indicated that the red boxes came from the model, the responsible_boxes function and the NMS function. Codes on line 08 and 13 of Cell Utility_fn(4/5) use the NMS function in Utility_fn(2/5) to obtain true and predicted bounding boxes for mAP calculations. An input of the NMS function is those responsible bounding boxes on an image. Other inputs of the function are an IOU threshold (=0.5) and a probability threshold (=0.4). With the code on line 02 of the NMS function, only those responsible bounding boxes with probability higher than the probability threshold are selected, and then these selected boxes are sorted reversely according to their probabilities by the code on line 03. In a while loop for those sorted boxes, the first one is popped out as the chosen box. Other sorted boxes are used to reconstruct a shorter list of sorted boxes if any of these boxes is in a different class; or if in the same class of the chosen box, they should have lower IOU values to the chosen box. In this way, many similar bounding boxes of each class are discarded, and only those best boxes are kept.

```
# Utility_fn(2/5): Non Max Suppression for better bboxes out of y_hat-----fn(2/5)
def NMS(bboxes, iou_threshold, threshold):
    #assert type(bboxes) == list   #--------[[class_idx, p, x1, y1, x2, y2], ...]
    bboxes = [box for box in bboxes if box[1] > threshold]      #---------line 02
    bboxes = sorted(bboxes, key=lambda x: x[1], reverse=True)  #---------line 03
    bboxes_after_nms = []
    while bboxes:
        chosen_box = bboxes.pop(0)
        bboxes = [box for box in bboxes if (
            box[0] != chosen_box[0] or IOU(torch.tensor(chosen_box[2:]),
                            torch.tensor(box[2:])) < iou_threshold)]
        bboxes_after_nms.append(chosen_box)
    return bboxes_after_nms
# Utility_fn(3/5) to pick out responsible pred_bboxes from y_hat=model(images) --
def responsible_boxes(y_hat):
    batch_size = y_hat.shape[0]    # N = batch_size
    y_hat = y_hat.to("cpu")        # y_hat.shape = N x 1127 for Chess Dataset
    y_hat = y_hat.reshape(batch_size, S, S, C+5*B)
    bboxes1 = y_hat[..., (C+1):(C+5)]              # 1st bbox in every grid cell
    bboxes2 = y_hat[..., (C+6):(C+10)]             # 2nd bbox in every grid cell
    scores = torch.cat((y_hat[..., C].unsqueeze(0),           # p for 1st bbox
                    y_hat[..., (C+5)].unsqueeze(0)), dim=0)  # p for 2nd bbox
                ) # a map of possibilities,  scores.shape = 2 x N x 7 x 7
    best_box = scores.argmax(0).unsqueeze(-1)    # best_box.shape = N x 7 x 7 x 1
    best_boxes = bboxes1 * (1 - best_box) + best_box * bboxes2   # N x 7 x 7 x 4
    column_indices = torch.arange(7).repeat(batch_size, 7, 1).unsqueeze(-1)
    row_indices = column_indices.permute(0, 2, 1, 3)
    W = best_boxes[..., 2:3]*488
    H = best_boxes[..., 3:4]*488
```

```
    Xc = (best_boxes[..., 0:1] + column_indices )*64    #----center coordinate Xc
    Yc = (best_boxes[..., 1:2] + row_indices)*64        #----center coordinate Yc
    converted_bboxes = torch.cat((Xc, Yc, W, H), dim=-1) # shape = N x 7 x 7 x 4
    pred_class = y_hat[..., :C].argmax(-1).unsqueeze(-1) # shape = N x 7 x 7 x 1
    best_confidence = torch.max(                        # shape = N x 7 x 7 x 1
                      y_hat[..., C],  y_hat[..., (C+5)]).unsqueeze(-1)
    converted_pred = torch.cat(            # converted_pred.shape=Nx7x7x6
            (pred_class, best_confidence, converted_bboxes), dim=-1)
    converted_pred = converted_pred.reshape(batch_size, S*S, -1)
    all_bboxes = [] #convert bbox tensor to a list: [[[c, p, Xc, Yc, W, H],...]]]
    for idx in range(batch_size):          # idx <= batch_size-1
        bboxes = []
        for bbox_idx in range(S * S):   # bbox_idx is an element in [0,1,..., 49]
            bboxes.append([x.item() for x in converted_pred[idx, bbox_idx, :]])
        all_bboxes.append(bboxes)
    return all_bboxes                      # np.array(all_bboxes).shape=N x 49 x 6
# Utility_fn(4/5) to mark pred_bboxes and true_bboxes with image idx in a dataset
def get_bboxes(loader, model, iou_threshold, threshold):
    img_idx = 0                    #-----img_idx <= (len(dataset)-1)
    all_true_boxes = []            # [[img_idx, class_idx, p, Xc, Yc, W, H],  ...]
    all_pred_boxes = []            # np.array(all_pred_boxes).shape=(-1, 7)
    model.eval()
    for batch_idx, (x, y) in enumerate(loader):    # batch_idx <= (len(loader)-1)
        batch_size = x.shape[0]
        true_bboxes = responsible_boxes(y.cuda())    #====================line 08
        with torch.no_grad():
            y_hat = model(x.cuda())                  #--------y_hat.shape = N x 1127
        bboxes = responsible_boxes(y_hat)            # np.array(bboxes).shape=Nx49x6
        for idx in range(batch_size):                # idx <= batch_size-1
            nms_boxes = NMS(bboxes[idx], iou_threshold=iou_threshold, #==line 13
                threshold=threshold)    # get a few better bboxes from 49 bboxes


            for nms_box in nms_boxes:        # mark pred_bboxes with img_idx
                all_pred_boxes.append([img_idx]+ nms_box)
            for box in true_bboxes[idx]:    # mark true_bboxes with img_idx
                if box[1] > threshold:
                    all_true_boxes.append([img_idx] + box)
            img_idx += 1
    model.train()
    return all_pred_boxes, all_true_boxes
# Utility_fn(5/5) for mean average precision function--------------------fn(5/5)
def mAP(pred_boxes, true_boxes, iou_threshold=0.5, num_classes=C):
    average_precisions = []
    for c in range(num_classes):
        detections = []              # --for pred_bboxes of class c in a dataset
        ground_truths = []           # for true bboxes of class c in the dataset
        for detection in pred_boxes:         # pick out pred_bboxes for class c
            if detection[1] == c:
                detections.append(detection)        #====================line 08
        for true_box in true_boxes:          # pick out true_bboxes for class c
            if true_box[1] == c:
                ground_truths.append(true_box)       #====================line 11
        amount_bboxes = Counter([gt[0] for gt in ground_truths]
```

```
            )   # a dictionary for true_bboxes number on each image
    for key, val in amount_bboxes.items():
        amount_bboxes[key] = torch.zeros(val) #===================line 15
    detections.sort(key=lambda x: x[2], reverse=True)  #==========line 16
    TP = torch.zeros((len(detections)))
    FP = torch.zeros((len(detections)))
    total_true_bboxes = len(ground_truths)     #total true_bboxes in class c
    if total_true_bboxes == 0:
        continue   # If no true_bboxes for class c, skip the following codes
    for detection_idx, detection in enumerate(detections):    #===line 22
        trueBboxesOn1Img = [   #Pick out all true bboxes on an image
            bbox for bbox in ground_truths if bbox[0] == detection[0]]
        num_gts = len(trueBboxesOn1Img)
        best_iou = 0
        for idx, gt in enumerate(trueBboxesOn1Img):          #======line 27
            iou = IOU(torch.tensor(detection[3:]),torch.tensor(gt[3:]))
            if iou > best_iou:
                best_iou = iou
                best_gt_idx = idx    #record the best true_bbox and its idx
        if best_iou > iou_threshold:            # =================line 32
            if amount_bboxes[detection[0]][best_gt_idx] == 0:
                TP[detection_idx] = 1 #if 2 more predicted bboxes on 1 img
                amount_bboxes[detection[0]][best_gt_idx] = 1   #===line 35
            else:                    # -------use each truth_bbox only once
                FP[detection_idx] = 1
        else:        # if IOU is lower then the iou_threshold
            FP[detection_idx] = 1             #=====================line 39
    TP_cumsum = torch.cumsum(TP, dim=0) #cumsum([1,0,1,0,1])->[1,1,2,2,3]
    FP_cumsum = torch.cumsum(FP, dim=0)
    recalls = TP_cumsum / (total_true_bboxes + epsilon)      #=====line 42
    recalls = torch.cat((torch.tensor([0]), recalls))
    precisions = TP_cumsum/(TP_cumsum + FP_cumsum + epsilon)
    precisions = torch.cat((torch.tensor([1]), precisions))  #=====line 45
    area = torch.trapz(precisions, recalls)                  #=====line 46
    # trapz for calculation of the area under the recalls-precisions curve
    average_precisions.append(area)
  return sum(average_precisions) / len(average_precisions)
#----------------------------------------------------------------------------
```

7.5 Applications of YOLOv3 for real-time object detection

It has been a long journey for us to finish the object detection project for the small chess dataset. From this simple project, we have ideas about grid cells, intersection over union, non max suppression, mean average precision and more for a YOLOv1 model. Now, it is possible for us to use more powerful YOLOv3 models without writing long codes from scratch, because YOLOv3 models have been packed in OpenCV (version $\geq$ 3.4.2), a library of programming functions for real-time computer vision. Two years after the first YOLO paper, Joseph Redmon and Ali Farhadi published their YOLOv3 paper (Redmon and Farhadi 2018). Compared with the YOLOv1 model's 24 convolutional layers, the YOLOv3 model has 106 convolutional layers. The new model is more accurate for object detection because of its three output branches at layer 79, 91 and 103 respectively. Each branch has three layers. Codes in Cell 01 of project 7.5 are used to import libraries and set hyperparameters for the project. MS COCO dataset's class names are obtained by reading a text file, as the

YOLOv3 model was trained by the dataset which has more than 200 000 images in 80 classes. The model's configuration files and pre-trained weight files can be found and downloaded from https://github.com/pjreddie/darknet for free. These files save a lot of time for people to train YOLOv3 models. The YOLOv3 configuration file can be opened and edited in MS Notepad. It is about the structure of the YOLOv3 model and its parameters. The last line of Cell 02 is about the three ends of the YOLOv3 model's three output branches: ['yolo_82', 'yolo_94', 'yolo_106']. Each grid cell for YOLOv3 has three anchor boxes (predicted bounding boxes), and each anchor box has 85 cubes. Parameters in cubes 0 to 3 are for center coordinates, width and height of an object in a grid cell. A parameter in cube 04 is for the probability of the object in the grid cell, and the remaining 80 cubes are used to hot encode the COCO class of an object. The maximum number of objects on an image for the YOLOv3 model to detect could be $3 \times (13 \times 13 + 26 \times 26 + 52 \times 52)$. The maximum number of objects for a YOLOv1 model is 49. Although so many calculations are added for the YOLOv3 model, it is still fast enough. The pre-trained YOLOv3 model can use GPU for model training (line 04–05 of Cell 02). It can also be set to use CPU if you want.

A function defined in Cell 04 is used to add bounding boxes, class names and probabilities to an image. Figure 7.4 shows object detection results of a pre-trained YOLOv3 model for a single image. The code on line 02 of Cell 04 modifies the image to a special format (blob) for the YOLOv3 model. These modifications are normalization, resizing and more. The formatted image is then processed by the model with the code on line 03, and the outputs of the model are obtained from the code on line 04. From

Figure 7.4. Results of object detection by a pre-trained YOLOv3 model for a single image.

the outputs, we have information of many bounding boxes. Using a function defined in Cell 03, only some bounding boxes matching ground truth well are picked out by the NMS module on line 16 of Cell 03. These good bounding boxes are then added to the original image by the codes in Cell 03. We can use the codes in Cell 05 to show all VOC images one by one with bounding boxes, class names and possibilities. Each image will be shown for 1000 milliseconds if you did not press any key on your key board, once any key except the Esc key is pressed, the next image will appear. The title of the image window indicates that if you press the Esc key, the program will be terminated.

```python
# Project 7.5 Applications of yolov3 for image slide show-------------Python v3.9
import cv2; import numpy as np; import glob; from tqdm import tqdm; import time
whT = 416    #resize original images to 416x416 for yolov3 model   ======line 02
iouThreshold = 0.5; nmsThreshold = 0.4  #for the NMS module
classesFile = 'D:/ImageSets/VOC/coco_classes.txt'      #=============line 04
classes = []  #a list with 80 class names from coco_classes.txt
with open(classesFile) as f:
    classes = f.read().rstrip(' ').split("\n")
# Cell 02: import trained yolo v3 with its configurations and weights-----------
modelConfiguration = "D:/ImageSets/VOC/yolov3.cfg"      #=============lin 01
modelWeights = "D:/ImageSets/VOC/yolov3.weights"        #=============lin 02
model   = cv2.dnn.readNetFromDarknet(modelConfiguration, modelWeights)
model.setPreferableBackend(cv2.dnn.DNN_BACKEND_CUDA)      # using GPU
model.setPreferableTarget(cv2.dnn.DNN_TARGET_CUDA)
#model.setPreferableBackend(cv2.dnn.DNN_BACKEND_OPENCV)    #or using CPU
#model.setPreferableTarget(cv2.dnn.DNN_TARGET_CPU)
layerNames = model.getLayerNames() #print(len(layerNames)) #=254  ==line 08
outputNames = [layerNames[i-1] for i in model.getUnconnectedOutLayers()]
# Cell 03: get bboxes from yolov3's output and add them to an image-------------
def findObjects(outputs, img):
    h, w, _ = img.shape      # sizes of an original image to show
    bbox = []                # a list of bounding boxes of bojects
    classIds = []            # a list of class indices of ojects
    confs = []               # a list of confidence of ojects
    for output in outputs:   # output = [xc,yc,w,h,p,c1,c2...,c20]
        for item in output:              #=============================line 07
            scores = item[5:]
            classId = np.argmax(scores)
            confidence = scores[classId]
            W, H = int(item[2]*w), int(item[3]*h)
            X, Y = int(item[0]*w-W/2), int(item[1]*h-H/2)
            bbox.append([X, Y, W, H])
            classIds.append(classId)
            confs.append(float(confidence))      #=====================line 15
    indices = cv2.dnn.NMSBoxes(bbox, confs, iouThreshold, nmsThreshold)
    for i in indices:                    #=============================line 17
        box = bbox[i]; X,Y,W,H = box[:]
        cv2.rectangle(img, (X,Y), (X+W, Y+H), (255,0,255), 1)   #=====line 19
        if Y < 10: Y=Y+H
        cv2.putText(img, f'{classes[classIds[i]]}{int(confs[i]*100)}%',
                    (X, Y), 0, 0.6, (255,0,255),2)          #=====line 22
```

```
# Cell 04: Add bounding boxes to images by yolov3 model------------------------
def yolov3(image):
    blob = cv2.dnn.blobFromImage(image, 1/255, (whT,whT), [0,0,0], 1, crop=False)
    model.setInput(blob)                   #==============================line 03
    outputs = model.forward(outputNames)   #==============================line 04
    findObjects(outputs, image)            #==============================line 05
    return image
import matplotlib.pyplot as plt
fig, ax = plt.subplots(figsize=(10,8))
ax.imshow(yolov3(plt.imread('d:/IMG_1071.jpg')));
#------------------------------------------------------------------------------
```

Watching carefully, you will find that some objects are not detected in the slide show. The pre-trained YOLOv3 model is not perfect, but is good enough. Using the following codes in Cell 06 to replace Cell 05, images from your laptop camera or from a video file would be used for object detection in real-time. You could also record the video processed by the YOLOv3 model. However, there is an issue about video recording. The number 30.0 on line 10 of Cell 06 is a parameter of video frame per second (FPS). From a green digit on the top-left corner of each video frame, you will find that the real FPS of the video recording was about 1 or 2. Because the YOLOv3 model is slow to process images, only a few frames are recorded in an output video file. When the video file is played by a video player with a normal speed, the play speed of the recorded video looks very fast. One solution is to reduce the FPS parameter from 30 to 4, so that you can watch your recorded video normally. The best solution is to use the latest YOLO models. Codes in Cell 07 are for a simplified version of Cell 06, with which video files are not recorded.

```
# Cell 05: to slide show images in a folder for depth estimation----------------
img_path = 'D:/ImageSets/VOC/VOCdevkit/VOC2012/JPEGImages/*'
img_list = glob.glob(img_path)[3000:3050]             #==================line 02
for file in tqdm(img_list):
    cv2.imshow("press Esc to stop the slid show", yolov3(cv2.imread(file)))
    if (cv2.waitKey(1000)&0xFF) == 27: break          #==================line 05
cv2.destroyAllWindows()
#------------------------------------------------------------------------------
# Cell 06: Object detection for camera or a video file with VIDEO RECORDING------
def output_video(source_file):
    if source_file.isnumeric():              #===========for a webcamera
        output_file = 'd:/' + source_file + '.mp4'
        source_file = int(source_file)
    else:
        output_file = source_file.split('.')[0]+'_new'+'.mp4'
    video_source = cv2.VideoCapture(source_file)
    w = int(video_source.get(3)); h = int(video_source.get(4))
    video_format = cv2.VideoWriter_fourcc(*'MP4V')
    video_data = cv2.VideoWriter(output_file,video_format,30.0, (w,h)) #line 10
```

```
    while True:
        (NotLastFrame, frame) = video_source.read()
        if not NotLastFrame or (cv2.waitKey(1)&0xFF) == 27: break
        start_time = time.time()
        out = yolov3(frame)
        fps = str(int(1/(time.time()-start_time+1e-5)))
        cv2.putText(out, fps, (7, 70), 0, 3, (100, 255, 0), 3, cv2.LINE_AA)
        video_data.write(out)
        cv2.imshow("press Esc to stop the video", out)
    video_source.release(); video_data.release(); cv2.destroyAllWindows()
source_file = '0'           #source_file = '0'  for webcam
output_video(source_file)                  #source_file = 'd:/traffic1.mp4'
#---------------------------------------The End---------------------------------
# Cell 07: Object detection for video without recording------------------------
def output_video(source):
    video_frame = cv2.VideoCapture(source)
    while True:
        (NotLastFrame, frame) = video_frame.read()
        if not NotLastFrame or (cv2.waitKey(1)&0xFF) == 27: break
        start_time = time.time()
        out = yolov3(frame)
        fps = str(int(1/(time.time()-start_time+1e-5)))
        cv2.putText(out, fps, (7, 70), 0, 3, (100, 255, 0), 3, cv2.LINE_AA)
        cv2.imshow("press Esc to stop the video", out)
    video_frame.release(); cv2.destroyAllWindows()
output_video(0)             # The source is 0 or 'd:/traffic1.mp4'
#---------------------------------------The End---------------------------------


# Cell 06: Object detection for camera or a video file with VIDEO RECORDING------
def output_video(source_file):
    if source_file.isnumeric():              #==========for a webcamera
        output_file = 'd:/' + source_file + '.mp4'
        source_file = int(source_file)
    else:
        output_file = source_file.split('.')[0]+'_new'+'.mp4'
    video_source = cv2.VideoCapture(source_file)
    w = int(video_source.get(3)); h = int(video_source.get(4))
    video_format = cv2.VideoWriter_fourcc(*'MP4V')
    video_data = cv2.VideoWriter(output_file,video_format,30.0, (w,h)) #line 10
    while True:
        (NotLastFrame, frame) = video_source.read()
        if not NotLastFrame or (cv2.waitKey(1)&0xFF) == 27: break
        start_time = time.time()
        out = yolov3(frame)
        fps = str(int(1/(time.time()-start_time+1e-5)))
        cv2.putText(out, fps, (7, 70), 0, 3, (100, 255, 0), 3, cv2.LINE_AA)
        video_data.write(out)
        cv2.imshow("press Esc to stop the video", out)
    video_source.release(); video_data.release(); cv2.destroyAllWindows()
source_file = '0'           #source_file = '0'  for webcam
output_video(source_file)                  #source_file = 'd:/traffic1.mp4'
#---------------------------------------The End---------------------------------
```

```
# Cell 07: Object detection for video without recording------------------------
def output_video(source):
    video_frame = cv2.VideoCapture(source)
    while True:
        (NotLastFrame, frame) = video_frame.read()
        if not NotLastFrame or (cv2.waitKey(1)&0xFF) == 27: break
        start_time = time.time()
        out = yolov3(frame)
        fps = str(int(1/(time.time()-start_time+1e-5)))
        cv2.putText(out, fps, (7, 70), 0, 3, (100, 255, 0), 3, cv2.LINE_AA)
        cv2.imshow("press Esc to stop the video", out)
    video_frame.release(); cv2.destroyAllWindows()
output_video(0)               # The source is 0 or 'd:/traffic1.mp4'
#----------------------------------------The End------------------------------
```

References

Everingham M, Gool L V, Williams C, Winn J and Zisserman A 2012 The PASCAL visual object classes challenge 2012 (VOC2012) results http://www.pascal-network.org/challenges/VOC/voc2012/workshop/index.html

Girshick R 2015 Fast R-CNN *Proc. of the IEEE Int. Conf. on Computer Vision* pp 1440–8

Girshick R, Donahue J, Darrell T and Malik J 2014 Rich feature hierarchies for accurate object detection and semantic segmentation *Proc. of the IEEE Conf. on Computer Vision and Pattern Recognition* pp 580–7

Ioffe S and Szegedy C 2015 Batch normalization: accelerating deep network training by reducing internal covariate shift *Int. Conf. on Machine Learning* (PMLR) pp 448–56

Liu W, Anguelov D, Erhan D, Szegedy C, Reed S, Fu C-Y and Berg A C 2016 Ssd: Single shot multibox detector *European Conf. on Computer Vision* (Berlin: Springer) pp 21–37

Redmon J, Divvala S, Girshick R and Farhadi A 2016 You only look once: unified, real-time object detection *Proc. of the IEEE Conf. on Computer Vision and Pattern Recognition* pp 779–88

Redmon J and Farhadi A 2018 Yolov3: an incremental improvement *arXiv preprint* arXiv:1804.02767

Ren S, He K, Girshick R and Sun J 2015 Faster R-CNN: towards real-time object detection with region proposal networks *Adv. Neural Inform. Process. Syst.* **28** 91–9

Roboflow, 2001. Chess Pieces Dataset https://public.roboflow.com/object-detection/chess-full

Wang C-Y, Bochkovskiy A and Liao H-Y M 2022 YOLOv7: trainable bag-of-freebies sets new state-of-the-art for real-time object detectors *arXiv preprint* arXiv:2207.02696

IOP Publishing

Mastering Computer Vision with PyTorch and Machine Learning

Caide Xiao

Chapter 8

YOLOv7, YOLOv8, YOLOv9 and YOLO-World

The subjects covered in this chapter are YOLOv7 and YOLOv8. Because YOLOv8 is easy to install and very fast, readers can just focus on YOLOv8. For a project of reading digits on images in a custom dataset MNIST4yolo constructed in this chapter, the model training time with YOLOv8, YOLOv7 and YOLO-NAS is 0.5, 12 and 4.0 h respectively. Pre-trained YOLOv8 models are used for object detection, image segmentation, image classification, human pose estimation, object tracking and counting.

After Wang *et al* 2022 published their YOLOv7 paper in July of 2023, we have faster and more accurate tools for real-time object detection. We can implement them without writing codes because YOLOv7 source codes can be downloaded and cloned from WongKinYiu's GitHub website to our computers. Kin-Yiu Wong is the first author of the YOLOv7 paper. It is easy to set an environment in VS Code with Python v3.9 by installing libraries and modules listed in a text file named 'requirements.txt' from the website. Running the code in a VS Code cell: *! python detect.py –conf 0.4 –nosave –view-img –source 0*, you will see yourself on your computer's screen with a bounding box. Holding a cellphone in front of your camera, you will see two bounding boxes on your screen. If you wanting to save the object detection video to a file, just delete the *–nosave* option from the code. When you want to terminate the video recording of your camera, just press the 'q' key on your keyboard. Replacing number 0 after the source by a video file name with its absolute path, such as *d:/traffic.mp4*, you will see cars with bounding boxes while you are playing the video file downloaded from YouTube. Of course, you can record the video with bounding boxes. On my laptop, YOLOv7 finishes these jobs about 10 times faster than YOLOv3. Changing the source to a single image file name or a batch of image files with an absolute path, such as d:/*.jpg, you will see objects with bounding boxes on your images. There is a small issue for the image object detection. Images with bounding boxes disappear on your screen too soon. Since the YOLOv7 codes were written in PyTorch, we can open the detect.py file in our VS Code editor. By replacing the waiting time of 1 millisecond in the waitKey() with 3000 milli-second on line 138 of the file, you would be able to watch those images comfortably. You need to changed the waiting time in waitKey() back to 1 millisecond for video, otherwise, your video playing speed will be very slow.

8.1 YOLOv7 for object detection for a custom dataset: MNIST4yolo

It is no surprise that we get very good object detection results with YOLOv7 applied to many well-known datasets. We also need YOLOv7 models to have the same ability to give us excellent results for custom datasets. Although Hugging Face, Roboflow and Kaggle provide many free public computer vision datasets, I would like to create and use my own dataset: MNIST4yolo. The resolution of each black and white image in the MNIST4yolo dataset is 448×448. The codes in Cells 01–04 of project 8.1 can generate samples based on MNIST images for YOLOv7. As usual, Cell 01 is used to import libraries and set hyperparameters for the project. On the last line of Cell 01, A string named 'xml_path' is just a folder name to save files of synthesized images and their plain text files for bounding boxes. Codes in Cell 02 should be familiar to us. From them, we get a MNIST train dataloader and a MNIST test dataloader.

Each batch of a MNIST dataloader has 256 MNIST images which are randomly picked out from a MNIST dataloader. In a 16×16 array, a total of 256 MNIST images are used to synthesize a bigger image with a resolution of 448×448 for the MNIST4yolov7 dataset. Then using a for-loop starting from line 06 in Cell 03, we mask around 245/256 MNIST images, and only about 10 digits are visible on a synthesized image in the new dataset. The location and the label of each visible MNIST digit are recorded for bounding box information: [label, x_c, y_c, w, h]. The image width and height of each MNIST image are the same: 28/448. A for-loop in Cell 05 calls the above functions to save 560 bigger images for a training dataset and 80 bigger images for a test dataset respectively. Of course, each image has a text file about bounding boxes. It is not necessary for us to encode those bigger images with their bounding boxes to construct datasets, because a pre-trained YOLOv7 model will take care of this work. Codes in Cells 01–05 should work in Python v3.6. Otherwise, each synthesized image would have a white border around it.

```python
# Project 8.1: Create a MNIST4yolov7 dataset for yolov7---------------Python v3.6
import torch; import torch.nn as nn; from torch.utils.data import DataLoader
from torchvision import transforms as T; from torchvision.datasets import MNIST
from torchvision.utils import make_grid; from skimage.io import imsave, imread
import numpy as np; import pandas as pd; import matplotlib.pyplot as plt
import cv2; from tqdm import trange; import time
batch_size = 256    # using 16x16 MNIST images to synthesize a yolov7 image
data_path = 'C:/Users/xiaoc/Python/Exercises/OCR/data/' # path of MNIST dataset
xml_path = 'D:/ImageSets/MNIST4yolo/'  #a path to save synthesized images&labels

# Cell 02: Input original MNIST datasets for two dataloaders--------------Cell 02
train_dataset = MNIST(data_path, train=True, download=False,
                    transform=T.Compose([T.ToTensor()]))  #len(train_dataset)=60k
test_dataset = MNIST(data_path, train=False, download=False,
                    transform=T.Compose([T.ToTensor()]))  #len(test_dataset)=10k
train_dataloader=DataLoader(train_dataset, batch_size=batch_size, shuffle=True)
test_dataloader =DataLoader(test_dataset, batch_size=batch_size, shuffle=False)

# Cell 03: Randomly select a few images for bbox information used in yolov7======
def bboxes4imgs(my_dataloader):
    for imgs, labels in my_dataloader:               #---------------line 02
        break            # randomly pick out 256 MINIST images
    locations = []  #indices of visible images as objects in synthesized images
    targets = []    #labels of visible images as tagets in synthesized images
    for i in range(batch_size):                      #------------------line 06
        rand = np.random.randint(256)
        if rand > 245:                               #------------------line 08
            locations.append(i) # randomly select images from 256 images
            targets.append(labels[i].item()) # find labels of selected images
        else:
            imgs[i] = 0*imgs[i]  #  around 245/256 MNIST images are masked
    loc = np.array(locations)    #location of each visible MINST object: [0:255]
    row_j, column_i = divmod(loc, 16)   #grid cell index --------------line 14
    obj_size = 28/448        # object's w and h relative to 448---------line 15
    df = pd.DataFrame(np.empty([len(row_j), 5]),     #for bboxes information
                    index = np.arange(len(row_j)),
                    columns=['label', 'x_c', 'y_c', 'w', 'h'])
    xmin, ymin = column_i*28/448, row_j*28/448       #------------------line 19
    df.iloc[:,0] = targets
    df.iloc[:,1] = xmin + obj_size/2          # x_c = xmin + w/2
    df.iloc[:,2] = ymin + obj_size/2          # y_c = ymin + h/2
    df.iloc[:,3] = obj_size         # bbox width:  w = 28/448 = 0.0625
    df.iloc[:,4] = obj_size         # bbox height: h = 28/448 = 0.0625
    return imgs, df   #imgs is a batch of 28x28 images, most of them are masked
# Cell 04: Show and save synthsized images ============================Cell 04
def synthesize_Images(my_imgs, img_name):
    fig, ax = plt.subplots(figsize=(5.934,5.934))
    input = make_grid(my_imgs, nrow=16, padding=0) #--------------------line 03
    ax.spines['bottom'].set_visible(False); ax.spines['left'].set_visible(False)
    ax.spines['top'].set_visible(False); ax.spines['right'].set_visible(False)
    ax.set(xticks=[], yticks=[])
    ax.imshow(input.permute(1,2,0)) #-------------------------------------line 04
```

```
    plt.savefig(img_name, bbox_inches = 'tight', pad_inches = 0, dpi=100)
    plt.show()
# Cell 05: Generate batch images and text files for yoolov7 (Python v3.9) Cell 05
for idx in range(0, 80): #range(0,560) for train; range(0,80) for test
    my_imgs, df = bboxes4imgs(test_dataloader)     #------choose a dataloader
    file_name = str(idx).zfill(4)
    synthesize_Images(my_imgs, xml_path+file_name+'.jpg')
    df.to_csv(xml_path+file_name+'.txt', index=False, sep=' ', header=False)
#-------------------------------------------------------------------------------
```

I created two sub-folders in a folder named 'MNIST4yolov7', one is named 'train' and the other is named 'test'. Each of them has two sub-folders: images and labels. The synthesized images and their text files generated in Cell 05 (in the xml_path folder) were moved to MNIST4yolov7's sub-folders respectively. The MNIST4yolov7 folder are then moved to a YOLOv7 folder cloned from WongKinYiu's GitHub website. Copy a data.yaml file in the YOLOv7 folder and paste it to the train folder of the MNIST4yolov7 folder. The file can be edited by MS Notepad or the VS Code with the following information.

    train: C:/Users/xiaoc/Python/Exercises/yolov7/MNIST4yolov7/train/images
    val: C:/Users/xiaoc/Python/Exercises/yolov7/MNIST4yolov7/test/images
    nc: 10
    names: ['0', '1', '2', '3', '4', '5', '6', '7', '8', '9']

While we are training the YOLOv7 model with the custom dataset, the *data.yaml* file provides information about where our images are, the number of classes (nc) and the names of the classes. Open a new VS code terminal with Python v3.9 and change the folder to yolov7 by a DOS command *cd yolov7*, because the pre-trained weight file yolov7.pt is there. Then run the following DOS command to train the YOLOv7 model with the custom data

   python train.py –weight yolov7.pt –data MNIST4yolov7/data.yaml –batch-size 4

There is an issue about the train.py, and many people have searched the internet to find a solution to the issue. For my computer, a solution is to add *os.environ ["KMP_DUPLICATE_LIB_OK"] = "TRUE"* after *import os* on line 4 in the *train.py* file in the yolov7 folder. There is another issue which has also caused problems for many people. The default batch size of the model training is 16. My laptop's memory is not big enough, so I reduced the batch size to four. Once the second issue was solved, the long training process started.

The default training epochs are 300. After about 2.3 h of model training, I saw that the training results were bad. The values of the numbers on the diagonal of a confusion-matrix (figure 8.1) were lower. The numbers for digit 3 and digit 5 were even less than 0.4. In an idea result, each number on the diagonal of the confusion-matrix should be equal to one. This means that every ground truth is predicted 100% right. I then used the best weight file *best.pt* from each previous training to train the model six more times and each time the epochs was set to be 200. The final results are shown in figure 8.1. The values of the 10 numbers on the diagonal of the confusion-matrix are above 0.9. It took 1.5 h to train the model with 200 epochs. The total training time was

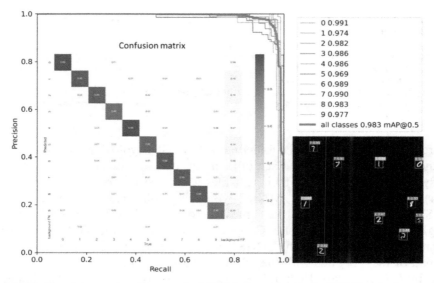

Figure 8.1. Model training results of a pre-trained YOLOv7 model with the MNIST4yolo dataset. On the blank center of the Recall-Precision curve is a Confusion-matrix. The black and white image in the lower-right corner was obtained by using the last training weight file to detect an image (0614.jpg).

about 12 h. With the following command in a VS Code terminal, I got the black and white image with digits shown on the lower-right corner of figure 8.1

python detect.py –weights best6MNIST.pt –conf 0.4 –img-size 448 –view-img –source 0614.jpg

The trained YOLOv7 model works for the MNIST4yolov7 dataset. Writing digits on paper and changing the source to 0 in the above DOS command, I was surprised that the trained model did not recognize any digits in my handwriting. Then I copied MNIST4yolov7 images to my cellphone and showed an image on my phone screen to the camera of my laptop, the trained model worked well. The Chess dataset is easy to train by the YOLOv7 model. With only in 300 epochs, the training results are very good. From a YouTube video published by Rob Mulla (www.youtube.com/watch?v=RX btSwZsoEU), you can learn more about how to train your own dataset with YOLOv7.

8.2 YOLOv7 for instance segmentation

Image segmentation is a computer vision task to partition an image or a video frame into different regions or segments. It can be used to help us to understand and analyze the content of the image at a more granular level. There are three kinds of image segmentation. The first one is semantic segmentation which marks all pixels of objects of a same class with the same color, and even pixels of background (sky, grass, trees) on the image are also marked with colors. The second one is instance segmentation which only marks pixels of countable objects on an image, and each object in the same class on the image is distinguished by different mask colors. The third one is panoramic segmentation which is a combination of the above two segmentations. Using libraries from Detectron2, YOLOv7 models can do instance segmentation for us. Detectron2 is the next generation open-source object detection framework from Facebook (Meta AI) Research.

On the website of WongKinYiu's GitHub repository, there is a mask branch. Codes in the mask branch integrate some modules of Detectron2 with YOLOv7. We can download a zip file from the mask branch and unzip the file into a folder named 'mask' in our VS Code workspace. The virtual environment for YOLOv7 can be used for the mask codes. We also need to download a zip file from Detectron2's GitHub repository and unzip it into a folder named 'detectron2'. The *detectron2* folder, the *mask* folder and the *yolov7* folder are on the same level in my VS code workspace. There are many YouTube videos to instruct us how to install Detectron2 on our computers. It is not an easy job, because Visual Studio 2022 is needed to compile some C++ files in the detectron2 folder. On my computer, most issues came from CUDA libraries. After solving issues of Detectron2 installation, we can stand on the shoulders of giants to do some great things. Open a new Jupyter notebook and save it using the name 'mask' in the mask folder in your VS code workspace, and then copy the following Cells 01–05 in project 8.2 to the notebook. Codes from line 04 to 06 in Cell 01 import libraries from files in the *../mask/utils* subfolder. Codes from line 07 to 10 import libraries from files in the *../detectron2* subfolder. A YOLOv7 model is then imported by codes in Cell 02 with pre-trained weights in a file: *yolov7-mask.pt*. From code on line 02 of Cell 02, many hyperparameters are also input from a file *hyp.scratch.mask.yaml*. You can check those parameters by using *print(hyp)* in an extra VS Code cell after Cell 02.

Codes in Cell 03 are used to do instance segmentation for any input image or video frame. These codes came from David Landup (https://stackabuse.com/instance-segmentation-with-yolov7-in-python/) and WongKinYiu's GitHub repository with modifications (https://github.com/WongKinYiu/yolov7/tree/mask). Without those codes from the two websites, it is almost impossible to know the model's output data structure (line 10–12 of Cell 03). The 'ROI Pooling' module on line 17 is an abbreviation of 'region of interest pooling', and comes from Detectron2. The output of Cell 03 is an image with instance segmentation, and the size of the image is the original image size (figure 8.2(A)). Codes on line 42–43 in Cell 03 are used to add colorful masks to objects on an image. You can deactivate them by adding a hash tag symbol in front of each of the two lines to see object detection results only (figure 8.2(B)). We can re-use the functions in Cells 05–07 of project 7.5 to display YOLOv7's outputs for images in a folder or from video. In

Figure 8.2. (A) Instance segmentation of an image. (B) Instance segmentation without masks. The video frame processing speed is about 20 FPS.

those display functions, 'yolov3' must be changed to 'yolov7'. The video frame processing speed of the pre-trained YOLOv7 model is about 20 FPS. There is an issue about the yolov7 function defined in Cell 03, and I found a solution from David Landup's YouTube video. We need to deactivate line 157 but keep the line's ")" in the file "C:\Users\xiaoc\miniconda3\Lib\site-packages\torch\nn\modules\upsampling.py". Of course, the user's name in the file path will be different.

```python
# Project 8.2: Yolov7 Instance Segmentations----------------------- Python v3.9
import torch; from torchvision import transforms
import numpy as np; import cv2; import time; import glob; from tqdm import tqdm
import matplotlib.pyplot as plt
from utils.datasets import letterbox; import yaml          #----------line 04
from utils.general import non_max_suppression_mask_conf
from utils.plots import output_to_keypoint, plot_skeleton_kpts
from detectron2.modeling.poolers import ROIPooler          #----------line 07
from detectron2.structures import Boxes
from detectron2.utils.memory import retry_if_cuda_oom
from detectron2.layers import paste_masks_in_image         #----------line 10
device = torch.device("cuda:0" if torch.cuda.is_available() else "cpu")
half = device.type != 'cpu'  # half precision only supported on CUDA
# Cell 02: load the pre-trained yolov7 model---------------------------------
with open('../mask/data/hyp.scratch.mask.yaml') as f:
    hyp = yaml.load(f, Loader=yaml.FullLoader)             #----------line 02
def load_model():
    model = torch.load('../mask/yolov7-mask.pt', map_location=device)['model']
    model.eval()
    if torch.cuda.is_available():
        model.half().to(device)
    return model
model = load_model()
# Cell 03: A function for instance image segmentation------------------------
def yolov7(my_img):
    image = cv2.cvtColor(my_img, cv2.COLOR_BGR2RGB)
    img_size = image.shape
    image = letterbox(image, 640, stride=64, auto=True)[0]
    image_ = image.copy()        # for an output image without objects----line 05
    image = transforms.ToTensor()(image)
    image = image.unsqueeze(0)  # for a batch of images with one image
    image = image.to(device)     # to use GPU to save time
    image = image.half() if half else image.float()  # for float16 to save time
    output = model(image) # bounding boxes info of  a segmented image----line 10
    inf_out = output['test']; attn = output['attn']
    bases = output['bases']; sem_output = output['sem'] #---------------line 12
    bases = torch.cat([bases, sem_output], dim=1)
    _, _, height, width = image.shape
    names = model.names
    pooler_scale = model.pooler_scale       #---------------------------line 16
    pooler = ROIPooler(output_size=hyp['mask_resolution'],scales=(pooler_scale,),
        sampling_ratio=1, pooler_type='ROIAlignV2', canonical_level=2)
    output, output_mask, _, _, _ = non_max_suppression_mask_conf(inf_out,
                attn, bases, pooler, hyp, conf_thres=0.25, iou_thres=0.65,
                merge=False, mask_iou=None)
    pred, pred_masks = output[0], output_mask[0]
    if pred is not None:                      # for an image with object(s)
        bboxes = Boxes(pred[:, :4])
        original_pred_masks = pred_masks.view(
                -1, hyp['mask_resolution'], hyp['mask_resolution'])
        pred_masks = retry_if_cuda_oom(paste_masks_in_image)(
```

```
                        original_pred_masks, bboxes, (height, width), threshold=0.5)
        pred_masks_np = pred_masks.detach().cpu().numpy()
        pred_cls = pred[:, 5].detach().cpu().numpy()
        pred_conf = pred[:, 4].detach().cpu().numpy()
        nbboxes = bboxes.tensor.detach().cpu().numpy().astype(int)
        output_img = image[0].permute(1,2,0)*255
        output_img = output_img.cpu().numpy().astype(np.uint8)
        output_img = cv2.cvtColor(output_img, cv2.COLOR_RGB2BGR)
        for one_mask,bbox,cls,conf in zip(
            pred_masks_np,nbboxes,pred_cls,pred_conf):
            if conf < 0.25:
                continue
            color = [np.random.randint(255), np.random.randint(255),
                     np.random.randint(255)]
            output_img[one_mask] = (output_img[one_mask]*0.5 +    # ====line -42
                np.array(color, dtype=np.uint8)*0.5)  # add masks == line -43
            label = '%s %.3f' %(names[int(cls)], conf)
            tf = max(1 - 1, 1)  #opt.thickness = 1
            t_size = cv2.getTextSize(label, 0, fontScale=1/3, thickness=tf)[0]
            c2 = bbox[0] + t_size[0], bbox[1] - t_size[1] - 3
            cv2.rectangle(output_img, (bbox[0], bbox[1]), (bbox[2], bbox[3]),
                        color, thickness=1, lineType=cv2.LINE_AA)
            cv2.rectangle(output_img, (bbox[0], bbox[1]),
                        c2, color, -1, cv2.LINE_AA) #filled label
            cv2.putText(output_img, label, (bbox[0], bbox[1]-2), 0, 1/2,
                        [255,255,255], thickness=tf, lineType=cv2.LINE_AA)
        else: output_img = image_      # to an image without any object
        output_img = cv2.resize(output_img, (img_size[1], img_size[0]))
        return output_img
%matplotlib inline
fig, ax = plt.subplots(figsize=(10,8)); ax.axis("off")
ax.imshow(yolov7(plt.imread('d:/STANPED1105.jpg'))); plt.show()
# Cell 04: Re-use Cell 05 of Project 7.5 for Slide show images in a folder-------
# Cell 05: Re-use Cell 06 or 07 of Project 7.5 for camera or a video file--------
#-----------------------------------The End-----------------------------------
```

8.3 Using YOLOv7 for human pose estimation (key point detection)

Human pose estimation is a computer vision task which is used to estimate the positions and orientations of human joints (key points) from images or video frames. There are numerous applications of pose estimation. By tracking the pose of a person over time, it is possible to analyze and recognize specific actions or gestures. Human key points are vital points in our bodies for movements. YOLOv7 traces 18 key points of our bodies. The human nose tip is point 0. The middle point of a line linking two shoulders is point 1. From left to right, six points are on joints of two arms and six points are on joints of two legs. Then two points are for two eyes and two points are for two ears. Usually, pose estimation needs expensive position tracking hardware. There is pose estimation software, such as Google DeepPose and MediaPipe. They work in two stages: person detection and key point detection. YOLOv7 pose is a one-stage multi-person key point detector. In WongKinYiu's YOLOv7 GitHub repository, there is a pose branch for us to download. After Unzipping a downloaded file from the branch to the 'mask' folder in our VS Code workspace, we can run a pre-trained key point detection model with a weight file *yolov7-w6-pose.pt* for human key point detection (Maji *et al* 2022).

Codes on line 02–04 in Cell 01 of project 8.3.1 import functions from Python files *datasets.py*, *general.py* and *plots.py* respectively. These files are in the *../mast/utils/* folder. A function defined in Cell 02 loads a YOLOv7 pose model and a pre-trained weight file. If GPU is available, the model will be moved to GPU memory and half floating numbers (float16) will be used to save time. You can print out the model to see the structure of the model, and you can also print the *model.yaml* file to see some of the hyperparameters of the model. The code on line 02 of Cell 03 is used to keep the size of the input image, so the size of the output image with key points can be resized to the original image size by the code on line 18 of Cell 03. The Code on line 03 of Cell 03 uses the *letterbox* function to modify the input image to fit the model. One modification is to resize the input image to 960×960. The output of the *process_img ()* function in Cell 03 is an image with key points. We can re-use Cells 04 and 05 in the last section to display images or video by changing *yolov7* to *process_img*. An image with processed results is shown in figure 8.3. The image processing speed of the YOLOv7 pose mode is around 15 FPS, and a pre-trained Detectron2 pose model is around 3 FPS (appendix F).

```python
# Project 8.3.1 Yolov7 for human pose estimation--------------------Python v3.9
import torch; from torchvision import transforms
from utils.datasets import letterbox               #====================line 02
from utils.general import non_max_suppression_kpt
from utils.plots import output_to_keypoint, plot_skeleton_kpts  #========line 04
import cv2; import glob; import numpy as np
import matplotlib.pyplot as plt; import time; from tqdm import tqdm
device = torch.device("cuda:0" if torch.cuda.is_available() else "cpu")
half = device.type != 'cpu'      #-------------------Using float16 to save time
# Cell 02: import pre-trained yolov7 model loading for pose estimation----------
def load_model():
    model = torch.load('../mask/yolov7-w6-pose.pt',map_location=device)['model']
    model.eval()
    if torch.cuda.is_available():
        model.half().to(device)
    return model
model = load_model()
# Cell 03: A function to process a batch of images------------------------------
def process_img(image):
    img_size = image.shape         #===============================line 02
    image = letterbox(image, 960, stride=64, auto=True)[0]  #=========line 03
    image = transforms.ToTensor()(image)
    image = image.half().to(device) if half else image.float()
    image = image.unsqueeze(0)  # a batch of images with one image    line 06
    with torch.no_grad():
      output, _ = model(image)
    output=non_max_suppression_kpt(output,0.25,0.65,nc=1,nkpt=17,kpt_label=True)
    #NMS thresh=0.25, IoU thresh=0.65, nc: Classes Number, nkpt: Keypoints Number
    with torch.no_grad():
        output = output_to_keypoint(output)
    output_img = image[0].permute(1, 2, 0) * 255
    output_img = output_img.cpu().numpy().astype(np.uint8)
    output_img = cv2.cvtColor(output_img, cv2.COLOR_RGB2BGR)
    for idx in range(output.shape[0]):
        plot_skeleton_kpts(output_img, output[idx, 7:].T, 3)
    output_img = cv2.resize(output_img, (img_size[1], img_size[0]))   #line 18
    return cv2.cvtColor(output_img, cv2.COLOR_RGB2BGR)
%matplotlib inline
fig, ax = plt.subplots(figsize=(10,8)); plt.axis('off')
ax.imshow(process_img(plt.imread('d:/Monkeys.jpg')));
#Re-use Cell 05-07 of Project 7.5 to show processed images, video or a video file
#----------------------------------The End-------------------------------
```

Figure 8.3. Outputs of Cell 03 about a pre-trained YOLOv7 pose model applied to an image. The model's video processing speed is around 15 FPS.

Aarohi Singla has a very helpful GitHub repository website to teach people how to use Detectron2. Based on her codes, I was able to import pre-trained Detectron2 models to my PyTorch codes for object detection, instance segmentation, panoptic segmentation and key point detection (codes are listed in appendix F). The image processing speed for object detection, instance segmentation, panoptic segmentation and key point detection are 3, 4, 2 and 3 respectively. Models based on YOLOv7 are faster. There are many other open-source libraries for image segmentation. Pixellib is one of them. With modules imported from Pixellib, codes with only five lines are needed for image and video segmentations, but you have to install tensorflow and keras. I tried to use a Pixellib model with a pre-trained weight file 'deeplabv3_x-ception65_ade20k.h5' for video semantic segmentation, and found its image processing speed was about 3 FPS. Using a Pixellib model for image instance segmentation with a pre-trained weight file named 'mask_rcnn_coco.h5', I saw that masks from the model are not as good as YOLOv7's masks. I also tried Apache MXNet for image segmentation. Image processing speed for video with pre-trained models of MNNet libraries is about 1 FPS. Detectron2 provides the best masks for instance segmentation. CVZONE is a computer vision package that makes its easy to run image processing and AI functions. The core of cvzone uses OpenCV and mediapipe libraries. Using the following codes and Cell 07 of project 7.5, we can use a CVZONE pose detector to process video frames from a camera, ant the speed is about 35 FPS.

```
# Project 8.3.2 Application of cvzone's Pose detector--------------- Python v3.9
from cvzone.PoseModule import PoseDetector; import cv2; import time
import glob; from tqdm import tqdm
detector = PoseDetector()
def poseDetector(img):
    img = detector.findPose(img)
    lmList, bboxInfo = detector.findPosition(img, bboxWithHands=False)
    if bboxInfo:
        center = bboxInfo["center"]
        cv2.circle(img, center, 5, (255, 0, 255), cv2.FILLED)
    return img
#----- Re-use Cell 07 of Project 7.5 for Video from a camera--------------The End
```

8.4 Applications of YOLOv8, YOLOv9 and YOLO-World models

8.4.1 Image object detection, segmentation, classification and pose estimation

On January 10, 2023, YOLOv8 was released by Glenn Jocher, the founder of Ultralytics who also launched YOLOv5 a few years ago. Built on the success of previous YOLO versions, YOLOv8 is designed to be faster, more accurate, and easier to use. If you had managed to install YOLOv3 in your computer, you would appreciate the work that YOLOv8 team have done for us. I spent one week compiling YOLOv3's darknet in my computer, because I had to find ways to coordinate VC++, OpenCV, Nvidia CUDA and other third-party software to share their libraries. For YOLOv8, just using a DOS command *pip install ultralytics* in a VS Code terminal, you can install YOLOv8 in a virtual environment of VS Code in a few minutes, depending on your internet speed to download files from YOLOv8 website. There are many models supported by pre-trained parameter files for us to download. Those files are not very big and are easy for people to use. On the home page of YOLOv8, there are detail instructions about how to install Ultralytics and use pre-trained models. DOS command line interface (CLI) of YOLOv8 lets us to train, validate or infer models on various tasks. The following is an example of a DOS code to take video for yourself by using your laptop's camera. Adding an exclamation mark '!' in front of the DOS code, you can even run it in a VS Code cell. If you set the save option in the following DOS command to be True, your video will be saved in a file. I downloaded a traffic video from YouTube and save the video to a file named *d:/traffic.mp4*. Changing the DOS command's source option from 0 to the video file name, I can watch video frames with bounding boxes, labels and probabilities. The video processing speed is about 100 FPS. With YOLOv3 and YOLOv7 models, the speed was 2 and 20 FPS respectively. Changing the source to an image file named *d:/dog.jpg*, you can see object detection results from the pre-trained yolov8 model. However, the image disappears quickly on my computer's screen. Changing the model to 'yolov8n-seg.pt', 'yolov8n-cls.pt', 'yolov8n-pose.pt' and other pre-trained models, we can use the single line code for instance segmentation, image classification and pose estimation. An alphabet following yolov8 in a model's name could be n, s, m, l and x to denote the size of a pre-trained YOLOv8 mode from nano, small, medium, large to extreme large respectively.

> *yolo task=detect mode=predict model=yolov8n.pt source=0 conf=0.25 iou=0.5 conf=0.15 show=True save=False*

It is more flexible to use YOLOv8 models in a Python environment of VS Code. Just using codes in 7 lines, the following project 8.4.1 could also be used for object detection, image semantic segmentation, image classification and pose estimation by changing the name of the pre-trained model on line 04 of Cell 01. Those models were trained with MS COCO dataset. Deleting [2030:2040] from line 05 in Cell 02, you would display all 17,125 VOC images one by one. It takes a long time to watch the slide-show. You can terminate the program at any time by pressing the Esc key on your keyboard, but be sure to let your computer to focus on the image window by click your mouse on the image window. By default, each image will be shown in 1000 milliseconds set by an option of the waitKey() on line 08. To accelerate the slid show, you can press any key (such as the space bar) other than the Esc key. Some objects ignored by yolo8n.pt could be detected by yolo8l.pt. Changing the code on line 04 of Cell 01 to 'yolov8 = YOLO('yolov8n.pt').track', you would see each detected object on an image has an ID number. However, the object tracking function does not work for classification models. In February of 2024, Chien-Yao Wang and his collaborators (Wang *et al* 2024) released YOLOv9 which was built on top of YOLOv7. After upgrading Ultralytics to the latest version (v8.1.24), I can test a pre-trained a YOLOv9 model by running codes in Project 8.4.1 by replacing 'yolov8n.pt' with 'yolov9c.pt' on line 04 of Cell 01. The video processing speed of the YOLOv9 model is 25 FPS. I also tested a pre-trained YOLO-World model 'yolov8s-world.pt' and found that its video processing speed was about 50 FPS. YOLO-World (Cheng *et al* 2024) models enable us to detect any object within an image based on descriptive texts. Codes on line 05-6 are used for the YOLO-World model. A string list in line 06 is for the descriptive texts which instructs the model to find objects listed in the string list.

```
# Project 8.4.1 Applications of YOLOv8 YOLOv9 and YOLO-World models---Python v3.9
from ultralytics import YOLO; import matplotlib.pyplot as plt
import cv2; import glob; from tqdm import tqdm; import time
model = YOLO("yolov8n.pt") # yolov8n-seg.pt, yolov8n-pose.pt, yolov8n-cls.pt
#model = YOLO('yolov9c.pt')                      #--------------------line 04
#model = YOLO('yolov8s-world.pt')                #--------------------line 05
#model.set_classes(["person", "cat", "horse"])  #for YOLO-World------line 06
source = 'd:/Stamped2023.jpg'
results = model.predict(source, verbose=False)[0].plot()
plt.imshow(cv2.cvtColor(results, cv2.COLOR_BGR2RGB));
# Cell 02: to slide-show images processed by a pre-trained YOLO models ---Cell 02
def slide_show(file_path):
    file_list = glob.glob(file_path)
    for file in tqdm(file_list[2030:2040]):
        image = cv2.imread(file)
        annotated_img = model(image, verbose=False)[0].plot()
        cv2.imshow('press Esc to stop the video', annotated_img)
        if (cv2.waitKey(1000)&0xFF)==27:
            break
    cv2.destroyAllWindows()
source = 'D:/ImageSets/VOC/VOCdevkit/VOC2012/JPEGImages/*.jpg'
slide_show(source)
# Cell 03: show video frames processed by a pre-trained YOLO modes--------Cell 03
def video_player(source):
    cap = cv2.VideoCapture(source)
    while True:
        (notLastFrame, frame) = cap.read()
        start_time = time.time()
        if not notLastFrame or (cv2.waitKey(1)&0xFF==27):
            break
        output = model(frame, verbose=False)[0].plot()
        fps = str(int(1/(time.time() - start_time + 1e-5)))
        cv2.putText(output, fps, (7, 70), 0, 3, (100, 255, 0), 3, cv2.LINE_AA)
        cv2.imshow('Esc', output)
    cap.release()
    cv2.destroyAllWindows()
video_player(0)      # The source is 0 or 'd:/traffic1.mp4'
#---------------------------------------The End---------------------------------
```

8.4.2 Object counting on an image or a video frame

In project 8.4.2, YOLOv8 models are used to count objects detected on a single image or video frame. An image in a NumPy array is used as a source of a YOLOv8 model in a function named 'yolov8' (line 06). You could use the code on line 07 to replace the code on line 06 to assign an object ID number to each detected object, and would find that many objects were not detected. It is convenient for us to obtain bounding box information from outputs of a YOLOv8 model (lines 08–10). Codes on lines 11–13 counter numbers of objects in a category of COCO dataset. The counting result is a dictionary using object names as its keys, and object numbers as its values. The dictionary is then converted to a text string by codes on lines 14–16. This string is then printed on the bottom of the image. The coordinates $(x1, y1)$ and $(x2, y2)$ of a bounding box are absolute pixel values relative to the top-left corner of an input image. We are able to write our own codes to add bounding boxes, class indices and probabilities on images. Codes in Cell 02 display a single image (figure 8.4) with bounding boxes obtained by the pre-trained YOLOv8 model *yolov8l.pt*. On the bottom of the image, you will see that six kinds of objects were detected. Change the pre-trained model on line 02 to see the difference in object counting. We can

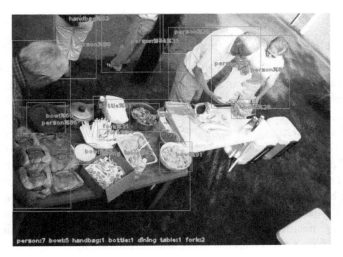

Figure 8.4. Object detection/counting by a pre-trained YOLOv8 model for an image. Video process speed is about 80 FPS.

re-use codes in Cells 05–07 of project 7.5 to display counting results for images from a folder or from video frames. The video processing speed of model 'yolov8n.pt' and 'yolov8l.pt' is 80 and 25 FPS respectively.

```python
# Project 8.4.2 Using Yolov8 to counter objects on an image ----------Python v3.9
from ultralytics import YOLO
import cv2; import numpy as np; import glob; from tqdm import tqdm
import matplotlib.pyplot as plt; from collections import Counter; import time
model = YOLO('yolov8n.pt')      #----------------------------------------line 04
def yolov8(image):
    outputs = model(image, conf=0.25, verbose=False)[0].boxes # --------line 06
    #outputs = model.track(image, conf=0.25, verbose=False)[0].boxes #---line 07
    boxes = outputs.xyxy
    P = outputs.conf
    labels = outputs.cls                    # labels are class ids------line 10
    objects_list = Counter(labels.cpu().numpy())    # counter objects----line 11
    objects_counter = {model.model.names[int(list_k)]: list_v for (
                            list_k, list_v) in objects_list.items()}
    counter_text = str()    # convert a dictionary to a text string------line 14
    for k,v in objects_counter.items():
        counter_text += (k+":"+str(v)+" ") # objects counter list to string
    cv2.putText(image, counter_text, (10, image.shape[0]-10), 1, 1, (0,255,0),2)
    for box, p, label in zip(boxes, P, labels):
        class_labels = f"{model.model.names[int(label.item())]}%{int(p*100)}"
        x1, y1, x2, y2 = [int(z) for z in box]
        xc, yc = [int((x1+x2)/2), int((y1+y2)/2)]
        cv2.rectangle(image, (x1,y1), (x2, y2), (255, 0, 255), 1)
        cv2.putText(image, class_labels, (xc, yc), 1, 1, (255, 0, 255),2)
    return image
# Cell 02: Single image show--------------------------------------------------
fig, ax = plt.subplots(figsize=(12,8)); plt.axis('off')
outputs = cv2.cvtColor(yolov8(cv2.imread('d:/Picnic.jpg')), cv2.COLOR_RGB2BGR)
ax.imshow(outputs);
#Re-use Cell 05-07 of Project 7.5 to show processed images, video or a video file
#-----------------------------------------------------------------------The End
```

8.4.3 Car tracking and counting for a video file

Object tracking and counting refer to processes of locating and monitoring objects in a video or an image sequence and then counting the number of objects belonging to a class of interest. Object tracking and counting find applications in many domains, such as surveillance, traffic monitoring, people counting, retail analytics, sports analysis, and wildlife monitoring, etc. There are three steps for this kind of computer vision task. The first one is object detection by YOLO or other object detection algorithms. The second is object tracking, and its aim is to associate objects detected in the current frame with the previously tracked objects on the previous frame. The final step is object counting. Applying the codes of the following project 8.4.3 to a video file, we will track and count cars running in opposite directions separately. Trucks running beside cars will be ignored in the video. The project codes are inspired by FREEDOM TECH's YouTube and his GitHub repository.

```
# Project 8.4.3 Tracking and counting cars for a video file----------Python v3.9
from ultralytics import YOLO; import cv2; import math; import time
model = YOLO('yolov8s.pt')      # a pre-trained YOLOv8 model------------line 02
green_y=340  # green line for a detection zone [green_y-dy,green_y+dy]---line 03
red_y=370    # red line for a detection zone [red_y-dy,red_y+dy]--------line 04
dy=6
vh_down = {}     # {1: 318, 0: 370...} Car IDs with y locations ----------line 06
n_down = []      # a list of car ids [1, 0,...] for counting of cars running down
vh_up = {}       # To register cars running up or away
n_up = []        # the length of the list is used to count cars running up
#---------------------------------------------------------------------------------
```

Before being processed by a pre-trained YOLOv8 model, each video frame is resized to 1024×512. A processed video frame shown in figure 8.5 is about vehicles running

Figure 8.5. Traffic tracking and counting for cars running down and up on video frames separately. The video file (~9 MB) came from my cellphone at a crossing of highway 1 and 36 St of North East of Calgary, Canada.

on a highway. The left-hand-side vehicles are moving towards the camera taking the video, and their directions are down: from the top to the bottom of the frame. The right-hand-side vehicles are moving away from the camera, and their directions are up: from the bottom to the top of the frame. Codes in Cell 01 import libraries and a small pre-trained YOLOv8 model. Seven hyperparameters are also set in the cell as usual. Two of them on line 03 and 04 set the y-axis locations of a green line and a red line as shown in the figure. Corresponding to the green line's position at $y=340$, a green zone on the frame with $340\text{-dy} \leqslant y \leqslant 340\text{+dy}$ is a detection zone for cars running up, where dy is set to be 6 pixels by a code on line 05. Also, the red line at $y=370$ sets a red zone of the same size area to detect cars running down. Other four hyperparameters will be explained later.

```
# Cell 04: Showing video for car tracking & counting--------------------Cell 04
vh_down={}; n_down=[]; vh_up={}; n_up=[]    # to empty counting data
def output_video(source):
    video_frame = cv2.VideoCapture(source)
    fm=1; FM = int(video_frame.get(cv2.CAP_PROP_FRAME_COUNT))    #FM: total frames
    while True:
        ret, frame = video_frame.read()
        if not ret or (cv2.waitKey(1)&0xFF) == 27: break
        start_time = time.time()
        out = yolov8tc(frame)
        fps = str(int(1/(time.time()-start_time+1e-5)))
        cv2.putText(out, f'FPS={fps}', (7,30), 0, 1, (255,0,255),2)
        cv2.putText(out, f'Frame={fm}%{FM}', (750,30), 0, 1, (255,0,255), 2)
        cv2.imshow("press Esc to stop the video", out)
        fm += 1
    video_frame.release(); cv2.destroyAllWindows()
output_video("d:/Project8_4_3.mp4")
#-------------------------------------The End-------------------------------------
```

We have to start to explain codes of the project from the last cell: Cell 04 which is almost the same as Cell 07 of project 7.5. Codes in this cell read a video file frame by frame. After a frame is processed by a function defined in Cell 03, information is added to the processed frame as shown on the above figure. The digit on the lower-left corner of the figure is the number of cars running down from the time of frame 0 to the time of current frame, and the digit on the lower-right corner is the number of cars running up. When a car is in a detection area, its bounding box center will be marked by a white dot, and its ID number will be shown beside the white dot. The color of the ID number is the color of the horizontal line for the detection zone. The top-left corner shows the image processing speed with a big variance. When there is no vehicle on the road, we may get a 'divided by zero' error. A small number (10^{-5}) is used in FPS calculations to prevent this issue. The current frame's sequence number and total frames of the video are shown on the top-right corner of the figure. At the time of frame 140/572 as shown in the figure, four cars had been found running up and two cars had been found running down. The image processing speed of the model was 57 FPS. At that moment, a black car with ID 229 was running down and was in the red zone.

```
#Cell 03: A function to pack a pre-trained YOLOv8 model for tracking and counting
def yolov8tc(frame):
    frame=cv2.resize(frame,(1024,512))       #----------------------------line 02
    outputs = model(frame, conf=0.25, verbose=False)[0].boxes # --------line 03
    boxes = outputs.xyxy
    labels = outputs.cls                    # labels are COCO class ids-------line 05
    car_list=[]
    for box, label in zip(boxes, labels):   #----------------------------line 07
        c = model.model.names[int(label.item())]  # cOCO class name -----line 08
        if 'car' in c:
            x, y, X, Y = [int(z) for z in box]
            car_list.append([x, y, X, Y])          #----------------------line 11
    cxcyIDs=tracker.update(car_list) #Call Tracker() in cell 02----------line 12
    for bbox in cxcyIDs:                    # moniter a car's y position--------line 13
        cx, cy, id = bbox
        if (cy > (green_y-dy)) and (cy < (green_y+dy)): #touchs the green zone
            cv2.circle(frame,(cx,cy),4,(255,255,255),-1)       #-------line 16
            cv2.putText(frame, str(id),(cx,cy),0,0.8,(0,255,0),2)
            vh_down[id] = cy              # register a car running down----line 18
        if id in vh_down:
            if (cy > (red_y-dy)) and (cy < (red_y+dy)):  #touchs the red zone
                if n_down.count(id)==0:     #if id is new ---------------line 21
                    n_down.append(id)     # only a new ID will be counted
        if (cy > (red_y-dy)) and (cy < (red_y+dy)):     #for a car running up
            vh_up[id] = cy               # register a car running up
            cv2.circle(frame,(cx,cy),4,(255,255,255),-1)
            cv2.putText(frame,str(id),(cx,cy),0,0.8,(0,0,255),2)
        if id in vh_up:
            if (cy > (green_y-dy)) and (cy < (green_y+dy)):
                if n_up.count(id)==0:       #if id is new
                    n_up.append(id)                    #---------------line 30
    cv2.putText(frame,f'-Car: {len(n_up)}',(910,490),0,0.8,(0,0,255),2)
    cv2.putText(frame,f'+Car: {len(n_down)}',(5,490),0,0.8,(0,255,0),2)
    cv2.line(frame,(200,green_y),(800,green_y),(0,255,0),1) #Green line
    cv2.line(frame,(135,red_y),(850,red_y),(0,0,255),1)   #Red line
    return frame
#-----------------------------------------------------------------------------
```

The name of the function defined in Cell 03: *yolov8tc* means that the function based on a pre-trained YOLOv8 model is used for object tracking and counting. The function is a modification of the yolov8 function defined in Cell 01 of project 8.4.2. A code on line 02 resizes an original video frame into a new frame to a size of 1024×512. The new frame is then processed by the YOLOv8 model to get each object's bounding box coordinates (boxes), and the bounding box's COCO class identity number (labels). We use codes on line 07–11 to pick out cars and pack four coordinates of each car's bounding box into a list which is then appended to a list named 'car_list'. A bounding box's four coordinates are for the box's top-left corner (x,y) and the lower-right corner (X,Y). On line 12 of Cell 03, the car list is processed by a function of an instance of a class Tracker defined in Cell 02, and the output of the track function is still a list named 'cxcyid'. The input list and the output list have the same length. However, each list inside the output list *cxcyid* has three elements: two center coordinates of a bounding box and an ID number assigned by the Tracker class. The two center coordinates are obtained by the two formulae: $cx=int((x+X)/2)$ and $cy=int((y+Y)/2)$. The Tracker is smarter enough to know if an object detected on the current frame was on the previous frame. If a car is new object on the current frame, it will be assigned a bigger ID number assigned by the Tracker.

On the current frame, we know each car with an ID number and its center coordinates. Codes on line 13–30 are used to check y-axis positions of cars. If a car is in the green zone (code on line 15), we will mark it with a white dot and print its ID number beside the dot on the current frame. The car is then registered in a dictionary named 'vh_down' for cars running down. For a car whose ID in the vh_down dictionary touches the red zone, and the car's ID is new (code on line 21) to a list named 'n_down', the car's ID will be appended to the list. The length of the list is the number of cars running down from the time of frame 0 to the time of current frame. In the same way, the number of cars running up can also be obtained by codes on line 23 to 30. We then print the two numbers on the two lower corners of the frame as shown in the figure. Also, two lines for the green and red zones are printed on the frame. The function yolov8tc returns a frame with the above information.

```python
# Cell 02: A class to calculate car center coordinates and assign car IDs--------
class Tracker():
    def __init__(self):
        self.center_points = {} #keep car center points on the previous frame
        self.id_count = 1 #keep the last car ID on the previous frame plus 1
    def update(self, car_list):
        cxcyIDs = []          #[[111,122, 1], [120, 200, 2], ...]   line 06
        for xyXY in car_list:      #----------------------------line 07
            x, y, X, Y = xyXY
            cx = int((x + X)/2)
            cy = int((y + Y)/2)
            same_object_detected = False   # check if the car was detected

            for id, pt in self.center_points.items():        #---------line 12
                dist = math.hypot(cx - pt[0], cy - pt[1])   #---------line 13
                if dist < 35:
                    self.center_points[id] = (cx, cy)   #update old ID center
                    cxcyIDs.append([cx, cy, id])      #------------line 16
                    same_object_detected = True
                    break  #the car is found on the previous frame----line 18
            if same_object_detected is False:   # assign an ID to new object
                self.center_points[self.id_count] = (cx, cy)        # line 20
                cxcyIDs.append([cx, cy, self.id_count])
                self.id_count += 1   #-------------------------------line 22
        new_center_points = {} # to delete repeated IDs--------------line 23
        for obj_bb_id in cxcyIDs:
            _, _, object_id = obj_bb_id
            center = self.center_points[object_id]
            new_center_points[object_id] = center
        self.center_points = new_center_points.copy()       #---------line 28
        return cxcyIDs#, self.center_points
tracker=Tracker()
#-----------------------------------------------------------------------------
```

When we use a code on the last line of Cell 02 to define an instance of the class Tracker, the instance is initialized by an empty dictionary named 'center_points' and a scalar named 'id_count'. A code on line 12 of Cell 03 only calls the instance's function 'tracker.update()' to process the current video frame. Center coordinates of cars on the previous frame are kept in center_points, and the maximum ID number on the previous frame was increased by 1 and saved in the *id_count*. Suppose the pre-trained YOLOv8 model found three cars on the first frame, and the tracker.update() function is used to process the car list. In a for-loop starting from line 07 of Cell 02, the first car's center points are obtained at first, and the car's same object detected property is set to be False. Since the center_points dictionary is empty at the time of the first frame, codes from line 12 to line 18 are skipped. The first car will be assigned with an ID number 1 by a code on line 20, and the *id_count* will be 2 then. Now the *center_points* dictionary has one element {1: (cx1, cy1)}, and the center_ids will be [[cx1, cy1, 1]].

We are still in the loop started from line 07 to calculate the second car's center. A sub-loop starting from line 12 to line 18 checks the Euclidean distance between the second car and the first car. If the distance is less than 35 pixels, the two cars are the same object. If they are not the same, the second car will be assigned with an ID number 2, and the *center_points* will have two elements {1: (cx1, cy1), 2:(cy2, cy2)}. After the third car is processed, we have the center_points {1: (cx1, cy1), 2:(cx2, cy2), 3:(cx3,cy3)} if their distances are longer than 35, and the id_count is 4. Occasionally, the distance between two cars is shorter than 35, so they have a same ID number. Codes from line 23 to 28 are used to keep only the latest car from many cars with a same ID number.

While the yolov8tc function is processing the second frame, the tracker.update() function will be called again. The *center_points* dictionary and the *id_count* scalar obtained from the first frame are kept in the ___int___( ) function of the Tracker class. They are used for processing of the second frame. If the second frame only has the same three cars and each of them move a distance less than 35 pixels, the Tracker's update function will identify each of the three cars with an old ID number on the first frame. The *id_count* will not be changed (=4), but the *center_points* dictionary for the three cars will be updated. In a condition that a car's moving distance is longer than 35 pixels in the time interval between two frames, the car will be assigned a new ID as a new object. But this is not right. The number 35 is a critical distance, a hyperparameter for the project. It is dependent on camera resolutions and many other hardware settings. Codes for a new version of project 8.4.3 are listed in appendix G. Codes in the new version can detect running objects in multiple COCO classes. Each object's COCO class label (an integer) detected by YOLOv8 is registered in the car list on line 07 of Cell 03 for codes of the new version. With the extra information, it is possible for us to count cars and trucks simultaneously.

8.4.4 Fine tuning YOLOv8 for objection detection and annotation for a custom dataset

YOLOv8 and YOLOv7 models use the same format of annotation files, and even a yaml file of the MNIST4yolo dataset can be used for both of them. Using codes in the following project 8.4.4, we will implement the pre-trained *yolov8n.pt* model to the

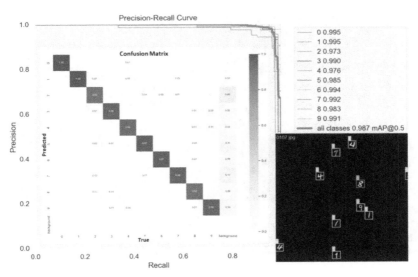

Figure 8.6. Fine tuning a YOLOv8 model for the MNIST4yolo dataset. On the blank center of the Recall-Precision curve is a confusion-matrix. The black and white image on the lower-right corner was obtained during model training.

MNIST4yolo custom dataset. In model training with 100 epochs, codes on lines 03–04 are deactivated by adding a hash tag # in front each of them. Model training finished in 20 min, and a best trained model was saved in the path shown on line 04. This trained model could be used for the next 100 epochs by removing the hash tags in front of line 03–04, and adding a hash tag in front of line 02. But no more model training is needed. I was surprised to get very good results (figure 8.6) just in 20 min. Those results shown in figure 8.1 from YOLOv7 took 12 h of model training for the same dataset.

```
# Project 8.4.4-1 Fine Tuning YOLOv8 for a custom dataset MNIST4yolo--Python v3.9
from ultralytics import YOLO
model = YOLO('yolov8n.pt')                          #-----------------line 02
#model = YOLO(                                       #-----------------line 03
#    'C:/Users/xiaoc/Python/Exercises/yolov7/runs/detect/train17/weights/best.pt')
results = model.train(
    data='C:/Users/xiaoc/Python/Exercises/yolov7/MNIST4yolov7/data.yaml',
    epochs=100,
    imgsz=448,
    batch=4)
#------------------------------The End of Model Fine Tuning-----------------------
```

The trained YOLOv8 model is very useful. In case we have 10 000 images we manually label 1000 images, and train a YOLOv8 model by the 1000 images. Then using the trained YOLOv8 model in the following Cells 2–3, we can automatically label the remaining 9000 images. A test image and its annotation table shown in figure 8.7 are outputs of Cell 03. The annotation table is predicted by the trained YOLOv8 model. Although the predicted and the ground truth are a little different, we can see that the prediction is very good, based on the bounding boxes on the left image of figure 8.7.

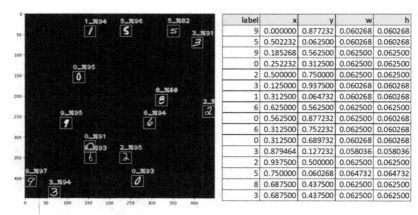

label	x	y	w	h
9	0.000000	0.877232	0.060268	0.060268
5	0.502232	0.062500	0.060268	0.060268
9	0.185268	0.562500	0.062500	0.062500
0	0.252232	0.312500	0.062500	0.062500
2	0.500000	0.750000	0.062500	0.062500
3	0.125000	0.937500	0.060268	0.060268
1	0.312500	0.064732	0.060268	0.060268
6	0.625000	0.562500	0.062500	0.062500
0	0.562500	0.877232	0.062500	0.060268
6	0.312500	0.752232	0.062500	0.062500
0	0.312500	0.689732	0.062500	0.060268
3	0.879464	0.127232	0.058036	0.058036
2	0.937500	0.500000	0.062500	0.062500
5	0.750000	0.060268	0.064732	0.064732
8	0.687500	0.437500	0.062500	0.062500
3	0.687500	0.437500	0.062500	0.062500

Figure 8.7. Using a trained YOLOv8 model to annotate the MNIST4yolo test dataset. (Left) A test image with predicted bounding boxes. (Right) A table of the predicted bounding boxes (x and y are coordinates of a bounding box's top-left corner; w and h are weight and height of the bounding box; the ground truth w=h=0.625).

```
# Cell 02 Evaluation of the best.pt model for images in the test dataset---------
from ultralytics import YOLO; import cv2
import pandas as pd; import numpy as np; import glob; from tqdm import tqdm
import matplotlib.pyplot as plt; import matplotlib.patches as patches
model = YOLO('../yolov7/runs/detect/train17/weights/best.pt')
classes = ['0', '1', '2', '3', '4', '5', '6', '7', '8', '9']
def yolov8(image):
    outputs = model(image, conf=0.25, verbose=False) # ------------------line 02
    boxes = outputs[0].boxes.xyxy
    P = outputs[0].boxes.conf
    labels = outputs[0].boxes.cls                    #------------------line 05
    bboxes = []
    for box, p, label in zip(boxes, P, labels):
        class_label = classes[int(label.item())]+'_%'+str(int(p.item()*100))
        x1, y1, x2, y2 = [z/448 for z in box.cpu()]
        bboxes.append([int(label.item()), x1, y1, x2-x1, y2-y1])

        x1, y1, x2, y2 = [int(z) for z in box]
        cv2.rectangle(image, (x1,y1), (x2, y2), (255, 0, 255), 1)
        cv2.putText(image, class_label, (x1, y1-5), 1, 1, (0, 255, 0),2)
    return image, pd.DataFrame(np.array(bboxes))
# Cell 03: show a single image and automatically labelled images----------------
source = '../yolov7/MNIST4yolov7/test/images/0638.jpg'
image = cv2.imread(source, 1)
%matplotlib inline
fig, ax = plt.subplots(figsize=(12,8))
output_img, bboxes = yolov8(image)
df = bboxes.astype({0: 'int'})             # ------bounding boxes information
print(df)
df.to_csv(r'd:/MNIST4yolov8.txt',          #-------to automatically label images
          header=None, index=None, float_format='%.6f', sep=' ')
outputs = cv2.cvtColor(output_img, cv2.COLOR_RGB2BGR)
ax.imshow(outputs);
#------------------------------------------The End-----------------------------
```

We still need to label some images of our own datasets. I found that labelImg is a very useful tool for image annotation. This tool was created by Tzutalin with the help of dozens of contributors. It is free software under MIT license. In a VS Code terminal running a DOS code: *pip install labelImg*, you can install the software in your computer in a few seconds. Then in the terminal running another DOS code: *labelImg*, you can use the software in a window interface. In June 2023, we have a new library tool Autodistill to label images automatically for YOLOv8. It is a Python package which allows us to transfer the knowledge of large foundation models to smaller models for building AI applications running in real-time. To use Autodistill, I tried a Roboflow project for milk bottle detection in Google Colab. Even 16 GB GPU memory in a Tesla T4 was not big enough to run the codes of the project.

In May 2023, Deci AI released YOLO-NAS models for object detection. The abbreviation NAS denotes 'Neural Architecture Search,' a technique invented by Deci to automate the design process of neural network architectures. On the GitHub repository of Deci/super-gradient, it is claimed that 'The new YOLO-NAS delivers state-of-the-art (SOTA) performance with the unparalleled accuracy-speed performance, outperforming other models such as YOLOv5, YOLOv6, YOLOv7 and YOLOv8.' SuperGradients is a PyTorch-based training library. Based on SuperGradients, Deci provides three pre-trained models: yolo_nas_s, yolo_nas_m, and yolo_nas_l under an open-source license with pre-trained weights available for non-commercial use. We can use 'pip install super-gradients' to install SuperGradients in a virtual environment of VS Code with Python v7-9 and PyTorch 1.9-1.10. The object detection speed of using the small, middle and large size model is 15, 10 and 10 PFS, respectively. From the last section, we know that the speed of model 'yolov8n.pt' and model 'yolov8l.pt' is 80 and 30 FPS, respectively. It is a surprise that YOLO-NAS is slower than YOLOv8 on my computer. A YouTube video from Nicolai Nielsen also shows that YOLOv8 is faster than YOLO-NAS. Inspired by codes from Aarohi Singla and Roboflow, I could write my codes to fine-tune the large YOLO-NAS model for my MNIST4yolov7 dataset. Model training of 100 epochs took more than four hours. YOLOv8 model's training time was 0.3 hour for 100 epochs, and codes for YOLOv8 model training were only a few lines. I do not show codes for fine-tuning the large YOLO-NAS model because they are very long.

References

Maji D, Nagori S, Mathew M and Poddar D 2022 YOLO-pose: enhancing YOLO for multi person pose estimation using object keypoint similarity loss *Proc. of the IEEE/CVF Conf. on Computer Vision and Pattern Recognition* pp 2637–46

Wang C-Y, Bochkovskiy A and Liao H-Y M 2022 YOLOv7: trainable bag-of-freebies sets new state-of-the-art for real-time object detectors *arXiv preprint* arXiv:2207.02696

Cheng T, Song L, Ge Y, Liu W, Wang X and Shan Y 2024 YOLO-World: Real-time open-vocabulary object detection arXiv preprint arXiv:2401.17270

Wang C-Y, Yeh I-H and Liao H-Y M 2024 YOLOv9: Learning what you want to learn using programmable gradient information arXiv preprint arXiv:2402.13616

IOP Publishing

Mastering Computer Vision with PyTorch and Machine Learning

Caide Xiao

Chapter 9

U-Nets for image segmentation and diffusion models for image generation

A U-Net is a kind of ResNet with a special architecture which is easy to train and needs few training samples. In section 9.1, a U-Net is used for retinal vessel segmentation. A WGAN-GP code using the U-Net as an image generator for the same task is listed in appendix H. Hugging Face's pre-trained diffusion models based on U-Nets were used to generate photorealistic images for an Oxford flower dataset in section 9.3. The mathematical principle is explained using codes to generate quadratic curves in section 9.2. Using Hugging Face's Stable Diffusion models, we can even instruct a computer to generate beautiful images according our text prompts.

YOLOv8 is very powerful for object detection and segmentations, but those objects must be countable. Many objects such as blood vessel systems in our bodies and river systems on Earth have fractal structures. To segment images obtained from microscopes or satellites about uncountable objects with fractal structures, we can use a U-Net, a residual convolutional network proposed by Olaf Ronneberger, Philipp Fischer, and Thomas Brox in their paper (Ronneberger *et al* 2015) published in 2015. The title of the paper is 'U-Net: Convolutional Networks for Biomedical Image Segmentation'. The U-Net architecture has proven to be effective in various image segmentation tasks, especially when the available training data is limited. With less than 100 images to train a U-Net, we could quickly get excellent segmentation results. It allows for accurate and detailed segmentation results, capturing both local and global information in images. U-Nets are also used in diffusion models for image generation. The fake images from diffusion models are of photorealistic quality.

doi:10.1088/978-0-7503-6244-3ch9   9-1

9.1 Retinal vessel segmentation by a U-Net for DRIVE dataset

The DRIVE Dataset is used to demonstrate the super power of a U-Net. The name of the dataset is an abbreviation of digital retinal images for vessel extraction (DRIVE). The dataset was introduced by Joes Staal *et al* in their paper (Staal *et al* 2004) titled 'Ridge-based vessel segmentation in color images of the retina'. We can download a zip file of the dataset from Kaggle. The size of the compressed file is less than 30 MB. After unzipping the file to a folder named 'd: \Retina', we can find a 'training' sub-folder and a 'test' sub-folder. Each of the two sub-folders has an 'images' sub-folder containing 20 TIF color fundus images (figure 9.1(A)). The resolutions of all the color images are the same: 565 × 584 pixels with eight bits per channel (three channels). According to Staal, these images were obtained from a diabetic retinopathy screening program in the Netherlands, and 7 out of 40 images are about abnormal pathology cases. In the training sub-folder, there is a folder named '1st_manual' with 20 black and white GIF images (figure 9.1(B)). They were manual segmentation results by an ophthalmological expert, and were used as ground truth for model training. From the images shown in figure 9.1, we have an idea about what we should to do with these images: to generate black and white images of blood vessels from those color fundus images automatically by a U-Net (figure 9.1(C)) in the following project 9.1. The U-Net architecture has several key features:

- The contracting path (the left-hand-side of figure 9.1(C)) consists of a series of convolutional and pooling layers that progressively reduce the spatial resolution while increasing the number of feature channels. This path captures the context and extracts high-level features from the input image.

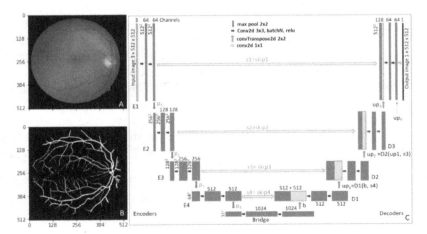

Figure 9.1. A color fundus image (A) and its mask (B) (cropped outputs of Cell 04). (C) The architecture of a U-Net.

- The expanding path (the right-hand-side of figure 9.1(C)) consists of a series of transposed convolutional and convolutional layers that increase the spatial resolution while decreasing the number of feature channels. It combines the low-level features from the contracting path with the high-level features to generate detailed segmentation maps.
- Skip connections (the horizontal arrows in figure 9.1(C)) between the corresponding layers in the contracting and expanding paths enable the network to use both local and global information for accurate segmentation. The skip connections are residual connections.
- Final layer: the last layer of the U-Net is a 1×1 convolutional layer.

As usual, we import libraries and set all hyperparameters in Cell 01 of project 9.1. A class defined in Cell 02 is used to pack images into a train dataset and a validation dataset. Only having 20 images in the train dataset for model training, we have to do many image augmentations: resize, rotation, horizontal flipping, vertical flipping and normalizations. The color image shown in figure 9.1(A) was vertically flipped, because a small color bulge on each original color image is at the position of 1:30 of an analog clock. The mask image of each color image should have the same augmentations. Codes starting from line 11 in Cell 02 do augmentations for both the color images and their masks simultaneously. The two datasets are then sliced into two dataloaders by codes in Cell 03. Codes in Cell 04 display a batch of images in the train dataloader. Because the image resolution is higher (512×512) in DRIVE, my computer can only handle a dataloader with a batch size of two.

The architecture of the U-Net used for the project is shown in figure 9.1(C). It is a little different from Olaf Ronneberger's U-Net (Ronneberger *et al* 2015) in which batch normalization (Ioffe and Szegedy 2015) was not used because this operator was not invented at that time. The input of the U-Net is a batch of color images with the shape $N \times 3 \times 512^2$, and the output of the U-Net is a batch of black and white images with the shape $N \times 1 \times 512^2$, where N is the batch size. The output images will be forced to match with masks of those color images by a BCE loss function with logits during model training. In PyTorch, this loss function 'combines a Sigmoid layer and the BCE Loss in one single class. This version is more numerically stable than using a plain sigmoid followed by a BCE Loss as, by combining the operations into one layer, we take advantage of the log-sum-exp trick for numerical stability.' Codes in the ExtraCell ONE are used to demonstrate how to calculate values of the loss function automatically and manually by the formula $L = -\frac{1}{N}\sum_{i=1}^{N}\left[y_i \ln(\sigma(\hat{y}_i)) + (1 - y_i)\ln(1 - \sigma(\hat{y}_i))\right]$.

```
#ExtraCell ONE: an example of the BCEWithLogitsLoss loss function----------------
import torch; import torch.nn as nn
loss = nn.BCEWithLogitsLoss()
input = torch.randn(3, requires_grad=True)
print('input=', input)  #---------[-1.3664, -0.3638, -1.3526]
target = torch.empty(3).random_(2)
print('target=', target)    #-----[1., 1., 0.]
output = loss(input, target)
print('BCEWithLogitsLoss=', output)    #----output= tensor(0.9050)
#------Manually Calculate BCEWithLogitsLoss--------------------------------------
s = 0
for i in range(3):
    sigma = 1/(1+torch.exp(-input[i]))
    s -= target[i]*torch.log(sigma) + (1-target[i])*torch.log(1-sigma)
s/3    #---- s/3 = tensor(0.9050)
#-------------------------------------------------------------------------------
```

The rectangles with different colors and sizes in figure 9.1(C) represent image data of different shapes, and the arrows with different colors represent operators to the image data. The width of each rectangle is proportional to channels of every batch of processed image data, and the height of each rectangle is proportional to the resolution of the batch of processed image data. Images in the datasets are resized to the same widths and heights, and we define the size of these images as their width or height (line 13 of Cell 01). There are four encoders (E1 to E4) on the left side of the U-Net, and four decoders (D1 to D4) on the right side of the U-Net. Each encoder has one input and two outputs. For example, encoder E4's output skip4 will be used as an input for decoder D1, and another output of E4 is p4: the results of a 2×2 MaxPool2d operator acted on a copy of skip4. The second output of E4 is then used as an input for the bridge which connects with decoder D1.

Each decoder has two inputs and one output. For example, decoder D1's first input is skip4 with the shape N×512 × 64^2, its second input is b: the bridge's output with the shape N×1024 × 32^2. Decoder D1 first acts on the second input by a transposed convolution operator, so that the output shape of the transposed convolution matches with the shape of the first input's shape for a concatenation along the channel direction. The result of the concatenation is a tensor with the shape N×1024 × 64^2. The tensor is then processed by a basic block to get up1: D1's output with the shape N×512 × 64^2. From a Basic class defined in Cell 06, you can see that each basic block has two convolution layers. The basic block will change its input's channels not its input's resolution. In the four encoders and the bridge, the basic block increases the image channels; in the four decoders, the basic block decreases the image channels. The four MaxPool2d operators in the four encoders halve image sizes. Using the four transposed convolutions in the four decoders, we get the resolution of the U-Net's output to match the input image's resolution. The channels of U-Net's output image could be any integers set by ourselves for our projects. For example, if our project is used to segment 10 objects in images of a dataset, the channels of the output image from our U-Net would be 10, and we must use a cross entropy loss function for model training.

```
# Project 9.1 Retinal Vessel Segmentation by a U-Net-----------------Python v3.6
import torch; import torch.nn as nn; import torch.nn.functional as F
from torch.utils.data import Dataset, DataLoader
import torchvision; from torchvision.utils import make_grid
from operator import add; from albumentations.pytorch import ToTensorV2
import os; import cv2; from glob import glob; import albumentations as A
from skimage.io import imsave, imread, imshow; from skimage import img_as_float32
from sklearn.metrics import precision_score, recall_score
from sklearn.metrics import accuracy_score, f1_score, jaccard_score
import numpy as np; import pandas as pd; import matplotlib.pyplot as plt
from tqdm import tqdm, trange
lr = 2e-4
batch_size = 2
n_epochs = 100
H = 512; W = 512     #resized image sizes for U-Net-------------------line 13
root = 'D:/imageSets/Retina/'
Train_img_dir = root + 'training/images/'
Train_mask_dir = root + 'training/1st_manual/'
Val_img_dir = root + 'test/images/'
Val_mask_dir = root + 'test/1st_manual/'
# Cell 02: Datasets and Dataloaders------------------------------------Cell 02
class MyDataset(Dataset):
    def __init__(self, image_dir, mask_dir, transform=None):
        self.images = sorted(glob(os.path.join(image_dir, "*.tif"))) #image files
        self.masks = sorted(glob(os.path.join(mask_dir, "*.gif")))   # mask files
        self.transform = transform
    def __len__(self):
        return len(self.images)
    def __getitem__(self, index):
        image = imread(self.images[index])
        mask = img_as_float32(imread(self.masks[index]))
        if self.transform is not None:  #---------------------------line 11
            augmentations = self.transform(image=image, mask=mask)
            image = augmentations["image"]
            mask = augmentations["mask"]
        return image, mask
# Cell 03: Datasets and Dataloaders------------------------------------Cell 03
train_dataset = MyDataset(Train_img_dir, Train_mask_dir,
        transform = A.Compose([
                A.Resize(height=H, width=W),
```

```python
            A.Rotate(limit=35, p=1.0, border_mode=cv2.BORDER_CONSTANT),
            A.HorizontalFlip(p=0.5),
            A.VerticalFlip(p=0.5),
            A.Normalize(mean=[0.5]*3,std=[0.5]*3, max_pixel_value=255.0,),
            ToTensorV2()]))
train_dataloader = DataLoader(train_dataset,batch_size=batch_size, shuffle=True)
valid_dataset = MyDataset(Val_img_dir, Val_mask_dir,
        transform = A.Compose([
            A.Resize(H, W),
            A.Normalize(mean=[0.5]*3,std=[0.5,]*3, max_pixel_value=255.0),
            ToTensorV2()]))
valid_dataloader = DataLoader(valid_dataset, batch_size=batch_size,shuffle=False)
# Cell 04: Display images and masks in a batch of a dataloader---------Cell 04
for images, masks in train_dataloader:
    masks = masks.unsqueeze(dim=1) # add the channel number 1 after batch size
    print("images.shape=", images.shape, '\tmax&min:',
                images.max().item(), images.min().item())
    print("masks.shape=", masks.shape, '\tmax&min:',
                masks.max().item(), masks.min().item())
    break
def denorm(img_tensors):    # Shift image pixel values to [0,1]
    return img_tensors * 0.5 + 0.5
def show_imgs(i, m):        # i for images and m for masks
    fig, ax = plt.subplots(2,1, figsize=(10,8), sharex=True, sharey=True)
    input0 = make_grid(i, nrow=batch_size).permute(1,2,0)
    i_plot = ax[0].imshow(input0)
    ax[0].set(xticks=np.linspace(0, 1024, 9), yticks=np.linspace(0, 512, 5))
    input1 = make_grid(m, nrow=batch_size)
    m_plot = ax[1].imshow(input1.permute(1,2,0), cmap='gray')
    plt.show()
show_imgs(denorm(images), masks)
# Cell 05: Model parameters initialization ----------------------------Cell 05
def weights_init(m):
    if(type(m) == nn.ConvTranspose2d or type(m) == nn.Conv2d):
        nn.init.normal_(m.weight.data, 0.0, 0.02)
    elif(type(m) == nn.BatchNorm2d):
        nn.init.normal_(m.weight.data, 1.0, 0.02)
        nn.init.constant_(m.bias.data, 0)
# Cell 06: U-net Model ------------------------------------------------Cell 06
class Basic(nn.Module):
    def __init__(self, in_ch, out_ch):
        super().__init__()
        self.net = nn.Sequential(
                    nn.Conv2d(in_ch, out_ch, 3, 1, 1, bias=False),
                    nn.BatchNorm2d(out_ch), nn.ReLU(True),
                    nn.Conv2d(out_ch, out_ch, 3, 1, 1, bias=False),
                    nn.BatchNorm2d(out_ch), nn.ReLU(True))
    def forward(self, images):
        return self.net(images)
class Encoder(nn.Module):
    def __init__(self, in_ch, out_ch):
        super().__init__()
```

```
            self.up = nn.ConvTranspose2d(in_ch, out_ch, 2, 2, 0)
            self.conv = Basic(out_ch*2, out_ch)
        def forward(self, inputs, skip):
            x = self.up(inputs)
            x = torch.cat([x, skip], dim=1)
            return self.conv(x)
class U_Net(nn.Module):
    def __init__(self):
        super().__init__()
        self.E1 = Encoder(3, 64)
        self.E2 = Encoder(64, 128)
        self.E3 = Encoder(128, 256)
        self.E4 = Encoder(256, 512)
        self.bottle_neck = Basic(512, 1024)
        self.D1 = Decoder(1024, 512)
        self.D2 = Decoder(512, 256)
        self.D3 = Decoder(256, 128)
        self.D4 = Decoder(128, 64)
        self.final = nn.Conv2d(64, 1, 1, 1, 0, bias=True)
    def forward(self, images):
        skip1, pool1 = self.E1(images) #s1.shape=Nx64x512^2    p1.shape=Nx64x256^2
        skip2, pool2 = self.E2(pool1)  #s2.shape=Nx128x256^2   p2.shape=Nx128x128^2
        skip3, pool3 = self.E3(pool2)  #s3.shape=Nx256x128^2   p3.shape=Nx256x64^2
        skip4, pool4 = self.E4(pool3)  #s4.shape=Nx512x64^2    p4.shape=Nx512x32^2
        b =self.bottle_neck(pool4)                #b.shape=Nx1024x32^2
        up1 = self.D1(b, skip4)          #up1.shape = Nx512x64^2
        up2 = self.D2(up1, skip3)        #up2.shape = Nx256x128^2
        up3 = self.D3(up2, skip2)        #up3.shape = Nx128x256^2
        up4 = self.D4(up3, skip1)        #up4.shape = Nx64x512^2
        return self.final(up4)           #putput.shape = Nx1x512^2
model = U_Net().cuda()
model.apply(weights_init)
optimizer = torch.optim.Adam(model.parameters(), lr=lr)
loss_fn = nn.BCEWithLogitsLoss()
# Cell 07: Calculate accuracy, IoU, precision, recall and f1-------------Cell 07
def metrics(y_true, y_hat):
    y_true = y_true.cpu().numpy()     #----------ground truth
    y_true = y_true > 0.5
    y_true = y_true.astype(np.uint8)
    y_true = y_true.reshape(-1)
    y_hat = y_hat.cpu().numpy()       #----------predictions
    y_hat = y_hat > 0.5
    y_hat = y_hat.astype(np.uint8)
    y_hat = y_hat.reshape(-1)
```

```
        acc = accuracy_score(y_true, y_hat)   #------metrics
        IoU = jaccard_score(y_true, y_hat)
        precision = precision_score(y_true, y_hat, zero_division=1)
        recall = recall_score(y_true, y_hat)
        Dice = f1_score(y_true, y_hat)
        return [acc, IoU, precision, recall, Dice]
# Cell 08 Model Training--------------------------------------------------Cell 08
def train(model, dataloader, optimizer, loss_fn):
    epoch_loss = 0.0
    metrics_score = [0.0, 0.0, 0.0, 0.0, 0.0]
    model.train()
    for x, y in dataloader:
        y = y.unsqueeze(1).cuda()
        y_pred = model(x.cuda())
        with torch.no_grad():
            y_hat = torch.sigmoid(y_pred)   #----------------------sigmoid
            score = metrics(y, y_hat)
            metrics_score = list(map(add, metrics_score, score))
        loss = loss_fn(y_pred, y)
        optimizer.zero_grad()
        loss.backward()
        optimizer.step()
        epoch_loss += loss.item()
    epoch_loss = epoch_loss/len(dataloader)
    return epoch_loss, np.array(metrics_score)/len(dataloader)
def evaluate(model, dataloader, loss_fn):
    epoch_loss = 0.0
    metrics_score = [0.0, 0.0, 0.0, 0.0, 0.0]
    model.eval()
    with torch.no_grad():
        for x, y in dataloader:
            #x = x.cuda()
            y = y.unsqueeze(1).cuda()
            y_pred = model(x.cuda())
            y_hat = torch.sigmoid(y_pred)   #----------------------sigmoid
            score = metrics(y, y_hat)
            metrics_score = list(map(add, metrics_score, score))
            loss = loss_fn(y_pred, y)
            epoch_loss += loss.item()
        epoch_loss = epoch_loss/len(dataloader)
    return epoch_loss, np.array(metrics_score)/len(dataloader)
def fit(epochs):
    torch.cuda.empty_cache()
    df = pd.DataFrame(np.empty([epochs, 12]),
            index = np.arange(epochs),
            columns=['train_loss', 'train_acc', 'train_IoU', 't_precision',
                    'train_recall', 'train_Dice',
                    'valid_loss', 'valid_acc', 'valid_IoU', 'v_precision',
                    'valid_recall', 'valid_Dice',])
    progress_bar = trange(epochs)
    for i in progress_bar:
        df.iloc[i, 0], df.iloc[i, 1:6] = train(
```

```
                    model, train_dataloader, optimizer, loss_fn)
        df.iloc[i, 6], df.iloc[i, 7:12]  = evaluate(
                    model, valid_dataloader, loss_fn)
        progress_bar.set_description("train_acc=%.4f" % df.iloc[i, 1])
        progress_bar.set_postfix({'valid_acc': df.iloc[i, 7]})
    return df
history = fit(n_epochs)
# Cell 09: Display model training history------------------------------Cell 09
df = history
fig, ax = plt.subplots(2,3, figsize=(12,6), sharex=True)
for i in range(2):
    for j in range(3):
        df.plot(ax=ax[i,j], y=[3*i+j,3*i+j+6], style=['r-', 'b-+'])
        ax[i,j].set(ylim=[0,1])
        ax[i,j].grid(which='major', axis='both', color='g', linestyle=':')
        ax[i,j].set(xlabel='Epoch')
#---------------------------------------------------------------------The End



# Cell 10: Save the trained model--------------------------------------Cell 10
File_name = 'd:/Unet4Retina2022Dec29.pth'
torch.save(model, File_name)
#model = torch.load(File_name)
#model.eval()
#model = model.cuda()
# Cell 11: Show the trained model acts on the valid_dataset------------Cell 11
for i, (images, masks) in enumerate(valid_dataloader):
        masks = masks.unsqueeze(dim=1)
preds=torch.sigmoid(model(images.cuda()))
#preds=model(images.cuda())
print('min, max:', preds.min().item(), preds.max().item())
show_imgs(denorm(images), preds.cpu())
#---------------------------------------------------------------------The End
```

Using the functions defined in Cell 07 and 08, I trained the U-Net to segment blood vessels from those fundus images. The training results puzzled me for a few months; the results I got at that time are shown in figure 9.2(D). You can see that many tiny vessels could not be found in figure 9.2(D), compared with the ground truth shown in figure 9.2(B). I tried to use a residual net in the basic block, added one more encoder to the contracting path, and one more decoder to the expanding path, but I still could not see any significant improvement for my model. Then I tried to use the U-Net as a generator in a WGAN-GP. In the WGANs in Chapter 5, our generator creates images from noises. In the WGAN U-Net, the generator generates black and white images from color fundus images. I got a very good result shown in figure 9.2(F) (WGAN-GP codes are listed in appendix H). To compare the outputs of my U-Net and my WGAN-GP U-Net, I shifted pixel values of the U-Net's output images linearly (figure 9.2(C)) and nonlinearly (sigmoid, figure 9.2(E)). WGAN-GP U-Net took 100 min for model training, but we did not really need it because figure 9.2(E) is better than figure 9.2(F). It seems that figure 9.2(C) is the best (model training time 25 min). The U-Net model training metrics are shown in figure 9.3.

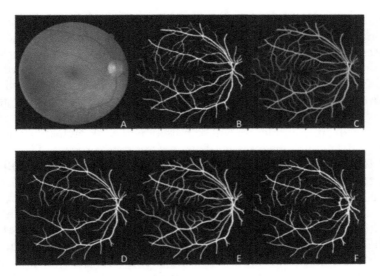

Figure 9.2. Vessel segmentation results of the U-Net. (A) a color fundus image in the valid dataset. (B) Ground truth. (C) Pixel values of the U-Net's output were linearly shifted to [0,1]. (D) The U-Net's output was displayed by VS Code with automatic clipping. (E) Pixel values of the U-Net's output were shifted to [0,1] by a sigmoid function. (F) The output of a WGAN-GP using the U-Net as an image generator.

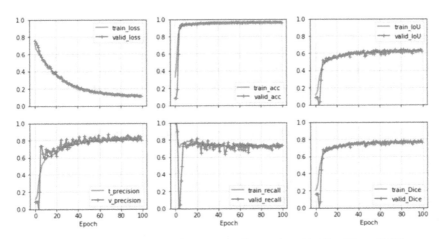

Figure 9.3. U-Net training metrics corresponding to sigmoid shift of figure 9.2(E).

9.2 Using an attention U-Net diffusion model for quadratic curve generation

Starting from noises, a denoizing diffusion probabilistic model (DDPM) can generate images, audios and even videos with good enough quality to fool us. A DDPM system is a type of generative model introduced by Jonathan Ho,

Ajay Jain, and Pieter Abbeel in their paper (Ho *et al* 2020) published in 2020. DDPMs are trained to find a conditional distribution function of clean images given noises and then to use the conditional distribution function for denoising tasks. The principle of DDPM is easy to understand. Suppose you have an image of the Mona Lisa at the bottom of a tank with clean water and you add black ink drop by drop to water in the tank. The ink drop is tiny, and the time interval between two drops is long enough to let each ink drop diffuse thoroughly in the tank. Drop by drop, your picture will be noised by the ink pigments, and finally at drop 1000, you picture disappears. This is a forward process. Then we use an advanced tool to take the ink out of the tank drop by drop. When all 1000 ink drops are removed from the water in the tank, we can see the Mona Lisa clearly again. This is a reverse process or denoising process. An advanced tool for image generation in the reverse process of DDPM is a U-Net model. After the model is trained with images in a dataset, the model can generate fake images from pure noises. These fake images are not the original images in the dataset, but are in the same style as the original images. For example, if you train your U-Net model with Pablo Picasso's paintings, you will obtain fake images in Picasso's painting style. Denoising diffusion probabilistic models have shown promising results in image denoising tasks. They provide a probabilistic framework for noise removal, allowing for effective handling of various types of noise and producing visually pleasing denoised images.

9.2.1 The forward process in a DDPM

An original image x_0 (a quadratic curve or a digital Mona Lisa image) is a sample with an unknown PDF q: $x_0 \sim q(x)$. In a forward process or diffusion process, noises from a standard normal distribution are added to x_0 to get a latent image x_1 with a conditional PDF: $q(x_1|x_0)$. This forward process is going on step by step based on a variance schedule $0 < \beta_1 < \beta_2 < \cdots < \beta_T \ll 1$. The variance schedule could be linear, quadratic, cosine, etc, just like a learning rate schedule. If the time step T is big enough ($\sim$1000), our final image x_T would be an isotropic Gaussian noise: $q(x_T|x_{T-1}) = N(x_T;0,I)$. All the latent images x_1, ..., x_T have the dimensionality of the original image x_0. At time step t, a latent image is obtained by $x_t = \sqrt{1 - \beta_t}\, x_{t-1} + \sqrt{\beta_t}\, \varepsilon$, where ε is a sample from a multivariant standard normal distribution $N(0,I)$ with the dimensionality of x_0. The PDF of the latent image at time step t is a normal distribution given by a latent image at a previous time step $t-1$

$$q(x_t \mid x_{t-1}) = q(x_t \mid x_{t-1}, x_0) = \mathbb{N}(x_t; \sqrt{1 - \beta_t}\, x_{t-1}, \beta_t I) \qquad (9.1)$$

We know that the combination of two independent normal distributions is still a normal distribution. If the two independent normal distributions are $x \sim \mathbb{N}(x;0, \sigma_1^2)$ and $y \sim \mathbb{N}(y;0, \sigma_2^2)$, then we have $z = x + y \sim \mathbb{N}(z;0, (\sigma_1^2 + \sigma_2^2))$. From that fact and with $\alpha_t = 1 - \beta_t$, $\bar{\alpha}_t = \prod_{i=1}^{t} \alpha_i$, the latent image $x_t = \sqrt{\bar{\alpha}_t}\, x_0 + \sqrt{1 - \bar{\alpha}_t}\, \varepsilon$ at time step t can be directly obtained from x_0 by a PDF:

$$q(x_t \mid x_0) = \mathbb{N}(x_t; \sqrt{\bar{\alpha}_t} x_0, (1 - \bar{\alpha}_t)I) \qquad (9.2)$$

The diffusion process is a Markov chain with an approximate posterior possibility distribution function shown in equation (9.2). At the end of the forward process, we get $x_T \sim q(x_T \mid x_0) = \mathbb{N}(x_T; 0, I)$, a pure noise.

$$q(x_{1:T} \mid x_0) = \prod_{t=1}^{T} q(x_t \mid x_{t-1}) = q(x_T \mid x_{T-1})...q(x_2 \mid x_1)q(x_1 \mid x_0) \qquad (9.3)$$

The quadratic curves in figure 9.4(A) are used as original images to demonstrate DDMP's power to generate images from noise in project 9.2. Four thousand batches of quadratic curves are used to train a U-Net model in a DDMP system. A batch of quadratic curves in figure 9.4(A) were generated by codes in Cells 01–03; these codes have been used many times in the previous chapters. There are 64 curves in a batch, and there are 64 points on each curve. A function for the forward process is defined in Cell 04. Hyperparameters for the function are set in front of this function. The total forward steps are set to be $T = 200$ for this simple project. A time embedding dimension for model training is set to be 100 on line 2 of Cell 04. With a linear schedule, betas increase from 0.001 to 0.2 in 200 steps (line 03 in Cell 04). Many other hyperparameters are also listed there, such as $\alpha, \bar{\alpha}, \sqrt{\bar{\alpha}}$, and $\sqrt{1 - \bar{\alpha}}$. Only one original curve is used to add noises at time step $t = 1, 25, 50$ and 199 for us to see the forward process in figure 9.4(B). At the end of the process, $\bar{\alpha}_{199} = 4.2 \times 10^{-10}$. According to equation (9.2), the contribution of the original image to the last latent image x_{199} can be ignored. Only a standard Gaussian noise ε exists in the last latent image. From an empirical rule, we know that 99.7% of the Gaussian noise values lie withing three standard deviations. That is why the values of x_{199} are between -3 and 3 along the y-axis in figure 9.4(B). In the q_sample function defined in Cell 04, a Pytorch function gather() is new to us. Running the following codes in an extra VS code cell, you will know how the function picks out elements in a 1D tensor z according to another 1D tensor t: $z = torch.tensor([1, 2, 3, 4, 9])$; $t = torch.tensor([2, 0])$; $z.gather(dim = -1, index = t)$. The output of these extra codes is $[3, 1]$, or $[z[t[0]], z[t[1]]]$.

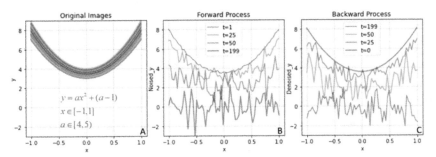

Figure 9.4. A DDPM's forward and backward processes. (A) A batch of quadratic curves (outputs of Cell 03). (B) Noised images or curves at time step 1, 25, 50 and 199 in a forward process (outputs of Cell 04). (C) Denoised images starting from $t = 199$ and ending at $t = 0$ (outputs of Cell 09).

```
# Project 9.2 DDPM for Quadric Curve Generation ----------------------Python v3.6
import torch; import torch.nn as nn; import torch.nn.functional as F
import torch.optim.lr_scheduler as lr_scheduler; import numpy as np
from tqdm import trange; import pandas as pd; import matplotlib.pyplot as plt
n_epochs = 40            # traing epochs
n_points = 64            # nummber of points on each curve
batch_size = 64          # total 64 curves in a batch
n_batch = 100            # batchs per epoch for model trainig
lr = 4e-4
# Cell 02: Creating training data from y=a*x^2+(a-1)----------------------Cell 02
def training_data():
    a = np.random.uniform(4, 5, batch_size).reshape(-1,1)
    points = a*x*x + (a-1)
    return points
x = np.linspace(-1, 1, n_points)        # x=[-1, -0.9,...,1]
y = training_data()
# Cell 03: Show curves------------------------------------------------------Cell 03
def show_curves(x, y):
    fig, ax = plt.subplots(figsize=(4,4)); ax.grid(color='g', linestyle=':')
    batch_size = y.shape[0]
    for i in range(batch_size):
        ax.plot(x, y[i,:])
    ax.set(xlabel='x', ylabel='y', title='Original Images', ylim=[-3,9],
        xticks=np.arange(-1.0, 1.1, 0.5))
    ax.yaxis.labelpad=-5;
show_curves(x,y)


# Cell 04: Hyperparameters and a function for the DDPM Forward Process ---Cell 04
T = 200                                 # total time steps
time_emb_dim = 100                      # time embedding dimension
betas = torch.linspace(0.001, 0.2, T)   # betas=[0.001, 0.002,..., 0.2]---line 03
alphas = 1. - betas                     # alphas=[0.999, 0.998,..., 0.800]
a_bar = torch.cumprod(alphas, axis=0)   # a_bar=[0.999,...,5.2e-10, 4.2e-10]
sqrt_a_bar = torch.sqrt(a_bar)          #sqrt_a_bar=[0.9995, 0.9985,..., 2e-5]
sqrt_one_minus_a_bar = torch.sqrt(1 - a_bar)   #=[0.0316, 0.0548,..., 1]
sqrt_recip_a = torch.sqrt(1/alphas)     # sqrt_recip_a=[1.0005, 1.001,..., 1.118]
alphas_cumprod_prev = F.pad(a_bar[:-1], (1, 0), value=1.0) #=[1,0.999,...5.2e-10]
posterior_variance = betas * (1. - alphas_cumprod_prev) / (1. - a_bar)
def q_sample(img_0, t, noise):
    return (sqrt_a_bar.gather(-1, t).unsqueeze(-1) * img_0 +
            sqrt_one_minus_a_bar.gather(-1, t).unsqueeze(-1) * noise)
img_0 = torch.FloatTensor(training_data())[:1]   # real image is a single curve
fig, ax = plt.subplots(figsize=(4,4)); ax.grid(color='g', linestyle=':')
for t in torch.tensor([1, 25, 50, 199]):
    time_step = t*torch.ones(img_0.size(0)).to(torch.int64)
    noise = torch.randn_like(img_0) #noise.shape=[1,64]
    noised_img = q_sample(img_0, time_step, noise).squeeze()
    ax.plot(x, noised_img, label=f"t={t.item()}")
ax.set(xlabel='x', ylabel='Noised_y', title='Forward Process')
ax.set(xticks=np.arange(-1, 1.1, 0.5), ylim=[-3,9])
ax.yaxis.labelpad=-5
ax.legend();
#--------------------------------------------------------------------------------
```

9.2.2 The backward process in the DDPM

In the physical world, it is easier to mix two materials than to separate them once mixed. It is the same in the digital world for a DDPM. The forward process is much easier than the backward process. The reverse or backward process is another Markov chain starting from a pure noise $x_T \sim p_\theta(x_T) = \mathbb{N}(x_T; 0, I)$ and the process is going backwards to get denoised latent images step by step: $x_{T-1}..., x_t, x_{t-1}, ... , x_0$, where θ represents parameters of a U-Net. Figure 9.4(C) shows the results of a backward process from a pure noise at $t = 199$. At time step $t-1$, the latent image x_{t-1} has a PDF $p_\theta(x_{t-1} \mid x_t) = \mathbb{N}(x_{t-1}; \mu_\theta(x_t, t), \beta_t I)$, where $\mu_\theta(x_t, t)$ coming from the trained U-Net model.

The backward PDF $p_\theta(x_{t-1} \mid x_t)$ corresponds to a reverse of the forward PDF, and it is equal to $q(x_{t-1} \mid x_t, x_0)$, which is referred to as 'forward process posterior distribution.' Detailed derivations can be found in the DDPM paper (Ho *et al* 2020). The following equations (9.3) and (9.4) come from appendix I for completeness

$$q(x_{t-1} \mid x_t, x_0) = \mathbb{N}(x_{t-1}; \tilde{\mu}(x_t, x_0), \tilde{\beta}_t I) = q(x_t \mid x_{t-1}, x_0)\frac{q(x_{t-1} \mid x_0)}{q(x_t \mid x_0)} \tag{9.4}$$

$$\tilde{\mu}(x_t, x_0) = x_t - \frac{1 - \alpha_t}{\sqrt{1 - \bar{\alpha}_t}}\varepsilon \tag{9.5}$$

$$\tilde{\beta}_t = \frac{1 - \bar{\alpha}_{t-1}}{1 - \bar{\alpha}_t}\beta_t \tag{9.6}$$

The above formulae will be used for variational lower bound loss of model training. The joint probability distribution of the backward process is:

$$p_\theta(x_{0:T}) = p_\theta(x_T) \prod_{t=1}^{T} p_\theta(x_{t-1} \mid x_t) = p_\theta(x_0 \mid x_1)p_\theta(x_1 \mid x_2)...p_\theta(x_{T-1} \mid x_T)p_\theta(x_T) \tag{9.7}$$

From the joint possibility distribution and $\int q(x_0)dx_0 = 1$, we have the negative log likelihood (loss function) of the system for model training: $L = -\log(p_\theta(x_0)) = -\log \int p_\theta(x_{0:T})dx_{1:T}$

$$L = -\left(\int q(x_0)dx_0\right) \log \int q(x_{1:T} \mid x_0)\frac{p_\theta(x_{0:T})}{q(x_{1:T} \mid x_0)}dx_{1:T} \tag{9.8}$$

Using Jensen's inequality, we can simplify the above formula to get the variational lower bound loss of the system (appendix I)

$$L < -\int q(x_0)dx_0 \int q(x_{1:T} \mid x_0) \log \frac{p_\theta(x_{0:T})}{q(x_{1:T} \mid x_0)}dx_{1:T} = L_{VLB}$$

$$L_{VLB} = D_{KL}(q(x_T \mid x_0)\|p_\theta(x_T)) + \sum_{t=2}^{T} D_{KL}(q(x_{t-1} \mid x_t, x_0)\|p_\theta(x_{t-1} \mid x_t)) - E_q\left[\log p_\theta(x_0 \mid x_1)\right]$$

$$L_{\text{VLB}} = L_T + \sum_{t=2}^{T} L_{t-1} + L_0$$

The variational lower bound for this process is a sum of losses at each time step, $L = L_0 + L_1 + \ldots + L_T$. Each D_{KL} term in the L_{VLB} (except for L_0) is about the difference between two Gaussian distributions and therefore they can be computed directly. L_T can be ignored during model training because it is a constant, and L_0 is also ignored because the authors of the DDPM paper got better results without this item. Based on $q(x_{t-1} \mid x_t, x_0) = \mathbb{N}(x_{t-1}; \tilde{\mu}(x_t, x_0), \tilde{\beta}_t I)$ and $p_\theta(x_{t-1} \mid x_t) = \mathbb{N}(x_{t-1}; \mu_\theta(x_t, t), \sigma_t^2 I)$, we have the following formula, where C is a constant which does not relate to model training, and t = 2,3..., T

$$L_{t-1} = D_{\text{KL}}(q(x_{t-1} \mid x_t, x_0) \| p_\theta(x_{t-1} \mid x_t)) = E_q\left(\frac{1}{2\sigma_t^2} \|\tilde{\mu}_t(x_t, x_0) - \mu_\theta(x_t, t)\|^2\right) + C$$

The authors of the DDPM paper (Ho *et al* 2020) set the predicted $\mu_\theta(x_t, t)$ to have the same format of $\tilde{\mu}_t(x_t, x_0)$ shown in equation (9.5), and ignored all that baggage in the formula to get a reweighted version L_{VLB} that emphasizes reconstruction quality, where ε_θ is a function approximator intended to predict ε from x_t

$$L_{t-1} = E_{x_0,\, \varepsilon}(\| \varepsilon - \varepsilon_\theta(x_t, t) \|^2) \tag{9.9}$$

We train our U-Net model to predict noises ε_θ at a time step t, and then calculate the difference between the predicted noises ε_θ and noises ε inside $x_t = \sqrt{\bar{\alpha}_t} x_0 + \sqrt{1 - \bar{\alpha}_t} \varepsilon$ with equation (9.9) in a MSE loss function. A function defined in Cell 06 is used to train the U-Net according to the above DDPM theory with a little modification. To save model training time, we do not use all time steps for each image in each batch. The code on line 10 of Cell 07 generates a batch of random integers from 0 to T-1 (included) as the time steps. From the code on line 12, we get a batch of latent images x_t at those time steps by adding a batch of noises ε generated by the code on line 11. The U-Net then predicts noises ε_θ for us to calculate the MSE loss according to equation (9.9).

The first function defined in Cell 05 is used for time stamps. The backbone of the U-Net is the same as the one in section 9.1 with many modifications. We have to mark latent images with time stamps by time embedding in the basic block (class Basic of Cell 06). We used label information embedding in section 3.3 for conditional GANs. Time embedding can be done in many ways. Codes of the 'sinusoidal_embedding' function defined in Cell 05 were inspired by codes in Brian Pulfer's GitHub repository. A multi-head self-attention class (MHSA (Petit *et al* 2021)) is used for the bridge. There are four self-attention heads inside the instance of the class. The inputs Q, K and V of the instance are the same: a layer normalized and reshaped bridge. Detailed information about multi-head self-attention will be provided in chapter 10. A single head cross attention class (Attention) is used to modify skips of the U-Net. I was able to write the single head cross attention codes after watching DigitalSreeni's YouTube video and reading an Attention U-Net paper (Oktay *et al* 2018). A U-Net with attention gives the relevant parts of an images larger weights. In the Basic class in Cell 06, a shortcut is used to construct a residual network, and also layer normalization is used. It took a long time to get the smooth quadric curve shown in figure 9.4(C). The function defined in Cell 09 is based on equations (9.5)–(9.6) to generate images from pure noises.

```
# Cell 05: time embedding function and attention classes----------------Cell 05
def sinusoidal_embedding(n, d):
    embedding = torch.tensor(
        [[i/10000 ** (2*j/d) for j in range(d)] for i in range(n)])
    sin_mask = torch.arange(0, n, 2)              # sin_mask=[0, 2, 4..., 198]
    embedding[sin_mask] = torch.sin(embedding[sin_mask])   # 1-sin_mask
    embedding[1-sin_mask] = torch.cos(embedding[sin_mask]) # =[1,-1,-3..., -197]
    return embedding    # embedding indices: [0, 1, 2, -197, 4,..., -3, 198, -1]
class MHSA(nn.Module):
    def __init__(self, channels, size):
        super().__init__()
        self.channels = channels
        self.size = size
        self.mha = nn.MultiheadAttention(channels, 4, batch_first=True)
        self.ln = nn.LayerNorm([channels, self.size, self.size])
        self.ff_self = nn.Sequential(
            nn.LayerNorm([channels]),
            nn.Linear(channels, channels),
            nn.GELU(),
            nn.Linear(channels, channels),)
    def forward(self, x):
        x_ln = self.ln(x).view(-1, self.channels, self.size * self.size)
        x_ln = x_ln.swapaxes(1, 2)
        y, _ = self.mha(x_ln, x_ln, x_ln)    #   Q = K = V = x_ln
        y = y + x.view(-1, self.channels, self.size * self.size).swapaxes(1, 2)
        y = (self.ff_self(y) + y).swapaxes(2, 1)
        return y.view(-1, self.channels, self.size, self.size)
class Attention(nn.Module):
    def __init__(self, s_ch, g_ch):
        super().__init__()
        self.conv_s = nn.Conv2d(s_ch, s_ch, 1,2,0)
        self.conv_g = nn.Conv2d(g_ch, s_ch, 1,1,0)
        self.out = nn.Sequential(
            nn.ReLU(),
            nn.Conv2d(s_ch, s_ch, 1, 1, 0),
            nn.Sigmoid(),
            nn.ConvTranspose2d(s_ch, s_ch, 2, 2, 0),)
    def forward(self, skip, gate):
        y = self.conv_s(skip)+self.conv_g(gate)
        y = self.out(y) * skip
        return y
# Cell 06: Attention U-Net Model  ---------------------------------------Cell 06
class Basic(nn.Module):
    def __init__(self, in_ch, out_ch):
        super().__init__()
        self.time_mlp =  nn.Linear(time_emb_dim, out_ch)
        self.relu = nn.ReLU()
        self.conv1 = nn.Conv2d(in_ch, out_ch, 3, padding=1)
        self.conv2 = nn.Conv2d(out_ch, out_ch, 3, padding=1)
        self.shortcut = nn.Conv2d(in_ch, out_ch, 1, padding=0)
    def forward(self, img, t):
        shortcut = self.shortcut(img)
```

```
        time_emb = self.time_mlp(t).unsqueeze(-1).unsqueeze(-1)
        y = self.relu(self.conv1(img)) + time_emb
        y = F.layer_norm(y, y.shape[1:])
        y = shortcut + self.relu(self.conv2(y))
        return y
class Encoder(nn.Module):
    def __init__(self, in_ch, out_ch):
        super().__init__()
        self.skip = Basic(in_ch, out_ch)
        self.pool = nn.Conv2d(out_ch, out_ch, 4, 2, 1)
    def forward(self, images, t):
        skip = self.skip(images, t)
        return skip, self.pool(skip)
class Decoder(nn.Module):
    def __init__(self, in_ch, out_ch):
        super().__init__()
        self.up = nn.ConvTranspose2d(in_ch, out_ch, 2, 2, 0)
        self.conv = Basic(out_ch*2, out_ch)
    def forward(self, inputs, skip, t):
        x = self.up(inputs)
        x = torch.cat([x, skip], dim=1)
        return self.conv(x, t)
class U_Net(nn.Module):
    def __init__(self):
        super().__init__()
        self.E1 = Encoder(1, 64)
        self.E2 = Encoder(64, 128)
        self.E3 = Encoder(128, 256)
        self.bottle_neck = Basic(256, 512); self.sa1=Attention(256, 512)
        self.D1 = Decoder(512, 256); self.sa2=Attention(128, 256)
        self.D2 = Decoder(256, 128); self.sa3=Attention(64, 128)
        self.D3 = Decoder(128, 64)
        self.final = nn.Sequential(nn.Conv2d(64, 1, 1, 1, 0,),
                        nn.Flatten(), nn.Linear(32*32, n_points))
        self.time_embed = nn.Embedding(T, time_emb_dim)     # Time embedding
        self.time_embed.weight.data = sinusoidal_embedding(T, time_emb_dim)
        self.time_embed.requires_grad_(False)
        self.fc_in = nn.Linear(n_points, 1024)  # 1024=32*32
        self.mhsa_b = MHSA(512, 4)
    def forward(self, noised_imgs, time_steps):
        t = self.time_embed(time_steps)                 # t.shape=N x 100
        imgs = self.fc_in(noised_imgs).view(-1, 1, 32, 32)   # [N,1,32,32]
        skip1, pool1 = self.E1(imgs, t)
        skip2, pool2 = self.E2(pool1, t)
        skip3, pool3 = self.E3(pool2, t)
        b =self.bottle_neck(pool3, t)   #b.shape=N x 512 x 4^2
        b = self.mhsa_b(b)
        skip3 = self.sa1(skip3, b)
        up1 = self.D1(b, skip3, t)              #up1.shape = N x 256 x 8^2
        skip2 = self.sa2(skip2, up1)
        up2 = self.D2(up1, skip2, t)            #up2.shape = N x 128 x 16^2
        skip1 = self.sa3(skip1, up2)
```

```python
        up3 = self.D3(up2, skip1, t)          #up3.shape = N x 64 x 32^2
        return self.final(up3)                #final.shape=N x 64
model = U_Net().cuda()
optimizer = torch.optim.Adam(model.parameters(), lr=lr)
criterion = nn.MSELoss()
scheduler = lr_scheduler.OneCycleLR(optimizer, max_lr=lr,
                steps_per_epoch=n_batch, epochs=n_epochs, pct_start=0.6)
# Cell 07: Training function---------------------------------------------Cell 07
x_0 = torch.FloatTensor(training_data())         # x_0.shape=[64, 64]
def fit(epochs):
    torch.cuda.empty_cache()
    df = pd.DataFrame(
        np.empty([epochs, 2]), index = np.arange(epochs), columns=['loss', 'lr'])
    progress_bar = trange(epochs)
    for i in progress_bar:
        Loss = 0.0
        for step in range(n_batch):
            t = torch.randint(0, T, (x_0.size(0), ))       #----------line 10
            noise = torch.randn_like(x_0)                  #----------line 11
            noisy_x = q_sample(x_0, t, noise)              #----------line 12
            noise_pred = model(noisy_x.cuda(), t.cuda()) #------------line 13
            optimizer.zero_grad()
            loss = criterion(noise_pred, noise.cuda())     #----------line 15
            Loss += loss.item()
            loss.backward()
            learn_rate = optimizer.param_groups[0]['lr']
            optimizer.step()
            scheduler.step()
            progress_bar.set_description("loss=%.4f" % loss.item())
            progress_bar.set_postfix({'lr': learn_rate})
        df.iloc[i, 0] = Loss/n_batch
        df.iloc[i, 1] = learn_rate
    return df
train_history = fit(n_epochs)
# Cell 08: Show the training history----------------------------------Cell 08
df = train_history
fig, ax = plt.subplots(1,2, figsize=(9,4), sharex=True)
df.plot(ax=ax[0], y=[0])
df.plot(ax=ax[1], y=[1])
for i in range(2):
    ax[i].set_xlabel('epoch')
    ax[i].grid(which='major', axis='both', color='g', linestyle=':')
ax[0].set_ylabel('Loss'); ax[1].set_ylabel('Learning rate')
ax[1].ticklabel_format(style='sci', axis='y', scilimits=(0,0));
# Cell 09: Generate and show images generated by a backward function-----------
@torch.no_grad()
def sample_plot_image():
    img = torch.randn(1, n_points) # Backward progress starting from pure noises
    fig, ax = plt.subplots(figsize=(4,4)); ax.grid(color='g', linestyle=':')
    for i in range(0,T)[::-1]:
        t = torch.full((1,), i, dtype=torch.long)
        alpha_t = alphas.gather(-1, t)
```

```
        beta_t = betas.gather(-1, t)
        sqrt_recip_a_t = torch.sqrt(1.0 / alpha_t)
        sqrt_one_minus_a_bar_t = sqrt_one_minus_a_bar.gather(-1, t)
        posterior_variance_t = posterior_variance.gather(-1,t)
        model_mean = sqrt_recip_a_t * (img - beta_t *
            model(img.cuda(), t.cuda()).cpu() / sqrt_one_minus_a_bar_t)
        if t[0] == 0:
            img = model_mean
        else:
            img = model_mean + torch.sqrt(
                posterior_variance_t) * torch.randn_like(img)
        if i==T-1 or i==50 or i==25 or i==0:
            y = img.squeeze()
            ax.plot(x, y, label=f"t={t.item()}")
    ax.set(xlabel='x', ylabel='Denoised_y', title='Backward Process',
        xticks=np.arange(-1, 1.1, step=0.5), ylim=[-3,9])
    ax.legend(); ax.yaxis.labelpad=-5
    print('std=', y.std())
sample_plot_image()
#------------------------------------------------------------------------
```

9.3 Using a pre-trained U-Net from Hugging Face to generate images

The attention U-Net in the last section is powerful enough for MNIST, but not smart enough for CIFAR10. To generate high-quality fake images for other datasets such as CelebA and STL10, we need more powerful U-Nets. Fortunately, Hugging Face provides a pre-trained U-Net model for different datasets. We just need to write a few code lines to generate beautiful images. Codes in the following project 9.3.1 are used to demonstrate the power of Hugging Face's diffusion model. Before running the codes, please use the DOS command pip install Hugging Face *diffusers* in a VS Code terminal of your workspace. The 'model_id' on line 02 is the name of a file with pre-trained parameters for a specific dataset. After starting to run the codes for the first time, a file of about 500 MB will be downloaded for a U-Net to a DDPMPipeline. You can find more files with pre-trained parameters from Hugging Face. The names of a few such files are listed on lines 02–3. The output of an instance of the *DDPMPipeline* on line 05 is a dictionary with a key named 'sample'. The value of the key is a list with only one element for an image generated from pure noises. The code on line 06 picks out and displays that image. Three fake images generated by three pre-trained U-Nets are shown in figure 9.5. I believe that the quality of the image generated by the program with only six lines can compete with the quality of images on a famous website: *This Person Does Not Exist*. You can try to run the short codes on your laptop or Google Colab. On my laptop with a RTX 2060 GPU, the program running time is about 2.5 min.

Figure 9.5. Fake images generated by pre-trained Hugging Face U-Net models: (A) 'google/ddpm-celebahq-256'; (B) 'google/ddpm-ema-church-256'; and (C) 'google/ddpm-ema-cat-256'.

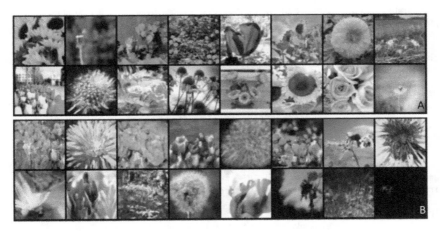

Figure 9.6. (A) Original flower images from the Kaggle Flowers Dataset with a license CCO 1.0. (B) Fake flower images generated from pure noises by a DDMP U-Net of Hugging Face in about 11 h model training.

```
# Project 9.3.1: Using pre-trained U-Net to generate images ----------Python v3.6
from diffusers import DDPMPipeline              #!pip install diffusers
model_id = "google/ddpm-celebahq-256" #"google/ddpm-ema-church-256" #--- line 02
# "google/ddpm-ema-cat-256" "google/ddpm-bedroom-256" "google/ddpm-cifar10-32"
image_pipe = DDPMPipeline.from_pretrained(model_id)
images = image_pipe()['sample'] #---generate images from  noises----line 05
images[0]                       #---display an image generated by DDPMPipeline
#-----------------------------------------------------------------------The End
```

It is more flexible to use Hugging Face's powerful U-Nets in our Pytorch codes for custom datasets, such as flower dataset downloaded from Kaggle. The dataset is about 215 MB with five kinds of beautiful flowers: daisy, dandelion, rose, sunflower and tulip. This dataset was released by DPhi Data Sprint #25: Flower Recognition under the Creative Commons By-Attribution License. The outputs of the following project 9.3.2 are shown in figure 9.6. After every 25 epochs, a trained model was saved for the next 25 epochs. Model training with a total of 25 × 11 epochs took about 11 h. The results are good enough, but still not as good as the original images. The codes of the flower project are almost the same as the codes for the quadratic curve project in section 9.2. Using only three lines in Cell 06, we can import a pre-trained U-Net from Hugging Face. After each 25-epoch model training, the model is saved by codes in Cell 10. The saved model would be loaded by Codes in Cell 06.

```python
# Project 9.3.2 DDPM image generation for Kaggle Flower Dataset-------Python v3.6
import os; import torch; import torch.nn as nn; import torch.nn.functional as F
from torch.utils.data import DataLoader
import torch.optim.lr_scheduler as lr_scheduler
from torch.utils.data.dataset import random_split as split
from torchvision import transforms; from torchvision.utils import make_grid
from torchvision.datasets import ImageFolder
from  matplotlib import pyplot as plt
import numpy as np; import pandas as pd; from tqdm import tqdm, trange
n_epochs = 25
img_size = 64
img_channels = 3
batch_size=16
lr =1e-4
data_path = 'C:/Users/xiaoc/Python/Exercises/OCR/data/FlowersDataset/flowers'
# Cell 02: Flowers Dataset ---------------------------------------------Cell 02
dataset = ImageFolder(root=data_path, transform=transforms.Compose([
                        transforms.Resize(img_size),
                        transforms.CenterCrop(img_size),
                        transforms.RandomHorizontalFlip(p=0.5),
                        transforms.ToTensor(),
                        transforms.Normalize([0.5,0.5,0.5], [0.5,0.5,0.5])]))
n_samples = len(dataset); n_train=3616; n_valid=n_samples-n_train  #4317
train_dataset, val_dataset = split(dataset, [n_train, n_valid])
# Cell 03: Flowers DataLoader-------------------------------------------Cell 03
train_dataloader = DataLoader(train_dataset, batch_size=batch_size, shuffle=True,
                num_workers=4, pin_memory=True, drop_last=True)
val_dataloader = DataLoader(val_dataset, batch_size=batch_size, shuffle=False,
                num_workers=4, pin_memory=True, drop_last=True)
n_batch = len(train_dataloader) #113
# cell 04: Display the 1st batch of the train_dataloader----------------Cell 04
for imgs, labels in train_dataloader:
    print(imgs.shape, '\nlables=', labels); break
def denorm(img_tensors): # Shift image pixel values to [0,1]
    return img_tensors * 0.5 + 0.5
def show_imgs(images):
    fig, ax = plt.subplots(figsize=(16,10))
    inputs = make_grid(denorm(images), nrow=8)
    ax.imshow(inputs.permute(1,2,0))
    ax.set(xticks=[], yticks=[]);
show_imgs(imgs)
# Cell 05: Constants and a function for forward image generation----------Cell 05
min_beta=1e-4; max_beta=0.02; T=1000; n_steps=T; time_emb_dim=100
beta = torch.linspace(min_beta, max_beta, T)
alpha = 1 - beta
a_bar = torch.cumprod(alpha, axis=0)
sqrt_a_bar = torch.sqrt(a_bar)
sqrt_one_minus_a_bar = torch.sqrt(1-a_bar)
a_bar_prev = F.pad(a_bar[:-1], (1, 0), value=1.0)
posterior_variance = beta * (1. - a_bar_prev) / (1. - a_bar)
sqrt_recip_a = torch.sqrt(1/alpha)
```

```python
def forwardIMG(x0, t):  # t is a batch of 1D integers  for time steps
    N = x0.size(0)
    noise = torch.randn_like(x0)
    sqrt_a_bar_t = sqrt_a_bar.gather(-1, t).reshape(N, *(1,)*3)
    sqrt_one_minus_a_bar_t=sqrt_one_minus_a_bar.gather(-1,t).reshape(N, *(1,)*3)
    img_t = sqrt_a_bar_t * x0 +sqrt_one_minus_a_bar_t * noise
    return img_t, noise
# Generate a batch of noised images at timestep (<T)
timestep = 99  # < T
t = timestep*torch.ones(batch_size).to(torch.int64)
imgs_t, noises = forwardIMG(imgs, t)
print(imgs_t.min(), imgs_t.max())
print(imgs_t.shape)
show_imgs(imgs_t)
# Cell 06: Import a U-Net from Hugging Face-----------------------------cell 06
from diffusers import UNet2DModel
repo_id = "google/ddpm-church-256"
model = UNet2DModel.from_pretrained(repo_id).cuda()
'''
File_name = 'D:/ddpmFlower.pth'
torch.save(model, File_name)   # to save trained model after each model training
#model = torch.load(File_name) # to load trained model for next model training
#model.eval()
'''
#-----------------------------------------------------------------------------


# Cell 07: Fitting function------------------------------------------Cell 07
optimizer = torch.optim.Adam(model.parameters(), lr=lr)
criterion = nn.MSELoss()
scheduler = lr_scheduler.OneCycleLR(optimizer, max_lr=lr,
                    steps_per_epoch=n_batch, epochs=n_epochs, pct_start=0.6)
def fit(epochs):
    torch.cuda.empty_cache()
    df = pd.DataFrame(np.empty([epochs, 2]),
                        index = np.arange(epochs), columns=['loss', 'lr'])
    progress_bar = trange(epochs)
    for i in progress_bar:
        Loss = 0.0
        for step, (imgs, _) in enumerate(train_dataloader):
            t = torch.randint(0, T, (batch_size,))
            imgs_t, noises = forwardIMG(imgs, t)
            noise_pred = model(imgs_t.cuda(), t.cuda())['sample']
            optimizer.zero_grad()
            loss = criterion(noise_pred, noises.cuda())
            Loss += loss.item()
            loss.backward()
            learn_rate = optimizer.param_groups[0]['lr']
            optimizer.step()
            scheduler.step()
            progress_bar.set_description("loss=%.4f" % loss.item())
            progress_bar.set_postfix({'lr': learn_rate})
        df.iloc[i, 0] = Loss/n_batch
        df.iloc[i, 1] = learn_rate
    return df
train_history = fit(n_epochs)
```

```
# Cell 08: Show the training history-----------------------------------Cell 08
df = train_history
fig, ax = plt.subplots(1,2, figsize=(12,5), sharex=True)
df.plot(ax=ax[0], y=[0])
df.plot(ax=ax[1], y=[1])
for i in range(2):
    ax[i].set_xlabel('epoch')
    ax[i].grid(which='major', axis='both', color='g', linestyle=':')
ax[0].set_ylabel('Loss')
ax[1].ticklabel_format(style='sci', axis='y', scilimits=(0,0));
# Cell 09: The backward process to generate images from pure noises------------
@torch.no_grad()
def backwardIMG():
    x = torch.randn(16, img_channels, img_size, img_size).cuda()
    for i in range(0,T)[::-1]:
        N = x.size(0)
        t = torch.full((N,), i, dtype=torch.long)
        beta_t = beta.gather(-1, t).reshape(N, *(1,)*3).cuda()
        sqrt_recip_a_t = sqrt_recip_a.gather(-1,t).reshape(N, *(1,)*3).cuda()
        sqrt_one_minus_a_bar_t = sqrt_one_minus_a_bar.gather(-1, t
                                    ).reshape(N, *(1,)*3).cuda()
        posterior_variance_t = posterior_variance.gather(-1,t
                                    ).reshape(N, *(1,)*3).cuda()


        model_mean = sqrt_recip_a_t * (x -
            beta_t * model(x, t.cuda())['sample'] / sqrt_one_minus_a_bar_t)
        if t[0] > 0:
            x = model_mean+torch.sqrt(posterior_variance_t)*torch.randn_like(x)
        else:
            x = model_mean
    return x.cpu()
my_img = backwardIMG()
show_imgs(my_img)
# Cell 10: save the trained model-----------------------------------model saving
File_name = 'D:/ddpmFlower.pth'
torch.save(model, File_name)
#-------------------------------------------------------------------The End
```

9.4 Generate photorealistic images from text prompts by stable diffusion

The flower images generated by the pre-trained Hugging Face U-Net model are really beautiful. However, it is impossible for us to control what kind of flower to generate. We could use a conditional DDMP model to generated images according to our settings. Even if our conditional DDMP model with codes in a thousand lines works very well, it only can generate images in categories limited by the dataset used to train our model. To obtain photorealistic images, model training time could be very long. How can we generate any high-quality images by using text prompts without model training?

We now (since 2022) have a generative model to generate any image from text prompts. It is Hugging Face's Stable Diffusion, a deep learning, text-to-image model with the name: latent diffusion model (LDM (Rombach *et al* 2022)). A dataset used to train Stable Diffusion is Laion-5B, an open-source dataset which provides more than 5.85 billion CLIP-filtered image-text pairs. Natural language processing (NLP) is a branch of computer science. Multi-head self-attention used in section 9.2 is an NLP method to obtain information from encoded text. Stable diffusion is an integration of computer vision and NLP. Hugging Face has a website for Stable Diffusion 2.1 Demo, in which there is a link to DreamStudio Beta. The second website generates images with higher loyalty to our text prompts. If you generate images of human faces, you will see a huge difference between the two websites. We can download libraries of Stable Diffusion and practice to generate images in VS Code. The file sizes of those libraries and pre-trained parameters are huge (>10 GB). To save computer hard disk space, you can run the following codes in Google Colab or Kaggle with free GPUs (figure 9.7). On January of 2024, Microsoft's Copilot and Google's Bard let people to generate photorealistic image with text prompts.

```
# Project 9.4: Text-to-Image generation with Stable Diffusion---------Python v3.6
#!pip install --upgrade diffusers transformers accelerate  #----install libraries
import torch
from diffusers import StableDiffusionPipeline # ---import a pipeline with a model
repo_id = "runwayml/stable-diffusion-v1-5"    #----import pre-trained parameters
pipe = StableDiffusionPipeline.from_pretrained(     # using 16-bits to save time
        repo_id, torch_dtype=torch.float16).to("cuda")
prompt = "a girl in a rose garden"       # text prompts from users
image = pipe(prompt).images[0]      # image generation in Kaggle or Google Colab
#image = pipe(prompt)['sample'][0] # image generation in VS Code
image
#--------------------------------------------------------------------The End
```

Figure 9.7. An image generated with the text prompt 'a girl in a rose garden' by a pre-trained Stable Diffusion in project 9.4 running in Google Colab.

References

Ho J, Jain A and Abbeel P 2020 Denoising diffusion probabilistic models *Adv. Neural Inform. Process. Syst.* **33** 6840–51

Ioffe S and Szegedy C 2015 Batch normalization: accelerating deep network training by reducing internal covariate shift *Int. Conf. on Machine Learning* (PMLR) pp 448–56

Oktay O, Schlemper J, Folgoc L L, Lee M, Heinrich M, Misawa K, Mori K, Mcdonagh S, Hammerla N Y and Kainz B 2018 Attention u-net: learning where to look for the pancreas *arXiv preprint* arXiv:1804.03999

Petit O, Thome N, Rambour C, Themyr L, Collins T and Soler L 2021 U-net transformer: Self and cross attention for medical image segmentation *Int. Workshop on Machine Learning in Medical Imaging* (Berlin: Springer) pp 267–76

Rombach R, Blattmann A, Lorenz D, Esser P and Ommer B 2022 High-resolution image synthesis with latent diffusion models *Proc. of the IEEE/CVF Conf. on Computer Vision and Pattern Recognition* pp 10684–95

Ronneberger O, Fischer P and Brox T 2015 U-Net: convolutional networks for biomedical image segmentation *Int. Conf. on Medical Image Computing and Computer-Assisted Intervention* (Berlin: Springer) pp 234–41

Staal J, Abramoff M D, Niemeijer M, Viergever M A and Ginneken B V 2004 Ridge-based vessel segmentation in color images of the retina *IEEE Trans. Med. Imaging* **23** 501–9

Chapter 10

Applications of vision transformers

Using models based on transformers but not convolution networks, computers are smart enough to understand human languages. Transformers used for computer vision tasks are vision transformers. The first section introduces the architecture of a basic vision transformer. Then, pre-trained vision transformers were used in the following four sections for image classification and objection detection without model training (Zero-shot) for custom datasets.

The birth of ChatGPT (Generative Pre-trained Transformer) from OpenAI is a breakthrough in computer science. People can chat with computers to discuss any subject. It seems that ChatGPT knows everything, and can reply to many questions asked by people. On the interface of the ChatGPT website, I used the text prompts 'please write Python codes about logistic regression for me'. Then in a few seconds, I was able to copy and paste codes from ChatGPT to a cell in VS Code and run the codes. Computers have passed the Turing Test, a method of inquiry in AI to determine whether or not a computer is capable of thinking like a human being. ChatGPT is a language model which uses a transformer (Vaswani *et al* 2017) for natural language processing (NLP) tasks such as language translation, text classification, and text generation. In the transformer, there is an encoder and a decoder. Words in a text prompt written in a natural language are digitalized as tokens in a high-dimensional vector space. A token is a small unit of information. These tokens embedded with sequence information of words in the text prompt are used as inputs of an encoder of the transformer. Self-attention mechanisms are used in the transformer to capture dependencies between different tokens in the paper. The use of the transformer has led to revolutionary improvements in NLP tasks. Vision transformers (ViT) are modified NLP transformers for computer vision tasks such as image classification and object detection. Vision transformers were introduced by Dosovitskiy *et al* in their 2020 paper (Dosovitskiy *et al* 2020) titled 'An Image Is Worth 16×16 Words: Transformers for Image Recognition at Scale.' Unlike traditional convolutional neural networks which use a series of convolutional and pooling layers to extract local features from images, a ViT based on a NLP transformer can capture spatial relationships among different parts of an image.

10.1 The architecture of a basic ViT model

In a basic ViT model based on the ViT paper (Dosovitskiy *et al* 2020), there is only a modified encoder, no decoder. Any color image input to the ViT model should be resized to $3 \times 224 \times 224$, and then split into a grid of patches with a specified patch size. If the patch size is 8 then the image is split into 784 ($=224/8 \times 28$) patches. Each color patch is then flattened into a 1D array as a token which has 192 ($=3 \times 8 \times 8$) elements. The key idea of a ViT is to treat an image as a sequence of tokens and then process these tokens by using a transformer's encoder. This allows ViT to capture global information of an entire image, rather than just local information in specific regions from CNN networks. Vision transformers have achieved state-of-the-art performance. They have also been used in a variety of applications, including image captioning, image generation, and video classification. Codes in the following project 10.1.1 are used to explain the architecture of the basic ViT model.

As usual, codes in Cell 01 import libraries for the project and set hyperparameters in a dictionary named 'config'. In a class defined in Cell 02, a tool or library named *einops* is used to reshape and permute an input image according to a text instruction: 'b c (h h1) (w w1) -> b (h w) c h1 w1', where b, c, h1 and w1 are batch size, image channels (=3), and patch size (= 8 pixels) in row and column directions respectively. Based on the known input image size (224), an instance of the class calculates another two parameters h and w (28 = 224/8). Einops is a powerful library for tensor operations in computer vision. The name 'einops' stands for 'Einstein operations' and is inspired by Einstein's notation used in physics to express tensor operations in his Theory of Relativity. Two parameters in a pair of parentheses of the text instruction are used for a parameter's value which is equal to the production of the two parameters. For example, (h h1) is for a parameter about the image height 224 which is equal to 28×8. Although we can do the same job by using PyTorch tools such as *reshape* and *permute*, *einops* is easy to understand with text prompts. Each color patch of the image is then flattened to a tensor with 192 elements ($D = 3 \times 8 \times 8$). With the above operations, a 2D image $x \in \mathfrak{R}^{C \times H \times W}$ is split into a series of flattened 2D patches $x_p \in R^{N \times (P^2 \cdot C)}$, where $H \times W$ is the resolution of the input image, C is the number of image channels, P is the patch size, and $N (= HW/P^2)$ is the number of patches. Each flattened patch is a token like a word token in NLP. The use of tokens enables ViT to learn relationships among different regions of an image and make predictions based on the overall context of the image (figure 10.1).

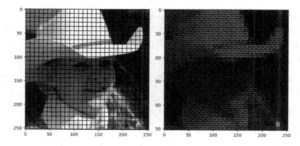

Figure 10.1. (A) An image with a resolution $3 \times 244 \times 244$ was directly divided into a grid with 28×28 patches by an einops operation in Cell 02. (B) The same image was split by a convolution operation and reshaped to [1, 786, 3, 8, 8].

```
# Project 10.1.1 The Architecture of a basic ViT model----- ----------Python v3.9
import torch; import torch.nn as nn; import numpy as np; import math
from torchvision.utils import make_grid; import torchvision.transforms as T
import matplotlib.pyplot as plt; import matplotlib.image as mpimg
import einops # Einstein operations for numpy arrays and torch tensors
config = {
    "image_size": 224,          # all images are resized to 224x224
    "num_channels": 3,          # color images
    "patch_size": 8,            # 8 pixels, n_patches=(224/8)^2=784
    "hidden_size": 192,         # 3x8x8=192 pixels: embedding_dims
    "intermediate_size": 768,   # = 192x4 used in MLP: mpl_size
    "num_attention_heads": 6,   # self attention heads in a multihead layer
    "num_hidden_layers": 12,    # Multihead self attention layers
    "num_classes": 10,          # num_classes of CIFAR10
    "hidden_dropout_prob": 0.1,
    "attention_probs_dropout_prob": 0.0,
    "qkv_bias": True,
    "use_faster_attention": True}
f0 = T.Resize(size = (224,224), antialias=True) # a function for image resize
path = 'd:/Stamped2016-Lady.jpg'          # for an image example
image = mpimg.imread(path)[:, 0:600, :] # [600,800,3] cropped to [600,600,3]
my_img = f0(torch.tensor(image).permute(2,0,1)).unsqueeze(0)/255
# Cell 02: A function to patch a batch of images by einops--------------Cell 02
class PatchedImgs(nn.Module):
    def __init__(self, config):
        super().__init__()
        self.patch_size = config["patch_size"]
    def forward(self, x):    # input x.shape=[N, 3, 244,244]
        x = einops.rearrange(x,
            'b c (h h1) (w w1) -> b (h w) c h1 w1',
            h1=self.patch_size, w1=self.patch_size)
        return x     #output x.shape=[b, 784, 3, 8, 8]
f1 = PatchedImgs(config)     #             input image.shape=[1, 3, 224, 224]
patched_img = f1(my_img)     #             patched_img.shape=[1, 784, 3, 8, 8]
def show_imgs(images):
    fig, ax = plt.subplots(figsize=(5,5))
    inputs = make_grid(images, nrow=28, padding=1)
    ax.imshow(inputs.permute(1,2,0))
    plt.show()
show_imgs(patched_img[0])
#---------------------------------------------------------------------------
```

With codes in the following Cell 03, a learnable token $z_{00} = x_{\text{class}}$ with a name 'cls' is then pre-pended to the sequence of the tokens for image classification. The dimensionality of the cls token is the same as that of a flattened patch. Since the sequence of image patches is as important as words in a paper, we need to add position embeddings to the tokens to retain positional information. The result of these operations is a tensor z_0 as an input of the ViT encoder shown in equation (10.1), where $E_{\text{pos}} \in \mathfrak{R}^{(N+1) \times D} E \in E_{\text{pos}}$ is a trainable position embedding tensor, and $E_{\text{pos}} \in \mathfrak{R}^{(P^2 \cdot C) \times D}$ is a learnable linear projection tensor from a convolution operation in the following Cell 02. The above Cell 02 with an einops operation is just used for visualization of image patches

$$z_0 = \left[x_{\text{class}}, x_{p_1}E, x_{p_2}E, \ldots, x_{p_N}E \right]^T + E_{\text{pos}} \tag{10.1}$$

In the forward function of a class defined in Cell 03, the input is a batch of images with the shape [b, 3, 224, 224], where the parameter b is batch size. From an instance of a class defined in the following Cell 02 with a convolution and a permute operations, the input image is split to a tensor with the shape [b, 784, 192]. A learnable *cls* token is created by the code on line 06 of Cell 03. It is then expanded for every image in a batch by the code on line 14. After the *cls* token is pre-pended to each image of the batch, we add a tensor for position embedding to each token of each image. PyTorch will take care of dimension difference between the two tensors by broadcasting. To reduce overfitting issues, we need a dropout operation for the output of Cell 03. By running codes inside the quotation makers `f2=Embeded_Imgs(config);emb_img=f2 (my_img); emb_img.shape` in an extra cell after Cell 03, we will know the shape of the output of Cell 03 is [1, 785, 192] for a batch with only one image.

```python
# Cell 02: A function to patch a batch of images by convolution-----------Cell 02
class PatchedImgs(nn.Module):
    def __init__(self, config):
        super().__init__()
        self.conv = nn.Conv2d(in_channels=config["num_channels"],
                              out_channels=config["hidden_size"],
                              kernel_size=config['patch_size'],
                              stride=config['patch_size'],
                              padding=0)
        self.flatten = nn.Flatten(start_dim=2)
    def forward(self, x):     # input x.shape=[b, 3, 244,244]
        x = self.flatten(self.conv(x)).permute(0,2,1)
        return x              # output x.shape=[1, 784, 192]
f1 = PatchedImgs(config)      # an instance to patch an image shape=
patched_img = f1(my_img)      #   my_img.shape=[1, 3, 224, 224]
def show_imgs(images):
    fig, ax = plt.subplots(figsize=(5,5))
    inputs = make_grid(images, nrow=28, padding=1)
    ax.imshow(inputs.permute(1,2,0))
    plt.show()
show_imgs(patched_img.view(1,784,3,8,8)[0])
# Cell 03: A function to embed tokens of a batch of images----------------Cell 03
class Embeded_Imgs(nn.Module):
    def __init__(self, config):
        super().__init__()
        self.num_patches = (config["image_size"] // config["patch_size"] ) ** 2
        self.patched = PatchedImgs(config)              #--------instance of a class
        self.cls_token = nn.Parameter(                  # ------------------line 06
                torch.randn(1, 1, config["hidden_size"]),requires_grad=True)
        self.position_embeddings = nn.Parameter(        # ------------------line 08
                torch.randn(1, self.num_patches + 1, config["hidden_size"]))
        self.dropout = nn.Dropout(config["hidden_dropout_prob"])
    def forward(self, x):                  # input x.shape=[b, 3, 244,244]
        batch_size = x.shape[0]
        x = self.patched(x).flatten(2)
        cls_tokens = self.cls_token.expand(batch_size, -1, -1)  # ------line 14
        x = torch.cat((cls_tokens, x), dim=1)        #x.shape=[b, 785, 192]
        x = x + self.position_embeddings      # ------------------------line 16
        x = self.dropout(x)
        return x              # output x.shape = [b, 785, 192]
#---------------------------------------------------------------------------
```

The architecture of a basic ViT model is shown on the left side of figure 10.2. Those tokens from Cell 03 or equation (10.1) are processed by 12 transformer encoder layers connected in series. They refine the representation of input images. The structure of an encoder layer is shown in the middle of the figure. Inside the encoder layer, there is a multi-head attention block which has six self-attention heads connected in parallel to process each batch of tokens. The structure of a single self-attention head is shown on the right-hand-side of the figure. The shape of the input and the output of each self-attention head are the same [b, 785, 192]. According to equation (10.2), we can write codes for the self-attention head in Cell 04. In the equation and the figure, a dot between two tensors means a dot product. Each of the three tensors Q, K and V is an output of three fully connected layers, respectively. The input of any fully connected layer is the same: a batch of tokens of images in a batch, and D is equal to 192 (the number of pixels of the color patch: $3 \times 8 \times 8$). The outputs of all six self-attention blocks are then concatenated into a bigger size tensor with the shape [b, 785, 192 × 6] by the code on line 18 of Cell 05. Then a fully connected layer is used to project the big size tensor to a tensor with the shape [b, 785, 192] by the code on line 21. After a dropout operation acts on the result of the projection, the final result is output as a tuple with two elements. The first element is an attention tensor for a batch of tokens, and the second element of the tuple is for attention probs. We can run codes 'f4=MultiHeadAttention (config); Y=f4(emb_img)[0]; Y.shape' to check if codes of the classes are functional

$$\text{Attention}(Q, K, V) = \text{softmax}\left(\frac{Q \cdot K^T}{\sqrt{D}}\right) \cdot V \qquad (10.2)$$

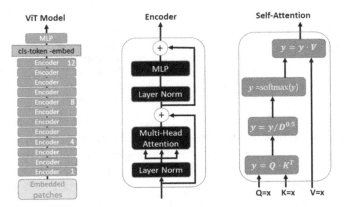

Figure 10.2. The architecture of a basic ViT model, an encoder layer or block inside the ViT model and a single self-attention head (right). The arrows indicate information flowing directions.

```
# Cell 04: A Class for Self Attention---------------------------------Cell 04
class AttentionHead(nn.Module):
    def __init__(self, config):
        super().__init__()
        self.hidden_size = config["hidden_size"]
        self.bias = config["qkv_bias"]
        self.p = config["attention_probs_dropout_prob"]
        self.query = nn.Linear(self.hidden_size, self.hidden_size, self.bias)
        self.key = nn.Linear(self.hidden_size, self.hidden_size, self.bias)
        self.value = nn.Linear(self.hidden_size, self.hidden_size, self.bias)
        self.dropout = nn.Dropout(self.p)
    def forward(self, x):    # x.shape=[b, 785, 192]
        Q = self.query(x); K = self.key(x); V = self.value(x)
        QxKT = torch.matmul(Q, K.transpose(-1, -2))
        attention_scores = QxKT / math.sqrt(self.hidden_size)
        attention_probs = nn.functional.softmax(attention_scores, dim=-1)
        attention_probs = self.dropout(attention_probs)      #shape=[b,785,785]
        attention_output = torch.matmul(attention_probs, V) #shape=[b,785,192]
        return (attention_output, attention_probs)
# Cell 05: A Class for Multihead Self Attention-------------------------Cell 05
class MultiHeadAttention(nn.Module):
    def __init__(self, config):
        super().__init__()
        self.hidden_size = config["hidden_size"]                    #192
        self.num_attention_heads = config["num_attention_heads"]    #6
        self.all_head_size = self.num_attention_heads*self.hidden_size #6*192
        self.qkv_bias = config["qkv_bias"]
        self.p = config["hidden_dropout_prob"]
        self.heads = nn.ModuleList([])  # Create a list of attention heads
        for _ in range(self.num_attention_heads):
            head = AttentionHead(config)
            self.heads.append(head)
        self.output_projection = nn.Linear(self.all_head_size, self.hidden_size)
        self.output_dropout = nn.Dropout(self.p)
    def forward(self, x):                       #input x.shape=[b, 785, 192]
        attention_outputs = [head(x) for head in self.heads]
        attention_output = torch.cat([    #output.shape=[b, 785, 192*6]--line 18
            attention_output for attention_output,_ in attention_outputs],dim=-1)
        attention_output = self.output_projection(attention_output) #----line 21
        attention_output = self.output_dropout(attention_output)
        attention_probs = torch.stack([attention_probs
                        for _, attention_probs in attention_outputs], dim=1)
        return (attention_output, attention_probs)
#----------------------------------------------------------------------------
```

The input of a transformer encoder is a batch of tokens of images. Because each token of an image is embedded with position information, we should not use batch normalizations, but layer normalizations in the encoder. Also, two residual connections are used in the encoder block (line 19, 21 in Cell 06). In the MLP (multi-layer perceptron) block of an encoder layer, there are two fully connected layers, and between them is an activation class $nn.GELU()$ (line 12 of Cell 06). Dropouts are also used in the MLP block.

Mathematical operations for each of the 12 (=L) encoder layers can be represented by equations (10.3) and (10.4) for Cell 07. To the first layer for example, the output of the first layer normalization to the input tokens z_0 is $LN(z_0)$, which is then processed by a multi-head self-attention block to get MSA(LN(z_0)). Using equation (10.3), we obtain a temporary output Φ_0 of the first residual block in the first encoder layer. Using Φ_0 as an input for the second residual block in the first encoder layer and equation (10.4), we get z_1, the output of the first encoder layer. The output of the last encoder layer is also a tuple with two elements about tokens and attention scores

$$\Phi_{\ell-1} = \text{MSA}(\text{LN}(z_{\ell-1})) + z_{\ell-1} \quad \ell = 1, 2, ..., L \tag{10.3}$$

$$z_\ell = \text{MLP}(\text{LN}(\Phi_{\ell-1}) + \Phi_{\ell-1} \quad \ell = 1, 2, ..., L \tag{10.4}$$

$$y = \text{MLP}(z_L[:, 0]) \tag{10.5}$$

We only use z_L[b, 0, 192] for image classification. The shape of z_L[:,0] in equation (10.5) is [b, 192]. A classification head is added on top of the final transformer layer to make predictions for image classification. We can make sure that codes in all the above classes are functional by run the codes 'f6=Vit(config); f6(my_img)' in an extra cell after Cell 07. Using codes in Cell 10 in project 2.1 of chapter 2, you would find there were a total of 14,443,018 parameters in the ViT model defined in Cell 07.

```
# Cell 06: A Class for the transformer encoder-------------------------Cell 06
class EncoderBlock(nn.Module):
    def __init__(self, config):
        super().__init__()
        self.hidden_size = config["hidden_size"]
        self.num_attention_heads = config["num_attention_heads"]
        self.dim_feedforward = config["intermediate_size "]
        self.p = config["hidden_dropout_prob"]
        self.norm = nn.LayerNorm(self.hidden_size)
        self.multihead = MultiHeadAttention(config)
        self.enc_MLP = nn.Sequential(
                    nn.Linear(self.hidden_size, self.dim_feedforward),
                    nn.GELU(),                    # ----line 12
                    nn.Dropout(self.p),
                    nn.Linear(self.dim_feedforward, self.hidden_size),
                    nn.Dropout(self.p))
    def forward(self, emb_img):
        firstnorm_out = self.norm(emb_img)     #emb_img.shape=[b, 785, 192]
        attention_out, attention_score = self.multihead(firstnorm_out)
        first_added = attention_out + emb_img     # ---line 19
        secondnorm_out = self.norm(first_added)
        output = first_added + self.enc_MLP(secondnorm_out) #----line 21
        return output, attention_score   # #attention_score.shape=[b,6,785,785]
# Cell 07: A Class for the basic ViT model----------------------------Cell 07
class Vit(nn.Module):
    def __init__(self, config):
        super(Vit, self).__init__()
        self.num_hidden_layers = config["num_hidden_layers"]
        self.hidden_size = config["hidden_size"]
        self.num_classes = config["num_classes"]
        self.embeded_Imgs = Embeded_Imgs(config)
        self.encStack = nn.ModuleList(          # Create a stack of encoders
            [EncoderBlock(config) for i in range(self.num_hidden_layers)])
```

```
        self.MLP_head = nn.Sequential(
                        nn.LayerNorm(self.hidden_size),
                        nn.Linear(self.hidden_size, self.hidden_size),
                        nn.Linear(self.hidden_size, self.num_classes))
    def forward(self, x):        # a batch of images   x.shape = [b, 3, 224, 224]
        enc_output = self.embeded_Imgs(x)
        for enc_layer in self.encStack:
            enc_output, attention_score = enc_layer(enc_output)
        cls_token_embed = enc_output[:, 0]     # cls_token_embed.shape=[b, 768]
        output = self.MLP_head(cls_token_embed) # output.shape=[b, 10]
        return output, attention_score  # #attention_score.shape=[b,6,785,785]
#-----------------------------------------------------------------The End
```

10.2 Hugging Face ViT for CIFAR10 image classification

I would like to use the above ViT model for CIFAR10 image classification. Since the model's parameter number is more than 10 million, the computation job of the ViT model training is too heavy for my laptop to handle 50 thousand images resized to 224 × 224. I have to use a pre-trained Hugging Face ViT model to demonstrate the power of vision transformers. Because the pre-trained model has about 86 million parameters, I have to freeze them and only train a few parameters in the last layer for image classification to save time. From YouTube, GitHub, Kaggle and Google Colab, we can find codes to demonstrate how to fine tune Hugging Face ViT models for CIFAR10. My codes are inspired by those people's codes. The accuracies of image classification of the following project 10.2 are 94.9%, 94.5% and 94.7% for the train, validation and test datasets respectively. Code running time is about 33 min in 10 epochs.

With a pre-trained Hugging Face ViT model named '*google/vit-base-patch16–224-in21k*', it is easy for us to write codes for project 10.2 where the code structure is almost the same as the one in project 2.3 of chapter 2. Hugging Face provides a library named 'datasets' to download datasets from internet (line 05 of Cell 01), and it is convenient to use. Datasets downloaded from internet are saved on my hard disk, and can be used without downloading again even when my laptop is restarted. In Kaggle and Google Colab, we have to download the codes again when we restart to use any of the two free GPU systems. Many libraries from Hugging Face work in Python with a version above 3.6. The codes for this project were tested and worked well in Python v3.9 of VS Code. If you print out *train_ds[0]* after Cell 01, you will see a dictionary with two keys: 'img' and 'label', not a tuple as in chapters 1–9.

A Hugging Face class named '*ViTImageProcessor*' on line 09 of Cell 01 can be used to modify images to a specific format for the pre-trained ViT model. Printing out the processor or using a code on the last line of Cell 02, you will see many image augmentations, such as normalize, rescale, resize, etc. A function defined in Cell 03 packs processed image datasets into dataloaders, and codes in Cell 04 display a batch of images in a train dataloader. From a for-loop on the first line of in Cell 04, you will find that each sample in a dataloader is a dictionary with a 'label' key and a 'pixel_values' key respectively.

```
# Project 10.2 CIFAR10 Image classification by a Hugging Face ViT-----Python v3.9
import torch; import torch.nn as nn
from torch.utils.data import DataLoader
import numpy as np; from tqdm import trange, tqdm
from datasets import load_dataset         # a new Hugging Face library-----line 05
from transformers import AdamW, ViTModel, ViTImageProcessor
from torchvision.utils import make_grid; import matplotlib.pyplot as plt
model_name = "google/vit-base-patch16-224-in21k"        # --------------line 08
processor = ViTImageProcessor.from_pretrained(model_name)    #-----------line 09
device = 'cuda' if torch.cuda.is_available() else "cpu"
epochs = 10
lr = 1e-5
batch_size = 20


# Cell 02: Load cifar10 from internet for three datasets------------------------
train_ds, test_ds = load_dataset('cifar10',split=['train[:10000]','test[:2000]'])
splits = train_ds.train_test_split(test_size=0.1)       # split for training + val
train_ds = splits['train']; val_ds = splits['test']
example = processor(train_ds[0:2]['img'], return_tensors='pt')       #----line 04
print(example['pixel_values'].shape )        # shape=[2, 3, 224, 224]
processor

#Cell 03: Processes images by a pre-trained ViT model for 3 dataloaders----------
def preprocess(batch):
    inputs = processor(batch['img'], return_tensors='pt')
    inputs['label'] = torch.tensor(batch['label'])
    return inputs
prepared_train = train_ds.with_transform(preprocess)
train_dataloader = DataLoader(prepared_train, batch_size=batch_size,shuffle=True)
prepared_val = val_ds.with_transform(preprocess)
val_dataloader = DataLoader(prepared_val, batch_size=batch_size)
prepared_test = test_ds.with_transform(preprocess)
test_dataloader = DataLoader(prepared_test, batch_size=batch_size)
#Cell 04: Display A batch of the train datalosder------------------------------
for batch in train_dataloader:
    labels = batch['label']; print(labels)
    images = batch['pixel_values']; print(images.shape)
    break
# Cell 04: Show images in a batch of dataloader-----------------------------
def denorm(img_tensors):    # Shift image pixel values to [0,1]
    return img_tensors * 0.5 + 0.5
def show_imgs(images):
    fig, ax = plt.subplots(figsize=(8,6))
    inputs = make_grid(denorm(images), nrow=10, padding=1)
    ax.imshow(inputs.permute(1,2,0))
    ax.set(xticks=[], yticks=[])
    plt.show()
show_imgs(images)
#Cell 05: ViT Image Classification Model, criterion, optimizers-------------
vit_model = ViTModel.from_pretrained(model_name)
for param in vit_model.parameters():           #--------------line 02
    param.requires_grad = False
```

```python
class ViTForImageClassification(nn.Module):
    def __init__(self, num_labels=10):
        super().__init__()
        self.vit = vit_model
        self.dropout = nn.Dropout(0.1)
        self.classifier = nn.Linear(self.vit.config.hidden_size, num_labels)
        self.num_labels = num_labels

    def forward(self, pixel_values):
        outputs = self.vit(pixel_values=pixel_values)
        output = self.dropout(outputs.last_hidden_state[:,0])
        logits = self.classifier(output)
        return logits
model = ViTForImageClassification()
model = model.to(device)
optimizer = AdamW(model.parameters(), lr = lr)
criterion = nn.CrossEntropyLoss()
#Cell 06: Training function for an epoch-------------------------------------
def train():
    model.train()
    total_loss = 0
    total_preds=[]
    for batch in train_dataloader:
        pix, lbl = batch.items()
        pix, lbl = pix[1].to(device), lbl[1].to(device)
        preds = model(pix)
        loss = criterion(preds, lbl)
        total_loss += loss.item()
        loss.backward()
        torch.nn.utils.clip_grad_norm_(model.parameters(), 1.0)
        optimizer.step()
        optimizer.zero_grad()
        total_preds.append(preds.detach().cpu().numpy())
    avg_loss = total_loss / len(train_dataloader)
    total_preds  = np.concatenate(total_preds, axis=0)
    return avg_loss, total_preds
#Cell 07: Evaluation for the val_dataloader to find overfitting--------------
def eval():
    total_loss = 0
    model.eval()
    for step,batch in enumerate(val_dataloader):
        pix, lbl = batch.items()
        pix, lbl = pix[1].to(device), lbl[1].to(device)
        preds = model(pix)
        loss = criterion(preds, lbl)
        total_loss += loss.item()
    return total_loss / len(val_dataloader)
# Cell 08: Fitting function-------------------------------------------------
progress_bar = trange(epochs)
for epoch in progress_bar:
    train_loss, _ = train()
    val_loss = eval()
```

```
    progress_bar.set_description("Loss_train=%.4f" % train_loss)
    progress_bar.set_postfix({'Loss_val': val_loss})
# Cell 09: Evaluation for the test dataloader-----------------------------
def test_eval():
    model.eval()
    y_pred = []; y_true = []
    with torch.no_grad():
        for _, batch in tqdm(
                enumerate(test_dataloader), total = len(test_dataloader)):
            pix, lbl = batch.items()
            pix, lbl = pix[1].to(device), lbl[1].to(device)
            outputs = model(pix)
            outputs = torch.argmax(outputs, axis=1)
            y_pred.extend(outputs.cpu().detach().numpy())
            y_true.extend(lbl.cpu().detach().numpy())
    return y_pred, y_true
y_pred, y_true = test_eval()
correct = np.array(y_pred) == np.array(y_true)
accuracy = correct.sum() / len(correct)
print("Accuracy of the model", accuracy)
#---------------------------------------------------------------------The End
```

10.3 Zero shot image classification by OpenAI CLIP

To understand what a 'zero shot' is, we need to recap image classification from chapter 2. To get good results for image classification projects, we have to use as many samples as possible to train a ResNet model. If the number of samples needed to train a model is N, the model needs N-shot learning. Zero shot image classification refers to the ability of a neural network system to classify images into categories without model training. How can OpenAI's CLIP (Radford *et al* 2021) make zero shot learning possible? CLIP is an abbreviation of 'contrastive language image pretraining', a name for a transformer-based framework developed by OpenAI. In a CLIP system there are two models. The first is a text transformer to encode text into a space with 512 dimensions, and the second is a vision transformer (ViT) to encode images in the same space. OpenAI has trained CLIP on a dataset with 400-million text-image pairs. Each pair of an image and its caption are two close points in the space. From an image we can find its caption text, and vice versa. Zero shot image classification does not need to train models because OpenAI has trained the CLIP system for us. This zero shot capability is a significant advantage of CLIP, as it eliminates the need for fine-tuning or retraining on specific classes. However, CLIP has its limitations. The accuracy of the predictions depends on the quality and diversity of the training data. Additionally, CLIP may struggle to describe a single image with a few words because 'a picture is worth a thousand words'.

The codes in the following two projects were inspired by codes from CLIP's GitHub repository. As usual, codes in Cell 01 of project 10.3.1 import the necessary libraries. Since there is no model training, there are no hyperparameter to set. CIFAR10's test dataset is used in the project. The code on line 06 of Cell 01 prints out the class labels of the dataset. We will use them to identify objects in the 10 000 images of the test dataset which has the same dataset structure in chapter 2. In an extra cell after Cell 01 running the code *clip.available_models( )*, you will see nine CLIP models. From model 'ViT-B/32' and 'ViT-L/14', I got accuracies of 88.79% and 95.32% with a program running time of 2 min and 3.5 min respectively. The *preprocess* code following *model* on the last line of Cell 01 is for image augmentations. In another extra cell, you can *print(preprocess)* to see many augmentations: resize(244), centerCrop ((224,224)), to RGB, ToTensor and normalize. With a fitting function defined in Cell 02, images in the test dataset are checked one by one in a for-loop. Before the loop, the dataset's 10 labels are encoded by *clip.tokenize* into a 10×512 tensor. In front of each label, a text string 'a photo of a' is pre-pended. According to the CLIP paper (Radford *et al* 2021), CLIP models have better performance with those extra words added to each label. The code on line 11 of Cell 02 encodes a single image in a batch into a 1×512 tensor. With a dot product on line 13 for the encoded image tensor and the encoded label tensor, we get the class identity of an object in a CIFAR10 image. The final results are shown in table 10.1, and the average accuracy of the zero shot classification is 95.3%. In chapter 2 for same test dataset, the accuracy is 92%.

Table 10.1. Zero shot image classification for CIFAR10 by CLIP.

Label	Airplane	Automobile	Bird	Cat	Deer	Dog	Frog	Horse	Ship	Truck	Acc (%)
Airplane	952	2	19	2	0	0	1	4	17	3	95.2
Automobile	0	965	0	0	0	0	0	0	0	35	96.5
Bird	1	0	957	8	24	1	1	8	0	0	95.7
Cat	1	1	13	947	7	23	2	5	0	1	94.7
Deer	0	0	9	4	957	3	1	26	0	0	95.7
Dog	0	0	4	35	3	954	0	4	0	0	95.4
Frog	0	0	47	39	30	8	867	8	1	0	86.7
Horse	0	0	5	1	5	3	0	985	1	0	98.5
Ship	11	11	5	0	0	3	0	0	965	5	96.5
Truck	1	13	0	0	1	0	0	1	1	983	98.3

```
# Project 10.3.1: Zero-shot Image Classification for CIFAR10---------Python v3.6
import clip; import pandas as pd; import numpy as np; from tqdm import tqdm
import torch; from torchvision.datasets import CIFAR10
data_path = './OCR/data/cifar10'
dataset = CIFAR10(root=data_path, download=False, train=False,)
labels = dataset.classes    #['airplane','automobile','bird','cat',
print(labels)                    #'deer','dog','frog','horse','ship','truck']
model, preprocess = clip.load('ViT-L/14', device="cuda") #'ViT-B/32' ----line 07
# Cell 02: Zero-shot classifier---------------------------------------------------
def fitting():
    df = pd.DataFrame(np.zeros([len(labels), 11]), index = labels,
                      columns=labels + ['acc'])
    text_inputs = torch.cat([clip.tokenize(          #text_inputs.shape = 10 x 77
              f"a photo of a {c}") for c in labels]).cuda()
    text_features = model.encode_text(text_inputs)        #---------------line 07
    text_features /= text_features.norm(dim=-1, keepdim=True)  #--shape=10 x 512
    with torch.no_grad():
```

```
        for _, (image, class_id) in tqdm(enumerate(dataset), total=len(dataset)):
            image_input = preprocess(image).unsqueeze(0).cuda() #--------line 10
            image_features = model.encode_image(image_input)   # shape = 1x512
            image_features /= image_features.norm(dim=-1, keepdim=True)
            similarity = (image_features@text_features.T).softmax(dim=-1)
            index = torch.argmax(similarity, dim=-1)
            df.iloc[class_id, index.cpu()] += 1
        for i in range(len(labels)):
            df.iloc[i, -1] = 100*df.iloc[i,i]/sum(df.iloc[i, :-1])
    return df
df = fitting(); print('accuracy=', df.iloc[:,-1].mean())
#df.to_csv('d:/CLIP4CIFAR10.csv')
df
#--------------------------------------------------------------------The End
```

The codes in project 10.3.1 work well for datasets with bigger color images. For small black and white images in MNIST dataset and Fashion MNIST dataset, the accuracies are around 60%. We can use a linear-probe evaluation classifier in the following project 10.3.2 to solve the issue. The classifier only uses CLIP to encode images in both the train dataset and the test dataset in Cell 02 of the project. Then in Cell 03, a logistic regression is performed for the train dataset's encoded images and their labels. A regression function obtained from the train dataset is then used to predict the class labels of images in the test dataset. If you print out the prediction results on line 04 in Cell 03, you will see a 1D array [3, 8, 8, ..., 5, 0, 7]. Each integer in the array is a class index for an image in the test dataset. With model 'ViT-B/32' or 'ViT-L/14', the accuracy for CIFAR10 is 95% and 98%, and code running time is 6 min and 25 min respectively. In section 2.3, the accuracy for CIFAR10 was about 92%. You can also use other datasets to confirm the power of the zero shot classifier.

```
train_features, train_labels = get_features(train)
test_features, test_labels = get_features(test)
# Cell 03: Perform logistic regression----------------------------------Cell 03
classifier = LogisticRegression(random_state=0, C= 0.316,
                                max_iter=1000, verbose=0, n_jobs=4)
classifier.fit(train_features, train_labels)
predictions = classifier.predict(test_features)      #-------------------line 04
accuracy = np.mean((test_labels == predictions).astype(np.float64)) * 100.
print(f"Accuracy = {accuracy:.3f}")
#--------------------------------------------------------------------The End
```

10.4 Zero shot object detection by Hugging Face's OWL-ViT

The state-of-the-art YOLOv8 models can be used for object detection, image classification, and instance segmentation. YOLOv8 is faster and more accurate than YOLOv7. No matter how advanced a YOLO model is, we have to spend a lot of time labeling images with bounding boxes. Suppose we have 10 000 pathological tissue slide photos from optical microscopes, and we want to construct a dataset to train an AI model for cancer diagnosis. You can guess how expensive it would be to hire at least two of the best pathologists to label those photos. Only after the long time (days even months) needed to train the model with a labeled dataset, would we get the model ready for applications. Later, we may need to add one or more classes to the dataset. For example, a new kind of cancer cell is found, so we must add an extra class label about this kind of cancer cells into the tissue slide dataset. In this scenario, we have to repeat the model training again.

Hugging Face provides us an alternative method for object detection. Using Hugging Face's OWL-ViT transformer library, we can detect objects without model training (zero shot). OWL-ViT is an abbreviation of 'vision transformer for open-world localization'. The name came from a paper (Minderer *et al* 2022) published by Matthias Minderer and his collaborators. With a pre-trained OWL-ViT model, it is not necessary to label datasets, and we also do not need to train models. Figure 10.3 shows a zero shot object detection result by a pre-trained OWL-ViT model. My codes came from codes on Owl-Vit's Google Colab website with modifications. Because we do not need model training, we do not need hyperparameters in Cell 01 of project 10.4. Among some libraries imported in Cell 01, *OwlViTProcessor, OwlViTForObjectDetection* are new. The first one is used to pack text prompts and images into a dictionary for data input to a pre-trained model, and the second is for the outputs of the model.

Using an instance of OwlViTProcessor with a code on line 03 of Cell 03, we pack a list of class names and images for a dictionary named 'inputs' for the pre-trained OWL-ViT model with many augmentations. One of those augmentations is to resize each image into a new image with a resolution of $3 \times 768 \times 768$. In the dictionary, there are three keys: 'input_ids', 'attention_mask' and 'pixel_values'. With a code *model(**inputs)*, we get the model's outputs, which is also a dictionary. From *outputs['pred_boxes']* and *outputs['logits']*, we obtain bounding boxes, labels and label scores (line 07–10 in Cell 03). In the photo shown in figure 10.3, there is a butterfly. But there is no such label in VOC and COCO classes. Just add 'butterfly' to the list of VOC classes in Cell 01, the OWL-ViT model can find and label the butterfly. Kaggle and Google Colab have an issue to dynamically show images with code *cv2.imshow()*.

I tried to install Hugging Face's transformer library on my laptop, but had an issue importing the OwlViTProcessor library. After a few days of exploration and searching, I discovered that the issue was caused by Python v3.6, and then installed the Hugging Face transformer library with OwlViTProcessor in a virtual environment using Python v3.9. The codes in project 10.4 can be used to slide-show images with bounding boxes, to detect objects from a camera or a video file. VOC dataset's classes are used for the model's text queries. The labels 'cup' and 'butterfly' are added to the text queries, so the model can detect cups and butterflies. IOU and NMS thresholds are set on the last line of Cell 01. Codes in Cell 02 for IOU and NMS came from chapter 7. Cell 03 takes an image as its input, and it outputs the image with bounding boxes/labels/probabilities. The H, W and C parameters on line 02 of Cell 03 are saved for bounding boxes. From the pre-trained model, we obtain

Figure 10.3. Results of using Hugging Face's OWL-ViT for zero shot object detection about a butterfly image.

576 bounding boxes on each image. Each bounding box has its probability and class label. Those probabilities came from a SoftMax function (line 07 of Cell 03) acting on an output of the pre-trained model. Relative bounding boxes are lists from a list on line 16. Each element of the list in the list is a bounding box's xc, yc, w, h, label and probability. The four coordinates are relative numbers between 0 to 1. I pack them into a list so that I can use the two functions defined in chapter 7 to pick out a few good bounding boxes from those 576 bounding boxes. OWL-Vit model is sensitive enough to detect many small objects in a background. The code on line 13 of Cell 03 is used to ignore very small objects. Codes in Cell 05–07 of project 7.5 are re-used to display images in a folder or video frames from a camera. The image processing speed is about 10 FPS. You can terminate the program at any time by pressing the Esc key while your computer is focused on the image window. The OWL-ViT object detection accuracy is lower than that of YOLOv8 models.

```
# Project 10.4: Zero shot object detection by Owl-Vit----------------Python v3.9
import torch; import glob; import cv2; from tqdm import tqdm
import matplotlib.pyplot as plt; import numpy as np; import time
from transformers import OwlViTProcessor, OwlViTForObjectDetection
model = OwlViTForObjectDetection.from_pretrained("google/owlvit-base-patch32")
processor = OwlViTProcessor.from_pretrained("google/owlvit-base-patch32")
device = 'cuda' if torch.cuda.is_available() else "cpu"
model = model.to(device)
model.eval()
classes = ['aeroplane', 'bicycle', 'bird', 'boat', 'bottle', 'bus',
           'car', 'cat', 'chair', 'cow', 'cup', 'butterfly',
           'diningtable', 'dog', 'horse', 'motorbike', 'person',
           'sheep', 'sofa', 'train', 'tvmonitor', 'cell
phone']    #'pottedplant',
img_dir = 'D:/ImageSets/VOC/VOCdevkit/VOC2012/JPEGImages/*'
img_file_names = sorted(glob.glob(img_dir))
image_size = 768  # resize image to 768 for OwlViT model
#iou_threshold=0.4; threshold=0.5   # Detect more objects for VOC images
iou_threshold=0.06; threshold=0.85

# Cell 02 IOU (a copy from Section 7.4) and NMS (a copy from Section 7.3.2)-----
def IOU(boxes_preds, boxes_labels): # boxes_preds=[[Xc, Yc, W, H],...]
def NMS(bboxes, iou_threshold, threshold):
# Cell 03 Add bounding boxes and labels to an image processed by Owl_Vit--------
def owl_vit(image):
    H, W, C = np.array(image).shape # keep original image sizes------line 02
    inputs = processor(       #pack text and images for Owl-Vit model---line 03
        text=classes, images=image, return_tensors="pt").to(device)
    with torch.no_grad():    #Using a pre-trained Owl-Vit model-------line 05
        outputs = model(**inputs) # outputs['logits'][0].shape = 1x512x20
    logits = torch.max(torch.softmax(outputs['logits'][0], dim=-1), dim=-1)
    scores = logits.values.cpu().detach().numpy()    #probaility-------line 08
    labels = logits.indices.cpu().detach().numpy()   #class label------line 09
    boxes = outputs['pred_boxes'][0].cpu().detach().numpy() #---------line 10
    pred_bboxes = []    #bboxes=[[xc,yc,w,h],[]...] relative to 1 and <= 1
    for label, score, box in zip(labels, scores, boxes):
        if box[2] * box[3] > 0.05: #delete small bounding boxes======line 13
            pred_bboxes.append([label, score, box[0], box[1], box[2], box[3]])
    pred_bboxes = [box for box in pred_bboxes if box[1] > threshold]
    relative_bboxes = NMS(pred_bboxes, 0.8, 0.3)
    absolute_bboxes = []#bboxes in pixels of the original image sizes line 17
    for j, bbox in enumerate(relative_bboxes):
        xc, yc, w, h = bbox[2:]
        x1 = int((xc-w/2) * W); y1 = int((yc-h/2) * H)  #lop-left corner
        x2 = int((xc+w/2) * W); y2 = int((yc+h/2) * H)  #lower-right corner
        absolute_bboxes.append([bbox[0], bbox[1], x1, y1, x2, y2])
    absolute_bboxes = NMS(absolute_bboxes, iou_threshold, threshold)
    for j, bbox in enumerate(absolute_bboxes):  #--------------------line 23
        class_label = classes[int(bbox[0])]+' P='+str(round(bbox[1],2))
        label, score, x1, y1, x2, y2 = bbox
        cv2.rectangle(image, (x1,y1), (x2, y2), (225, 0, 225), 1)
        cv2.putText(image, class_label, (x1, y2-5), 1, 1, (225, 0, 225))
```

```
    return image
source = 'D:/ Butterfly0.jpg'
image = plt.imread(source)
plt.imshow(owl_vit(image));
# Cell 04: Slide show of object detection for images from a folder--------------
def output_img(img_dir):
    img_list = glob.glob(img_dir)[7050:7090]  #[m: m+n] to select some images
    for file in tqdm(img_list):
        my_img = cv2.imread(file, 1)
        cv2.imshow("press Esc to stop the slid show", owl_vit(my_img))
        if (cv2.waitKey(1000)&0xFF) == ord(chr(27)):
            break
    cv2.destroyAllWindows()
output_img(img_dir)
#Cell 05 Re-use Cell 07 in Project 7.5 for a video file or video from camera-----
#----------------------------------- The End -----------------------------------
```

10.5 RT-DETR (a vision transformers-based real-time object detector)

On July 6 of 2023, Wenyu Lv and his colleagues in Baidu of China published a paper (Lv *et al* 2023) about the development of a vision transformers-based real-time object detector, RT-DETR, which does not need post-processing, such as non-maximum suppression (NMS). The detector's efficient hybrid encoder reduces computational costs for real-time object detection. They claimed that the detector 'outperforms the state-of-the-art YOLO detectors of the same scale in both speed and accuracy.' From the ultralytics website, we can download two pre-trained weight files for a large RT-DETR model and an extra-large RT-DETR model. Their file sizes are around 100 MB. Using codes in the following Project 10.5, we can apply a pre-trained RT-DETR model for objection detection about a single image file, multiple images in a folder, and video frames from a camera or a video file. If you delete the code on line 05, the label for each object displayed on an image will be an integer about an index of a COCO class. Re-using Cell 02-03 in Project 8.4.1 for this project, you need to change the model's name from 'model' to 'baidu' in those two cells. The extra-large model is better than the large model with a sacrifice of speed. The video frame processing speed is about 15 and 10 FPS for the large and the extra-large model, respectively. You would get four labels for three persons and three labels for three horses in the image shown in figure 10.4 if the large model is used.

```
# Project 10.5: Use a pre-trained RT-DETR model for object detection Python v3.9
from ultralytics import RTDETR, YOLO
import matplotlib.pyplot as plt
import cv2; import glob; from tqdm import tqdm; import time
baidu = RTDETR('rtdetr-x.pt')                    # 'rtdetr-l.pt', 'rtdetr-x.pt'
baidu.model.names = YOLO("yolov8n.pt").model.names  #for object labels---line 05
source = 'd:/Stamped2023-5.jpg'      # use your image file path in your computer
results = baidu(source, verbose=False, save=False)[0].plot()
plt.imshow(cv2.cvtColor(results, cv2.COLOR_BGR2RGB));
# Re-use Cell 02 and 03 in Project 8.4.1 for batch images and video frames
#------------------------------------The End------------------------------------
```

Figure 10.4. Object detection results for a single image by a pre-trained extra-large RT-DETR model from BAIDU of China. Video frame processing speed of the model is about 10 FPS.

References

Dosovitskiy A, Beyer L, Kolesnikov A, Weissenborn D, Zhai X, Unterthiner T, Dehghani M, Minderer M, Heigold G and Gelly S 2020 An image is worth 16x16 words: transformers for image recognition at scale *arXiv preprint* arXiv:2010.11929

Lv W, Xu S, Zhao Y, Wang G, Wei J, Cui C, Du Y, Dang Q and Liu Y 2023 Detrs beat yolos on real-time object detection *arXiv reprint* arXiv:2304.08069

Minderer M, Gritsenko A, Stone A, Neumann M, Weissenborn D, Dosovitskiy A, Mahendran A, Arnab A, Dehghani M and Shen Z 2022 Simple open-vocabulary object detection with vision transformers *arXiv preprint* arXiv:2205.06230

Radford A, Kim J W, Hallacy C, Ramesh A, Goh G, Agarwal S, Sastry G, Askell A, Mishkin P and Clark J 2021 Learning transferable visual models from natural language supervision *Int. Conf. on Machine Learning* (PMLR) pp 8748–63

Vaswani A, Shazeer N, Parmar N, Uszkoreit J, Jones L, Gomez A N, Kaiser Ł and Polosukhin I 2017 Attention is all you need *Adv. Neural Inform. Proces. Syst.* **30** 6000–10

Chapter 11

Knowledge distillation and its applications in DINO and SAM

In the year 2023, Facebook released many computer vision models based on vision transformers. Although they are very powerful, their sizes are too big for real-time usage on resource/power limited devices. Knowledge distillation is used to transfer intelligence from a pre-trained jumbo model to a small model. In section 11.1 there is a demonstration of knowledge distillation from ResNet9 to ResNet6 used in chapter 2. Examples in sections 11.2–4 show the intelligence of Facebook's DINO, DINOv2 and SAM models in self-supervised learning to find object characteristics in images or video frames. Since SAM needs 8 GB GPU memory, I have to run it in CPU and it is very slow. A fastSAM model from China enables us to segment anything with a speed 50× faster than SAM.

11.1 Knowledge distillation for neural network compression

According to Moore's Law, the number of transistors in IC (integrated circuit) chips doubles approximately every two years. This has enabled the development of faster processors, increased memory capacity, and improved performance in various computing devices. The number of parameters of neural networks in computer vision projects and machine learning projects has also increased significantly for more powerful and functional models. In the model of a linear regression (project 1.3.1), there are only two parameters; in the model of project 10.1.1 about a basic vision transformer model for image classification, there are 14,443,018 parameters. The model of ChatGPT (based o GPT 3.5) has 175 billion parameters. However, as the parameter number of a model increases from millions to billions, model training and deployment will be computationally more expensive. With the rise of smart mobile devices such as smart phones, smart watches, and various other devices, we need a small neural model (student) to have the functions of a jumbo model (teacher). Knowledge distillation (Hinton *et al* 2015) refers to a technique in machine learning where a teacher model transfers its knowledge to a student model by using 'soft targets' during the training process for the student model. The goal of knowledge distillation is to compress the knowledge contained in a large model into a smaller model that can be deployed on resource-limited devices. Knowledge distillation has been successfully applied in many domains, including computer vision, natural language processing and speech recognition. It is a popular technique for model compression and transfer learning, allowing for the transfer of knowledge from large models to smaller models which can be used in real-world applications.

Soft targets are outputs of a teacher model. A pre-trained ResNet9 model from project 2.3 for CIFAR10 image classification was saved as a teacher model for the following project 11.1. Its prediction accuracies for the classification of images in the train, validation and test datasets are 99.5%, 92.6% and 92.3% respectively. From Cell 10 of project 2.3, we see that an output y_hat of the trained ResNet9 to a batch of only one image in the test dataloader is [[−103.4488, −113.6267, −95.8173, −90.3314, −70.0091, −96.2804, −94.8856, −100.3270, −113.8334, −108.6170]]. Each of the 10 elements in y_hat is a logit v_i which produces a soft target probability p_i at a temperature T for the pre-trained teacher model, where $i = 0, 1...,9$

$$p_i = \frac{e^{v_i/T}}{\sum\limits_{j=1}^{C} e^{v_j/T}} \tag{11.1}$$

A modified ResNet6 model from section 2.2 will be used as a student model in project 11.1. Replacing ResNet9 by the modified ResNet6 in project 2.3, you will find the prediction accuracies for the train, validation and test datasets are 95.9%, 88.4% and 88.4% respectively. The output z of the modified ResNet6 applied to a batch of one image also produces probabilities q at a temperature T. Normally, the value of the temperature is set to be equal to 1. We will use a higher T value to produce a softer probability distribution over classes

$$q_i = \frac{e^{z_i/T}}{\sum\limits_{j=1}^{C} e^{z_j/T}} \tag{11.2}$$

The student model is then trained with a loss function which has a hard loss and a soft loss. The hard loss is a cross-entropy about predicted probabilities of the student model at $T=1$ and labels of the train dataloader. The soft loss is a cross-entropy about p and q at a high temperature: $L_{\text{soft}} = -\sum\limits_{j=1}^{C} p_j \log(q_j)$. Using some approximations (Hinton *et al* 2015), the soft cross-entropy gradient $\partial L_{\text{soft}}/\partial z_i$, with respect to each logit z_i of the student model can be simplified to:

$$\frac{\partial L_{\text{soft}}}{\partial z_i} = \frac{1}{T}(q_i - p_i) \approx \frac{1}{NT^2}(z_i - v_i) \tag{11.3}$$

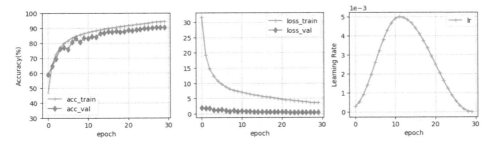

Figure 11.1. Model training results of knowledge distillation from ResNet9 to ResNet6.

At a high temperature, distillation is equivalent to minimizing $0.5(z_i - v_i)^2$. Since the magnitudes of the gradients produced by the soft targets are proportional to $1/T^2$, it is important to multiply them by T^2 when using both hard and soft targets to train the student model. According to equation (1.7), we have $L_{soft} = D_{KL}(p\|q) + H(p)$. Because the Shannon entropy $H(p)$ is a constant to z, we will use $L_{soft} = T^2 D_{KL}(p\|q)$ to train the student model. There is a PyTorch class nn.KLDivLoss for $D_{KL}(p\|q)$ calculations. How do we choose the value of T? One approximation to obtain equation (11.3) is $e^{z_i/T} \approx 1 + z_i/T$ in a condition $|z_i| \ll T$. We can find the absolute element value of y_hat from ResNet9 or ResNet6 is about 100, so we set $T=10\,000$. With the above information, we can write the codes for project 11.1. After running the codes to transfer knowledge from the pre-trained ResNet9 to ResNet6, we get that the prediction accuracies for the train, validation and test datasets are 94.3%, 90.1% and 90.2% respectively. The knowledge distillation increases the ResNet6 model's prediction accuracies by about 2% for the validation and test datasets. However, using $T = 100$ to train the student model, I found the results were almost the same as those shown in figure 11.1 for $T = 10\,000$.

```
#Project 11.1 Knowledge distillation (ResNet9->ResNet6) for CIFAR10---Python v3.9
# Cell 01-04: Re-use codes in Cell 01-04 from Project 2.3----------------------
# Cell 05: ResNet9 model, criterion, optimizer and learning rate scheduler------
def basic(in_channels, out_channels):
    return nn.Sequential(
        nn.Conv2d(in_channels, out_channels,
                kernel_size=3, padding=1, bias=False),
        nn.BatchNorm2d(out_channels),
        nn.ReLU(inplace=True))
class Rs_Block(nn.Module):          # a class for the teacher model
    def __init__(self, in_channels):
        super().__init__()
        self.resnet = nn.Sequential(
                basic(in_channels, in_channels),
                basic(in_channels, in_channels))
    def forward(self, x):
        return x + 0.5*self.resnet(x)
```

```
class ResNet9(nn.Module):          # a class for the student model
    def __init__(self, in_channels=img_channels, num_classes=n_class):
        super().__init__()
        self.net =  nn.Sequential(
                basic(in_channels, 64),            #batch_size x 64 x 32^2
                basic(64, 128), nn.MaxPool2d(2),   #batch_size x 128 x 16^2
                Rs_Block(128),   #batch_size x 128 x 16^2
                basic(128, 256), nn.MaxPool2d(2),  #batch_size x 256 x 8^2
                basic(256, 512), nn.MaxPool2d(2),  #batch_size x 512 x 4^2
                Rs_Block(512),   #batch_size x 512 x 4^2
                nn.MaxPool2d(4),                   #batch_size x 512 x 1^2
                nn.Flatten(),
                nn.Linear(512, num_classes))       #batch_size x 10
    def forward(self, images):
        output = self.net(images) #images.shape=batch_size x 3 x 32^2
        return output             #output.shape = batch_size x 10
class ResNet6(nn.Module):
    def __init__(self, in_channels=img_channels, num_classes=10):
        super().__init__()
        self.net =  nn.Sequential(
                basic(in_channels, 64), nn.MaxPool2d(2), # Nx64x16^2 layer 01
                basic(64, 128), nn.MaxPool2d(2),    # Nx128x8^2       layer 02
                Rs_Block(128),  nn.MaxPool2d(2),    # Nx128x4^2  layer 03-04
                basic(128, 256), nn.MaxPool2d(4),   # Nx256x1^2       layer 05
                nn.Flatten(),
                nn.Linear(256, num_classes))        # Nx10            layer 06
    def forward(self, x):
        return self.net(x)
teacher = ResNet9().cuda()         # acc=92.7% for the test dataloader
student = ResNet6().cuda()         # acc=88.6% for the test dataloader
kl_div_loss = nn.KLDivLoss(log_target=True, reduction='sum')   #soft loss_fn
criterion = nn.CrossEntropyLoss(reduction='sum')               #hard loss_fn
temperature = 10000.0              # knowledge distillation temperature
File_name = 'C:/Users/xiaoc/Python/Exercises/GroundingDINO/teacher.pth'
big_model = torch.load(File_name)       # load the pre-trained teacher model


big_model.eval()
# Cell 06: Model Training for the train_dataloader----------------------Cell 06
def training(my_dataloader, model, optimizer, scheduler, big_model):
    total_loss = 0.0; n_correct = 0.0
    n_samples = len(my_dataloader.dataset)
    model.train()
    for i, (images, labels) in enumerate(my_dataloader):
        images = images.cuda()
        labels = labels.cuda(non_blocking=True)
        outputs = model(images)
        hard_loss = criterion(outputs, labels)
        #--------------knowledge disttllation------------------------------
        soft_prob = nn.functional.log_softmax(outputs / temperature, dim=-1)
        with torch.no_grad():
            big_logits = big_model(images)
        soft_targets = nn.functional.log_softmax(big_logits/temperature, dim=-1)
        soft_loss = kl_div_loss(soft_prob, soft_targets)*temperature**2
        loss = hard_loss + soft_loss
        #------------------------------------------------------------------
```

```
        predictions = torch.argmax(outputs, dim=1)
        n_correct += torch.sum(predictions==labels).item()
        total_loss += loss.item()
        loss.backward()
        nn.utils.clip_grad_value_(model.parameters(), clip_value=0.1)
        optimizer.step()
        scheduler.step()
        optimizer.zero_grad()
    return total_loss/n_samples, 100*n_correct/n_samples
# Cell 07: Model Evaluation or val_dataloader and test_dataloader------Cell 07
def evaluation(my_dataloader, model):
    n_samples = len(my_dataloader.dataset)
    with torch.no_grad():
        total_loss = 0.0; n_correct = 0
        model.eval()
        for i, (images, labels) in enumerate(my_dataloader):
            images = images.cuda()
            labels = labels.cuda(non_blocking=True)
            outputs = model(images)
            loss = criterion(outputs, labels)
            predictions = torch.argmax(outputs, dim=1)
            n_correct += torch.sum(predictions==labels).item()
            total_loss += loss.item()
    return total_loss/n_samples, 100*n_correct/n_samples
# Cell 08: The main training function -----------------------------Cell 08
def distillation(epochs, model, big_model):
    df = pd.DataFrame(np.empty([epochs, 5]),
            index = np.arange(epochs),
            columns=['loss_train', 'acc_train', 'loss_val', 'acc_val', 'lr'])
    optimizer = torch.optim.SGD(model.parameters(), lr=lr)
    scheduler = lr_scheduler.OneCycleLR(optimizer, max_lr=lr,
                    steps_per_epoch=s_p_e, epochs=n_epochs, pct_start=0.4)
    progress_bar = trange(epochs)

    for i in progress_bar:
        df.iloc[i,0], df.iloc[i,1] = training(train_dl, model, optimizer,
                                        scheduler, big_model)
        df.iloc[i,2], df.iloc[i,3] = evaluation(val_dl, model)
        df.iloc[i,4] = optimizer.param_groups[0]['lr']
        progress_bar.set_description("train_loss=%.5f" % df.iloc[i,0])
        progress_bar.set_postfix(
                    {'train_acc': df.iloc[i,1], 'val_acc': df.iloc[i,3]})
    return df
train_history = distillation(n_epochs, student, big_model)
# Cell 09: Graphs of Model training outputs-------------------------Cell 09
df= train_history
fig, ax = plt.subplots(1,3, figsize=(12,3), sharex=True)
df.plot(ax=ax[0], y=[1,3], style=['r-+', 'b-d'])
df.plot(ax=ax[1], y=[0,2], style=['r-+', 'b-d'])
df.plot(ax=ax[2], y=[4], style=['r-+'])
for i in range(3):

    ax[i].set_xlabel('epoch')
    ax[i].grid(which='major', axis='both', color='g', linestyle=':')
#ax[0].set_ylabel('accuracy(%)')
ax[0].set(ylim=[30, 100.0], ylabel='accuracy(%)')
ax[2].ticklabel_format(style='sci', axis='y', scilimits=(0,0));
# Cell 10: Using test dataloader to test the trained student model------Cell 10
loss, accuracy = evaluation(test_dl, student)
print('test dataloader accuracy (%)=', accuracy)
#---------------------------------------The End---------------------------------------
```

11.2 DINO: emerging properties in self-supervised vision transformers

Although the image classification results of using ViT model for CIFAR10 in section 10.2 are good enough compared with the results from CNN models in section 2.3, there is no benefit, because ViT model training is computationally expensive. To use the ViT model for data processing, we have to resize each CIFAR10 image from 32×32 to 224×224. It is almost impossible for a personal laptop to handle computational tasks of ViT model training. We had to use the pre-trained Hugging Face ViT Model for Project 10.2.

The multi-head self-attention class in Cell 05 of project 10.1.1 returns a tuple with two elements. One is 'attention output' and the other is 'attention probs'. For image classification, we only use the first one. Using the second one, Mathilde Caron (Caron *et al* 2021) and collaborators in Facebook found a unique property of vision transformers: self-supervised learning. To train a YOLOv8 model for objection detection and image segmentation in chapter 8, we have to use labeled datasets. The traditional supervised learning approach requires a large amount of labeled data, which can be expensive and time-consuming to obtain. In contrast, self-supervised learning aims to learn representations by solving pre-text tasks on unlabeled data. This approach has gained attention in recent years due to its ability to leverage the vast amount of freely available unlabeled data.

DINO, which stands for 'self DIstillation with NO labels,' is a method that focuses on self-supervised learning for vision transformers. DINO models can discover and segment objects on an image or video frame without supervision and without being given any segmentation-targeted objects. This means that this kind of model is capable of a higher-level of image understanding. DINO technology is based on knowledge distillation between a teacher model and student model. Both models use the same ViT model, but with different parameters and each of them is trained in a different way. Any image input to a DINO system is cropped into two global patches and eight local patches. The global and local crop scales are above 40% and below 40% respectively. Global patches are resized to 224×224, and the local patches are resized to 96×96. All patches are processed by the student model, but only the two global patches are input to the teacher model. Figure 11.2(A) shows an original image in which there is a rabbit scratching its chin. Two global patches and eight local patches are also shown in the figure. These patches were obtained by

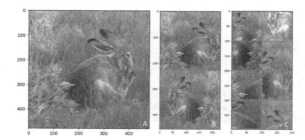

Figure 11.2. An original image (A) is cropped and resized into two global patches (B) and eight local patches (C) for DINO model training.

the codes in project 11.2.1. A class defined in Cell 02 came from Facebook's DINO GitHub repository. In a normalization transform of the class, Facebook's special numbers are not used for simplification.

```python
# Project 11.2.1 Crop an image into 2 globe and 8 local patches-------Python v3.9
import torch.nn.functional as F
import torchvision.transforms as T; from torchvision.utils import make_grid
import matplotlib.pyplot as plt
global_crops_scale=(0.4, 1)
local_crops_scale=(0.05, 0.4)
n_local_crops=8
from PIL import Image
image = Image.open('d:/rabbit.jpg')
plt.imshow(image);
# Cell 02: Define a class for image augmentations----------------------Cell 02
class DataAugmentation:
    def __init__(self):
        self.n_local_crops = n_local_crops
        RandomGaussianBlur = lambda p: T.RandomApply(
                    [T.GaussianBlur(kernel_size=5, sigma=(0.1, 2))], p=p)
        flip_and_jitter = T.Compose([
                T.RandomHorizontalFlip(p=0.5),
                T.RandomApply([T.ColorJitter(
                    brightness=0.4,contrast=0.4,saturation=0.2,hue=0.1,)]),
                T.RandomGrayscale(p=0.2)])
        normalize = T.Compose([T.ToTensor(),
                        T.Normalize((0.5, 0.5, 0.5), (0.5, 0.5, 0.5))])
                        #((0.485, 0.456, 0.406), (0.229, 0.224, 0.225))
        self.global_1 = T.Compose([
                T.RandomResizedCrop(224, scale=global_crops_scale,
                            interpolation=Image.Resampling.BICUBIC),
                flip_and_jitter, RandomGaussianBlur(1.0), normalize])

        self.global_2 = T.Compose([
                T.RandomResizedCrop(224, scale=global_crops_scale,
                            interpolation=Image.Resampling.BICUBIC),
                flip_and_jitter, RandomGaussianBlur(0.1),
                T.RandomSolarize(170, p=0.2), normalize])
        self.local = T.Compose([
                T.RandomResizedCrop(96, scale=local_crops_scale,
                            interpolation=Image.Resampling.BICUBIC),
                flip_and_jitter, RandomGaussianBlur(0.5), normalize])
    def __call__(self, img):        #Input img : PIL.Image
        all_crops = []
        all_crops.append(self.global_1(img))
        all_crops.append(self.global_2(img))
        all_crops.extend([self.local(img) for _ in range(self.n_local_crops)])
        return all_crops
# Cell 03: Show 2 globe patches and 8 local patches----------------------Cell 03
f = DataAugmentation()       # the instance of the DataAugmentation class
cropped_imgs = f(image)      # get 2 globe patches and 8 local patches
def denorm(img_tensors):
    return img_tensors*0.5 + 0.5
def show_imgs(imgs):
    all_crops = imgs
    fig, ax = plt.subplots(figsize=(10,8))
    input = make_grid(all_crops, nrow=2, padding=3) # nrow=1 for globe patches
    ax.imshow(denorm(input).permute(1,2,0))
    plt.show()
show_imgs(cropped_imgs[2:])      # show_imgs(cropped_imgs[:2]) for globe patches
#----------------------------------------The End----------------------------------
```

It is not necessary to copy and paste Facebook's DINO codes here, and it is impossible for my laptop to train any DINO model. There are many GitHub and YouTube sources to explain DINO. I have to use a pre-trained Facebook DINO ViT model to demonstrate the power of DINO. Five pre-trained Facebook DINO models are listed in Cell 01 of project 11.2.2. The name of the model used in the project is 'facebook/dino-vits8' in which 's' denotes a small model and 8 is the patch size. If an image's resolution is 480×480, the image is then split and embedded into $(480/8)^2+1$ tokens for a ViT model similar to that in section 10.1, and they are different from those global and local patches. To understand how the codes in project 11.2.2 work, we need to print out the ViT parameters in DINO by *print (model.config)*. There are 12 encoder layers in the DINO ViT and each layer has six self-attention blocks. The last layer of the DINO ViT outputs 3601 tokens and an 'attentions' tensor which is a $1 \times 6 \times 3601 \times 3601$ tensor for a batch of one image in Cell 02 in project 11.2.2. The shape of the attentions tensor is decided by the second output of Cell 05 in project 10.1.1 with operations of $\mathrm{softmax}(Q \cdot K^T/\sqrt{D})$. We use attention scores related to the [cls] token selected by attentions[0, :, 0, 1:] in the following Cell 02. The selected attention score tensor with a shape 6×3600 is then reshaped into $6 \times 60 \times 60$ and interpolated to $6 \times 480 \times 480$ in Cell 03. Then, we can plot the six black and white images shown in figure 11.3. Each black and white image's resolution is 480×480. From the bright spots in the six images, we see that different self-attention heads focus on different objects in the image.

```
ViTConfig {"_name_or_path": "facebook/dino-vits8",
          "architectures": ["ViTModel"], "attention_probs_dropout_prob": 0.0,
          "encoder_stride": 16, "hidden_act": "gelu","hidden_dropout_prob": 0.0,
          "hidden_size": 384,
          "image_size": 224,
          "initializer_range": 0.02, "intermediate_size": 1536,
          "layer_norm_eps": 1e-12, "model_type": "vit",
          "num_attention_heads": 6,
          "num_channels": 3,
          "num_hidden_layers": 12,
          "patch_size": 8,
          "qkv_bias": true, "torch_dtype": "float32","transformers_version": "4.27.4"}
```

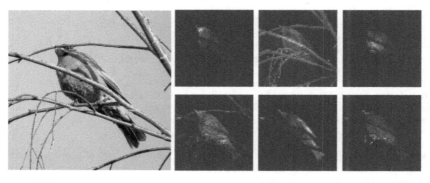

Figure 11.3. (Left) Input: an image processed by the pre-trained DINO model. (Right) Outputs: the self-attention of the [CLS] token of the last layer. There are six multi-head self-attention blocks in each encoder layer of the ViT model.

```
# Project 11.2.2 Hugging Face ViT Attention Score Visualization ------Python v3.9
from PIL import Image
import torch.nn as nn
import torch.nn.functional as F
import matplotlib.pyplot as plt
from transformers import ViTImageProcessor
from transformers import ViTModel
model_name = "facebook/dino-vits8" #"facebook/dino-vitb8","facebook/dino-vits16"
#model_name = "facebook/dino-vitb16", "Ramos-Ramos/dino-resnet-50"
model = ViTModel.from_pretrained(model_name, add_pooling_layer=False)
feature_extractor = ViTImageProcessor.from_pretrained(model_name, size=480)
image = Image.open('d:/robin.jpg')
image
# Cell 02: Using the pre-trained ViT model to get attention scores---------------
input = feature_extractor(images=image, return_tensors="pt").pixel_values
outputs = model(input,
                output_attentions=True, interpolate_pos_encoding=True)
attentions = outputs.attentions[-1] #multihead attention scores in the last layer
print('last layer attention score shape:', attentions.shape)
h_patches = input.shape[-1] // model.config.patch_size   #480/8=60
w_patches = input.shape[-2] // model.config.patch_size   #480/8=60
n_heads = attentions.shape[1] # number of head = 6
attentions = attentions[0, :, 0, 1:]   #attention score related to the cls token
print('cls attention score shape:', attentions.shape)
# Cell 03: Visualization of ViT attention ------------------------------------------
attentions = attentions.reshape(n_heads, w_patches, h_patches)
attentions = F.interpolate(attentions.unsqueeze(0),
               scale_factor=model.config.patch_size, mode="nearest")[0].cpu()
attentions = attentions.detach().numpy()
fig, axs = plt.subplots(2, 3, figsize=(7, 5))
for i in range(n_heads):
    ax = axs[i//3, i%3]
    ax.imshow(attentions[i])
    ax.axis("off")
fig.tight_layout()
#-----------------------------------The End-----------------------------------
```

11.3 DINOv2 for image retrieval, classification and feature visualization

In April 2023, Meta AI released four pre-trained DINOv2 models: a ViT-g model trained from scratch, and three models (ViT-s, ViT-b, ViT-l) distilled from the ViT-g. A large, curated, diverse dataset (LVD-142M) was used to train these models with a method described in a paper (Oquab *et al* 2023): 'DINOv2: Learning Robust Visual Features without Supervision'. Unlike other pre-training models whose algorithms rely on labeled data or manual captions to interpret image meanings, DINOv2 can learn from any image dataset without requiring accompanying metadata. By avoiding the omission of crucial background information, DINOv2 has a comprehensive grasp of image details to pixel level. DINOv2 stands out by eliminating the need for fine-tuning. Its outputs of high-performance features can be directly employed with classifiers as simple as linear layers on a variety of computer vision tasks. Each DINOv2 model takes an image as input and returns a class token and patch tokens. DINOv2 models can be used for image classification, image segmentation, image retrieval, object detection and object depth estimation.

With a pre-trained small DINOv2 model named 'dinov2_vits14', the codes in project 11.3.1 can retrieve flower images in the flower dataset used in chapter 9. From the outputs of the project, you would find that a caption with a few words is not enough to describe a photo, because 'a picture is worth a thousand words'. Codes in Cell 04 output a batch of flower images from a train dataloader with a batch size of six (figure 11.4(A)). By choosing an integer (n) between 0 to 5 in Cell 06, we can select a query image for a type of flower, and then the remaining codes of the project will pick out six flower images from a validation dataset. The retrieved flowers and the query flower should be the same type. In figure 11.4(A), there are two dandelion images at $n = 1$ and 5. Using an image at any of these two positions as a query image, we got figures 11.4(B) and (C). The pre-trained DINO2 model can distinguish images of dandelions at different life stages: yellow flowers and white seeds. One English word 'dandelion' is not enough to distinguish them.

Figure 11.4. Image instance retrieval by a small pre-trained DINOv2 model. (A) A batch of images in the train dataloader of the flower dataset. (B) Retrieved images with a query image (*n*=1). (C) Retrieved images with a query image (*n*=5). All retrieved images are in the validation dataset. Images in the first row reproduced from Flowers Dataset with a license CC0 1.0.

```
#Project 11.3.1 Image instance retrieval by DINOv2-------------------Python v3.9
import faiss      # a library for similarity search and clustering of dense vectors
import torch      # pip install faiss-gpu.
from torch.utils.data import DataLoader
from torch.utils.data.dataset import random_split as split
from torchvision.datasets import ImageFolder
from torchvision.utils import make_grid
import torchvision.transforms as T
import matplotlib.pyplot as plt
img_size = 224
batch_size = 6
data_path = 'OCR/data/FlowersDataset/flowers'
model = torch.hub.load('facebookresearch/dinov2', 'dinov2_vits14').cuda()
model.eval()
# Cell 02-04: Flowers Dataset------------------Re-use Cell 02-04 in Project 9.3.2
# Cell 05: Image Features in a dataset extracted by a pre-trained DINOv2 model---
def feature(my_dataset):
    dataset_features = []
    for _, sample in enumerate(my_dataset):
        img, _ = sample
        with torch.no_grad():
            features = model(img.unsqueeze(0).cuda())
        dataset_features.append(features)
    return torch.cat(dataset_features, dim=0)
dataset_features = feature(val_dataset)
dataset0features = dataset_features.clone().cpu().numpy()
dataset0features.shape        # a clone for re-use dataset_features [701, 384]
# Cell 06: Features of a querry image in a batch of train_dataloader in Cell 04--
n = 1          # select n <= (batch_size - 1) for an image in imgs to query
query_img = imgs[n]
print(f'My querry_img flower is {classes[labels[n]]}.')
with torch.no_grad():
    query_features = model(query_img.unsqueeze(0).cuda())
print(f'The shape of query_features is {query_features.shape}')
Faiss_index = faiss.IndexFlatL2(query_features.shape[1])
Faiss_index.add(dataset0features)    # Convert features to a Faiss index
# Cell 07: Perform nearest neighbor search in the Faiss_index -----------Cell 07
k = batch_size*1   # k: number of neighbors to retrieve
distances, indices = Faiss_index.search(query_features.cpu().numpy(), k)
indices      # retrieved image indices in the val_dataset
# Cell 08: Display the retrieved images-------------------------------------------
def retrival_imgs(my_dataset):
    my_imgs = []
    for i in range(k):
        img, _ = my_dataset[indices[0][i]]
        my_imgs.append(img)
    my_imgs = torch.cat(my_imgs, dim=0).view(k, 3, img_size, img_size)
    return my_imgs
my_imgs = retrival_imgs(val_dataset)
print(f'My instance retrieval images for {classes[labels[n]]} flowers.')
show_imgs(my_imgs)
#------------------------------The End-------------------------------------------
```

When you run the code in Cell 01 for the first time, the small pre-trained DINOv2 model will be downloaded from Facebook automatically. The file size is about 21 MB. The size of a large DINOv2 model is about 300 MB. Codes in Cell 06 process each image in the validation dataset to get a 1D tensor with 384 elements for detailed object information about the image. The shape of the output tensor of the cell is 701×384, because there are 701 images in the validation dataset. We use Cell 06 to select a query image, and then use the model to extract image features. A Facebook library faiss (Johnson *et al* 2019) is used for image similarity search. It assumes that vectors of image features can be compared with L2

(Euclidean) distances or dot products. Vectors that are similar to a query vector are those that have the lowest L2 distance or the highest dot product with the query vector, according to the introduction on the faiss GitHub repository. The output of Cell 07 is a list with batch size elements. Each element is an integer for a position index (<701) of a retrieved image in the validation dataset. The retrieved images are then displayed by the codes in Cell 08. Codes of three small DINOv2 projects in this section were inspired by codes from Purnasai Gudikandula's GitHub repository. I met an issue from the FAISS library after my Python and Pytorch were updated. An improved version of Project 11.3.1 was listed in Appendix J, in which Euclidean distances are calculated directly without using a third party library.

Since the DINOv2 models are so powerful that they are able to learn image features without human instructions, we can use these models for image classification with the codes listed in project 11.3.2. To save space, I re-use Cells 02–04 from project 9.3.2 for the flower image dataset, and Cells 06–09 from project 2.3 for model training without the learning rate scheduler. A class for the classification model is defined in Cell 05. The backbone of the model is the pre-trained big DINOv2 model. Two fully connected layers are appended to the DINOv2 model for image classification. In less than 8 min for model training of five epochs, image classification accuracies for the train dataset and the validation dataset are 99.5% and 95.5% respectively.

```
# Project 11.3.2 Using DINOv2 for Flower Image Classification---------Python v3.9
import os; import torch; import torch.nn as nn; import torch.nn.functional as F
from torch.utils.data import DataLoader
import torch.optim.lr_scheduler as lr_scheduler
from torch.utils.data.dataset import random_split as split
from torchvision import transforms; from torchvision.utils import make_grid
from torchvision.datasets import ImageFolder
from  matplotlib import pyplot as plt
import numpy as np; import pandas as pd; from tqdm import trange
n_epochs = 5
img_size = 224
img_channels = 3
batch_size=4
lr =1e-6
data_path = 'OCR/data/FlowersDataset/flowers'
# Cell 02-04: Flowers Dataset. -------Re-use codes of Cell 02-04 of Project 9.3.2
# Cell 05: Modifiy the small DINOv2 model for image classification -------Cell 05
dinov2s = torch.hub.load('facebookresearch/dinov2', 'dinov2_vits14')
class Dino2ViTclassifier(nn.Module):
    def __init__(self):
        super().__init__()
        self.transformer = dinov2s
        self.fc = nn.Sequential(
                nn.Linear(384, 256),nn.ReLU(),nn.Linear(256, 6))
    def forward(self, x):
        x = self.transformer(x)
        x = self.transformer.norm(x)
        x = self.fc(x)
        return x
model = Dino2ViTclassifier().cuda()
criterion = nn.CrossEntropyLoss()
optimizer = torch.optim.Adam(model.parameters(), lr=lr)    #lr=0.000001
# Cell 06-09: Model Training -----------Re-use codes of Cell 06-09 in Project 2.3
#---------------------------------------The End-----------------------------------
```

DINOv2 models can extract image features which can be used for image retrieval and image classification. We can visualize the high dimensional features by using a mathematical tool PCA (principal component analysis) in project 11.3.3. A pre-trained large DINOv2 model 'dinov2_vitl14' is used in the project, and the outputs of the project for a color image with four deer are shown in figure 11.5. The original size of the image is $800 \times 533 \times 3$. A transformer function defined in Cell 02 processes the original image to get a tensor with a resolution of $1 \times 3 \times 518 \times 518$. Using a patch size of 14, the model splits the image into 1369 ($=518/14 \times 37$) patches with an embedding dimension of 1024. The outputs of the model are a class token and 1369 patch tokens. Using *model.forward_features(img_transformed)* but not *model.(img_transformed)* in Cell 02, we obtain a dictionary with four keys, but only one key's value is used in the project as a tensor *batch_total_features* of the image, and the tensor's shape is $1 \times 1369 \times 1024$. Using PCA, codes in Cell 03 reduce the dimensions of a *total_features* tensor with a shape of 1369×1024 to get a *pca_features* NumPy array with a shape of 1369×3. Only the zeroth channel of the pca_features array is normalized and displayed by Cell 04. To save space, I overlayed the first PCA image on the top-left corner of the original photo shown in figure 11.5.

Figure 11.5. Image feature visualization by using PCA to a pre-trained DINOv2 model's outputs.

```
# Project 11.3.3 Using 2-step PCA to Visualize DINOv2 features--------Python v3.9
import torch
import torchvision.transforms as T
from sklearn.decomposition import PCA
import matplotlib.pyplot as plt
from PIL import Image
model = torch.hub.load('facebookresearch/dinov2', 'dinov2_vitl14').cuda()
patch_pixels = model.patch_size # patch_size = 14 pixels
n_patch = 520//patch_pixels     # 520//14=37
embed_dim = 1024
img_path = 'd:/deer4.jpg'
img = Image.open(img_path)
img
# Cell 02: Using the DINOv2 model to extract image features--------------Cell 02
f = T.Compose([T.Resize(520, interpolation=T.InterpolationMode.BICUBIC),
               T.CenterCrop(518),
               T.ToTensor(),
               T.Normalize(mean=0.5, std=0.2),
               ])
with torch.no_grad():
    img_transformed = f(img).unsqueeze(0).cuda()
    features_dict = model.forward_features(img_transformed)
    batch_total_features = features_dict['x_norm_patchtokens']
batch_total_features.shape        #batch_total_features.shape=[1, 1369, 1024]
# Cell 03: Using 1st PCA to reduce dimensions of image features for visualization
total_features = batch_total_features[0].cpu() #total_features.shape=[1369, 1024]
pca = PCA(n_components=3)
pca_features = pca.fit_transform(total_features)  # pca_features.shape=[1369, 3]
# Cell 04: Normalization and visualization of the 1st channel PCA features-------
pca_features[:, 0] = (pca_features[:, 0] - pca_features[:, 0].min()) / (
                      pca_features[:, 0].max() - pca_features[:, 0].min())
plt.imshow(pca_features[0 : n_patch*n_patch, 0].reshape(n_patch, n_patch),
           cmap='gray')
plt.colorbar();
# Cell 05: Choose and visualize background from the 1st channel of PCA features--
pca_features_bg = pca_features[:, 0] > 0.35 # from first histogram
plt.imshow(pca_features_bg.reshape(n_patch, n_patch), cmap='gray');
# Cell 06: Get and visualize foreground from the 1st channel of PCA features-----
pca_features_fg = ~pca_features_bg  # reversed background image
plt.imshow(pca_features_fg.reshape(n_patch, n_patch), cmap='gray');
# Cell 07: Using the 2nd PCA only for the foreground patches --------------------
f_features = pca.fit_transform(total_features[pca_features_fg])
for i in range(3):
    f_features[:, i] = (f_features[:, i] - f_features[:, i].min())/(
                        f_features[:, i].max() - f_features[:, i].min())
attention_rgb = pca_features.copy()  #pca_features.shape = (1369, 3)
attention_rgb[pca_features_bg] = 0        # mask black background
attention_rgb[pca_features_fg] = f_features
attention_rgb = attention_rgb.reshape(n_patch, n_patch, 3)
plt.imshow(attention_rgb)
plt.colorbar();
#-----------------------------------The End-----------------------------------
```

The pixel values of the first PCA image are between 0.0 to 1.0 as shown by a gray bar of the gray image. The background is brighter than the foreground (deer). With a threshold value of 0.35, codes in Cell 05 convert the gray image into a black and white image shown on the top-right corner of figure 11.5. We name the black and white image 'background'. The value of each white pixel in the background image is equal to 1, and the value of each dark pixel is equal to 0. We use Cell 06 to reverse the background image, and name a new image 'foreground'. The foreground image is shown on the lower-left corner of figure 11.5.

A NumPy array *pca_features_fg* before being reshaped for the foreground image in Cell 06 is an 1D array with 1369 elements. Printing out the array's summation, you will see that it is equal to 580. This means that there are 580 'true' values in the 1D array. The shape of the total_features tensor is 1369 × 1024. The code on the first line of Cell 07 uses *pca_features_fg* to mask *total_features*. The result is an array *f_features0* with a shape of 580 × 1024. The criterion to pick out a row in the tensor *total_features* is that with the index of the row, we should find 'true' in the 1D array *pca_features_fg*. Then we use the second PCA transformer to obtain an array *f_features* with a shape of 580 × 3. This array is then linearly normalized by code on three lines starting from line 03 of Cell 07.

An array *attention_rgb* on line 06 of Cell 07 is a copy of the array *pca_features*, the output of the first PCA transformer, and the array is masked by the 1D array of the background image. The normalized second PCA output is then assigned to the array *attention_rgb* which is displayed as a color image on the lower-right corner of figure 11.5. You can see the deer heads are shown in green, the necks are orange, their feet are blue, and bodies are pink. DINOv2 models can not only detect objects but also distinguish the components of each object.

11.4 Segment anything model: SAM and FastSAM

People with experience of using Photoshop to remove image backgrounds would be very happy to have a new tool: the segment anything model (SAM), which was released by Meta AI on April 15, 2023. Users without any computer code knowledge can upload their photos to Meta's SAM website, and use their mouse to click or draw a box on a photo. Objects on the photo selected by users with those mouse prompts would be segmented from the photo in a few milli-seconds, and the pixels of those objects are separated from the photo's background. People can then use the pixels of those objects to edit images and analyze photos. Figure 11.6(A) shows a photo of a mother deer standing on ground covered by snow in my garden. The photo was segmented into 74 objects by codes in Cell 01 of project 11.4.1 with a model and pre-trained parameters loaded from a check point file *sam_vit_h_4b8939.pth*. Because the size of the file is more than 2.5 GB, my laptop's 6 GB GPU memory is not big enough to handle the codes which needs 8 GB. Luckily, I can run the codes in CPU, but code run-time is about 130 seconds. With a free GPU from Google Colab, the code run-time is about 4 seconds. Although I can run my codes on my laptop's GPU with a smaller check point file *sam_vit_b_01ec64.pth* (0.37 GB), the outputs of the codes are trashy. The biggest check point file from the SAM GitHub website is *sam_vit_l_0b3195.pth*. I tried it with my codes, and couldn't see a significant quality improvement comparing with the middle size one. My codes were inspired by Piotr Skalski's Colab codes, in which Roboflow supervision module (version ⩾ 5.0) is used to display SAM masks (figure 11.6(B)).

Figure 11.6. (A) Original image. (B) Panoramic segmentation by SAM. (C) Objection detection by OWL-ViT.

```
#Project 11.4.1 Application of SAM for image segmentation-------------Python v3.9
from segment_anything import sam_model_registry, SamAutomaticMaskGenerator
import supervision as sv #ROBOFLOW supervision ver>=5.0 for displaying SAM masks
import cv2; import numpy as np; import matplotlib.pyplot as plt
#device = torch.device("cuda:0" if torch.cuda.is_available() else "cpu")
checkpoint = 'C:/Users/xiaoc/Python/Exercises/SAM/sam_vit_h_4b8939.pth'
model_type = "vit_h"
model = sam_model_registry[model_type](checkpoint=checkpoint)
mask_generator = SamAutomaticMaskGenerator(model)
img_bgr = cv2.imread('d:/deer0.jpg')                    # input an image with cv2
img_rgb = cv2.cvtColor(img_bgr, cv2.COLOR_BGR2RGB)
sam_result = mask_generator.generate(img_rgb)      # analyze image masks by SAM
#Cell 02: Display the first six masks-------------------------------------------
print('number of objects:', len(sam_result))
print(sam_result[0].keys())
masks = [mask['segmentation'] for mask in sorted(
                    sam_result, key=lambda i: i['area'], reverse=True)]
sv.plot_images_grid(images=masks[:6], grid_size=(1, 6), size=(8, 4))
#Cell 03 Display a few important SAM masks for instance segmentation------------
mask_annotator = sv.MaskAnnotator(color_map = "index")
detections = sv.Detections.from_sam(sam_result=sam_result.copy()[:3])
annotated_image = mask_annotator.annotate(
            scene=img_bgr.copy(), detections=detections)
sv.plot_images_grid(images=[img_bgr, annotated_image], grid_size=(1, 2))
#Cell 04: Remove the background from the original image-------------------------
my_img = np.expand_dims(masks[0], axis=2)*img_rgb.copy()
plt.axis('off')
plt.imshow(my_img);
#------------------------------------The End-----------------------------------
```

The output of the SAM mask generator on the last line of Cell 01 is a list, and each element in the list is a dictionary for an object. Codes on the first two lines Cell 02 print out the number of objects segmented from the image, and the dictionary keys of each object are: 'segmentation', 'area', 'bbox', 'predicted_iou', 'point_coords', 'stability_score', 'crop_box'. The 'segmentation' key is for a mask of a SAM segmentation, and the shape of the mask is the resolution of the original image: 480×480. The two keys 'point_coords', and 'crop_box' are mouse prompts set by users. Since we set SAM to use automatic mask generator in Cell 01, the values of the two keys are set by the model automatically. The key 'stability_score' is used to pick out an object from its background. We can display 72 masks with a grid size (9, 8) by the code on the last line of Cell 02. You will see many masks are for the same object, and many meaningless shade spots are segmented as objects on the image. Codes in Cell 02 sort masks reversely according to their areas, and only display the first six masks as black and white images. Codes in Cell 03 show the original image and a processed image with only three major masks. The deer and the snow are separated from the background. Codes in Cell 04 use the major mask masks[0] to pick out the deer from the background.

SAM has no object detection function. By taking the output image from Cell 04 to project 8.4.2, we can use YOLOv8 to detect the object in the image: a cow with a percentage of 79%. It is wrong because YOLOv8 uses classes of COCO dataset to identify objects, but there is no deer class in COCO dataset. Then I used codes in project 10.4 to analyze the image by Owl-Vit Zero shot object detection. After adding a 'deer' item in the class list of Cell 01 in project 10.4, the Owl-Vit program was able to find the deer in the image as shown in figure 11.6(C). There is nothing special in SAM models (Kirillov *et al* 2023), but a ViT as an image encoder, a prompt encoder for points, box and text, and a masks decoder. Meta AI trained SAM modes with 11 million images and 1 billion masks. People are saying that SAM from Meta AI will have the same impact on our world as ChatGPT from Open AI.

The SAM proposed by Meta AI is becoming a foundation for many computer vision tasks, such as image segmentation, image caption, and image editing. However, SAM needs heavy computation resources because SAM's architecture is based on the vision transformer mentioned in Section 10.1. Xu Zhao and his collaborators in June 2023 proposed FastSAM (Zhao *et al* 2023) based on YOLOv8. With FastSAM, they achieved a comparable performance with the SAM method at 50× higher run-time speed. They released their codes on their GitHub website. According to their instructions, I downloaded and unzipped their codes in a folder named 'FastSAM' into my current working folder named 'Exercises' in a VS Code virtual environment with Python v3.9. In a VS Code cell, running the codes in the quotation marks *'import os; os.getcwd( ); %cd fastsam'*, I can run codes in project 11.4.2 which uses some Python files in the FastSAM folder. With these setting, we can import some libraries with the code on line 03 of Cell 01: *from fastsam import FastSAM, FastSAMPrompt.*

```
class FastSAMPrompt:      #------------ modify codes in FastSAM/fastsam/prompt.py
    def __init__(self, img, results, device='cuda') -> None:    #-img_path -> img
        self.device = device
        self.results = results
        #self.img_path = img_path                          #------------deactivated
        self.ori_img = img    #cv2.imread(img_path) if img_path else None
```

The original FastSAMPrompt library only accepts a string of an image file name path as an image source. To use FastSAM for camera frames, we have to modify codes from line 23 to 27 in FastSAM/fastsam/prompt.py, so a NumPy array can be used as an image source for the library FastSAMPrompt. I found this solution from Nicolai Nielsen's YouTube video. Roboflow also has a helpful YouTube video about FastSAM. In Cell 02, codes deactivated on line 06–08 are for a box prompt, a point prompt and a text prompt. They work, but the results may not be what we expected. For example, with the text prompt 'lady', we only have one lady in the image of figure 11.7 segmented. Re-use codes in Cell 05 and 07 and replace 'yolov3' by 'fastsam', we can use the function defined in Cell 02 to process images in a folder, frames from a camera or a video file. The speed of the video is about 3 FPS.

Figure 11.7. Implement of a pre-trained FastSAM model to a single image with a prompt for everything. (left) The original image with bounding boxes from the model. (right) Objects of the image were segmented by the model, and each object with a blue edge was marked with different colors.

Although FastSAM's quality of image segmentation is not as good as SAM's quality, we have to sacrifice a little quality for speed.

```
#Project 11.4.2 Application of FastSAM for image segmentation--------Python v3.9
import cv2; import glob; from tqdm import tqdm; import numpy as np; import torch
from PIL import Image; import matplotlib.pyplot as plt; import time
from fastsam import FastSAM, FastSAMPrompt   #----------------------line 03
model = FastSAM('./weights/FastSAM-x.pt')
DEVICE = torch.device('cuda:0' if torch.cuda.is_available() else 'cpu')
# Cell 02: A function to annotate an image with any of 4 prompts----------Cell 02
def fastSAM(frame):
    outputs = model(source=frame, device=DEVICE, retina_masks=True,
                    imgsz=512, conf=0.4,iou=0.9, verbose=False)
    prompt_process = FastSAMPrompt(frame, outputs, device=DEVICE)
    masks = prompt_process.everything_prompt()
    #masks = prompt_process.box_prompt(bbox=[0, 0, 200, 700])    #------line 06
    #masks = prompt_process.point_prompt(points=[[700,300]], pointlabel=[1])
    #masks = prompt_process.text_prompt(text='lady')             #------line 08
    annotated_img = prompt_process.plot_to_result(annotations=masks) #--line 09
    my_boxes = outputs[0].boxes.xyxy
    for box in my_boxes:       # add bounding boxes to a frame------line 11
        x1, y1, x2, y2 = [int(z) for z in box]
        cv2.rectangle(frame, (x1,y1), (x2, y2), (0, 255, 0), 1)
    img_list = [frame, annotated_img]
    new_image = np.array(Image.fromarray(   #---------------------------line 15
                    np.concatenate([x for x in img_list], axis=1)))
    return new_image
# Cell 03: Implement the fastSAM function to a single image--------------Cell 03
fig, ax = plt.subplots(figsize=(16,8))
img = cv2.imread('D:/STANPED1105.jpg')  #'D:/STANPED1105.jpg'
image_RGB = cv2.cvtColor(fastSAM(img), cv2.COLOR_BGR2RGB)
ax.imshow(image_RGB);
# Cell 04: to slide show images in a folder for depth estimation----------------
file_path = 'D:/ImageSets/VOC/VOCdevkit/VOC2012/JPEGImages/*'
img_list = glob.glob(file_path)[7000:7030]           #=================line 02
for file in tqdm(img_list):
    cv2.imshow("press Esc to stop the slid show", fastSAM(cv2.imread(file)))
    if (cv2.waitKey(1000)&0xFF) == 27: break          #=================line 05
cv2.destroyAllWindows()
# Cell 05: Re-use Cell 07 of Project 7.5 for video frames from a camera or a file
#----------------------------------The End---------------------------------
```

References

Caron M, Touvron H, Misra I, Jégou H, Mairal J, Bojanowski P and Joulin A 2021 Emerging properties in self-supervised vision transformers *Proc. of the IEEE/CVF Int. Conf. on Computer Vision* pp 9650–60

Hinton G, Vinyals O and Dean J 2015 Distilling the knowledge in a neural network *arXiv preprint* arXiv:1503.02531

Johnson J, Douze M and Jegou H 2019 Billion-scale similarity search with {GPUs} *IEEE Trans. Big Data* **7** 535–47

Kirillov A, Mintun E, Ravi N, Mao H, Rolland C, Gustafson L, Xiao T, Whitehead S, Berg A C and Lo W-Y 2023 Segment anything *arXiv preprint* arXiv:2304.02643

Oquab M, Darcet T, Moutakanni T, Vo H, Szafraniec M, Khalidov V, Fernandez P, Haziza D, Massa F and El-nouby A 2023 DINOv2: learning robust visual features without supervision *arXiv preprint* arXiv:2304.07193

Zhao X, Ding W, An Y, Du Y, Yu T, Li M, Tang M and Wang J 2023 Fast segment anything *arXiv preprint* arXiv:2306.12156

Chapter 12

Applications of NeRF and 3D Gaussian splatting for synthesis of 3D scenes

This chapter is about the latest computer vision development by the end of 2023 for synthesis of 3D scenes. In the first section, MiDaS is used for image depth estimation. From Nvidia instant NeRF in the second section, the principle of neural radiance field (NeRF) is introduced about how to synthesize 3D scenes from a set of images by ray tracing. In the last section, a 2D Gaussian splatting program is used to introduce 3D Gaussian splatting for real-time rendering of 3D scenes by rasterization.

We are in a great age to develop machine learning algorithms for computers to have 3D vision about our world. Image depth estimation is a fundamental task in computer vision that enables machines to perceive the 3D structure of a scene from 2D. By accurately extracting objects' depth information on images or video frames, computers can understand the spatial layout of objects on each image, and make the right decisions for actuators to interact with the environment effectively. NeRF (Mildenhall *et al* 2020) and 3D Gaussian splatting (Kerbl *et al* 2023) are two different techniques for creating 3D models from 2D images. NeRF is a novel technique that uses deep learning to model 3D scenes from a set of photos. It represents a scene as a continuous 3D function that predicts the color and opacity of each point in 3D space. NeRF aims to capture complex 3D scenes by training a neural network model to learn the underlying scene representation from multiple 2D images, allowing for the synthesis of novel views of 3D scenes. It has gained popularity for its ability to generate high-quality 3D reconstructions and novel views of scenes. However, NeRF takes heavy computations to synthesize 3D scenes, and it is not quick enough for real-time projects. A technique called '3D Gaussian

doi:10.1088/978-0-7503-6244-3ch12

splatting' allows us to create photo-realistic 3D models from a set of images. It works by representing any scene with millions of 3D Gaussian particles. Each particle has a rugby ball shape whose size and orientation are decided by a 3D Gaussian covariance matrix with nine parameters. Each rugby ball has its own 3D position coordinates, RGB colors and opacity. These particles are then projected onto a 2D plane and blended together to create an image. 3D Gaussian splatting has several advantages over other radiance field methods, such as faster training and rendering, higher visual quality, 3D editability and better handling of empty space. A limit of 3D Gaussian splatting is its model training need a huge amount of GPU memory (24 GB).

12.1 Using MiDaS for image depth estimation

Traditionally, depth estimation relied heavily on expensive hardware, such as stereo cameras. The advent of machine learning has revolutionized the field of computer vision, including image depth estimation. In recent years, researchers have invented many techniques for image depth estimation. Some techniques use supervised learning, such as MiDaS (Ranftl *et al* 2020), whose models have been trained on 10 distinct datasets using multi-objective optimization to ensure high quality on a wide range of inputs. Using self-supervised vision transformers, Facebook's DINOv2 models can be used for image classification, instance retrieval, video understanding as well as semantic segmentation and depth estimation.

Before using any complex AI model to estimate image depth information, I would like to demonstrate a simple project about measuring distance between your face and your laptop camera by using libraries of OpenCV, cvzone and mediapipe. We also need a keychain tape to do some measurements for calibrations. We treat a laptop camera as a thin lens with a focal length (f). Usually, the value of f is about a few millimeters, and the object distance (u) of my face to the camera is around 500 mm. For example, my cellphone's focal length is 3.5 mm. With a condition $u \gg f$, we get the image distance of the object $v = f$ according to the thin lens equation shown in figure 12.1. If the height or width of an object is H, and the image

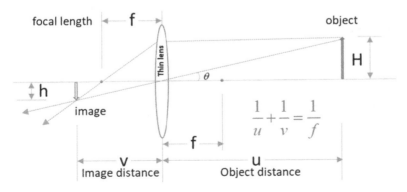

Figure 12.1. Parameters of a thin lens system for measuring face distance in front of a laptop camera.

height or width is h, we have an equation $\tan(\theta) = H/u = h/f$, from which we have a formula to measure the object distance for my codes in Project 12.1.1.

$$u = \frac{f}{h}H. \tag{12.1}$$

I measured the distance (H) between my two eye pupils with the keychain tape in front of a mirror, and found $H = 65$ (mm). Using a cvzone module FaceMeshModule in the following Python codes, I can measure the image width (h) of my two eye pupils in pixels. Of course, the value of h changes with the distance of my face to the camera. The cvzone module can measure coordinates of 468 points on a face. The left eye is point 145, and the right eye is point 374. If you change an option on line 06 from False to True, you can see all 468 points. With the keychain tape to set the distance (u) between my face and my laptop camera to 220 mm, I found the value of h was 155 pixels. From equation (12.1), it is easy to estimate the focal length of my camera $f = 525$ (pixel). Two of the three parameters on the right sight of equation (12.1) are known constants now, and it is possible to use equation (12.1) to automatically measure my face distance to my laptop camera. Running codes in Project 12.1.1 to measure the distance, I read the distance values on screen and compare them with my keychain tape's measurements. After the calibration, I need to adjust the focal length to 600 pixels on line 14. My codes were inspired by Murtaza's YouTube video.

```
# Project 12.1.1: Measurement of face distance to webcam-------------Python v3.9
import cvzone        # pip install cvzone and pip install mediapipe
import cv2; import time
from cvzone.FaceMeshModule import FaceMeshDetector
detector = FaceMeshDetector(maxFaces=1)
def faceMesh(img):           # a function to process video frames
    img, faces = detector.findFaceMesh(img, draw=False)       #-------line 06
    if faces:
        face = faces[0]     # 468 face points
        L_eye = face[145]; R_eye = face[374]
        cv2.line(img, L_eye, R_eye, (0,200,0), 1)
        cv2.circle(img, L_eye, 2, (255,0,255), cv2.FILLED)
        cv2.circle(img, R_eye, 2, (255,0,255), cv2.FILLED)
        h, _ = detector.findDistance(L_eye, R_eye)  # h: distance betweew 2 eyes
        u = f'u={int(65*600/(h + 1e-4))}mm'         # u = H*f/h  ---line 14
    return img, u           # u: distance between  your face and your webcam (mm)

def output_video(source):         # a function to display outputs
    video_frame = cv2.VideoCapture(source)
    while True:
        (NotLastFrame, frame) = video_frame.read()
        if not NotLastFrame or (cv2.waitKey(1)&0xFF) == 27: break
        out, u = faceMesh(cv2.flip(frame, 1))
        cv2.putText(out, u, (7, 70), 0, 2, (100, 255, 0), 3, cv2.LINE_AA)
        cv2.imshow("press Esc to stop the video", out)
    video_frame.release(); cv2.destroyAllWindows()
output_video(0)
#-------------------------------------------The End-----------------------------
```

Codes of Project 12.1.1 work well to measure the absolute distance between your face and your webcam in real time, but make an issue. If I cover one eye while the codes are running, the program will crash, because the program cannot find the standard object to measure its length for calculations of the absolute distance. Using a monocular camera to extract image depth information is not an easy job. It is dependent on optical settings of cameras. MiDaS models released by Intelligent Systems Lab Organization give us power to estimate relative image depth information about images and videos from different sources for many kinds of objects. The right-side image in figure 12.2 is an output image of Project 12.1.2. The names of three pre-trained models are listed on line 04. Only a small-size model (82 MB) was used in the project. The size of a big model is more than 1.2 GB. There is no significant visual difference between the outputs of the two models in my laptop, and it is much slower to use the big model. The right leg of a woman on the right of the original image was close to my camera, so the pixels of the leg are brighter on the relative depth image. Since two women on the left side of the original image were far away from my camera, their pixels are not as bright as the pixels of the right woman on the relative depth image. Copy Cell 05 and 07 in Project 7.5 and paste them after Cell 02 (change function name 'yolov3' to 'midas'), we can use the function defined in Cell 02 to process images in a folder or video frame from a camera. The speed for processing video is about 30 FPS. I met an issue in running codes in the project. After using *pip install timm* to install *safetensors* and *timm* in my VS Code virtual environment with Python v3.9, the codes then work well.

Figure 12.2. (Left) original image; (right) relative depth image extracted by a pre-trained small MiDaS model.

```
# Project 12.1.2 Image depth estimation by MiDaS---------------------Python v3.9
import torch; import torch.nn.functional as F; import cv2
import matplotlib.image as mpimg; from tqdm import tqdm; import numpy as np
import matplotlib.pyplot as plt; import time; from PIL import Image; import glob
model_name = 'MiDaS_small'  # "DPT-Large", "DPT_Hybrid"
model = torch.hub.load('intel-isl/MiDaS', model_name).cuda(); model.eval()
processor_name =torch.hub.load("intel-isl/MiDas", "transforms")
processor = processor_name.small_transform
#processor = midad_transformers.dpt_transform #for  "DPT-Large", "DPT_Hybrid"
# Cell 02: A function for using MiDaS to get depth estimation images------------
def midas(img):
    image = processor(img).cuda()
    with torch.no_grad():
        depth_map = F.interpolate(model(image).unsqueeze(1),
                                  size = img.shape[:2],
                                  mode='bicubic',
                                  align_corners=False
                                  ).squeeze().cpu().numpy()
        depth_map = cv2.normalize(depth_map, None, 0, 1,
                        norm_type=cv2.NORM_MINMAX, dtype=cv2.CV_64F)
        depth_map = (depth_map*255).astype(np.uint8)
        depth_map = cv2.applyColorMap(depth_map, cv2.COLORMAP_MAGMA)
        img_list = [img, depth_map]
        new_image = np.array(Image.fromarray(
                        np.concatenate([x for x in img_list], axis=1)))
    return new_image
my_img = mpimg.imread('D:/STANPED1105.jpg')
fig, ax = plt.subplots(figsize=(16,8)); ax.axis("off")
ax.imshow(midas(my_img));
# Cell 03: to slide show images in a folder for depth estimation----------------
img_path = 'D:/ImageSets/VOC/VOCdevkit/VOC2012/JPEGImages/*'
img_list = glob.glob(img_path)[3040:3050]
for file in tqdm(img_list):
    cv2.imshow("press Esc to stop the slid show", midas(cv2.imread(file)))
    if (cv2.waitKey(1000)&0xFF) == 27: break
cv2.destroyAllWindows()
# Cell 04: Re-use Cell 07 of Project 7.5 for video frames from a camera or a file
#---------------------------------------The End-----------------------------------
```

12.2 Neural Radiance Fields (NeRF) for synthesis of 3D scenes

There is another computer vision technique called Neural Radiance Fields (Li *et al* 2022) (NeRF) which can also be used for image depth estimation. However, the most impressive function of NeRF is to synthesize a 3D model of objects from a set of 2D images taken around these objects, and the data of the 3D model can then be used by other software such as Meshlab for 3D print. From high school mathematics, we can derive formulae to extract 3D information of objects from two images taken by a camera in two positions. That is why many kinds of animals and insects have two eyes to get stereo vision of our world as a result of evolution. Using 20~100 images taken by a camera around objects, NeRF has enough data to synthesize 3D scenes with smart algorithms. The original NeRF paper (Mildenhall *et al* 2020) was published in August 2020. Since model training time of NeRF is very slow (many hours or even days), many models based on the original NeRF were proposed in recent years. Nvidia's instant NeRF (Müller *et al* 2022) can synthesize 3D scenes from images in a few seconds. We do not even need to install Python files from Nvidia's GitHub website, because Nvidia provides an executable binary file instant-ngp.exe to download for a Windows operating system. According to the instructions of the GitHub website, I used my cellphone to take 35 photos around a sculpture about a bull and a cow shown in figure 12.3. To save computer time, I resized the resolution of these images from 4096×2304 to 843×474. Using Colmap and colmap2nerf.py, I obtained a *transforms.json* file about *Intrinsic parameters* of my camera listed below. In the file, each image has a 4×4 *Transform Matrix* which is used to convert pixel coordinates of each image to 3D world coordinates for each object in the image.

```
{
    "camera_angle_x": 1.152519572061334,
    "camera_angle_y": 0.701556594290402,
    "fl_x": 648.6253845698438,    # focal length in pixel along xc-axis
    "fl_y": 647.6989307782064,    # focal length in pixel along yc-axis
    "k1": 0.10088013173403937,    #1st radial distorial parameter
    "k2": -0.19027652003996334,   #2nd radial distorial parameter,
    "k3": 0,   #3rd radial distorial parameter for OPENCV_FISHEYE
    "k4": 0,   #4th radial distorial parameter for OPENCV_FISHEYE
    "p1": 0.0013280007985792053,  #1st tangential distortion parameter for OPENCV
    "p2": 0.002065113778747612,   #2nd tangential distortion parameter for OPENCV
    "is_fisheye": false,
    "cx": 425.93108187095646,     #principal point x
    "cy": 250.79174974746948,     #principal point y
    "w": 843.0,     #image width
    "h": 474.0,     #image height
    "aabb_scale": 16, #Axis-Aligned Bounding Box-------camera intrinsic parameters
  "frames": [
      {"file_path": "./smallcows/IMG_20230722_141116.JPG",
        "sharpness": 404.0864748965511,
        "transform_matrix": [
          [0.34142994000, -0.11060363748, 0.933376896790, 3.329634792894],
          [0.92710410628, 0.202980248113, -0.315082520923, -1.5237185883],
          [-0.1546078011, 0.972916159939, 0.1718446204182, 0.97689645579],
          [0.0,0.0,0.0,0.0,1.0]]
      },
```

Figure 12.3. One of 35 photos of a 3D sculpture for NeRF to synthesize 3D scenes.

12.2.1 Camera intrinsic and extrinsic matrices

We used a lot of photos from digital cameras for model training in computer vision projects. A digital camera projects objects in our 3D world to its 2D photon sensor (a CCD or CMOS array) to create digital images. With NeRF techniques, we could use a set of images to reconstruct or synthesize 3D scenes of objects in the 3D world. To understand NeRF, we need to know four Cartesian coordinate systems in a digital camera. As shown in figure 12.4, they are the world coordinate system, the camera coordinate system, the image coordinate system and the sensor coordinate system. In the first one, the z_w-axis direction is upward and the x_w–y_w plane is horizontal. Relative to the fixed real-world coordinate system, a movable camera coordinate system's z_c-axis is parallel with the y_w-axis before the camera is moved and rotated, and its x_c-axis could be in any direction. For simplicity, I set the x_c-axis and the x_w-axis in opposite directions. To a 3D world vector $\vec{X}_w = [1,1,1]^T$, we are sure that the vector in the camera coordinate system is $\vec{X}_c = [-1,1,101]^T$ if the camera is at a position set by a real-world vector $\vec{C}_w = [0, -100,0]^T$. From the vector $\vec{C}_w$, we know the distance between the two coordinate systems is 100. The unit of these coordinates could be millimeter (mm). From the figure, we have an equation to calculate the coordinates of the 3D world point $[1,1,1]$ in the camera system $\vec{X}_c = R \cdot (\vec{X}_w - \vec{C}_w) = R \cdot \vec{X}_w + \vec{t}$, where R is an orthonormal matrix about rotation operations, and $\vec{t} = -R \cdot \vec{C}_w = [0,0,100]^T$ is about a transposition operation of the camera coordinate system to the real-world system. From the coordinates of $\vec{t}$, we know the position of the origin of the world coordinate system in the camera system. We also have $R^{-1} = R^T$ and $RR^T = R^T R = 1$.

$$R = \begin{bmatrix} r_{11} & r_{12} & r_{13} \\ r_{21} & r_{21} & r_{23} \\ r_{31} & r_{32} & r_{33} \end{bmatrix} = \begin{bmatrix} \vec{x}_c \cdot \vec{x}_w & \vec{x}_c \cdot \vec{y}_w & \vec{x}_c \cdot \vec{z}_w \\ \vec{y}_c \cdot \vec{x}_w & \vec{y}_c \cdot \vec{y}_w & \vec{y}_c \cdot \vec{y}_w \\ \vec{z}_c \cdot \vec{x}_w & \vec{z}_c \cdot \vec{x}_w & \vec{z}_c \cdot \vec{x}_w \end{bmatrix} = \begin{bmatrix} -1 & 0 & 0 \\ 0 & 0 & 1 \\ 0 & 1 & 0 \end{bmatrix} \qquad (12.2)$$

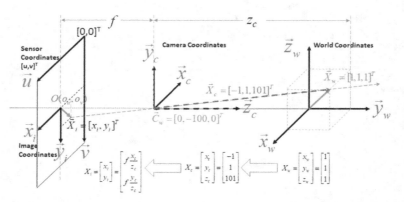

Figure 12.4. A digital camera's four Cartesian coordinate systems for NeRF. From right to left, they are the world coordinate system, the camera coordinate system, the image coordinate system and the sensor coordinate system.

For mathematical convenience, we use a 4D vector to represent a 3D vector in the world and camera coordinate systems: $\tilde{\chi}_w = \left[x_w, y_w, z_w, 1 \right]^T$ and $\tilde{\chi}_c = \left[x_c, y_c, z_c, 1 \right]^T$. The 4D vector is a homogeneous representation of a 3D vector, and the fourth coordinate is a fictitious number not equal to zero. A relationship between the two new vectors is set by equation (12.3), where the 4×4 matrix is called an *Extrinsic Matrix* of the camera for a photo.

$$\tilde{\chi}_c = \begin{bmatrix} x_c \\ y_c \\ z_c \\ 1 \end{bmatrix} = \begin{bmatrix} r_{11} & r_{12} & r_{13} & t_x \\ r_{21} & r_{22} & r_{23} & t_y \\ r_{31} & r_{32} & r_{33} & t_x \\ 0 & 0 & 0 & 1 \end{bmatrix} \begin{bmatrix} x_w \\ y_w \\ z_w \\ 1 \end{bmatrix} = \begin{bmatrix} R_{3\times3} & t \\ 0_{1\times3} & 1 \end{bmatrix} \tilde{\chi}_w \quad (12.3)$$

The vector $\overline{X}_c$ is then projected to the 2D image coordinate system by the camera, as shown in figure 12.4. Since the focus of the camera is only a few millimeters ($f << z_c$), the image coordinate system is on the focal plane of the camera. Based on Optics, we have the coordinates of the image in the images coordinate system $x_i = \frac{x_c}{z_c}f$ and $y_i = \frac{y_c}{z_c}f$. A digital camera uses millions of tiny CCD or CMOS sensors to detect photons. The sensor densities on the u-axis and the v-axis are m_x and m_y, respectively. The unit of sensor density is the number of sensors per millimeter. It is possible that m_x and m_y are not the same. The origin point of a digital image is usually set at the top-left corner of the image (view from the back of the 2D image sensor chip). In the sensor coordinate system, each pixel's coordinates (u, v) are integers: $u = m_x f \frac{x_c}{z_c} + o_u = f_x \frac{x_c}{z_c} + o_u, v = m_y f \frac{y_c}{z_c} + o_v = f_y \frac{y_c}{z_c} + o_v$, where f_x, f_y, o_u, o_v are the camera's intrinsic parameters. They have a same unit: pixel. The coordinates of the principle center of the 2D image sensor chip are $O(o_u, o_v)$ in the sensor coordinate system. If an image's resolution is 1024×768, the principle center of the image could be $O(512\ 384)$.

For the same reason, we use a 3D homogeneous representation for the 2D sensor coordinates in equation (12.4), where M_{int} is the *Intrinsic Matrix* of the camera. With equation (12.3) and (12.4), we get equation (12.5), which is used to project a real-world vector to the sensor coordinate system, where P is the *Projection Matrix* of the camera with 12 unknown parameters.

$$\tilde{\zeta} = \begin{bmatrix} u \\ v \\ 1 \end{bmatrix} \equiv \begin{bmatrix} \tilde{u} \\ \tilde{v} \\ \tilde{w} \end{bmatrix} = \begin{bmatrix} uz_c \\ vz_c \\ z_c \end{bmatrix} = \begin{bmatrix} f_x & 0 & o_u & 0 \\ 0 & f_y & o_v & 0 \\ 0 & 0 & 1 & 0 \end{bmatrix} \begin{bmatrix} x_c \\ y_c \\ z_c \\ 1 \end{bmatrix} = M_{int} \cdot \tilde{\chi}_c \quad (12.4)$$

$$\tilde{\tilde{\zeta}} = M_{int} \cdot \tilde{\chi}_c = M_{int} \cdot M_{ext} \cdot \tilde{\chi}_w = \begin{bmatrix} P_{11} & P_{12} & P_{13} & P_{14} \\ P_{21} & P_{22} & P_{23} & P_{24} \\ P_{31} & P_{32} & P_{33} & P_{34} \end{bmatrix} \begin{bmatrix} x_w \\ y_w \\ z_w \\ 1 \end{bmatrix} = P \cdot \tilde{\chi}_w \quad (12.5)$$

Using an image of an object with six (or more) known real-world coordinates, it is possible to get their pixel coordinates in the sensor coordinate system. For example, the first real-world coordinates $[x_{w1}, y_{w1}, z_{w1}]^T$ is projected to the sensor coordinate system as $[u_1, v_1]^T$, and they are known by measurements. Taking them to equation (12.4) for all six points, we got the following equation $A \cdot p = 0$.

$$
\begin{bmatrix}
x_{w1} & y_{w1} & z_{w1} & 1 & 0 & 0 & 0 & 0 & -u_1 x_{w1} & -u_1 y_{w1} & -u_1 z_{w1} & -u_1 \\
0 & 0 & 0 & 0 & x_{w1} & y_{w1} & z_{w1} & 1 & -v_1 x_{w1} & -v_1 y_{w1} & -v_1 z_{w1} & -v_1 \\
x_{w2} & y_{w2} & z_{w3} & 1 & 0 & 0 & 0 & 0 & -u_2 x_{w2} & -u_2 y_{w2} & -u_2 z_{w2} & -u_2 \\
0 & 0 & 0 & 0 & x_{w2} & y_{w2} & z_{w2} & 1 & -v_2 x_{w2} & -v_2 y_{w2} & -v_2 z_{w2} & -v_2 \\
\cdots & \cdots & \cdots & \cdots & \cdots & \cdots & \cdots & \cdots & \cdots & \cdots & \cdots & \cdots \\
x_{w6} & y_{w6} & z_{w6} & 1 & 0 & 0 & 0 & 0 & -u_6 x_{w6} & -u_6 y_{w6} & -u_6 z_{w6} & -u_6 \\
0 & 0 & 0 & 0 & x_{w6} & y_{w6} & z_{w6} & 1 & -v_6 x_{w6} & -v_6 y_{w6} & -v_6 z_{w6} & -v_6
\end{bmatrix}
\begin{bmatrix}
p_{11} \\ p_{12} \\ p_{13} \\ p_{14} \\ p_{21} \\ p_{22} \\ p_{23} \\ p_{24} \\ p_{31} \\ p_{32} \\ p_{33} \\ p_{34}
\end{bmatrix}
=
\begin{bmatrix}
0 \\ 0 \\ 0 \\ 0 \\ 0 \\ 0 \\ 0 \\ 0 \\ 0 \\ 0 \\ 0 \\ 0
\end{bmatrix}
$$

This is a homogeneous least squares problem (Inkilä, 2005). The 12 unknown parameters in the matrix p can be obtained by solving an eigenequation $A^T A p = \lambda p$ under two conditions: $\|A \cdot p\|^2 = \min$ and $p^T \cdot p = 1$. We can us Colmap and colmap2nerf.py to calculate the 12 parameters for each image automatically.

12.2.2 Using MLP with Gaussian Fourier feature mapping to reconstruct images

In any NeRF project, the hardest part is pre-processing image pixels $[u, v]$ to get 3D world coordinates $[x_w, y_w, z_w]$ of objects. NeRF models and model training are easy. We would like to work on easy jobs at first. A fully connected multi-layer neural network is called a multilayer perceptron (MLP). We have used MLPs in transformer models in chapter 10; two fully connected layers were used in chapter 2 for nonlinear regressions to numerically simulate any functions. Using an image's pixel coordinates (u, v) and RGB colors (r, g, b) as two datasets, an MLP model can even simulate and reconstruct the image. Pre-processing raw input data is very important for any machine learning project, often crucial for model training results. If an image's resolution is 512×512, we need to normalize each pixel's u and v values from [0, 511] to [-1, 1], and its RGB values from [0, 255] to [0, 1].

We have an issue about the quality of the reconstructed or predicted image, because a standard MLP model fails to learn image details in high frequencies (Tancik *et al* 2020). Comparing the ground truth image shown in figure 12.5A, you can see that it is impossible to find a single hair on the head of a tamias shown in figure 12.5B, which is the output of Cell 10 in the following Project 12.2.1 without position encoding. By using Fourier features for positional encoding of the ground truth $[u, v]$ coordinates with codes in Cell 04, we have the output of the same MLP model shown in figure 12.5C which is almost the same as the ground truth. We use a metrics PSNR (peak signal- to-noise ratio) to indicate the similarity of two images. In equation (12.6), MSE is the mean squared error of RGB colors between the reconstructed image and the ground truth, and the MSE loss function is used for model training.

$$PSNR = -10 \log_{10}(MSE) \tag{12.6}$$

Figure 12.5. (A) Ground truth image; (B) a predicted image without position encoding; (C) a predicted image with Gaussian Fourier feature mapping for image position encoding. Model training time is less than 10 min.

```
# Project 12.2.1: Using MLP to restore a tamias image---------------Python v3.90
import torch; import torch.nn as nn
from torch.utils.data import Dataset, DataLoader
import torch.optim.lr_scheduler as lr_scheduler
import kornia; from kornia import create_meshgrid; import imageio
from einops import rearrange; import numpy as np; import pandas as pd
import matplotlib.pyplot as plt; from tqdm import trange
batch_size = 4096
lr = 1e-3
n_epochs = 500
# Cell 02 Import an image and display the image which is used in Cell 10 for PNSR
image_path = "Tamias.jpg"        # "myfox.jpg"   "Squirrel.jpg" "Tamias.jpg"
image = imageio.v3.imread(image_path)[..., :3]/255.
H, W, C = image.shape
image = kornia.utils.image_to_tensor(image, keepdim=True)
print(image.shape)
plt.title('Ground Truth'); plt.imshow(image.permute(1,2,0));
# Cell 03: Construct 2 datasets and 2 dataloaders for model training--------3/10
class ImageDataset(Dataset):
    def __init__(self, image_path: str, split: str):
        image = imageio.v3.imread(image_path)[..., :3]/255.  # shape=[512,512,3]
        self.uv = create_meshgrid(*image.shape[:2], True)[0] # shape=[512,512,2]
        self.uv = rearrange(self.uv, 'h w c -> (h w) c')     # shape=[262144, 2]
        self.rgb = torch.FloatTensor(image)
        self.rgb = rearrange(self.rgb, 'h w c -> (h w) c')   # shape=[262144, 3]
        if split == 'train':                 #using 75% pixels for model training
            self.uv = [item for idx, item in enumerate(self.uv) if idx%4 !=0]
            self.rgb = [item for idx, item in enumerate(self.rgb) if idx%4 !=0]
        elif split == 'val':                 #using 25% pixels for model validation
            self.uv = [item for idx, item in enumerate(self.uv) if idx%4 ==0]
            self.rgb = [item for idx, item in enumerate(self.rgb) if idx%4 ==0]
    def __len__(self):
        return len(self.uv)
    def __getitem__(self, idx: int):
        return {"uv": self.uv[idx], "rgb": self.rgb[idx]}
```

```
train_dataset = ImageDataset(image_path=image_path, split="train")
train_dataloader = DataLoader(train_dataset, shuffle=True, batch_size=batch_size)
n_samples = len(train_dataset)    #n_samples=196608
s_p_e = int(n_samples/batch_size) #steps per epoch = 48 for lr_scheduler
val_dataset = ImageDataset(image_path=image_path, split="val")
val_dataloader = DataLoader(val_dataset, shuffle=False,  batch_size=batch_size)
# Cell 04: Encode the normalized image coordinates [u,v] with sin and cos---4/10
B = 10*torch.randn((2, 256), device="cuda")     #B.shape=[2,256]
class PE(nn.Module):
    def __init__(self, B):
        super().__init__()
        self.B = B
    @property
    def out_dim(self):               # for other functions to get B.shape[1]*2
        return self.B.shape[1]*2     # PE(B).out_dim=512
    def forward(self, uv):           # uv.shape=Batch_size x 2
        x = 2*np.pi*uv@self.B
        encoded_uv = torch.cat([torch.sin(x), torch.cos(x)], 1)
        return encoded_uv            # encoded_uv.batch_size = Batch_size x 512
pe = PE(B).cuda()
#---------------------------------------------------------------------------
```

Codes in Cell 01–02 are used to import libraries, set hyperparameters, input and display an image named 'Tamias.jpg'. The Kornia library is 'a differentiable library that allows classical computer vision to be integrated into deep learning models'. A class defined in Cell 03 uses 75% pixels of the image for a train dataset, and 25% pixels for a validation dataset. Each of the datasets is then sliced into a dataloader with a batch size of 4096 pixels. Codes in Cell 04 are used to encode [u, v] coordinates in each batch (v) of a dataloader with Gaussian Fourier feature mapping according to the following formulae, in which the matrix B was sampled from an isotropic Gaussian distribution. The constant 10 on the first line of Cell 04 is a critical hyperparameter according to Matthew Tancik. You can try to use 1 or 100 to replace 10 to generate B to see the quality of the reconstructed image. The input for equation (12.7) is a batch of image coordinates with shape [4096, 2], and the output shape is [4096, 256]. A sin function and a cos function element-wisely acted on the output, respectively, and they are then concatenated into a matrix with shape [4096, 512] as shown in equation (12.8). The code '@property' in Cell 04 is for a function named 'out_dim' which will be used in the MLP model's first fully connected layer. If you do not want position encoding in the project, replace the code 'x=pe(uv)' by 'x=uv' in the forward function of the MLP model class defined in Cell 05, and also replace 'n_in=pe.out_dim' by 'n_in=2' in the model instance. Codes in Cell 10 use all pixels in the image to construct a dataloader with only one batch. The trained model uses the batch to predict or reconstruct a predicted image shown in figure 12.5C.

$$2\pi*v \cdot B = 2\pi*\begin{bmatrix} u_1 & v_1 \\ u_2 & v_2 \\ \cdots & \cdots \\ u_{4096} & v_{4096} \end{bmatrix} \cdot \begin{bmatrix} B_{1,1} & B_{1,2} & \cdots & B_{1,256} \\ B_{2,1} & B_{2,2} & \cdots & B_{2,256} \end{bmatrix} \tag{12.7}$$

$$\gamma(v) = cat[\sin(2\pi*v \cdot B), \cos(2\pi*v \cdot B)] \tag{12.8}$$

```
# Cell 05: A MLP model with 4 fully connected layers to restore an image-----5/10
class MLP(nn.Module):
    def __init__(self, n_in=2, n_layers=4, n_hidden_units=256):
        super().__init__()
        self.net = nn.Sequential(
            nn.Linear(n_in, n_hidden_units), nn.ReLU(True),
            nn.Linear(n_hidden_units, n_hidden_units), nn.ReLU(True),
            nn.Linear(n_hidden_units, n_hidden_units), nn.ReLU(True),
            nn.Linear(n_hidden_units, 3), nn.Sigmoid(),
        )
    def forward(self, uv):   #uv: (B, 2) # pixel uv (normalized)
        x = pe(uv)  # -----------------none position embedding: x = uv
        predicted_rgb = self.net(x)
        return    predicted_rgb      # predicted_rgb.shape = (B, 3)
model = MLP(n_in=pe.out_dim).cuda() # none position embedding: (n_in=2)
optimizer = torch.optim.Adam(model.parameters(), lr=lr)
criterion = nn.MSELoss(reduction='sum')
scheduler = lr_scheduler.OneCycleLR(optimizer, max_lr=lr,
                   steps_per_epoch=s_p_e, epochs=n_epochs, pct_start=0.7)
# Cell 06: Model Training for the train_dataloader-------------------------6/10
def training(my_dataloader):
    total_loss = 0.0; n_samples = len(my_dataloader.dataset)
    model.train()
    for batch in my_dataloader:
        uv = batch['uv'].cuda()
        rgb = batch['rgb'].cuda()
        y_hat = model(uv)
        loss = criterion(y_hat, rgb)
        total_loss += loss.item()
        loss.backward()
        optimizer.step()
        scheduler.step()
        optimizer.zero_grad()
    return total_loss/n_samples
# Cell 07: Model Evaluation for val_dataloader and test_dataloader----------7/10
def evaluation(my_dataloader):
    total_loss = 0.0; n_samples = len(my_dataloader.dataset)
    with torch.no_grad():
        model.eval()
        for batch in my_dataloader:
            uv = batch['uv'].cuda()
            rgb = batch['rgb'].cuda()
            y_hat = model(uv)
            loss = criterion(y_hat, rgb)
            total_loss += loss.item()
    return total_loss/n_samples
# Cell 08: The fitting function -------------------------------------------8/10
def fitting(epochs):
    df = pd.DataFrame(np.empty([epochs, 3]),
        index = np.arange(epochs),
        columns=['loss_train', 'loss_val', 'lr'])
    progress_bar = trange(epochs)
```

```
    for i in progress_bar:
        df.iloc[i,0] = training(train_dataloader)
        df.iloc[i,1] = evaluation(val_dataloader)
        df.iloc[i,2] = optimizer.param_groups[0]['lr']
        progress_bar.set_description("lr=%.5f" % df.iloc[i,2])
        progress_bar.set_postfix(
                    {'train_loss': df.iloc[i,0], 'val_loss': df.iloc[i,1]})
    return df
train_history = fitting(n_epochs)
# Cell 09: Graphs of Model training outputs------------------------------9/10
import matplotlib.pyplot as plt
df= train_history
fig, ax = plt.subplots(1,3, figsize=(12,2.5), sharex=True)
df.plot(ax=ax[0], y=[0,1], style=['r-', 'b-'])
df.plot(ax=ax[1], y=[2], style=['r-'])
ax[2].plot(range(n_epochs) ,-10*np.log10(df['loss_train']), 'r-')
ax[2].plot(range(n_epochs), -10*np.log10(df['loss_val']), 'b-')
for i in range(3):
    ax[i].set_xlabel('epoch')
    ax[i].grid(which='major', axis='both', color='g', linestyle=':')
ax[0].set_ylabel('loss'); ax[1].set(ylabel='learning rate');
ax[2].set(ylabel='PSNR')
ax[1].ticklabel_format(style='sci', axis='y', scilimits=(0,0));
# Cell 10: Construct a dadaloader of 1 batch to predict an image by the model---
class IMG_uv(Dataset):
    def __init__(self, image_path):
        image = imageio.v3.imread(image_path)[..., :3]/255.  # shape=[512,512,3]
        self.uv = create_meshgrid(*image.shape[:2], True)[0] # shape=[512,512,2]
        self.uv = rearrange(self.uv, 'h w c -> (h w) c')
    def __len__(self):
        return len(self.uv)
    def __getitem__(self, idx: int):
        return self.uv[idx]
img_uv = IMG_uv(image_path)
uv_dataloader = DataLoader(img_uv, shuffle=False,  batch_size=len(img_uv))

def restore_img(my_dataloader):
    with torch.no_grad():
        for batch in my_dataloader:
            uv = batch.cuda()
            predicted_img = model(uv).reshape(H, W, C)
    return predicted_img
predicted_img = restore_img(uv_dataloader)
loss = criterion(predicted_img.cpu(), image.permute(1,2,0))/(H*W)
psnr = -10*np.log10(loss.item())
print(f'psnr={psnr.item():.2f}', f'loss={loss.item():.5f}')
plt.title(f'Predicted image: PSNR={psnr:.2f}')
plt.imshow(predicted_img.cpu().detach().numpy());
#---------------------------------The End-------------------------------------
```

12.2.3 The physics principle of render volume density in NeRF

In order to get compatible results with Colmap, I will use the coordinate systems shown in figure 12.6. There is a virtual ray starting from each pixel $[u, v]$ on an image. After passing through the camera center (the origin of the camera coordinate system), the ray penetrates through objects like an x-ray. There are infinite points on each ray. To save computer time, we have to set a near threshold (L_n) and a far

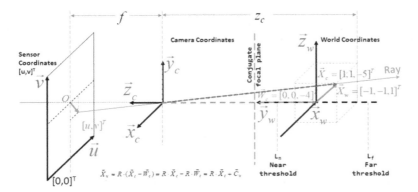

Figure 12.6. NeRF coordinate systems in their initial orientations. The camera can move around the fixed world coordinate system. The angle of the camera moving around z_w-axis has a name theta: $\theta \in [0, 2\pi]$ on the x_w-y_w plane, and the angle of the camera moving around the x_w-axis has a name phi: $\varphi \in [-\pi, \pi]$ on the y_w-z_w plane. ($r = 4$; $z_c//y_w$: $\theta = 0$, $\varphi = 0$; $z_c//x_w$: $\theta = 90^o$; $z_c//z_w$: $\varphi = -90^o$).

threshold (L_f) on the z_c-axis, and choose N points on the line between the two thresholds. The sample number N could be 32, 64, 128, ..., 1024, or any other integers. The bigger the sample number N, the better NeRF results would be, but the model training time would be longer. The distance between two neighbour points on the z_c-axis is $d = (L_f - L_n)/(N - 1)$. We will then get a point on the ray corresponding to a point on z_c-axis between L_n and L_f. Those points on the ray are query points. In the case where our image resolution is 100×100, and number of samples on each ray is 32, we would have 320 000 query points for each image in model training.

In Cell 05 of Project 12.2.2 listed in appendix K, a tiny NeRF model's output has a name, *radiance_field*, and the shape of the radiance field is [100, 100, 32, 4] for each of 10 000 pixels with 32 query points per ray. Each radiance field point on the ray corresponds to a query point. The four parameters of a radiance field point are for three colors (r, g, b) and a density (σ). Now we treat each radiance field point as a tiny LED light source with RGB colors. The light intensity emitted by a point with a density (σ) is proportional to $\alpha = 1 - e^{-\sigma \cdot d}$. If there is nothing at the query point, a tiny space or volume around the point is transparent and its density is $\sigma = 0$. This point will not emit light because of $\alpha = 0$. The contribution of the first radiance field point to a pixel on a predicted image is $[\alpha_1 r_1, \alpha_1 g_1, \alpha_1 b_1]$. If σ_1 is a bigger positive number, the second radiance field point's light will be partially blocked by point 1. The blocking percentage is equal to α_1, and the remain percentage is equal to $\beta_1 = 1 - \alpha_1$. The contribution of the second point to the pixel's color on the predicted image is $[\alpha_2 r_2, \alpha_2 g_2, \alpha_2 b_2]\beta_1$. The contribution of the last query point to the pixel's color is $\left[\alpha_{32} r_{32}, \alpha_{32} g_{32}, \alpha_{32} b_{32} \right] \prod_{i=1}^{31} \beta_i$. The following table is a summery of the above explanations. The sum of each color column in the table is a color of a pixel on the predicted image. A function *render_volume_density* defined in Cell 06 of the Project is used to do the above calculations. An MSE loss function is used in Cell 05 to compare color difference between ground truth and the predicted image during model training.

Point	Red color	Green color	Blue color	Density
01	$\alpha_1 r_1$	$\alpha_1 g_1$	$\alpha_1 b_1$	σ_1
02	$\alpha_2 r_2 \beta_1$	$\alpha_2 g_2 \beta_1$	$\alpha_2 b_2 \beta_1$	σ_2
03	$\alpha_3 r_3 \beta_1 \beta_2$	$\alpha_3 g_3 \beta_1 \beta_2$	$\alpha_3 b_3 \beta_1 \beta_2$	σ_3
...	...	...	...	...
32	$\alpha_{32} r_{128} \prod_{i=1}^{31} \beta_i$	$\alpha_{32} g_{32} \prod_{i=1}^{31} \beta_i$	$\alpha_{32} b_{32} \prod_{i=1}^{31} \beta_i$	σ_{32}

When we use α or β to calculate light blockage of a query point to its neighbour query point on a ray, the distance of the two points should be along the ray. How can we find world coordinates of 32 points on each ray starting from an image pixel at $[u, v]$? There are two steps. The first step is to convert $[u, v]$ of a pixel in the sensor coordinate system to $[x_c, y_c, z_c]$ in the camera coordinate system, and the second step is to convert $[x_c, y_c, z_c]$ to $[x_w, y_w, z_w]$ in the world coordinate system. For simplicity, we suppose that the principle center of the 2D image sensor chip is at $O(W/2, H/2)$, where W and H are the width and height of the image sensor chip in a unit of pixel. The camera in figure 12.6 has a conjugate focal plane at $z_c = -f$. We project the camera's focal plane at $z_c = f$ to the conjugate focal plane, on which the u-axis is parallel with the x_c-axis and the v-axis is in opposite direction to y_c-axis. An angle between the ray and the x_c-axis is equal to $\arctan\left[\left(u - \frac{W}{2} + 0.5\right)/f\right]$, and an angle between the ray and the y_c-axis is equal to $-\arctan\left[\left(v - \frac{H}{2} + 0.5\right)/f\right]$. At a plane with $z_c = -1$ in the camera coordinate system, the $[u, v]$ is converted to $[x_c, y_c, z_c] = [\left(u - \frac{W}{2} + 0.5\right)/f, -\left(v - \frac{H}{2} + 0.5\right)/f, -1]$. A set of these camera coordinates has a name 'ray_directions' in the *get_ray_bundle* function defined in Cell 04. Each query point on the ray has a depth value: $d_i = L_n + i*d$, where $i \in [0, (N - 1)]$. Using a query point's depth values to multiply the ray_directions, we will get all the query point's camera coordinates: $[x_c, y_c, z_c] = [\left(u - \frac{W}{2} + 0.5\right)d_i/f, \left(u - \frac{H}{2} + 0.5\right)d_i/f, -d_i]$. To convert camera coordinates $[x_c, y_c, z_c] = [1,1,-5]$ in the figure, we need to use a formula: $\vec{X}_w = R \cdot (\vec{X}_c - \vec{W}_c) = R \cdot \vec{X}_c - R \cdot \vec{W}_c = R \cdot \vec{X}_c + \vec{C}_w$, where $\vec{W}_c$ is a vector for the origin of the world coordinate system in the camera system, and $\vec{C}_w$ is a vector for the camera origin in the world coordinate system.

$$\begin{bmatrix} x_w \\ y_w \\ z_w \end{bmatrix} = \begin{bmatrix} \vec{x}_w \cdot \vec{x}_c & \vec{x}_w \cdot \vec{y}_c & \vec{x}_w \cdot \vec{z}_c \\ \vec{y}_w \cdot \vec{x}_c & \vec{y}_w \cdot \vec{y}_c & \vec{y}_w \cdot \vec{z}_c \\ \vec{z}_w \cdot \vec{x}_c & \vec{z}_w \cdot \vec{y}_c & \vec{z}_w \cdot \vec{z}_c \end{bmatrix} \cdot \begin{bmatrix} x_c \\ y_c \\ z_c \end{bmatrix} = \begin{bmatrix} -1 & 0 & 0 \\ 0 & 0 & 1 \\ 0 & 1 & 0 \end{bmatrix} \cdot \begin{bmatrix} 0 \\ 0 \\ -r \end{bmatrix}$$

You would see that the world coordinates of the camera are equal to the last column of R multiplied by the distance (r) between the two coordinate systems. The set of the world coordinates of the camera has a name 'ray_origins' in the 'get_ray_bundle' function defined in Cell 04. Because the image is virtually projected on the conjugate focal plane, we can ignore the focal plane, so that all rays of the image start from the camera's center (ray_origins). In the initial NeRF coordinate systems shown in figure 12.6, the camera can move around the fixed world coordinate system. The angle of the camera moving around z_w-axis has a name theta: $\theta \in [0,2\pi]$ on the x_w-y_w plane, and the angle of the camera moving around the x_w-axis has a name phi: $\varphi \in [-\pi, \pi]$ on the y_w-z_w plane $(z_c//y_w$: $\theta = 0$, $\varphi = 0$; $z_c//x_w$: $\theta = \pi/2$; $z_c//z_w$: $\varphi = -\pi/2)$. In the case where the camera rotates an angle φ around the x_w-axis, and then an angle θ around the z_w-axis, the coordinates of the $\overline{X}_w$ in the world coordinate system can be found by a new rotation matrix R:

$$R = \begin{bmatrix} \cos(\theta) & \sin(\theta) & 0 \\ -\sin(\theta) & \cos(\theta) & 0 \\ 0 & 0 & 1 \end{bmatrix} \cdot \begin{bmatrix} 1 & 0 & 0 \\ 0 & \cos(\varphi) & \sin(\varphi) \\ 0 & -\sin(\varphi) & \cos(\varphi) \end{bmatrix} \cdot \begin{bmatrix} -1 & 0 & 0 \\ 0 & 0 & 1 \\ 0 & 1 & 0 \end{bmatrix}$$

$$pose = c2w(\theta, \varphi, r) = \begin{bmatrix} -\cos(\theta) & \sin(\theta)\sin(\varphi) & \sin(\theta)\cos(\varphi) & r\sin(\theta)\cos(\varphi) \\ \sin(\theta) & \cos(\theta)\sin(\varphi) & \cos(\theta)\cos(\varphi) & r\cos(\theta)\cos(\varphi) \\ 0 & \cos(\varphi) & -\sin(\varphi) & -r\sin(\varphi) \\ 0 & 0 & 0 & 1 \end{bmatrix}$$

The 3×3 sub-matrix on the top-left corner of the *pose* matrix is equal to the new rotation matrix R. From the top 3×1 sub-matrix in the last column of the *pose*, we get a ray origin, or the camera's world coordinates after the camera is rotated, where r is the distance between the two coordinate systems. We use the *pose* matrix to convert $\overline{X}_c$ to $\overline{X}_w$ for query points. During model training, all query points and ray origins are position-encoded by a function defined in the last function of Cell 04. A hyperparameter L is the number of encoding functions. The value of L for query points and ray origins is set to be 6 and 4, respectively. In the following equation, q is a batch of query points with a batch size B, where $L = 6$ is the number of encoding functions. After the coordinates of q are multiplied by $2\pi 2^0$, a sin function acts on them element-wisely, and a cos function also acts on them element-wisely. The operations of the two triangular functions are appended to q to construct a list with nine elements: $[q, \sin(2\pi 2^0 q), \cos(2\pi 2^0 q)]$ at frequency 2^0.

$$\sin(2\pi 2^{i*} q) = \sin\left(2\pi 2^{i*} \begin{bmatrix} q_{x1} & q_{y1} & q_{z1} \\ q_{x2} & q_{y2} & q_{z2} \\ \cdots & \cdots & \cdots \\ q_{xB} & q_{yB} & q_{zB} \end{bmatrix}\right) i \in [0, (L-1)]$$

The list of position encoding results of q are concatenated to get a tensor with shape $B \times (3 + 3 \times 2 \times L)$ as one of two inputs of an MLP model defined in Cell 05. With the above background information, it should be easy to understand the codes of the tiny NeRF project listed in appendix K. My codes are inspired by Bmild. Model training time is about 125 min for 128 query points on each ray, and PSNR value is around 28.5. The trained MLP model is then saved by codes in Cell 13. The size of the saved model file is 301 kB. Running code in Cell 14, we can load the saved model to synthesize a Lego image at any θ and φ angles for a distance r around 4. The right

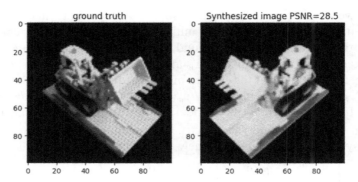

Figure 12.7. Using a trained tiny NeRF model to synthesize a tiny Lego image at any θ and φ angles with a distance *r* around 4. (left) Image of the ground truth; (right) a synthesized tiny Lego image with theta, phi, *r* = 135°, -45°, 4.The tiny Lego image is reproduced with MIT license from Mildenhall *et al* (2020) (the authors of the original NeRF paper) and Yen-Chen Lin, the owner of 'NeRF-pytorch' GitHub repository.

image shown in figure 12.7 is the output of the following codes. You can change the values of theta, phi and *r* on the first line of following function to see different synthesized images. To improve the quality of the synthesized images, we need to increase the sample points on each ray, but we will have issues about the limit of GPU memory and model training time. Now we have many new NeRF algorithms enabling us to reconstruct photorealistic videos in real time. The development of computer vision is very fast. Some techniques in the book are obsolete when you are reading the book.

```python
# Functions to obtain a c2w pose for a camera at (theta, phi, r) in the world----
theta, phi, r = 280, -45, 4  #Try to change these parameters to synthesize images
def r_phi(phi):             # phi: the camera rotation angle around Xw axis
    phi = np.pi*phi/180
    array = np.array([[1, 0, 0],
            [0, np.cos(phi), np.sin(phi)],
            [0, -np.sin(phi), np.cos(phi)]] )
    return array
def r_theta(theta):          # theta: the camera rotation angle around Zw
    theta = np.pi*theta/180
    array = np.array([[np.cos(theta), np.sin(theta), 0],
            [-np.sin(theta), np.cos(theta), 0],
            [0, 0, 1]])
    return array
def c2w_pose(theta, phi, r):
    pose = torch.eye(4).to(torch.float32)
    Rotation = r_theta(theta)@r_phi(phi)
    base = np.array([[-1,0,0], [0,0,1], [0,1,0]]) #Camera initial orientation
    R = torch.FloatTensor(Rotation@base)
    pose[:3,:3] = R
    pose[:3,-1] = r*R[:,-1]   #r: distance of the camera to the world center
    return pose
R = c2w_pose(theta, phi, r); print(R)
# Using R for the trained model to synthesize a tiny Lego image----------------
with torch.no_grad():           #num_samples = 128
    rgb_predicted = run_one_iter_of_tinynerf(R.cuda())
    fig, ax = plt.subplots(1,2, figsize=(8, 4))
    ax[0].imshow(testimg.detach().cpu().numpy())
    ax[0].set(title='ground truth')
    ax[1].imshow(rgb_predicted.detach().cpu().numpy())
    ax[1].set(title='Synthesized image')
    plt.show()
#-----------------------------------The End----------------------------------
```

12.3 Introduce 3D Gaussian splatting by 2D Gaussian splatting

Model training for 3D Gaussian splatting is easy. In fact, there is no neural network model for the new technique. We just need to train a fitting function with many parameters which are updated during model training. You can start your 3D Gaussian splatting project by using a cellphone or a drone to take photos around something, such as a sculpture, an Egyptian pyramid, the Eiffel tower, or even buildings in downtown Vancouver. Then, you can use Colmap or other free software to get a point cloud file from your photos about 3D points on the surface of your objects. The codes of a 3D Gaussian splatting project will initialize those points as 3D Gaussian rugby balls. During model training, millions of rugby balls will be projected to a confocal plane according to equation (12.5) for a camera at a position. This process is called 'rasterization'. GPUs would be used to sort distance of all rugby balls to the confocal plane. Each 'tile' with 16x16 pixels on the confocal plane is a batch for GPUs to get a predicted image on a tile. An image taken by the camera at the position is used as a ground truth. An L1 loss function and a Structural Similarity Index (SSIM) loss function are used to calculate the difference between the predicted image and the ground truth. During model training, each rugby ball's position, size, orientation, color and opacity will be updated according to gradients of the loss function to some of the rugby balls' parameters. If a rugby ball's opacity is low enough (or transparency is high enough), the rugby ball will be deleted; if the norm of the gradient of the loss function to the position coordinates of a rugby ball is big enough, the rugby ball will be cloned, and in the case when the cloned rugby balls' sizes are big enough, the sizes of the two same rugby balls will be scaled down. This process will be repeated for all ground truth images to adjust each rugby ball's position, size, orientation, color and opacity. By the end, we can see photorealistic predicted images at any view angle around those objects.

The only problem is that model training needs a huge amount GPU memory for using millions of 3D Gaussians to reconstruct photorealistic 3D scenes. My RTX 2060 GPU with 6 GB memory can only handle 3536 2D Gaussians in the following Project 12.3.1. At the time while I am writing this chapter, LUMA AI provides free web service for people to upload their photos so they can download 3D Gaussian splatting models trained by their photos. I have to use a 2D Gaussian splatting project to give you some ideas about the new technique. My codes were inspired by OutofAi. A ground truth image in figure 12.8A was processed by codes in Project 12.3.1 to obtain a synthesized image with 3536 2D Gaussians. It took me around 1x5 hours to get the good enough output with the structural similarity index (SSIM) to be equal to 0.882. SSIM was first introduced in the 2004 by an IEEE paper (Wang *et al* 2004). It is better than PSNR used in the last section for image quality assessment, because its value is in the range [0,1]. A SSIM loss function defined in Cell 02 is based on an instance of a class in kornia library. The value of the loss function is

Figure 12.8. (A) A ground image, the output of Cell 01; (B) a synthesized image with 3536 2D Gaussians, the output of Cell 06. Model training time is 1x5 hours (SSIM=0.882, PSNR=26.223).

equal to (1-SSIM)/2. In case a predicted image completely matches with its ground truth, we have SSIM = 1 and loss = 0. The maximum SSIM loss value is 0.5.

On line 11 of Cell 02, 5000 pixels are randomly selected as cloud points for the squirrel image input in Cell 01. Using coordinates of these points, a function defined in the cell returns RGB colors and normalized coordinates of each cloud point. The values of these normalized coordinates are in the range [−1, 1]. With an inverse hyperbolic tangent function on line 16, the range of these cloud points' coordinates are extended to [−∞, ∞] in order to reduce gradients of a loss function to the coordinates for smooth model training. Otherwise, the splitting of Gaussians is too quick to get good model training results because of an 'out of memory' issue. Codes on line 12 to 14 of the cell randomly set each 2D Gaussian's sigma, rho and color density. All these parameters are packed as a weight tensor with a shape [5000,9]. During model training, the weight tensor will be updated, so that some Gaussians will be cloned, deleted, resized, moved. In the process, these Gaussians' RGB colors will also be changed. For a 2D Gaussian with σ_x, σ_y and a correlation coefficient ρ, the covariance matrix and its inverse of the 2D Gaussian will be set by equation (12.9). These matrices are used in Cell 03 to calculate a batch of 2D Gaussians in Cell 03. PDF contours of three 2D Gaussians would be printed on screen as examples. The third Gaussian's PDF contours are ellipses because its x and y variables are not independent. The orientation of those ellipses is decided by the correlation coefficient ρ. The PDFs of the three 2D Gaussians are colorized and integrated into a color image by a function defined in Cell 04. A 2D affine matrices named 'theta' is used to transpose each Gaussian to its center (the coordinates of a cloud point) with colors. Using codes on the last three lines of Cell 04, we would see a color image just for the three 2D Gaussians. This model function will be used in model training to generate color images with thousands of Gaussians.

$$\Sigma = \begin{pmatrix} \sigma_x^2 & \rho\sigma_x\sigma_y \\ \rho\sigma_x\sigma_y & \sigma_y^2 \end{pmatrix} \qquad \Sigma^{-1} = \frac{1}{\sigma_x^2\sigma_y^2(1-\rho)} \begin{pmatrix} \sigma_y^2 & -\rho\sigma_x\sigma_y \\ -\rho\sigma_x\sigma_y & \sigma_x^2 \end{pmatrix} \qquad (12.9)$$

Codes in Cell 05 are used for model training. In the first 2000 epochs, model training speed is about 1.5 s per epoch. As more and more Gaussians are optimized for the synthesized image, the speed will be very slow. The program would be interrupted by an 'out of memory' issue. Or you can interrupt the program at any time if you find the program is very slow. Codes in Cell 05 save a check point for us in every 100 epochs if the number of Gaussians are more than 1000 in the output. By moving those three single quotation marks at the end of line 25 to the front of line 11 in Cell 02, we can train the model from a previous check point for the next 1000 epochs. At the time when we use the first check point, we need to change the *densification interval* parameter in Cell 01 to 100. Using a check point can accelerate model training speed. I tried to use float 16 to solve the 'out of memory' issue, but found the output image quality was poor. While 3D Gaussian splatting technique is still in its baby stage, its promise is undeniable in the domain of computer vision for 3D graphics. The original 3D Gaussian splatting can only handle static 3D scenes. Three months after Gaussian splatting was introduced, there are seven papers published with smart algorithms for animatable (Luiten *et al* 2023, Li *et al* 2023) 3D Gaussian splatting. SuGaR (Guédon and Lepetit 2023) is a novel method for efficient 3D mesh reconstruction and high-quality mesh rendering from 3D Gaussian splatting representations. SuGaR enables easy editing, sculpting, rigging, animating, compositing and relighting of the Gaussians using traditional software by manipulating the mesh instead of the Gaussians themselves. Retrieving such an editable mesh for realistic rendering is done within minutes with SuGaR, while providing a better rendering quality. There is no limit for human intelligence. We are in a great age to build a digital Babel tower in the virtual world, from which we would know how to use atoms to synthesize big molecules, to construct nano-robots, to grow human organs, and even to build human bodies with intelligence.

```
# project 12.3.1 Using 2D Gaussian Splatting to describe an image----------------
import os;os.environ['KMP_DUPLICATE_LIB_OK']='True' #solution of a matplotlib bug
from einops import rearrange, repeat, reduce
from kornia.losses import SSIMLoss
from skimage.io import imread, imshow; import time
import matplotlib.pyplot as plt
import numpy as np; from tqdm import trange; import gc
import torch; import torch.nn as nn; import torch.nn.functional as F
device = torch.device('cuda' if torch.cuda.is_available() else 'cpu')
PI = torch.tensor(np.pi, device=device) #PI=3.1415926
num_epochs = 1000
learning_rate = 0.01
kernel_size = 101           # for 2D Gaussian PDF space resolution (101, 101)
image_size = (256, 256, 3)  # input and output image resolution: (256, 256, 3)
primary_samples = 1000      # Initial 2D Gaussians number: 1000
backup_samples = 4000       # Rreserved for cloning and splitting 2D Gaussians
densification_interval = 200 # In every 300 epochs to clone and split Gaussians
display_interval = 100      # In every 100 epochs to display a generated image
grad_threshold = 0.002      # for the norm of gradient of Loss to pixel coods
gauss_threshold = 0.75      # for the norm of the 2D Gaussian sigmoids
num_samples = primary_samples + backup_samples  # total number of 2D Gaussians
PADDING = kernel_size // 2  # Padding 2D Gaussian PDF space to (256, 256)
width, height = image_size[:2]
image_file_name = 'd:/Squirrel.jpg'      # File path for a ground truth image
image_array = np.array(imread(image_file_name))/255 # Normalize pixel values
target_tensor = torch.tensor(image_array, dtype=torch.float32, device=device)
target = target_tensor.permute(2,0,1).unsqueeze(0) #Ground truth in loss function
plt.axis('off')
plt.imshow(target_tensor.cpu().numpy());    # Display the ground truth image

#Cell 02: Randomly generate (1000+4000) 2D Gaussians to prepare cloud points----
def give_required_data(input_coords):  #Normalize pixel coords' values  to [-1,1]
  coords = torch.tensor(input_coords / [width, height], device=device).float()
  coords_shifts = torch.tensor([0.5, 0.5], device=device).float()
  coords = (coords - coords_shifts) * 2.0  # normalize to [-1,1]
  # Fetching pixel colors of each coordinate
  color_values = [image_array[coord[1], coord[0]] for coord in input_coords]
  color_values_np = np.array(color_values)
  color_values_tensor = torch.tensor(color_values_np, device=device).float()
  return color_values_tensor, coords
# Initialization Parameters (coords.shape=[5000,2], 0 <= coords[0] <= 255) ------
coords = np.random.randint(0, [width, height], size=(num_samples, 2))  #--line 11
sigma_values = torch.rand(num_samples, 2, device=device)      # shape=[5000, 2]
rho_values = 2*torch.rand(num_samples, 1, device=device) - 1 # for covariances
alpha_values = torch.ones(num_samples, 1, device=device)  # pixel color density
color_values, pixel_coords = give_required_data(coords)
pixel_coords = torch.atanh(pixel_coords)   #---------------------------- line 16
weights = torch.cat([sigma_values, rho_values,
                     alpha_values, color_values, pixel_coords], dim=1)
W = nn.Parameter(weights) # parameters in W to be updated during model training
'''
checkpoint = torch.load('Gaussian2DSplatting.pth')  #----------line 21
primary_samples = checkpoint['primary_samples']
backup_samples = checkpoint['backup_samples']
output = checkpoint['output']
W = checkpoint['weights']                                  #------------line 25'''
```

```
starting_size = primary_samples # 1000 pixels are used for training at epoch=0
left_over_size = backup_samples # the rest 4000 pixels in W are set to zeros
persistent_mask = torch.cat([torch.ones(starting_size, dtype=bool), #--line 29
                            torch.zeros(left_over_size, dtype=bool)], dim=0)
current_marker = starting_size  # model training starting point
optimizer = torch.optim.Adam([W], lr=learning_rate) #update W in model training
ssim_loss = SSIMLoss(window_size=11, max_val=1.0)
l1_loss = nn.L1Loss()                    # torch.abs((network_output - gt)).mean()
mse_criterion = nn.MSELoss(reduction='sum')   # for psnr calculations
def combined_loss(pred, target):
    loss = l1_loss(pred, target) + ssim_loss(pred, target)
    return loss
# Cell 03: 2D Gaussian PDF Generator --------------------------------------------
def mesh_grid_generator(kernel_size, device):
    x = torch.linspace(-5,5, kernel_size, device=device)
    X, Y = torch.meshgrid((x,x), indexing='ij')
    xy = torch.stack([X, Y], dim=-1).unsqueeze(0)
    return X, Y, xy              # xy.shape = [1,101,101,2] X.shape=[101,101]
def gaussian2dPDFs(kernel_size, sigma_x, sigma_y, rho,
device=device):
    batch_size = colors.shape[0]
    sigma_x = sigma_x.view(batch_size, 1, 1)
    sigma_y = sigma_y.view(batch_size, 1, 1)
    rho = rho.view(batch_size, 1, 1)
    covariances = torch.stack(
        [torch.stack([sigma_x**2, rho*sigma_x*sigma_y], dim=-1),
         torch.stack([rho*sigma_x*sigma_y, sigma_y**2], dim=-1)],
        dim=-2)
    inv_covariances = torch.inverse(covariances)
    # construct a mesh grid in a square 2D probability space-------------------
    _, _, xy = mesh_grid_generator(kernel_size, device) # xy.shape=[1,101,101,2]
    # Calcualtions for 2D Gaussian PDFs for a batch of images------------------
    p = torch.einsum('b...i, b...ij, b...j -> b...',xy, -0.5*inv_covariances,xy)
    c = (2 * torch.tensor(np.pi, device=device) *
            torch.sqrt(torch.det(covariances)).view(batch_size, 1, 1))
    kernel = torch.exp(p) / c
    return kernel                        #Z.shape=[3, 101, 101]
# Plot two 2D Gaussian PDFs------------------------------------------------------
sigma_x = torch.tensor([2, 0.5, 0.5], device=device)
sigma_y = torch.tensor([2, 0.5, 1.5], device=device)
rho = torch.tensor([0.0, 0.0, -0.5], device=device)
mus = torch.tensor([(0, 0.0), (-0.5, -0.5), (0.5, 0.5)], device=device)
colors = torch.tensor([[(1.0, 0.0, 0.0),
                        (0.0, 1.0, 0.0),
                        (0.0, 0.0, 1.0)], device=device)
batch_size = len(rho)
Z = gaussian2dPDFs(kernel_size, sigma_x, sigma_y, rho, device=device)
fig, ax  = plt.subplots(1,batch_size, figsize=(10,6))
for i in range(batch_size):
```

```python
    ax[i].contourf(X.detach().cpu().numpy(),
                   Y.detach().cpu().numpy(),
                   Z[i].detach().cpu().numpy(), cmap='hsv')
    ax[i].set(xlabel='x', ylabel='y', xticks=np.arange(-5, 5, 1),
              yticks=np.arange(-5, 5, 1))
    ax[i].grid( color='g', linestyle=':'); ax[i].set_aspect('equal')
plt.show()
# Cell 04: 2D Gaussian Splatting Generator which is a model to be trained--------
def model(kernel_size, sigma_x, sigma_y, rho, coords,  # coords: Gaussian center
                colors, image_size=image_size, device=device):
    kernel = gaussian2dPDFs(kernel_size, sigma_x, sigma_y, rho,
device=device)
    max_eachChannel= reduce(kernel,'b h w->b','max').view(len(rho),1,1)
    Z = kernel/(max_eachChannel) #channel normalization
    kernel_rgb = repeat(Z, 'b h w->b c h w', c=3)
    # Padding to make the kernel size equal to the image size--------------------
    pad_h = image_size[0] - kernel_size
    pad_w = image_size[1] - kernel_size
    padding = (pad_w // 2, pad_w // 2 + pad_w % 2,  # padding left and right
               pad_h // 2, pad_h // 2 + pad_h % 2)  # padding top and bottom
    kernel_rgb_padded = F.pad(kernel_rgb, padding, "constant", 0)
    # Creating a mesh grid to transform images by shifting [tx, ty] ------------
    b, c, h, w = kernel_rgb_padded.shape    # Extracting shape information
    theta = torch.zeros(b, 2, 3, dtype=torch.float32, device=device)
    theta[:, 0, 0] = 1.0; theta[:, 1, 1] = 1.0;
    theta[:, :, 2] = coords       # Create 2D affine matrices from the coords
    grid = F.affine_grid(theta, size=(b, c, h, w), align_corners=True)
    kernel_rgb_padded_translated = F.grid_sample(kernel_rgb_padded,
                                                 grid, align_corners=True)
    # Colorize each 2D Gaussian splatting with alpha density
    rgb_values_reshaped = colors.unsqueeze(-1).unsqueeze(-1)
    final_image_layers = rgb_values_reshaped * kernel_rgb_padded_translated
    final_image = final_image_layers.sum(dim=0)
    final_image = torch.clamp(final_image, 0, 1)
    final_image = final_image.permute(1,2,0)
    return final_image                          #final_image.shape=[105, 105, 3]
final_image = model(kernel_size, sigma_x, sigma_y, rho, mus,
                    colors, image_size)
plt.imshow(final_image.detach().cpu().numpy());
# Cell 05: Upgrade parameters in W to use Gaussians to synthesize an image -----
for epoch in trange(num_epochs):
    if epoch % (densification_interval + 1) == 0 and epoch > 0:
      indices_to_remove=(torch.sigmoid(W[:,3]) < 0.01).nonzero(as_tuple=True)[0]
      if len(indices_to_remove) > 0:
        print(f"number of pruned points: {len(indices_to_remove)}")
      persistent_mask[indices_to_remove] = False
      W.data[~persistent_mask] = 0.0 # Zero-out parameters of transparent pixels
    gc.collect()
    torch.cuda.empty_cache()
    output = W[persistent_mask]
    batch_size = output.shape[0]
```

```python
sigma_x = torch.sigmoid(output[:, 0])
sigma_y = torch.sigmoid(output[:, 1])
rho = torch.tanh(output[:, 2])
alpha = torch.sigmoid(output[:, 3])
colors = torch.sigmoid(output[:, 4:7])
pixel_coords = torch.tanh(output[:, 7:9])    # ------------------------lin 17
colors_with_alpha = colors * alpha.view(batch_size, 1)
g_tensor_batch = model(kernel_size, sigma_x, sigma_y, rho,
                       pixel_coords, colors_with_alpha, image_size, device)
pred = g_tensor_batch.permute(2, 0, 1).unsqueeze(0)
loss = combined_loss(pred, target)
optimizer.zero_grad()
loss.backward()
# Apply zeroing out of gradients at every epoch
if persistent_mask is not None:
    W.grad.data[~persistent_mask] = 0.0
if epoch % densification_interval == 0 and epoch > 0:
  # Calculate gradient norms and gaussian norms for 2D Gaussian selections--
  gradient_norms = torch.norm(#gradient norm of loss to pixel coords-line 30
                      W.grad[persistent_mask][:,7:9],dim=1,p=2)
  gaussian_norms = torch.norm(      # Gaussian sigmoid norms---------line 32
                  torch.sigmoid(W.data[persistent_mask][:,0:2]), dim=1,p=2)
  sorted_grads, sorted_grads_indices = torch.sort(gradient_norms,
                                            descending=True)
  sorted_gauss, sorted_gauss_indices = torch.sort(gaussian_norms,
                                            descending=True)
  large_gradient_mask = (sorted_grads > grad_threshold) # 0.002 -----line 38
  large_gradient_indices = sorted_grads_indices[large_gradient_mask]
  large_gauss_mask = (sorted_gauss > gauss_threshold)   # 0.75 ------line 40
  large_gauss_indices = sorted_gauss_indices[large_gauss_mask]
  common_indices_mask = torch.isin(large_gradient_indices,
                            large_gauss_indices)
  common_indices = large_gradient_indices[common_indices_mask]    #--line 44
  distinct_indices = large_gradient_indices[~common_indices_mask] #--line 45
  # Split and descale Gaussians with big gradient_norms & big sigmoid norms
  if len(common_indices) > 0:
    print(f"number of splitted points: {len(common_indices)}")
    start_index = current_marker + 1
    end_index = current_marker + 1 + len(common_indices)
    persistent_mask[start_index: end_index] = True
    W.data[start_index:end_index, :] = W.data[common_indices, :]
    scale_reduction_factor = 1.6
    W.data[start_index:end_index, 0:2] /= scale_reduction_factor
    W.data[common_indices, 0:2] /= scale_reduction_factor
    current_marker = current_marker + len(common_indices)
  # Clone Gaussian with big gradient_norms and small sigmoid norms----------
  if len(distinct_indices) > 0:
    print(f"number of cloned points: {len(distinct_indices)}")
    start_index = current_marker + 1
    end_index = current_marker + 1 + len(distinct_indices)
    persistent_mask[start_index: end_index] = True
    W.data[start_index:end_index, :] = W.data[distinct_indices, :]
```

```
        current_marker = current_marker + len(common_indices)
    # Clone Gaussian with big gradient_norms and small sigmoid norms----------
    if len(distinct_indices) > 0:
        print(f"number of cloned points: {len(distinct_indices)}")
        start_index = current_marker + 1
        end_index = current_marker + 1 + len(distinct_indices)
        persistent_mask[start_index: end_index] = True
        W.data[start_index:end_index, :] = W.data[distinct_indices, :]
        current_marker = current_marker + len(distinct_indices)
    optimizer.step()
    # Display the genereated image and save a checkpoint for every 100 epochs---
    if epoch % display_interval == 0:
        if len(output) > 1000:
            train_results={'weights': W,'output': output,
                        'primary_samples': len(output),
                        'backup_samples': 5000-len(output)}
            torch.save(train_results, 'Gaussian2DSplatting.pth')
        fig, ax = plt.subplots(figsize=(12, 6))
        my_generated_img = g_tensor_batch.cpu().detach().numpy()
        ax.axis('off')
        plt.imshow(my_generated_img)
        plt.show(); plt.clf(); plt.close()
        print(f"Epoch {epoch+1}/{num_epochs}, Loss: {loss.item()}, \
            {len(output)} points",)
# Cell 06: Evaluation of model training results-----------------------------
batch_size = output.shape[0]              # Gaussians from model training
sigma_x = torch.sigmoid(output[:, 0])
sigma_y = torch.sigmoid(output[:, 1])
rho = torch.tanh(output[:, 2])
alpha = torch.sigmoid(output[:, 3])       # color densities
colors = torch.sigmoid(output[:, 4:7])
pixel_coords = torch.tanh(output[:, 7:9])
colors_with_alpha  = colors * alpha.view(batch_size, 1)
g_tensor_batch = model(kernel_size, sigma_x, sigma_y, rho,
                    pixel_coords, colors_with_alpha, image_size, device)
pred = g_tensor_batch.permute(2, 0, 1).unsqueeze(0)      #shape=[1, C, H, W]
l1_loss = l1_loss(pred, target); print('l1_loss:', l1_loss.item())
ssim_loss = ssim_loss(pred, target); print('ssim_loss:0', ssim_loss.item())
ssim = 1-2*ssim_loss; print('ssim:', ssim.item())
mse_loss = mse_criterion(pred, target)/(width*height)
psnr = -10*np.log10(mse_loss.item())
print('psnr:', psnr)
plt.axis('off'); plt.imshow(g_tensor_batch.cpu().detach().numpy());
#---------------------------------The End-----------------------------------
```

References

Guédon A and Lepetit V 2023 SuGaR: Surface-aligned Gaussian splatting for efficient 3D mesh reconstruction and high-quality mesh rendering *arXiv preprint* arXiv:2311.12775

Inkilä K 2005 Homogeneous least squares problem *Photogramm. J. Finland* **19** 34–42

Kerbl B, Kopanas G, Leimkühler T and Drettakis G 2023 3d Gaussian splatting for real-time radiance field rendering *ACM Trans. Graph. (ToG)* **42** 1–14

Li L, Shen Z, Wang Z, Shen L and Tan P 2022 Streaming radiance fields for 3d video synthesis *Adv. Neur. Inform. Process. Syst.* **35** 13485–98

Li Z, Zheng Z, Wang L and Liu Y 2023 Animatable Gaussians: learning pose-dependent Gaussian maps for high-fidelity human avatar modeling *arXiv preprint* arXiv:2311.16096

Luiten J, Kopanas G, Leibe B and Ramanan D 2023 Dynamic 3d Gaussians: tracking by persistent dynamic view synthesis *arXiv preprint* arXiv:2308.09713

Mildenhall B, Srinivasan P P, Tancik M, Barron J T, Ramamoorthi R and Ng R 2020 Nerf: Representing scenes as neural radiance fields for view synthesis *Commun. ACM* **65** 99–106

Müller T, Evans A, Schied C and Keller A 2022 Instant neural graphics primitives with a multiresolution hash encoding *ACM Trans. Graph. (ToG)* **41** 1–15

Ranftl R, Lasinger K, Hafner D, Schindler K and Koltun V 2020 Towards robust monocular depth estimation: mixing datasets for zero-shot cross-dataset transfer *IEEE Trans. Pattern Anal. Mach. Intell.* **44** 1623–37

Tancik M, Srinivasan P, Mildenhall B, Fridovich-Keil S, Raghavan N, Singhal U, Ramamoorthi R, Barron J and Ng R 2020 Fourier features let networks learn high frequency functions in low dimensional domains *Adv. Neur. Inform. Process. Syst.* **33** 7537–47

Wang Z, Bovik A C, Sheikh H R and Simoncelli E P 2004 Image quality assessment: from error visibility to structural similarity *IEEE Trans. Image Process.* **13** 600–12

IOP Publishing

Mastering Computer Vision with PyTorch and Machine Learning

Caide Xiao

Appendix

A Kullback–Leibler divergence of two multivariate normal distributions

$$p(X = x) = \prod_{i=1}^{k} \frac{1}{\sqrt{2\pi\sigma_i^2}} e^{-\frac{1}{2}\left(\frac{x_i - \mu_i}{\sigma_i}\right)^2} = \frac{1}{(2\pi)^{k/2} \mid \Sigma \mid^{1/2}} e^{-\frac{1}{2}(x-\mu)^T \Sigma^{-1}(x-\mu)}$$

$$q(X = x) = \frac{1}{(2\pi)^{k/2} \mid I \mid^{1/2}} e^{-\frac{1}{2}(x^T I^{-1} x)}$$

$$X = [x_1, x_2, \ldots, x_k]^T, \ \mu = [u_1, u_2, \ldots, u_k]^T, \ \mu_2 = [0, 0, \ldots, 0]^T$$

$$\Sigma = \begin{bmatrix} \sigma_1^2 & 0 & \ldots & 0 \\ 0 & \sigma_2^2 & \ldots & 0 \\ \cdots & \cdots & \cdots & \cdots \\ 0 & 0 & \ldots & \sigma_k^2 \end{bmatrix}, \ \Sigma^{-1} = \begin{bmatrix} \sigma_1^{-2} & 0 & \ldots & 0 \\ 0 & \sigma_2^{-2} & \ldots & 0 \\ \cdots & \cdots & \cdots & \cdots \\ 0 & 0 & \ldots & \sigma_k^{-2} \end{bmatrix}, \ \Sigma_2 = I = \begin{bmatrix} 1 & 0 & \ldots & 0 \\ 0 & 1 & \ldots & 0 \\ \cdots & \cdots & \cdots & \cdots \\ 0 & 0 & \ldots & 1 \end{bmatrix}$$

$$(x - \mu)^T \Sigma^{-1}(x - \mu) = [x_1 - \mu_1 \ \cdots \ x_k - \mu_k] \begin{bmatrix} \sigma_1^{-2} & 0 & \ldots & 0 \\ 0 & \sigma_2^{-2} & \ldots & 0 \\ \cdots & \cdots & \cdots & \cdots \\ 0 & 0 & \ldots & \sigma_k^{-2} \end{bmatrix} \begin{bmatrix} x_1 - \mu_1 \\ x_2 - \mu_2 \\ \cdots \\ x_k - \mu_k \end{bmatrix} = \sum_{i=1}^{k} \frac{(x_i - \mu_i)^2}{\sigma_i^2}$$

$$D_{KL}(p(X) \| q(X)) = \iiint_x p(x)[\ln p(x) - \ln q(x)] dx$$

$$= \iiint p(x) \left[\frac{1}{2} \ln \left(\frac{\mid \Sigma_2 \mid}{\mid \Sigma \mid} \right) + \frac{1}{2}(x - \mu_2)^T \Sigma_2^{-1}(x - \mu_2) - \frac{1}{2}(x - \mu)^T \Sigma^{-1}(x - \mu) \right] dx$$

$$= \iiint p(x)\left[\frac{1}{2}\ln\left(\frac{|I|}{|\Sigma|}\right) + \frac{1}{2}(x-0)^T I^{-1}(x-0) - \frac{1}{2}\sum_{i=1}^{k}\frac{(x_i - \mu_i)^2}{\sigma_i^2}\right]dx$$

$$= -\frac{1}{2}\ln(|\Sigma|) + \frac{1}{2}\iiint p(x)[x^T x]dx - \frac{1}{2}\iiint p(x)\sum_{i=1}^{k}\frac{(x_i - \mu_i)^2}{\sigma_i^2}dx$$

$$= -\frac{1}{2}\ln(|\Sigma|) + \frac{1}{2}\iiint p(x)(x_1^2 + x_2^2 + \ldots + x_k^2)dx - \frac{k}{2}$$

$$= -\frac{1}{2}\ln\left(\prod_{i=1}^{k}\sigma_i^2\right) + \frac{1}{2}\iiint \prod_{i=1}^{k} p_i(x_i)(x_1^2 + x_2^2 + \ldots + x_k^2)dx_1 dx_2 \ldots dx_k - \frac{k}{2}$$

$$= -\frac{1}{2}\sum_{i=1}^{k}\ln(\sigma_i^2) - \frac{k}{2} + \frac{1}{2}\iiint \prod_{i=1}^{k} p_i(x_i)(x_1^2 + x_2^2 + \ldots + x_k^2)dx_1 dx_2 \ldots dx_k$$

$$= -\frac{1}{2}\sum_{i=1}^{k}\ln(\sigma_i^2) - \frac{k}{2} + \frac{1}{2}\int p_1(x_1)x_1^2 dx_1 + \frac{1}{2}\int p_2(x_2)x_2^2 dx_2 + \ldots + \frac{1}{2}\int p_k(x_k)x_k^2 dx_k$$

$$= -\frac{1}{2}\sum_{i=1}^{k}\ln(\sigma_i^2) - \frac{1}{2}\sum_{i=1}^{k}1 + \frac{1}{2}\sum_{i=1}^{k}\left(\mu_i^2 + \sigma_i^2\right)$$

$$= \frac{1}{2}\sum_{i=1}^{k}[\mu_i^2 + \sigma_i^2 - \ln(\sigma_i^2) - 1]$$

B Expectation-maximization algorithm

$$L = -\ln(P(X)) = -\ln\prod_{j=1}^{n} p(x_j) = -\sum_{j=1}^{n}\ln\left(\sum_{i=1}^{3} p(x_j \mid z_i)p(z_i)\right)$$

$$\frac{\partial L}{\partial \mu_1} = -\frac{\partial}{\partial \mu_1}\sum_{j=1}^{n}\ln(p(x_j)) = -\sum_{j=1}^{n}\frac{1}{p(x_j)}\frac{\partial p(x_j)}{\partial \mu_1} = -\sum_{j=1}^{n}\frac{1}{p(x_j)}\frac{\partial}{\partial \mu_1}\sum_{i=1}^{3} p(x_j \mid z_i)p(z_i)$$

$$\frac{\partial L}{\partial \mu_1} = -\sum_{j=1}^{n}\frac{1}{p(x_j)}\frac{\partial}{\partial \mu_1}\sum_{i=1}^{3}\frac{1}{\sqrt{2\pi\sigma_i^2}}e^{-\frac{1}{2}\left(\frac{x_j - \mu_i}{\sigma_i}\right)^2}p(z_i) = -\sum_{j=1}^{n}\frac{1}{p(x_j)}\frac{p(z_1)}{\sqrt{2\pi\sigma_1^2}}e^{-\frac{1}{2}\left(\frac{x_j - \mu_1}{\sigma_1}\right)^2}\frac{x_j - \mu_1}{\sigma_1^2}$$

$$\frac{\partial L}{\partial \mu_1} = -\frac{1}{\sigma_1^2}\sum_{j=1}^{n}\frac{p(x_j, z_1)}{p(x_j)}(x_j - \mu_1) = -\frac{1}{\sigma_1^2}\sum_{j=1}^{n}p(z_1 \mid x_j)(x_j - \mu_1) = 0$$

$$\mu_1 = \frac{\sum_{j=1}^{n} x_j p(z_1 \mid x_j)}{\sum_{j=1}^{n} p(z_1 \mid x_j)}$$

$$\mu_i = \frac{\sum_{j=1}^{n} x_j p(z_i \mid x_j)}{\sum_{j=1}^{n} p(z_i \mid x_j)}$$

$$\frac{\partial L}{\partial v_1} = -\frac{\partial}{\partial v_1} \sum_{j=1}^{n} \ln\left(p(x_j)\right) = -\sum_{j=1}^{n} \frac{1}{p(x_j)} \frac{\partial p(x_j)}{\partial v_1} = -\sum_{j=1}^{n} \frac{1}{p(x_j)} \frac{\partial}{\partial v_1} \sum_{i=1}^{3} p(x_j \mid z_i) p(z_i)$$

$$\frac{\partial L}{\partial v_1} = -\sum_{j=1}^{n} \frac{1}{p(x_j)} \frac{\partial}{\partial v_1} \sum_{i=1}^{3} \frac{1}{\sqrt{2\pi v_i}} e^{-\frac{1}{2v_i}(x_j - \mu_i)^2} p(z_i) = -\sum_{j=1}^{n} \frac{1}{p(x_j)} \frac{\partial}{\partial v_1} \left(\frac{1}{\sqrt{2\pi v_1}} e^{-\frac{1}{2v_1}(x_j - \mu_1)^2} \right) p(z_1)$$

$$\frac{\partial L}{\partial v_1} = -\sum_{j=1}^{n} \frac{p(z_1)}{p(x_j)} \left[\frac{-1}{2v_1^{3/2}\sqrt{2\pi}} e^{-\frac{1}{2v_1}(x_j - \mu_1)^2} + \frac{1}{\sqrt{2\pi v_1}} e^{-\frac{1}{2v_1}(x_j - \mu_1)^2} \frac{1}{2v_1^2}(x_j - \mu_1)^2 \right]$$

$$\frac{\partial L}{\partial v_1} = -\sum_{j=1}^{n} \frac{p(z_1)}{p(x_j)} \left[\frac{-1}{2v_1} p(x_j \mid z_1) + p(x_j \mid z_1) \frac{1}{2v_1^2}(x_j - \mu_1)^2 \right]$$

$$\frac{\partial L}{\partial v_1} = -\sum_{j=1}^{n} \frac{p(x_j \mid z_1)p(z_1)}{p(x_j)} \left[\frac{-1}{2v_1} + \frac{1}{2v_1^2}(x_j - \mu_1)^2 \right]$$

$$\frac{\partial L}{\partial v_1} = \frac{-1}{2v_1^2} \sum_{j=1}^{n} p(z_1 \mid x_j) \left[v_1 - (x_j - \mu_1)^2 \right] = 0$$

$$v_1 = \sigma_1^2 = \frac{\sum_{j=1}^{n} (x_j - \mu_1)^2 p(z_1 \mid x_j)}{\sum_{j=1}^{n} p(z_1 \mid x_j)}$$

$$v_i = \sigma_i^2 = \frac{\sum_{j=1}^{n} (x_j - \mu_i)^2 p(z_i \mid x_j)}{\sum_{j=1}^{n} p(z_i \mid x_j)}$$

$$\frac{\partial L}{\partial p(z_1)} = -\frac{\partial}{\partial p(z_1)}\sum_{j=1}^{n}\ln\left(p(x_j)\right) = -\sum_{j=1}^{n}\frac{1}{p(x_j)}\frac{\partial p(x_j)}{\partial p(z_1)}$$

$$p(z_3) = 1 - p(z_1) - p(z_2)$$

$$\frac{\partial L}{\partial p(z_1)} = -\sum_{j=1}^{n}\frac{1}{p(x_j)}\frac{\partial}{\partial p(z_1)}\sum_{i=1}^{3}p(x_j\mid z_i)p(z_i) = -\sum_{j=1}^{n}\frac{1}{p(x_j)}\left[p(x_j\mid z_1) - p(x_j\mid z_3)\right] = 0$$

$$\frac{\partial L}{\partial p(z_1)} = -\sum_{j=1}^{n}\left[\frac{p(z_1)}{p(x_j)}\frac{p(x_j\mid z_1)}{p(z_1)} - \frac{p(z_3)}{p(x_j)}\frac{p(x_j\mid z_3)}{p(z_3)}\right]$$

$$\frac{\partial L}{\partial p(z_1)} = -\sum_{j=1}^{n}\left[\frac{p(z_1\mid x_j)}{p(z_1)} - \frac{p(z_3\mid x_j)}{p(z_3)}\right]$$

$$\frac{\partial L}{\partial p(z_1)} = -\frac{1}{p(z_1)}\sum_{j=1}^{n}p(z_1\mid x_j) + \frac{1}{p(z_3)}\sum_{j=1}^{n}p(z_3\mid x_j) = 0$$

$$p(z_1) = p(z_3)\frac{\sum_{j=1}^{n}p(z_1\mid x_j)}{\sum_{j=1}^{n}p(z_3\mid x_j)}$$

$$p(z_2) = p(z_3)\frac{\sum_{j=1}^{n}p(z_2\mid x_j)}{\sum_{j=1}^{n}p(z_3\mid x_j)}$$

$$p(z_3)\frac{p(z_1)}{\sum_{j=1}^{n}p(z_3\mid x_j)} + p(z_3)\frac{p(z_2)}{\sum_{j=1}^{n}p(z_3\mid x_j)} + p(z_3) = 1$$

$$p(z_3)\frac{1}{\sum_{j=1}^{n}p(z_3\mid x_j)}\left[\sum_{j=1}^{n}p(z_1\mid x_j) + \sum_{j=1}^{n}p(z_2\mid x_j) + \sum_{j=1}^{n}p(z_3\mid x_j)\right] = 1$$

$$p(z_3)\frac{1}{\sum_{j=1}^{n}p(z_3\mid x_j)}\sum_{j=1}^{n}\sum_{i=1}^{3}p(z_i\mid x_j) = p(z_3)\frac{1}{\sum_{j=1}^{n}p(z_3\mid x_j)}\sum_{j=1}^{n}1 = 1$$

$$p(z_3) = \frac{1}{n}\sum_{j=1}^{n} p(z_3 \mid x_j)$$

$$p(z_2) = \frac{1}{n}\sum_{j=1}^{n} p(z_2 \mid x_j)$$

$$p(z_1) = \frac{1}{n}\sum_{j=1}^{n} p(z_1 \mid x_j)$$

C Gradients of MSE loss function to weights in a linear regression

$$\begin{bmatrix} 1 & x_{0,1} & \cdots & x_{0,m} \\ 1 & x_{1,1} & \cdots & x_{1,m} \\ \cdots & \cdots & \cdots & \cdots \\ 1 & x_{n,1} & \cdots & x_{n,m} \end{bmatrix} \cdot \begin{bmatrix} w_0 \\ w_1 \\ \cdots \\ w_m \end{bmatrix} = \begin{bmatrix} \hat{y}_0 \\ \hat{y}_1 \\ \cdots \\ \hat{y}_n \end{bmatrix}, \; Y = \begin{bmatrix} y_0 \\ y_1 \\ \cdots \\ y_n \end{bmatrix}, \; (i = 0,1\ldots n, j = 0,1\ldots m)$$

Model: $X \cdot w = \hat{Y}$

Model prediction: $\hat{y}_i = \sum_{j=0}^{m} x_{i,j} w_j$

Loss function: $L(X, w) = \frac{1}{(n+1)}\sum_{i=0}^{n}(\hat{y}_i - y_i)^2$

$$J_{i,j} = \frac{\partial \hat{y}_i}{\partial w_j} = \frac{\partial}{\partial w_j}\sum_{k=0}^{m} x_{i,k} w_k = x_{i,j}$$

$$\nabla L(X, w) = \left(\frac{\partial L}{\partial w_0}, \frac{\partial L}{\partial w_1}, \ldots, \frac{\partial L}{\partial w_m} \right)^T$$

$$\frac{\partial L}{\partial w_j} = \frac{\partial}{\partial w_j}\frac{1}{(n+1)}\sum_{i=0}^{n}(\hat{y}_i - y_i)^2 = \frac{2}{(n+1)}\sum_{i=0}^{n}(\hat{y}_i - y_i)\frac{\partial \hat{y}_i}{\partial w_j} = \frac{2}{(n+1)}\sum_{i=0}^{n}x_{i,j}(\hat{y}_i - y_i)$$

$$\begin{bmatrix} \frac{\partial L}{\partial w_0} \\ \frac{\partial L}{\partial w_1} \\ \cdots \\ \frac{\partial L}{\partial w_m} \end{bmatrix} = \frac{2}{n+1}\begin{bmatrix} 1 & 1 & \cdots & 1 \\ x_{0,1} & x_{1,1} & \cdots & x_{n,1} \\ \cdots & \cdots & \cdots & \cdots \\ x_{0,m} & x_{1,m} & \cdots & x_{n,m} \end{bmatrix} \cdot \begin{bmatrix} \hat{y}_0 - y_0 \\ \hat{y}_1 - y_1 \\ \cdots \\ \hat{y}_n - y_n \end{bmatrix}$$

$$\nabla L(X, w) = \frac{2}{n+1}X^T \cdot (\hat{Y} - Y)$$

D Application of a VAE-GAN to generate fake Anime-faces dataset images

```
# Project 4.5.1 Cell 01: Libraries and hyperparameters-------------------Cell 01
import torch; import torch.nn as nn; from torch.utils.data import DataLoader
from torchvision.utils import make_grid; import torchvision.transforms as T
from torchvision.datasets import ImageFolder; from tqdm import trange
import pandas as pd; import numpy as np; import matplotlib.pyplot as plt
n_epochs = 25    # model training time ~210 min
batch_size = 64
img_channels = 3
img_size = 64
img_dim = img_size * img_size
z_dim = 128
lr = 1e-4
alpha = 10            # D_lr = alpha*lr
data_path = './OCR/data/AnimeFaces'
# Cell 02: Anime-faces Dataset-------------------------------------------Cell 02
train_dataset = ImageFolder(data_path,
          transform=T.Compose([T.Resize(img_size),
                          T.CenterCrop(img_size),
                          T.ToTensor(),
                          T.Normalize([0.5]*3, [0.5, 0.5, 0.5])]))
n_samples = len(train_dataset) #n_sample=63566
# Cell 03: Dataloader----------------------------------------------------Cell 03
train_dataloader = DataLoader(train_dataset, batch_size=batch_size,
                          shuffle=True, num_workers=2, pin_memory=True)
n_batch = len(train_dataloader) #n_batch=994
for imgs, _ in train_dataloader:
    print("imgs_batch.shape=", imgs.shape)
    break
# Cell 04: Show images of in the 1st the batch of train_dataloader--------Cell 04
def denorm(img_tensors):
    return img_tensors*0.5 + 0.5
def show_imgs(images):
    fig, ax = plt.subplots(figsize=(16,12))
    input = make_grid(denorm(images[:42]), nrow=14)
    ax.imshow(input.permute(1,2,0))
    ax.set(xticks=[], yticks=[])
    plt.show()
show_imgs(imgs)
# Cell 05: Model parameters initialization ------------------------------Cell 05
def weights_init(m):
    if(type(m) == nn.ConvTranspose2d or type(m) == nn.Conv2d):
        nn.init.normal_(m.weight.data, 0.0, 0.02)
    elif(type(m) == nn.BatchNorm2d):
        nn.init.normal_(m.weight.data, 1.0, 0.02)
        nn.init.constant_(m.bias.data, 0)
# Cell 06: Encoder Class----------------------------------------Model Q------Cell 06
def conBL(in_channels, out_channels, f=4, s=2, p=1):
    return nn.Sequential(
            nn.Conv2d(in_channels, out_channels,
                    kernel_size=f, stride=s, padding=p, bias=False),
            nn.BatchNorm2d(out_channels),
            nn.LeakyReLU(0.2, inplace=True))
```

```python
class Encoder(nn.Module):
    def __init__(self):
        super().__init__()
        self.net = nn.Sequential(
            conBL(img_channels, 64, 4, 2, 1),  #shape=batch_size x 64 x 32^2
            conBL(64, 128, 4, 2, 1),           #shape=batch_size x 128 x 16^2
            conBL(128, 256, 4, 2, 1),          #shape=batch_size x 256 x 8^2
            conBL(256, 512, 4, 2, 1))  #layer 04 shape=batch_size x 512 x 4^2
        self.mu = nn.Conv2d(512, z_dim, 4, 1, 0, bias=False)
        self.logvar = nn.Conv2d(512, z_dim, 4, 1, 0, bias=False)
    def forward(self, images):              #images.shape=batch_size x 3 x 64^2
        output = self.net(images)           #output.shape=batch_size x 512 x 4^2
        mu = self.mu(output).squeeze()          #mu.shape=batch_size x z_dim
        logvar = self.logvar(output).squeeze()  #logvar.shape=batch_size x z_dim
        std = torch.exp(0.5*logvar)         #std.shape=batch_size x z_dim
        z = (mu + std*torch.randn_like(std))      #rand_like(std): ~N(0, I)
        return z, mu, logvar
Q = Encoder().cuda()
Q.apply(weights_init)
# Cell 07: Definition of an image discriminator class-------Model D-------Cell 07
class Discriminator(nn.Module):
    def __init__(self):
        super().__init__()
        self.net = nn.Sequential(
            nn.Conv2d(img_channels, 32, 4, 2, 1),
            nn.LeakyReLU(0.2, inplace=True),    # shape=batch_size x 32 x 32^2
            conBL(32, 64, 4, 2, 1),             # shape=batch_size x 64 x 16^2
            conBL(64, 128, 4, 2, 1),            # shape=batch_size x 128 x 8^2
            conBL(128, 256, 4, 2, 1),           # shape=batch_size x 128 x 4^2
            conBL(256, 512, 4, 2, 1)) #layer 05 shape=batch_size x 512 x 2^2
        self.scalar = nn.Sequential(nn.Conv2d(512, 1, 2, 1, 0),
            nn.Flatten(),
            nn.Sigmoid())               # layer 06 output.shape=batch_size x 1
    def forward(self, images):          #images.shape = batch_size x 3 x 64^2
        output = self.net(images)       #output.shape = batch_size x 512 x 2^2
        scalars = self.scalar(output)   #scalars.shape = batch_size x 1
        return scalars, output.view(-1, 512*2*2)
D = Discriminator().cuda()
D.apply(weights_init)
# Cell 08: Decoder Class----------------------------------Model P------Cell 08
def basic_P(in_channels, out_channels, p=1):
    return nn.Sequential(
        nn.ConvTranspose2d(in_channels, out_channels, 4, 2, padding=p,
bias=False),
        nn.BatchNorm2d(out_channels),
        nn.ReLU(True))
class Decoder(nn.Module):
    def __init__(self):
        super().__init__()
        self.net = nn.Sequential(
            basic_P(z_dim, 512, p=0),           #shape = batch_size x 512 x 4^2
            basic_P(512, 256),                  #shape = batch_size x 256 x 8^2
```

```
            basic_P(256, 128, p=1),              #shape = batch_size x 128 x 16^2
            basic_P(128, 64, p=1),               #shape = batch_size x 64 x 32^2
            nn.ConvTranspose2d(64, img_channels, 4, 2, 1),
            nn.Tanh())          #layer 05 output.shape = batch_size x 3 x 64^2
    def forward(self, z):
        input = z.view(-1, z_dim, 1, 1)      #z.shape=batch_size x z_dim
        output = self.net(input)          #input.shape=batch_size x z_dim x 1^2
        return output                #output.shape=batch_size x 3 x 64^2
P = Decoder().cuda()
P.apply(weights_init)
# Cell 09: Criterion and optimizers----------------------------------------Cell 09
criterion=nn.BCELoss(reduction='sum') # 'sum' is better than 'mean', for Model D
loss = nn.MSELoss(reduction='sum')     # for Model Q and P
optimizer_Q=torch.optim.RMSprop(Q.parameters(), lr=lr) #RMSprop Adam
optimizer_P=torch.optim.RMSprop(P.parameters(), lr=lr)
optimizer_D=torch.optim.RMSprop(D.parameters(), lr=alpha*lr)
# Cell 10: Loss functions-----------------------------------------------------Cell 10
def loss_gan(inputs, z):                #GAN loss
    batch_size = inputs.shape[0]
    preds_real = D(inputs)[0]
    one_targets = torch.ones(batch_size, 1, device='cuda')
    loss_real = criterion(preds_real, one_targets) #BCELoss for real images
    pred_fake = D(P(z))[0]
    zero_targets = torch.zeros(batch_size, 1, device='cuda')
    loss_fake = criterion(pred_fake, zero_targets) #BCELoss for fake images
    z_p = torch.randn(batch_size, z_dim, device='cuda')
    x_p =D(P(z_p))[0]
    loss_noises = criterion(x_p, zero_targets)     #BCELoss for noise z_p
    loss_gan = loss_real + loss_fake + loss_noises
    return loss_gan
def loss_rec(inputs, z):                #Reconstruction loss
    pixel_real = D(inputs)[1]
    pixel_fake = D(P(z))[1]
    #rec_loss =((pixel_real - pixel_fake)**2).sum()
    rec_loss = 0.5*loss(pixel_real, pixel_fake)
    return rec_loss
# Cell 11: Definition of a fitting function---------------------------Cell 11
def fit(epochs):
    torch.cuda.empty_cache()
    # The DataFrame df is a recorder of the training history
    df = pd.DataFrame(np.empty([epochs, 3]),
                    index = np.arange(epochs),
                    columns=['D_loss', 'P_loss', 'Q_loss'])
    for i in trange(epochs):                #tqdm's trange is for progressing bar
        loss_q = 0.0; loss_d = 0.0; loss_p = 0.0
        for real_images, _ in train_dataloader:
            inputs = real_images.cuda()
            z, mu, logvar = Q(inputs)
            D_loss = loss_gan(inputs, z)     #---- Discriminator Loss
            loss_d += D_loss.item()
            optimizer_D.zero_grad()
            D_loss.backward(retain_graph=True)
    optimizer_D.step() #--------------------Training for model D
```

```
            D_loss = loss_gan(inputs, z)
            rec_loss =loss_rec(inputs, z)
            P_loss = rec_loss - D_loss        # ----------Decoder Loss
            loss_p += P_loss.item()
            optimizer_P.zero_grad()
            P_loss.backward(retain_graph=True)
            optimizer_P.step() #--------------------Training for model P

            Dkl = mu.pow(2) + logvar.exp()- logvar - 1
            prior_loss = torch.mean(Dkl)
            rec_loss =loss_rec(inputs, z)
            Q_loss =  rec_loss + prior_loss # --Encoder Loss
            loss_q += Q_loss.item()
            optimizer_Q.zero_grad()
            Q_loss.backward(retain_graph=True)
            optimizer_Q.step() #--------------------Training for model Q

        df.iloc[i, 0] = loss_d/n_samples
        df.iloc[i, 1] = loss_p/n_samples
        df.iloc[i, 2] = loss_q/n_samples
        if i==0 or (i+1)%5==0:
            print('Dkl=', prior_loss.item())
            print(
                "Epoch={}, D_loss: {:.4f}, loss_P: {:.4f}, loss_Q: {:.4f}"
                .format(i+1, df.iloc[i,0], df.iloc[i,1], df.iloc[i,2]))
            show_imgs(real_images)
            fake_images = P(z)
            show_imgs(fake_images.detach().cpu())
    return df
train_history = fit(n_epochs)
# Cell 12: Show the training history-------------------------------------Cell 12
df = train_history[1:].copy()
df.iloc[:,0] =100*df.iloc[:,0]
fig, ax = plt.subplots(figsize=(4.5,3))
#history.plot(ax=ax, style=['-','-', '+'], color=['r','b','g'])
df.columns=['100*D_loss', 'P_loss', 'Q_loss']
df.plot(ax=ax, style=['-','-', '+'], color=['r','b','g'])
ax.grid(which='major', axis='both', color='g', linestyle=':')
ax.set(xlabel='epoch')#, ylim=[0, 800])
plt.show()
# Cell 13: Show 14x3 Real images and a14x3 fake images------------------Cell 13
z, mu, logvar = Q(imgs.cuda())
show_imgs(imgs)
fake_images = P(z)
show_imgs(fake_images.detach().cpu())
#-----------------------------------------------------------------------The End
```

E Applications of a cWGAN-GP system to MNIST or fashion MNIST

```
# Project 5.4.2 WGAN-GP for FashionMNIST ==============================Cell 01
import torch; import torch.nn as nn; from torch.utils.data import DataLoader
from torchvision import transforms as T; from torchvision.utils import make_grid
from torchvision.datasets import FashionMNIST; from tqdm import trange
import numpy as np; import pandas as pd; import matplotlib.pyplot as plt
n_epochs = 30
batch_size = 100
latent_size = 100
z_dim = 126          # Dimensions of the latent space
lr = 3e-4            # Learning rate in cell 08  lr = 1e-4
lamda_gp = 10
n_critic = 1
fixed_latent = torch.randn(batch_size, z_dim).cuda() # Get a batch of noises
#Generate fake_labels: [0,0,0,0,0,0,0,0,0,1, ..., 8,9,9,9,9,9,9,9,9,9]
fixed_labels = torch.LongTensor([i for i in range(10) for j in range(10)]).cuda()
# Cell 02: MNIST of Fashion DataSet -----------------------------------Cell 02
path = './OCR/data/' #path = 'D:/ImageSets'
train_Dataset = FashionMNIST(path, train=True, download=False,
            transform=T.Compose([T.ToTensor(),
T.Normalize([0.5],[0.5])]))
test_dataset = FashionMNIST(data_path, train=False, download=False,
            transform=T.Compose([T.ToTensor(), T.Normalize([0.5],[0.5])]))
n_samples = len(train_Dataset) #len(trainData)=60000
# Cell 03: Create a DataLoader (train_dataloader)----------------------Cell 03
train_dataloader = DataLoader(train_Dataset, batch_size=batch_size, shuffle=True)
test_dataloader=DataLoader(test_dataset, batch_size=batch_size, shuffle=False)
n_batch = len(train_dataloader) #n_batch=n_sample/batch_size=600
# Cell 04: Show the images in a batch of the train dataloader----------Cell 04
for imgs, labels in train_dataloader: # for the 1st batch on the train dataloader
    print('imgs_batch.shape=', imgs.shape)
    #print('labels=', labels[:40])
    break
def denorm(img_tensors):         # Shift the value of each image pixel to [0,1]
    return img_tensors * 0.5 + 0.5
def show_imgs(imgs):
    fig, ax = plt.subplots(figsize=(12,8))
    input = make_grid(denorm(imgs), nrow=20, padding=2)
    ax.imshow(input.permute(1,2,0), cmap='gray')
    ax.set(xticks=[], yticks=[])
    plt.show()
show_imgs(imgs)
# Cell 05: Model parameters initialization ---------------------------Cell 05
def weights_init(m):
    if(type(m) == nn.ConvTranspose2d or type(m) == nn.Conv2d):
        nn.init.normal_(m.weight.data, 0.0, 0.02)
    elif(type(m) == nn.BatchNorm2d):
        nn.init.normal_(m.weight.data, 1.0, 0.02)
        nn.init.constant_(m.bias.data, 0)
# Cell 06: Image discriminator Class with labels
```

```
class Discriminator(nn.Module):
    def __init__(self):
        super().__init__()
        self.model = nn.Sequential(# input.shape = batch_size x2x 28^2
            nn.Conv2d(2, 64, kernel_size=4, stride=2, padding=1),
            nn.LeakyReLU(0.2, inplace=True),
            # layer 01 output.shape = batch_size x 64 x 14^2
            nn.Conv2d(64, 128, kernel_size=4, stride=2, padding=2, bias=False),
            nn.BatchNorm2d(128),
            nn.LeakyReLU(0.2, inplace=True),
            # layer 02 output.shape = batch_size x 128 x 8^2
            nn.Conv2d(128, 256, kernel_size=4, stride=2, padding=1, bias=False),
            nn.BatchNorm2d(256),
            nn.LeakyReLU(0.2, inplace=True),
            # layer 03 output.shape = batch_size x 256 x 4^2
            nn.Conv2d(256, 1, kernel_size=4, stride=1, padding=0),
            nn.Flatten()
        )   # layer 04 output.shape = batch_size x 1
        self.label_emb = nn.Embedding(10, 784)
        # Encode a batch of labels as an extra channel of images
    def forward(self, imgs, labels):
        x = imgs.view(imgs.shape[0], 784)  # x.shape= batch_size x 784
        c = self.label_emb(labels)             # c.shape= batch_size x 784
        imgs_labels = torch.cat([x, c], dim=1)
        input = imgs_labels.view(c.shape[0], 2, 28, 28)
        out = self.model(input)   #input.shape = batch_size x 2 x 28^2
        return out                #output.shape = batch_size x 1
D = Discriminator().cuda()
D.apply(weights_init)
# Cell 07: Image Generator Class with label information---------------Cell 07
class Generator(nn.Module):
    def __init__(self):
        super().__init__()

        self.model = nn.Sequential(    # input.shape=batch_size x 110 x 1 x 1
            nn.ConvTranspose2d(z_dim+10, 256,
                    kernel_size=4, stride=1, padding=0, bias=False),
            nn.BatchNorm2d(256),
            nn.ReLU(True),
            # Layer 01 output.shape = batch_size x 256 x 4^2
            nn.ConvTranspose2d(256, 128,
                    kernel_size=3, stride=2, padding=1, bias=False),
            nn.BatchNorm2d(128),
            nn.ReLU(True),
            # Layer 02 output.shape = batch_size x 128 x 7^2
            nn.ConvTranspose2d(128, 64,
                    kernel_size=4, stride=2, padding=1, bias=False),
            nn.BatchNorm2d(64),
            nn.ReLU(True),
            # Layer 03 output.shape = batch_size x 64 x 14^2
            nn.ConvTranspose2d(64, 1,
                    kernel_size=4, stride=2, padding=1),
```

A-11

```
            nn.Tanh()
        )    # Layer 04 output.shape = batch_size x 1 x 28^2
        self.label_emb = nn.Embedding(10, 10)
        # Encode each label in a batch into 10 trainable random numbers
    def forward(self, z, labels): # z is a batch of noises for fake images
        z = z.view(z.shape[0], z_dim)   # z.shape = batch_size x z_dim
        c = self.label_emb(labels)      # c.shape = batch_size x 10
        z_c = torch.cat([z, c], dim=1)  # z_c.shape = batch_size x 110
        input = z_c.view(z.shape[0], z_dim+10, 1, 1)
        out = self.model(input) #input.shape = batch_size x 110 x 1^2
        return out              #  out.shape = batch_size x 1 x 28^2
G = Generator().cuda()
G.apply(weights_init)
# Cell 08: Choose optimizers
optimizer_D = torch.optim.Adam(D.parameters(), lr=lr, betas=(0.5, 0.999))
optimizer_G = torch.optim.Adam(G.parameters(), lr=lr, betas=(0.5, 0.999))
# Cell 09 Gradient-penalty function-----------------------------------cell 09
def gradient_penalty(D, real_data, fake_data, fake_labels):
    batch_size = real_data.size(0)     #real_data.shape = batch_size x 1 x 28^2
    eps = torch.rand(batch_size, 1, 1, 1).cuda() #eps.shape=batch_size x 1 x 1^2
    eps = eps.expand_as(real_data)            #eps.shape=batch_size x 1 x 28^2
    # Sample Epsilon from a uniform distribution
    interpolation = eps * real_data + (1 - eps) * fake_data
    # Interpolation of real data and fake data,    shape = batch_size x 1 x 28^2
    interp_logits = D(interpolation, fake_labels)
    # get logits for interpolated images
    gradients = torch.autograd.grad(
        outputs=interp_logits,
        inputs=interpolation,
        grad_outputs=torch.ones_like(interp_logits),
        create_graph=True,
        retain_graph=True,
    )[0]    # Compute Gradients
    # Compute and return Gradient Norm
    gradients = gradients.view(batch_size, -1)
    grad_norm = gradients.norm(2, dim=1) #----dim=1
    gradient_penalty = torch.mean((grad_norm - 1) ** 2)
    return gradient_penalty
# Cell 10: Definition of a train function for the discriminator
def train_D(inputs, labels, optimizer_D):
    for _ in range(n_critic):
        #for parm in D.parameters():
        #        parm.data.clamp_(-0.01, 0.01)
        real_preds = D(inputs, labels)  #input.shape=batch_size x 1 x 28^2
        real_score = torch.mean(real_preds)

        # create fake images and labels with random numbers
        latent = torch.randn(inputs.shape[0], z_dim).cuda()
        fake_labels = torch.LongTensor(
                torch.randint(0, 10, (inputs.shape[0],))).cuda()
        fake_images = G(latent, fake_labels)
        fake_preds = D(fake_images.detach(), fake_labels.detach())
        fake_score = torch.mean(fake_preds)
        # Train the optimizer_D with real_loss and fake_loss
        gp = gradient_penalty(D, inputs, fake_images, fake_labels)
        loss = fake_score - real_score + lamda_gp*gp   #lamda_gp=10
        optimizer_D.zero_grad()
        loss.backward()
        optimizer_D.step()
    return loss.item(), real_score.item(), fake_score.item()
```

```python
# Cell 11: Train the generator to fool the discriminator
def train_G(optimizer_G):
    # Create fake images and labels
    latent = torch.randn(batch_size, z_dim).cuda()
    fake_labels = torch.LongTensor(
        torch.randint(0, 10, (batch_size,))).cuda()
    fake_images = G(latent, fake_labels)

    # Try to fool the discriminator
    preds = D(fake_images, fake_labels)
    loss = -torch.mean(preds)
    optimizer_G.zero_grad()
    loss.backward()
    optimizer_G.step()
    return loss.item()
# Cell 12: Definition of a fitting function to train D&G
def fit(epochs):
    torch.cuda.empty_cache()
    # The DataFrame df is a recorder of the training history
    df = pd.DataFrame(np.empty([epochs, 4]),
        index = np.arange(epochs),
        columns=['Loss_G', 'Loss_D',
                'D(X)', 'D(G(Z))'])
    for i in trange(epochs):
        loss_G = 0.0; loss_D = 0.0; real_sc = 0.0; fake_sc = 0.0
        for real_images, labels in train_dataloader:
            inputs = real_images.cuda()
            labels = labels.cuda()
            loss_d, real_score, fake_score = train_D(inputs, labels, optimizer_D)
            loss_D += loss_d; real_sc += real_score; fake_sc += fake_score
            loss_g = train_G(optimizer_G)
            loss_G += loss_g
        # Record losses & scores
        df.iloc[i, 0] = loss_G/n_batch
        df.iloc[i, 1] = loss_D/n_batch
        df.iloc[i, 2] = real_sc/n_batch
        df.iloc[i, 3] = fake_sc/n_batch

        if i==0 or (i+1)%2==0:
            print(
            "Epoch={:2}, Ls_G={:.2f}, Ls_D={:.2f}, D(X)={:.2f}, D(G(Z))={:.2f}"
            .format(i+1, df.iloc[i,0], df.iloc[i,1], df.iloc[i,2], df.iloc[i,3]))
            fake_images = G(fixed_latent, fixed_labels)
            show_imgs(fake_images.detach().cpu())
    return df
history = fit(n_epochs)
# Cell 13: Show the training history----------------------------------Cell 13
df = history
fig, ax = plt.subplots(1,2, figsize=(9,4), sharex=True)
df.plot(ax=ax[0], y=[0,1], style=['r-', 'b-+'])
gp = df.iloc[:,1] - df.iloc[:,3] + df.iloc[:,2]
ax[0].plot(10*gp, label='10*Gradient Penalty', color='k', linestyle=':')
ax[0].set(ylabel='loss')
ax[0].legend()

df.plot(ax=ax[1], y=[2,3], style=['r-+', 'b-'])
for i in range(2):
    ax[i].grid(which='major', axis='both', color='g', linestyle=':')
    ax[i].set(xlabel='epoch')
plt.show()
# -------------------------------The End----------------------------------
```

F Four applications of pre-trained Detectron2 models

```
# Appendix C: Using Detectron2 for object detection=====================Cell 01
import torch
from detectron2 import model_zoo
from detectron2.config import get_cfg
from detectron2.data import MetadataCatalog
from detectron2.engine import DefaultPredictor
from detectron2.utils.visualizer import Visualizer
import cv2; import glob; import time; from tqdm import tqdm
import matplotlib.pyplot as plt; import matplotlib.image as mpimg; import os
# Cell 02-1: Pre-trained object detection model===use either of one Cell 02======
cfg = get_cfg()
cfg_file = "../detectron2/configs/COCO-Detection/faster_rcnn_R_101_FPN_3x.yaml"
weights_file = os.path.join('detectron2://COCO-Detection/' +
                'faster_rcnn_R_101_FPN_3x/137851257/model_final_f6e8b1.pkl')
cfg.merge_from_file(cfg_file)
cfg.MODEL.ROI_HEADS.SCORE_THRESH_TEST = 0.5
cfg.MODEL.WEIGHTS = weights_file
cfg.MODEL.DEVICE = "cuda"
predictor = DefaultPredictor(cfg)
# Cell 03: Slide show of processed images for VOC dataset----------------------
def output_img(img_path):
    img_list = glob.glob(img_path)[3040:3050]
    for file in tqdm(img_list):
        img = cv2.imread(file, 1)
        outputs = predictor(img)
        v = Visualizer(img[:, :, ::-1],
                    MetadataCatalog.get(cfg.DATASETS.TRAIN[0]), scale=1.2)
        out = v.draw_instance_predictions(
                    outputs["instances"].to("cpu")).get_image()[:, :, ::-1]
        cv2.imshow('image', out)
        if (cv2.waitKey(3000)&0xFF) == ord(chr(27)):
            cv2.imwrite('d:/output_img.jpg', out)    #save an image
            break
    cv2.destroyAllWindows()
img_path = 'D:/ImageSets/VOC/VOCdevkit/VOC2012/JPEGImages/*'
output_img(img_path)
# Cell 04: Show and record video from camera or a video file------Replace Cell 03
def output_video(source_file):
    if source_file.isnumeric():                #==========for a web camera
        output_file = 'd:/' + source_file + '.mp4'
        source_file = int(source_file)
    else:
        output_file = source_file.split('.')[0]+'_new'+'.mp4'
    video_source = cv2.VideoCapture(source_file)
    w = int(video_source.get(3)); h = int(video_source.get(4))
    video_format = cv2.VideoWriter_fourcc(*'MP4V')
    video_data = cv2.VideoWriter(output_file, video_format, 30.0, (w, h))
    prev_frame_time = 0; new_frame_time = 0            # for fps calculations
    while True:
```

```
            (NotLastFrame, frame) = video_source.read()
            if not NotLastFrame or (cv2.waitKey(1)&0xFF) == ord(chr(27)):
                break
            new_frame_time = time.time()
            fps = str(int(1/(new_frame_time-prev_frame_time)))
            prev_frame_time = new_frame_time
            outputs = predictor(frame)
            v = Visualizer(frame[:, :, ::-1],
                        MetadataCatalog.get(cfg.DATASETS.TRAIN[0]), scale=1.2)
            out = v.draw_instance_predictions(
                        outputs["instances"].to("cpu")).get_image()[:, :, ::-1]
            out = cv2.resize(out, (w, h))
            cv2.putText(out, fps, (7, 70), 0, 3, (100, 255, 0), 3, cv2.LINE_AA)
            video_data.write(out)
            cv2.imshow("press Esc to stop the video", out)
        video_source.release()
        video_data.release()
        cv2.destroyAllWindows()
source_file = '0'              #source_file = '0'  for webcam
output_video(source_file)      #source_file = 'd:/traffic1.mp4'
# -------------------------------The End------------------------------------


# Cell 02-2: Pre-trained pose model---- Try either of one Cell 02-------Cell 02-2
cfg = get_cfg()   # get a fresh new config
cfg.MODEL.DEVICE = "cuda"
cfg.merge_from_file(model_zoo.get_config_file(
                "COCO-Keypoints/keypoint_rcnn_R_50_FPN_3x.yaml"))
cfg.MODEL.ROI_HEADS.SCORE_THRESH_TEST = 0.7  # set threshold for this model
cfg.MODEL.WEIGHTS = model_zoo.get_checkpoint_url(
                        "COCO-Keypoints/keypoint_rcnn_R_50_FPN_3x.yaml")
predictor = DefaultPredictor(cfg)


# Cell 02-3: Pre-trained instalce segmentation model*******************Cell 02-3
cfg = get_cfg()
cfg.MODEL.DEVICE = 'cuda' #"cpu"
cfg.merge_from_file(model_zoo.get_config_file(
                "COCO-InstanceSegmentation/mask_rcnn_R_50_FPN_3x.yaml"))
cfg.MODEL.ROI_HEADS.SCORE_THRESH_TEST = 0.5
cfg.MODEL.WEIGHTS = model_zoo.get_checkpoint_url(
                        "COCO-InstanceSegmentation/mask_rcnn_R_50_FPN_3x.yaml")
predictor = DefaultPredictor(cfg)


# Cell 02-4: Pre-trained Panoptic segmentation model ------------------Cell 02-4
cfg = get_cfg()
cfg.MODEL.DEVICE = "cuda"
cfg.merge_from_file(model_zoo.get_config_file(
                    "COCO-PanopticSegmentation/panoptic_fpn_R_101_3x.yaml"))
cfg.MODEL.WEIGHTS = model_zoo.get_checkpoint_url(
                    "COCO-PanopticSegmentation/panoptic_fpn_R_101_3x.yaml")
predictor = DefaultPredictor(cfg)
    # -------------------------------The End------------------------------------
```

G Traffic tracking and counting for objects in multiple COCO classes

```
# Project 8.4.3-2 Tracking and counting cars & trucks for a video file-Python 3.9
from ultralytics import YOLO; import cv2; import math; import time
model = YOLO('yolov8s.pt')      # a pre-trained YOLOv8 model------------line 02
green_y=340  # green line for a detection zone [green_y-dy,green_y+dy]---line 03
red_y=370    # red line for a detection zone [red_y-dy,red_y+dy]--------line 04
dy=6
vh_down = {}    # {1: 318, 0: 370...} Car IDs with y locations ----------line 06
n_down = []     # a list of car ids [2, 1,...] for counting of cars running down
class_down=[]   # a list of class indices of objects running down
vh_up = {}      # To register cars running up or away
n_up = []       # the length of the list is used to count cars running up
class_up=[]     # a list of class indices of objects running up
from collections import Counter
def list2dic2str(list):
    counter_text = str()
    objects_list = Counter(list)
    objects_counter = {model.model.names[int(list_k)]: list_v for (
                        list_k, list_v) in objects_list.items()}
    for k,v in objects_counter.items():
        counter_text += (k+":"+str(v)+" ")
        return counter_text
# Cell 02: A class to calculate car center coordinates and assign car IDs--------
class Tracker():
    def __init__(self):
        self.center_points = {} #keep car center points on the previous frame
        self.id_count = 1 #keep the last car ID on the previous frame plus 1
    def update(self, car_list):
        cxcyIDs = []        #[[111,122, 1], [120, 200, 2], ...]   line 06
        for xyXY in car_list:      #----------------------------line 07
            x, y, X, Y, label = xyXY
            cx = int((x + X)/2)
            cy = int((y + Y)/2)
            same_object_detected = False   # check if the car was detected
            for id, pt in self.center_points.items():        #--------line 12
                dist = math.hypot(cx - pt[0], cy - pt[1])    #--------line 13
                if dist < 35:
                    self.center_points[id] = (cx, cy, label)#update old ID center
                    cxcyIDs.append([cx, cy, label, id]) #------------line 16
                    same_object_detected = True
                    break  #the car is found on the previous frame----line 18
            if same_object_detected is False:   # assign an ID to new object
                self.center_points[self.id_count] = (cx, cy, label) # line 20
                cxcyIDs.append([cx, cy, label, self.id_count])
                self.id_count += 1    #-----------------------------line 22
        new_center_points = {} # to delete repeated IDs--------------line 23
        for obj_bb_id in cxcyIDs:
            _, _, _, object_id = obj_bb_id
            center = self.center_points[object_id]
            new_center_points[object_id] = center
        self.center_points = new_center_points.copy()         #--------line 28
        return cxcyIDs
tracker=Tracker()
```

```
        frame=cv2.resize(frame,(1024,512))        #------------------------------line 02
        outputs = model(frame, conf=0.25, verbose=False)[0].boxes # --------line 03
        boxes = outputs.xyxy
        labels = outputs.cls                # labels are COCO class ids-------line 05
        car_list=[]
        for box, label in zip(boxes, labels):   #----------------------------line 07
            c = model.model.names[int(label.item())]  # cOCO class name -----line 08
            if 'car' in c or "truck" in c:
                x, y, X, Y = [int(z) for z in box]
                car_list.append([x, y, X, Y, int(label)])       #------------line 11
        cxcyIDs=tracker.update(car_list) #Call an instance of Tracker() -----line 12
        for bbox in cxcyIDs:            # moniter a car's y position--------line 13
            cx, cy, label, id = bbox
            if (cy > (green_y-dy)) and (cy < (green_y+dy)): #touchs the green zone
                cv2.circle(frame,(cx,cy),4,(255,255,255),-1)       #-------line 16
                cv2.putText(frame, str(id),(cx,cy),0,0.8,(0,255,0),2)
                vh_down[id] = cy           # register a car running down----line 18
            if id in vh_down:
                if (cy > (red_y-dy)) and (cy < (red_y+dy)):  #touchs the red zone
                    if n_down.count(id)==0:    #if id is new --------------line 21
                        n_down.append(id)      # only a new ID will be counted
                        class_down.append(label)    #+++++++++++++++++++++++++++++++++

            if (cy > (red_y-dy)) and (cy < (red_y+dy)):    #for a car running up
                vh_up[id] = cy             # register a car running up
                cv2.circle(frame,(cx,cy),4,(255,255,255),-1)
                cv2.putText(frame,str(id),(cx,cy),0,0.8,(0,0,255),2)
            if id in vh_up:
                if (cy > (green_y-dy)) and (cy < (green_y+dy)):
                    if n_up.count(id)==0:     #if id is new
                        n_up.append(id)                #----------------line 30
                        class_up.append(label)     #+++++++++++++++++++++++++++++++++
        objects_up = list2dic2str(class_up)
        cv2.putText(frame,f'UP {objects_up}',(800,490),0,0.8,(0,0,255),2)
        objects_down = list2dic2str(class_down)
        cv2.putText(frame,f'DOWN {objects_down}',(100,490),0,0.8,(0,255,0),2)
        cv2.line(frame,(200,green_y),(800,green_y),(0,255,0),1) #Green line
        cv2.line(frame,(135,red_y),(850,red_y),(0,0,255),1)  #Red line
        return frame, objects_up, objects_down
# Cell 04: Showing video for car tracking & counting----------------------Cell 04
vh_down={}; n_down=[]; class_down=[]; vh_up={}; n_up=[]; class_up=[]
def output_video(source):
    video_frame = cv2.VideoCapture(source)
    fm=1; FM = int(video_frame.get(cv2.CAP_PROP_FRAME_COUNT))   #FM: total frames
    while True:
        ret, frame = video_frame.read()
        if not ret or (cv2.waitKey(1)&0xFF) == 27: break
        start_time = time.time()
        out, objects_up, objects_down = yolov8tc(frame)
        fps = str(int(1/(time.time()-start_time+1e-5)))
        cv2.putText(out, f'FPS={fps}', (50,30), 0, 1, (255,0,255),2)
        cv2.putText(out, f'Frame={fm}%{FM}', (700,30), 0, 1, (255,0,255), 2)
        cv2.imshow("press Esc to stop the video", out)
        fm += 1
    print(f'objects_up({objects_up})')
    print(f'objects_down({objects_down})')
    video_frame.release(); cv2.destroyAllWindows()
output_video("d:/Project8_4_3.mp4")
#-----------------------------------The End-----------------------------------
```

H U-Net Wasserstein generative adversarial networks for retina

```
# Project 9.01-2 Retinal Vessel Segmentation ------------------------Python v3.6
import torch; import torch.nn as nn; import torch.nn.functional as F
from torch.utils.data import Dataset, DataLoader
import torchvision; from torchvision.utils import make_grid
from operator import add; from albumentations.pytorch import ToTensorV2
import os; import cv2; from glob import glob; import albumentations as A
from skimage.io import imsave, imread, imshow; from skimage import img_as_float32
from sklearn.metrics import precision_score, recall_score
from sklearn.metrics import accuracy_score, f1_score, jaccard_score
import numpy as np; import pandas as pd; import matplotlib.pyplot as plt
from tqdm import tqdm, trange
lr = 2e-4
batch_size = 2
n_epochs = 100
H = 512; W = 512    #resized image sizes for U-Net
root = 'D:/imageSets/Retina/'
Train_img_dir = root + 'training/images/'
Train_mask_dir = root + 'training/1st_manual/'
Val_img_dir = root + 'test/images/'
Val_mask_dir = root + 'test/1st_manual/'
# Cell 02: Datasets and Dataloaders------------------------------------Cell 02
class MyDataset(Dataset):
    def __init__(self, image_dir, mask_dir, transform=None):
        self.images = sorted(glob(os.path.join(image_dir, "*.tif"))) #image files
        self.masks = sorted(glob(os.path.join(mask_dir, "*.gif")))   # mask files
        self.transform = transform
    def __len__(self):
        return len(self.images)
    def __getitem__(self, index):
        image = imread(self.images[index])
        mask = img_as_float32(imread(self.masks[index]))
        if self.transform is not None:  #----------------------------line 11
            augmentations = self.transform(image=image, mask=mask)
            image = augmentations["image"]
            mask = augmentations["mask"]
        return image, mask
# Cell 03: Datasets and Dataloaders------------------------------------Cell 03
train_dataset = MyDataset(Train_img_dir, Train_mask_dir,
        transform = A.Compose([
                A.Resize(height=H, width=W),
                A.Rotate(limit=35, p=1.0, border_mode=cv2.BORDER_CONSTANT),
                A.HorizontalFlip(p=0.5),
                A.VerticalFlip(p=0.5),
                A.Normalize(mean=[0.5]*3,std=[0.5]*3, max_pixel_value=255.0,),
                ToTensorV2()]))
train_dataloader = DataLoader(train_dataset,batch_size=batch_size, shuffle=True)
valid_dataset = MyDataset(Val_img_dir, Val_mask_dir,
```

```
        transform = A.Compose([
                A.Resize(H, W),
                A.Normalize(mean=[0.5]*3,std=[0.5,]*3, max_pixel_value=255.0),
                ToTensorV2()]))
valid_dataloader = DataLoader(valid_dataset, batch_size=batch_size,shuffle=False)
# Cell 04: Display images and masks in a batch of a dataloader---------Cell 04
for images, masks in train_dataloader:
    masks = masks.unsqueeze(dim=1) # add the channel number 1 after batch size
    print("images.shape=", images.shape, '\tmax&min:',
                images.max().item(), images.min().item())
    print("masks.shape=", masks.shape, '\tmax&min:',
                masks.max().item(), masks.min().item())
    break
def denorm(img_tensors):     # Shift image pixel values to [0,1]
    return img_tensors * 0.5 + 0.5
def show_imgs(i, m):         # i for images and m for masks
    fig, ax = plt.subplots(2,1, figsize=(10,8), sharex=True, sharey=True)
    input0 = make_grid(i, nrow=batch_size).permute(1,2,0)
    i_plot = ax[0].imshow(input0)
    ax[0].set(xticks=np.linspace(0, 1024, 9), yticks=np.linspace(0, 512, 5))
    input1 = make_grid(m, nrow=batch_size)
    m_plot = ax[1].imshow(input1.permute(1,2,0), cmap='gray')
    plt.show()
show_imgs(denorm(images), masks)
# Cell 05: Model parameters initialization -----------------------------Cell 05
def weights_init(m):
    if(type(m) == nn.ConvTranspose2d or type(m) == nn.Conv2d):
        nn.init.normal_(m.weight.data, 0.0, 0.02)
    elif(type(m) == nn.BatchNorm2d):
        nn.init.normal_(m.weight.data, 1.0, 0.02)
        nn.init.constant_(m.bias.data, 0)
# Cell 06: U-net Model  ------------------------------------------------Cell 06
lamda_gp = 20
n_critic = 5
n_batch = int(len(train_dataset)/batch_size)
class Basic(nn.Module):
    def __init__(self, in_ch, out_ch):
        super().__init__()
        self.net = nn.Sequential(
                        nn.Conv2d(in_ch, out_ch, 3, 1, 1, bias=False),
                        nn.BatchNorm2d(out_ch), nn.ReLU(True),
                        nn.Conv2d(out_ch, out_ch, 3, 1, 1, bias=False),
                        nn.BatchNorm2d(out_ch), nn.ReLU(True))
        #self.shortcut = nn.Conv2d(in_ch, out_ch, 1, 1, 0)
    def forward(self, images):
        #shortcut = self.shortcut(images)
        #return shortcut + self.net(images)
        return self.net(images)
class Encoder(nn.Module):
    def __init__(self, in_ch, out_ch):
        super().__init__()
        self.skip = Basic(in_ch, out_ch)
```

```
            self.pool = nn.MaxPool2d(2)
    def forward(self, images):
        skip = self.skip(images)
        return skip, self.pool(skip)
class Decoder(nn.Module):
    def __init__(self, in_ch, out_ch):
        super().__init__()
        self.up = nn.ConvTranspose2d(in_ch, out_ch, 2, 2, 0)
        self.conv = Basic(out_ch*2, out_ch)
    def forward(self, inputs, skip):
        x = self.up(inputs)
        x = torch.cat([x, skip], dim=1)
        return self.conv(x)
class U_Net(nn.Module):
    def __init__(self):
        super().__init__()
        self.E1 = Encoder(3, 64)           #-------------color image channels = 3
        self.E2 = Encoder(64, 128)
        self.E3 = Encoder(128, 256)
        self.E4 = Encoder(256, 512)
        self.bottle_neck = Basic(512, 1024)
        self.D1 = Decoder(1024, 512)
        self.D2 = Decoder(512, 256)
        self.D3 = Decoder(256, 128)
        self.D4 = Decoder(128, 64)
        self.final = nn.Conv2d(64, 1, 1, 1, 0, bias=True) #output channel=1
        self.active = nn.Tanh()        # Tanh-Sigmoid
    def forward(self, images):              #images.shape=N x 3 x 512^2
        skip1, pool1 = self.E1(images)  #s1.shape = N x 64 x 512^2
        skip2, pool2 = self.E2(pool1)   #s2.shape = N x 128 x 256^2
        skip3, pool3 = self.E3(pool2)   #s3.shape = N x 256 x 128^2
        skip4, pool4 = self.E4(pool3)   #s4.shape = N x 512 x 64^2
        b =self.bottle_neck(pool4)   #b.shape=N x 1024 x 32^2
        up1 = self.D1(b, skip4)          #up1.shape = N x 512 x 64^2
        up2 = self.D2(up1, skip3)        #up2.shape = N x 256 x 128^2
        up3 = self.D3(up2, skip2)        #up3.shape = N x 128 x 256^2
        up4 = self.D4(up3, skip1)        #up4.shape = N x 64 x 512^2
        return self.active(self.final(up4))     #final.shape = N x 1 x 512^2
G = U_Net().cuda()
G.apply(weights_init)
# Cell 07: Definition of an image discriminator class-------Model D-------Cell 07
def basic_D(in_channels, p=1):
    return nn.Sequential(nn.Conv2d(in_channels, 2*in_channels, kernel_size=3,
                                   stride=2, padding=p, bias=False),
                     nn.InstanceNorm2d(2*in_channels),
                     nn.LeakyReLU(0.2, inplace=True)
        )
class Discriminator(nn.Module):
    def __init__(self):
        super().__init__()
        self.net = nn.Sequential(
            nn.Conv2d(1, 64, kernel_size=4, stride=2, padding=1),
```

```
            nn.LeakyReLU(0.2, inplace=True),  #shape=batch_size x 64 x 256^2
            basic_D(64),                      #shape=batch_size x 128 x 128^2
            basic_D(128),                     #shape=batch_size x 256 x 64^2
            basic_D(256),                     #shape=batch_size x 512 x 32^2
            nn.Conv2d(512, 1, kernel_size=1, stride=1, padding=0),
            nn.Flatten(),
            nn.Linear(1024,1)
        )
    def forward(self, images):
        output = self.net(images)    # input.shape=batch_size x 1 x 512^2
        return output                # output.shape=batch_size x 1
D = Discriminator().cuda()
D.apply(weights_init)
# Cell 08: Definitions of optimizers, criterion, learning rate scheduler
optimizer_D = torch.optim.RMSprop(D.parameters(), lr=lr)
optimizer_G = torch.optim.RMSprop(G.parameters(), lr=lr)
# Cell 09 Gradient-penalty function------------------------------------------cell 09
def gradient_penalty(D, real_data, fake_data):
    batch_size = real_data.size(0)      #real_data.shape = batch_size x 1 x 28^2
    eps = torch.rand(batch_size, 1, 1, 1, device='cuda') # batch_size x 1 x 1^2
    eps = eps.expand_as(real_data)                   #eps.shape=batch_size x 1 x 28^2
    # Sample Epsilon from a uniform distribution
    interpolation = eps * real_data + (1 - eps) * fake_data
    # Interpolation of real data and fake data,    shape = batch_size x 1 x 28^2
    interp_logits = D(interpolation)
    # get logits for interpolated images
    gradients = torch.autograd.grad(
            outputs=interp_logits,
            inputs=interpolation,
            grad_outputs=torch.ones_like(interp_logits),
            create_graph=True,
            retain_graph=True,
        )[0]     # Compute Gradients
    # Compute and return Gradient Norm
    gradients = gradients.view(batch_size, -1)
    grad_norm = gradients.norm(2, dim=1)
    gradient_penalty = torch.mean((grad_norm - 1) ** 2)
    return gradient_penalty
# Cell 10: Model D's training function--------------------------------------Cell 10
def train_D(masks, fake_masks, optimizer_D):
    for _ in range(n_critic):
        batch_size = masks.shape[0]
        real_preds = D(masks)
        real_score = torch.mean(real_preds)

        fake_preds = D(fake_masks.detach())
        fake_score = torch.mean(fake_preds)
        gp = gradient_penalty(D, masks, fake_masks)
        loss = fake_score - real_score + lamda_gp*gp
        optimizer_D.zero_grad()
        loss.backward(retain_graph=True)
        optimizer_D.step()
```

```
        #scheduler.step()
    return loss.item(), real_score.item(), fake_score.item()
# Cell 11: Model G's training function-----------------------------------Cell 11
def train_G(fake_masks, optimizer_G):
    preds = D(fake_masks)
    loss = -torch.mean(preds)
    optimizer_G.zero_grad()
    loss.backward()
    optimizer_G.step()
    return loss.item()
# Cell 12: The main training function-------------------------------------Cel2
def fit(epochs):
    torch.cuda.empty_cache()
    df = pd.DataFrame(np.empty([epochs, 4]), index = np.arange(epochs),
            columns=['loss_G', 'loss_D', 'real_scores',
'fake_scores'])
    progress_bar = trange(epochs)
    for i in progress_bar:
        loss_G = 0.0; loss_D = 0.0; real_sc = 0.0; fake_sc = 0.0
        for color_imgs, masks in train_dataloader:
            masks = masks.unsqueeze(dim=1).cuda()
            fake_masks = G(color_imgs.cuda())
            loss_d, real_score, fake_score = train_D(masks, fake_masks,
optimizer_D)
            loss_D += loss_d
            real_sc += real_score
            fake_sc += fake_score
            loss_g = train_G(fake_masks, optimizer_G)
            loss_G += loss_g
        df.iloc[i, 0] = loss_G/n_batch
        df.iloc[i, 1] = loss_D/n_batch
        df.iloc[i, 2] = real_sc/n_batch
        df.iloc[i, 3] = fake_sc/n_batch
        progress_bar.set_description("loss_G=%.4f" % df.iloc[i, 0])
        progress_bar.set_postfix({'loss_D': df.iloc[i, 1]})
    return df
history = fit(n_epochs)
# Cell 13: Show the training history-------------------------------------Cell 13
df = history[3:]
fig, ax = plt.subplots(1,2, figsize=(9,4), sharex=True)
df.plot(ax=ax[0], y=[0,1], style=['r-', 'b-+'])
gp = df.iloc[:,1] - df.iloc[:,3] + df.iloc[:,2]
ax[0].plot(gp, label='Gradient Penalty', color='k', linestyle=':')
ax[0].set(ylabel='loss')
ax[0].legend()

df.plot(ax=ax[1], y=[2,3], style=['r-+', 'b-'])
for i in range(2):
    ax[i].grid(which='major', axis='both', color='g', linestyle=':')
    ax[i].set(xlabel='epoch')
plt.show()
# Cell 14: Show the trained model acts on the valid_dataset------------Cell 12
for i, (images, masks) in enumerate(valid_dataloader):
        masks = masks.unsqueeze(dim=1)
fake_masks = G(images.cuda())
print('fake_masks min, max:', fake_masks.min().item(), fake_masks.max().item())
show_imgs(fake_masks.detach().cpu(), masks)
# --------------------------The End------------------------------------
```

I DDPM forward process posterior distribution and L_{VLB}

$$q(x_{t-1} \mid x_t, x_0) = \frac{q(x_{t-1}, x_t, x_0)}{q(x_t, x_0)} = \frac{q(x_t \mid x_{t-1}, x_0)q(x_{t-1}, x_0)}{q(x_t \mid x_0)q(x_0)}$$

$$q(x_{t-1} \mid x_t, x_0) = \frac{q(x_t \mid x_{t-1}, x_0)q(x_{t-1} \mid x_0)q(x_0)}{q(x_t \mid x_0)q(x_0)} = q(x_t \mid x_{t-1}, x_0)\frac{q(x_{t-1} \mid x_0)}{q(x_t \mid x_0)}$$

$$q(x_{t-1} \mid x_t, x_0) = \mathbb{N}\left(x_{t-1}; \tilde{\mu}(x_t, x_0), \tilde{\beta_t} I\right) = q(x_t \mid x_{t-1}, x_0)\frac{q(x_{t-1} \mid x_0)}{q(x_t \mid x_0)}$$

$$\propto \exp\left(-\frac{1}{2}\frac{(x_t - \sqrt{\alpha_t}x_{t-1})^2}{\beta_t} - \frac{1}{2}\frac{(x_{t-1} - \sqrt{\bar{\alpha}_{t-1}}x_0)^2}{1 - \bar{\alpha}_{t-1}} + \frac{1}{2}\frac{(x_t - \sqrt{\bar{\alpha}_t}x_0)^2}{1 - \bar{\alpha}_t}\right)$$

$$= \exp\left(-\frac{1}{2}\left[\frac{x_t^2 - 2\sqrt{\alpha_t}x_t x_{t-1} + \alpha_t x_{t-1}^2}{\beta_t} + \frac{x_{t-1}^2 - 2\sqrt{\bar{\alpha}_{t-1}}x_0 x_{t-1} + \alpha_t x_0^2}{1 - \bar{\alpha}_{t-1}} - \frac{(x_t - \sqrt{\bar{\alpha}_t}x_0)^2}{1 - \bar{\alpha}_t}\right]\right)$$

$$= \exp\left(-\frac{1}{2}\left[\left(\frac{\alpha_t}{\beta_t} + \frac{1}{1 - \bar{\alpha}_{t-1}}\right)x_{t-1}^2 - \left(\frac{2\sqrt{\alpha_t}}{\beta_t}x_t + \frac{2\sqrt{\bar{\alpha}_{t-1}}}{1 - \bar{\alpha}_{t-1}}x_0\right)x_{t-1} + \left(\frac{x_t^2}{\beta_t} + \frac{\alpha_t x_0^2}{1 - \bar{\alpha}_{t-1}} - \frac{(x_t - \sqrt{\bar{\alpha}_t}x_0)^2}{1 - \bar{\alpha}_t}\right)\right]\right)$$

$$= \exp\left(-\frac{1}{2}\left[\left(\frac{\alpha_t}{\beta_t} + \frac{1}{1 - \bar{\alpha}_{t-1}}\right)x_{t-1}^2 - 2\left(\frac{\sqrt{\alpha_t}}{\beta_t}x_t + \frac{\sqrt{\bar{\alpha}_{t-1}}}{1 - \bar{\alpha}_{t-1}}x_0\right)x_{t-1} + C_0(x_t, x_0)\right]\right)$$

$$= \exp\left(-\frac{1}{2}\left(\frac{\alpha_t}{\beta_t} + \frac{1}{1 - \bar{\alpha}_{t-1}}\right)\left[x_{t-1}^2 - 2\left(\frac{\alpha_t}{\beta_t} + \frac{1}{1 - \bar{\alpha}_{t-1}}\right)^{-1}\left(\frac{\sqrt{\alpha_t}}{\beta_t}x_t + \frac{\sqrt{\bar{\alpha}_{t-1}}}{1 - \bar{\alpha}_{t-1}}x_0\right)x_{t-1} + C_1(x_t, x_0)\right]\right)$$

In the above formula, $C(x_t, x_0)$ is a function not involving x_{t-1} and details are omitted. Following the standard Gaussian density function with $\alpha_t = 1 - \beta_t$, $\bar{\alpha}_t = \prod_{i=1}^{t} \alpha_i$, the mean and variance of $q(x_{t-1} \mid x_t, x_0)$ can be parameterized as follows:

$$\tilde{\beta_t} = \left(\frac{\alpha_t}{\beta_t} + \frac{1}{1 - \bar{\alpha}_{t-1}}\right)^{-1} = \left(\frac{\alpha_t(1 - \bar{\alpha}_{t-1}) + \beta_t}{\beta_t(1 - \bar{\alpha}_{t-1})}\right)^{-1} = \left(\frac{1 - \bar{\alpha}_t}{\beta_t(1 - \bar{\alpha}_{t-1})}\right)^{-1}$$

$$\tilde{\beta_t} = \frac{1 - \bar{\alpha}_{t-1}}{1 - \bar{\alpha}_t}\beta_t$$

$$\tilde{\mu}(x_t, x_0) = \left(\frac{\alpha_t}{\beta_t} + \frac{1}{1 - \bar{\alpha}_{t-1}}\right)^{-1}\left(\frac{\sqrt{\alpha_t}}{\beta_t}x_t + \frac{\sqrt{\bar{\alpha}_{t-1}}}{1 - \bar{\alpha}_{t-1}}x_0\right)$$

$$\tilde{\mu}(x_t, x_0) = \left(\frac{\sqrt{\alpha_t}}{\beta_t} x_t + \frac{\sqrt{\bar{\alpha}_{t-1}}}{1 - \bar{\alpha}_{t-1}} x_0 \right) \frac{1 - \bar{\alpha}_{t-1}}{1 - \bar{\alpha}_t} \beta_t$$

$$\tilde{\mu}(x_t, x_0) = \frac{\sqrt{\alpha_t}(1 - \bar{\alpha}_{t-1})}{(1 - \bar{\alpha}_t)} x_t + \frac{\beta_t \sqrt{\bar{\alpha}_{t-1}}}{1 - \bar{\alpha}_t} x_0$$

$$\tilde{\mu}(x_t, x_0) = \frac{\sqrt{\alpha_t}(1 - \bar{\alpha}_{t-1})}{(1 - \bar{\alpha}_t)} x_t + \frac{\beta_t \sqrt{\bar{\alpha}_{t-1}}}{1 - \bar{\alpha}_t} \frac{1}{\sqrt{\bar{\alpha}_t}} (x_t - \varepsilon \sqrt{1 - \bar{\alpha}_t})$$

$$\tilde{\mu}(x_t, x_0) = \frac{\sqrt{\alpha_t}(1 - \bar{\alpha}_{t-1})}{(1 - \bar{\alpha}_t)} x_t + \frac{\beta_t \sqrt{\bar{\alpha}_{t-1}}}{1 - \bar{\alpha}_t} \frac{x_t}{\sqrt{\bar{\alpha}_t}} - \frac{\beta_t \sqrt{\bar{\alpha}_{t-1}}}{1 - \bar{\alpha}_t} \frac{\varepsilon}{\sqrt{\bar{\alpha}_t}} \sqrt{1 - \bar{\alpha}_t}$$

$$\tilde{\mu}(x_t, x_0) = \left(\frac{\sqrt{\alpha_t}(1 - \bar{\alpha}_{t-1})}{(1 - \bar{\alpha}_t)} + \frac{1}{\sqrt{\alpha_t}} \frac{\beta_t}{1 - \bar{\alpha}_t} \right) x_t - \frac{\beta_t}{\sqrt{1 - \bar{\alpha}_t}} \frac{\varepsilon}{\sqrt{\alpha_t}}$$

$$\tilde{\mu}(x_t, x_0) = \frac{1}{\sqrt{\alpha_t}} \left(\frac{(\alpha_t - \bar{\alpha}_t)}{(1 - \bar{\alpha}_t)} + \frac{1 - \alpha_t}{1 - \bar{\alpha}_t} \right) x_t - \frac{\beta_t}{\sqrt{1 - \bar{\alpha}_t}} \frac{\varepsilon}{\sqrt{\alpha_t}}$$

$$\tilde{\mu}(x_t, x_0) = \frac{1}{\sqrt{\alpha_t}} \left(x_t - \frac{1 - \alpha_t}{\sqrt{1 - \bar{\alpha}_t}} \varepsilon \right)$$

The variational lower bound loss L_{VLB}

$$L_{VLB} = - \int q(x_0) q(x_{1:T} \mid x_0) \log \frac{p_\theta(x_{0:T})}{q(x_{1:T} \mid x_0)} dx_{0:T}$$

$$L_{VLB} = E_{q(x_{0:T})} \left[\log \frac{q(x_{1:T} \mid x_0)}{p_\theta(x_{0:T})} \right] = E_q \left[\log \frac{\prod_{t=1}^{T} q(x_t \mid x_{t-1})}{p_\theta(x_T) \prod_{t=1}^{T} p_\theta(x_{t-1} \mid x_t)} \right]$$

$$= E_q \left[-\log p_\theta(x_T) + \log \frac{\prod_{t=1}^{T} q(x_t \mid x_{t-1})}{\prod_{t=1}^{T} p_\theta(x_{t-1} \mid x_t)} \right] = E_q \left[-\log p_\theta(x_T) + \sum_{t=1}^{T} \log \frac{q(x_t \mid x_{t-1})}{p_\theta(x_{t-1} \mid x_t)} \right]$$

$$= E_q \left[-\log p_\theta(x_T) + \sum_{t=2}^{T} \log \frac{q(x_t \mid x_{t-1})}{p_\theta(x_{t-1} \mid x_t)} \right] + \log \frac{q(x_1 \mid x_0)}{p_\theta(x_0 \mid x_1)}$$

$$= E_q \left[-\log p_\theta(x_T) + \sum_{t=2}^{T} \log \frac{q(x_{t-1}|x_t)}{p_\theta(x_{t-1}|x_t)} \frac{q(x_t|x_0)}{q(x_{t-1}|x_0)} + \log \frac{q(x_1 \mid x_0)}{p_\theta(x_0 \mid x_1)} \right] \text{according to equation(9.4)}$$

$$= E_q \left[-\log p_\theta(x_T) + \sum_{t=2}^{T} \log \frac{q(x_{t-1}|x_t, x_0)}{p_\theta(x_{t-1}|x_t)} \frac{q(x_t|x_0)}{q(x_{t-1}|x_0)} + \log \frac{q(x_1|x_0)}{p_\theta(x_0|x_1)} \right]$$

$$= E_q \left[-\log p_\theta(x_T) + \sum_{t=2}^{T} \log \frac{q(x_{t-1}|x_t, x_0)}{p_\theta(x_{t-1}|x_t)} + \sum_{t=2}^{T} \log \frac{q(x_t|x_0)}{q(x_{t-1}|x_0)} + \log \frac{q(x_1|x_0)}{p_\theta(x_0|x_1)} \right]$$

$$= E_q \left[-\log p_\theta(x_T) + \sum_{t=2}^{T} \log \frac{q(x_{t-1}|x_t, x_0)}{p_\theta(x_{t-1}|x_t)} + \log \prod_{t=2}^{T} \frac{q(x_t|x_0)}{q(x_{t-1}|x_0)} + \log \frac{q(x_1|x_0)}{p_\theta(x_0|x_1)} \right]$$

$$= E_q \left[-\log p_\theta(x_T) + \sum_{t=2}^{T} \log \frac{q(x_{t-1}|x_t, x_0)}{p_\theta(x_{t-1}|x_t)} + \log \frac{q(x_T|x_0)}{q(x_1|x_0)} + \log \frac{q(x_1|x_0)}{p_\theta(x_0|x_1)} \right]$$

$$= E_q \left[-\log p_\theta(x_T) + \sum_{t=2}^{T} \log \frac{q(x_{t-1}|x_t, x_0)}{p_\theta(x_{t-1}|x_t)} + \log \frac{q(x_T|x_0)}{p_\theta(x_0|x_1)} \right]$$

$$= E_q \left[\log \frac{q(x_T|x_0)}{p_\theta(x_T)} + \sum_{t=2}^{T} \log \frac{q(x_{t-1}|x_t, x_0)}{p_\theta(x_{t-1}|x_t)} - \log p_\theta(x_0 \mid x_1) \right]$$

$$= \int q(x_{0:T}) \log \frac{q(x_T|x_0)}{p_\theta(x_T)} dx_{0:T} + \sum_{t=2}^{T} E_q \left[\log \frac{q(x_{t-1}|x_t, x_0)}{p_\theta(x_{t-1}|x_t)} \right] - E_q \left[\log p_\theta(x_0 \mid x_1) \right]$$

$$= D_{\mathrm{KL}}(q(x_T \mid x_0) \| p_\theta(x_T)) + \sum_{t=2}^{T} D_{\mathrm{KL}}\big(q(x_{t-1} \mid x_t, x_0) \| p_\theta(x_{t-1} \mid x_t)\big) - E_q \left[\log p_\theta(x_0 \mid x_1) \right]$$

$$= L_T + \sum_{t=2}^{T} L_{t-1} + L_0$$

J An Improved Version of Project 11.3.1 to Avoid a FAISS Issue

```python
#Project 11.3.1 Image instance retrieval by DINOv2--------------------Python v3.9
import torch
from torch.utils.data import DataLoader
from torch.utils.data.dataset import random_split as split
from torchvision import transforms as T
from torchvision.utils import make_grid
from torchvision.datasets import ImageFolder
import matplotlib.pyplot as plt
img_size = 224
batch_size = 6
data_path = 'OCR/data/FlowersDataset/flowers'
classes = ['daisy', 'dandelion', 'rose', 'sunflower', 'tulip']
model = torch.hub.load('facebookresearch/dinov2', 'dinov2_vits14').cuda()
model.eval()
# Cell 02-04: Flowers Dataset. -------Reuse codes in Cell 02-04 of Project 9.3.2
# Cell 05: Extracted Image Features by a pre-trained DINOv2 model-------Cell 05/7
def feature(my_dataset):
    dataset_features = []
    for _, sample in enumerate(my_dataset):
        img, _ = sample
        with torch.no_grad():
            features = model(img.unsqueeze(0).cuda())
        dataset_features.append(features)
    return torch.cat(dataset_features, dim=0)
dataset_features = feature(val_dataset).cpu().numpy()
dataset_features.shape      # dataset_features.shape=(701, 384)
# Cell 06: A querry image's Features in train_dataloader---------------Cell 06/7
n = 1      # select n <= (batch_size - 1) for an image in imgs to querry
query_img = imgs[n]
print(f'My querry_img flower is {classes[labels[n]]}.')
with torch.no_grad():
    query_features = model(query_img.unsqueeze(0).cuda())
expanded_query_features = query_features.expand(701, -1).cpu()
L1 = expanded_query_features - dataset_features          # L1 distance
L2 = torch.sqrt(torch.sum(L1*L1, dim=-1))                # L2 distance
values, indices = torch.sort(L2)     # image indices in my_dataset of Cell 05
print('The most close flower indices in my_dataset: ', indices[:batch_size])
# Cell 07: Display retrieved images by the pre-trained DINOv2 mode------Cell 07/7
def retrival_imgs(my_dataset):
    my_imgs = []
    for i in range(batch_size):
        img, _ = my_dataset[indices[i]]
        my_imgs.append(img)
    my_imgs = torch.cat(my_imgs, dim=0).view(batch_size, 3, img_size, img_size)
    return my_imgs
my_imgs = retrival_imgs(val_dataset)
print(f'My instance retrieval images for {classes[labels[n]]} flowers:')
show_imgs(my_imgs)
#---------------------------------The End----------------------------------
```

K Tiny NeRF codes for lego 3D scene synthesis

```python
# Project: Using a tiny NeRF model to restore an image of 3D Lego---Python v3.90
from typing import Optional
import torch; import torch.nn as nn
import torch.optim.lr_scheduler as lr_scheduler
import numpy as np; import pandas as pd
import matplotlib.pyplot as plt
from tqdm import tqdm, trange
import cv2
device = torch.device("cuda" if torch.cuda.is_available() else "cpu")
data_path = 'D:/ImageSets/NeRF/tiny_nerf_data.npz'
n_epochs = 10000
lr = 5e-3
randomize = True
seed = 9458        # using the seed to get repeatable results
torch.manual_seed(seed); np.random.seed(seed)
# Cell 02: input images and poses of a camera to convert [u,v] to [xw,yw,zw]----
data = np.load(data_path)
images = torch.from_numpy(data["images"][:100]).to(device) #shape=[100,100,100,3]
poses = torch.from_numpy(data["poses"][:100] ).to(device)  #shape=[100, 4, 4]
focal_length = torch.from_numpy(data["focal"]).to(device)   # f=138.8889 pixels
height, width = images.shape[1:3]    # H and W of each image: 100 pixels
H, W = height, width
near_thresh = 2.    # near and far clipping thresholds for depth values.
far_thresh = 6.     # Using -6 <= zc <= -2 to calculate [xw,yw,zw] on each ray
num_samples = 128   # distance between 2 points in a ray: d=(6-2)/31 for N=32
n_encodeF4q_p = 6  # for encoding [xw,yw,zw] with 2^0, 2^1...,2^9
n_encodeF4dic = 4   # for encoding ray direction with 2^0, 2^1...,2^3
chunksize = 8192   # Use chunksize of 8*4096 ray points for model training------
testimg = torch.from_numpy(data['images'][101]).to(device)  #shape=[100,100,3]
testpose = torch.from_numpy(data['poses'][101]).to(device)  #shape=[4, 4]
plt.title("Ground truth: test image")
plt.imshow(testimg.detach().cpu().numpy());
'''
# Cell 03: to slide-show 100 images used for model training------------------3/14
for image in tqdm(images):
    img = cv2.resize(image.cpu().numpy(), (600,600))
    img = cv2.cvtColor(img, cv2.COLOR_BGR2RGB)
    cv2.imshow("press Esc to stop the slid show", img)
```

```
        if (cv2.waitKey(1000)&0xFF) == 27: break
cv2.destroyAllWindows()'''
# Cell 04: Functions to convert image [u.v] to ray [xw,yw,zw] encoded by position
def meshgrid_xy(tensor1: torch.Tensor, tensor2: torch.Tensor):
  ii, jj = torch.meshgrid(tensor1, tensor2, indexing='xy')
  return ii, jj
# example: meshgrid_xy(torch.linspace(-1,1,5), torch.linspace(-1,1,9))
def cumprod_exclusive(tensor: torch.Tensor):
  cumprod = torch.cumprod(tensor, -1)      #dim = -1
  cumprod = torch.roll(cumprod, 1, -1)
  cumprod[..., 0] = 1.
  return cumprod
# example: cumprod_exclusive(torch.tensor([0.1,0.2,0.3,0.2,0.5]))
def get_ray_bundle(pose):
  H = height; W = width; f = focal_length
  u, v = meshgrid_xy(torch.arange(W).to(pose), torch.arange(H).to(pose))
  uv2cam = torch.stack( #[u,v] to camera [xc,yc] at zc=-1, shape=[100,100,3]
              [(u-W/2+0.5)/f, -(v-H/2+0.5)/f, -torch.ones_like(u)], dim=-1)
  ray_directions = torch.sum(uv2cam[..., None, :] * pose[:3, :3], dim=-1)
  ray_origins = pose[:3, -1].expand(ray_directions.shape) #world [xw,yw,zw]
  return ray_origins, ray_directions
def query_points_on_rays(ray_origins, ray_directions):
  depth_values = torch.linspace(                   #[2.0000, 2.1290, ..., 6.0]
                    near_thresh, far_thresh, num_samples).to(ray_origins)
  shape = [height, width, num_samples]             #shape=[100, 100, 32]
  d = (far_thresh - near_thresh) / (num_samples-1)  # distance of 2 points
  depth_values = depth_values + torch.rand(shape).to(ray_origins)*d
  query_points = (ray_origins[..., None, :] +    #32 points [xw,yw,zw] on a ray
                  ray_directions[..., None, :] * depth_values[..., :, None])
  return query_points, depth_values
def positional_encoding(x, L):  # x: query_points or ray_directions
  if x.shape[2] == 3:           # for ray_directions
    x = x[..., None, :].expand(H ,W, num_samples, 3)
  x = x.reshape(-1,3)
  pe = [x]
  for i in range(L):
      x = 2* np.pi * 2**i * x
      pe.append(torch.sin(x))
      pe.append(torch.cos(x))
  return torch.cat(pe, dim=-1)
#Cell 05: A MPL model to process date encoded with position information------5/14
class VeryTinyNeRFMLP(nn.Module):
    def __init__(self, n_hidden=128):
        super().__init__()
        dim4q_p = 3 + 3 * 2 * n_encodeF4q_p
```

```python
        dim4dic = 3 + 3 * 2 * n_encodeF4dic
        self.net1 = nn.Sequential(
                    nn.Linear(dim4q_p, n_hidden), nn.ReLU(),
                    nn.Linear(n_hidden, n_hidden), nn.ReLU(),
                    nn.Linear(n_hidden, n_hidden), nn.ReLU(),
                    nn.Linear(n_hidden, n_hidden + 1), nn.ReLU())
        self.net2 = nn.Sequential(
                    nn.Linear(n_hidden + dim4dic, n_hidden), nn.ReLU(),
                    nn.Linear(n_hidden, 3))
    def forward(self, query_points, ray_directions):
        output = self.net1(query_points)
        sigma = output[:, 0].unsqueeze(-1)
        rgb = self.net2(torch.cat([output[:, 1:], ray_directions], dim=-1))
        radiance_field = torch.cat([rgb, sigma], dim=-1)
        return radiance_field
model = VeryTinyNeRFMLP().to(device)
optimizer = torch.optim.Adam(model.parameters(), lr=lr)
criterion = nn.MSELoss()
#Cell 06: contribution of all 128 points on a ray to color of a pixel on an image
def render_volume_density(radiance_field, ray_origins, depth_values):
  sigma = torch.nn.functional.relu(radiance_field[..., 3])      # density of point
  rgb = torch.sigmoid(radiance_field[..., :3])              #rgb.shape=[100,100,3]
  one_e_10 = torch.tensor([1e10], dtype=depth_values.dtype,    #shape=[100, 100, 1]
              device=depth_values.device).expand(depth_values[..., :1].shape)
  dists = torch.cat((depth_values[..., 1:] - depth_values[..., :-1],
                  one_e_10), dim=-1)                #dists.shape=[100,100,32]
  alpha = 1.0 - torch.exp(-sigma * dists)  #light intensity emitted by a point
  beta = 1.0 - alpha    #light intensity left after light passing through a point
  weights = alpha * cumprod_exclusive(beta + 1e-10) #contribution of each point
  rgb_map = (weights[..., None] * rgb).sum(dim=-2)  # predicted image color
  return rgb_map
# Cell 07: One iteration of TinyNeRF model to predict an image---------------7/14
def run_one_iter_of_tinynerf(pose):
  ray_origins, ray_directions = get_ray_bundle(pose)
  query_points, depth_values = query_points_on_rays(ray_origins, ray_directions)
  pe4q_p = positional_encoding(query_points, n_encodeF4q_p)    #shape=[320000,39]
  pe4dic = positional_encoding(ray_directions, n_encodeF4dic) #shape=[320000,39]
  N = pe4q_p.shape[0]    # total query points for an image
  batchs4q_p = [pe4q_p[i:i + chunksize] for i in range(0, N, chunksize)]
  batchs4dic = [pe4dic[i:i + chunksize] for i in range(0, N, chunksize)]
  predictions = []
  for b4q_p, b4dic in zip(batchs4q_p, batchs4dic):
    predictions.append(model(b4q_p, b4dic))
  radiance_field_flattened = torch.cat(predictions, dim=0) # shape=[320000, 4]
  unflattened_shape = list(query_points.shape[:-1]) + [4]  # [100, 100, 32, 4]
```

```
    radiance_field = torch.reshape(radiance_field_flattened, unflattened_shape)
    rgb_predicted=render_volume_density(radiance_field, ray_origins, depth_values)
    return rgb_predicted
# Cell 08: Model Training for the train_dataloader--------------------------8/14
def training(idx):
    model.train()
    target_img = images[idx].to(device)
    target_pose = poses[idx].to(device)
    rgb_predicted = run_one_iter_of_tinynerf(target_pose)
    lr = optimizer.param_groups[0]['lr']
    loss = criterion(rgb_predicted, target_img)
    loss.backward()
    optimizer.step()
    #scheduler.step()
    optimizer.zero_grad()
    #psnr = -10. * torch.log10(loss)
    return loss.item(), lr
# Cell 09: Model Evaluation for val_dataloader and test_dataloader-----------9/14
def evaluation():
    model.eval()
    with torch.no_grad():
        rgb_predicted = run_one_iter_of_tinynerf(testpose)
        loss = criterion(rgb_predicted, testimg)
        #psnr = -10. * torch.log10(loss)
    return loss.item()
# Cell 10: The main training function ------------------------------------10/14
def fitting(epochs):
    df = pd.DataFrame(np.empty([epochs, 3]),
        index = np.arange(epochs),
        columns=['loss_train', 'loss_val', 'lr'])
    progress_bar = trange(epochs)
    for i in progress_bar:
        idx = np.random.randint(images.shape[0]) # Randomly pick an image
        df.iloc[i,0], lr = training(idx)
        df.iloc[i,1] = evaluation()
        df.iloc[i,2] =lr
        progress_bar.set_description("lr=%.5f" % lr)
        progress_bar.set_postfix(
                {'loss_train': df.iloc[i,0], 'loss_val': df.iloc[i,1]})
    return df
train_history = fitting(n_epochs)
# Cell 11: Graphs of Model training results--------------------------------11/14
df= train_history
fig, ax = plt.subplots(1,3, figsize=(12,2.5), sharex=True)
df.plot(ax=ax[0], y=[0,1], style=['r-', 'b-'])
```

```
df.plot(ax=ax[1], y=[2], style=['r-'])
ax[2].plot(range(n_epochs) ,-10*np.log10(df['loss_train']), 'r-', label='train')
ax[2].plot(range(n_epochs), -10*np.log10(df['loss_val']), 'b-', label='val')
for i in range(3):
    ax[i].set_xlabel('epoch')
    ax[i].grid(which='major', axis='both', color='g', linestyle=':')
ax[0].set_ylabel('loss'); ax[2].set(ylabel='PSNR')
ax[1].ticklabel_format(style='sci', axis='y', scilimits=(0,0))
ax[2].legend();
# Cell 12: Comparison of the ground truth and the predicted image-----------12/14
with torch.no_grad():          #num_samples = 128
        rgb_predicted = run_one_iter_of_tinynerf(testpose)
        psnr = -10*np.log10(df['loss_val'][n_epochs-1])
        fig, ax = plt.subplots(1,2, figsize=(8, 4))
        ax[0].imshow(testimg.detach().cpu().numpy())
        ax[0].set(title='ground truth')
        ax[1].imshow(rgb_predicted.detach().cpu().numpy())
        ax[1].set(title=f'preditcted image pnsr={psnr:.1f}')
        plt.show()
# Cell 13: save a trained model----------------------------------------model saving
File_name = 'tinyNeRF-model-20K.pth'
torch.save(model, File_name)
'''
# Cell 14: load a saved model---------------------------- saved model loading--
model = torch.load('tinyNeRF3.pth')
model.eval()
print(model.state_dict())'''
#--------------------------------The End-------------------------------------
```

Printed in the USA
CPSIA information can be obtained
at www.ICGtesting.com
CBHW081240060824
12632CB00004B/17

9 780750 362429